WESTMAR COLLEGE
W9-CDC-216

MAN IN REVOLT

MAN IN REVOLT

A CHRISTIAN ANTHROPOLOGY

By

EMIL BRUNNER

Professor of Theology in Zürich

TRANSLATED BY

OLIVE WYON

LUTTERWORTH PRESS

LONDON and REDHILL

233
B897

BT
701
.B72
1939

ALL RIGHTS RESERVED

First published in English 1939
Second impression 1942
Third impression 1947

PRINTED IN GREAT BRITAIN BY UNWIN BROTHERS LIMITED, WOKING

71044

From this we see how necessarily our Self is rooted and grounded in Him who created it, so that the knowledge of our Self does not lie within our own power, but that in order to measure the extent of the same, we must press forward into the very heart of God Himself, who alone can determine and resolve the whole mystery of our nature.

HAMANN

CONTENTS

MAIN SECTION II

DEVELOPMENT OF THE THEME

CONTENTS

APPENDICES

PREFACE TO THE GERMAN EDITION

WHAT is Man? This question is the point at which the passionate interest of men and the divine message of the Bible meet and come into conflict. Primarily, man regards himself as the natural centre of his life and of his world. Even where in theory he thinks that he has overcome this 'naïve anthropocentricism,' in practice, in life itself, he does not cease to assert himself as this centre. A world with as many centres as there are human beings—that is the cause of all the chaos and disintegration in the world of men. The message of the Bible, therefore, is this: God, not man, is the centre; this truth must be expressed not only in theory but in practice. Hence this message is not concerned with 'God in Himself,' but with 'God for us,' the God who manifests His nature and His will in the Son of Man, in order that in man this centre may once more become the true centre. The great obstacle to this, however, is that view of himself held by man; to overcome this 'misunderstanding' of man about himself, to which he clings as a supreme good, is the revealed will of God, and the act in which this resistance is overcome is faith. The understanding of man's being is decided in faith or unbelief; in the fact, that is, whether God or man is the centre.

Thus in itself the truth of faith involves discussion, the Gospel is essentially—not accidentally—controversial. It is an attack on man who is his own centre. Divine truth wrestles with human falsehood, and man conceals himself behind his 'self-knowledge' in order to defend himself against the Divine claim. Hence a Christian doctrine of man must be beaten out on the anvil of continual argument with man's own view of himself. If faith simply means that human thought and will finally capitulate to the truth and the will of God, then theology can never be anything other than an attempt, in some way or another, to 'transcribe' this controversy between the Word of God and the thought of man. Hence all genuine theology is dialectical and not orthodox. It is aware that its 'transcript' reflects the imperfection of our human effort of thought as much as the glory of divine truth. Above all, it is aware that its task is never finished.

Thus this book also is an unfinished piece of work, and would still be so even if I were to work on it for many more years. Its first beginnings lie in the past, more than fifteen years ago, when it became clear to me, under the deep impression made by the anthropological work of Kierkegaard, that the distinction between modern Humanism and the Christian faith must be made at this point: in the understanding of man. Acquaintance with the thought of Ebner, Gogarten, and Buber helped me further along the path which I had begun to follow. Here too, however, I learned still more from the new light thrown on the teaching of the Reformers; I learned most from Luther, for I came to see that in this question, of all the Reformers his teaching is the most Scriptural and the most profound. Yet as I probed more deeply into the subject I saw that it would be impossible simply to re-affirm the Reformation position and to go no further. I saw too why this was inevitable. In the central anthropological question of freedom versus unfreedom, in particular, the inadequacy of the teaching of the Reformers was evident. There is a great deal to learn from Augustine the thinker which escaped the notice of Luther the fighter. Above all, it became plain to me that the whole ecclesiastical tradition was burdened with certain fundamental axioms, wrongly regarded as Biblical truth; it is these ideas, regarded as axioms, which frequently provide a handle for attacks on the ecclesiastical doctrine on the part of its opponents. In the attempt to reformulate the Christian doctrine of man I took it for granted that I should utilize the results of Biblical criticism, and also, even though less directly, of modern discoveries in the field of natural science. Since we are now at the beginning of a theological era of increasing rigidity in orthodoxy, it is particularly important to preserve the faculty of criticism, although this too has its own peculiar dangers.

The book which I here present has passed through a number of preliminary stages. The germ of the whole was an article on *Law and Revelation* which I published in March 1925 in *Theologische Blätter*; the second stage was a lecture on *Christian Psychology* which I gave in the winter of 1927, which, completely recast in 1934, forms the foundation of the present work. A chapter on Biblical psychology in my small book *God and Man* provided a preliminary outline for the structure of the whole; but most of the other papers which were published, both before and afterwards, turned on the question of anthropology, especially those entitled *Die andere Aufgabe der Theologie* (the Other Task of Theology) and *The Point of Contact* (*Anknüpfungspunkt*).

With the publication of this book I hope that I have redeemed the promise made in the foreword to the second edition of *Natur und Gnade*, namely, that only a completely theological anthropology, which begins with the great central truths of the Christian faith—the Trinity, Election, and Incarnation—and is directed towards the final Redemption, will be in a position, without causing new misunderstandings, to show clearly my concern, as against Karl Barth, namely, man's responsibility. It is that alone, and not any weakening of the doctrine of the *sola gratia*, which causes me to hold fast to the Biblical doctrine of a general or "natural" revelation of God, in spite of all that may be said to the contrary. The fundamental idea of my book is this: that even the unbeliever is still related to God, and therefore that he is responsible, and that this responsibility is not put out of action even by the fullest emphasis upon the generous grace of God, but, on the contrary, that God requires it. This fundamental idea is illustrated in a number of ways throughout the book as a whole. It is concerned with a Biblical doctrine of man, whom the Word of God—as a word of judgement and of promise—addresses and apprehends. One 'theme with variations' will always be exposed to the reproach of repetition—especially if there are a good many of them. In my justification I would point to the illustration of the winding tunnels in our Swiss mountain railways, which continually present us with the same view seen from another aspect and from a greater height. The same, if said in a different context, is not simply the same.

Owing to my conception of the task of theology, all technical discussions are relegated to the notes and the appendices. Real theology is not only for experts, but it is for all to whom religious questions are also problems for thought. Hence I have tried to deal with difficult theological questions in such a way that they can be followed by those who have no special theological equipment. There are many ways of faith to Him who alone is the Way; theological reflection also may be such a way, although it certainly is not the way most people would choose. Among all the problems of theology that of anthropology is one of the most important. It is only through the study of this question that many a person comes to understand the Christian message itself, simply because he has learned to think more deeply about himself. Even thought may lead us into 'the cell of self-knowledge,' but this real self-knowledge is the point at which faith comes into being. Rightly understood, therefore, to begin at this point is genuine missionary effort.

In conclusion, there are two things I wish to say. I would like to express my cordial thanks to all those who have helped me, especially those who have helped me in the arduous labour of proof correction. And I would like to ask the reader to forgive me for not saying what I had to say in briefer compass. In spite of all my resolutions to the contrary this has developed into a big book after all, and yet I have left a great deal of material untouched. May the readers of this book regard its length as a parable showing that, in the last resort, we human beings cannot fully express even that vision of the truth which we have seen.

EMIL BRUNNER

ZÜRICH
March 1937

TRANSLATOR'S NOTE

The present work is an unabridged translation of the book which was first published in German in 1937, by the *Furche-Verlag, Berlin*, under the title: *Der Mensch im Widerspruch*, with the sub-title: *Die christliche Lehre vom wahren und vom wirklichen Menschen* (*Eng.* Man in Contradiction. The Christian Doctrine of the true (or ideal) man, and of man as he actually is).

The English title: *Man in Revolt*, has been chosen by Dr. Brunner himself.

For the English version the author has slightly altered the text on page 360 (page 372 in the German original).

The translator desires to offer her cordial gratitude to the many friends who have helped her, in various ways, during the course of this work. For assistance with the revision of the manuscript she would thank particularly: Dr. H. Boobyer, Dr. L. Frankl, Miss L. Goodfellow, and Miss Edith Sandbach-Marshall, M.A., B.D. For the elucidation of some difficult passages she is grateful to Edwyn Bevan, Esq., D.Litt., and to the Rev. John Oman, D.D.

OLIVE WYON

LONDON
May 1939

INTRODUCTION

THE QUESTION OF MAN

CHAPTER I

THE RIDDLE OF MAN

It is not self-evident that man should inquire into his own nature, or even that he should ask questions at all. To ask questions and to take things for granted are incompatible attitudes; when man begins to inquire, he can no longer take things for granted. A mysterious movement has begun, and none can tell whither it may lead. Moreover, once the question of his own nature has been raised, man seeks an answer to a second, still more disquieting question. The earlier questioning had made only his surroundings, the shell of his existence, seem insecure; now, however, he himself feels insecure. Not only is the world full of riddles; he himself, who asks the riddles, has become a riddle. Small wonder, then, that man tries to evade this upheaval. He feels the danger of inquiry, and tries to avoid it by persuading himself that it does not really matter. A sane human being, he says, has something more sensible to do than to look at himself in a mirror. In any case, man should not consider himself so very important. What is there in him so outstanding—this speck of dust, this none too successful late product of Nature? In the world of antiquity it was perhaps allowable that man, with his restricted view of the world and his geocentric outlook, should consider himself to be specially important; but we modern men, for whom astro-physics has shattered the familiar and homely picture of the world, and has opened up to our gaze the infinity of the universe, can no longer ascribe any special importance to man and his problems. Man must accustom himself to the idea that he is only one problem among many others, and by no means the most important.

But the riddle of man cannot be shelved like this. This riddle is not the fruit of our opinions; it springs from its own inward necessity, as the question above all others. Other problems may seem to us to be greater or more important, but they are still *our* problems. It is *we* who probe into the remote recesses of the world's existence; it is for *us* that the phenomena of the universe become questions. All our problems are focused in this one question: Who is this being who questions—the one behind all questions? Who is this who perceives the infinity of the world? Who is this who is tortured by all life's problems—whether in human existence or outside it? Who is this being who sees himself as a mere speck in the universe, and yet, even while so doing, measures the infinite horizon with his mind? We are here confronted by the problem of the *subject*, separated by a great gulf from all problems of the objective world. What is this to which things are objects, which they are 'set over against'? What is this unextended point, like the inapprehensible originator of waves behind a field of electro-magnetic force, its emissive and receptive centre—the soul?

'Go hence; the limits of the soul thou canst not discover, though thou shouldest traverse every way; so profoundly is it rooted in the Logos,'[1] says the great sage of Ephesus, he who was the first to utter the proud word: 'I have inquired of myself.'[2] Hence the soul is separated, as by a deep gulf, from all that man can know or discover by search and inquiry, because the soul itself, which makes itself known, is that which knows; because in the very act of laying something upon the dissecting table for examination, the soul looks away beyond it. It is the inquiring eye, the intelligence, that makes what is examined into a unity; this it is that knows the problems and seeks to solve them. But the soul does not only think and examine; it also wills and feels, makes estimates, loves and hates. It gives its rightful place within the intellectual life as a whole to research, science, thought—to all, indeed, that has value and meaning. Only he who forgets this can overlook the fact that the question of man as subject is not one among many others; it is a new dimension of questioning, and the soul is an 'object' whose particular problems consist in the very fact that it is not an 'object' at all. We cannot assign any place to the soul—that is, to man—because the soul itself is that which puts everything else in its right place. Hence man is unfathomable in a way different from everything else, because he himself fathoms things; he is the discoverer of that

[1] In Diels, *Fragmente der Vorsokratiker*, Fr. 45. [2] Ibid., Fr. 101.

which is unfathomable. If to fathom anything means to get to the other side of it, then the soul is unfathomable because it is that which penetrates to the other side. The fact, however, that man, who can include in his gaze the whole horizon of the world, is at the same time a minute point in the world, an object of infinite smallness in space, does not reduce, but rather increases, the riddle of his being. The difference—indeed, the unfathomable gulf—between the subject and the object, the soul and the world of things, between soul and body, is one problem; a second problem, and one with which thinkers have wrestled in vain for thousands of years, is that of the relation between both, and the way in which both exist alongside of one another—the problem of body and soul.

Even the 'man in the street' is aware of this dualism, although he does not give it much thought. He knows that he ought to treat human beings differently from things, not only because they 'react differently,' but because he has no right to treat them as things. A purely objective attitude where human beings are concerned is not only impossible; it is not right, and is therefore forbidden. It is precisely this sense that he has no right to dispose of himself and of his fellow-creatures in such a way that gives man the consciousness of his peculiar nature—of his being as man. This 'thou shalt' and 'thou shalt not' is not something added externally to human existence; it constitutes the heart of man's being. Man's being is inseparable from his sense of obligation.

Once again a new depth in human existence is disclosed. Man is not merely what he is; his peculiar being is characterized by that inward and higher 'something' which confronts him either with a challenge or at least with pressure from without. But this element which confronts him does so as that which is 'over against' him, and not as an 'object.' It is genuinely 'over against' him, whereas objects are not really 'over against' but 'beneath' us. This challenge, then, is not foreign to man's life, but it comes as a call to one's own nature, as the call to accept responsibility for one's own life,[1] to be truly oneself,

[1] The original word is *Eigentlichkeit*—an allusion to one of the leading ideas in the philosophy of Martin Heidegger. If 'one' accepts responsibility for one's life, if a person desires to be what he *is*, and to decide on his own

and yet it exercises a kind of compulsion. Man is not only one who can ask questions because he is subject; but he is one who *must* ask them—one who is constrained to do so because he does not yet know, and is not yet what he would be. Whether he will or not, in some way or other he must reach out beyond himself; he must transcend himself; he must measure his thinking, willing, and acting by something higher than himself. As the butterfly is attracted by the light, so irresistibly is he drawn by this 'higher' element, whether it be the 'truth' which he does not yet know, and by which he tests his thought, or by 'righteousness,' 'the good' or 'the beautiful,' 'the perfect' or 'the holy,' or even that which is 'truly human.' However he may explain this 'higher' element to himself, he cannot escape from it, and the disturbance which it causes is so intimately connected with his existence that without it the nerve of his existence as man would be cut, and he himself would sink to the sub-human level. Just as the tension of the bow-string makes the bow—apart from this it is merely a piece of wood—so it is this tension between him and this 'higher' element which constitutes the essential human quality in human existence, without which man would be only a particular kind of animal. Man is not merely what he is; he is the being which first seeks himself. All that man creates by his own works, which express his nature, is at the same time a manifestation of the fact that he seeks to understand himself.

Man is not at home with himself; as he is, he cannot come to terms with himself. He desires to be and to express himself as that which he is; yet at the same time he does not want to be what he is. Hence he conceals himself behind his ideals. He is ashamed of his naked existence as it is. He cannot tolerate it; he feels that in some way or other he must live for a future existence in order to endure his own view of himself. In some way or other he counts that 'higher' element

responsibility, then he is *eigentlich* (literally 'proper,' 'true,' 'real'). If, on the other hand, man allows himself to be concealed by conventional fictions about himself (idealistic, traditional, etc.), he does not accept responsibility for his own life, and is therefore *un-eigentlich*. On Heidegger's philosophy, see Werner Brock's *Contemporary German Philosophy* (Cambridge University Press, 1935).—*Translator.*

as his own, in order to be able to say 'yes' to himself, and yet he knows that this 'higher' element is not real. Thus—in a far deeper sense than in the dualism of body and soul—he is a divided being, and is always conscious of this division. The 'harmonious human nature' completely at rest within itself is an extreme instance which does not really exist, whereas the other extreme instance certainly does exist—that of the man who is so divided that his inner nature no longer finds any unity at all, the schizophrenic, the insane. The sense of division, however, owing to the contrast between that which he is and that which he ought to be or would like to be, forms part of the very essence of all human life known to us. We are all aware of this defect in the bell, and of the discords which it causes. Man is a contradictory creature in a threefold sense: he contains contradictions within his own nature, he knows that this is so and suffers accordingly, and, on account of this very contradiction, opposes himself to and vainly tries to free himself from this contradiction.

Or can it be that 'man with his conflict' is fortunately an exceptional instance? Is it true to say that 'man' as such exists at all? Is not that an unreal abstraction, and can it be that the illusion of the contradiction is created by the fact that in a quite unallowable way, which completely falsifies reality, the various qualities of the individual man, as we observe him, have been ascribed to a common denominator, in order that we may then exclaim: 'See, what a monster is man?' If this were so, then we should be dealing not with a contradiction but with *individual differentiation.* The one *genus humanum* is presented to us in a variety of species, sub-species, varieties and individuals, each uniform in itself, but impossible to reduce to a common denominator. How can we possibly speak of 'man' in view of the immense differences between the races and historical epochs—from the cave-dweller of the Stone Age to the Athenian of the days of Pericles, from St. Francis to the man of the age of ferro-concrete and of the wireless; in view of the differences which separate the civilized world of the East from that of the West; or again, in view of the fundamental differences which are brought out by the psychological study of types and of character? Does what we say about the old apply also to the young man, and what is true of man to woman as well? This at least is true, that to speak of man as a whole without taking these differences into account would mean that one was talking not of man as he actually is, but of an empty abstraction.

But the converse is also true. All these human beings are bound to one another not only by a very far-reaching common element in their physical and mental endowments, but also by that 'something' which makes man *man*, the 'mind' or the 'reason'; so that, in spite of all differences, they can speak with one another, work together, create and tend common goods and hand them down to succeeding generations. The term 'man' not only denotes a zoological species, but, in contradistinction from all names of zoological species, it also seems to denote an independent whole, something which is distinctive, in contrast to all that can be conceived from the biological point of view; that is to say, the *humanum*. Indeed, is it not a fact that it belongs to this common element—common, that is, to all human beings, but to them alone—continually to deny the reality of that *humanum* which distinguishes it from all other creatures? Is it not part of the picture of man that he is the being who can deny his nature, his human existence, and continually turn into his opposite, the inhuman? Is it not in this *humanum* itself that the cause of the conflict from which man suffers resides? Is it not a fact that the mind, the very element which teaches human beings to understand one another, is also the main cause of their being brought into conflict with one another? Indeed, is it not true that the more we learn to understand man the more we see that it is impossible to understand him?

Then perhaps, though for a different reason, we are not justified in speaking of 'man' in general. When we do so, we think involuntarily of the individual human being, even if at the same time we also think of the common element present in all. May it be, after all, for this reason, that 'man' is an abstraction, since he cannot in any way be understood as an individual? Possibly what leads us astray in the line of thought which starts with the contrast between the subject and the object is this: that it isolates the individual human being as though it were something which could be understood as an independent entity, whereas man in his concrete actuality not only does not occur as an individual, or cannot exist physically, but precisely in his peculiar existence as human can only be conceived and understood in his relation to the other. The decisive, distinctive element is not the 'I' which confronts the object, the 'It,' but the 'I' which confronts the 'Thou'—or rather does not confront the 'Thou,' but in its very existence as an 'I' is also determined by the 'Thou.' However unfamiliar this view of human nature may be, may it not be the correct view? Has it not always been familiar in some way or other to non-reflective thought—to thought which has not been corrupted by the abstractions of philosophy?[1]

The fact that man is a *zoon politikon*, a social being, was already taught by Aristotle in a decisive passage.[2] The fact that the individual can only be understood in the context of a larger whole was indeed, although in an entirely opposite way, brought afresh to our consciousness by Darwin and Hegel; the former, by treating seriously the idea of the *zoon*, and the latter, by dealing seriously with the idea of the *politikon*: the individual human being a dependent member in the series of his species, and further in the series of living creatures in general; the individual man a more or less unimportant point of transition in the universal history of Spirit, which attains its highest point in the State. In both views the individual is understood as a collective being, as a dependen part of a larger whole.

But the idea that the 'I' can only be understood in the light of the 'Thou' means something quite different. It is not the member of a species, not the *zoon*, and not man as the more or less indifferent transitional point in the history of civilization and of Spirit, the spirit-being, which knows the 'Thou,' but solely the human being who, in the 'Thou' of the 'Other,' comes to realize that his being a Self means his being a person, which

[1] The 'thou' as the theme of anthropology and philosophy dates from Kierkegaard's philosophy of existence, though in the narrower sense only since Buber and Ebner (in spite of appearances to the contrary, Feuerbach cannot be mentioned in this connexion). On this cf. Cullberg, *Das Du und die Wirklichkeit* (Uppsala, 1933).

[2] Aristotle's *Politics*, 1253a.

is not subordinated to any higher 'something,' but is itself the ultimate meaning—that which alone gives to every mental object, to all culture and civilization, and to all life in political communities, its meaning and its right. By this we do not mean merely Goethe's conception that 'the highest happiness of earth's children is in personality alone'; for this saying again suggests that the individual is the ultimate and final point of reference. What is meant is the person, which only arises and exists in inseparable union with the 'Thou' of the 'Other' as 'I-Myself.' Just as man, as the subject of all science, stands over against all objects of knowledge, and cannot be included among them as a member of a series, so man as person stands over against all his intellectual objects, his science, his art, his civilization, his political life, as their source, the one who gives them meaning, and their measure, and is neither incorporated with nor subordinated to them. Man does not exist for the sake of culture or civilization, he is not a means to an end, but he is an end for himself, precisely because, and in so far as, he, as person, is a self which is related to and bound up with a 'Thou.' A new depth of human existence and of the riddle of man has disclosed itself to our gaze. Can it be that this is ultimate and final?

Man is part of this world; he is a physical body, a conglomeration of chemical compounds, a *zoon* with a vegetative and sensory-motor system; he is a species of the great order of mammals. He is also the *homo faber*, the maker of tools—and what a monstrous tool he has created for himself in modern technique! He is, however, also the *humanus*, that is, the being who not only makes signs, but can and does speak; the being who not only maintains his own physical existence, but creates and shapes culture and civilization. As this individual human being, he is an individuality which cannot be compared with any other. Hence, in spite of all human resemblances, and in spite of his power to communicate with others through the medium of speech, in the depths of his being he is incomprehensible to every other human being. He is the person who only becomes an 'I-Self' in union with the 'Thou.' And he is also the little creature who is for ever seeking himself, and therefore also fleeing from himself; one who is for ever being drawn and attracted by something higher, and yet is ever seeking to release himself from this higher element; the creature who is both aware of his contradiction and yet at the same time denies it; a creature so great and again so pitifully small that he can measure the universe and yet can be attacked by a bacillus and die. Man is a spirit which dreams of 'eternity' and creates 'eternal' works—and then the loss of a little thyroid gland makes him an idiot. Man is all this. Is this all?

There is one final depth in man which we have hitherto ignored. Man has gods, and he renders them homage. He has *religion.* Whatever may be said of the dividing-line between him and the other living creatures known to us, this at any rate is his special preserve; it has been characteristic of him from his earliest beginnings, and seems to be an inseparable part of his existence. Whether he adored his totem animal or the gods of the sun, the moon and the stars; whether by the practice of magic he tries to gain control of supernatural forces; whether by the practices of asceticism and of Yoga he achieves union with the 'Wholly-Other'; or whether in union with his fellow-countrymen he brings a solemn sacrifice to the high gods, or somewhere in solitude he approaches the Ground of all being in mystical contemplation; one thing remains the same, namely, that just as man is *homo faber*, so also he is *homo religiosus.* He is this even when he renounces all mythology, all ideas of a supernatural being, and becomes an agnostic or an atheist. The dimension of the infinite, of the absolute, of the unconditioned, is not empty for any human being, even when he has cut himself adrift from all traditional religious ideas. If he no longer has any personal gods, all the more surely he has one or more impersonal gods[1]—something which he regards as taboo, something which may not be touched at any cost, whether it be his Communism or his Nationalism, his civilization or 'life.' 'Man always has God or an idol.'[2] He can no more rid himself of this dimension of his existence than he can rid himself of the dimensions of time: past, present, and future. Just as little as he can get rid of his past by ceasing

[1] Cf. Th. Spoerri, *Die Götter des Abendlandes.*

[2] "Der Mensch hat immer Gott oder Abgott," Luther.

to take it into account, can he get rid of his relation to God by denying it. And just as little as he can get rid of anxiety about the future by shutting his eyes to it, can he escape from the unrest of the unconditioned and the longing for perfection by renouncing 'religious mythology.' This too belongs to the nature of man, and he has as little power over it as he has over the fact of his existence. He can 'do away with himself'—but can he? Is this so certain? Anyone who has tried to do this has always begun to wonder whether it was so simple, after all, to evade the riddle of man and the torment of his existence. The dimension of eternity remains, never unoccupied, even if only by the sense of insecurity and the anxiety which accompanies it. Even the extreme instance confirms the truth that this ultimate depth which calls everything else in question, and possibly constitutes the ground of everything, forms an integral part of human existence.

And now, what is man? In view of the wealth, the variety, and the obscurity of the problems upon which we have touched in our rapid survey, is there any possibility of solving the riddle of man? Is anyone able to demonstrate the point from which multiplicity can be reduced to a unity, and presented as an intelligible whole? Attempts to do this have never been lacking. Aristotle must have been the first to undertake to bring together all the particular knowledge of man into a systematic order, and to present from one central point of view an interpretation of man. His attempt has had an incalculable influence upon the whole of Western thought. The Aristotelian anthropology has been part of the supporting structure of European history. This immense influence should not be regarded as due to an unusual depth of thought, but to the fact that in him—in a way which has never been repeated—philosophical, scientific and psychological thought was combined with the non-reflective knowledge and understanding of the ordinary, non-philosophical and non-scientific human being. It is, of course, also true that he owes a great deal of his enormous influence to the fact that behind him stood the greatest thinker the world had known up to that time—Plato, his master and teacher. But neither Plato nor Aristotle mastered the problem of man. Although even to-day no one who wishes to deal seriously with this question can afford to ignore them, yet no one can take his stand on the views of either of them. Two thousand years of history are no small matter, even—and particularly so—for thought about man. The man of the twentieth century not only knows other things about man; he himself, too, is different, not finally because he knows, or thinks he knows, fresh things about himself. It is characteristic, if not of our own day, at least of the period which immediately preceded it, that 'anthropology' had become a branch of natural science, and that a book with the title 'Man' was as a rule either a scientific or a medical book. In the nineteenth century, humanity tried once more, and with more material than at any previous time, to solve the riddle of man from the point of view of objective research. The effort has not been without result; an immense amount of material about man —I might almost have said, of incriminating material against man—has been collected, and to some extent sifted. But the main result must still be regarded as this, that the decisive questions of human existence are not even perceived by objective scientific research; still less does it contribute anything to their solution. By anthropology, then, to-day, men begin to understand something which, at any rate in general outline and in its main features, far more resembles the attempt of an Aristotle or a Plato than of a Darwin.

But between the extremes of a purely materialistic and a purely spiritual, a purely individualistic and a purely collectivistic, a purely positivistic and a purely religious or theological way of looking at the subject, there lie also to-day all the hundred and one different possibilities of method and combination which have emerged in the history of the past two thousand years, after it has been proved that the problem cannot be solved from the point of view of objective scientific research, in spite of all the resources of scientific method. Naturalistic anthropology is to-day one among several others, and, if I am not mistaken, it is no longer the predominating one. At the present time, therefore, we seem to be as far as ever from being able to give a clear answer to the question: What is Man?

And yet we *ought* to have an answer. We are not concerned

with science and its achievements. We are concerned with ourselves. We are concerned with our life. How can man live if he does not know what his life means? And how can he understand what his life means if he does not know what he, man, is? The question of man is not one which can be pushed aside at will, like that concerning the character of a species of animal or of a spiral mist. Knowledge of oneself forms part of human existence; but human existence is not something optional, which one can take or leave at will, it is the one thing which is not optional but obligatory. It will be worth while to devote some thought to this problem.

CHAPTER II

MAN'S OWN VIEW OF HIS SIGNIFICANCE

THERE exists, at least apparently, a certain kind of human life which asks no questions; a human existence which, at least apparently, knows nothing about itself, and has no desire to know—that non-reflective existence which Goethe, for instance, admired and envied so much in the poetry of Homer, and which is such a favourite subject to-day with poets who are weary of civilization. Yet even the 'Homeric' man, and he particularly, does not lack a quite definite, clearly defined anthropology; he believes that he knows what genuine human existence is. The question lies behind him; he has found an answer, and he is expressing it in his life.[1] The naïve human being is not distinguished from the reflective human being by the fact that he neither knows nor cares about human existence, but by the fact that he regards his knowledge of human existence as settled. In this sense alone is there an existence which does not raise questions. Above all, however, there is a longing for such existence; it is there as a postulate, as the romantic idealization of some kind of primitive existence. The man who is weary of his intellectuality and his culture, the man who is weary of activity, longs for the repose of 'simple existence'; the man who is tormented by the unrest of questioning dreams of immediacy. But to know oneself is always reflection, 'turning in upon one's self'; therefore we must do away with self-knowledge. Reflection is unhealthy; the healthy human being does not reflect, he lives. He does not let his left hand know what his right hand is doing; he is man, without knowing or asking any questions about himself.

The reasons for this longing, as we shall see in a moment, are not superficial, nor are they merely a sign of weariness; but this does not alter the fact that this longing produces a deceptive picture. The human being who knows nothing about his human existence, and does not inquire into it, is not a human being; this existence freed from all questioning is not

[1] Cf. Nägelsbach, *Homerische Theologie*; Rohde, *Psyche*; W. Jäger, *Paideia.*

human but animal existence, and those who consider this to be the correct view would do well not to write clever books about 'the mind as the enemy of the soul.'[1] For who will believe that it is possible to find the way back to this unquestioning kind of existence simply by reading books?

Knowledge of human existence and the desire to have this knowledge is indissolubly connected with the nature of will. The fact that 'I will this or that' cannot possibly be separated from the fact that 'I am this or that' and 'I will be this or that.' My understanding of myself is reflected in my will. Self-understanding and self-determination are two aspects of one original fact; willing and doing are always at the same time a demonstration and an exposition of one's understanding of oneself, whether this understanding be genuine or sham. The purposes and ends which determine my practical attitude are not only related to one another, either secretly or openly, but they are also connected with the picture which I make to myself of the right or happy or true or good 'life'; and this always means, of human life. Even a human being who one day decides that he will take no more trouble about questions of human existence does this upon the basis of a picture—although this may be unconscious—of the right life; and what he henceforth does or 'lives' is, so far as he does not sink to the unquestioning level of the animals, still, and continually, determined by that secret connexion.

This connexion of thought is, however, only one of the component parts which determine our actual existence. Man is not absolutely what he wills and what he loves—as Fichte thinks he is—he is also that which he does not will to be and that which he does not love; he is also something 'accidental,' through birth and destiny, through the play of obscure forces, often borne with reluctance, of the surrounding reality which influences him. But that element of deliberate volition which determines the ends and purposes for which man lives is never absent from human life, and it is this which gives to our life its distinctiveness and its specifically human character. There is a system of our ends and purposes which cannot be evaded.

[1] An allusion to the chief work of Ludwig Klages, *Der Geist als Widersacher der Seele* (in three vols.).—*Translator.*

I will this or that, because I will that particular thing, and I will it because I will something still more fundamentally different. I may give to this final basis any name—happiness, meaning, value, divine destiny, whatever I choose—yet in so doing I have not yet expressed that controlling content of my purposes which determines my will and my action. This content, however, comes from that which I regard as the truly human, or happy, or divinely destined, or significant life, that is, human life, even though this 'thought' may be quite in the background and largely unconscious—something which is rather 'felt' or pictured than a clearly formulated idea.[1]

Still another point should be noted. If, having become aware of this inward system of practical active life, of this hierarchical order of ends and purposes, we name the highest point in this hierarchy which determines all the rest, the dominant, we must not be led into thinking that the conscious, so to speak official, dominant must be the actual one. There are human beings with an elaborate system of conscious aims which they acknowledge and even proclaim as 'official,' with a very ideal ultimate end or dominant, who in their actual life do not live in the very least in accordance with these proclaimed ends and purposes—perhaps without being altogether conscious of the inconsistency. This does not prevent their having a certain secret but nevertheless close inner connexion, but it is of a quite different kind, because it is dominated by another 'unofficial' dominant. Karl Marx's view of history, his theory of ideologies, and his systems of values which are not in the least in harmony with them, are based upon the proof of this dualism. With exactly opposite methods, the psychological background of Nietzsche does the same; this is the method he employs in order to try to get to the bottom of the 'official' lies of human history. But Marx as well as Nietzsche cannot help regarding the actual behaviour of human beings, not, it is true, from the point of view of the 'official' values, but from that of one which is equally ordered in a hierarchical manner, and ultimately ends in a definite view of man. Here, therefore, we may leave this distinction between the 'official' and the

[1] Cf. my book *Das Gebot und die Ordnungen* (English translation: 'The Divine Imperative'), Chap. I.

'unofficial' system of values, and the self-understanding of man, since all we are aiming at here is to prove the presence of some such system as a presupposition and an impelling force in human life and action. Human life is always—not exclusively but also, and essentially—determined by this system of values, which again is rooted in man's view of himself.

Indeed, how could it be otherwise? For our loving and our hating, our desires and our fears, our longings and our detestations, do not constitute a fortuitous bundle of instincts, but—so far as they are human at all—they all flow from one source. Man wills 'something as a whole,' and he determines the details of his life in accordance with this purpose. Even in the extreme instance of the man or woman who drifts through life, at least a trace of this can be found; that is, in the constancy of this determination to drift, which is rightly, if paradoxically, described with an active verb, 'to let oneself drift.' An animal does not let himself drift; he cannot do so, for in him the presuppositions are lacking, namely, the possibility of not letting himself go, of acting according to any other logic than that of his instincts.

History shows us to how great an extent man's understanding of himself—even when conscious and explicit—actually influences and shapes society. Thus, the Stoic view of man influenced Roman law, and through that the whole development of law in Europe, right down to Rousseau's *Contrat Social* and the ideas of the French Revolution, and beyond that to modern Socialism and Communism.[1] Thus, too, the civilization of China is—or was—dominated by the classic ideals of filial piety and fraternal subordination created by the great teachers of antiquity, and, through the system of education which they brought into being, handed down from generation to generation. What a rigid form has been stamped upon Indian society, and indeed upon the life of India as a whole, by the religious doctrine of man standardized in the Code of Manu![2] Finally, how firmly the Christian view

[1] Troeltsch, *The Social Teaching of the Christian Churches*, I, 64–9; 150 ff.; IV, p. 726. Dilthey, *Ges. Schriften*, II, pp. 246–82.

[2] Cf., e.g., A. Geiger, *Die indoarische Gesellschaftsordnung*, 1935, and Max Weber's *Religionssoziologie*. vol. ii.

of man, in spite of all the forces ranged against it both inside and outside the Church, has been imprinted upon the peoples of Europe!

These are only a few examples which show how a definite view of human existence—whether it be empirical or ideal—is able to determine historical reality for thousands of years, and indeed has actually done so. The fact that alongside these 'official' views considerable influence is exercised by the 'unofficial' views of man proclaimed by Marx, Nietzsche and Freud, of man as determined by hunger, power and sex, does not contradict this statement, but is only another proof, along a different line, of the same truth, namely, that man's view of himself determines his life. I would, however, repeat that this truth must be modified by the following qualification: it determines his life along with the 'accidental' elements of his existence and his environment.

Every culture has its own special aspect, and behind this aspect its soul. It is possible that Spengler's assertion that religion is the soul of every civilization may be too strong; but it is impossible to refute his argument that every civilization possesses a relative, systematic unity, and that this unity is determined by its 'soul.' It would, however, be more correct to say that we find this 'soul' rather in man's view of himself than in religion. The culture of the Renaissance, for instance, certainly has its own clear characteristics, and the power by which this was shaped is its 'soul.' But who would claim that this was due to the religion of the Renaissance, and not rather to its 'feeling for life'—which means precisely man's view of himself—which gave it its dominant laws and its dominant aspect through all the varying forms of expression, in actual contrast to the religious forces which preceded and followed it?[1] Similarly, scarcely anyone will say that our machine age possesses its distinctive—though relative—essential unity in its religion, and not rather in man's particular understanding of himself as the *homo faber*, as the man of technique and of natural science. The fact, however, that man's view of himself may also be a religious and even an ecclesiastical or

[1] Cf. Jakob Burckhardt, *Die Kultur der Renaissance*, especially *Die Entdeckung des Menschen.*

theological one, is shown easily enough by the history of other epochs, such as the twelfth and the sixteenth centuries. At a second point, too, Spengler is right, namely, when he says that the vitality of that which is specifically human, the humanity-content of a civilization, is determined by its connexion with a living religious tradition. For every civilization, for every period in history, it is true to say: 'Show me what kind of a god you have, and I will tell you what kind of a humanity you possess.' A purely secular civilization will always lack this deeper kind of humanity; and the converse of this statement would be that the purest humanity is to be found where God, not man, is at the centre of all. The truth of this statement will be examined later on.

From some outstanding modern instances, we can see how largely a definite view of the nature of man is able to determine the practical reality of human life, both of the individual and of groups. They show us that the 'solution' of definite practical problems of a period—as, for instance, those of race, economics and sex—is always based upon definite views of the nature and the destiny of man. The fact that binds together the most influential thinkers of recent generations, those whose thought was capable of determining the thought not only of other thinkers, but also of the masses, and through them of determining the whole course of political development—Charles Darwin, Friedrich Nietzsche and Karl Marx—was this: that each of them gained power, directly or indirectly, over a considerable section of mankind by his view of man, by his 'anthropology.' Whether they were aware of it or not, it was not their scientific systems or their systems of philosophy which made history, but their view of man.

Darwin, if not the first, is still the most impressive of the thinkers who placed the life of man under biological categories. I am not speaking here of the importance of Darwin's work for natural science—no one questions that, whatever else they may think about the views of Darwin—but for us that is a matter of only indirect importance. It was not the origin of the species as a scientific theory of the genesis of the forms of life, but the inclusion of man in the biological process of evolution, and the explanation of human forms of life in terms of biological laws of growth, which made Darwin's theory a force in the life of our day. Man understands himself as a 'living being' in continuity with all other living beings, and the laws of his life are biological in character. This is an argument which even the ordinary man can understand, which appeals to something familiar to him, and justifies it. The theme itself is not new, but the general acceptance which it gained in an era of natural science, owing to its 'scientific' character, is certainly new. Those who popularized this theory found people willing and even eager to listen, both among the educated classes and among the people at large. The period of humanism was succeeded by the period of biology; the *humanum*—that which distinguishes man from all that is sub-human—disappears in the view that man is essentially an animal 'like all other living creatures.' One of the most practical conclusions drawn from this general thesis is the understanding of man from the standpoint of 'race.' The unity of the human race becomes doubtful, the varied types and values of particular races come to the fore and become a guiding principle in politics, especially in a political theory of civilization. The anthropology of Darwin, in the conclusions which he himself did not draw, became a main factor in political legislation and action.[1]

Nietzsche's picture of man, and its historical influence, is far more complicated. But whatever may be the elements of humanistic idealism and humanistic romanticism contained in his idea of man, here too the main element is naturalistic. That which became influential in the thought of Nietzsche was essentially his vitalistic dynamism, his theory of man as a creature governed by impulse and instinct. The justification for this theory is not scientific but philosophical, we might almost say prophetic. Nietzsche is aware of himself as one who proclaims a new man—namely, that man who gives first place not to the mind (or spirit) but to life itself, and indeed to a 'life' which is understood essentially as strength of impulse, sureness of instinct, and 'self-expression.'

[1] The following well-known book is typical: Günther, *Rassenkunde des deutschen Volkes*. Cf. the book of Hertwig, *Zur Abwehr des ethischen, des sozialen, des politischen Darwinismus*, which is still instructive.

Here, too, simplifications and transformations had to take place before useful slogans for the political conflict could be gained from the ideas of the over-cultivated and ultra-sensitive humanistic philosopher. But they were acquired, and they have made history. Both Italian Fascism and German National Socialism are unthinkable apart from Nietzsche. The direct influence of Nietzsche upon the thought of the Duce is well known; his influence upon the German Führer is less direct. National Socialism springs from a view of man which may be described as Vitalism, and among its chief creators Friedrich Nietzsche may be considered supreme, whether or not many of his views agree with those held in the Third Reich.[1]

The third and still more outstanding example is that of Karl Marx, as regards both the significance of his view of man as such, and its direct influence in the political sphere. Marxism is not primarily an economic or sociological theory; it is above all an anthropology, a definite attempt to define the nature of man. In spite of all the differences between Marxism and the views of Darwin and Nietzsche, the former has this at least in common with them: the refusal to admit any transcendental, metaphysical or religious basis for his view of man. It is not his political economy and his theories of value and capital, and the scientific arguments on which they are based, or even the proofs of the economic conception of history—the so-called 'historical materialism'—but the ideal of man and of society taught by Karl Marx which has created modern Socialism, and has made Marxism an historical force of the first rank.

This ideal of man and of society, which at the same time provides the standard for the criticism of bourgeois society, is itself a structure which cannot easily be understood or analysed. Various threads have here been interwoven: Jewish, Christian, Stoic rationalism as well as modern naturalism.

[1] The work of Nietzsche shows an increasing preponderance of the naturalistic over the classical-humanistic elements, while certainly the formal element, the prophetic consciousness and the imperative character of the doctrine of values, cannot be understood either from naturalism or from humanism, but only from the Biblical background. Nietzsche draws his strength and his nourishment from his opponent, Jesus Christ.

The ideas of human dignity and of justice, that of the identity of the idea of man and the ideal of society, and lastly the understanding of the historical nature of human existence, may be regarded as its main elements. But whatever may be its content or its origin, it is this idea of man which has roused the masses of the proletariat, and has welded them into a unity of desire and action which, at least in one of the great states of the world to-day, has achieved great political success. The actual impelling power of the proletarian revolution is faith in oneself, in the common man, in his ideas, his powers, and his rights. Karl Marx has made history, not as an academic economist, but as an anthropologist.[1]

A fourth illustration may be added which shows the effect of anthropology not so much in the sphere of political and public life as in that of private life and of custom—Sigmund Freud's theory of sex and of the unconscious. Here again what concerns us is not its medical and therapeutic aspect, nor its psychological and scientific aspect, but its significance as a general theory of man. Man is essentially sex-instinct—in the view of Adler, desire for power, in the view of Jung, *libido*, in a broader and more indefinite sense of the word—and is above all to be understood from the point of view of the unconscious.[2] The new scientific theory shows not only that this is so, but that it is meaningless and dangerous to play off any sense of obligation against this existence. This theory justifies man as a sex being, it gives him the right to understand himself primarily from the point of view of his sexuality. Here again, as in other instances, the simple thesis is embedded in a complicated system of scientific and in part also of philosophical arguments. It is not, however, these arguments which exert an influence, but the thesis itself, the view of man which is able to become a leading idea, and indeed has already to a very large extent become so. The sexualistic—in the broader sense the erotic—view of man is a force in the literature of to-day, both literature proper and merely popular

[1] Cf. *Orient und Okzident*, June 1936; *Die biblische Botschaft und Karl Marx*, by Lieb and Berdyaev. Also Allwohn, *Die marxistische Anthropologie und die christliche Verkündigung* in *Imago Dei*, published by Bornkamm, 1932.

[2] G. Adler, *Entdeckung der Seele*. From Freud and Adler to Jung, 1934.

writings, which to a large extent determines the practical life of man.[1]

Although these four thinkers are very different from one another, and although at many points their views and their methods of teaching may be opposed, yet they have three elements in common. Firstly, they show that it is through the interpretation of man that ideas make history. Secondly, they show that deliberately positivist or even atheistic views of man have done most to influence the thought of our day. Thirdly—and this should be added to what has gone before—they show that even these theories could only become factors in the formation of history when they themselves, in some way or another, became either a religion or a substitute for religion. To-day, as in pre-Christian days, there is once again a religion of blood, of power, and of sex. So long as the idea of man—of whatever kind—is not elevated to the plane of the absolute, of the unconditioned, it is not really able to shape history, and it remains more or less a private concern; it remains academic, and has little power to influence actual life. As we suggested in the previous chapter, this is how the matter stands: the dimension of the Absolute does not remain unoccupied, even when it has been deliberately cleansed from all religious mythology. The various views of man are distinguished from one another not by the fact that man posits an absolute when he tries to understand himself, but by what kind of an absolute he posits, and of what kind his relation to it is. Man has always either a god or an idol (*Gott oder Abgott*).

At the close of this brief survey, however, we must also remind ourselves of the fact that all these modern views of man, which we must describe primarily as positivist and atheistic, although they have brought pressure to bear upon the two main older traditions which have formed our civilization—those of Biblical Christianity and of Platonic Idealism—have by no means got rid of them. The individual and the social ethos is still nourished by their deep roots. No one has yet attempted to discover in any detail how much there is in our legal institutions and our social services, in our views of good

[1] Illustrative of this whole tendency: D. H. Lawrence for English literature, and (the later) Gerhard Hauptmann for German literature.

and evil, of what is and is not permitted, is noble and base, sacred and despicable, that gains its vitality from these sources. The question whether this element is diminishing or not is as a rule one rather of personal conviction than of proof. The new usually attracts more attention than the old. Here it is not our concern to try to weigh one against the other; all that we have tried to do is to remind ourselves that the Christian and the ancient humanistic views of man have as much right to exist, to-day as in other ages, as the new views of man.

CHAPTER III

THE VARIETY OF THE VIEWS OF MAN

We must know what man is; for in all that we do we answer, we are obliged to answer, the question of how we understand ourselves, our life. But where shall we find the right answer? An almost unlimited variety of views and theories opens up before us as we look. Which of them is the right one? Can it be possible that there is no right view, that there are only fragments, here a little and there a little, but nothing which binds all these individual perceptions into a unity? There is a good deal to be said for this opinion and it would be in harmony with a view of man which regards him not as a unity, but as composed of various elements which are co-ordinated but not united. Man is, indeed, an entity which belongs to the most varied spheres of existence: to the inorganic, vegetable, animal, psychical, spiritual, and perhaps to some transcendent sphere of reality. Can it be that from each of these standpoints there is a particular view which in itself is always correct, and yet can never be the only view, but must always be complemented by others? Why not? Why should we not let the experts in each of these spheres speak for themselves?

Man, a part of the physico-chemical world, subject to the law of gravity like everything else, is a portion of matter composed of hydrogen, carbon, nitrogen, phosphorus, calcium, and other elements. It will not do to regard this physico-chemical substratum as a mere trifle, as merely the outer shell within which the real human being lives. Not only does a little thyroid-gland secretion more or less determine the whole of a man's bodily existence; it also affects his psycho-spiritual existence as well. A blow upon the head—that is, a purely physical movement, the shifting of a molecule—may turn a genius into an idiot, and bring to an end the existence of the strongest man. It is not surprising that, from the days of Democritus until now, attempts have been made again and again to explain man as a whole from this point of view of his physical nature. This attempt is particularly active to-day as a result of our research into chromosomes and hormones. It is easy to understand that the physician, who every day observes the physico-chemical limitations of human life, and who finds that he must exert his influence almost exclusively at this point, constantly falls a prey to the temptation to ignore other aspects of man. It is indeed a temptation; if he seeks to understand the whole nature of man by studying the physico-chemical aspect only, he is chasing a will-o'-the-wisp, although it is quite true that this aspect should be studied.

Side by side with and above the materialistic theory there is the organic-zoological theory—that of man as an animal having a peculiarly complicated structure, in particular a highly differentiated central nervous system which gives him his biological superiority over the other species. The modern idea of evolution which has changed the rigid distinction of the species into a fluid *continuum* is supported by such a mass of observations and established facts that no one with insight can fail to be convinced by its arguments. Man, the final—perhaps from some points of view the highest—offshoot of the mammals? Why not? The fact that man has a soul, and that it is impossible to identify this 'soul,' without further consideration, with an organism, need not on that account be denied. Then has the animal, for instance, no soul? Are the instincts of man—even though the one-sided development of the brain and intellect may have weakened them—essentially different from those of the higher mammals? The ancient traditional view that the intellect forms the boundary between the animal and man can be held no longer. Even though the intellectual faculties of man may surpass a hundredfold the intellectual faculties of the animal, it is still impossible to fix a boundary-line; everywhere we see points at which continuity exists. Is it not particularly true that man to-day has no cause to elevate himself too high above his fellow-creatures, his own animal nature and bondage to his instincts being only too evident? The fact that man has even conceived himself recently as a degenerate animal may at least be noted as a sign of the times, nor must we overlook the grain of truth which exists even in this strange theory.

But in spite of all these attacks of modern naturalism, the view still exists, well established and not confuted, that man differs from the animal, not only in degree but in principle, by a 'something' which the animal lacks at all stages of his development—and in an unconditional sense, not merely to a certain degree; and that down to the present time no traces of this 'something' have ever been discovered in an animal—the reason or the mind, in the sense of the power to grasp ideas and to express them. 'Man alone, in so far as he is person, is able to rise above himself as an animal, and, from a centre beyond the world of time and space, to make everything—including himself—the object of his knowledge.' 'Thus man is the being which is superior to himself and to the world. . . . As such a being, he is also capable of irony and of humour, which always include an elevation above one's own existence.' 'The capacity for the separation between existence and nature constitutes the main sign of the human mind.' 'Man is able to separate "three-ness" as a number of three things from these things, and to operate with the number three as an independent object according to the inner law of production of the series of such objects. The animal can do nothing of this kind.'[1]

By means of his mind, his reason, man is able to create culture and civilization;[2] this is his *humanitas*—that which distinguishes him from all other living creatures, from all other *zoa*—his distinctive characteristic. The animal may have the rudiments of technique and civilization—that is, the artificial means of preserving life—but it never has the slightest beginning of culture. Man alone has science, that is, research for the sake of truth alone; he alone has art, that is, creation of beauty in form and colour, for the sake of beauty alone; he alone has religion, that is, worship and adoration for the sake of the Holy. Man alone has speech; the system of signs used by animals, wrongly called the language of animals, is—as William von Humboldt has shown us once for all[3]—something fundamentally

[1] Scheler, *Der Mensch im Kosmos*, pp. 57 ff.

[2] Ger. *Kultur*—practically untranslatable; but W. von Humboldt's definition may be quoted: 'Civilization (*Zivilisation*) is the humanizing of the nations in their external organization, and in the spirit and temper to which this is related; to this culture (*Kultur*) adds science and art.'—*Translator.*

[3] W. von Humboldt, *Sprachphilosophische Werke*, published by Steintal, p. 51.

different from human speech. For speech is formed precisely by that which the animal lacks—the general conception, the idea. This contrast is sharp; it is the direct line of division between the human and the sub-human. The animal remains connected with that which constitutes sense-existence, and his interest does not extend beyond his biological sphere of existence. Man, however, even when he makes no use of this capacity, is capable of going beyond this sphere through his mind, his reason. This capacity constitutes his humanity. This humanity, however, is the distinctively human element. Thus, whoever desires to speak of man must speak of his humanity, his capacity for culture, and his spiritual destiny.

Here, then, we reach the position which the philosophical doctrine of man, since its first splendid outline by Plato and Aristotle, has triumphantly maintained, in opposition to all attempts to understand man from the point of view of natural science or of psychology, from the levels of sense-existence and of that which can be experienced physically: the *humanistic idealistic understanding* of man. In the spirit a new dimension of existence is opened up: the truth that our life *here* is determined by a life *beyond*, that which is conditioned by that which is unconditioned, that which is accidental by a norm of necessity, the imperfect by the perfect, the changing by that which is eternally valid. In all that is specifically human there is this relation to a realm beyond, a transcendental realm—whether in the formal logical laws of thought, in the content of the idea of Truth, in the idea of Justice or of the Good, in the idea of Beauty, of that which is full of absolute meaning. Man is the bearer of ideas, the shaper of ideas; the actual *nature* of man, in contrast to his 'accidental' appearance, is the Idea itself.

From the first creative suggestion of Plato down to Leibniz, Kant, Fichte, Hegel, and their modern successors, the ways in which this one fundamental idea has been expressed have been most varied, and their influence within history has been immeasurable. But the creed of Idealism is always the same: essentially man is spirit, and therefore immortal, eternal, divine, in the deepest part of his nature. All that is mortal, perverted, meaningless, limited, is 'non-essential'; it is a kind of foreign addition, perhaps even a mere illusion. Although apparently in accordance with his empirical aspect, man may be un-free, as *homo noumenon* he belongs to a wholly different world, the world of freedom, eternity, and perfection. Indeed, from the Far East, where one comes to terms more easily with this tiresome irrational actuality than in the realistic West, this gospel is proclaimed still more boldly and completely; *Atman is Brahman*,[1] the spirit in us—the being-subject—is the same as the All-spirit; *tat tvam asi*, 'that'—namely, the All, the Deity, the One—'art thou,' the man who knows.[2]

This perception arises not only out of the intellectual labour of the philosophers, but also out of the contemplation of the mystics. He who in this contemplation severs himself from illusion, he who 'detaches' himself from the world, who sinks down into the inmost ground of the soul, or into 'ecstasy,' who in mystical rapture forsakes the prison of his bodily nature, he also experiences it thus. He beholds his unity with the principle of all existence and of all life, with changeless, eternal being; he knows no contradiction and no separation any longer between the One and the Self; he has reached the point where the Wholly Other and the 'I' are the same. This mysticism is tied neither to time nor place; whether India be its country of origin or not, it has found a home everywhere, in pre-Christian and Christian Europe as well as in Asia; it has its parallels in Africa and among the 'primitive' people of America. To-day it is the religion of the educated and the learned, just as it was three thousand years ago; it is combined to-day with the most recent modern psychology as in the days of the first yogis. And its varieties, as countless as those of Idealism, yet display one fundamental form of the view of man or of the soul.[3]

One variety we must not overlook, owing to its special influence in modern times and at the present day—the romantic view, which lies midway between the organological and the mystical views. Its starting-point and its fundamental principle is the 'soul,' as distinguished from the 'spirit.' This 'soul,' through the medium of the unconscious and psychical, is the formative power of the organism; it is that which makes it a

[1] Deussen, *Allgemeine Geschichte der Philosophie*, I, pp. 79 ff.
[2] Ibid., p. 37.
[3] Otto, *West-Östliche Mystik*; Lévy-Bruhl, *L'âme primitive.*

living whole. On the other hand, it is the mother-source from which springs the life of the spirit. But it is more original, deeper, more profound than the spirit. In the spirit arise contradictions, harsh opposition; in the soul, however, is the original totality and unity. Nature and Spirit, subject and object, reality and ideality, are one in the deepest experience of the soul, in that obscure darkness of the unconscious into which division has not yet entered, which only arises in the garish light of the spirit. Here in the realm of the unconscious and the psychical, the realm of the mothers, is the origin of all genius as well as of all creative dreams. Here in the fiery centre all is still fluid, which on the surface forms into solid shapes. Here the truth has not yet been solidified into sharp masculine conceptions, but everything is still maternally soft, in symbols, intuitions and emotional awareness. Here in the deep centre, in this seeing, this awareness, this feeling, we are close to the primal reality, to that existence and life which has no contradictions, which has not yet been differentiated, the 'immediate.'[1] Hence the soul and not the spirit is the true centre of man, in such a way, however, that the contrast between man and nature, the arrogant elevation of the son above the mother, is regarded as the primal sin. It will not be necessary for me to produce documentary historical evidence for this view from the mother cults of the ancient world down to the romantics of last century[2]—down to the 'Psyche' of Carus, and the *Kosmogonische Eros* of Klages, and the metaphysical psychology of Jung. All I wish to do at this point is to describe briefly a typical and important interpretation of the riddle of man.

Nor must we forget the 'wisdom of the man in the street.' Even the simple man, who is neither a scientist nor a philosopher nor a mystic, has his own view of man. There is an anthropology of the *sensus communis*, difficult as it is to discover it among all the historical *débris* of the various religions. It lives in the wisdom literature of the various nations, and reveals in it its *sensus*, its meaning, as well as its *communis*, its universal expansion. But we can only speak of it with extreme caution, for at every step we perceive definite and distinctive historical opinions which are

[1] H. Kutter, *Das Unmittelbare.*
[2] Cf. Baeumler's *Introduction to Bachofen's Works.*

now regarded simply as 'common sense.' To-day we no longer believe in those *notiones communes* in the sense in which Cicero used the words—which were the basis of the whole of the medieval and modern anthropology until modern historical research swept it away. And still this characteristic wisdom of the man in the street, which Oetinger loved so dearly and described so beautifully, does exist. What does *it* say about man?[1]

First, it says everything in an un-academic way; it makes no appeal to 'principles.' Quite deliberately it does not attempt to go too deeply into these problems. It knows that man is body, soul, and spirit, and that he is both an independent individual, with his own responsibility, and a being who is bound to the community and intended for community. It is aware of man's freedom and also of man's bondage; of the higher element in man and of his pitiful need; of the unity of his personality and of the contradiction which it contains. Further, it is aware of man's eternal destiny, and yet also that man dies, and that all his life is in some way determined by the fact of death, and tends towards death. It is aware of the necessity of becoming conscious, but also of the dangers which this involves, and of the power of the unconscious. It is aware of the peculiar character of each individual, and also of the common element which binds all individuals together. This 'wisdom' knows all these things, but it cannot be grasped at any particular point. The more eagerly we try to seize it, the more elusive it becomes, this extraordinarily intelligent and reflective, and yet at the same time superficial and incomplete kind of knowledge. If we inquire into it too boldly and eagerly, it waves its hand and turns its back on the questioner—just like mother-wit, that keen, merry, profound, lighthearted thing.

Before and behind all scientific, philosophical and theological anthropology there lies this ordinary, universally human, naïve, pre-reflective understanding of man, very variously interwoven, concealed, enriched and distorted by those other views, and

[1] Oetinger, *Die Wahrheit des Sensus communis oder des allgemeinen Sinnes in den nach dem Grundtext erklärten Sprüchen und Prediger Salomo*. Also A. Auberlen, *Die Theosophie F. C. Oetingers*.

yet independent of them.[1] All that the poets and artists tell us about man usually comes from this source. It is possible that genius consists mainly in a specially high degree of such naïveté, which is able to maintain itself against all that is conventional, against all *clichés*, against all the established forms which have been set up by tradition. But wherever a poet or a thinker in a special degree probes into the depths, there, to the extent in which he moves away from this *sensus communis*, he comes under the influence of a scientific, philosophical, or definitely religious anthropology which both enriches and distorts, deepens and injures his view of man. As naïveté disappears the 'isms' become powerful—Realism, Idealism, Pantheism, each of which makes one element of human nature the principle of interpretation, and in so doing possibly brings to light truths which are not accessible to the others, but at the price of a one-sidedness which distorts the picture of man. There seems to be only one exception to this rule. Where the poetic naïveté of this view of human nature has been combined with the Christian faith, there has arisen—for instance, in Pascal, Kierkegaard, Dostoevsky, Gotthelf—a penetrating view of man which has no rival. That which the non-reflective simple human being, whose highest point is attained in the genuine poet, knows about man seems to be fulfilled in the Christian faith alone. This, however, means that we have already entered the sphere of religion.

Every religion has its own view of man, which springs out of its own nature—the Homeric as well as the Egyptian, the Iranian as well as the Vedic or Hindu, the Jewish or the Mohammedan. Each of these religious anthropologies is based upon the view of *common sense*—which, as we have already seen, must be regarded as something very indefinite—but it deepens or broadens or transforms it in a way that springs out of the fundamental nature of the religion in question, often leading

[1] The ontology of Heidegger is very largely a philosophical interpretation of 'ordinary' human existence, the non-philosopher's view of himself expounded in philosophical terms. In it there are interwoven elements of Fichte's philosophy (*Eigentlichkeit*), Neo-Platonist mysticism (*das Nichts*), and of Christian thought (guilt, conscience, death); these form a unity which is more impressive than inwardly articulated. The really important element in Heidegger is his respect for 'simple' human existence, which he has learned from Kierkegaard.

to caricatures, to strange and curious structures which are scarcely intelligible, but also often in a way which cannot fail to make a deep impression upon us.[1]

In spite of the infinite variety of the views of man, it is possible to distinguish certain directions in which the doctrine of man experiences a further development in religion. Man, in some way or another, is a dependent being, conditioned by those higher powers which he adores. In so far as they are the guardians of the sacred law of life, he is responsible to them, and must give an account of himself to them. Through the gods, or through the Divine Being, the individual human being is in some way united with his people or his tribe; but in his relation to the divinity he also experiences a heightening of his own value and an intensification of his own nature. It is in the sphere of religion, not in that of philosophy, that the view of the immortality of the soul, of a transcendent reward, of a higher world for which man is destined, arises. All these statements must, however, be qualified by the observation that scarcely one of them is acknowledged in *all* religions. At this point it becomes very clear that the idea of the Enlightenment—the idea that behind all historical religions there lies a 'natural religion' or the 'essence of religion'—is untenable. The Enlightenment doctrine of 'natural religion' is a misunderstanding which has arisen out of the age-long union, beginning in the early days of Christianity, between Christianity and the ancient humanism of the philosophy of religion, in which both these unique historical forces were welded into a more or less artificial unity.[2]

In spite of its apparent similarity to the religious philosophical humanism of the ancient world handed on to us, for instance, by Cicero, the Christian doctrine of man, as far as both its content and its origin are concerned, is completely unconnected with it, unless we regard as an affinity the fact that it goes beyond that which is obvious to everyone. But to class both

[1] Cf. Stratton, *Psychology of the Religious Life*, a book which provides a valuable comparative religious anthropology from, unfortunately, rather a dull and formal psychological point of view. Cf. also the anthropological sections of the comparative *Phänomenologie der Religion* by van der Leeuw.

[2] Cf. Scheler, *Mensch und Geschichte*, 1928.

together as a unity, as Scheler does in 'the classic theory,'[1] can only succeed in the hands of one who looks at the whole subject from such a distance that even the most obvious contradictions have become blurred and indistinct.

* * * * *

The first thing that must be said of the Christian doctrine of man is that it is not a 'theory' or a *philosophumenon*, but a *statement of faith*. Thus even the expression 'doctrine' is misleading, or at least it needs some explicit qualification. It is the essential element in the Christian faith—and it is this which distinguishes it from all religions, as well as from all mysticism, philosophy, and science—that its statements do not spring from a process of analysis or meditation or reflection upon existence, but from their relation to an historical event, in which it itself, as one element, participates, and in so doing itself becomes historical. One is tempted to contrast the Christian faith as a metaphysic of history with the non-historical philosophies or religions—that is, with those which have no essential relation to the historical. But again, to do so would be to miss the whole point and distinctive character of the Christian statement. For every metaphysic must, as the great example of Hegel shows us, derive the historical from a super-historical which, as such, is accessible to thought; whereas the Christian faith, while it derives, it is true, the historical from a super-historical—namely, the eternal will and counsel of God—goes back to a super-historical which only makes itself known within history. Every attempt to derive the historical to which the Christian faith is related from a system of timeless truths and a system of truths which is independent of the historical—as was done by all the great German Idealists—falsifies its substance. The principle of Fichte that it is only the metaphysical, and not the historical, which saves us, is diammetrically opposed to the fundamental creed of Christianity: 'Grace and truth came by Jesus Christ . . . No man hath seen God at any time; the only Begotten Son, which is in the bosom of the Father, He hath declared Him.'[2] This, which would make every good Platonist's

[1] Cf. Scheler, *Der Mensch im Kosmos*, p. 73.

[2] John i. 17, 18, R. V.

hair stand on end, is the central article in the Christian theory of knowledge.

This statement, however—in order to make it quite clear that it is not a 'theory'—needs to be supplemented by another. 'But we received, not the spirit of the world, but the spirit which is of God; that we might know the things that are freely given to us by God.'[1] This knowledge, which is given to us by the Spirit of God, of that which has been historically revealed by God, is called in the New Testament 'faith,' or, to put it more exactly, the 'obedience of faith,'[2] the decision of faith. Faith is not a neutral, objective, intellectual or even ecstatic or intuitive view; faith is the act of obedience, of decision, in face of the historical revelation. But just as the Christian faith is not related to the historical in general, but has to do with a definite point in history—namely, with the historical in which the truly super-historical is revealed—so also the decision in which faith consists is not any decision, but *that* decision in which man completely surrenders to the Divine Will which is disclosed to him in that historical. In this decision is fulfilled the new understanding of human existence; in this self-surrender man experiences the meaning of his existence. Thus we see how little we have to do here with an anthropological theory. What matters here is the meaning of human existence, which can only be perceived and acquired at the price of the surrender of self to the will of God.

In the Christian doctrine of man we are concerned with the true knowledge of responsible existence. One who has understood the nature of responsibility has understood the nature of man. Responsibility is not an attribute, it is the 'substance' of human existence. It contains everything: freedom and bondage, the independence of the individual and our relation to one another and the fact of community, our relation to God, to our fellow-creatures and to the world, that which distinguishes man from all other creatures, and that which binds him to all other creatures. Thus even the knowledge of responsibility is that which makes every human being a real human being—although otherwise he may be and think or believe, what he wills—thus it is the absolutely universal human element. Yet responsibility

[1] 1 Cor. ii. 12. [2] Rom. i. 5.

is at the same time that which no man rightly knows, unless he holds the Christian faith.

It is, of course, true that every human being is aware of responsibility; if this were not so, he would be either a god or a devil. 'Christ and the Devil have no conscience.' The consciousness of sacred obligation is indestructible; it outlasts all destructive developments of human thought. Even the atheist or the cynic is aware of it, although he may deny it in his theory; it is not wise to charge him with irresponsibility. The boundary of the knowledge of responsibility coincides with the boundary of human existence; if a human being had lost all sense of responsibility, he would have ceased to be a human being. But the converse is equally true: that the basis, depth, and ultimate meaning of responsibility are concealed from man until they are revealed to him through the Christian faith. Ignorance of the real significance of responsibility is inseparably connected with not being responsible. Here existence and perception are indistinguishable. Man is not fully aware of responsibility because he does not live in a truly responsible manner. He lives in that irresponsibility and in that misunderstanding of responsibility which the Bible calls 'sin' and 'life under the law.' The moral consciousness is still far from being a knowledge of the meaning of responsibility. On the contrary, there is no clearer proof of the fact that man does not fully know what responsibility is than the moral. The moral is the substitute for the loss of responsibility, in the meaning both of existence and of knowledge. The moral is the misunderstanding of responsibility which arises when the meaning of responsibility has been lost, and when one does not live in a truly responsible manner. True responsibility is the same as true humanity; the moral, however, which would preserve the human character of existence by setting up dykes to check the inrush of the flood of the sub-human, actually has something inhuman about it. The existence of the moral behind these dykes is the human life which has already lost its truly human character; human existence, that is, which has lost the knowledge of its origin and of its meaning

It is the Christian faith—or rather it is the Divine revelation in history—which once again discloses to us the meaning of responsibility, and with it restores to us true humanity. It reveals to us the meaning and origin, the nature and the content of human existence as responsibility, by unveiling to us the origin of man in the Divine Word; the answer to the Divine Word, the possibility and the necessity of this answer as the meaning of life—that is, genuine responsibility, and at the same time genuine humanity. We have lost this Word, in which, from which, and for which we have been created; we have become alienated from it. No Platonist *anamnesis*, no mystical or philosophical contemplation, can give it back to us again. Genuine humanity has been taken away from our life. A sinister inhumanity clouds all life. We have forgotten who we are, and no remembrance of an absolute obligation brings us back to our lost origin; all obligation simply intensifies the gulf which lies between us and our origin in the Word of God. Responsibility and love, which were formerly a unity, have been turned into a contradiction. The way to man's original destiny has been blocked—from the point of view of knowledge as well as from that of existence.

Then, however, the way is re-opened, both in knowledge and in existence. Faith as the renewed knowledge of man's lost origin through the re-establishment of the beginning in the centre of history, is both existence and knowledge. It is a new understanding of our nature as man, and a new life. It means that man, who had been separated from his origin, has been re-united, both in knowledge and in love.

The Christian faith is so utterly simple; it is nothing less than the renewed understanding of the meaning of responsibility. But in order that this 'simple' thing should take place, the most tremendous events had to happen. God had to become man, in order to restore to man his original existence and knowledge, his responsibility. We can express the whole meaning of the truth of the Christian revelation with the one word *love*. But in order to define this word for ourselves so that its inmost content be revealed, it was necessary to have all the miracle of the history of salvation. All that matters really is this: 'We love, because He first loved us.'[1] But only one who has been reconciled to God by Jesus Christ knows what this means, and only to

[1] 1 John iv. 19.

him can this demand be made with any meaning. All that matters is something excessively simple—responsibility; but this extremely simple thing is the same as the revelation of the Triune God. Responsibility is existence in the Word of God as an existence which is derived from and destined for the Word of God. If any human being were ever to respond to God in harmony with His Word, and upon the basis of His Word, in believing love, he would be truly human. He would know what human existence means, and he alone would express and represent this knowledge in his life. In this human being the riddle of humanity would be solved, both in theory and in practice. All other attempts to solve the riddle of man are only fragments of meaning, broken and distorted parts of the whole, which cannot be fitted together again because they are distorted. They are all significant, because they reveal traces of the Divine Origin, of the Divine Purpose; but they are useless as solutions. Hence it would be futile to add one more attempt to the thousand efforts which have already been made. Our aim in this book is entirely different. It is this: to show, as clearly as possible, the Divine solution of this problem.

MAIN SECTION I

FOUNDATIONS

CHAPTER IV

THE PRESUPPOSITIONS OF THE CHRISTIAN DOCTRINE OF MAN

(*a*) THE WORD OF GOD AS THE SOURCE OF KNOWLEDGE

1. KNOWLEDGE WITHOUT PRESUPPOSITIONS?

ONE of the most important chapters in Jakob Burckhardt's *Kultur der Renaissance* bears the pregnant title: 'The Discovery of Man.' In point of fact the men of the Renaissance, that is, the leading minds in the art, philosophy and science of that day, were filled with the proud consciousness that they had either discovered man, or that they were about to do so. It is true of course that even in the Middle Ages man was in the centre of thought, but the 'man' of that day was not man as he really is, but—so ran the agreed criticism of medieval anthropology—man as he was conceived, postulated, believed to be. His actuality was concealed under the speculations of metaphysical philosophy, the dogmas of the Church or the mythologies of the Bible. The thinkers of the Renaissance felt it incumbent upon them to clear away all this rubbish, just as they felt it incumbent upon them to set nature, in its reality, free from the trammels of the teaching of Aristotle and St. Thomas Aquinas. In both instances the programme was understood in the same sense: a knowledge of reality which was empirical, free from all presuppositions, non-metaphysical and non-theological.[1] The task begun then by a few thinkers was carried forward by others in the centuries which followed, and, with the aid of a vast scientific apparatus, the thinkers of the nineteenth century tried to complete it, the task, namely, of constructing an empirical anthropology and psychology, a direct, unambiguous knowledge of man as he actually is, based on a knowledge which is free from all presuppositions.

When we look back over the path that has been trodden for these past four hundred years, and when we weigh up the

[1] Cf. Dilthey, *Ges. Schriften*, II, especially *Die Funktion der Anthropologie in der Kultur des 16. und 17. Jahrhunderts*, pp. 416 ff.

result of these gigantic efforts, the comparison between that which has been attained and that which was expected is absolutely grotesque; at any rate, at the best it has a very sobering effect. While natural science moved forward from one revolutionary discovery to another, the knowledge of man—apart from that of his body as a part of nature as a whole—has not made progress in essentials, although it has done so at particular points. The psychological laboratories of our universities, which were opened fifty years ago with the highest expectations, and even twenty years ago were full of activity, are to-day deserted, and passers-by merely glance at them with gentle amusement. Why has the programme of a science free from all presuppositions, which in the one case revolutionized the world, not proved successful in the other? The answer is easy. Because neither in the one case nor in the other was there any real procedure apart from all presuppositions. In both cases men worked on the one and the same presupposition; only in the one instance it was suitable and in the other it was not. In both cases the presupposition which was really operative—although usually people were not aware of this—was that man, like nature, was accessible to the methods of objective-causal research. Modern anthropology was no more 'free from presuppositions' than the anthropology of the Middle Ages or of antiquity, only the actual presupposition was different: the parallelism between nature and man, the knowledge of nature and the knowledge of man, proved to be unsuitable for human nature, or at least applicable only to one 'part' of human nature. Where this presupposition was effective, that is, in so far as man is really part of the natural world, the anthropology of natural science has gained just as brilliant and amazing and indeed revolutionary results as in any other branch of natural science. Only this knowledge affected the *zoon homo sapiens* rather than the *humanus*, that is, it did not touch the essential element in human nature.

This perception, from the point of view of method, is of the highest significance. It shows that anthropology, even when it desires to be wholly disinterested, cannot be so; indeed, that then in particular it makes specially irrelevant presuppositions, which are remote from its subject. Man is *not* only a part of nature; indeed, essentially that is not what he is, and therefore this apparently impartial research, which in reality only applies the presupposition of natural science to this sphere, never touches the essential element in man or in human existence at all. All 'empirical' research is definitely limited when it touches man, for the following reasons: because, whether he is aware of it or not, man is always aspiring after something beyond himself, or perhaps it would be truer to say that he is 'apprehended' by a world beyond himself; because, further, man, in contradistinction from all 'other animals,' is the 'animal' who has ideas, who seeks Beauty, Truth, Goodness, Justice, or the Holy—or else he flees from them—because man has mind and conscience; and, finally, because man is aware of, or at least dreams of, the Infinite, the Perfect, the Absolute. The more that this fact is forgotten by anthropology the more meaningless and misleading will be its results.

Moreover, the empiricism of the period of the Renaissance and of the two succeeding centuries was not 'pure'; that is precisely why, at that time, people were able to see man afresh, and to say all sorts of new things about him. The concept of nature of that day, namely—especially when one spoke of human nature—included within itself such a wealth of determinations, that at the present time they would no longer be reckoned as belonging to 'nature' but either to 'spirit,' to the 'super-sensible,' or to the realm of 'metaphysics.' The idea of nature of those days—at least so far as man was concerned—was still a long way from the physics of Galileo; it was rather that of Stoic philosophy, that 'natural system' whose nature and significance for the whole modern world was first brought home to us by Wilhelm Dilthey.[1] Thus the anthropologists of those days, although they believed that they were working on purely empirical lines, were working

[1] W. Dilthey, op. cit., *Das natürliche System der Geisteswissenschaften im 17. Jahrhundert*, pp. 90–245. Cf. also B. Groethuysen, *Philosophische Anthropologie*, part ii, in the *Handbuch der Philosophie* of Baeumler and Schröter. Dilthey, like Troeltsch, tends to undervalue the influence of Christian ideas, because he is not aware that the Biblical conception of the orders of creation (cf. Matt. xix. 1–8) forms an analogy to the *lex naturae*, and is often concealed under Stoic terminology.

with a fundamental capital of supra-empirical presuppositions which had been bequeathed to them by Plato, Aristotle, Roman Stoicism and also by Christianity, which they calmly included in their 'conception of nature,' and thus in their 'freedom from all presuppositions.' This 'transcendental' element the anthropologists of that day, still supported by the tradition of the previous centuries, imported in a quite naïve way into that which already existed, that which empirically existed of human 'nature.' Thus their picture of man still remained impregnated with humanity. The sharp division, however, which the last two hundred years made between the causal world of nature and all non-causal spiritual existence and transcendence, makes it the more imperative for us to emphasize very clearly that all purely empirical views of man, in the sense of objective science, do not touch man himself, but only the framework of man. The problem is not whether man, in order to be understood, must be seen in the light of that realm beyond, but what this standpoint beyond himself is? The understanding of man always leads us—we may dispose of it as we will—either into the region of metaphysics or into that of faith; whether this metaphysic be that of materialism, idealism or of mystical pantheism, or whether this faith be the Christian faith or some other form of religion.

2. THE PRINCIPLE OF EMPIRICAL CRITICISM

Yet the empiricist reaction of the Renaissance against the dogma and the metaphysic of the Middle Ages contains an element of truth, which we ought not to lose, the principle of criticism in the light of experience. By this we mean that no statement about man, whatever its source, may contradict experience, and, on the other hand, that all that can be learned about man from experience ought to be included in any doctrine of man. This requirement was obviously contradicted by the anthropology of the Middle Ages, in spite of the depth of its knowledge. From the point of view of its theological presuppositions it set up postulates about man which could not be reconciled with the knowledge gained from experience, and up to the present time theological anthropology has done the same. The fact, however, that under the cover of 'impartial research' much materialistic metaphysic has been set before an unsuspecting public is equally true and unfortunate; but it does not in any way weaken the postulate of the criticism of experience which is quite formal, and is opposed to all that goes beyond the facts, even from the materialistic point of view. This principle also applies, to the fullest extent, to Christian anthropology, and the Christian doctrine of man should unhesitatingly adopt this principle as its own.

The Christian doctrine of man maintains that, although it understands man from the point of view of the truths of revelation, which are not accessible to experience, yet it does not in any way contradict what can be known of man in and through experience; on the contrary, it incorporates this knowledge gained by experience into its rightful context. The Christian doctrine of man itself requires that all its statements about man—so far as they have any connexion with actual experience at all—should be in harmony with man's 'natural' experimental knowledge, and should indeed absorb it.

At this point, as at all others, the Christian truth includes 'natural' knowledge; this means, all that man can know from observation and thought apart from faith. The Christian does not claim that he has a special brand of mathematics, physics or chemistry, zoology, botany or anatomy. Christian theology operates with the same formal logic as any other science, and in preaching or in teaching the Christian Church depends upon the validity of the psychological laws, like any other body which has something to teach or explain. The old theologians, even our Reformers, summed up this dualism in a simple formula: in secular matters—both in science and in practice—the reason is competent; in spiritual matters, faith.[1] This simple division of labour is useful as a starting-point, but —as we see in ethics, for instance—it contains great dangers. The relations between the 'natural' and the 'spiritual' sphere cannot be presented quite so simply.

[1] Lau, *Äusserliche Ordnung und weltlich Ding in Luthers Theologie*. Above all, Luther's Disputations, especially *De homine*, 1536, and the disputations about the graduation of *Palladius* and *Tilemann* in Drew's *Disputationen Dr. Martin Luthers*, pp. 90 ff., 110 ff.

There are problems of anthropology which belong equally to the 'natural' and the 'supernatural' spheres, that is, they belong both to the realm of scientific philosophy and to that of religion. Such problems are, for instance, those concerned with the human mind, the conscience, and free will. It is impossible to make a clear distinction between the spheres in which the different problems arise; for it is in these very questions that we can trace, all through the history of the development of Christian thought, the way in which both the Christian and religious view and the philosophical and rational view are intertwined; sometimes they run along parallel lines, at other times they are interwoven, while again they may sometimes be opposed to one another. No simple delimitation of spheres will do justice to this state of affairs. The only possible attitude is a dialectical one, which—if I may say so—takes into account, from the very outset, the theological nature of man.

It is of course self-evident that there is practically no conflict between mathematics and theology, between physics, chemistry and theology, because here the autonomy of the sciences, even from the point of view of the Christian faith, is almost complete; but the nearer we come to the personal centre of man the more the situation changes. We may reject the postulate of a 'Christian psychology,' if by 'psychology' we mean the doctrine of sensation and other elementary processes. But we shall recognize it immediately as a necessary and integral part of Christian theology as soon as it is understood to include the doctrine of the human soul as the bearer of personal life, as indeed the best Christian teachers of all ages have always done. The more we have to do with man as a personal whole, the more—from the Christian point of view—does the autonomy of the empirical-rational view decrease, and the more important and definite does the claim of Christian truth become. The point, however, at which both necessarily come into conflict, and where the question of priority necessarily arises, is the problem of responsibility. This too all the great Christian teachers—from Paul to Kierkegaard—have recognized. The natural knowledge is aware of a divine law, an obligation.

The perception of the Divine law as law, that is, the *cognitio legalis*, also belongs in principle, according to the most strict

Reformation view, to the realm of 'natural' knowledge.[1] No one is without some sense of responsibility, and there is no Christian missionary or spiritual adviser who does not make this sense of responsibility his point of contact. According to Kierkegaard the sense of 'guilt' belongs, in contradistinction to the knowledge of sin, to the sphere of immanence.

On the other hand, it is clear that the contact of the Christian message with the natural moral sense, with the knowledge of the law, is at the same time the most fundamental contradiction. Man's understanding of himself from the point of view of the law is opposed by man's understanding of himself from the point of view of grace; this takes place, however, in such a way that his knowledge of the law is not removed but is greatly heightened and intensified. This is the dialectic of the Christian knowledge of man, which is most intimately connected with the centre of the Christian truth as a whole, with the message of the Cross. Thus at this point the 'natural' truth and the 'religious' truth about human existence lie very close to one another; indeed, at some points they cross each other in this dialectic. The 'natural' knowledge of responsibility—of the law—is the point at which the rational and the religious self-knowledge of man come closest together and yet are farthest apart. The natural understanding of responsibility is, on the one hand, the source of 'natural' humanity, and at the same time—as we shall see more clearly later on—the place of the greatest contradiction between divine destiny and human self-will, just as the 'natural' knowledge of human freedom is at the same time the presupposition and the opposite of the Christian doctrine of freedom and un-freedom.[2] Why this is so, and how this should be understood in greater detail, will be the subject of the next chapter.

3. MAN VIEWED FROM 'ABOVE' HIS PRESENT EXISTENCE

The fact that man as a whole cannot be understood from himself, but that, in some way or another, in addition, he

[1] So Luther. See Seeberg, *Lehrbuch der Dogmengeschichte*, IV, first half, pp. 202 ff., and Theodosius Harnack, *Luthers Theologie*, I, *Gott in seiner Doppelbeziehung zur Welt*, pp. 69–112.

[2] See Appendices II and III (pp. 516 and 527).

must be regarded from a point of view which is 'above' man, is the presupposition common to all anthropologies. This conviction lies in the conception of understanding itself. All understanding is co-ordination and sub-ordination.[1] But what this standpoint 'above' man may be, from which we may come to understand his nature as a whole, gives rise to views which are radically and irreconcilably opposed to one another. Some postulate this 'above' as Nature—conceived more or less in a purely causal and material manner; others postulate it as Spirit or the Idea, others again as a Deity which in some way or another we can learn to know by ourselves. The Christian doctrine of man posits this standpoint as God, as He makes Himself known to us and teaches us to know ourselves in His revelation, the Word of God. Thus it takes its standpoint 'above' man in the one and only genuine 'above,' in God Himself. Its first article of belief is that man cannot be known from himself but only from God. As the materialist maintains that man must be understood from the point of view of matter, and as the Idealist tries to understand human existence from the point of view of spiritual existence or from that of the Idea, so the Christian faith asserts that we can only understand him in the light of the Word of God.[2] Thus by this statement we do not mean merely that the Bible is the fundamental basis of the correct doctrine of man, although certainly this suggestion is included in that first statement;[3] but we mean

[1] Cf. Dilthey, *Die Entstehung der Hermeneutik* (*Ges. Schriften*, V, pp. 317 ff.).

[2] I can accept the thought expressed by Schlink in his book, *Der Mensch in der Verkündigung der Kirche*: 'Philosophical anthropology does not attain to knowledge of man but it only succeeds in establishing certain particular (isolated) truths about man' (p. 173). But this phrasing is not altogether happy, in so far as 'philosophical'—Schlink is thinking evidently only of non-Christian philosophy—that is, rational anthropology, not only has all kinds of individual things to say about man, but it is able for its part to grasp important aspects of human existence which should also be acknowledged by theology. On this whole question, see Appendix IV on philosophical and theological anthropology, p. 542.

[3] That is the difference between a 'Biblical psychology,' as it has been conceived by Beck and Delitzsch and others, and that which is here presented. They all conceive the relation to the Word of God only in a formal way, although they—and Delitzsch in particular—come very

something far more fundamental, namely, that the way of human existence, the being of man itself, that in which it is different from all other forms of being, can only be understood in the light of its relation to the divine Word, namely, as being in the Word and from the Word of God.

This means that man can only understand himself when he knows God in His Word. All merely natural understanding of man is a misunderstanding. Not only the man who believes, but also the man who does not believe, the 'godless' human being, can only be understood in his human existence in the light of God, or more exactly in that of the Divine revelation, from the point of view of the Word of God which demands an answer, through which he is responsible. Man is the 'theological' being, the creature whose peculiar characteristic it is that his existence is in the Word of God, whose greatness and misery, whose destiny and guilt, possibilities and limits, freedom and bondage, meaning and meaninglessness can only be rightly seen from that point of view, in the light of that origin. In all that man is, does, says, and thinks, he gives an answer to the word of creation, the word of destiny; indeed, he not only gives an answer, he himself is an answer. Human existence, in contrast to every other form of existence, is responsive existence, that is, existence which must and can answer, and in so doing is free and yet bound. But the answer which man gives, the answer which he is himself—like all other answers—is not intelligible in the light of his own nature, but only in that which precedes it—a primal truth. Man's independence is based upon and in this dependent human existence, and it is only in the light of this primal origin that we can comprehend the end for which he has been created; it is only in this light that we can understand the aim of man's existence and the meaning of his failure to attain this aim. The truth of man is more original than his untruth, but the source of knowledge of the truth and the untruth of human existence is the Word of God, in accordance with the principle: *verum est judex sui et falsi.*

The fact that this Word of God, in which we have been

near to the truth in the fact that they take seriously the origin of man in Christ, the Eternal Word. Cf. Delitzsch, *System der biblischen Psychologie*, p. 27.

created, the Word of our origin in Jesus Christ, has been restored to us, is the reason why we are able to understand our human existence in faith; why, for instance, as is necessarily the case outside the Christian faith, we are not obliged to misunderstand ourselves. The Word of God which has been given back to us, is Jesus Christ; in Him God reveals to us both His being and our being, His truth and the truth of man. The truth of human existence is disclosed to us not by an *anamnesis* which we ourselves can accomplish, but only by an *anagennesis* which is based upon faith in the Incarnate Word of God; thus it is only an act of knowledge which is at the same time an act of life—and indeed an act of life in which God is the One who gives, and we are those who receive—which discloses to us the truth of human existence. This new knowledge is at the same time a new being, the true being of man.

Even in the Greece of Pericles something was discovered, once for all and irrevocably, about the true being of man. A visitor to the British Museum who passes from the Sphinx art of Egypt and the Lion pictures of Babylon, and stands for the first time before the frieze from the Parthenon, may still experience something of that emancipation which came to man at that time in classical Athens. And yet that which was then released was not the distinctive element in man; therefore that release was a deliverance which at the same time was bound to lead to the self-destruction of man. If genius, the creative power of thought and influence, was the distinctively human element, then the Greeks ought to have the first prize, both for discovery and for emancipation. But genius, the creative mind and spirit, is only the possibility, not the reality of human life. But the reality is: love. It is not creativeness but responsibility which constitutes the truly human. This, however, has been disclosed and given to us, not upon the Acropolis, but upon Golgotha, where God reveals to us the truth about Himself, and about ourselves, as love.

4 THE FORMS IN WHICH THE WORD OF GOD IS EXPRESSED

We can only speak of the Divine Word and of existence in Him to Him and from Him, because He has revealed Himself to us in Jesus Christ. As the incarnate Logos we only possess Him in the word of His witnesses, the word of the Scripture. He Himself is the Word,[1] the Word of the Bible is the witness to Him as the Word.[2] *Christus dominus et rex scripturae* (Luther). But the Divine Word revealed in the flesh is identical with the Word in the beginning, with the Word in which all that is has been created, with the light 'which lighteth every man, coming into the world.'[3] The revelation of Christ points back to the revelation in the Creation, to the Word 'in whom all things cohere,[4] in whom also, in a very special way, man has the ground of his being, as man. His responsible being is based upon the Word of the Origin; but although man's being is perverted both in its meaning and in its content by sin, it does not cease, on that account, to be responsible being. Even the being of the sinner is a being in God's Word, or being 'in the sight of God'—otherwise how could it be sinful? But it is a perverted being-in-the-Word-of-God.[5]

On the other hand, the Word of Scripture, which points back to Jesus Christ and the Word in the Beginning, is not given to us except through the message of the Church, which hands down to us, translates and explains the Bible as the Word of God. But one link in the chain is still missing. It is not a matter of course that in Jesus Christ we should know the truth of God and the truth of man. This knowledge is something which we can in no wise guarantee or enforce. God Himself wills to speak to us; we can only perceive that truth in so far as God Himself actually speaks to *us*. The Bible expresses this double truth by the two phrases: the witness of the Holy Spirit, and the faith of the heart. Only where God Himself speaks to me can I have faith, and only in my faith does God Himself speak to me. God Himself must speak His Word to *me*, if it is to become mine. I myself must say 'yes' to Him if I want to hear God's distinctive Word.

The Word of God and the word of faith are inseparable. It is not God who believes but I myself who believe; yet I do not believe of myself, but because of God's speech, which is

[1] John i. 1. [2] John v. 39. [3] John i. 9.
[4] Col. i. 17. [5] See below, p. 169.

a gift, and because of His gift which is a Word.[1] In this faith He gives me not only Himself, but He also gives me knowledge of myself. In this faith He decides about my existence, so that I decide for myself. Outside this decision there is no true self-knowledge, no true knowledge of human existence. There is no theoretical and neutral knowledge of God and of the true man; for knowledge of the Word of God is at the same time the basis of true responsibility. To know God's Word means: to perceive and accept, and therefore to obey, the Lord's Word *as* the Word of the Lord.

At this point we have reached the limits of the validity of a Christian doctrine of man. In so far as every doctrine presupposes an objective and detached attitude, a theoretical severance from the process of decision, the Christian doctrine too, as doctrine, is no longer the truth, but simply the human attempt to grasp the truth. Man's true understanding of himself takes place only in the process of the divine self-testimony and of human self-decision. Every doctrine shares in the errors which arise when theoretical forms are imposed upon that which cannot be conceived in theoretical terms. Hence we must always be aware that Christian doctrine, although it grasps *divine* truth, because it does so—that is, because it becomes incorporated and bound up with *human* knowledge—it always stands in need of correction.

5. NATURAL KNOWLEDGE AND THE KNOWLEDGE OF FAITH

In all that has been said up to this point, we have only had in mind that which makes man *man*, that which is decisive and distinctive about him, not that which unites man with other creatures and with all creaturely existence. Man, however, is not only the being who is responsible to God; he is also dust of dust, *zoon*, a psychical and rational being. Man is a hierarchical whole.[2] In every hierarchy the understanding

[1] Cf. my pamphlet, *Vom Werk des Heiligen Geistes*, 1935, pp. 29 ff.

[2] See below, p. 409, in the chapter "Man in the Cosmos." Haecker lays much stress upon this 'hierarchical' element in his fine Catholic anthropology, *Was ist der Mensch?* But when he reiterates 'we are "hierarchists"' and in this refrain expresses opposition to Protestantism and

goes from higher to lower, not from lower to higher. To the understanding of man's responsibility to God it is possible to add also the 'lower' elements, material, biological, psychical and rational nature—but not contrariwise. The meaning of a whole can only be understood in the light of its ultimate and final meaning, even in its material aspect; but the meaning cannot be understood from the material end. This makes it clear that the understanding of man from the point of view of the Word of God does not exclude, but includes, the partial understanding of these lower aspects in their own context.

The dust out of which man has been created is not dust of some special kind, but 'the dust of the ground.'[1] It is therefore not only possible that a Christian anthropology should be connected with a physico-chemical anthropology; so long as it remains within its own proper bounds, it is necessary. All the possible and necessary light on the anatomy and the chemical elements of the human organism, however, we shall seek not in the Bible but in natural science.

In principle the same is true of the biological, psychical and rational nature of man. We shall seek not only the laws of biology and psychology, but also the logical and the other nöetic laws—like those of science, art, law, morality—precisely where these laws, which belong to human nature, are studied with the means and methods which are suitable for them. Therefore we are not concerned with declaring war upon a philosophical anthropology from the point of view of the Christian faith. On the contrary, this too is required from the point of view of the Christian faith. But it will certainly always be a sphere of frequent conflict.[2] These conflicts will be due first of all to the fact that the human reason will claim more than its due, only with great reluctance will it allow itself to be limited and corrected from the point of view of faith. This is why so many of the best Christian

connects his belief in the ecclesiastical hierarchy with the idea of the hierarchical order of human existence, he evidently forgets that there is also a Neoplatonic, and thus non-Christian 'hierarchical' theory, that of Dionysius the Areopagite: 'Of the Celestial Hierarchy,' which had a good deal of influence upon the formation of the medieval view.

[1] Gen. ii. 7.

[2] See Appendix IV, p. 542.

theologians are so distrustful of all philosophical anthropology, and, within limits, their distrust is justified.

But these conflicts may equally well arise out of a mistaken action on the part of theology; that is, theology may go beyond its province, and, forgetting the inadequacy of all human formulations of Divine truth, it may proclaim as a Divine revealed truth what is solely a human and erroneous conception of Divine truth. In the course of history the natural sciences and philosophy have had just as much reason to complain of these encroachments on the part of theology as theology has to complain of encroachments upon *its* sphere. Hence both sources of error must continually be watched, and the opinion must not be allowed to gain ground that it is a special sign of Christian conviction to ignore philosophical and scientific knowledge, or that it is a special sign of scientific accuracy to ignore Christian truth. We should remember that saying of the Apostle, 'what man knoweth the things of a man, save the spirit of man which is in him?'[1] but 'the things of God knoweth no man, but the Spirit of God. Now we have received . . . the spirit which is of God,'[2] in so far as we have perceived the truth and affirmed it in His Word. The greatest teachers of the Church have allowed themselves to be guided by this distinction, and we do well to follow their example, without believing that this exhausts our responsibility. How little this is the case will soon become clear.

(*b*) THE WORD OF GOD AS THE SOURCE OF BEING

I. THE WORD OF GOD AS THE GROUND OF BEING

The fundamental article of the Christian faith is this, that God is the Creator. In this statement a Christian, Biblical, religious doctrine of being is opposed to all other forms of ontology. Its main thesis is that all being is either of God or has been created and established by Him. But the Biblical

[1] I Cor. ii. 11. Here Paul merely sets a fundamentally natural and a spiritual knowledge alongside of one another, and admits that the former—within its limits—is justified, but he does not reflect upon the dialectical relation between the two.

[2] I Cor. ii. 12, A.V.

ontology is not content with this. It states that God has created all that is outside Himself through HIS Word. The Word of God therefore, according to the teaching of the Bible, is the ground of being of all created existence, not merely in the sense that all created being has its origin in the Word of God, but in the sense that in the Word 'all things cohere,'[1] that all that God has created He upholds 'by the Word of His power.'[2] Thus between the Word of God and creaturely being there exists not merely the relation that it is only possible to perceive the origin and the truth of created existence from the Word of God—the cognitive relation, with which we were dealing in the last section—but further there exists, and fundamentally for that cognitive relation, the ontological relation, which grounds all being in the Word of God.

Now this is true in a special way of the being of man. Man has a quite special relation of being to the Word of God, because in man being and perception stand in a peculiar relation to one another. All things have been created by the Word of God: 'All things were made by Him, and without Him was not anything made that was made.'[3] But only of man is it said that this Word is also the Light, the true Light, which 'lighteth every man.'[4]

The specific being of man, which distinguishes him from all other creatures, is not only known from the Word of God but it is also based upon the Word of God. Since all created existence is based upon the Word of God, human existence is based upon a special relation to the Word of God. Man is man by the fact that he is a creature who stands in a special relation to the Word of God, a relation of being grounded in and upheld by the Word. This is no mere phrase or figure of speech, but a simple and realistic expression of the fact that man lives 'by every word that proceedeth out of the mouth of God.'[5] Just as the new man is generated by the Word of God, so also the original man in the divine original act of Creation was generated by the Word of God. But just as this generation in the Word of God includes the hearing of the Word and belief in the Word—and thus a spiritual

[1] Col. i. 17. [2] Heb. i. 3. [3] John i. 3.
[4] John i. 9. [5] Matt. iv. 4.

relation to the Word of God—so also the original Creation includes such a process, which makes man not merely a product but a receiver of the Divine Word. This is the content of the doctrine of the Image of God with which we shall be dealing in detail in the next chapter.

In this original, ontological relation between the being of man and the Word of God lies the reason that man can only understand himself in God, or to put it more exactly, in the Word of God.[1] The Word of God, as revealed to us through the Holy Scriptures, is thus not merely the ground of knowledge, but it is also the ground of man's being. This is what Calvin means in the famous sentence with which he opens his Institutes, 'Our wisdom, in so far as it ought to be deemed true and solid wisdom, consists almost entirely of two parts: the knowledge of God and of ourselves. But as these are connected together by many ties, it is not easy to determine which of the two precedes and gives birth to the other.'[2] There exists, Calvin continues, a reciprocal relation between the understanding of God and of Man. But this is not meant in the sense of a rational and speculative doctrine of God—as if it were just as possible to discern God from the nature of man as to discern man from the nature of God. On the contrary, only from the knowledge of the revealed Word of God can both the nature of God and the nature of man be perceived, but in such a way that we understand: 'Our existence itself is simply *subsistentia in uno deo.*' But this is true of man as he actually is, of the being whose *miserabilis ruina* Calvin describes. This actual, sinful man (that is, we ourselves, as we are) is to be understood in God and in God alone; this actual man has his continued existence and the ground of his being in the Word of God. Even in his perverted condition, even in his opposition to the Word of Creation, man can only be under-

[1] Thus Luther says of Adam's original condition: *ipsa natura adeo fuit pura et plena cognitione Dei, ut verbum Dei per se intelligeret et videret* (WA. 42, 50). J. Gerhard, *Loci theologici: posuit Deus intra ipsummet hominem suam imaginem, quam homo intuens cognosceret, qualis sit Deus* (IV, 247); and: *creaturae omnes stabant in ordine suo . . . homo ex earum et sui inspectione Deum creatorem cognoscebat*; ibid., 294.

[2] Calvin, *Institutio I*, i, 1. (*Institutes of the Christian Religion,* translated by Henry Beveridge (p. 47), 1845.)

stood as existing in the Word of Creation as that being which not only has his existence—like all other creatures—in the Word, but also as a being which, in his special relation to the Word, has a special nature, that is, human nature.

We will now express this—without waiting to develop it further—by a conception which indicates this special relation to the Word and the special form of being which is grounded in it, namely: man is the being who is responsible. Human responsibility has no other ground than that of the Word of God, that is, that man, in contrast to all other creatures, is not only borne by this Word of God, but is borne by Him in such a way that he is in some way or other aware of it. 'In some way or other' every human being is aware of his responsibility, just as every human being—to the extent in which he is really a human being—is responsible. Every human being knows that he is responsible; how and why he is responsible he should and could know, were it not for the intrusion of the fact of sin.[1] Responsibility is the presupposition of the fact that man is able to be a sinner. Only the human being who is responsible is able to sin. Responsibility and the knowledge of it—however obscure and distorted it may be—the responsibility precisely of the 'godless' human being, can only be understood from man's special relation to God, to the Word of God.

We shall understand this connexion more clearly if instead of the formal conception of responsibility we use the pregnant idea of love. The meaning of all responsibility is love; for love is the fulfilling of all law. Hence man can only be understood as issuing from love and made for love. Love is both the source and the meaning of his life. Again, every human being

[1] Rom. i. 19. The meaning of the passage is evidently this: to lay bare human guilt and human responsibility through the relation of man—pagan man—to the revelation of Creation. Cf. on this point the good exposition by Schlier, *Evangelische Theologie*, 1935, pp. 9 ff., and Gutbrod, *Die paulinische anthropologie*, pp. 12 ff.: 'The connexion between the fact of man's createdness and his responsibility in the sight of God, as it is expressed especially in Rom. i. 18 ff.,' 'precisely because man is always in the sight of God, the question of just—unjust is so significant,' p. 22, against Kuhlmann's curious exposition in his work, *Die Theologia naturalis bei Philo und Paulus.*

is aware of this to some extent, even if only dimly; but what he cannot and does not know from himself is why this is so, and what the real content and meaning of love is. This is indeed the content of the revelation of God in Jesus Christ. Only in this revelation is the meaning of the word 'love' rightly 'defined' for us by the Divine action; and in it alone is this love revealed to us as the ground and the end of our life. In it we perceive why, to whom, and for what purpose we are responsible. We understand ourselves only when we understand ourselves in the light of the Divine love—even in our very godlessness. For only so do we understand that godlessness and lovelessness are the same thing. The being of man has its ground in the Being, the will and the work of God.

2. THE BEING OF GOD: THE TRINITY

Being-for-love is not one attribute of human existence among others, but it is human existence itself. Man is man to the exact extent in which he lives in love. The degree of his alienation from love is the degree of his inhumanity. The distinctively human element is not freedom, nor intellectual creative power, nor reason. These are rather the conditions of realization of man's real human existence, which consists in love. They do not contain their own meaning, but their meaning is love, true community. It is not the degree of genius which determines the degree of humanity of human existence, but the degree of love. But all this is true only and in so far as we understand love in the New Testament sense as the fulfilling of responsibility, the one explaining the other, and maintaining its right meaning. Both these words can only be understood in their unity when we understand responsibility and love in the light of their origin, the love of God. Only as an answer to the divine love is human love the fulfilment of responsibility and the realization of humanity. The love of God, the Primal Word, with which God calls man into existence, and in so doing gives him the meaning and the stability of his existence, is the ground from which human existence comes into being. Hence we must first of all speak of God if we want to speak about man. But we can only speak of God because and in so far as He has revealed Himself to us.

God, who discloses Himself to us in His revelation in His unfathomable being, God who shows Himself to us in His revelation as He is in Himself, so that His revelation is not something different from Himself but is Himself: this is the Triune God, Father, Son and Holy Spirit. We can only understand who man is and what human existence is, being-in-responsibility, being-for-love, when we know that God is the Triune God. He is the God of the Christian faith.

First of all we mean only this one simple truth, that God in His open historical revelation, in His Son Jesus Christ, and in His secret and inward revelation, in the Holy Spirit, is no other than He is in Himself, in His eternal Father-Mystery. It is really God Himself who as the Holy Spirit implants His Word in our hearts. The God who reveals His love to us in Jesus Christ and in it His holy, inviolable, sovereign will, in so doing really shows us *Himself*, not merely something of Himself, not merely an apparent form of His existence. No, we may now know that 'God is love; and he that dwelleth in love dwelleth in God, and God in Him.'[1] This love is God and God is this love. Existence which springs from this love is from God, and only existence which springs from God is really existence in love.

But this first statement also contains a second: God is not only one who loves us, whose love is connected with us; *in Himself*, quite apart from the existence of any creatures, apart from the existence of man, He is the One who loves, otherwise He would show Himself to us as other than He is in Himself. His love to us, to men, is the outflow of His being, of the fact that He is Himself loving, and that He loves. It is the radiation of His love which He has to His Son from all eternity.[2] So also the love which the Son shows us, is the outflow of the love which He has for His Father, from all eternity.[3] And as He makes this His love our own through the Holy Spirit—for 'the love of God is shed abroad in our hearts by the Holy Spirit'[4]—so in God Himself is the Primal source and ground of this inwardness. The Father loves the Son and the Son loves the Father through the Holy Spirit. *One* God—

[1] 1 John iv. 16.
[2] John xvii. 24.
[3] John xvii. 5.
[4] Rom. v. 5.

who in Himself is the truly loving. We know that we are stammering when we say this. But we must say as much as this in order to bind together indissolubly both the idea that God is love and that He is an unfathomable mystery. Thus, this is the nature of God from which we are to understand the nature of man, our essential being. It is not any kind of love from which, in which and for which we have been created, but it is this love, the unfathomable mystery of God, cut off from all that is natural by the abyss of the mystery of the Trinity. It is this God who makes us responsible, and as the content of our responsibility—of our response—gives us Himself, His Primal Word, His love. The God who in Himself is loving, who has need of no creature in order to be able to love, He alone can freely and groundlessly love the creature in His spontaneous generous way which seeks nothing in return. In Him alone is the source of all unfathomable, generous love.

3. THE WILL OF GOD: THE DECREE OF ELECTION

The Christian doctrine of the Will of God is the doctrine of the divine 'decree.' This means that all that exists has its origin in God's thought and will, but that this will and thought of God is not arbitrary but is in harmony with His nature. The Bible knows nothing of a 'double decree,'[1] but it knows one alone, the decree of election, and thus no twofold will, but only one, the will revealed to us as love. But it reminds us of the fact—and this is the truth in the mistaken, unscriptural doctrine of the double decree—that this will of love, of God, is His Holy Will, against which he who opposes His love is shattered. Thus all that is creaturely has its origin not in the

[1] To Calvin the doctrine of election is rightly the centre of theology. The doctrine of a twofold predestination, on the contrary, lies on the fringe of his thought; we see this indeed from the fact that Calvin scarcely ever preached this view, which has however been constantly asserted by theologians since Schneckenburger and Alex. Schweizer. This doctrine of a twofold predestination is not even Scriptural; it is an unallowable conclusion drawn from Scriptural premisses, in the nature of the case a philosophical idea—that of necessity—dragged into theology by Augustine. Cf. the Zürich dissertation of P. Jacobs, *Prädestination und Ethik bei Calvin.*

nature of God—as an outflow of His nature—but in His will, which stands over against the one who has been created.

From this it follows that all that has been said hitherto about the nature of man in its connexion with the nature of God, must not be understood as meaning that man is of one nature with God. Man, although he has been created out of love, in love and for love, is not of divine nature, as though he had a share in the being of God; but he is a product of His will, he is a creature. But this will of love which God imparts in His word to man, is certainly the eternal will of God; so that the nature of man, although it is created and thus has a beginning, has its ground in the eternal will of God. It is not man and his nature that is eternal, but the ground of his being in the eternal will of love, the eternal election of God. The man who knows his true being can only understand himself in the eternal will, in the free, gracious election, not in a state of eternal independence.[1]

Once again, however, this means that man ought not to understand himself in the light of his own nature, nor should he regard himself as due to 'something,' but that he must understand himself in the light of the Eternal Word, which precedes man's existence, and yet imparts Himself to him. Man possesses—and this is his nature—One who stands 'over-against' him, One whose will and thought are directed to him, One who loves him, One who calls him, in and from and for: love. And this One who confronts man, and imparts Himself to him, is the ground of man's being and nature. Thus the Bible bases the responsibility of man upon the doctrine of

[1] The connexion between the doctrine of the *Imago* and the doctrine of election is expressed most clearly in the New Testament in Rom. viii. 29; cf. also Eph. ii. 10 and all that refers to the connexion between the Creation and Christ, Creation and the plan of salvation. The understanding of eternal election from the point of view of judgement, which inevitably leads to the idea of a twofold predestination, cannot be proved from the Scriptures. Why? That would have to be seen in the light of a Biblical view of Time, of the dialectic of 'before' and 'after' which takes Time seriously. Here that can merely be suggested. Those are rejected who reject the eternal election in Christ which is proclaimed to them. It is the task of theology at the present time to free the Scriptural idea of election from the Augustinian-Neoplatonic misunderstanding, which also overshadows to some extent the theology of the Reformation.

election. Only he who is aware of this eternal call of election knows what he should answer; he alone is able to respond.[1]

The word of Divine election is the call to human destiny, the call which at once makes us free and binds us; makes us free from the world, and binds us to God, makes us responsible to God, and therefore free from the compulsion of things. There is no other freedom than that which is grounded in this responsibility, and no other responsibility than that which is based upon the divine election. He who overlooks this, and fails to listen to this Call, does not cease to be responsible, it is true—just as little as failure to hear the call annihilates the call itself—but he ceases to understand his responsibility aright. Above all, he ceases to live in this responsibility. The responsible life, the right knowledge of responsibility, and life in the love of God, are all the same.

The eternal election is the divine will, of which the so-called moral law is only a reflection, the reflection in which God shows Himself even to fallen man. The eternal election for communion with God, and through that for communion with all creatures, is the primal form and the primal reality, which still lies behind the moral law, even though there it is concealed. Hence the possibility and the reality of the Good, of true humanity and love, is not obedience to the Law but the believing knowledge of election. Election is the way in which God allows us to participate in His being, in His eternal love, and in so doing gives us our own human existence. We know of this eternal election, however, only through the historic Word of God, through Jesus Christ, but in such a way that we understand it as the Primal Word in which we were created.[2]

4. THE WORK OF GOD: CREATION AND REDEMPTION

The work of God in which the being of the actual man has its origin and its continued existence is the word and work

[1] Cf. P. Jacobs, loc. cit., where it is shown that this connexion between election and responsibility is the fundamental structure of Calvin's theology. Especially it might be shown from the Old Testament how the whole 'ethic' is based upon Israel's election, and the remembrance of election is constantly the main ethical motive.

[2] Col. i. 15 ff.

of creation and preservation; but the ground of knowledge of this first work is the second: the work and word of reconciliation and redemption, the historical Word of revelation which discloses eternity. In the second work of God we perceive His first as first, as that in which we already always had our life. For in it, in the word and work of creation everything has its continued existence, not merely its origin.[1] The fact that man has been created by God means that he, the actual man, even in his godlessness, is upheld by the Word of God. Hence although creation and preservation must be distinguished from one another, they must never be severed from one another. Man *was* not, in his origin, a responsible being, but he *is* still a responsible being, even in his irresponsibility, there, where he denies his responsibility and sets himself in opposition to his origin. Hence he does not cease to be man, even when his human existence is distorted qualitatively into 'inhumanity.' He could not be a perverted human being, he could not act irresponsibly, he could not be a sinner and commit sins, unless, even now, his 'continued existence' was still in the Word of God, unless the 'true light' was still illuminating him who has been blinded.[2] As he in the midst of his apostasy from the Creator is still borne and guided by the Divine Providence, so also is he borne by the Word, 'which upholds all things.'[3] And he as man, in contradistinction from all other creatures, is so borne by the Word that, although his spiritual vision is obscured, he is aware of this fact, even if in a distorted manner. Even distorted knowledge is knowledge, and is infinitely more—and at the same time infinitely less—than ignorance. Hence man is the being who is above and at the same time also below all the rest of creation known to us; he is above by his responsibility, and below because he denies his responsibility and acts against it. Man never ceases to be the work of God and to live by the power of God's operation. 'In Him we live and move and have our being'[4]—that was spoken to pagans and is true without any qualification at all. The Divine Creation and Preservation is

[1] Col. i. 17.

[2] John i. 9. This is how Calvin understands the passage: xlix, xliv; xlvii. 7; xxiii. 39.

[3] Heb. i. 3.

[4] Acts xvii. 28.

greater than the godlessness of man. The desire of man to be independent of God has indeed been suggested to him by the Serpent and is therefore a deception. Man remains in the Hands and in the workshop of God, even when he is perverted, and moreover, if I may put it so, when he feels the pressure of the Divine Hand to be 'against the grain' of his own desires.

Like the Creation and the Preservation of man, so also the nature of man can only be understood in the light of the perfected work of God, the Redemption. It is not as though the redemption was merely the restoration of the creation; the formula *Urzeit gleich Endzeit* ('the End reproduces the Beginning') applies to pagan mythology, but not to the revelation of the Bible; for it describes the world-process as an eternal cycle. The goal which has been shown to us in Jesus Christ is indeed also and first of all the restoration of that which was at the beginning, but it is much more than that; it is the eternal consummation which goes far beyond the Creation. Thus also that which is 'proper' to man, according to the Divine plan of Creation, can only be understood in the light of the End which is disclosed in Jesus Christ, the aim of the Kingdom of God. It is at that point that the destiny of man is shown to us;[1] the destiny however belongs to the nature of man. That is reflected in the fact that in the present sinful and godless condition of man, man must never be understood merely in the light of his being, but also in the light of what he ought to be. This sense of obligation is a fragmentary trace of the original aim of life for man. In faith in the redemption through Jesus Christ what is and what ought to be are once again united, through grace the aim of the Creation is once more ascribed to us as our reality, and its realization has begun. He who is called the Incarnate Word, He in whom God reveals to us the aim of His Kingdom, life in perfect communion with God and man as the whole meaning of existence, is also the One in whom we perceive the meaning of our existence—both that which is in accordance with the original purpose of Creation and with man's present opposition to the aim of Creation—and of our sense of obligation and our destiny.

[1] 1 John iii. 2.

Man does not only perceive, he actually has his origin and his goal in the Divine Word; for the Word of God is not imitative but creative; 'all things have been made by Him';[1] hence the Word not only promises, it creates anew. Hence, as we have already said, the knowledge of true human existence is no mere matter of knowledge, it is at the same time also a new being. Only in this new existence—what the Bible calls being 'in Christ'—can man truly understand himself; since only in Him, in the Word of God, man himself becomes true, can perceive the truth about himself, and also the great lie which we call sin. This opens up the further way for our inquiry.

[1] John i. 3.

CHAPTER V

THE ORIGIN: THE IMAGO DEI

(*a*) THE PROBLEM

1. THE STARTING-POINT

We all feel that there is something distinctive about man, that he belongs to a 'higher' category than the rest of creation. Even the cynic who denies this in theory does not allow himself to be classified as an animal without protest, and he also expects other people to treat him in 'human' fashion. Even when he expatiates upon his nihilistic views, in which he pours ridicule upon this 'distinctive' element in man, he demands a hearing as one who proclaims valid, absolutely valid truth—an attitude which is not very fitting for a being who is nothing more than a 'degenerate cerebrating animal.' No man is a cynic where his own claim to be considered is concerned. But, on the other hand, if man really belonged to this 'higher' category there would be no room for cynicism. The idealistic mystic who makes man into a god, but loses his temper because he has toothache, is the exact opposite of the cynic who ardently defends his nihilistic views, and is just as amusingly inconsistent. The ordinary simple man is neither a cynic nor a mystic. He is aware of this distinctive, 'higher' element in man, but he is also aware of the 'misery of man.' He knows—and yet he does not know; for he knows neither the ground nor the limits, nor the origin of this 'higher' element, and he does not know the origin of the contradiction in human nature.

Of ourselves we cannot know either this 'higher' element or the contradiction, because they are within ourselves, because we ourselves are entangled in the contradiction between the two. Indeed, the sinister thing about this contradiction is the fact that we cannot perceive it because we are involved in it, because it is not 'something within us' but is our very existence, because we are wholly in it, and do not stand above it. To see truly we need to be at a distance, or at a certain elevation; if we were above the contradiction we would be able to perceive both it and the source of the 'higher' element in man.

As Christians we say that we can know ourselves, our origin and the contradiction, only 'in Christ.' Jesus Christ, the Word of God, is indeed not a symbol of our nature, of that 'higher' element by which we interpret the 'higher' element within us; no, Jesus Christ is God's Word to us; this 'Word' does not spring out of the depths of our own being, but descends to us from the heights of God, and lays hold of us from beyond ourselves, from beyond the contradiction to which we have fallen a prey, in order to show us what we have lost through the contradiction. He shows this however only to him who is 'in Him,' to him who in faith accepts this Word of God, and in so doing allows himself to be lifted to this higher plane, and thus attains that elevation above himself from which he can henceforth perceive himself both in his origin and in his contradiction. The Word of God, which is itself the Origin, allows us to perceive that of which every human being is dimly aware; at the same time this light shows us that our 'dim perceptions' are merely a groping in the dark. Hence the Christian doctrine of man is threefold: the doctrine of man's origin, the doctrine of the contradiction, and the doctrine of the actual state of man as life in conflict between his origin and the contradiction. The Christian doctrine of man is therefore quite different from all other anthropologies, because it alone takes this conflict seriously, and does not try to explain it away or to neutralize it in any direction.

The phrase with which the Christian doctrine describes the origin of man, and in so doing the ground, the character, and the limits of that higher element, is the parabolic expression of the Creation narrative: namely, that man has been created 'in the image of God.' What this means, however, the Church ought to make clear, not by arbitrary interpretations, but by explaining this phrase in the light of a second, New Testament expression, namely, that we, in so far as we are in Jesus Christ, are 'being renewed unto knowledge after the image of Him that created him.'[1] We must gain a clear idea of the

[1] Col. iii. 10. On the doctrine of the *Imago Dei* in the Old and the New Testament, see Appendix I, p. 499.

meaning of the *Imago Dei* by reflecting on what is said to us in Jesus Christ about our origin, and not by speculating upon the deeper meaning of that mysterious expression in the Creation narrative. It is not the Old Testament narrative as such, but its meaning fulfilled in Jesus Christ, which is the 'Word of God' in which alone we can understand ourselves.

2. THE CLASSICAL DOCTRINE

If the Church had followed this rule it would have been preserved from teaching that the original existence of man was an actual state which could be described, in the sense of a *status integritatis*. The fact that it has done so has burdened the simple Bible narrative with its own views—in themselves absolutely necessary and highly significant—and in so doing it created a picture of 'the first man' which, the more it was theologically correct, the more it was in opposition to its historical form. Whereas in the pre-Augustinian Church the picture of the first man oscillated between a being at a still wholly undefined, childlike and primitive stage of human development, and that of a being which was not of earth at all but of heaven,[1] Augustine, for religious reasons, created that picture of the Primitive State which has remained the classical ecclesiastical doctrine ever

[1] The Apostolic Fathers do not mention the Primitive State (apart from an allusion to the Biblical narrative in the Epistle of Barnabas); Justin Martyr knows a doctrine of the Fall (*Dial. c. Trypho*, chap. 88) without any closer definition of the Primitive State; Theophilus emphasizes the childlike, undeveloped condition of Adam (*ad Autol.* II, 24 ff.). The same may be said of Irenaeus, who deals with the question in detail; Adam's advantage was innocence, not righteousness (IV, 38), his condition was primitive; we find the same attitude in *Clem. Al Strom.* IV, 23, 623. For the quite different theory of Origen, see p. 74. The Greek Fathers say less about the Primitive State than about the *Imago*, which they regard as more characteristic of the nature of man than the historic Primitive State. On the other hand, with Athanasius the later orthodox view begins to emerge. Adam is described as a fully contemplative soul, with a mind detached from earth (cf. Harnack, *Dogmengeschichte*, II, p. 146). Gregory of Nyssa oscillates between Origen and Athanasius; to him the most important point is that before the Fall Adam had not been tainted by sexual intercourse (ibid., p. 150). This oscillation between a monistically evolutionary theory and the dualistic theory of Origen was the prevailing attitude; it was not until Augustine, and the Pelagian controversy in particular, that this oscillation ceased; and even then, only in the West.

since. The first human pair was not only endowed with the *justitia originalis*, that is, with full obedience to their Creator in faith and love; but also with all the perfection of human endowments in body, mind and spirit. Their complete innocence therefore was not merely that of children or of primitive man; rather it was that of fully mature human beings in union with God, who possessed, to an unlimited extent, the *liberum arbitrium*, that is, a freedom of the will which was limited by nothing save the Command of God. Later on in this book we shall consider the important differences which, in spite of this common ecclesiastical doctrine, arose within the different confessions. At first, in any case, they completely disappear behind the common dogma: the first historical human beings, inhabitants of this earth, those who constitute the first generation of this history—in contrast to the Gnostic doctrine of Origen (which was rejected) of a state of pre-historical or supra-historical pre-existence—were practically in every respect perfect human beings. It was not the distinction between these 'perfect' beings and Primitive man which created difficulties, but the distinction between them and those redeemed by Christ, because the starting-point of the former was already so high. The more purely a theology grasped the Christian central idea the higher it placed this point of view,[1] in so far as this was compatible with the distinction between the first man and the redeemed man.

3. THE SCIENTIFIC SITUATION AND TASK

This whole historic picture of 'the first man' has been finally and absolutely destroyed for us to-day.[2] The conflict between the teaching of history, natural science and palaeontology, on the origins of the human race, and that of the ecclesiastical doctrine, waged on both sides with the passion of a fanatical concern for truth, has led, all along the line, to the victory of the scientific view, and to the gradual but inevitable decline of the ecclesiastical view. Upon the plane of empirical research, whether that of history or of natural science, which in the wide

[1] Even Luther can scarcely say enough about the perfections of the Primitive State. But in the main he is only concerned with one thing: the *justitia originalis*, WA. 42, 45 ff.

[2] Cf. Chap. 17, p. 390.

field of pre-history often merge into one another, no facts have been left which could support the Augustinian ecclesiastical view of the historical 'first man,' or which could prove that the empirical origin of the human race was to be sought on a specially elevated plane of spiritual existence. It is true, of course, that we shall have occasion to realize that we must not forget the hypothetical character of the theory of evolution, and that we must leave much room for future modifications of our present state of knowledge; we shall also set aside those views of Primitive Man which give too dogmatic a picture from the point of view of natural science, since we regard them as the products of an uncritical scientific dogmatism. But all this does not alter the fact that the more deeply scientific knowledge probes into the obscurity of pre-history, the picture of man becomes still more 'primitive,' and the fewer are the traces of a higher form of existence corresponding to the distinctively 'higher' nature of man. The pitiable comedy which is produced when theology claims that a 'higher, more perfect' human existence of the first generation existed in a sphere not accessible to research, as it retires before the relentless onward march of scientific research, should be abandoned, once for all, since it has for long provoked nothing but scorn and mockery, and has exposed the message of the Church to the just reproach of 'living at the back of beyond.'

Far more important than this external reason for giving up the story of Adam and Eve is an inner one. By clinging to the historical framework the actual fundamental content of the Christian doctrine of the origin of man has been either concealed or buried. So long as the historico-theological interest was maintained on the plane of empirical history, the central Biblical truth remained concealed behind a story which was perceived to be impossible. To one who thought in scientific terms there remained only the two other alternatives which do not conflict with historical research: a theory of evolution conceived in either naturalistic or idealistic terms; that is, a modified Darwinian or Hegelian view—and from the very outset the Hegelian view was only possible for a small circle of philosophical thinkers. Thus to-day we are confronted by the fact—and preachers of the Gospel would do well at last to confess that this is the fact, and to realize its meaning—that the average man of to-day knows or believes about the origin of man only that which remains in his memory from his instruction in natural history about the 'origin of man.' The ecclesiastical doctrine of Adam and Eve cannot compete with the impressive power of this scientific knowledge.

The 'modern theology' of the nineteenth century perceived this situation, and drew its own conclusions. Schleiermacher, (as usual) under the cloak of a re-formulation of the Christian doctrine, actually gives up the fundamental Christian view of the origin of man, and substitutes for it an idealistic, evolutionary theory with a strongly naturalistic bent; for the idea of the origin in Creation he substitutes that of the goal of evolution of a universal spiritual process.[1] Hase shows this change of view quite plainly when he says that, in his opinion, the doctrine of the origin 'deals not so much with a lost past as with an intended future.'[2] Rothe, with an evident Hegelian tendency, thinks that 'the concept of the Creation itself contains the idea that at first the personal creature could not emerge otherwise than from matter, and was then immediately tainted and defiled by matter; thus even its personality became changed, or, in short, sinful.'[3] Pfleiderer believes that after the traditional doctrine has been given up it is possible to retain, as its core, the idea that the dignity of man does not lie behind us but before us as the goal of evolution.[4] Similarly Troeltsch declares that 'the doctrine that man was made in the Image of God does not mean the loss of an original condition, but a goal to be reached through historical development.'[5]

All along the line, therefore, the Christian doctrine, because its historical form has become impossible, is renounced and is replaced by an idealistic evolutionism which—as also took place at other points—was then stated to be the 'real content' of the Christian view. The real core of the Christian doctrine, however, quite apart from its historical form, differs fundamentally both

[1] Schleiermacher, *Glaubenslehre*, § 60

[2] Hase, *Evangelische Dogmatik*, § 52.

[3] Rothe, *Theologische Ethik*, § 480, p. 46.

[4] Pfleiderer, *Religionsphilosophie auf geschichtlicher Grundlage*, p. 537.

[5] Troeltsch, *Glaubenslehre* (postum), p. 295.

from the naturalistic and from the idealistic evolutionary theory; it consists in this truth, that man is in conflict between his divine origin in creation and his opposition to the latter, that is, sin. It is not our concern to modify our theology to meet the increasing pressure of secular knowledge, because we cannot do anything else, hoping that we may at least save a 'core' of truth; our position rather is this: the fact that the increasing pressure of secular knowledge has awakened us to the nature of this problem leads us to reflect upon the real meaning and content of our own message; in the light of this reflection we then deliberately renounce a form of belief which was never any real part of Christian theology, which only obscured its meaning, and burdened it with dubious suggestions.

The abandonment of the historical form of the doctrine is not a loss, nor is it a trifle, but it is a necessary purification of the Christian doctrine for its own sake, not for the sake of science.[1] Science stimulates us to find a positive and adequate form for the Biblical message of the origin of Creation and the Fall of man. Only thus, too, will it be possible to clarify and intensify our opposition to metaphysical evolutionism.[2] Above all, by this new formulation it will become clear that when we talk about the origin of man we are not speaking of a certain man called Adam, who lived so many thousand years ago, but of myself, and of yourself, and of everyone else in the world. Only in this way will the Christian doctrine cease to be bad metaphysics; for in its old historical form, without intending it, it was a metaphysic of history, and thus bad theology.

[1] Karl Barth's answer to the question: 'Did the serpent in Paradise really speak?' (*Credo*, pp. 163 ff.; English translation, p. 190): 'We should rather inquire what the serpent said,' is a clever evasion of a problem which, in Holland in particular, ought not to be evaded. There is more at stake here than a desire for enlightenment which has little theological importance; it is not a mere question of apologetics. For theological reasons the Adam narrative ought to be abandoned, since it is the main source of that 'determinism' with which even Barth reproaches the classic ecclesiastical doctrine.

[2] The scientific doctrine of evolution is something different; metaphysical evolutionism is something different. Cf. Chap. 7.

(*b*) MAN AS CREATION

'For Thou hast possessed my reins:
Thou hast covered me in my mother's womb.
I will give thanks unto Thee; for I am fearfully
and wonderfully made:
Wonderful are Thy works;
And that my soul knoweth right well.
My frame was not hidden from Thee
When I was made in secret,
And curiously wrought in the lowest parts of the earth.
Thine eyes did see mine unperfect substance,
And in Thy book were all my members written,
Which day by day were fashioned,
When as yet there was none of them.'

So speaks the Psalmist[1] of his origin in God's Creation. He is aware of the 'natural story of creation,' he is aware that man arises through procreation in his mother's womb, and passes through remarkable stages of embryonic development before he reaches human form and receives human existence.[2] But he is also aware that this is only the visible side of his nature. The invisible side of this same process of growth, however, is the fact that God 'sees' and 'knows' him, that he has been predetermined and created by God. Directly, not by reflecting upon a 'first man,' he knows that he has been created by God; the creative act of God, accessible only to faith, and the natural genesis of man which everyone knows, are directly related to one another. He is aware of his empirical *beginning*; that is, the process of procreation in his mother's womb. But he is also aware of his *origin*; that is, the thought, the will and the creation of God. The fact that he may set his beginning in the light of this origin is to him an occasion for praise and adoring thanksgiving. But he reflects upon his origin—and that is the significance of Psalm cxxxix—in his worship of the Omnipresent Deity. The Christian doctrine of Creation does not give us any peculiar view of the beginning of man, but it takes over a view which is well known to everyone; yet it is itself the doctrine of the invisible Divine origin behind, above and within this visible and earthly beginning. The doctrine of Creation does not

[1] Psa. cxxxix. 13–16 (R.V.).

[2] Cf. Job x. 8.

compete with secular science, which deals with the visible beginnings which can be discovered by the processes of research, but it points to a quite different dimension, the dimension of the origin, of which, in principle, science knows as little as the chemistry of colour knows of the beauty of a picture, or physical acoustics of the content of a symphony.

The original Biblical word 'Creation' means first of all, that there is an impassable gulf between the Creator and the creature, that for ever they stand over against one another in a relation which can never be altered. There is no greater sense of distance than that which lies in the words Creator—Creation. Now this is the first and the fundamental thing which can be said about man: He is a creature, and as such he is separated by an abyss from the Divine manner of being. The greatest dissimilarity between two things which we can express at all—more dissimilar than light and darkness, death and life, good and evil—is that between the Creator and that which is created. For all other dissimilarities are ranged below this fundamental difference. They are related to that which has been created, and thus they are included in the fundamental similarity which they possess as that which has been created. God, however, is the Uncreate, the Creator. Man, whatever may distinguish him from all other creatures, has this in common with them, which distinguishes him from God: *like them, he has been created.*

This truth banishes any arrogance, which may be a temptation to man when he thinks of his peculiar nature, when he is conscious of his selfhood or of himself as spirit.[1] If man may rightly assert that he is not a bit of the world, that, indeed, he is not the world at all, yet he has this at least in common with this world with which he contrasts himself, that he too is a creature, like the world, and thus stands over against the Creator. Like all other creatures, he is a dependent being, a being who not only came into being from another region, but whose continued existence depends upon this further dimension. That which has been created has not only been created by God once for all; the same Creative Word by which the Creator created it also supports it, and thus preserves its existence.

[1] Hence belief in the Creation is the great stumbling-block to Idealistic Monism, and at the same time the protest against all metaphysical dualism.

Just as the concept of 'creation' or 'creature' places man and God at a distance from one another, so also it binds man fast to God. The created world is not simply the world, but the world-from-God, the world in which God is present and operating. When the Psalmist speaks of the Creation he is speaking at the same time of the inescapable, operative presence of God. The idea of Creation is not only the protest against every form of Pantheism, which blurs the boundary line between God and the world, but also against all Deism, which separates God and the world, as though there was a form of existence which could exist absolutely apart from God.[1] Creaturely being is a form of being which—for blessedness or judgement, for joy or torment—is indissolubly united with God, and is always an instrument and a manifestation of Him who operates. There is no divine creation which is not as such also a divine manifestation and a divine presence at work. The phrase (which sounds rather pantheistic): 'In Him we live and move and have our being,' is a fundamental statement of Scripture; it distinguishes the creation from the secular world. In truth there is no secular world; there is only a created world which has been secularized. The very idea of 'the secular' is an abstraction, a view of actuality apart from Him who acts. All reality is actuality, the actuosity of God.

(c) THE IMAGE OF GOD[2]

1. THE HISTORICAL HERITAGE

Although man has his created nature in common with all other creatures, he has been created in a different manner, and

[1] Karl Barth in his *Credo* (pp. 33 ff.)—probably to the astonishment of a good many people—has clearly accepted this 'immanence of the God who so absolutely transcends the world.' But there is no immanence of the Creator which is not at the same time His manifestation. This is the root of the revelation of the Creation, so obstinately contested by Barth, which is an integral element of the Bible. According to Luther, God spoke with Adam His Word through the creatures (see above p. 72); this connexion has been destroyed by sin, but—at least in part—like the *Imago*, it is restored by the New Birth. Hence the summons to behold God in His works (Rom. i. 19 ff.).

[2] On this whole section, see Appendix I (p. 499).

he is a 'creature' in a different way. Commentators have not been playing with words, but they have been true to their expository aim, when from time immemorial they have always laid stress on the fact that in the Bible narrative of Creation something *new* begins with the creation of man. After the whole cosmos has come into existence, even if in different ways, yet always under the same Divine imperative: 'And God said, Let there be . . . and there was . . .' it is as though the Lord of Creation paused for a while before the last great die was cast, and then began a new kind of creation. 'And God said: Let us make man in our image, after our likeness. . . .' A new kind of creative act, a wholly different relation between the creature and the Creator, corresponds to the new form of existence of that which is about to be created: man. Here the Creator does not create by means of an imperative word,[1] but—as Michelangelo has magnificently expressed this thought in pictorial form—in stooping down towards the human being whom He creates. Man, in contrast from all the rest of creation, has not merely been created by God and through God, but in and for God. He is, what he is originally, by God and through God; he is also in and for God. Hence he can and should understand himself in God alone. Just as it is said of no other creatures, 'let us make,' so also it is said of no other that it has been created 'after His likeness' or 'in His image.' What does this mean? The whole Christian doctrine of man hangs upon the interpretation of this expression—but on the interpretation which is drawn from the New Testament, from the point of view of Jesus Christ. The history of this idea is the history of the Western understanding of man, in which both the great spiritual forces of the past two thousand years, Greek philosophy and the Christian faith, have, so to speak, an equal share. Here the question was, and indeed still is, of the relation between Christianity, humanity and humanism. When Max Scheler—in the passage which has already been quoted—ranges both the Christian and the Idealistic Greek view under the one concept as the 'classical theory,' he is justified in so far as even in the

[1] With this exposition cf. Tertullian: the creation of man took place *non imperiali verbo ut cœtera animalia, sed familiari manu, etiam praemisso blandiente illo verbo, faciamus*, etc. *Adv. Marc.* 4[2]; so also Luther, WA. 42, 41.

early Christian days it was this very concept of the *Imago Dei* which formed a synthesis between the Platonist-Aristotelian-Stoic view and the Christian view of man, which dominated the whole of the Patristic period and the Christian Middle Ages, and has been, and still is, operative.

How can man, how can the *humanum*, that is to say, that which distinguishes man—whether he is a believer or an unbeliever—from the non-human creation, be so understood from the point of view of the divine creation, that this view will also express the contrast between man in his present sinful condition and his original creation? The understanding of the meaning of being 'created in the likeness of God' determined from the first—and still determines—the statement of the relation between reason and revelation, the Church and civilization, faith and humanity. Irenaeus outlined the path the Church was to follow for nearly fifteen hundred years, and his solution is still that of the Catholic Church. Supported by the double expression 'image' and 'likeness'—

Hebrew	*Zälem* and *Demuth*
Greek	*εἰκών* and *ὁμοίωσίς*
Latin	*imago* and *similitudo*[1]

the first great theologian of the early Catholic Church distinguishes a double element in man: the *image of God*, which consists in the freedom and rationality of his nature, and *the likeness* to God, which consists in his self-determination according to the divine destiny, in the *justitia originalis* as a special divine gift, the gift of supernatural communion with God. While sin has destroyed this second element, which was added to nature, man has retained the first, the human nature, the *humanum*. This is a simple and brilliant solution of the central problem of anthropology—the solution upon which the whole edifice of Catholic theology and conception of culture is based; a synthesis of immeasurable consequences.

It was not until Luther came that this 'two-storey' edifice was destroyed and also its systematic basis, Irenaeus' doctrine

[1] On these expressions and the whole question of the Old Testament cf. Eichrodt, *Theologie des Alten Testaments*, II, pp. 60 ff. Cf. Appendix I (p. 499).

of the *Imago* and the *Similitudo*. Luther, with his sure feeling for exegesis, recognized the nature of Hebrew parallelism, and saw that the distinction between the *Imago* and the *Similitudo* was untenable. But he was concerned with more than exegesis; he saw plainly that the actual unity of human nature was involved, or, to put it more exactly, the unity of the theological and religious views of human nature. In full accordance with the spirit of Scripture he saw that man must be interpreted in the light of *one* principle, that of the Original Word and Image of God.

Man's being as man is both in one, nature and grace. The fact that man is determined by God is the original real nature of man; and what we now know in man as his 'nature' is de-natured nature, it is only a meagre relic of his original human nature. Through sin man has lost not a 'super-nature' but his God-given nature, and has become unnatural, inhuman. To begin the understanding of man with a neutral natural concept—*animal rationale*—means a hopeless misunderstanding of the being of man from the very outset.[1] Man is not a 'two-storey' creature, but—even if now corrupted—a unity. His relation to God is not something which is added to his human nature; it is the core and the ground of his *humanitas*. That was Luther's revolutionary discovery. But this process of piercing through the thirteen-hundred-year-old falsely-synthetic tradition was not fully completed.

In order to make a complete formulation of the doctrine of Original Sin, Luther abandoned the Catholic dualism. The *Imago Dei*, man's original nature—not merely the added element of 'super-nature'—has been destroyed. What then is to be said of man's persisting rational nature, of his humanity, in short, of all that now distinguishes him from the animal creation? On the plane of the traditional historical view there was only a double possibility: either, not to equate this *humanum* with the original Creation, and thus with the divine destiny of man; or, in some way or other, to acknowledge this relation afterwards. The Reformation took the second path. It introduced the confused and dogmatically extremely doubtful concept of a

[1] The same is true of a neutral structure idea, as required by Bultmann, op. cit.

'relic' of the *Imago Dei*: essentially, it is true, the image of God in man has been destroyed, but a certain 'relic' has remained, just enough to enable man to understand the *humanum*—that which differentiates man from the animal—in the light of his origin, that is, from the point of view of theology. The second, more radical way, has been taken, so far as I know, first of all by Karl Barth: the bond between the *humanum* and man's relation with God has been severed; the fact that 'man is man and not a cat' is 'quite unimportant,'[1] the *humanum* has become a *profanum*. This dualism between revelation and reason would, if logically carried out, lead to the destruction of all theology and to an extreme 'Puritanism' in our attitude to culture and civilization.

Hence none of the Reformers dared to do what Karl Barth, with apparently greater logic, has done.[2] In spite of their conflict with the humanism of their own day they were 'humanistic' enough to know that the difference between man and a cat is neither banal nor secular, but a matter of the highest theological importance. Deeply as they were impregnated with the idea of man's 'total depravity,' they refused to go to the extreme length of severing the *humanum* from man's relation with God. Rather reluctantly they admitted that a 'relic' of the *Imago* still remained in man's nature. But whether they did this willingly or not, the fact remains, they *did* it. Thus by means of an only semi-legitimate conception they saved the connexion between the *humanitas* and the *Imago*, between Reason and the Word of God. But this confused idea of the 'relic' of the *Imago* (which had only been smuggled in, as it

[1] Karl Barth, *Nein!* pp. 25, 27.

[2] The fact that the Confessional Writings only speak of the complete loss of the *Imago*, but make no mention of the 'remnant' of the *Imago* on which the *humanum* is based, is due to their polemical and ecclesiastical purpose. For that period the doctrine of the 'remnant' of the *Imago* was—so to speak—merely a *theologumenon*. Yet not only Melanchthon and Calvin, but Luther too, wherever he speaks of the *lex naturae*, of the heathen knowledge of God, or of the *justitia civilis*, come back finally to this idea of a 'remnant' of the *Imago*. There can be no shadow of doubt that Luther, when he speaks of 'conscience,' 'reason,' *theologia naturalis*, etc., regards them as relics of man's original relation with God, in spite of the hopeless 'corruption' into which he has fallen. (Cf. Appendices II and III, pp. 516 and 527.)

were) prevented the actual clarification of the problem. It conceded both too much and too little to humanism; this was the point at which, at the time of the Enlightenment, the whole Reformation front was pierced and crumpled up. This, too, is the point at which we must start our work afresh. What we need to do is to think out, quite logically, the idea of the unity of human nature taught in the Bible and by the Reformers. This means, however, that we must avoid all the three solutions which have been previously suggested: the separation between the *Imago* and the *Similitudo*, the concept of the 'relic' of the *Imago*, and the view which depreciates or secularizes humanity; or, to put it positively, we must recognize that the *humanitas* which sinful man still possesses, and the *justitia originalis* which he has lost, both spring from the same source. This, however, is only possible by abandoning the historico-mythical form of the traditional doctrine, and by relating each human being both to his origin in the Word of God and to the Fall; and, on the other hand, under the guidance of the New Testament, we must conceive the idea of the *Imago Dei* in a completely personalistic and actual manner, which means that we must do away with the Aristotelian idea of the *animal rationale*.

. THE FUNDAMENTAL TERMS OF THE IMAGO DOCTRINE

'Created in His Image, in His Likeness' is a parable, hence its meaning does not lie on the surface. First of all, it says that the nature of man—in his origin or in general—is nothing in itself, and that it is not intelligible from itself, but that its ground of existence and of knowledge is in God. If we understand this phrase in the light of the specifically New Testament doctrine, we would do well to understand 'image' in the sense of reflection, that is, as an existence which points back or refers back to something else. 'But we all, with unveiled face reflecting as a mirror the glory of the Lord, are transformed into the same image from glory to glory.'[1] Man's meaning and his intrinsic worth do not reside in himself, but in the One who stands 'over against' him, in Christ, the Primal Image, in the Word of God. And the fact that man 'has' intrinsic value—that is, his distinctive being—consists in 'having' the Word, that is, that he knows

[1] 2 Cor. iii. 18. Cf. Rom. viii. 29.

himself to be in God, and also knows that God knows and recognizes him.[1] God creates man through the Word, but—all the passages of the New Testament which deal with this *imago* agree in this—He creates him in such a way that in this very creation man is summoned to receive the Word *actively*, that is, he is called to listen, to understand, and to believe. God creates man's being in such a way that man knows that he is determined and conditioned by God, and in this fact is truly human. The being of man as an 'I' is being from and in the Divine 'Thou,' or, more exactly, from and in the Divine Word, whose claim 'calls' man's being into existence. The expression, that God 'calls' the creature into existence,[2] is solely applicable to man in the literal sense, and is then also transferred from man to the rest of the created universe. From the side of God this twofold relation is known as a 'call,' and from that of man as an 'answer'; thus the heart of man's being is seen to be: responsible existence.

The being of man, in contrast to all other forms of creaturely being, is not something finished, but it is a being-in-self-knowledge and a being-in-self-determination, but in a self-knowledge and in a self-determination which is not primary but secondary; it is self-knowledge and self-determination on the basis of being known and determined. Figuratively speaking, God produces the other creatures in a finished state; they are what they ought to be, and this they remain.[3] But God retains *man* within His workshop, within His hands. He does not simply make him and finish him; human nature, indeed, consists in the fact that we may and must remain in the hands of God. The creatures which have not been endowed with reason are turned out as 'finished articles.' The characteristic imprint of man, however, only develops on the basis of the

[1] Luther understands the being of man in the Word of God thus: "Where or with whom God speaks, whether in wrath or in grace, the same is certainly immortal. The Person of God who there speaks, and the Word, indicate that we are creatures with whom God wills to speak on into eternity, and in an immortal manner." WA. 43, 481.

[2] Gen. i; Rom. iv. 17; 2 Cor. iv. 6.

[3] Naturally that is not opposed to the fact of that growth which also takes place in the world of nature. It is not gradual growth which is excluded by the 'finished article,' but the responsive relation, self-determination of such a kind that in it alone a divine destiny is realized.

Divine determination, as an answer to a call, by means of a decision. The necessity for decision, an obligation which he can never evade, is the distinguishing feature of man. It implies therefore—in contrast to all sub-human existence—a form of being which at every moment posits itself, thinking-willing being, the kind of being which is being for self. But it is at the same time—in contrast to the Divine Being—not *actus purus*, not a being which arises out of itself, not one which originally posits itself, but is responsive, 'answering,' responsible being. It is a being for self it is true, but it is not self-originated; it is the creaturely counterpart of His Divine Self-existence, posited by God Himself; it is the being created by God to stand 'over-against' Him, who can reply to God, and who in this answer alone fulfils—or destroys—the purpose of God's creation.

But this responsibility—and here the Biblical understanding of man finally parts company with the Idealistic understanding of man—is not first of all a task but a gift; it is not first of all a demand but life; not law but grace. The word which—requiring an answer—calls man, is not a 'Thou shalt' but a 'Thou mayest be.' The Primal Word is not an imperative, but it is the indicative of the Divine love: 'Thou art Mine.'

The original Divine Word therefore is not first of all a demand, because it is self-communication, a Divine word of love which summons man to communion with Him, the Creator, as the destiny of man. With this Word God turns to man, imparts Himself to him, and in so doing gives him his life. But He gives it him in such a way that man must receive it. He does not fling it at him—for that would mean that he was a 'finished article'—but He offers it to him through His call: so man must answer by accepting the gift of life from His Hands. He must 'repeat' the original Divine Word—he must not make a word of his own, but of his own accord he must give it back saying: 'Yes, I am Thine.' Man is destined to answer God in believing, responsive love, to accept in grateful dependence his destiny to which God has called him, as his life. Thus here we are concerned not with an 'image' and a 'reflection' but with a 'word' and an 'answer'; this is the exposition which the New Testament gives of the Old

Testament story of Creation, the idea of the *Imago Dei.* The intrinsic worth of man's being lies in the Word of God, hence his nature is: responsibility from love, in love, for love.

3. HISTORICAL RETROSPECT

Current anthropology also knows something about responsibility, even—in one way or another—of a relation between man and God. But it regards this simply as accidental, as something which has been added to the nature of man. Man is, to take the first point first, something for himself, a substance,[1] a soul-entity, or a body-entity. Where however—as in Idealism—man is understood as spirit, he is understood as the subject of this spirit, as a spirit-centre which is self-sufficing. It is true of course that Plato has some dim sense of the responsive character of the soul and its relation to God; according to Platonic doctrine, the soul only attains its true nature by the contemplation of the Divine Idea. But this Idea is neutral, it is not an acting subject; it does not lay hold of man, it does not give itself to man but man lays hold on it. The Idea does not love man and give itself to him, but man alone loves and thus acquires the divine life. Because Plato does not know the God who is self-giving love, his Eros, in which he defines the real nature of the soul, is something utterly different from that which the New Testament calls love; it is not self-surrender, belonging to another, and responsibility, but it is contemplative delight, enjoyment of the Supreme. In the thought of Aristotle even this relic of a relation with God has been deleted; man is the being who is endowed with reason, intelligible as he is in himself. The Platonic longing has become alien to him, man in the Aristotelian sense has his own law within himself.[2] The doctrine

[1] The current anthropology is summed up by Aristotle in philosophical ideas; the scholastic distinction between 'substance' and accident' which arose under his influence also penetrated into the Confessional Writings of the Reformation. Another source of this fatal terminology, which causes hopeless confusion in the problem, is the Augustinian idea that all being is, as such, good, and thus that evil is only *privatio boni*. Cf. for instance *Enchiridion*, iv. 12.

[2] 'With Aristotle there is achieved the return of man to himself. Man becomes something positive—man, like all other natural beings, bears his

71044

of the autonomous Self, of the autonomous reason, is dawning on the horizon, which was then worked out by the Stoics and handed down to succeeding generations. No longer do God and man stand 'over against' one another, but instead there is the one Reason, in which man, as the *animal rationale*, participates. Conversation must become conversation with oneself. The time has come to say the highest things that one has to say *εἰς ἑαυτόν*, in conversation with oneself.

This concept of the Divine Reason, in which man, as the *animal rationale*, has a share—through the concept of the *Imago Dei*, as understood by Irenaeus—now penetrates into Christian theology itself. To be 'in the image of God' has now become an attribute of human nature; the view now prevails that it is of the essence of rational being to resemble the being of God. Man is now 'also a rational being,' as God is a rational being, only with this difference, that God is Infinite Reason and man is only finite reason. The actuality and the relation to the Thou of the New Testament conception of the *imago* (*εἰκών*) has been forgotten and its place has been taken by the idea of analogy. The nature of man is now something quite different from his relation to God; the original essence of man, his original nature, is 'rational even as God is rational,' and it is no longer: 'to stand in a responsive relation to God.' Communion with God is now a secondary, additional, 'supernatural' element, which may disappear, owing to sin, without altering the essence or the nature of man. Thus Greek rationalism has suppressed Biblical personalism.

Among the philosophers it was Kant who first shook this

meaning within himself' (Groethuysen, op. cit., I, p. 39). Aristotle describes man as that living creature to whom the *νοῦς* is its distinctive element (*De. an.* II, 1, 2). In this connexion it is decisive that for him the *νοῦς is* the Divine: *τὸν νοῦν μόνον θύραθεν ἐπεισιέναι καὶ θεῖον εἶναι μόνον* (de gen. et corr. B.3.736*b*). The real question is not the one which is usually asked—that is, whether Aristotle, whether Greek philosophy as a whole, in some way or another makes a distinction between the human and the divine *νοῦς*—but whether it places the human *νοῦς* over against the divine *νοῦς* as 'I' and 'Thou.' To put this question is to answer it. Where God and man stand over against one another as 'Thou' and 'I,' there the philosophy of immanence ceases, there begins revelation and faith; or rather, this 'over-againstness' only takes place from the point of view of faith, not from that of reason.

thousand-year-old tradition by his definition of the person as a responsible being; the Christian idea—here as in other points—forced its way into his philosophy; but the notion of the one, autonomous reason left no room for this idea to develop. The responsible human being finally became the *homo noumenon*, responsible to himself alone; the monistic idea of reason conquered.[1] In another direction Fichte revolted violently against tradition. He disposed of the traditional idea of a soul-entity or a mind-entity and replaced it by the idea of the actual 'I'—with an intellectual energy for which the world owes him a debt of permanent gratitude. But he was dominated by the will to autonomy, to which he gave the most audacious titanic expression in the idea of the world-creative and self-creative Ego.[2] Hamann alone—that solitary thinker who dared to make the Bible the starting-point of his thinking—as he brooded long over human language and its relation to reason, began to perceive the fundamental scriptural idea of the Image of God, and of the opposition which it contains to all ideas of the autonomy of reason. Once more he knew that the human 'I' has its origin in the divine 'Thou,' and in the Divine Word, and that the idea of autonomy is its

[1] It is true of course that the obscurity of the concept of the 'intelligible ego' and the ambiguity of the meaning of the relation between empirical (human) and transcendental or pure reason has always been pointed out (cf. Kroner, *Von Kant bis Hegel*; Sannwald, *Der Begriff der Dialektik und die Anthropologie*). But this obscurity is not accidental; it is inherent in the principle of transcendental philosophy itself. Whether critical Idealism is possible upon the basis of the belief in the Creation may perhaps still be an open question. But wherever the idea of Creation is based upon philosophical argument (as for instance recently in the Gifford lectures of the Archbishop of York, *Nature, Man and God*, by W. Temple), either the idea of Creation or the rational process of proof is not used strictly enough.

[2] To how great an extent this kind of Ego-God philosophy is active within the Idealism of the present day—even if it does not venture to express itself quite so plainly as Fichte—comes out in the following passage from Hermann Schwarz, quoted by Sannwald: 'The remote infinity disappeared from him (Fichte), that spiritual infinity arises within ourselves. The name for this spirituality we may choose as we will, so long as we are conscious of this one thing: it is as much more than our empirical Ego as the heaven is higher than the earth. Most people may call it God, or eternal Life, or infinite consciousness . . . the Supra-Ego within us' (loc. cit., p. 114).

own tragic and sinful 'confusion of reason with itself.' Through Kierkegaard we have learned to know Hamann's thought, and to re-interpret it in its connexion with Scriptural revelation.

4. THE IMAGO DEI AND THE BEING OF MAN

Man may be described as an hierarchical system. In him there is an 'above' and a 'below'; hence as a whole he should be understood from above, and then downwards; not vice versa. On this point common sense, idealistic Humanism and the Christian faith agree. Difference of opinion only arises when we try to define the nature of this 'above.' Idealism posits it as the Divine Reason in which man participates; the Christian faith posits it as the Word of God, that self-bestowing, challenging Word, in Whom man as man has his ground. The first thing said about man in the Bible is that his relation to God is like that of a picture to its model. Man must first of all be defined theologically; only then may the philosopher, the psychologist and the biologist make their statements. The fact that man is what he is is not a merely human but a 'theological' concern; he is not to be understood in himself, nor from that reason which is in him. He can be understood only in the light of that which stands 'over against' him, the Word of his Creator. His relation to God, not his reason, is the summit of the pyramid, the highest point in the hierarchy; this is the way in which man is built, and this is how man can be understood. Reason is, so to speak, only the organ of man's relation to God, as the soul is the organ of the reason, and the material body is the organ of the soul. The summit of man, purely from the point of view of man, is the 'I-Self.' The 'I-Self,' however, is what it is, and what it ought to be, through the Divine 'Thou.'

Man's relation to God is not to be understood from the point of view of reason, but reason is to be understood from the point of view of man's relation to God. Responsibility is not an attribute, or an enrichment of the rational man, but from the very outset reason is directed towards the perception of the Divine Word. It is—so to say—the material, the substratum of man's relation to God. Because God creates man as one who can hear His call and can answer it, He also creates him as a rational being. The reason is the organ of perception, but the meaning of this organ, its final 'Whence' and 'Whither,' that which determines its structure, is the Word of God. Because in creating man God creates one who stands 'over against' Himself, one to whom He wills to impart Himself, He creates man as a rational creature, as a being who is able to receive His Word. Hence the concept of the Logos is the highest and final conception which even the reason alienated from the Word of God is able to conceive. The reason is so prepared and disposed for the perception of the Word of God, and man's relation with God is so deeply implanted, that even in his godlessness the reason must conceive God—although certainly a rational deity, who is not the Living God; for we cannot conceive the Living God; we can only perceive Him in His Word. The metaphysical idea of the Logos may be described as an impotent and strained attempt of a mutilated organ to fulfil its function, which, owing to its mutilated condition, it can no longer fulfil.[1]

Thus we ought not to understand man, who has been created in the Image of God, as of a rational nature, like unto God—to which the 'supernatural' element, his relation to God, is added, as something secondary; no, we should understand man as one created by God 'over against' Himself, as a creature to whom He imparts Himself through His Word, whom therefore He endows with reason as the organ for the reception of the Word. But because this call of God is first of all an act of self-communication, an act of the Divine love, and not first of all a demand, a law, the 'Primitive State,' even if it is not an historical fact, should be understood primarily not as an obligation but as a form of being. Being according to the

[1] The ultra-Reformation theology, which does not allow for a relation between the *humanum* and man's relation with God, cannot even concede a *fundamentum in re* to the speculative idea of God. But precisely from this point of view does the connexion of the *deus nudus* (*absolutus*), the wrath of God, the law and the speculative knowledge of God become plain in Luther (cf. Th. Harnack, op. cit., pp. 84 ff.). The God to Whom one comes by way of speculative immanentism is always—whether we know this or not—the *deus nudus*, the wrathful God, to Whom the 'majesty of the creature is intolerable.' Both the Divine Thou and the human I are swallowed up in an abstract conception of the All-One.

Imago Dei is a divine gift, it is communicated life, not merely an aim. Seen from a negative point of view: that from which sin turns away is not merely a demand, but a God-given being. The life originally given to man is being in the love of God. This gift, not merely a divine task, is prior to our empirical sinful existence. Human existence was originally disposed for the reception of this gift, not for meeting an obligation by means of our own efforts. It is thus that we come to understand ourselves once more—our being according to the *Imago Dei*—in the light of the New Testament, since we are renewed unto this image, through the Word which gives, through the self-sacrificing love of God, through a purely receptive faith.

Since then the gift comes first, and not the task—'Let us love Him because He first loved us'—the original, God-created state of life is to be understood as an existence in love, as a *justitia originalis*. It is not that we think that a 'first man' of this type actually ever lived anywhere at any time—this idea is merely the historical husk concealing the kernel of the Biblical message—but this original righteousness—being in the love of God who gives and who loves us first—is that for which God creates man. When man turns away from this divine gift, he turns away not merely from a task, a destiny, an aim which is to be attained by our own efforts, but from the gift of God. Life as God gives it is existence in His love; if this is not the character of man's actual empirical life, the fault lies not with God but with man.

Thus the original nature of man is being in the love of God, the fulfilment of responsible being, the responsibility which comes not from a demand but from a gift, not from the law but from grace, from generous love, and itself consists in responsive love. From the point of view of God this is His intention for human life, and this is the reason for which He created it. The human character of existence consists in the very fact that it is related to God, and indeed in the reception of the divine love. The Reformers defended this truth of man's fulfilment in God, and its responsive character when they insisted that the *Imago Dei*, which determines the nature of man, is to be understood as *justitia originalis* and not as reason, freedom or creative capacity. Man is to be understood from the point of view of his being-in-God, of his derivation from God, and not in the light of his own efforts and achievements.

What, then, is the position of that being of man which even the godless man, who has turned away from God, sinful, fallen man—man, that is, in the empirical sphere, to which we all belong—still possesses? From all that I have said already it is evident that we must abandon the dubious idea of a 'relic' of the *Imago,* which was introduced by the Reformers. For it says both too much and too little; too much, because it seems to suggest that there is a sphere in human existence which is not affected by sin; and too little, because it does not take into account the fact that man—precisely in his sin—bears witness to his original relation with God, that also, and particularly in sin, he manifests his 'theological' nature, as one who 'stands before God,' and is related to God. We ought to say rather that the original state of life, the *justitia originalis* has been completely lost—owing to sin—and that in point of fact man is not living in accordance with the love of God; man is not loving God who 'first loved' him; yet the 'theological' structure of human existence, as it has been created by the Creator, is not annihilated by the hostility of man to the will of the Creator, although it is perverted in its operation. Even as a sinner man can only be understood in the light of the original Image of God, namely, as one who is living in opposition to it. Let us not forget that when we speak of an 'Image of God' and of its 'destruction' we are speaking figuratively. So far as clear-cut ideas are possible in this realm, what we can say is this: man's relation with God, which determines his whole being, has not been destroyed by sin, but it has been perverted. Man does not cease to be the being who is responsible to God, but his responsibility has been altered from a state of being-in-love to a state of being-under-the-law, a life under the wrath of God. But this whole question can only be fully treated in the context of the next chapter.

5. COMMUNITY IN THE CONCRETE

Responsibility-in-love first becomes real in man's relation with his fellow-men. For alongside the first commandment of the love of God there is a second which is 'like unto it'[1]—a second and yet not a second—the love of man. Here too, however, it is not the commandment which comes first, but the gift; the fact of the Divine 'Thou' means that the human 'Thou' is also given to man as the possibility of his selfhood. Man cannot be man 'by himself'; he can only be man in community. For love can only operate in community, and only in this operation of love is man human.[2] The human 'Thou' is not an accident of human existence, something which gives to his present human existence a new content and richness; but it is that which conditions his human existence. Only if he is loving can he be truly man. This means the discovery of a new idea of humanity, which does not find the distinctively human element, the core of humanity, in the creative or perceptive reason, but in community, as the fulfilment of responsibility. 'Love is the fulfilling of the Law'[3]—not merely of the moral law, but of the law of life. Human life is characterized as human, not by its attainments in the realm of reason, but by the union of human beings in love. That is the content of human existence, which is in accordance with man's original divine destiny, and is an earthly reflection of the divine nature itself. 'In Himself' the Triune God is love; in His relation to the world He is Creator. Therefore He reveals Himself in His Incarnation, not as creative genius, but as perfect love; in the Incarnation we perceive both the original nature of God and the reflected original nature of man. True community is the ground and the content of Christian 'humanity'; it is fundamentally different from that of individualistic humanism.[4] Where man is regarded as a rational being, as a participator in the *one* reason, his humanity consists in his rational thought and activity. Whether in so doing he remains alone or not is of no importance. The Stoic sage as well as the Platonic contemplator of Ideas is self-sufficient. The fact that other human beings exist may perhaps

[1] Matt. xxii. 39.

[2] Hence rationalism, even in its speculative idealistic form, is necessarily individualistic or abstractly universalistic; in both instances it has no 'Thou.'

[3] Rom. xiii. 10; Matt. xxii. 40.

[4] Cf. below pp. 324 ff.

lead him to undertake a task of political ethics or of philanthropic obligation.

6. THE 'THOU' AS THE BOUNDARY

In the Christian conception, however, community is not only a concrete working out of man's destiny; it is also the concrete limitation of the 'I.' The Divine 'Thou' is not confronted by a single human 'I'—for if this were so, such a self would not be responsible, a being with genuine ties—but by a number of selves who recognize that the bond which unites them with God also unites them with one another. As the Creator gives to man the humanity of his life in community, in love, so also He assigns to him his limitations in his connexion with others. From the outset the human 'I' is limited by a concrete 'Thou,' and only so does it become a concretely responsible Self. The fact that this is so rules out both the self-sufficiency and the arrogance of the autonomous reason.

The self which understands itself as autonomous reason, once it has 'discovered' its divine nature, has no limits, for no one stands 'over against' it. Hence too the boundary between it and God fades away. This individualism leads not only to autarchy but to metaphysical solipsism and to self-deification; to that titanic idea of the self which has been most strongly expressed in the West by Fichte, which, however, in all its intensity could only be worked out to its extremest limits in the East. There the self does not know itself as created being, hence it knows neither responsibility nor limitation. No other being stands 'over against' it, either human or divine; fantastic as this may sound to our realistic Western ears, it is: the Divine Self. The rationalistic West, however, precisely in its rationalism, has preserved at least one element of this audacious claim to unlimited powers: the deification of reason, the unbounded claim of reason to be recognized as valid and supreme.

7. THE BODY AND THE WORLD

Yet again, however, in the Christian truth concerning man's origin, man is given a possibility of self-expression which is at the same time placed within certain definite limits. The material body is given to man, with his actual responsible self-determination, in order that it may be quite plain that he is a 'creature,' and that he may be aware of his 'creaturely' character. The body is given that he may come into contact with the world, empirically, and also that he may shape the world; the body has been set as the creaturely boundary of the individual between himself and the Creator, and also between himself and other individuals. According to the anthropology of the Bible, man is not only of this world, but he is also a bit of this world, 'dust of the ground.'[1] In spite of the vehement protest made by Fichte, he is a localized self, bound to a definite spot in this world of time and space. His corporeal nature ought to make him aware of his distance from the Creator Spirit, and of the fact of his dependence on other human beings, on the 'Thou.' The clearest expression of this bond by means of the body is: procreation and birth. Here, in so far as he does not in his abstractions transcend reality, man experiences the fact that his life is bound up with and conditioned by the existence of other human beings. He experiences it also in his bodily nature and in the way in which his mind and spirit are connected with his body. But in this he experiences not only a limitation but also his creative capacity. Through the body he shapes matter, and in thus shaping it he is imitating the Creator. As a physical shaper of matter he is able to manifest his spirit in a reflected manner, just as the Creator does in His creation.

8. THE CITIZEN OF TWO WORLDS

From this point of view there is one final thing to be said. According to his origin man is a being composed of body and spirit; he belongs to two spheres of being. In two ways he has a share in the Divine Spirit: through the fact that he springs from God and that he is made for God. This is not meant, however, in the sense in which it is understood in speculative rationalism, that is, as substantial, as *particula Dei*,[2]

[1] Gen. ii. 7.

[2] The account in the story of the Creation (Gen. ii. 7) of the divine in-breathing of the breath of life was of course from the time of Philo a favourite occasion for the idealistic allegorization of the Bible. Here the Bible seemed to come into contact with the fundamental idea of ancient

but as functional, in the sense of dependence and responsibility. But through God's giving he has a share in the life of God. He is so created that he can perceive God's eternal Word, and can answer it as the reason which perceives, and as a self-determining will. The false element in the definition of rationalism and Idealism is not the fact that man is a rational being and can determine himself, but their error consists in saying that he is an *autonomous* rational being, and that he of himself determines his own life. The fundamental error of the non-Christian doctrine of Reason is this: it implies reason without anyone to perceive, self-determination without any Divine determination, an irresponsible rational self without any other being 'over against' it.

Through this participation in the divine life and in spiritual existence man, for his part, stands 'over against' the world, as its master—in accordance with the divine appointment.[1] As a rational being who is able to think about that which presents itself to his consciousness, man is able to look at the world from a distance, with the detachment of an outside observer; he is able to know it, and through this knowledge he is able to master it. This does not take place in the sense in which God does so, as absolute, sovereign Lord, but in a limited, imitative manner, in a relative sense. But this man can do, and this is his destiny assigned him by the Creator, just as responsibility for love is his destiny so far as his fellow-man is concerned. In this position of spiritual domination man is something other than the world, namely, a spiritual being, and this is why he creates within it something which is other than the world, namely, culture, the work of the mind and spirit. He is a citizen of two worlds, a being who stands midway between two spheres, in virtue of his divine destiny. Therefore it is not arrogance when he takes a position above the world. He ought to do so, and he may do so—so long as

Humanism, participation in the divine spirit (*particula Dei*) or the *Nous*. Doubtless this personal in-breathing indicates a special nearness of God to the man whom He has created (cf. Eichrodt, op. cit., p. 99); but there is not the remotest connexion between this Hebrew idea and that spirit-immanence of the Greek philosophers. Cf. Calvin on this passage, opp. 23, 35: it is life as a whole which man thus receives.

[1] Gen. i. 26, 28; Psa. viii. 7 ff.

all this takes place within the limits which have been appointed him, and he himself remains aware of his 'creaturely' character. He may know that he stands above other created beings, in virtue of his mind and spirit; he may know therefore that he is a higher creature, the crown of creation, although as a corporeal being he is a mammal, without any specially distinctive character. His distinctiveness as a physical being refers only to that which makes him capable of expressing his mind in an effective way, and, by means of his spirit, to rule; or to that which is serviceable to his responsible relation to his fellow-creature. In several other relations man is not the crown of creation, but rather he is heavily handicapped. And why should he not be? His distinctiveness is not based upon the power of his muscles or the acuteness of his sense-organs, but upon the fact that he participates in the life of God, God's thought and God's will, through the Word of God.

This distinctive position of man in the cosmos was not unobserved by the thinkers in the ancient world.[1] Their perception of and insistence on this fact is the common ground of the principle of humanity both in Christian thought and in the thought of antiquity; but its basis and its limitation are utterly different. It is precisely this perception of being something higher and distinctive which serves the speculative philosopher as the starting-point of his concept of the autonomous reason. Conversely, Idealistic Humanism (both ancient and modern) regards the corporeal nature of man as the *partie honteuse*, indeed as a 'prison' which is incompatible with the spiritual nature of man. To it the body is a kind of survival —whatever one may do with its instincts, or however one may use them, so far as this is possible, for self-glorification! The idea that the body could be an instrument to do the will of God is an idea which is as alien to this mode of thought as it is natural to the thought of the Bible.[2]

9. THE NEW DOCTRINE AND THE ANCIENT DOCTRINE

At two points we have been obliged to criticize the traditional doctrine of the *Imago* and the Primitive State. The first

[1] Cf. Appendix V, *On the ancient idea of Humanity* (p. 547).
[2] Rom. xii. 1.

point is concerned with the historical form of the doctrine. It is not some human being who happened to live in the far-off and dim ages of pre-history who is the Adam created in the Image of God; it is you, and me, and everybody. The Primitive State is not an historical period, but an historical moment, the moment of the Divinely created origin, which we only know in connexion with its contrast, with sin. The question of the historical origins of humanity leads into a quite different dimension, in which there is no hope of finding an answer to our question. Pre-historic man, whoever he may have been, has no closer relation to Adam than any of the rest of us. The question of the 'first man' leads us into the impenetrable obscurity of palaeontology, of which all that is clear is that from the theological point of view it contains nothing to guide us on this point.[1] We must face this quite seriously; the fact that in so doing we not only do justice to the scientific conscience, but also to the fundamental Biblical view of the responsible human being, will come out still more clearly in the next chapter.

The second point is still more important. The fact that even the sinful and fallen man is still a human being led ancient theology to regard this apparently neutral humanity as the distinctively human nature, and to interpret this in the spirit of Greek rationalism as a rational nature. It is this rationalism and naturalism which dominates the whole history of theology, which we contest. There is no nature of man as man, to be understood first of all as rational, no human nature which is to be understood apart from man's relation to God, to which man's relation to God may then be added as 'supernature.' The distinction between *imago* and *similitudo* is bad exegesis. The whole 'nature' of man is supernatural—that of the sinner no less than that of the redeemed. Man is fundamentally misunderstood when, by a method of subtraction, that which is common to fallen man and to man as originally created is contrasted as 'nature' with that which has been lost as 'supernature.'

The Reformers fought against this error by teaching that the whole nature of man—and nothing else—is corrupt, and

[1] Cf. Chap. 17.

that this original nature is identical with communion with God, with the *justitia originalis*. But the pseudo-historical doctrine of the Primitive State prevented the full result of their revolutionary perception from being gained. Because they did not venture to identify us with the original Adam, they did not know how to relate the undeniable *humanum* of fallen man to the *imago*, which was supposed to have been lost; hence on the one hand they went back to the rationalistic idea of the *animal rationale*, and on the other hand they introduced the confusing concept of the 'relic' of the *Imago*, without being able to unite both with each other, and with the original conception of the lost *Imago*. The abandonment of the historical character of the 'Adam' narrative alone made possible for us the logical carrying through of the strictly theological, because actual and personalistic concept of the *Imago*, and in so doing to think through to its conclusion the Biblical and Reformation idea of man as created in the Image of God, whose destiny we know through Jesus Christ alone.

10. RELIGIOUS OR RATIONALISTIC MYTHOLOGY?

So long as the doctrine of the Primitive State was burdened with the Adam narrative, rationalistic criticism could make short work of it. The impossible historical form concealed the true contradiction: between an understanding of man as due to the Word of God and an understanding of man from the point of view of the autonomous reason. Seen from the standpoint of the autonomous reason, every strictly theological doctrine, that is, every doctrine which takes into account the Word of God as the Word from 'over against' man, must be condemned as 'mythological.' For if the human reason with its 'divine' character is the highest court of appeal, how can the Christian doctrine be other than a reversal of truth, an anthropomorphism projected into the transcendent sphere? The logical result of this anthropomorphic idea of God is then, so runs the conclusion, the theomorphic idea of man, in consequence of which there lies the further necessity for a revelation, and thus the necessity for a mythology.

So long as the idea of the autonomous reason is maintained, it is impossible to escape from the logic of this idea. Every time the frontier of that which can be attained by reason is exceeded, it must appear to be mythology, or to use the language of Kant, 'extravagance.' But Kant himself never got rid of this 'extravagance'; the simple Christian within him was always wrestling with the transcendental philosopher,[1] and this struggle was still going on in his later works which were published after his death. At many points in his theoretical philosophy, in the *Kritik der reinen Vernunft*; above all, in his reflection on the problem of responsibility, he came to the extreme limits of his rationalistic doctrine. Once he stepped over this boundary, namely, where without taking into consideration the postulates of the doctrine of autonomy he examined the phenomenon of responsibility in its most critical form, in the form of evil. In his doctrine of radical evil, amid the protests of his contemporaries, he abandoned the Idealistic line of thought and went part of the way with the Bible. Then, however, he turns back resolutely; he cannot and will not renounce the claim of the autonomous reason, the idea of the intelligible human being as our real self. Such a surrender indeed is not to be achieved by way of thought. This surrender would be what in the New Testament is called 'Repentance': the self which ceases to be its own judge, and recognizes the Judge who is above and beyond himself. At this point alone, and this means once again in the sphere of real responsibility, the question is decided which of the two is mythology: the Christian thought which is derived from the Word of God, or the Greek, which deifies the human reason.

[1] On this point cf. my book, *Religionsphilosophie protestantischer Theologie* in Bäumler's *Handbuch der Philosophie*, pp. 25 ff.

CHAPTER VI

THE CONTRADICTION: THE DESTRUCTION OF THE IMAGE OF GOD

1. THE PROBLEM: THE CONTRADICTION

THE Christian message of the reconciliation and redemption of mankind contains, as its negative presupposition, the doctrine that man, who has been created in the image of God, has set himself in opposition to his origin, and that it is this opposition which determines the contradiction in his nature, the conflict between his true nature and his actual, empirical nature. In the perception of this truth—which is only disclosed to those who believe in God's Word through Jesus Christ—the Christian doctrine maintains that it is the only realistic doctrine of man, that is, the only one which is in touch with reality, the only one which understands and explains man aright.[1]

Just as everyone knows something of the higher and distinctive element in man—even the cynic—so also everyone knows something of the contradiction in man—even the idealistic mystic. The thesis that man is identical with the Deity, or that his nature is divine, cannot be made plausible to anyone without certain reservations which take some account of the contradiction in human nature. The mystic is forced to admit that man is only identical with Deity, or divine, in the 'depths of his being,' in his 'real' nature, which has somehow become unreal, or concealed, or at least appears to be so. On the other hand, the sceptic is embarrassed by the 'higher' element in man when it appears in a negative form, as a sign of conflict, as, for instance, an accusing conscience. In romantic Pantheism the contradiction comes out

[1] In his otherwise most informing article on 'the Question of Theological Anthropology' (in the work, *Um Kirche und Lehre*, pp. 78 ff.) K. F. Schumann confuses anthropology as a statement about myself with the statement as one which is made by me myself (p. 89); hence he maintains that what preaching (or the Bible) says decisively about man is not an anthropological statement, but Christological, pneumatic, theological anthropology.

in all that is opposed as the enemy of immediacy; in the mind as the adversary of the soul,[1] in intellectualistic reflection which destroys naïveté, and the like. Common sense, however, is simply aware of the contradiction in the fact of evil, which it does not attempt to deny, but is unable to explain.[2]

In point of fact, evil is the open wound where the disease breaks out and can no longer be concealed. Evil, however, at least in practical life—especially when one has to suffer from it—is recognized by everyone, even if denied in theory. The contrast between good and evil, different as the content may be, which will be given to these two concepts, is a perception common to all human beings and to all races.[3] Even the content of these ideas, as soon as one examines the various interpretations more closely, is comparatively a common one: good is what furthers life; bad is what hinders, corrupts or destroys life. But 'good' or 'evil' only mean that which furthers or destroys life where it is combined with the idea of responsibility. Evil (*das Böse*) is different from misfortune (*Übel*);[4] evil is the destructive action of a responsible being. Thus evil is the negative aspect of responsibility. Here—in responsibility—the contradiction becomes evident.

But as soon as we try to give a more exact definition of the origin and the nature of this contradiction which comes out in evil, opinions become very confused. Some maintain that the contradiction springs from the dual character of our nature, that is, the fact that we are both body and mind; or it is supposed to be due to our fatal entanglement with earthly-

[1] L. Klages, *Der Geist als Widersacher der Seele*; Bergson, *Évolution créatrice* and *Introduction à la métaphysique*.

[2] Cf. what Heidegger has to say about 'Uneigentlichkeit' and guilt in *Sein und Zeit* (pp. 280 ff.). Here in particular we see what was said above: the value and the limit of value of Heidegger's observations on guilt are precisely those of the *sensus communis*. (Cf. Translator's Note on p. 19.)

[3] Cf. Cathrein, *Die Einheit des sittlichen Bewusstseins der Menschheit*, where, quite apart from the Catholic interpretation, there is a mass of anthropological material for evidence.

[4] *Übel*, almost = misfortune or disaster. It is 'evil' without a moral element; it contains the idea of 'evil' as a 'defect' or 'imperfection'; it is partly negative, because 'evil' (in this sense) is not regarded as due to the individual.—*Translator*.

cosmic existence; or it is a tragic Fate, due to the will of supernatural forces; or it is the act of the will determined by the sense-nature; or it is the result of man's animal nature which has not yet been overcome by culture and civilization —the natural expression of primitive human nature, which is still undeveloped.[1] In all these 'explanations' the attempt is made to derive evil from a kind of fate, and thus to relieve man of responsibility for his existence. In contrast to all these views is the purely moral theory, namely, that evil has no other origin than the free will of man, who is able to decide equally well for evil as for good. Here the whole responsibility for evil is ascribed to man, without any attempt to explain how it comes to pass that sometimes he decides for evil and at other times for good. Thus we are confronted by the fact that in the one instance the deep cleavage in the nature of man is recognized but responsibility for it is disclaimed, while in the other case, although responsibility is admitted, the cleavage is denied. Evidently it is not possible for us to visualize at the same time both the fact of the fatal cleavage in human nature and the fact of full responsibility.

The Biblical revelation, however, shows us both in one, since it tells us that we are sinners, that means human beings who not only sin now and then, occasionally—that is, every time we do not do the good—but whose very being is defined as sin; but this also means human beings who are fully responsible for all the evil they do, and for the evil in their nature as well.[2] Thus the Biblical revelation permits the contradiction

[1] On all these theories (as well as on the whole chapter) of evil, cf. the work—hitherto unsurpassed—of J. Müller, *Christliche Lehre von der Sünde*, 2 vols., 1838–44, 1877[6].

[2] Possibly there is significance in the fact that both the Old Testament and the teaching of Jesus in the Synoptic Gospels always speak of sin (or, more correctly, of *sins*) in the sense of *act*, and scarcely ever in the sense of state of being. Sin is rebellion, disobedience, disloyalty towards God and the transgression of His commands. Even where, as in the story of the Fall and in the parable of the Prodigal Son, sin is the subject, it is always presented to us in the form of a story, that is, sin is shown us as *act*. Only against this background can the Johannine, and still more the Pauline, doctrine of sin be rightly understood, in which sin is mainly spoken of in the singular, as a state of being, as a force which dominates man. This deeper view is really deeper only if the character of sin as *act* has been

in man's being to be seen without weakening it; at the same time too it allows the whole responsibility in action to be seen without weakening it.[1] It recognizes the fatal sense of the inevitable, the sense of Fate in evil; it calls us 'slaves of sin,' who have no free choice not to commit sin or not to be sinners; but it also recognizes man's absolute responsibility, and does not attempt to ascribe it to some impersonal force in the form of a destiny outside our own will. It conceives sin, the contradiction, wholly ontologically, so that the whole nature of the individual human being, as well as the numerical totality of all human beings, is affected by it, and it is quite impossible to isolate the individual moment, or act, or individual human being; at the same time it conceives it as wholly personal and deliberate, so that nothing neutral, no natural element, is admitted as a ground of explanation. It defines the contradiction in ontological terms, to such an extent that the whole character of human existence, even that which lies far removed from the moral sphere, is affected by it, and again it defines it so personally that it consists simply in a personal relation, namely, in the relation between God and myself, which works out in my relation to my fellow-man. This paradox, which cannot be grasped by thought, shows itself in faith as the actual condition of man, which man cannot perceive just because he is so deeply entangled in it. It is of sin in this sense that Luther speaks when he says that it is 'such a deep and evil corruption of nature that no reason understands it, but that it must be believed from the revelation of

secured; because unless this is done the personal knowledge of sin is replaced by an impersonal metaphysic of sin—however profound this may be—and this has actually been the case in the ecclesiastical doctrine of Original Sin. The Augustinian scholastic distinction between sin as *actus* and as *habitus* is unscriptural. Sin, even as Original Sin, is always *actus*, even if it is not a momentary act which can be isolated, but a wholly personal act, an act which determines the being of the person as a whole. Cf. below p. 148. And also on this point the word ἁμαρτία in Kittel's *Wörterbuch*.

[1] Even J. Gerhard, who as a rule does not hesitate to use very crude naturalistic concepts to describe Original Sin (see p. 121 note), says: '*ita cohaerent peccatum originale et actualia, ut non facile sit homini contentioso ostendere punctum mathematicum, in quo distinguantur*' (op. cit., v. 17).

the Scriptures.'[1] In this view that which every man recognizes as 'evil' is regarded merely as a symptom, as the open eruption of the 'sickness unto death,'[2] while it unveils the source of the disease, the contradiction itself which lies behind the difference between good and evil. The contradiction—this is obvious from what has already been said—is not simply 'something contradictory' in man, but it is a contradiction of the whole man against the whole man, a division within man himself. And this division, if what has been said about man's origin be correct, can only consist in the fact that man, who was originally created to decide in accordance with the divine determination, has decided against this determination, so that, just as the original determination gave him his true life, this hostility to it robs him of his true life, and allows him to fall a prey to an unreal life. It is with this contradiction to his true origin, which becomes a kind of fate which man has brought upon himself by his own fault, that Christian doctrine is concerned.

2. THE ECCLESIASTICAL DOCTRINE

The traditional ecclesiastical doctrine deals with this contradiction under the twofold conception of the Fall and of Original Sin: the idea of the Fall suggests that the 'contradiction' consists in apostasy from man's origin; the idea of Original Sin maintains that this 'contradiction' is a fateful determination of man's actual condition. Primarily there is no objection to this twofold view; indeed it is entirely relevant

[1] Schmalk. Art. (WA. 50, 221), Luther certainly uses the customary ecclesiastical terminology, *corruptio naturae*, etc., but he immediately transforms it into personalistic terms. Where he himself formulates what sin is he uses expressions such as: to be under the devil, or outside of Christ, under the wrath of God, enmity against God, contempt of God, disobedience, *curvitas cordis*, unbelief. 'And thus briefly and barely there is included in this word sin what one lives and does outside faith in Christ' (EA. 12, 111). 'Unbelief is in all men the chief sin, even in Paradise it was the beginning and the first of sins, and it probably remains the last of all sins.' It is this 'unbelief which has been implanted in human nature by Adam' (WA. 46, 41). This results from the relation of man to the Word of God: *Quam magnum igitur est verbum, tam magnum etiam est peccatum quod contra verbum admittitur* (WA. 42, 122).

[2] Kierkegaard, *Die Krankheit zum Tode*, *Werke*, Jena, vol. 8.

and must not be abandoned. The question, however, is only this: is the way in which these two aspects of the same fact are seen together in accordance with reality? And does it succeed in expressing the two intentions—necessity and responsibility, totality and individuality—equally clearly?

To this question the only answer can be 'No.' The ecclesiastical traditional doctrine is forced by its historical form to sever the unity of the two points of view. It destroys the unity between responsibility and necessity, since it distributes it first of all to different persons, and then afterwards removes the unity into the sphere of nature instead of keeping it in the sphere of the person.

The classical doctrine of sin, too, the doctrine of the Fall of Adam, and of the Original Sin handed down from him to all succeeding generations, starts, like the doctrine of the *Imago*, from the Old Testament narrative, as it is stated in Genesis iii, but in such a way that the narrative, interpreted in the light of the New Testament doctrine of sin,[1] with the

[1] To what extent can the Augustinian doctrine appeal to Romans v. 12 ff.? The exegesis of this *locus classicus* of the doctrine of Original Sin may indeed be regarded as one of the most difficult tasks of Biblical theology. Here I will only touch upon some of the chief points: (*a*) The use of the story of the Fall as an explanation of the sinfulness of man is foreign to the Old Testament itself; it does not appear until the time of Jewish Apocalyptic (cf. N. P. Williams, *The Idea of the Fall and of Original Sin*, 1929). (*b*) In the New Testament indeed, even with Paul himself, the story of Adam plays no part in connexion with the doctrine of sin, apart from Rom. v. 12 ff. and 1 Cor. xv. 21. The idea of sin in the New Testament, indeed, even the Pauline doctrine, is in its general sense independent of the story of Adam. The story of Adam is *one* of the means by which Paul interprets the universality and the power of sin. (*c*) Even in the Epistle to the Romans the real theme is not Original Sin, but death as the result of the sin of Adam. 'Paul first calls death that which the one has made to be the lot of all' (Schlatter, *Theologie der Apostel*, p. 264). (*d*) From the outset it is explicitly emphasized that this has happened 'on the ground that all have sinned.' The condemnation of all is not directly attributed to the fall of Adam but to the sin of all. The Augustinian doctrine of Original Sin, in the narrower sense of the word, was based upon the questionable exegesis: ἐφ' ᾧ = *in quo* = *in lumbis Adami*. The condemnation of all as a result of the sin of Adam does not annul the first-mentioned presupposition, but it silently presupposes it. (*e*) The exegetical evidence is not sufficient to deny that Paul taught something like a doctrine of Original Sin; on the contrary, in this one passage Paul comes very near to such a doctrine. But

aid of dogmatic postulates, is systematized and is stated in terms which cannot be excelled. After the early Christian theologians had developed very contradictory and different views of the Fall, and the extent of its effects upon the human race,[1] it was Augustine who gave to the ecclesiastical doctrine its standard form, in which it determined not only the history of Roman Catholic theology but the development of Protestant theology as well.

For our generation, the fact that this narrative is no longer historically credible means that the convincing power of this imposing doctrine, which dominated the thought of Europe for fifteen hundred years and—although modified in different ways—has formed the solid substance of the doctrine of sin of all Christian churches, has completely disappeared. For most of our contemporaries Adam is a kind of legendary figure; it can no longer play any part in the thinking of the succeeding generations as a historical force.

But what we said in connexion with the question of man's origin is still more true here: the re-formulation to which we are forced by scientific knowledge is not a retraction which cannot, 'unfortunately,' be avoided, but it is an inner necessity, inherent in the very truth apprehended by faith. It is not for scientific reasons, in the main, that the historical form of the doctrine of the Fall is questionable, but for religious reasons; it has led to serious distortions of the faith, of the understanding of sin, and of man's responsibility in the sight of God. The protest against it has not sprung only from a

it is just as inadequate to provide a convincing argument for such a doctrine. What Paul wants to express here is this: with the means at his disposal he wants to assert both the solidarity and unity of humanity in sin (see below p. 139) and the responsibility of each individual; the power which sin exerts over humanity as a whole, and also the personal character of sin. In 1 Cor. xv. 21 he is speaking not of sin but of death.

The Apostle's idea clearly is this: that where the redeeming power of the Risen Lord is not operative, sin now dominates man and humanity as a whole; that man, and humanity, at present not only 'sins' but is 'in sin'; here for once, and for once only, he expresses this view, which he never uses again, which also is not known in the rest of the New Testament. The theme of the Bible is not the historical *origin* of sin, but the universal and irresistible *power* of sin as affecting man's being.

[1] Williams, op. cit., pp. 167 ff.

rationalistic, 'Pelagian' way of thinking—although of course it is perfectly true that this is one of the chief reasons for the protest—but it is also due to the fact that men have seen that this wording of the contradiction emphasizes the necessity of sin at the expense of responsibility.

What Augustine wanted, and what he defended against the liberalism of his day—Pelagianism—inspired by the sense of a divine commission and the truth of the Scriptures, using the whole force of his powers of thought and faith, was this: the unity of inescapable necessity and responsibility which cannot be shaken off, sin as a totality which determines the person, and at the same time sin as a personal act. But his actual solution of the problem fell very far short of his intention. We do not say this in order to criticize him—his contribution to the solution has no rival. But his solution can no longer satisfy us, once our feeling for personal responsibility has been awakened. The solution which Augustine gives, that Adam's deed makes us sinful and guilty, is supported by two arguments of very unequal value and of different origin. Adam is the physical father of the race; sin is inherited sin (*Erb*[1]-*sünde*).[2] The German translation of *peccatum originis* by *Erb-*

[1] *Erbe* = inheritance.—*Translator.*

[2] It is only logical that the best teachers of the Church should be those who—to the extent in which they took up a position upon the doctrine of Original Sin—should represent the most massive doctrinal forms. Augustine: the *peccata* of Adam are our *contagione propagationis* (*contra Jul.c.m.*4); Anselm: *ex parentibus leprosis generantur leprosi, ita ex primis parentibus*, etc. (*De conc. virg.* Chap. 2); *peccatum intimis visceribus ac fibris arctissime per omnem vitam adharens* (Gerhard, IV, 334). A sinister part was played in this connexion by a wrong translation of Job xiv. 4: *quis faciet mundum de immundo conceptum semine?* (Gerhard knows that the translation is incorrect, but in spite of this he continually uses it. IV, 326.) *In primo conceptionis ardore peccati venenum una cum ipso calore a matre sit in ipsum transfusum* (Gerhard, IV, 349). The same tendency appears—in contradistinction from Augustine—when the earlier Lutheran theologians felt obliged to attribute to infants not merely Original Sin but actual sin, just as they had to ascribe actual faith to them in order to be able to uphold the view that their baptism was a genuine sacrament (cf. Hutter, *Loci communes*, X, 1, 3, quoted by Müller, op. cit., p. 51). This idea of transference shows further to how great an extent the dualistic view of sexuality in Augustine has also affected the formation of Protestant doctrine. Without this element the doctrine of Original Sin is inconceivable.

sünde has given to this one element—it is by far the less important of the two—the main emphasis, and as a rule even the whole emphasis: we are sinners because we have inherited sin through our natural descent from the sinful father of our race. Something which in its meaning is purely personal, sin, disobedience to the will of God, is ascribed to a purely natural fact, that of physical descent. We must take over the responsibility for guilt, for something in which we have actually no part. It is of course possible to 'believe' such a thing in the sense of the *sacrificium intellectus*; but it is impossible to believe it in the sense in which I may and ought to believe that Jesus Christ is my Lord and my Saviour. Here faith had to take the character of a false heteronomy, which is contrary to its nature.

The second argument—which is far more valuable and relevant—was this: Adam is the representative of the human race as a whole.[1] In Adam we have all sinned; we are all sinners in Adam. Here the point to be emphasized is not the physical fact of inheritance but our solidarity in sin as act and guilt. But, in order to make this phrase, 'sinners in Adam,' as concrete as possible, Augustine once more interpreted it in a physical manner: *in lumbis Adami*. In germ, physiologically, we were 'represented' in Adam. Thus in the concrete development of this doctrine this second *motif* also leads back to the first, and intensifies its fatal supremacy.

If we reject this conception of the Christian understanding of sin as insufficient and dangerous, since a personal relation ought not to be explained by a physical fact, thus when we describe as questionable precisely that element in

[1] *Adam non ut privatus homo, sed ut caput totius humani generis peccavit.* This is the phrase used by J. Gerhard following Augustine. This doctrine has more right than the doctrine of Original Sin, to appeal to Romans v, where nothing is said of a physical transference, where, on the contrary, it is said that through the disobedience of the one the many are 'treated' (by God) as sinners, or 'represented' as such. What is meant here is not physical but legal transference, and thus something which comes very near to that which we call 'solidarity-in-sin.' Further, Harnack has rightly pointed out that even the words *in quo* are to some extent a contradiction of the doctrine of Original Sin, inasmuch as this expression is intended to express our personal participation in the sin of Adam (*Lehrbuch der Dogmengeschichte*, III, p. 215).

the doctrine of *peccatum originale*, which leads to the rendering *Erbsünde*, this does not mean that the fact of procreation and of the relation between the generations should be excluded from the group of factors which are to be considered. The *peccatum originis* is certainly *also* inherited sin. The solidarity of being involved in sin manifests itself also in 'inheritance.' What we reject is this: the one-sidedness with which this one element is made the prevailing and, finally, the only element in the doctrine.

3. THE REACTION OF MODERN THEOLOGY

Just as in the question of the origin of man, modern theology has tried to find a new solution of the problem, in which the impossibilities of the historical conception should be avoided. If we examine these 'solutions' more closely we find that they can be divided into two groups, as modifications of two leading ideas. In the one group the idea of fateful necessity, in the other that of personal responsibility is re-formulated; but this is done in such a manner that in each case such scant attention is paid to the second aspect of the idea that the latter always comes off badly.

In Schleiermacher, for instance, in harmony with his thought as a whole, the aspect of fateful necessity, of determinism is expressed very impressively. His doctrine of 'Original Sin' comes to this, that at every new stage in his development man is hindered by the previous stages. These obstacles are determinations which always spring from the 'sense-nature,' which Schleiermacher, completely distorting the language of the Bible, describes by the Biblical expression, the 'flesh.'[1] In his thought the conflict between the spirit and the flesh, of which the Bible speaks, becomes a dynamic dialectic of the development of the natural, or sense element, and the ideal, or spirit element, instead of a personal decision. Original Sin is a kind

[1] For Schleiermacher sin is 'an arrestment of the determinative power of the spirit due to the independence of the sensuous functions' (*Der christliche Glaube*, § 66, 2). As Original Sin it asserts itself by the 'advantage which the flesh at that time (that is at the beginning of the spiritual activity) had already gained' (§ 67, 2). Hence Schleiermacher praises the first part of the word *Erbsünde* and criticizes the second (§ 69; addition).

of atavism; it means that the spirit has not kept pace with the rest of human development which is proceeding from the sphere of sense to that of spirit. Thus the problem of Original Sin (*Erbsünde*) is 'solved' afresh, that is, turned in a completely new direction, by means of an idealistic evolutionism with a strong naturalistic tinge—here we can only repeat the formula which has already been used. Schleiermacher is not dealing with sin at all, but with stages of development. The problem is 'solved' by those theologians who are influenced by Hegel in the same scheme of idealistic evolutionism although with somewhat different concepts.[1]

The attempts which were made to deal with this question from the Kantian point of view—for instance, by Ritschl—were the very opposite. Ritschl, as a good Kantian, starts from the problem of responsibility. Sin—and in his thought there can be no doubt at all about this—is the responsible act of the individual. In his thought the moral character of sin is preserved. But how does he approach the other aspect of the problem, that is, necessity—with this primarily purely moralistic, Pelagian and rationalistic conception? His attempt does not lack originality; but this originality, when we look at it closely, consists only in the fact that he applies the psychological theories of 'environment' to the problem of sin. The will of the individual, he says, is no isolated fact. The individual is always affected in his resolves by his environment. Now in so far as in this world there are always a number of forces which are operative, in which evil is expressed and exercises an influence—both personal forces, that is, human beings who do and will evil, and also impersonal forces such as institutions, customs, literature, catchwords, etc.—which influence the individual in the sense of evil, he lives in a 'kingdom of sin' and is exposed permanently to the influences of the latter. In this fact of a 'kingdom of sin,' which contains within itself the whole historical experience of evil, and thus brings a universal-historical power of sin to bear upon the

[1] Thus for instance Biedermann, *Dogmatik*, II, § 769. The fact of Original Sin 'has its natural basis in the nature of man as a finite spirit,' especially 'in the fact that from the very essence of his nature the single instincts of life . . . in their natural immediacy individually form the motives.'

individual and allows it to influence him, Ritschl believes that he is able to conceive the true content of the doctrine of Original Sin.

This idea of a 'kingdom of sin' certainly corresponds to a reality. It sums up a number of facts in one definite and impressive concept, and is therefore valuable. But its relation to that which Christian doctrine means by *peccatum originis* is very remote. For its content is purely psychological; it could equally well be expressed by the proverb: 'evil communications corrupt good manners.' For the way in which my environment influences me is not any necessity which lies in myself, but it is an urgent temptation to evil. The power of the temptation may be as great as possible; there is no necessity to succumb to it. The insidious, contagious power of evil in the world may be very great; but there is still the possibility of saying *No*, of remaining independent.[1] So Ritschl allows for the possibility of resisting temptation, and in so doing he eliminates the main element from the Christian doctrine, that of totality.[2] When this doctrine is examined more closely, it proves to be simply a form of Pelagianism, intensified by social psychology.

4. RADICAL EVIL

Kant's effort to define the nature of 'radical evil' goes far deeper than all other attempts to solve the problem.[3] His strictly personal idea of responsibility permits him to separate himself sharply from the contrast between the sense nature and the idealistic emphasis on Spirit, which dominates the whole tradition of Idealism. Evil is not to be sought in the sphere of sense but solely in the will. The origin of evil is not the fact that man is finite, the metaphysical constitution of man, but a personal decision. Evil must not be traced back

[1] 'The working together of the many in these forms of sin leads to an intensification of the same in common habits and principles. . . . Thus there arises an almost irresistible power of temptation . . . the kingdom of sin . . .' Ritschl, *Unterricht in der christlichen Religion*, § 30.

[2] Ritschl, op. cit., §§ 27, 28.

[3] Kant, *Die Religion innerhalb der Grenzen der blossen Vernunft*, first part. Cf. on this point, too, my book *The Mediator*, pp. 126 ff.; Sannwald, op. cit., pp. 93 ff.

to any impersonal neutral entity but it has its origin in the centre of personality, just as in its working out it injures personality. It is still possible, however, to combine these ideas with the rationalistic, Pelagian conception, with its individualism and indeterminism.

But Kant now takes an important step, beyond this position. He is not unaware that the evil act, the evil decision of the will, which is the final element for the rationalist, is not itself an ultimate, but rather that it points back to an ultimate, an origin. He describes this origin of the evil act as the 'tendency to evil.' This tendency, this reservoir of evil which lies in the person itself, from which alone every evil decision springs, he establishes as a fact, and indeed as a fact of unrestricted totality. All human beings have in themselves this tendency to evil. Likewise he recognizes the impossibility of discovering a temporal beginning of this tendency, of this evil personal quality in the empirical life of the individual, or indeed of even thinking of any such; for every beginning would indeed presuppose this tendency. Thus Kant is confronted finally by the insoluble mystery of 'inborn evil,' by which he does not regard physical birth as the beginning—the idea 'inborn' is to be understood solely negatively, evil has no beginning in the empirical course of life—but only the fact that it is impossible to derive evil from any source, with, at the same time, the fact of unconditional personal responsibility. Kant is quite aware that he is faced by the paradox of an insoluble, impenetrable mystery, and points explicitly to the story of the Fall as the only relevant, although certainly symbolic expression of the fact which he has perceived.

With this view of evil Kant came so near to the Christian view that all his Idealistic contemporaries charged him with treachery and hypocrisy. He then himself became unfaithful to his own perception (in the third part of his book), and, in order to be able to maintain his concept of the autonomous reason, he gave up the doctrine of radical evil, surrendering it for the idea that the intelligible man is the better self of man, from which standpoint evil can be overcome by the force of one's own efforts. But this does not belong to our subject. Kant's idea of radical evil remains the most serious attempt ever made by any philosopher—who does not bring his system into conformity with the Christian revelation—about evil.[1] In spite of this, however, his doctrine certainly cannot be considered as the re-formulation of the Christian truth about sin. It is the expression of that which the man who reflects seriously upon evil can discover for himself. It is a 'borderline' truth; that is, the man who perceives it—as the example of Kant shows—cannot stand still at this point; he is forced to do one of two things: either to turn back to a rational 'explanation,' thought out from the point of view of the concept of the autonomous reason, and then to give up the idea itself, or, finally leaving the sphere of the autonomous reason, he must himself become a Christian believer.[2]

We must not forget that Kant never speaks of *sin* but of *evil* (*das Böse*). This means that the subject which he has in mind is not set in opposition to God, the Creator and Giver of life, but to the abstract law of reason. Thus Kant is not concerned about the fact that man, who has been created by God in responsibility, for love, contradicts the life-giving purpose of God, that is, that he sets himself in opposition to his divine origin, that he rebels against God, and thus sets himself up against the Lord as his own master, and in so doing perverts the good creation of God. Thus—and this is the heart of the matter—in his understanding of evil Kant is not concerned with the fact that man takes his life into his own hands, breaks away from God and desires to do the good in the strength of his own will, so that both his 'doing good' and his 'doing evil' are sin. Kant is not and cannot be concerned about all

[1] I cannot describe Schelling's *Philosophische Untersuchungen über das Wesen der menschlichen Freiheit* (*Werke*, vol. iv, p. 223, Münchner Neudruck) (against Jul. Müller, op. cit., pp. 126 ff.) as in every direction a deepening of the Kantian doctrine of evil, since it seeks the solution of the problem in the Gnostic view of a dual divine nature. Cf. further Müller's excellent criticism, op. cit., pp. 131 ff.

[2] This significance of the idea of autonomous reason is clearly seen by Sannwald (op. cit.) and by all the thinkers who have rediscovered the 'Thou,' especially Ebner, Gogarten and Grisebach. The excellent Jul. Müller is also aware of it: *Autonomy—Theonomy* (op. cit., I, p. 107). 'Ever if the autonomy of the human spirit were no contradiction in itself it would still be a contradiction to the concept of the creature' (I, p. 114). Müller only lacks insight into the dialectic of the law.

this, because his view lacks both the starting-point and the point of view of man's original relation with God.

Just as Kant's conception of 'person' is derived from the law, the 'Thou shalt'—that means (on the one hand) a responsibility which is on this side of the contradiction to the generous Creator, God, and (on the other hand) a personality which no longer knows anything about being 'over against' God—so also his 'radical evil' is only *one* manifestation of sin, whose other far more dangerous manifestation is precisely that which in the thought of Kant is regarded as the Good: the fact that man does good by his own efforts. The fact that through the Fall alone man 'knows what is good and evil,' that already the difference between good and evil is itself the product of the contradiction, and therefore is only a relative contradiction—of all this Kant can know nothing, since on the plane on which he stands such things cannot be perceived.[1]

But since we must finally say farewell to Kant, let us at least recall his observations on what he rightly describes as the perversion of the problem. This applies to doctrine of all kinds, even the traditional Christian one. The contradiction, he points out, ought not to be traced back to an objective, neutral, impersonal entity, neither to sense, nor to the fact that man is finite, nor to the imperfection of the stage of development, nor to ignorance—the Socratic modification of the doctrine of imperfection—nor to the weakness of the spirit, nor—as in the ecclesiastical view—to inheritance. By all these formulations the concept of sin is corrupted in its centre, in responsibility. If there is one element in the Biblical message which from time immemorial has been clear and beyond all doubt, it is this: sin and responsibility are inseparably connected, and there is no ascription of responsibility, no verdict of guilt, without accusation and proof of responsibility, that is, no one is pronounced guilty for something which he has not

[1] Harnack (op. cit., p. 216) is perfectly right when he says that Augustine's doctrine of the Primitive State is Pelagian. Here, as in the fathers of Calvinistic theology in their doctrine of the *foedus operum*, Aristotle's rationalistic idea of man comes out ('A relation between man and God which is based upon mutuality.' Heppe, *Dogmatik der reformierten Kirche*, p. 204).

done.[1] This is the postulate which clearly emerges from our survey of the history of the problem.

5. THE PRIMAL CONTRADICTION: THE FALL

The first thing that the Bible tells us about Primal Sin is that it is the revolt of the creature against the Creator; thus it is not something negative, it is a positive negation. Sin is defiance, arrogance, the desire to be equal with God, emancipation, a deliberate severance from the hand of God. This is the explanation of the nature of sin and its origin, not only in the story of the Fall[2] but also in the parable of the wicked husbandmen—the stewards who wanted to make themselves masters,[3] and in the parable of the Prodigal Son.[4] The son who lives with the father goes to him with the request: 'Father, give me my inheritance!' He wants to be independent. When André Gide, in his booklet, *L'enfant prodigue*, extols this will to independence as the birth of human freedom and of man's responsibility for his own life, he is speaking out of the depths of the modern mind, severed from God, which believes that an independent human existence can only be attained by being freed from God, just as N. Hartmann postulates atheism[5] for the sake of freedom. The fact that true freedom is the same as dependence on God, that man is only free when he is united with God, is an idea which lies outside the horizon of the emancipated autonomous reason. Indeed, it *will* not understand this idea, for if it were to do so it would have to die.

And this is the very origin of sin: the assertion of human independence over against God, the declaration of the rights of man's freedom as independent of God's will, the constitution of the autonomous reason, morality, and culture, that 'misunderstanding of reason in itself' (Hamann) where reason refuses any longer to apprehend, but wants to give and to have, where it no longer reflects upon existing truth, but desires 'to think things out for itself,' to initiate, to create, to

[1] Cf. Jer. xxxi. 30, and Ezek. xviii. 5, 9.
[2] Gen. iii.
[3] Matt. xxi. 33 ff.
[4] Luke xv. 11 ff.
[5] Nik. Hartmann, *Ethik*, p. 735.

produce its own thoughts in its own way, a human self-initiated creation made by 'man in his own strength.'[1]

This sin would not be possible if man had not actually been created to be master, to be independent, to be superior—namely, over the world, over the 'earth' which is to be 'made subject unto him.' To this end he has been endowed by the Creator with spirit and reason, with powers of creativeness and thought. 'All things are yours'[2]—so is it said in the story of the Garden of Eden as well as in the First Epistle to the Corinthians. But to this is added: 'Ye are God's,' or—in the parable—'Of every tree of the garden thou mayest freely eat; but of the tree of the knowledge of good and evil thou shalt not eat.'[3] The whole world is yours, but its centre is not yours. Its centre is God Himself. To infringe His sovereign rights, His divine privilege, is to 'desire' to be 'like God.' What happens then, if you still insist on doing it? The Lord says, 'Thou shalt surely die';[4] the serpent says, 'Ye shall be as God.'[5] The story of autonomous humanity may well show us which was speaking the truth.

But it is precisely this which attracts man: to measure himself against God. That is presumption, arrogance. It is the actual, primal sin. Sin in its developed form is this presumption of the son who rebels against the father. In this pure form it may rarely appear; in spite of this, however, it lies at the bottom of all sin, even the most pitiful sins of weakness, as arrogance, defiance and the illusion of independence, as the will to be independent of the will of God. Man never sins purely out of weakness but always also in the fact that he 'lets himself go' in weakness. Even in the dullest sinner there is still a spark of decision, of active positive negation which is not merely 'negative.'

[1] The Formula of Concord (sol. decl. art. I) defines Original Sin as *corruptio superiorum et principalium animae facultatum*. When Joh. Gerhard asserts, against Bellarmine, that unbelief and not arrogance is the origin of sin (IV, 308), he is right from the point of view of dogmatics, and wrong from the point of view of psychology. From the dogmatic point of view, the severance from the Word is the first thing; but from the psychological point of view it is precisely this severance from the Word which is arrogance. Luther often expresses the same view.

[2] 1 Cor. iii. 22; Gen. ii. 16.

[3] Gen. ii. 17.

[4] Gen. ii. 17.

[5] Gen. iii. 5.

The decisive and distinctive element in the Biblical doctrine of sin is that sin is not described as something negative, but as a positive negation, whereas the non-Christian doctrine, especially that of Greek philosophy, which also determines modern Western philosophy, understands evil absolutely as a lack, a defect, as something in the spirit which is 'not yet.'[1] Not the spirit, but the lack of the spirit, is made responsible for evil. How could 'the divine reason' be able to sin? All non-Biblical doctrine makes evil harmless and excuses man, whereas the Bible shows up sin in all its terrible character and makes man 'inexcusable.' No Fate, no metaphysical constitution, no weakness of his nature, but himself, man, in the centre of his personality, is made responsible for his sin.

And yet we must not exaggerate this idea to the extent of making human sin 'satanic.' It is the story of the Fall itself which prevents us from accepting this interpretation. Man does not sin like Satan himself, purely out of defiance and rebellion.[2] He is led astray by sin. Evil forces were already there before him; man is not great enough to discover sin and introduce it into the world. But man is led astray in such a way that once desire is aroused, it militates against confidence in God. The sin of man is no purely spiritual matter, but it always takes place through the medium of the desires of the senses. Man begins to suspect that his connexion with God does not give full satisfaction to his hunger for life. All human sin has an element of weakness; it is mingled with anxiety for one's life, a fear of losing something by obedience to God; thus it is a lack of confidence, a fear of venturing all on God

[1] Augustine's unfortunate theory that evil is defect comes mainly from the fact that he does not make a distinction between moral good and actual good (the impossibility of making a distinction between *malum* = evil (*böse*) and *malum* = disastrous (*übel*)), logically, from the failure to make a distinction between contrary and contradictory, and this means, in the last resort, from the fact that nature is ranked higher than personality. The negative theory of evil completely dominates pre-Christian thought, especially in the modification of sin to mean 'not knowing.' Cf. Kierkegaard: 'That sin is not negative but positive' (*Krankheit zum Tode*, p. 94).

[2] Luther: 'In the devil there is a far greater enmity against God . . . than there is in man' (WA. 42, 107).

alone; it is not simply impudence, but anxiety about oneself; it is not merely rebellion, it is a kind of dizziness which attacks those who ought to step over the abyss leaning only on God. *Superbia* pure and simple is satanic, not human sin. Man's arrogance consists in believing that he can look after himself better than God can, that he knows what is good for him better than his Creator. His sin is composed of the mingled elements of distrust, doubt, and defiant desire for freedom. It is impossible for us to reduce it to a single formula; even in its inmost centre it is tainted with ambiguity. It is only pure spirits, not man with his psycho-physical nature who can sin simply from pure arrogance. This mixed character of primal sin is described in an inimitable way in the story of the Fall. It is a fruit that attracts, it is a whispered doubt which stirs, it is the dream of being like God which turns the scale.

But neither Satan's whispering nor the craving awakened from without is meant to explain the origin of sin. Only he who understands that sin is inexplicable knows what it is.[1] Sin—human sin, and not only satanic sin—is the one great negative mystery of our existence, of which we know only one thing, that we are responsible for it, without the possibility of pushing the responsibility on to anything outside ourselves. We believe this, not because the Bible says so, but we perceive this when God in Christ shows us our Origin and our Fall. Through the Word of God we ourselves know that it is so; we accept our guilt, freely acknowledging it in the evidence of the knowledge of faith, and to the judgement of God we say an unambiguous 'yes.' The final ground of sin is this, that we love ourselves more than our Creator—that is, self-will, incomprehensible as it is, yet known to us all in the depths of our being.

Thus man's distinctive endowment, his by the fact of his creation, namely, the fact that he has been made in the image of God, is the presupposition of sin. Sin itself is a manifestation of the image of God in man; only he who has been created in

[1] 'Rather we must recognize evil as in its very nature incomprehensible, since it only comes to be through caprice, and caprice on the other hand means breaking away from the ground and context of reason.' Jul. Müller, II, 234.

the image of God can sin, and in his sin he shows the 'supernatural,' spirit-power, a power not of this world, which issues from the primal image of God. Even when he commits sin man shows his greatness and his superiority. No animal is able to sin, for it is unable to rebel against its destiny, against the form in which it has been created; it has not the power of decision. The Creator has given this dangerous power to His last and highest earthly creature, since He created him not simply *through* His Word, but *in* His Word, and therefore responsible. And it is this very distinctiveness which becomes a temptation to man. The copy wants to be the model itself, the one who ought to answer wishes to be the 'word itself,' the planet wants to be the sun, a star in its own light. Man 'can' do this, thanks to the gift of the Creator. But if and when he does so, he destroys the possibility of doing what he could have done.

This is the mystery of the irreparable.

6. THE IRREPARABLE

The ego exists not as substance but as activity, as Fichte knew. Yet the human ego, in contradistinction to the Divine, exists not as pure activity, but as re-active, or, as we say, responsive activity, relation. Man exists originally for God, in accordance with the fact that he comes from God. But sin is the reversal of this position, turning direction towards God into aversion from God. Then, if the view holds that 'being is equal to relation,' the reversal of the relation must be at the same time the perversion of the being. This does not mean that man has received a different structure of being, for instance, from that of the animal or the thing; he is and he remains man, he is and he remains, in contradistinction from all other creatures known to us, in that particular, special relatedness to God which is called responsibility; his being is, both before and after, responsible and responsive existence; both before and after his distinctive element is the quality of decision. Both before and after man remains one whose existence is not only *through* the Word, but *in* the Word of God—otherwise how could he be responsible? But sin means that this relation—this particular and indissoluble relation—is now qualified in a negative manner. This is precisely the lie behind the original rebellion, the lie of the Serpent; man thinks that he can set himself free from God. He cannot indeed be God, he remains dependent, he remains in responsibility; but his responsibility is now determined in a negative manner. He was destined to say 'Yes' and he has said 'No'; he was destined for community and he has broken community; he was destined for love, and now through his defiance he has fallen away from love. The 'mind of the flesh'—this means, in the language of the Bible, the desire of the creature which is severed from union with God—'is enmity against God.'[1] For the defiant human being there is no loving God but only a hostile one. And again it is in the centre of his being, in the consciousness of responsibility, that this enmity breaks out: in the bad conscience.

Adam is afraid of God and hides from Him, when the Fall has taken place. Previously he had no fear of this kind; it does not belong to the original Creation as established by God. It is the sign of distance from God, it is the manner in which distance from God becomes conscious to man. To the bad conscience God is the angry God; man as sinner 'has' God only in the form of one who is angry, distant, accusing and 'condemning.'

This is no merely subjective illusion, but a reality. This is the effect of Holiness and Righteousness, the 'logic' of God. 'God is not mocked, for whatsoever a man soweth that shall he also reap.'[2] God accepts man's emancipation from Himself; He burdens him with it. The broken relation with God sets between God and the sinner: guilt. What has happened is not something passing; the past cannot be shaken off, it belongs to me. Sin, in so far as it stands between me and God as something which is both past and present, is guilt. In the concept of guilt the seriousness of the happening is objectified, something has taken place which can never be undone; it is lost for ever.[3] Innocence, once it has been lost, cannot be regained. The loss of innocence is irreparable;

[1] Rom. viii. 7.
[2] Gal. vi. 7.
[3] Cf. the connexion between guilt, the irreparable, and the wrath of God in Luther (Theodosius Harnack, *Luthers Theologie*, I, pp. 197 ff.).

the breach cannot be healed. Man is able to destroy his life, but he cannot restore it again. He is able to blind his vision, but he cannot restore his sight. He is able to destroy his communion with God, but he cannot restore it. The way of return to Paradise is barred, the angels with flaming swords stand on guard at its gates; it is impossible to go back; between us and God there lies guilt, an obstacle which we cannot remove, something which cannot be set aside and cannot be got over. The avalanche has fallen and has blocked access to God. Hence the problem of guilt—the problem of how guilt can be removed—is the central problem of the Christian Faith. Guilt binds us to the irreparable past, it identifies us with this which has once happened, which can never be undone. The knowledge of this, the central knowledge, the knowledge at the place of responsibility, is the bad conscience. The bad conscience preaches the angry God.

7. THE PERVERSION OF MAN'S NATURE

But that is only one aspect of the question. It is not as though sin could be repaired if this one obstacle, guilt, were removed, as though we, ourselves, would return, if only the way were not blocked by guilt. The real situation is that the perversion of man's relation with God carries with it the perversion of his nature as it actually is. We have not only become debtors but sinners. That is what we now are, once we have become so. 'Everyone that committeth sin is the bond-servant of sin';[1] we have destroyed the picture; we cannot mend it. We have taken too much upon ourselves. Like someone who has shrieked too loudly and has lost his voice, so we have been boastful in our freedom, and now freedom—not all kinds of freedom but our primal freedom—has been lost. *This* freedom has been destroyed by sin, for it was based upon man's relation to God, as God had established it. When we lost that status we also lost that freedom. When as children we 'pulled faces' our mother would warn us: 'Don't do that, or you may be "fixed" like that!' This 'grimace'—emancipation from God, rebellion, the lie of independence—has remained with us. It has become the permanent form of our

[1] John viii. 34.

present existence. We are sinners; we do not only commit sins. We are those who 'commit sins,' who have become 'slaves of sin.'

And the rest? what does 'the rest' mean here? As person man is a whole. His personal being is based upon that *imago*. The breaking of man's relation to God means that the image of God in man has also been broken. This does not mean that it no longer exists, but that it has been defaced. The person has not been removed, but the personal content of the person, the personal being, the being in the love of God, fellowship, has gone. Or rather it has not simply gone, but it has been perverted. Hate does not mean that love has gone, but that love has been turned into its opposite. The wine of the divine love has become the vinegar of enmity towards God. In virtue of the divine creation, we are irrevocably bound to this form of existence: we must either love or hate, we cannot leave this dimension of love-hate. Thus the primal form has disappeared since it has been turned into its negative form. But this means that we cannot speak of 'the rest.' The fact that the nature has been perverted means that the whole is perverted. Existence is now turned in the opposite direction. God has been removed from the centre, and we are in the centre of the picture; our life has become 'ec-centric.' The lie that we are the centre is characteristic of our present life. We 'revolve round ourselves.' The dominant note in our life is now no longer the *dominus* but the rebel: the 'I' itself. *Cor incurvatum in se*, the self which is bent back upon itself, Luther[1] calls it; in saying this he is not using an exaggerated expression but the one exact formula, by means of which the reality of man's life can be seen right down to the smallest detail. He discovers the 'I' which seeks itself not where everyone sees it, in crude egoism, but where we generally see the Good, in our virtue, in our 'striving after the Highest,' in our piety, in our mysticism—we shall follow it further in our art, science and philosophy. In every chorus of this life the self which seeks itself is the leader of the chorus. The broken relation

[1] Luther (*Römerbrief*, Ficker, II, 184, 136): *Incurvatum in se adeo, ut non tantum corporalia, sed et spiritualia bona sibi inflexit et se in omnibus querit. Curvus es totus in te et versus in tui amorem*, II, 337.

with God means the perversion and poisoning of all the functions of life. As we shall see later, this statement of the complete corruption of man does not mean that there is no longer 'any good' in man at all. All is good in him because it has been created by God,[1] but all this good which proceeds from God's creation, stands under a law of evil, or rather, sin. The order of the whole, the final motive, the final connexion, the unity, the fundamental direction, is not good because everything has been dislocated. As upon a chess-board which has been shaken, all the individual chessmen are still there, unbroken, 'good,' as they came out of the workshop of the turner; yet at the same time everything is confused and displaced and meaningless—so is the nature of man. We shall be dealing with this later on however; all that we need to stress here is the point of view of the totality of sin as such, not its individual manifestations. By sin the nature of man, not merely something in his nature, is changed and perverted.[2]

But there is *one* manifestation of man's perverted relation

[1] It is not the fact that Augustine (see above, p. 131) calls being, as such, good, which is Neo-Platonic and unscriptural, but the fact that he does not—or does not always—distinguish between the non-being of something—as *defectus*—and the *defectio* as act, between the *privatio boni* as an ontological, and the *privatio boni* as an ethical or existential statement; and secondly, that even where he speaks of love to God he always seems inclined to regard this in the sense of the Platonic Eros. Luther's doctrine of the divine preservation of the world (*apud Deum idem est creare et conservare*, WA. 43, 233; God remains with His creatures with His Word, the Only-Begotten Son) comes to the same result as the statements above; cf. Note (1) on the next page.

[2] This is the relative truth in the heresy of Flacius; in point of fact the *Imago Dei* is no mere 'accident,' and the loss of the *Imago* is not the loss of something 'accidental,' but the *Imago Dei* is being and its perversion is a perversion of one's being. The idea of perversion corresponds far more closely to the contradictory character—that is, the relation of sin to the Word—than the idea of *corruptio* which has more of a contrary and therefore natural character. The controversy between Flacius and his opponents can never be settled, because it contains a false antithesis. Flacius could appeal to the fact that even Luther spoke several times of sin as the 'image of the devil': 'Man must be an image either of God or of the Devil. For he is like that according to which he orders his life' (WA. 24, 51). His opponents were able to appeal to the fact that man, even as a sinner, is still always the creation of God: *Omnis substantia est a Deo creatore* (Gerhard, op. cit., IV, 335).

to God of which we must speak, when we are dealing with man in the Biblical view: the perversion of his relation to his fellow-man. Here if anywhere we must prove what has been said about the effect of sin. Man, so we said, was created in and for community, in and for love. Sin does not alter the fact that this is the meaning of his existence. This is what ought to be, as every one knows. And even in sin it does not cease to be so, so far as God's work is concerned.[1] Even now man is a social being—not a collective being like an animal, nor an individual being in the sense in which he is conceived in the abstract reason. His whole existence, from birth onwards, where through the union of two the new third comes into being, is impregnated with social relations. The individual becomes what he is in community and through others, and what he is also has its effect upon others. This—if I may put it so—formal structure of creation of man's being has remained as well as formal responsibility. Indeed, at bottom both are one, since community is simply responsibility in its concrete form. But: the quality of community, the love-content of this community-existence has been destroyed. Quite other forces than love—that love which is described in the Thirteenth Chapter of Corinthians—determine its reality. So far as motive is concerned, this 'community' is called *bellum omnium contra omnes*, whether in a coarser or a more refined form, physically, mentally or spiritually. *Cor incurvatum in se*—that is the secret formula, even when the opposite, love and justice, seems to be the case. Once again, this does not mean that there is no love and no justice anywhere in existence—who could be so blind to facts as to assert this![2]—but that there is no love or justice which is not tainted with egoism, behind which as the

[1] Luther: *merito autem hoc in loco* (Gen. ii. 29) *id observamus, quod inter morbum naturae per peccatum viciatae, et suum opus . . . spiritus sanctus discernit . . . etiam in viciata natura . . . donum generationis nobis commendat, tanquam insignem benedictionem* (WA. 42, 433). We must always distinguish between the *creatura* and its (recognizable) orders on the one hand, and the *peccatum originale*—something which to-day especially is forbidden in the name of the Reformation doctrine of sin. Cf. on this H. Thielicke, *Geschichte und Existenz*, 1935.

[2] Cf. what is said below about the good in ethics and the *justitia civilis*, p. 154.

final reality there is not the 'heart which is turned in upon itself.'

8. SOLIDARITY IN SIN

Ego totus, I wholly, that is the truth with which we have been dealing up to the present. *Nos toti*, we all—what that means is the next and perhaps the most difficult question. For the question cannot be that, so to say, accidentally, 'it has happened to all as to me the individual' so that when we learn to know ourselves, we learn to know each as 'one like ourselves.' It may perhaps happen like this empirically; but the problem why it is so remains hidden behind this statement of the facts. What did Augustine really want to say—without being able to say it aright—when he summed us all up in the one Adam? Certainly nothing of that which everyone who studies life with close attention is able to perceive, neither that 'kingdom of sin,' nor any kind of neutral actuality which seems to be due to Fate, for which we bear no responsibility. Only from the Word of God, and that means only when we take the Biblical idea that we are created in the Word seriously, can we gain any light upon this, the greatest mystery of all.

Who is 'man' who has originally been created by God after His Image? Is it I or you? Or someone else? Each for himself? Certainly, it is I, and you, and everyone for himself as this individual, with his own particular life, his I-self, which cannot be exchanged for any other.[1] But is it not strange that when we speak of the peculiar element, the central element in ourselves, we know that we might just as well be speaking of others as of ourselves? It is of course always true that I can only speak of myself; but I know that while I am doing so not only can the other understand it, but that it is equally applicable to him and to myself. This, we note, is the pre-

[1] Cf. the remarkable passage in Ezekiel, where the prophet receives a commission to address the King of Tyre: 'Thou sealest up the sum, full of wisdom and perfect in beauty. . . . Thou hast been in Eden the garden of God; every precious stone was thy covering. . . . Thou wast perfect in thy ways from the day that thou wast created, till iniquity was found in thee . . . therefore I will cast thee as profane out of the mountain of God. . . . Thine heart was lifted up because of thy beauty. . . . I will cast thee to the ground . . .' (Ezekiel xxviii. 12 ff.).

supposition of the fact that we are able to understand one another. But we do not know the reason for this. The Word of God tells us the reason, since it shows us that the 'man whom God created, is always both this individual and humanity' (Kierkegaard).[1] For, as we have already seen, this is the Biblical idea of man, that God, since He creates me as responsible, creates me in and for community with others. The isolated individual is an abstraction, conceived by the reason which has been severed from the Word of God. 'The other' is not added to my nature after my nature, after I myself, as this particular individual, have been finished. But the other, the others, are interwoven with my nature. I am not man at all apart from others. I am not 'I' apart from the 'Thou.' As I cannot be a human being without a relation to God, without the Divine 'Thou,' so also I cannot be man without the human 'Thou.' And were all human beings upon the earth to die and leave me alone alive: my life, in its impaired and solitary condition, in so far as it is still a human life, would still be related to the 'Thou' in remembrance, in longing and in hope. Robinson Crusoe's whole longing was to mingle once again with human beings, in order to become a human being once more.

In the Creation we are an individualized, articulated unity, one body with many members. 'Whether one member suffereth, all the members suffer with it; or one member is honoured, all the members rejoice with it.'[2] We are a unity bound together in a solidarity, bound together not as members of a species, like the individuals of a zoological species—that we may be, but this does not concern our existence as human beings—but we are bound together in a quite unique way, in that way which is called mutual responsibility, which is,

[1] Kierkegaard, *Der Begriff der Angst*, p. 22: '. . . the essential determination of human existence, that man is individual, and as such is both himself and the whole race, so that the whole race participates in the individual and the individual in the whole race (thus if an individual could fall away wholly and entirely from the race his fall would at the same time determine the race in a different way; if, however, an animal falls away from the species this would make no difference at all). . . . The perfecting of the individual in himself is at the same time, and in so doing, the perfect participation in the whole.'

[2] 1 Cor. xii. 26.

however, to be understood not as a task but as a gift, as a God-given life, not as an aim to be realized by us in the future, but as our Creation and Beginning in God. God has created us as this whole—so that only and precisely in this being-in-the-whole, in this personal existence which is based upon our relation from and to one another can each become that for which he is destined, a responsible person, a human man.[1]

If that is our origin, then our opposition to this origin cannot be an experience, an act, of the individual as an individual. The sin of Adam is the destruction of communion with God, which is at the same time the severance of this bond; it is that state of 'being against God' which also means 'being against one another.' Certainly each individual is a sinner as an individual; but he is at the same time the whole in its united solidarity, the body, actual humanity as a whole. As we know ourselves in Christ as this original community-in-the-Word, as those who have been elected not to be individuals but for the Body of Christ, as the community of the elect, so we perceive in Him also sin as the opposition to the electing Word and the dissolution of this community intended and prepared in the fact of election. 'All one in Christ'—that is not only the goal but also the origin, and it also applies to the perversion of the origin. As the man who has been created in the Word of God is at the same time both the individual and humanity, so also the man who has fallen away from the original Creation is both the individual and the community. In sin we are bound together as a united body, just as we are bound together in the Creation, only with this difference, that—and this belongs to sin—we deny this solidarity in sin.

Hence the Divine revelation, in which He reveals to us Himself and our origin—the true God and the true man—is the revelation of a love which is a complete solidarity, which does not do what we all do: reproach the other with guilt and in a Pharisaical way separate ourselves, as innocent, from the guilty. If Jesus Christ is the Word of God, who reveals to us the meaning of true human existence, then His solidarity with our guilt in the counterpart of His solidarity with all,

[1] Cf. the observations of Kähler on the historical character of human existence in the *Wissenschaft der christlichen Lehre*, pp. 271 ff.

reveals the true character of our guilt, and at the same time the character of our sin: the breach of solidarity.

9. THE ELEMENTS OF TRUTH AND ERROR IN THE ECCLESIASTICAL DOCTRINE

In Adam all have sinned—that is the Biblical statement; but how? The Bible does not tell us that. The doctrine of Original Sin is read into it.[1] In the doctrine of the New Testament all that matters is this: the unity of the human race in sin as the counterpart of the unity of redeemed humanity in Christ—type and anti-type. But more than that: the anti-type of Adam, the 'second Adam,' Christ, is at the same time the Origin; the Redeeming Word of God is at the same time the Creator-Word, in Whom, through Whom and for Whom we have been—not only redeemed—but created. Only out of this unity of the Creator- and Redeemer-Word[2] does there come an understanding of the unity of all individuals which also expresses itself as a unity in sin. But just as the origin cannot be visibly represented—the historical presentation of the ecclesiastical doctrine of the Primitive State leads to the most unfortunate and erroneous definitions—so also the unity of all in the contradiction cannot be visibly represented. Just as in respect of the Creation we ask in vain: How, where and when has this taken place? so also is it with the Fall. The Creation and the Fall both lie behind the historical visible actuality, as their pre-suppositions which are always present, and are already being expressed in the historical sphere.[3]

[1] Cf. above, p. 119, Note (1).

[2] 'God the Father has begun the creation o all creatures by His Word, and He has finished it, and still preserves it for ever through the same, and He remains with His work which He creates as long as He chooses, until the time comes when it shall no longer be' (Luther on John i. 3). He says the same of Christ: '. . . and all is still ruled and sustained by Him to the end of the world, for He is the beginning and the end of all creatures'; 'that through the same Word also all things which are thus created are preserved in their nature, otherwise they would not remain so long created' (WA. 46, 558, 560, 561).

[3] Julius Müller's theory of 'a sinfulness which lies beyond our individual and temporal existence, which . . . must have its origin in our personal self-decision,' the 'idea of a manner of existence of the created personality outside time, on which its life in time is dependent' (op. cit., II, 496),

The truth and the error in the traditional ecclesiastical doctrine is exactly determined by what is actually meant on the one hand, and by its historico-visible expression on the other. What it *means*, is the union of all in creation and sin. But what it *says*, in order to make clear or to 'explain' what is meant, in order to report what took place originally and what was done in opposition to this origin as an historical event, is something quite different: the responsible act of an individual, whose guilt, for incomprehensible reasons, is fastened on us, and whose sin is transferred to us in a manner which is quite incompatible with the nature of sin, namely, through natural inheritance. To confuse *this* stumbling-block with that stumbling-block which always lies alongside the possibility of faith as the possibility of unbelief, means a sinister misinterpretation of what is revealed to us in the New Testament as faith and 'stumbling-block.' In the New Testament the 'stumbling-block' is always: the desire to evade responsibility towards God, or the evasion of complete dependence upon His action. The 'stumbling-block' of the ecclesiastical doctrine, however, consists in this, that we are made responsible for a sin which someone else has committed. For when the ecclesiastical doctrine tries to right its mistake by teaching that we all commit sin *now* owing to the inherited sin of Adam, this certainly does not apply to the sin for which we are held responsible: the *peccatum originis*. And the sins which we ourselves commit are, according to the ecclesiastical doctrine, the necessary consequences of that transference, thus once again something for which honestly we cannot accept responsibility. What is the reason for this confusion? Simply historical demonstration, the idea that it is possible to present an historical report about this. This led to the fact, as Kierkegaard

springs from very similar considerations to those which are made here, but it is a metaphysical and speculative transgression of the boundary which is set for our knowledge, even for our knowledge in faith, and—in spite of Müller's modification (II, 102)—leads into paths trodden by the speculations of Origen. The particular question which could most easily lead to such a doctrine of the Original Fall, that of the basis of solidarity in sin, is not solved by Müller's theory, whereas Origen does solve it—in his own platonic dualistic way—by a combination of the Fall and (physical) humanity.

points out, that the first man is singled out in a fantastic way from the series of all the human beings who follow him,[1] and —what is far worse—the human beings who follow him in the course of history are in a fantastic way de-humanized. I would repeat: we may be grateful to historical science that it has eliminated the historical element from the story of the Creation and of the Fall, and in so doing has forced us to seek once more for the Divine Word concerning the Creation and the Fall of man.

By all this I do not mean to say that this idea of Original Sin (*Erb-Sünde* = inherited sin) in this narrower, ecclesiastical, traditional sense has no truth in it at all. As one of the manifestations of the solidarity of sin, we must take into account the connexion of individuals through the fact of physical descent, which, obscure though it may be, is forced upon us by experience. The transmission of the spiritual nature, of the 'character,' from parents to children is such an evident and tragically powerful experience that it would be strange if it were not brought into connexion with the idea of the *peccatum originis*. But it was an error to see in this fact an explanation of the primal fact of solidarity in sin itself. Upon this plane the doctrine—rejected by the Church as Pelagian—that this element of inheritance should be understood as merely a pre-disposition, that is, as an occasion for, but not as the ground of sin, had as much justification as the ecclesiastical doctrine itself. For in face of this physical determinism its denial for the sake of responsibility has a certain amount of quite solid justification. Both facts, the relative fact of being conditioned by one's heritage and the relative freedom over against it, are indeed manifestations on the one hand, of necessity, and on the other, of responsibility; but they do not actually constitute either necessity or responsibility.[2] The fact that we are to some extent conditioned by our heredity is no

[1] Kierkegaard, *Begriff der Angst*, p. 22.

[2] Karl Barth says too, in a similar vein: 'The Pelagian doctrine of freedom and the fatalistic doctrine of necessity . . . are in principle all similar distortions of the freedom in which the Divine Providence recognizes, encompasses and governs the contingency of the creature, the freedom of the human will, as such' (*Credo*, p. 35).

proof of Original Sin (*Erb-Sünde*), nor does the relative freedom we possess to resist this inherited tendency provide a proof against Original Sin (*Erb-Sünde*); but both facts are important, though not absolutely clear indications which point towards sin, in its fateful character and its responsibility. Among these indications, upon the relative plane, even that theory of the 'Kingdom of sin,' the ethical theory of environment, gains its relative justification; this, too, shows how the invisible, opaque solidarity of sin comes out visibly, in an historical and psychological way. Conversely, however, upon this relative plane also the perception of a moral freedom, of a capacity for the Good due to free resolve, as is taught by ethical rationalism, is not to be absolutely rejected, if we remind ourselves of the fact that this Good lies within the sphere which includes the concept of sin. There is sin within good as well as within evil, in virtue as well as in vice,[1] and to deny the reality of this Good, this virtue, this highmindedness and this ideal disposition, would be just as wrong as to play it off against the fact of universal and total sinfulness. This confronts us with a problem which needs more detailed explanation, the question of the relation between the *peccatum originis* and *actual* 'sins' which can be directly perceived. This explanation must also give us more detailed information in answer to the question: In what sense is the *peccatum originis* accessible to experience or not?

10. ORIGINAL SIN AND SINS OF ACT

The fact that we are sinners means that sin is not only an occasional, perhaps even a frequent act, always arising out of the wrong decision of the moment, but that it is a perverted tendency of our nature. The assertion, however, that sin has become 'our nature' has been rightly condemned, even by Lutheran theology, within which this terrible view arose, as a 'Manichean' distortion and exaggeration of the idea of the

[1] It is this which idealistic Humanism, and also religious moralism of every kind—in short, what the man who is outside the Christian revelation does not know—the Pharisaism which necessarily inheres in the moral human being, the 'Pharisaism of the idea' as Kutter so profoundly calls it.

peccatum originis.[1] But even without this extreme exaggeration the Christian statement remains difficult enough. 'Thou art a sinner' means: 'thou must sin, thou canst not act otherwise than in opposition to the will of God.' How are we to understand this 'being unable,' this 'must,' this 'necessity'? How can we understand it without destroying the character of decision and the responsibility of our present life in its actual experience? How can we, on the other hand, make room for this element without cutting the nerve of that fundamental statement, that 'must'? In opposition to the usual uncritical respect for the Reformers it must be said that in this question their doctrine is very far from being the final word, and that on this point Augustine[2] has thought through the problems involved far more thoroughly, and, I would repeat—in this question—he has done more for their solution than either Luther or Calvin. There can be no doubt that the Reformers, in their desire to preserve the fact of man's sinfulness at all costs, have often done so in such a way that we cannot wholly absolve them from the reproach of having fallen into a crude form of Determinism. The traditional, historical conception of the doctrine of Original Sin has indeed done far more than give 'occasion' for this; so long as this rigid doctrine held sway only two courses were open: either, to reduce the sense of obligation to the merely psychological level of a 'semi-necessity,' or, on the other hand, to accept the view of a natural causal determination. And yet in Augustine's searching discussions of the various meanings of the *non posse*, of necessity, the rudiments of a solution of this fatal dilemma might have been found. Who would want to reproach the Reformers for not having solved this problem? We are not raising this question in order to depreciate them, but in order to show clearly the nature of our present task. The phrase, man 'is' a sinner, he 'must' sin, must on no account be understood to mean that the sinful action which takes place at any particular moment

[1] Cf. what was said above on p. 137 about Flacius.

[2] Cf. the valuable presentation and interpretation of Augustine's doctrine of freedom by Heinrich Barth, *Die Freiheit der Entscheidung im Denken Augustins*; and H. Diem, *Augustins Interesse in der Prädestinationslehre*, *Festschrift für K. Barth*, pp. 379 ff.

'follows' like a final conclusion from certain premises, or as a physical effect follows its causes. The analogy of the tree and its fruits[1] ought not to be expounded in such a way. The statement, 'man is a sinner,' is neither the major term for the logical conclusion: thus all his acts are sinful, nor is the fact which it describes, the fact of being a sinner, the cause of his individual sinful actions. This word 'must' can have neither the logical-consecutive nor the physico-causal meaning. For every sin, which man commits, is a fresh decision against God; hence the Bible regards it just as seriously as the fact of man's general sinfulness. Indeed—however remarkable this may at first appear—between the two statements that man is the slave of sin, and that every sin is an actual decision, there does not seem to be in the Bible even a relation of tension; both statements are set alongside each other, each in its own place, and are given equal and full weight. Nothing is further from the thought of the Bible—Paul included—than determinism, unless it were indeterminism! How is this to be understood?

It would only be possible to give a comparatively satisfactory answer at the close of this whole book, since all the inquiries which follow are intended to be contributions to such an answer. Here all we can do, anticipating the result, is to sum up the most important points. All the hopeless confusion which characterizes the ideas on this question—and especially also the classical ecclesiastical ideas—is due to the fact that man was not understood in his essential relation to the Word of God, but was conceived as a soul-entity or rational being, existing independently, and the relation of the Divine Will to him had to be conceived either in a deterministic-causal manner (*Seelen-ding*), or in an indeterministic and autonomous manner (*Vernunft-wesen*). Thus from the very outset the relation between divine and human freedom is definitely insoluble. And even such a remarkably Scriptural thinker as Luther was not able wholly to free himself from this Greek habit of thought. In the last resort, however, by means of his paradoxes he always retrieves the Biblical understanding of man; but in these paradoxes—which do not arise out of the matter itself but out

[1] Matt. vii. 17.

of inadequate means of thought—he expects from us an inner force of tension which as a rule we do not possess, which also we should not need, if the truth were not expressed by such unsuitable means.

Man 'is' a sinner; but this 'is,' because it refers to man, must not be confused with any other 'is.' Man's 'being' never ceases to be a 'being-in-decision.' Even as sinner man is not a soul- or reason-entity of some kind. Man 'is' not a sinner in the way in which an elephant 'is' a mammal or the sum of the angles in a triangle 'is' 180 degrees. The whole problem of human existence is contained in the copula of this predicate, in the 'is,' while the philosophers and theologians usually seek it in the predicate. To be a sinner means: to be engaged in rebellion against God. Sin never becomes a quality or even a substance. Sin is and remains an act. The doctrine of the Church which, through the idea of inherited sin, has slipped into the physical sphere, has overlooked this permanent quality of the actuality of sin or at least—through its physical emphasis—it has obscured it; for it equates the state of 'being a sinner' with, for instance, a child's 'being blue-eyed' because his father had blue eyes.

Hence, because this actuality of the 'is' was not understood, but was confused with the logical ('is' 180 degrees) or with the physical ('is' blue-eyed), the relation between the actuality of primal sin and so-called 'sins' of act was not understood. Sin is never a state, but it is always act. Even being a sinner is not a state but an act, because it is being person. Being person is actual being, even if it is 'permanent being.' The application of concrete, physical natural categories to sin can only fundamentally corrupt the understanding of it. Even 'flesh' in the New Testament is not a natural but a personal definition:[1] the permanent act of being turned away from God, the fact that the person has become rigid in this negative action. In the Bible—not only in the Old Testament, but also in the New, and not only in the Synoptic Gospels but also in the writings of Paul—there is nothing said about sin which means anything other than the act of turning away from God. But in the very concept of 'being a sinner' this act is conceived

[1] See below p. 254, note.

as one which determines man's *whole* existence.[1] If Pelagius had only asserted this against Augustine his position would have been impregnable. But he asserted something quite different; he maintained that man is always able to decide this way or that, for or against God. But if this statement were true, the whole Christian message of redemption would be annulled; and Augustine was obliged, with all the means at his disposal—and if he had no other, then by means of the doctrine of Original Sin—to banish this destructive error from the Church. In the main, all the right was upon his side; but he was not wholly right. It is with this point that we are now concerned.

Man's apostasy from God is not simply something which happened once for all, and is over and done with; man is doing it continually. The contradiction is not a fatal tragic disaster which has taken place behind us and an equally disastrous quality within us. The contradiction remains—how could it ever be anything else?—contradiction, turning away, apostasy. Hence we, each one of us, are 'Adam,' just as we all together are 'Adam.' The statement that we are sinners, that we are fallen creatures, does not tell us anything about the 'cause' of this apostasy; for here there are no 'causes.' What it does express is the truth that all man's personal being is involved in this act of turning away from God. It states that he who commits this apostasy can do no other than repeat it continually, not because it has become a habit, but because this is the distinctive character of this act. It is because the foundation of the Creation, the truth and reality of the Creation

[1] Gutbrod (*Die Paulinische Anthropologie*, p. 135) has expressed very well the difference between being a sinner and sinning: 'Because man sins he is a sinner, and because he is a sinner he sins.' The fact that in the thought of Paul sin appears as a force which dominates men is not in the least in opposition to our contention that sin, and being a sinner, is never to be understood as a state but always as an act. Precisely the personification of sin as a force is an attempt to assert its (negative) actuality. It points in the same direction as the analogy of sin and 'constitution' in the text (p. 150). 'Constitution' is here—as there 'power'—understood as *principium activum*. Only once in the New Testament is 'nature' connected with sin: 'by nature children of wrath' (Eph. ii. 3); but φύσις is here rather an historical than a metaphysical definition: being, outside the revelation of salvation.

of our being is denied in this act, that in this act—in its continual repetition—our nature is altered, perverted. It does not cease to be an actuality, nor does it cease to be a related or responsive actuality; but it now lives as a negative actuality, in permanent opposition to itself and to God's original intention. Luther touches the spot—although he is unable to express it adequately with the means of thought at his disposal—when he always emphasizes the fact that the person is sinful; hence the person can do no good works. This is his clue to the labyrinth, by means of which he strides forward with confidence.[1] To him the doctrine of Original Sin is the means provided by tradition to visualize this in his mind. The method of expression is often questionable, but the truth which he is trying to express, namely, that the whole person is sinful, is indeed the whole point at issue. The Bible says this, and nothing else. To be person is a total act; but the total act can have no other content save that of the relation to God. The being of the person is constituted in the whole personal act, which must express itself henceforward in all that the person 'does.'

I will try to explain this by an illustration which is also something more than an illustration. A state is a state by means of its constitution. The constitution takes place, it is not a natural event, but an historical event; and, as certainly as it has a beginning, it is always *in actu*. A state decays, or at least

[1] 'Original sin, or natural sin, or personal sin, the real chief sin; if this were not there would be no real sin. This sin is not committed like all other sins, but it is, it lives, and it commits all sins, and it is the essential sin, which does not sin for an hour or for a time; but where and for how long the person is, there too is the sin' (WA. X, I, 508 ff.). Luther says directly of his doctrine of the person: *est autem haae doctrinae nostrae summa quod docemus et profitemur personam prius Deo acceptam esse quam opus et personam non fieri justam ex opere justo, sed opos fieri justum et bonum ex persona justa et bona* (on Gen. iv. 4, WA. 42, 190). In another passage (*Disput. Drews*, pp. 20–2) the conceptions *tota persona, cor* and *imago Dei* are related to one another: *Redime, hic dicitur, ad personam totam. Igitur primo requiritur cor. Opus fit per cor. Cor debet primo credere. . . . Rex vero credit et fit nova persona. Iam ergo non est amplius larva diaboli, sed imago Dei.* Further there appears in this connexion *tota vita* (22), *actus primus; oportet prius adesse personam quae credat. Persona, imago, cor, totus homo* are equivalents, and are all to be conceived in an actual manner: *relatio ad verbum* (cf. also Schott, *Fleisch und Geist nach Luthers Lehre unter besonderer Berücksichtigung des Begriffes totus homo*, 1928).

it *begins* to decay, as soon as the original constitution is no longer a living thing. A living state constitutes itself ever anew in the will of the people (here I am not thinking of the *contrat social* or of any other form in which a state comes into being). The state 'is' not in the way in which a building 'is,' but it 'is' in the manner of actuality. But out of this actuality of the constitution which gives it its character there now follow other subordinate acts: the legislation as a relatively total act, the decrees as further subordinate acts, and finally the current government business. These differentiated subordinate acts do not 'follow' with logical and causal necessity. In a living state, it is true, the legislation, the decrees and the individual proceedings do 'follow' out of the living constitution of the State, that is, out of the constitution which is constantly establishing itself afresh; this, however, does not take place from causal necessity or from logical necessity, but in a special manner. The constitution manifests itself ever afresh in these more or less comprehensive individual acts, and at the same time in them it is continually being reconstituted; the constitution is a permanent act. Thus there is something quite distinctive about the constitution in relation to the laws, decrees and proceedings of government. The actuality of the constitution determines and includes those other acts in a manner which makes them into manifestations; but the constitution does not invalidate the acts as acts. On the contrary, only in the genuine actuality of these acts, in the fact that they are not logical conclusions and causal consequences from the constitution, is the ever living constitution of the State attained.

To some extent the act which constitutes the person, and the individual 'acts' or 'works' of the person, resemble the procedure which has just been described. The constituting of the person is attained—and can only be attained—by the determination of his relation to God. Man is, so we said, what his attitude towards God is, or, to put it even more correctly, he is that as which he determines his attitude to God. But in this fact he is not free in the way in which we have imagined the constituting state to be. The attitude of man to God is determined by the Creation; it is given to man. It is, irrevocably, so created that man is grounded in the Word of God, that he has been created in and for love. Now if man decides against the Word of God, in so doing he does not simply give himself another constitution—for this power he simply does not possess—but he sets himself in opposition to his constitution. Thus his constitution—to continue the parable—is a permanent revolution.[1] As in all revolutions the situation, however, is this, that they do not come to an end of themselves, but only through the fact that a powerful man comes and creates order, by simply sweeping away the revolutionary 'government' which was no government at all. It is the same with the human revolution against God; of itself it cannot bring itself to an end. This it cannot do, for the curse of the opposition to God's constitution of man is this: man's self-made, rebellious, pseudo-constitution does not suffice for a real order. For the principle of revolution is disorder, chaos, the inability to create order. But this disorderly constitution, this revolutionary government—which is no government—is the very essence or characteristic of the constitution of man as sinner. The man, who is a sinner, cannot be a non-sinner, not because he now has the 'quality' of 'being a sinner,' but because this negatively total act brings about a quite peculiar state of affairs, which cannot be compared with any other (save with something which resembles the personal—like the State), namely, that this act can never be reversed, but can only continue to repeat itself afresh.

Kant was upon right lines when he maintained that radical evil cannot be overcome 'by gradual reform . . . but must be overcome by a revolution in the disposition.'[2] But his

[1] It may be assumed that it is clear that the view here represented has only a very remote connexion with the philosophical theory of the 'intelligible character' as it was developed in different ways by Kant, Schelling and Schopenhauer. The contrast lies above all in the starting-point: no creation in the Word of God; it lies, secondly, in the fact that that theory (in accordance with the starting-point) is completely individualistic; thirdly, that so far as the empirical is concerned, it is completely deterministic. What is held in common, however, is this, that what the Church means by the Fall and Original Sin we do not seek in the region of that which can be empirically proved, but 'beyond'; not in a timeless or supra-temporal sense, however, but in a created primal existence, which like the Creation can only be 'seen' from the point of view of the Word of God, and not from the point of view of experience.

[2] Kant, *Religion innerhalb der Grenzen der Vernunft*, Ausgabe Kehrbach, p. 49.

mistake was that he thought that the possibility of such a revolution lay in man himself. He came to this view because he did not rightly perceive the totalitarian and revolutionary character of evil. Indeed, he would not see it; because, if he had done so, he would have been forced to give up his immanental philosophy and his doctrine of the autonomous reason. But that he did not wish to do; he wanted to hold fast to the conviction that man himself, as *homo noumenon*, is his own creator and re-creator.

II. GREATER AND LESSER SINS: THE ETHICALLY GOOD

The second point which we perceive as a result of thinking out this question afresh is this, that this act which affects man as a whole must continually re-emerge in particular acts of greater or lesser intensity. This relative difference in intensity, which has always been noticed by man, is the basis for the distinction between greater and lesser sins, which is taken for granted throughout the Bible.[1] They are all manifestations of the one rebellion; so far as primal sin is concerned there is no 'greater' or 'lesser.' But it would be a sign of complete blindness to reality, of an obstinately doctrinaire spirit, were we to refuse to acknowledge that it does make a difference whether a man kills a fellow-creature in cold blood, or makes an unkind remark to a dear friend, which hurts him a little. Both are manifestations of the one and the same original fact in which there are no degrees; but from it there follows—in accordance with the extent of the sphere affected by the action, in accordance with the extent in which the person as a whole is 'in' it—the greater or lesser sinfulness of the 'sin of act.' Failure to perceive these distinctions has caused a great deal of useless controversy and—what is worse—has created a terrible amount of confusion of conscience.

Indeed, we must go a step further. Within Original Sin the distinction between 'good' and 'evil' has not been obliterated. The fact that we are 'all sinners'[2] does not mean that we can

[1] *Peccata alia aliis graviora esse docet Christus*. The Stoics alone have ventured to remove this difference *contra omnem sensum generis humani* (Gerhard, op. cit., V, 59). Cf. Matt. xii. 31; 1 John v. 18; Luke xii. 47; John xix. 11, etc.

[2] Rom. iii. 23.

do nothing good—in the usual ethical sense of the word—that we can only do evil. Such an assertion contradicts both experience and the clear Biblical doctrine. The Reformers, too, frankly admitted this fact—although they obstinately and passionately resisted the inferences which Catholic theology drew from it—and to this sphere they gave the name of the *justitia civilis.*[1]

Within the great circle of sinful existence which includes us all, there is an obvious difference between faithful and unfaithful married partners, between officials who are conscientious in the performance of their duties and those who are careless and unreliable, between people who give themselves pains to do good and who do achieve a large measure of goodness, and those who have gone to the dogs, to whom all that is moral is a matter of complete indifference, indeed, who find it rather ridiculous. A doctrinaire theology must have become very extreme if it has reached a position in which it is able to deny the reality of these differences and their significance; in any case, those who take this position cannot appeal to any important theological tradition, and least of all to Luther or Calvin. It is perfectly possible to combine being a sinner with being 'good' in the ethical sense; indeed, in the last resort the fact of being or not being a sinner has nothing to do with the difference between the morally 'good' and the morally 'evil'; the publicans and the harlots will enter into the Kingdom of Heaven before the righteous Pharisees—whose moral righteousness no one would dream of impugning. This is not because the Pharisees are morally good—as though it were an advantage to be a moral rascal—but because those who are morally good are always tempted to try to evade the truth that they too are sinners. The morally good—always

[1] The idea of the *justitia civilis* suggests the state of affairs indicated in Rom. ii. 14. Luther went a very long way in the recognition of pagan virtue, because to him this 'moral righteousness' was not in opposition to 'sin.' Systematically this possibility was based upon those *tenues quaedam reliquiae* of the *Imago Dei*, which have been left us as *rectrices externae disciplinae* (another term for *justitia civilis*) and as a point of contact for the divine grace *qua velut paedagogia quadam Deus utitur ad instaurationem imaginis* (Gerhard, op. cit., IV, 292), and with that *externa illa paedagogia in Christum locum habere posset, quae in diabolis non est* (Gerhard, op. cit., V, 202).

understood in this relative sense, which indeed is expressed in the word 'moral'—is in itself, objectively, naturally in closer correspondence with the will of God than the morally bad. When God commands: 'thou shalt not commit adultery,' He actually wills that adultery should not be committed, in the solid everyday sense in which the word is used by everyone. This is what God wills, this is what His Commandment means; only it means infinitely more than this, and it is this 'infinitely more' that remains hidden from the eyes of the Pharisee, the legalistic person. In order to understand this aright, there is still a final aspect of the problem of sin to consider, that is, the law.

12. THE ORIGIN, THE CONTRADICTION, AND THE LAW

Man in his divine origin, man who has been created in the image of God, is the truly responsible man, that is, the man who answers God's call of love with grateful love, the man who lives in communion with the Creator, and in consequence also with his fellow-creatures. True responsibility is identical with this love, which is grounded in the love of God. In this love alone can man fulfil the destiny of his creation; in this love alone does he live and act responsibly towards his Creator; since he knows that he is bound in this way to his neighbour, and since he makes this bond the law of his life,[1] he is a truly *human* being.

Such a human being does not exist, he has only existed once in the whole course of history, in the form of the One who could say: "The Son of Man came not to be ministered unto but to minister, and to give His life a ransom for many.'[2] But all the rest of us are 'sinners,' which means that we all live, we all are, in opposition to our origin. We perceive that we are in this opposition to our origin in the very fact that the origin is once more placed before our eyes. There, where the depth of the divine love is revealed, there, where at the same time true human love does its incomprehensible utmost, in the Cross of Christ, we become aware of our opposition to our origin. There alone do we perceive how irresponsibly we live.

[1] Law of faith, Rom. iii. 27; Law of the spirit of life, Rom. viii. 2; Law of freedom, Jas. i. 25.

[2] Mark x. 45.

This practical and actual denial of responsibility, this self-determination in opposition to it, *this* is *sin.*

Now, however, we see plainly that the divine determination in the Creation is far higher than our negative self-determination; in other words, that the two elements in our being, the divine (positive) and the human (negative), are not in equal proportions; this comes out in the fact that although, through sin, we cease to express our responsibility, we do not cease to be responsible. We do not even cease to be aware of responsibility. Responsibility still remains the characteristic formula for the nature of man, for fallen man as well as for man in his origin. But responsibility is now no longer the formula of his reality, but only the formula of his obligation, and through this fact its meaning is profoundly changed. It is true that man does not love God and his neighbour, but himself; yet he ought to love God and his neighbour. The divine law of nature has become a law of obligation. Instead of an existence derived from, and lived in love, life has become the dualism of what is and what ought to be. It is this law of obligation which Paul means when he speaks of the 'law.' Being under the law is thus the way in which man exists as sinner. Therefore being under the law is just as clear an expression of the contradiction as sin itself. Both are the same, seen from two different aspects. Sin means: man no longer does what God wills but what he wills. Law means: even the man who does what he wills, does not cease to live under the will of God, only now this will of God is for him no longer a gift of life but a death-bringing demand.[1] Hence the law, as Paul says, 'has come in between.'[2] The fact that we ought to do the good is the sign that we no longer live in the good. The knowledge of 'good and evil,' the knowledge of God's will in this form of the contradiction, is the effect of the Fall.[3]

[1] Cf. Stange, *Die ältesten ethischen Disputationen Luthers*; F. V. Baader, *Philosophische Schriften*, I, p. 17.

[2] Gal. iii. 19, 'The law . . . was added'; Rom. v. 20, 'The law entered . . .'; Luther too: 'Adam was thus created that he needed no commandment' (WA. 24, 72). The will of God becomes 'a law unto man in the real sense of the word only after the entrance of sin, as then it ceases to be law once sin has been removed' (Theod. Harnack, op. cit., 382).

[3] Gen. iii. 5.

Sin is the manner in which man emancipates himself from God, takes himself out of the hands of God; but the law is the way in which God still holds the rebel—the man who has tried to sever his connexion with God—in His hands. Man cannot escape from the law of responsibility; this iron ring surrounds his whole existence; it cannot be broken, thus it preserves for man's existence a vestige of humanity.[1]

Not only is the man who has become separated from his origin responsible, but also, even though dimly and obscurely, he *knows* that he is responsible. The law is indelibly written in his heart; some knowledge of this, in some form, constitutes an essential part of human nature and one that can never be lost. Every human being knows that he is responsible.[2] But it is in the very nature of the law as such that there cannot be any 'perfect knowledge' of the law. The will of God, in so far as it is understood as 'law,' is always misunderstood from the outset, although no one comes to the knowledge of the will of God except through the knowledge of the law. Hence the law and the knowledge of the law is the really "critical" point in the relation between God and man. In the understanding of the law the decision is made.[3] This was clearly seen, first of all by Paul, and then by Luther. Redemption does not mean simply that man is set free from the 'curse of the law,' from the punishment of guilt, and that he receives strength to fulfil the law; it also means that he ceases to regard his life in terms of 'law' at all; once more he has learned to regard it as a divine gift

[1] Cf. the idea of the divine 'protective custody' contained in Gal. iii. 23.

[2] Luther: 'The knowledge from the law is known to the reason, and the reason has firmly grasped and tasted God; for from the Law it has seen what is right and what is wrong, and the Law is written in our hearts. . . . Although it is more clearly given through Moses, still it is probably true to say that by nature all rational beings come so far that they know that it is wrong to be disobedient to father or mother or to the authorities, etc. . . . so far the reason comes to the knowledge of God, that it has *cognitionem legalem*, that it knows God's command. . . . And the philosophers have also had this knowledge of God, but it is not the right knowledge of God which takes place through the law, whether through that of Moses or that which is written in our hearts' (WA. 46, 667 ff.).

For Calvin cf. now: Bohatec, *Calvin und das Recht.*

[3] See Appendix II.

and grace. Only in freedom from the law is the meaning of the law fulfilled, because love—the meaning of the law—is in opposition to the law as a statutory demand. Hence the perfect will of God cannot be perfectly summed up in any law, not even in the law of love. The meaning of love is simply this: freedom from the law through being united and grounded in the divine love.

The law, however, places between the Divine 'Thou' and 'myself,' and likewise between the human 'thou' and 'myself,' a 'something,' an abstract rule, whatever its content may be. Attention is directed to this 'something' which is required to be done, through the law as 'law,' and in so doing man's relation to God, to his fellow-creatures, and to life, becomes rigid and abstract. The law as a statute necessarily contains an impersonal element. The law interposes between person and person, so that a direct relation is impossible. Even where the law is conceived quite formally, as in Kant's Categorical Imperative, where it expresses the pure form of responsibility itself and renouncing all content loses its statutory character, it does not cease to be abstract and impersonal because it remains a law of obligation. It does not put me in contact with the 'Thou'—whether divine or human—but with the abstract entity 'reason.' The final motive therefore in legal morality is self-respect; responsibility to God and to one's neighbour has been distorted into the self-responsibility of the rational self towards itself. I, the empirical human being, am responsible to my own higher self, the intelligible self or the *noumenon*-I, to the autonomous rational self. In the last resort legalistic responsibility is self-responsibility, thus it is not a relation to the 'Thou' but to the 'I.' Hence it is not surprising, but is its necessary consequence, that Kant will have nothing to do with the idea of a love-commandment. To him whatever goes beyond rational respect is erroneous; the boundary of the sphere of the self-contained reason must not be crossed; ethics must not become truly personal.

But even where the law has a more personal character, in the religious ethic of the various peoples, in their sacred law-books and decalogues, the conception of responsibility remains impersonal. Here, it is true, it is not, as in philosophy, the abstract reason which constitutes the impersonal character of responsibility; it is its statutory element. You must do this or that, this or that is commanded you by the gods or by God —this 'something' comes in between me and the Thou. The ritual and ceremonial element, the magical-technical element, the whole apparatus of the cultus, is connected with the ethical element. It is precisely this confusing mixture which is characteristic of the religious world outside the Bible. Even where, for instance, the command to love God and man emerges, it is not recognized as the 'fulfilling of the law,' as the one great twofold commandment which really says everything. This radical intensification of the law as law only takes place in the New Testament, where the law, since it is fulfilled, is at the same time abrogated. This brings us once again to the question of Law and Revelation.

Everyone knows that we are responsible, but not everyone knows the content, the basis and the meaning of responsibility. The law of God is written in our hearts; this does not mean that we really know the will of God. On the contrary! It is precisely the law which hides the will of God from us—the same law which continually reminds us sinners of the will of God and keeps us to it. Even the cynic or fanatic who denies God does not escape from God—in so far as he is always forced, in some way or another, to recognize the fact of responsibility. But the interpretations which he gives of this responsibility show how far he is from God, just as the fact that in some way or another he feels bound to interpret the phenomenon of responsibility indicates that he is connected with God. But where is the law rightly interpreted? The right of interpretation of responsibility is the love-commandment, and indeed the twofold love-commandment: 'Thou shalt love the Lord thy God with all thy heart . . .' and the second, which 'is like unto it,' 'Thou shalt love thy neighbour as thyself.'[1] The commandment of the love of man is not specifically Scriptural; even the truth that the commandment to love our neighbour sums up all law, is a truth which is not wholly lacking outside the Biblical revelation.[2] Indeed, even

[1] Matt. xxii. 37 ff.

[2] Haas, *Idee und Ideal der Feindesliebe in der ausserchristlichen Welt*, 1927.

the commandment to love God and the unity of the love of God and man is well known, in some way or other, in the non-Christian sphere of religion. But the phrase, 'in some way or other' is characteristic. This belongs to the nature of the law. Even in its purest form, in the form of the twofold love-commandment, the law is at the same time both the disclosure and the concealment of the divine will. The Hebrew conception shows this clearly.

The great twofold commandment is not a discovery of Jesus. Every pious Jew knew,[1] in some way or other, that these two commandments contained the whole law, although of course it was not so clearly seen and expressed as in the New Testament. The same is true of the Stoic sage. For the Jew, the personal meaning of this commandment lay beyond all discussion, whereas for the Stoic it was problematic; on the other hand, for the Stoic the humane meaning of this commandment was clearer than for the Jew, for whom it was burdened with national religious orthodoxy, and therefore with a great deal of the statutory element. But Jew and Stoic sage alike were equally full of the thought that this commandment could be fulfilled, because it was commanded. The fulfilment of the commandment was, for both, the way to right existence and to the right relation to God and man. Neither of them understood that the mere form of the imperative 'Thou shalt love' manifests the whole contradiction in man. The 'Thou shalt,' the commandment as law, only exists for him who is no longer in communion with God and therefore does not take love to be the most natural thing in the world. The law already manifests the breach which has been made; thus it conceals while it announces the will of God. It gives a God to man with whom it is possible to enter into right relations through the correct fulfilment of the law. But this view is not only erroneous, it is sinful: it is false human independence, self-righteousness. The very man who thinks that through the fulfilment of this commandmen t he is doing the will of God

[1] Cf. ἀγάπη in Kittel's *Wörterbuch*: 'The love of which the Rabbis speak is neither only love between God and man, nor solely love between man and man, nor both side by side, but both at once and in one' (I, p. 43). Cf. the Appendix.

shows by this very fact that he has no idea of the will of God; true as it is, on the other hand, that the love of God and man is the will of God. The confidence of man in himself—of the legalistic type of man that is, the Pharisee or the Stoic—his certainty that he is able to achieve this obedience by his own efforts, and in so doing to place himself in right relation to God and man, this autarchy of the religiously moral man is precisely the full measure of sin—alongside of which the moral degradation of the 'publicans and harlots' seems almost insipid, because to them at least their incapacity to do this is to some extent apparent, and they are free from the danger of considering themselves righteous. The moralistic and legalistic understanding of responsibility, which leaves me dependent on myself, is the very acme of the misunderstanding of responsibility.

In such a dialectical way is the 'natural' and the revealed understanding of responsibility, and therefore of human existence, interwoven. Only through the extreme intensification of the law do we come to the understanding of grace. But we come to the understanding of grace only when we perceive that the legalistic relation to God itself is sin. The point of greatest nearness to God is at the same time the point of greatest distance from God, the most direct point of contact is at the same time the greatest point of contradiction. The meaning of the law can only be understood in the overcoming of the law. What the law desires and should achieve, can be seen only from the farther side of the law, from that point at which man breaks down under the divine law, where the man who relies upon himself and his own efforts perceives that the realization of his responsibility is not possible, that he always falls short of what he ought to do, that guilt-obligation and obligation-guilt are the same. It is only when man takes the law seriously that he comes to the point at which, broken down under the law, he is at last able to perceive the fundamental perversion of his whole existence, his false independence. Thus the law is not only the critical, but the diacritical point in the right understanding of God and oneself. The command 'Thou shalt love God and thy neighbour' is the most accurate knowledge that man can have of himself.

But when he takes this seriously this commandment drives him to despair, from which only forgiving grace, the incomprehensible generous love, *sola gratia*, can save him.

From all this it is plain why the question of the relation between the law and revelation cannot be answered unambiguously. The law of God is implanted in the hearts of all men; but, as comes out plainly enough in historical and in daily experience, it is at the same time covered by the rubbish of sin. Hence it must be revealed anew; but this revelation is not the proper one. In so far as the 'law' is revealed in the Old Testament it belongs (according to Gal. iv.) to the Old Covenant, to the 'Jerusalem which now is.' For in principle it does not lead further than the *lex naturae*; it always remains at that *cognitio legalis* which, as such, is not the truth of the true God and of the true will of God. In so far, however, as the Old Testament is really a revelation, in the same sense as that of the New ('the Jerusalem which is above') as the same passage in Galatians says clearly: it is a promise, a revelation, not of the God who first of all demands something, but of the God who first of all *gives*. The Sermon on the Mount, although in itself it is certainly the highest intensification of the 'law,' is not to be understood essentially as law but as a Messianic order of life; given to those who know the grace of God in Jesus the Christ, who do not live in strivings after God, but who live in the grace which they receive from God. The real meaning of this law lies beyond all 'law'; it is revealed where it is abrogated, in that it is fulfilled: in the Cross of Christ.

We only know what love is when we know it in the sense of the thirteenth chapter of the First Epistle to the Corinthians; and no one knows this love from the law, not even from the Sermon on the Mount[1]—if it is conceived as law—but we only perceive this love from Him who is the sole Object of the Christian Message: Jesus Christ, and Him Crucified. Here alone is disclosed the meaning of responsibility, its source and its goal; but here it is not merely disclosed but also given, as the new

[1] Cf. Thurneysen, *Die Bergpredigt*, the main argument of which I would like to support with all my power, while the detailed exposition, on the other hand, seems to me very often to do violence to the text.

life which is love, through faith. Here also the whole legalistic understanding of human existence and of man's relation to God reveals itself as the profound 'misunderstanding of reason within itself,' namely, as sin itself. For here it is shown that the legalistic understanding of God and of the self belongs to the primal perversion; the God who is known thus is the angry God.

13. THE WRATH OF GOD AND EXISTENCE-UNTO-DEATH

As the original being of man is existence in the love of God, so also the existence of fallen man is existence in the wrath of God. Man never escapes from God, not even in hell. Indeed, this is the very essence of hell—that one would like to be free from God at last, and it is impossible. But certainly: it is the 'strange' God whom one has in hell, not the real God; the God with the 'altered Face,' not He who as the Triune God is in Himself what He is. For in Himself He is pure love. But this ought not to be understood to mean that the wrath of God is something purely subjective, or a kind of misunderstanding. In point of fact, in an ultimate profound sense of course this is so, it is a misunderstanding; namely, in the sense in which sin too is a misunderstanding, that unhappy 'misunderstanding of reason within itself,' the fact that one misunderstands God and oneself. But just as this misunderstanding is an objective reality, the perversion of human nature, so also its correlate, the wrath of God, is an objective reality. This is the God of the man who is in sin; he cannot and must not have any other. He can only have a different God—the true God, God as He really is—when he is brought back to his origin through the reconciliation which proceeds from God alone and takes place solely through Him. Here it is not our business to occupy ourselves with the transcendent aspect of this problem. The doctrine of the wrath of God, the penalty of God's anger, and the doctrine of release from this penalty does not belong directly to our theme.[1]

[1] On this above all Theodosius Harnack, op. cit., *The Dialectic of the Wrath and the Love of God*, which corresponds on the one hand to that of the Law and the Gospel, and on the other hand to that of the *Deus nudus, absolutus* and *Deus Revelatus*, has since then not been seen again in this

But that doctrine is the point of view which gives the right perspective for all that can be said about man as sinner, if it is to be seen aright. Our question therefore must be expressed thus: What is the nature of the existence which man has under the wrath of God? In what does this our existence, known to us all as the existence of man as he actually is, manifest itself? Is existence under the wrath of God? The answer is as follows: it is existence-unto-death. That is the effect of the wrath of God in sinful existence. 'The wages of sin is death.'[1]

Not in vain have we held obstinately to the statement which sounds so paradoxical: in His word of love God gives man life. We must not understand the life of man first of all as a biological fact (unless we are to misunderstand it hopelessly), to which then 'all kinds of things' are added, for instance, consciousness, mind and, finally, religion. The genetic view may show us this picture a thousand times; but a real understanding of man can only be gained if we begin wholly from above. The being of man is being in the love of God. In the love of God alone is the bond of unity which holds all the parts together, as the love of God is also the origin itself, the basic ground for human existence. For that very reason the opposite, existence in the wrath of God, is the dissolution of this bond of unity, existence-unto-death. Here, it is true, we are not dealing merely with a negation. This is excluded by the very fact that is an existence in the wrath of God, that is, an existence unto death. The positive statement, the 'Yes,' has the priority against the negative statement, the 'No'; for God's Creation is not annihilated by sin. Even as a sinner man does not cease to be in God; that in particular, if I may put it so, is the negative miracle of sin. This is why there is no

manner. Cf. further *Der verborgene Gott bei Luther* by Blanke, my book *The Mediator*, and my article *Der Zorn Gottes und die Versöhnung durch Christus* in *Zwischen den Zeiten*, 1927, pp. 93 ff.

[1] Rom. vi. 23. The expression 'Sein zum Tode' comes from Heidegger, who has taken it and transformed it from Kierkegaard's *Krankheit zum Tode*, which again has been taken from 1 John v. 16. What Heidegger means by this idea is—more or less—that knowledge of oneself and of death of the *sensus communis*, in the sense in which it is used by Oetinger. Luther regarded death quite differently; see Stomps, *Die Anthropologie Martin Luthers*.

such thing as a neutral secular *humanum* which, as such, would have nothing to do with God. Even the sinner stands in a relation to God, but it is a perverted relation, since the sinner himself has been perverted. The perversion of human existence corresponds to the alteration of God. God 'alters His Face.'[1] And that again is the same as existence under the law. The law and the wrath of God belong together. For the law, as the ground of existence understood as the basis of life, that is, as the correlate of legalistic existence or of legalism, is the perversion of the will of God. God, who stands in relation to man first of all as the one who makes demands, not as the one who gives, is the God whose face has been disfigured, the angry God. The curse of the law is existence-under-wrath and existence-unto-death.

By existence-unto-death we do not mean the fact that human life tends towards death and is aware of this in all its expressions. That is certainly part of it; but it is only the surface. It is because man is above all subject, not merely object, because he has been created in God's eternal Word, that his death is entirely different from the death of any other creature. We shall be dealing with this later on.[2] Hence also existence-unto-death is something quite different from the mere fact that all human life is moving towards the fact of physical death. It is not the knowledge beforehand of physical death, of the end of earthly existence, which characterizes existence-unto-death, but rather the 'unknowing' knowledge of an 'afterwards.' It is the 'unknowing' knowledge of the sinner; the bad conscience is combined with the thought of the unknown 'afterwards.' Here, if anywhere, sinful man meets the wrath of God, in a dim pre-awareness of the possibility of eternal punishment.[3]

[1] This is how Luther translates Jer. iii. 12, probably incorrectly. On the other hand, the expression that God 'hides' His face is frequently used, and always means the withdrawal of the gracious revealed Presence (Isa. lxiv. 7). Especially characteristic are the words: 'Your sins have hid His face from you' (Isa. lix. 2). Similarly 2 Cor. iii. 13 ff.

[2] See below p. 462.

[3] Cf. the observations on the connexion between the wrath of God, conscience and the fear of death in Luther in Günther Jacob, *Der Gewissensbegriff in der Theologie Luthers*, pp. 23 ff. The conscience is 'in such anxiety and would like to flee from the world and from the face of God

This 'unknowing' knowledge, this undefined anxiety about what is coming, throws its shadow over all human life. It is the downward current of the river which is hurrying towards the cataract, and is already swirling from its effects.

But existence-unto-death has not only this subjective aspect. The dissolution of the bond of life is, it is true, not yet achieved, but it is in process of being achieved. Human life is objectively a dying. From the physiological point of view this statement has no meaning; for we have no concept of positive life, by which death and dying as something negative might be measured but that one which is given to us; hence there is no sense in calling this a dying. But we are not speaking of the biological phenomenon, but of human life. In the human act of life as such, as we know it, there is always given with it a dissolution, an act of death, a division. In all our acts of life there can be perceived a disassociation, the breaking up of that which was intended to be a unity, but never becomes a unity. The central expression of this disassociation is: division, which will be the subject of the following chapter. The more we are concerned with the person as a whole the more clearly evident does this disassociation become. In the being of the subject being and consciousness can no longer be separated. Human personal life—so far as it is known to us empirically—is always divided. Christian theosophists speak of the *turba* as a result of the Fall, and an effect of the wrath of God.[1] Just as glory corresponds to the Divine love, so the *turba*, the revolt within the creature, corresponds to the Divine wrath. Through sin man has become 'ec-centric,' and through this eccentricity he has fallen into confusion. With all his efforts he is unable to unite those elements which really belong to one another. In everything there is an element of division, of dissolution; all that is empirically human has in it something like a clot, just as blood clots when it no longer circulates in the bloodstream.

if it could; that is the greatest fear, that of a bad conscience, that will also be the pains of Hell, that the damned will want to flee away and hide themselves in order that God may not see them, and they cannot' (p. 33).

[1] Cf. Delitzsch, *System der biblischen Psychologie*, p. 94.

This 'clot,' seen from the centre, is legalism. Life and legalism are enemies. Law is rigidity, life is adaptability. Love alone has this adaptability which is at the same time unity; it is the bond which holds everything together without forcing it.[1] Legalism, however, is hard as iron. It does not make the heart strong, like real faith;[2] it makes the heart hard. It does not really bind one to one's neighbour; it separates. Above all, it does not unite us with God, but makes us independent. It is the independence of death, of division. The separation of the leaf from the living tree is its death. The curse of the law is not only, as is so often said in books on dogmatics, the result of punishment, but first of all and most profoundly: existence-in-the-wrath-of-God, existence-unto-death, and thus existence which is divided within itself and separated both from the love of God and also from one's fellow-creatures. We will now turn to the study of this divided existence in its manifestations in greater detail.

[1] Eph. iv. 3, 16; Col. iii. 14.
[2] Heb. xiii. 9.

CHAPTER VII

THE CONFLICT BETWEEN THE ORIGIN AND THE CONTRADICTION IN MAN: MAN AS HE ACTUALLY IS

I. THE NEW STATE OF THE PROBLEM

THE real enigma of man is the conflict within his own nature, not the fact that he is composed of body and soul; the real problem does not lie in the fact that man is part of the world and is yet more than the world; the real problem is that the unity of all these elements—given by the Creation—has been lost, and that instead of complementing and aiding one another, they are in conflict with one another. Non-Christian anthropology tries to deal with this conflict in two ways: either by ascribing it to the constitutional conflict between sense and spirit, or it seeks to resolve the discord by suggesting that the difficulties are merely successive phases in a process of development, continuous stages in self-realization. The Christian doctrine takes this conflict seriously: man, by his own act of self-determination, contradicts the divine determination in the Creation. It is this duality which gives its particular imprint to human life as it actually is. Because man has been created in the image of God, and yet has himself defaced this image, his existence differs from all other forms of existence, as existence in conflict.

The traditional doctrine assigned the Original Creation and the Fall, on the one hand, and man's actual sinful state, on the other, to two different subjects—in the one case to Adam, and in the other to myself. This, as we have already seen, meant that it could give only a partial expression to the fact of the conflict in human nature. The result was that either human nature was regarded as uninjured, and man's apostasy from God was regarded as something external to human nature; or that the corruption of human nature was emphasized to such a degree that justice was not done to the fact of the distinctively 'human' element. All that could then be done was to argue that this quality of 'humanity' was due to 'relics of the original image of God.' When we renounce the historical view of the Creation and the Fall we are set free from this dilemma, and we are able once more to see the contradiction in man as an actual conflict. Man as sinner is in permanent revolt, in a rebellion (which he cannot now renounce by his own efforts) against his divine determination as intended in the Creation, and thus against the nature given him by God. The divine Creation still exists in man, not in the shape of 'relics,' but as the primal element in human nature, inevitably but continually being denied afresh.

Man is and remains one who has his nature and existence in the Word of God, and is therefore, and for this reason alone, responsible. He does not cease to be in the Word of God, called by God and summoned to responsibility. But through his contradiction his attitude to the God who calls him is perverted; hence also the call itself has been transformed from a call of generous love into that of a demanding and accusing law. The law as the really determinative element of human existence is the sign of both these facts: that the call of God does not cease, and that man's hearing is perverted. It is not the law that is perverted, and it is not the God who reveals Himself in the law who is perverted, an idol; but man's understanding of the law, and therefore his legalistic understanding of God and man, is perverted, and the God which he makes for himself is an idol. Luther reveals profound insight when he reduces the whole of paganism—including false Christianity—to the one common denominator: legalistic religion.[1] The God who is understood from a legalistic point of view is an idol, that is, a God with whom we ourselves can deal; and the legalistic understanding of man is, in its deepest sense, self-deification, since it seeks in man that which can only be found in God: the truly human possibility of life.

Hence there is nothing human which does not suggest the *Imago Dei*, and there is nothing human which does not indicate the perversion of human nature. Even now, on this side of the Fall, there is a *humanum* which distinguishes man from all

[1] Cf. Vossberg, *Luthers Kritik aller Religion*, pp. 46 ff. Also Seeberg. *Lehrbuch der Dogmengeschichte*, IV, pp. 201 ff.

other creatures known to us. But this specifically human element is not uncorrupted human nature, as is taught by the Roman Catholic Church; nor is it merely a 'relic' of the original human nature, as is represented by the Reformers. It is rather the whole of human nature created in the image of God, but in a completely perverted form. The human element as form, as structure—namely, as responsible being—has remained; the human element as content, that is, as being in love, has been lost. Man does not cease to be 'in the sight of' God; but he is in the sight of God as a perverted being, and therefore God also appears to be perverted to him.

Hence the temptation continually arises to regard this form of humanity in itself, and the idea of man[1] which it contains, as the real nature of man, as is done by Idealism. The responsibility of man which is distinctive of him, which he cannot evade or throw off, is understood in such a way that the law is interpreted as the law of his nature and is thus made the basis of the idea of autonomous humanity. Instead of man asking himself whether he is fulfilling this law, he deludes himself into thinking that this law is 'in him.' He ascribes what is God's claim on him and God's witness against him, to himself as the witness of his nature, and in so doing he conceals his own reality.[2] Responsibility becomes

[1] Schott (op. cit., p. 28) expresses in an excellent manner the contrast between the rational-philosophical and the religious anthropology according to the view of Luther: 'Philosophy shows what might have become of man, theology shows what he has become.' That which we here describe as 'formal' Luther calls *secundum substantium metaphisice* (WA. II, 464).

[2] Plato's myth of the soul is most intimately connected with his theory of Eros and the Ideas: the ascending movement of the Eros corresponds to the 'Fall' out of the world of the Ideas into that of material corporeality. The *anamnesis* is that which leads back from the one to the other. The myth of the soul is differently conceived in the *Phaedrus*, the *Phaedo*, the *Symposium*, the *Republic* and the *Timaeus*, but the fundamental idea remains the same. On this cf. Zeller, *Die Philosophie der Griechen*, vol. ii, pp. 690 ff.; Heinrich Barth, *Die Seele in der Philosophie Platons*, 1921. In Aristotle the fundamental idea of the myth is transferred to the intellectual sphere, the Unmoved moved in the way of being loved: *κινεῖ ὥς ἐρώμενον* (*Metaph.*, 1072, b, 3); at the same time, however, this ethico-religious principle has a tinge of natural philosophy: this ascent is the graded movement of the whole world of nature. Neo-Platonism again has a genuine myth of the soul; it is distinguished from the theory of Plato, on the one hand, by the

divinity; this is the humanistic misinterpretation of formal 'humanity.'

On the other hand, on account of the corruption of the original Creation there is the danger of depreciating or secularizing the specifically human element which has remained even in sinful man,[1] that is, of forgetting that even fallen man is still always in the sight of God, and that even in sinful existence the 'theological' nature of man, that is, the nature which is related to God, is manifested. When man as sinner is severed from his imperishable relation to the Word of God, he becomes a *truncus et lapis* which is absolutely passive under the Divine Word, like an object which bears the divine operation without any willed response of its own, as a stone bears the blows of the stone-mason. A false humanism therefore brings with it a false, de-humanizing view of man.

According to the true Scriptural doctrine it is precisely that in man which indicates his sin which also indicates his divinely created nature, because both are understood in their actual contradiction to one another, and not in a neutral quality of nature which has, so to say, become full of dross. Man is a rebel against his divine destiny; he is the steward who pretends to be the master of the vineyard and then kills his lord's messengers. He is the prodigal son who has demanded 'the portion of goods that falleth to him' and now squanders it. Not only has he done all this in the past, but the revolution is still in full swing. The fatality of the Fall does not consist in the fact that man was once created by God, and now, some thousands of years later, is nothing but the heir of the sin of

idea of emanations, and, on the other, by the mystical-gnostic theory of the One and of 'becoming one'; we might also add, by the preponderance of the aesthetic and speculative element over the moral. The Beauty of the All-One is that which moves all. Cf. Zeller, op. cit., pp. 600 ff.

[1] Karl Barth has often and with a certain satisfaction pointed out that German Idealism finally led to Feuerbach, Strauss and Marx; he does not even allow that an Idealistic anthropology may be relatively superior to a purely naturalistic one; to him, indeed, the *humanum* as a whole is a *profanum*, and man, 'even within the created world, is something trifling and insignificant' (*Credo*, p. 30). In this view Barth is clearly moving away from the standpoint of the Reformers, who frequently mention Plato's myth of the soul with approval, contrasting it favourably with the 'animal' conception of Epicurus, although—apart from Zwingli—they do not make this relative distinction into a principal difference.

Adam; the fatality of the Fall consists rather in the fact that every human being, in his own person, and in union with the rest of humanity, every day renews this Fall afresh, and cannot help doing so, that he is in process of falling and cannot escape from it, that he cannot get back to his origin. Hence the fact that he has been created in the image of God as his origin, which he is always denying, is always present in the accusing law which man always knows, somehow or other, as truth and yet in practice denies. If man is to be understood as he really is, he must be seen in this actual contradiction, which is the real conflict.

The traditional anthropology of the Church contradicts, however, not merely the Bible but the actual experience of man. Not as though experience as such could show us the real man; we know that every empirical programme is derived from hidden axioms. But the doctrine and message of the Church must be such that experience cannot charge it with falsehood. We must not hide behind the paradoxical character of the ecclesiastical doctrine, accessible only to faith, in order to hold fast statements which ought not to be regarded as true because experience proves them to be false. The genuine paradoxes of the Bible never contradict the truth of experience, however little they themselves may be accessible to experience. The Bible does not postulate any other kind of man than the one known to us by experience; but it interprets the enigma presented by man as we know him from experience, the enigma which no system of philosophy or psychology can solve. The conflict in man comes out in definite phenomena, although the background of these phenomena, the conflict between the origin and the contradiction, between creation and sin, does not itself 'appear,' but can only be grasped by faith. In the following pages facts of this kind are treated from three points of view: as manifestations of the image of God in man, of sin, and of the conflict between the two.

2. THE TRACES OF THE IMAGE OF GOD AND OF THE 'GREATNESS OF MAN'

There must certainly be something distinctive in man in the fact that, without being absolutely mad, he can confuse himself with God. Fichte is certainly not an idle talker; nor is even the most amazing audacity of the teaching of the Vedanta with its identification: '*Atman* equals *Brahman*, I equal God,' *sine fundamento in re*. It is precisely this apex of the 'misunderstanding of reason with itself' which is at the same time the clearest manifestation of the fact that man has been created in the image of God, and that this original divine destiny is still present with him in the midst of his perversion.[1] The most daring of all sins, that of self-deification, is only possible through the divine destiny of creation, which raises man above the whole of the rest of the created world. What indeed is sin as a whole save this misunderstanding of man's God-given freedom? And is not this a sign of his Divine Origin? Man alone is a spiritual subject, like God. As spirit, he stands over against the whole world as a being which is not of this world. This superiority to the world he experiences in his power of perception. He 'has' the world only because he stands away from it, at a distance, because he is 'over against' it. As the subject of all knowledge, he cannot be compared with anything there is to be known. How could he to whom all is made subject, to whom it was said: 'all is thine, of all trees shalt thou eat,' he who alone might name the creatures, not be exposed to the temptation to touch the tree in the midst of the garden and to confuse it with the other trees, to wish to be like God? This sinful confusion, by which the copy makes itself the original, is only possible because it *is* a copy. The original relation of man to God lives in every spiritual act—in the very fact that it is a spiritual act. The spiritual is spiritual through the relation to the absolute, infinite, unconditioned.[2]

[1] 'A mesure qu'on a plus de lumière, on découvre plus de grandeur et plus de bassesse dans l'homme' (Pascal, *Pensées*, Fr. 443). 'La grandeur de l'homme est si visible, qu'elle se tire même de sa misère. Car ce qui est nature aux animaux, nous l'appelons misère en l'homme. . . . Car qui se trouve malheureux de n'etre pas roi, sinon un roi dépossédé?' (ibid., Fr. 409). 'Il est dangereux de trop faire voir a l'homme combien il est égal aux bêtes, sans lui montrer sa grandeur' (ibid., Fr. 418).

[2] 'The first part, the spirit, is the highest, the deepest, the noblest part of man, by which he is enabled to grasp incomprehensible, invisible and eternal things; and this is indeed the house in which there dwells faith and the Word of God' (Luther, WA. 8, 550).

Why does man seek for truth? Not merely because the knowledge of truth is useful to him, but because the idea of unconditioned truth leaves him no peace. He is seeking for his lost home, although he does not know it. The absolute nature of this idea of Truth contains the absoluteness of the Word of the Creator. He seeks and he must seek 'what it is that holds the world together at its heart,' the deepest ground, the primal Cause, the connexion; and his perceptive spirit bows before the law of the true, before the demands of 'absolute,' 'objective' Truth, before truth for truth's sake. So great is the power of this idea of pure truth that for its sake he will even sacrifice his life. Who will deny that in this search for truth there is something holy? This search for truth cannot be understood in terms of biological concepts of self-preservation or of the preservation of the species. The idea of the unconditioned, of validity, of truth-in-itself, cannot be grasped from any instinctive copy of actuality. It is not derived from anywhere except from the divine origin, the Primal Word, in which the spirit of man is based, even after he has fallen.

This, too, is the truth which lies in the Ontological Proof for the Existence of God. The idea of God which the human mind necessarily forms, can only be explained from God Himself,[1] true as it is that this self-formed idea of God is not the living God but an '*Abgott*' (idol) and gives man occasion for self-deification. Because man has been created in the Word of God, even as a sinner he cannot escape from the idea of God. He cannot escape from it, indeed, even when he denies it. Even in his denial of God, namely in its claim to validity, there lives, unconsciously to himself, faith in unconditioned truth.

[1] 'Such light and understanding (that there is a God) is in the hearts of all men and does not allow itself to be obscured or extinguished. There may have been some, of course, like Epicurus, Pliny and the like, who deny this with their lips . . . and who desire to obscure the light in their hearts. But it does not help them at all, their conscience tells them a different story. For Paul does not deny that God has revealed to them that they know something of God' (Luther, WA. 19, 205). What Augustine says about the connexion between God and *veritas* (cf. Gilson, *Der heilige Augustin*, pp. 135 ff.; Heim, *Das Gewissheitsproblem*, pp. 49 ff.) remains extremely important, even after all the specific elements of Neo-Platonism have been eliminated from his statements.

The actual man, not only when he is thinking, but also when he is creating, lives on his divine origin in the Word. When the beaver 'creates' his house, he does not go further than is useful to him. Man, however, even in the sphere of mere technique and civilization, always transcends the boundary of that which is merely useful. He experiences and seeks in technique at the same time dominion over Nature, not merely the utilization and exploitation of her material treasures. He desires to prove himself, to show his superiority over nature, he desires to triumph over it. But his divinely-created nature comes out still more clearly in his own 'creative' acts, in which he consciously and willingly goes far beyond the borders of mere utility. Art in its historical beginnings may have arisen out of technical, or magical motives, or out of motives connected with self-preservation: but in any case its nature is independent of interest in the preservation of life; it is the shaping of the beautiful for the sake of beauty. Man contrasts the imperfect world of actual experience, as he knows it, with a perfect existence, a heightened, intensified, ideal existence, freed from the contingent and accidental, the sight of which gives him a satisfaction which is wholly different from that of the experience of any reality in this world as it is. Art is always—whatever else it may be—the child of the longing for perfection. But perfection is an 'idea' which does not spring out of any observation of the existing world. Rather this idea is an original standard by which we measure all that now exists. Plato's argument that the idea of Perfection—even if it were only the idea of the perfect circle—does not spring out of any perception, but that, on the contrary, it precedes all perception, and alone makes it possible, has never been controverted from that day to this. The Perfect is not an 'intensification of the imperfect'; for the intensification of the imperfect would be only that which is still more imperfect. It is also no 'abstraction,' the 'elimination of the imperfect'; for in order to eliminate the imperfect I must use the idea of Perfection as the rule for elimination. Only complete stupidity can entertain the idea that the Idea can be derived from the perception. But art lives on the Idea—not on that which is thought, but on that Perception which it inwardly beholds, and for which it longs. All genuine creativeness comes from such a vision and such a longing, and this vision and longing comes from the Original Creation in the Word.

When the first Greek philosophers felt impelled to describe the ground of all as the Logos they must still have been dimly aware of the connexion between reason and the Word, an awareness which was lost by later rationalism. The fact that man can speak, and that he must speak, that he has the power of speech, of the word, has always and rightly been regarded as the most characteristic token of humanity. Animals have no language; moreover, they are unable to hold in their minds truth which is independent of an object or situation accessible to sense-perception. Speech is the expression of reason, not merely of the intellect. But speech is far more than this; speech is the expression of the fact that human existence consists of the relation between one human being and another. The fact that even when we are 'by ourselves' we cannot do without speech, and that something has only really been thought out when it has been formulated in speech, is a sign that human existence is not a solitary rational existence but that it is a common existence in which we impart to one another.[1] Speech is reason-in-community. We may indeed turn the current phrase, speech is the means of reason (which is derived from the idea of rational autonomy with its lack of community), the other way round and say: reason is the means of speech. We have been created in order that we may have 'something to say to one another.' However that may be, among all the indications of the creation of man in the Word of God, speech is the plainest. It was not the 'Deed' but the 'Word' which was 'in the beginning'; for God has not created a world which is without meaning and without community. In the Word He created the World: this is the basis for the truth that He created it in and for love. Speech is not to be understood from the point of view of reason; but both reason and speech should be understood from the point of view of the Word of God, as the two most powerful indications of a lost divine origin, in which we still live, though

[1] This is the fundamental idea of the epoch-making work of Ferdinand Ebner, *Das Wort und die geistigen Realitäten.*

in a perverted manner. That is why God reveals Himself and our origin through the Incarnation of the Word, and this again through the proclamation of the Message: thus by means of human speech.

But it is not only speech which points to the fact that in his origin man is destined for community. We can certainly make the attempt—and it has been made often enough—to understand all forms of community-life from the point of view of instinct. But all these attempts break down on the facts. The elements which compose instinct are not adequate to explain friendship, marriage, the unity of a people, the consciousness of humanity. In all these existing facts an ideal element is coupled with that of instinct: the idea of community, the capacity for community, the willingness for, and the longing for, community. Give a human being all that he longs for, 'pressed down and running over,' and take community away from him; he will be the most miserable of creatures. Even in his flight from community man seeks community: in the cloister. Behind the formation of states, the loud, dominating theme of world history, the will to gather all men into community, of the most comprehensive and concentrated kind, is at work as the secret, impelling force. Man is not a ζῶον πολιτικόν, but *humanus*. No πόλις, no nation-state can satisfy him, because beyond these boundaries dwell human beings who also belong to him. In the ancient imperialist or pacifist dream of the one kingdom of humanity there lives the 'remembrance' of an original paradisaical unity of all mankind[1] as the destiny of humanity.

The most direct evidence for this truth is the ethico-religious consciousness. No human community now exists, or ever has existed, which has not had its moral code; no community has ever existed in which—in spite of constant changes—the distinction between the ethically 'good' and that which is merely conventional or 'utilitarian' has not been a vital part of its consciousness. In spite of the doctrinaire assertions of theo-

[1] Perhaps the most impressive instance of this is that of Alexander the Great; it may be true, of course, that in this connexion we can speak of a sense of a universal cultural mission for humanity; but the elemental scope of his reach was deeper than his Greek conception of humanity.

logians, it is a fact that the moral sense extends far beyond the circles affected by the Christian ethic, and has a profound influence. The sense of responsibility is the really primal human phenomenon, which is not wholly absent from anyone; sometimes it attains an immense power, or again an incredible delicacy. In its negative form, particularly, as the sense of guilt, as the bad conscience, it is a force which mocks at all rationalizing views and does not care a fig for theoretical denials. It is simply there, and witnesses against us—to our lost origin.[1] For there is nothing more profoundly human than the sense of guilt; nothing in which the lost image of God manifests its presence more clearly. It is the sense of responsibility and its power which stamps the life of man with that 'humanity' which reason, even that of the greatest genius, can never give it, and, indeed, of which it often robs it. It is not man's creative power expressed in varying degrees of genius, nor his play and his laughter which make the life of man 'full of human dignity'—even Hell has its geniuses, and there is a devilish laughter and play—but only unity in love and loyalty. The most richly endowed and the freest spirit could also be quite inhuman; the devilish element is not checked by creativeness but by unity-in-responsibility. But this union and this unity does exist always and everywhere to an unexpected and astonishing degree.[2] In it we are not confronted by the riddle but by the mystery of man. Fidelity, where all the advantage would be on the side of infidelity; this is the miracle of the water which flows uphill. This miracle does happen. Here 'supernature' is revealed in the nature of man, of fallen, sinful man. Here, in the midst of apostasy and contradiction, its origin is revealed as a sacred presence.

And yet the sense of the Holy, the religious element, is at first of quite distinct origin, and its development is to a large extent independent of ethics. Why must human beings wor-

[1] Cf. Kähler, *Das Gewissen*, especially pp. 139 ff.; Cathrein, op. cit. Calvin: *Certe conscientia, quae inter bonum et malum discernens Dei iudicio respondet, indubium est immortalis spiritus signum* (*Institutio*, I, 15, 2).

[2] Calvin, *Exempla igitur ista monere nos videntur, ne hominis naturam in totum vitiosam putemus, quod eius instinctu quidam non modo eximiis facinoribus excellerunt, sed perpetuo tenore vitae honestissime se gesserunt* (*Institutio*, II, 3, 3).

ship gods? All the positivist theories of religion—its derivation from fear, from the desire and need for an explanation, from wonder at that which is unintelligible and the like—do not answer the question: Why does man acknowledge something holy, which, often against his own desire and advantage, he feels he must worship and serve? Modern theories of religion may throw a great deal of light upon the more detailed content and *raison d'être* of religion, but the original fact itself, the recognition of a sacred power before which man must bow in adoration, not because he gets anything out of it, but because he is inwardly overwhelmed by the Holy, because he feels he 'must not' do otherwise—'must' and 'must not' are fundamentally religious words—defies all explanations, just as its intellectual correlate, the idea of the Absolute, of the Unconditioned and the Perfect, cannot be derived from any finite content.

According to the present state of ethnography, there never have been, anywhere, peoples without religion.[1] This does not mean that it would be impossible for sinful man to be without religion. There is indeed, alongside of religion, also atheism and agnosticism, to-day perhaps for the first time as a mass-phenomenon. But even in the denial of God there is an awareness of God, and the motives for the denial of God are often more religious than those of the particular empirical religion whose content is denied. The religious instinct also expresses itself, unfailingly, in the godless disposition: as an impulse to posit something—however absurd—as unconditioned and to worship it as divine.[2]

[1] Cf. the monumental work of P. Wilhelm Schmidt, *Der Ursprung der Gottesidee* (especially the last of the six volumes), which, whatever one may think about the author's interpretation, presents an incomparable collection of material, which has been well sifted, of primitive religion, by means of which certain positivistic prejudices have been destroyed once for all.

[2] Here, as in all questions which concern the 'nature' of man, we must make a distinction between the 'official' consciousness and the forces which actually control the inner life. Atheists are always more religious (or more superstitious) than they will admit, and as a rule religious people are less religious than they are aware—both of these not in the sense of a value-judgement but in actual practice. Jung has shown how religion which has been suppressed in the conscious life comes out in the unconscious. Cf. for instance the interesting case which he records in *Die Beziehungen zwischen dem Ich und dem Unbewussten* (pp. 24 ff.).

In the history of religions the Holy is always, in some way or another, separated from the Good; divinity and humanity lie apart. It is the distinctive element of the Christian idea of God that, although these two are not one, they are revealed in one; the Revealer of perfect humanity is at the same time the Revealer of the true Divinity, the Holy is also the Good, because the Holy, God, is revealed as love, which as such is the Good. But even if this unity remained concealed from the religious consciousness outside the Bible, yet in all religions there exist fragments, crooked, defaced, but yet undeniable traces of this primal mystery in which man has his origin. For that 'Word which was in the beginning' is also the 'Light which lighteth every man coming into the world.' Hence the history of religion, whatever else it may be, is also, and above all else: a witness—even if perverted—to the relation of man to God. It witnesses to the fact that man can never get away from God, but that, in the midst of his flight from God, he must always turn to Him again and again; and that man, even when in turning away from God he distorts the picture of his nature, even in this perverted nature still preserves a remembrance of his origin, which manifests itself effectively in him and in his life. This is the Biblical doctrine: that although man through his apostasy is 'far' from God, God Himself is 'not far from every one of us,' but that 'in Him we live and move and have our being.'[1] 'Because that which may be known of God is manifest in them; for God manifested it unto them.'[2] He has not left Himself without witness unto man. But that which He shows them they have 'changed' into idols.[3]

Thus even the most horrible idol tells us something of the secret of the Holy, and the most abominable cultus tells us something of the fact that we have been created by God for God.[4] Hence religion always produces, in spite of the non-

[1] Acts xvii. 27 ff.; xiv. 17 ff. [2] Rom. i. 19. [3] Rom. i. 23.

[4] This dialectic of the history of religions, which corresponds to the dialectic of the natural man as a whole, has been misunderstood by J. Witte—influenced by Karl Barth—in his book, *Die Christusbotschaft und die Religionen*. He appeals (wrongly) to Luther for support; whereas the latter, as the very quotations used by Witte show, perceived and acknow-

morality which it may contain, the sense of a holy bond and of a sacred unity, which makes life human. Therefore, to use the words of an unbeliever, religion, whatever it may be, is the soul of all human culture; and where it dies, there culture declines into mere civilization and technique (Spengler).

3. THE MANIFESTATIONS OF THE CONTRADICTION AND THE 'MISERY OF MAN'[1]

There is no stronger proof of the actuality and depth of that contradiction, which we called 'primal sin,' than the self-deification of man. Only rarely is this innermost tendency of our *cor incurvatum in se ipsum* consciously and openly manifested. The formula 'God and I are one' designates a 'summit' of mystical religiosity. It presupposes a complete severance from the concrete world of experience. For in this world of experience man is not given much opportunity to confuse himself with the Almighty. What man experiences primarily is his impotence and nothingness. The end of his Faustian way of knowledge is 'and I see that we can know nothing' *ignoramus ignorabimus*, *docta ignorantia*, the despair of all knowledge—not merely of its attainment—scepticism.

What do we really know, if we do not know the whole? What is a knowledge that immediately changes itself into fresh problems? Is our progress in knowledge simply like the movement of people stranded on a moving ice-floe, who do not know whence it comes or whither it is going? Is it anything more than the aimless 'progress' of the Wandering Jew?

Certainly, our knowledge is useful in the technical sphere; for it helps us to control and use the forces of nature. At least

ledged this dialectic. Luther regards idols, in particular, as proofs both of the general revelation of God and the sinful perversion of man. But perversion does not mean annihilation. The fact that man must always have either a god or an idol shows that man's being is 'theological.'

[1] The '*misère de l'homme*' is one of the main themes of the *Pensées* of Pascal; but for him—in contradistinction to Barth and his followers—this *misère* is a dialectical idea: *la misère se concluant de la grandeur et la grandeur de la misère* (416). *L'homme connaît donc qu'il est misèrable . . . mais il est bien grand puisqu'il le connaît* (ibid.). *Toutes ces misères-là mêmes prouvent sa grandeur. Ce sont misères de grand seigneur, misères d'un roi dépossédé* (398). It is the knowledge of this dialectic which distinguishes Pascal from Montaigne.

in the world of facts our knowledge helps us to find our way about in practical matters. But does this mean: to *know*? Do we know what an atom is, what matter or force is, time or space, life or impulse? It is true of course that knowledge is moving forward in *one* direction; once for all we have left behind us the view of the universe held in the ancient world. But where will the next century be? And does not all progress in knowledge also bring with it an increasing alienation from reality? Is not the very abstraction which makes things useful to us in the technical sphere also that which separates us from the intimacy of the knowledge of nature which is possessed by the primitive man, the artist, and the child? Does not the simple human being know better what fire and water are than the scholar who gives us the formula for it?[1] And further, are not those who know the most, most inclined to fall a prey to the completest scepticism, since with every advance in knowledge the question 'What *is* that which *is*?' has only become more perplexing? 'And I see . . . that we can know nothing. . . .' Is not perhaps that very objectivity, which is the pride of our knowledge, that which most thoroughly separates us from reality? All our modern progress in knowledge has not brought us any nearer to essential truth; indeed, it has only led us still further into the feeling that we know nothing, that everything is dim and obscure, that we are strangers in the universe. Ultimately does not an honest little sparrow know more about the mystery of nature than we who are so clever? O irony of *homo sapiens*, O the tragi-comedy of man, who confuses himself with God!

But the *misère de l'homme* does not only become evident in the sphere of knowledge. The creative human being has to-day brought things to such a pass that he has learned to understand the story of the *Magician's Apprentice*[2] as his own.

[1] It is above all the Romantic theory of knowledge which points out the one-sidedness of this conceptual rational knowledge which so distorts reality. Cf. Bergson, *Evolution créatrice; Introduction à la métaphysique.* To this also belongs Scheler's emotional theory of knowledge, and in principle too that of Nietzsche (cf. *Wille zur Macht als Erkenntnis*), although actually he does not get away from the intellectually positivistic picture of reality of his own day. See likewise H. Kutter, *Das Unmittelbare.*

[2] An allusion to a poem by Goethe.—*Translator.*

He falls into imminent danger through all the serviceable spirits which he has created for himself; the thousandfold strengthening of his sense-organs, of his hands and feet through technique, has not really made him richer; in any case, it has not made him happier and freer.[1] He has become the slave of his own machine. He must—what irony—'serve' it (Haecker),[2] must live for it; human life must be adapted to its laws. While mankind has come a hundred times closer together, so far as space is concerned, inwardly, in the same degree, it has become more remote and far more divided.

In the sphere of cultural, actual creation, this is less impressively felt; but perhaps this is still more dangerous. The outcry, 'the intellect the enemy of the soul,' is not a chance outburst; the flight into the primitive is not merely a natural symptom of fatigue, but a deep despair of this whole mental activity which we call education, art, culture. The intellectual, the bearer of culture, is somehow essentially an enemy of man, because through a system of intellectual values or goods he conceals, masters, or destroys the distinctively human element. Was Ferdinand Ebner wrong when he described all this intellectuality as a mere 'dream of the intellect'?[3] Do we not see again and again that somehow this intellectuality makes people unfit for life? We long for simplicity, for that which is wholly natural. But it seems as though man, and man alone, were condemned never to find the simple and the natural. Every wild rabbit can live his own rabbit-life quite naturally and fully; man cannot do so, as a civilized being; from the very outset he is burdened with a kind of insanity which makes all his attempts to be natural, and to enjoy existence in a simple way, unsuccessful.

Whether we regard man as an individual or as a social being, it is all the same. Since history has been in existence this has been its theme: the contrast between individualism and collectivism, freedom and authority, independence and

[1] Scarcely anyone has ever said anything more significant than Berdyaev in his book, *The Fate of Man in the Modern World*, and in his profound *Cinq méditations sur l'existence* (Solitude and Society).

[2] Th. Haecker, op. cit., p. 37.

[3] Ferdinand Ebner, *Das Wort und die Geistigen Realitäten*, p. 20.

submission, the predatory man and the herd-man. Every movement which aims at helping the individual to attain his rights ends in libertinism and the dissolution of community—the Athenians knew quite well why they gave Socrates the cup of hemlock; and every reaction which tries to assert community, authority, order, the whole over against the caprice and the egoism of the individual, ends in oppression, violence, and dull stupidity. The movements for freedom, full of vitality at the outset, and splendid in their leaders, shatter community, and the movements for community, at first full of a deep sense of responsibility and of service, trample on the individual and his rights. It is not the observation of the processes of nature, but the contemplation of this tragic element in human history, which is the school of pessimism, of despair of man, and of his destiny.

Man has a *conscience*, which an optimistic Enlightenment declared to be the 'Voice of God.' What has not this conscience already commanded man to do! The blood-feud as well as the Inquisition, with its tortures and its burnings, anarchy as well as tyranny, cynical frankness as well as diplomatic lies, all appeal to this 'Voice of God.' Have there ever been greater tormentors of mankind than the conscientious, the moralists, the 'Pharisees of the idea'?[1] Instinctive sadism is simple compared with the cruelty of those who are doctrinaire, who sacrifice all human happiness, rights, freedom and heart to the idea, the principle, the 'great cause.' *Fiat justitia, pereat mundus!* The divine Moral Law within us—what arrogance, what an insane assumption of divinity has already arisen from this source! Which is worse: the chaos of lawlessness and immorality or the slavery of custom and the hostility to life of a rigid morality? Which is more terrible, the morally degraded, the 'publican,' or the morally 'just,' the 'Pharisee'?

Humanity: the battlefield of demons; the human spirit: the arsenal of the instruments for the destruction of life. How impotent is human reason in construction, how almighty in destruction! With a few bombs man destroys in a few seconds the work of centuries, and no one knows whether the next war will sweep away, in a few days, the culture of thousands

[1] Hermann Kutter, in his little pamphlet, *Ich kann mir nicht helfen . . .*

of years, for ever. It is not the animal instincts, but the mind of man which is the origin of all evil, the same mind which creates, builds, carries on research, strives, which seeks truth and loves righteousness, which longs after love and community; this same mind, this same 'heart which glows with a sacred fire' is the fiery abyss whence issues all that is demonic and destructive.

The same mind which worships the divinity also flees from it. What is the history of religion itself but the story of the way in which man, who cannot get rid of God, tries to get off as easily as he can? This origin of the development of the religious imagination lies far behind all conscious motives.[1] No one consciously tries to escape from the Lord God, the Living God, by his pantheistic idea of God; and yet this is the case. Religious symbols, and also the real formative forces of metaphysical thought, arise out of the unconscious. But the unconscious is not something to which man is helplessly exposed. The unconscious, also, is a sphere for which man is responsible—even though, like Original Sin, it may lie behind all that we have at our spiritual disposal, even though it may seem to us to be a kind of Fate.

Many and varied are the ways by which guilty man tries to evade the Divine Gaze. They are summed up in the history of religions, of their cults and mythologies. Its principle is the deification of the world, whether in the primitive imaginative form of pagan polytheism, or in the conceptually abstract form of pantheistic metaphysics; or it may take the opposite form: the banishment of God from the world, the impotent, dethroned, distant Divine Being, the fallen dynasty of the gods, the shadowy First Cause, the Creator-God of Deism, who 'only pushes from without, Celestial bodies, driving them about';[2] and finally atheism, which says bluntly: 'God is

[1] This is where the naturalistic theory of religion—Hume, Spencer, Comte, Feuerbach—down to Freud's *Die Zukunft einer Illusion* is relatively right (Jung's psychology of religion takes into account a metaphysical depth which opens up in the collective unconscious); but it sees equally one-sidedly only the background, the all too evident instinctive aspect of religion, just as Idealism only sees the foreground. Cf. my *Religionsphilosophie* (pp. 64 ff.) and my paper *Die Christusbotschaft im Kampf mit den Religionen*.

[2] Goethe, *Sprüche im Reimen: Gott, Gemüth, und Welt.—Translator*.

dead' (Nietzsche), which imagines that with its theoretical denial of God it has got rid of God for ever. It would be an undertaking of more than theoretical value to write a Christian mythology, or theory of idols, a doctrine of the formation of idols written from the point of view of faith in God. In the first chapter of the Epistle to the Romans Paul has sketched in the main features of such a Christian doctrine of the creation of idols. The idol arises through man's apostasy from the Creator and the transference of the homage which is His due to the creature. The motive for this apostasy and this false transference of homage is ingratitude and disobedience. It is so much easier for man to worship idols than to worship God. Even when the idol demands much from man, it does not demand the man himself; even where one offers all to the god, in so doing one does at least gain his favour. And again: where the god or the gods gain full power over man, man falls into demonic dependence which destroys responsibility. Even Pantheism and Deism, these more abstract and reflective forms of mythology, are also efforts to escape from the claim of God.

The idol has an infinite number of faces; it appears as one and as many, in personal or in wholly impersonal form, as a transcendental concept or even as something finite which, unawares, has been treated as infinite. But the idol is always a power to which man is enslaved, without being truly responsible to it—'carried away unto these dumb idols,' says Paul[1] —a power which binds without setting free, or which sets free without binding, which one cannot truly, in the sense of reverence, fear. The idol is always a secularized God and a deified world, a humanized God who is not truly human, or a deified man who is not truly divine. The idol is always as much like the devil as the true God; it is never both the Holy and the Merciful, the Absolute and the Personal, the Lord

[1] Schelling's *Philosophie der Mythologie* cannot provide any substitute for that, however much there is still to learn from it even to-day; for ultimately its starting-point is not that of the Christian faith, but that of a more or less dualistic gnosis. An important corrective to Schelling is offered by E. Reisner, *Die Geschichte als Sündenfall und Weg zum Gericht*, 1929, pp. 208 ff.: *Das mythische Vergangenheitsbild.*

of All and the Good Shepherd who lays down His life for the sheep. The idol is always—and this describes his nature most fully: the godlessness of man projected into the unconditioned, whether this god is called Zeus or the All-Self, the All-One, Nothing; or else 'Reason,' 'culture,' 'Man,' 'Humanity,' 'the ideal society' or anything else. As a mountain climber at evening may suddenly perceive his own figure reflected upon a sea of cloud beneath him, but enlarged and distorted, so the idol is my godless self projected on to the plane of the unconditioned, and distorted in the mist of my fanciful imagination. We can, indeed, truly say that man creates his idol in his own image. But there is one thing we must never forget: the fact that man is able to do this, and that he feels impelled to do so, he derives from God.

Single out any part of human life that you may choose, whatever you examine will always be a product of the original perversion, of the primal sin! But when you see sin you also see the image of God. Only where there is the *Imago Dei* is there also *peccatum*; sin itself is a testimony to the divine origin of man. Even where man revolts against God in titanic rebellion, and with great daring and insolence 'gets rid' of Him, or deifies himself, even there, behind the human perversion, the Divine image itself looks forth. Man could not be godless without God; he could not curse God if he were not first of all loved by God. The wrath of God under which the idolatrous, sinfully perverted man stands is simply the divine love, which has become a force opposed to him who has turned against God. The wrath of God is the love of God, in the form in which the man who has turned away from God and turned against God, experiences it, as indeed, thanks to the holiness of God, he must and ought to experience it.

4. THE MANIFESTATIONS OF THE CONTRADICTION AS SUCH

(*a*) *The Conflict of Opinions and the Attempt to construct a synthesis*

The conflict in human nature is so evident that it is scarcely possible to overlook it. Hence the manifestations of this conflict are phenomena which everyone knows; everyone who has reflected upon them connects them, in some way or other, with the conflict in man. From the point of view of the Christian truth about man, what we say is not that such phenomena of the conflict exist, and what they are, but that these phenomena, which are so well-known, manifest *the* contradiction of which we speak as Christians, which alone in the strict sense of the word can be called contradiction. The contradiction to which we allude here is the co-existence of the divine purpose of Creation and the opposition thereto of the sinful self-determination of man. This is not the commonplace truth that every man possesses a 'lower and a higher self,' of the 'two souls which dwell, alas! within my breast'; no, what we maintain is this: it is this definite contradiction between man's Origin in the Creation and sin, which comes out in these manifestations.

The first thing that strikes us is the fact that man can no longer understand himself as a unity. But in so far as he strives after unification as scientist, philosopher, or thinker, he usually forces this unification by over-emphasizing one aspect and depreciating the other aspect of the nature of man. For thousands of years the idealistic and the materialistic conceptions of man have been wrestling with one another.[1] Idealism starts from the reason, from the spirit, and regards the corporeal aspect of man, the sense and material nature of man, as an accident, as something which does not concern his 'essential' nature. It sees only the *grandeur de l'homme*, all that suggests his divine origin; but because it does not reckon the sense nature as part of man proper, the boundary between human and divine being in general becomes fluid. The 'intelligible man' is identified with the purely divine, autonomous reason; the spirit of man, or the reason of man, is the divine world-reason itself. The ugly raw material which arises 'from below'—since Plato's myth of the soul there have been in Idealism the most varied theories about the way in which

[1] A Christian-dialectical theory of the non-Christian conceptions of God, Man and the World was hovering—as is well known—at the back of Pascal's mind; in his conversation with de Saci he outlined it. On the same lines, only fuller, is the dialectic of the understanding of existence outside the sphere of Christianity offered by the whole work of Kierkegaard—from the *Entweder-Oder* (Either-Or) to the *Krankheit zum Tode* (Sickness unto Death).

this takes place—is not able to obscure this glorious picture of human nature. Man is divine.[1]

Materialism, on the other hand, sees in the sense or material nature of man the 'real' nature of man, whereas the so-called 'spirit' is only an epiphenomenon of the material life-process. Essentially man is an animal, his instincts as well as his physico-psychical organism are the same; the only difference is that through the special development of his brain and of the central nervous system the life-process gains new possibilities of differentiation. It is from such differentiation that 'culture' is to be understood, as a superstructure—biologically necessary—of the vital functions. The spiritual element serves to regulate the life of this highly developed animal, and to keep its course as even as possible; owing to the special character of this animal, it needs these special measures to protect it.

Man a god, man an animal—even at the present day these two theories are striving with one another about the nature of man; each, especially the idealistic theory, in many ways modified and refined, but the fundamental features of both are quite clear. Common to both of them, however, is this view: they understand man from the point of view of an impersonal 'something,' whether it be from that of 'spirit in general,' or 'nature in general'; both therefore ignore the fact of responsibility. Materialism transforms responsibility into an impulse towards altruism for the preservation of the species; Idealism turns it into the responsibility of the self to itself.[2]

[1] The synthesis between Christianity and Idealism which is still represented in England—upon the Continent this was tried for the last time by Eucken—is achieved by a modified fusion of genuine Idealism with genuine Christian faith, as for instance in the works of Dean Inge.

[2] The most serious approach to the idea of true responsibility is presented in Kant's Categorical Imperative; but it too—through the idea of the intelligible, autonomous self—finally ends in self-responsibility without any feeling for the 'Thou,' whereby we cannot even say that the empirical self is responsible to the intelligible self; for the empirical self is not capable of responsibility because it is causally determined. For Fichte it is still more difficult to construct a view of responsibility; in its stead he sets first of all the consciousness of freedom and the claim of freedom as autonomy (cf. for instance Fichte, *System der Sittenlehre*, *Werke*, *Medicus*, II, 401 ff.). In Heidegger's terminology: the ideal of existence of *Eigentlichkeit* (or 'accepting responsibility for one's life').

Because both theories neither recognize nor acknowledge man's origin in the Word, they cannot perceive existence-in-responsibility, existence-in-personal-responsibility, and thus man's destiny for love. Hence they are also obliged to give a different meaning to the fact of sin, of evil and of guilt, whether they do this by calling it a disturbance of the process of evolution, or of adaptation, or as an error caused by the obscuring of the spirit by physical instincts and sense-perceptions. Thus it is either 'arrested development' of the spirit by physical causes, or it is an organic-functional disturbance of the life-process. Because man in his self-knowledge lacks the centre—the fact that he has been created in the Word of God—everything in him breaks away from every other element, and then he tries to knit together that which has broken away by means of artificial, forcibly abstract schemata.

This conflict of opinion, however, then extends to the whole, to the whole world-view or philosophy of life. If faith is lacking a 'world-view' is necessary; we have either a world-view or faith, that is, either we understand existence from the point of view of responsibility, or theoretically. World-views may be grouped in pairs: materialism-idealism; Pantheism-Deism; rationalism-sensualism; dogmatism-scepticism; monism-dualism (pluralism, etc.). Of course there have been many efforts to construct a synthesis; but the history of philosophy shows us that the syntheses were always weaker than the one-sided systems. It is evident that upon the plane of theory the synthesis is only possible by a compromise between both the principles which constitute the starting-points of the theory. Possibly the most magnificent synthesis is that of Hegelianism; yet—or it would not be so magnificent—this is not really a synthesis at all, but the gradual overcoming of the contradictions by means of the dialectic of Spirit, the presentation of all antitheses as only apparent contradictions, as phases of development of the one Spirit. The final contradiction which is here to be overcome is that between the finite (human) and the absolute divine spirit; and the overcoming takes place, according to Hegel, in the religious consciousness, in the sense of the unity of nature with God, in the achievement of the fundamental idea of speculative mysticism. Thus this apparent synthesis turns out to be absolute Idealism, the closest spiritual relation of the Indian mysticism of identity. This 'solution' therefore is only possible by ultimately declaring the contradiction in man to be an illusion, something which, seen in the light of higher reflection, is seen to be no contradiction at all, but merely different stages in a course of spiritual development. Where thought has the final word the contradiction is soon dealt with; for thought is determined to get rid of the contradiction at all costs. As the devil fears the crucifix, so thought fears the contradiction; it cannot rest till it has got rid of it.[1] This is the lie in thought; this, we might say, is the despairing self-assertion of man in his thought: he denies the contradiction in which he lives by continuing the process of thought until the contradiction disappears.[2]

(*b*) *The Recognition and the Interpretation of the Contradiction in non-Christian Thought*

But thought does not always 'succeed' in doing this. There are people who are quite unable to persuade themselves by this kind of argument that the contradiction in their existence which they experience, from which they suffer, and for which in some way or other they feel responsible, does not exist. A courageous attitude of this kind is characteristic of the religion of Zarathustra. To it the conflict between light and darkness, good and evil, lie and truth, is the primal fact which confronts us. It is to be traced back to two primal powers, the good and the bad God, but in such a way that man has a share

[1] Of course, the removal of the contradiction is a task, and indeed an ethical postulate for thought; but this formal postulate is limited by the material one: respect for reality, that which we called the 'experience-critical postulate.' The monism of thought alone does violence to reality, and above all to that primal reality: the 'over-againstness' of 'Thou' and 'I.'

[2] It is the great philosophical achievement of Kierkegaard to have stressed the idea of contingency (of that which cannot be thought) and of the contradiction as a contradiction of existence as against Hegel. Here Grisebach has stepped in and has shown the connexion between Idealism and the principle of identity. But Kierkegaard has seen more clearly that both contingency and contradiction can only be rightly perceived in the Christian faith (Creation, Sin), whereas Grisebach has continually surrendered to the ideas of a neutral philosophy (lastly in his paper, *Freiheit und Zucht*).

in responsibility for the evil. The conflict therefore cannot be overcome by means of any theory or explanation but only through an act, and only through the act of the good God, in which, however, man also must participate by means of his good deeds. This is, indeed, a most courageous attempt to grapple with the problem of the contradiction! If there is anything in the history of religions which might claim to be a 'parallel' to Christianity, then certainly it would be this dualistic and ethical eschatology of Zarathustra. And yet the difference is evident. Man is only confronted by the decision, the contradiction does not yet penetrate his whole nature; hence in virtue of his good intervention, he can, as one who is himself uninjured, help to heal the contradiction which is in the cosmos. He himself does not need healing, he does not need the *restitutio imaginis*, but only the exercise of his God-given powers. The conflict is in the world, certainly, but it is not in man himself.[1]

Of another kind, and perhaps still more profound, is the Platonic myth of the soul, which, on its part, again, is connected with the conception of tragedy. The contradiction certainly goes right through human nature, it is the result of a 'fall.' This 'fall' however is not a rebellion against the Creator and the severance of man's connexion with Him, but it is the fall out of the heavenly world, which was caused by the 'bad horse' in the double harness, through the sense nature. What the exact meaning of the Platonic myth is, it is difficult to say;[2] but one thing is certain: the fall out of the heavenly world is caused by the sense nature; that means, that the sense nature is made responsible for evil. This point of view finally leads to the idealistic view which has already been mentioned, namely, that the contradiction does not affect the spirit itself, but that it comes from the fact that the ignoble part, sense existence or corporeality, is allied with the noble

[1] Cf. Lommel, *Die Religion Zarathustras, nach dem Awesta dargestellt*, 1930.

[2] Rohde's exposition seems to me the most relevant: the pre-existent soul descends into the material world on account of a 'weakening of the perceptive part of the soul.' 'Thus it is not, as in Empedocles, a religio-moral transgression that leads to the incarnation of the souls, but a failure of intellect, an intellectual Fall in sin.' Cf. Rohde, *Psyche*, II, pp. 271 ff. (p. 480 in English translation).

part. The spirit is the victim of the delusion of the senses. Thus this view is not dealing with an actual contradiction, defiance, rebellion of man against the Creator, but with an unfortunate combination of the elements of which human nature is composed.

The greatest and the most profound things outside the Bible that have been said about the contradiction are connected with the Greek idea of tragic guilt. Man falls into guilty opposition to the Will of God, but this guilt is his Fate. Like a blind man he falls into this,[1] not knowing, not willing, a plaything of circumstances, a sacrifice to the 'tragic entanglement of circumstances.' Therefore one has sympathy with a hero who has become guilty in so tragic a manner. In this sympathy man has compassion upon his own tragic guilt. Self-pity and the tragic element are inseparably united, for the very reason that the guilt is not genuine, incurred by man himself. Man does not take the guilt really upon himself, he explains it as due to Destiny. This tragic aspect may also be transferred to the cosmos as a whole, and it then becomes the pessimistic doctrine of the sorrow of the world and its tragic Fate.

With this cosmological doctrine of disharmony (which again is dissolved in the subjective idealism of the Brahman-Atman speculation) there is combined in India, in a manner which to us is incomprehensible, a doctrine which has a certain resemblance to that of Original Sin: the doctrine of Karma. Guilt for any particular earthly situation, which seems appointed by destiny, is due to an act of the individual in a previous stage of existence. Each individual, in his previous existence, determines his own later destiny in the chain of re-birth. Here determinism and Fate and moral indeterminism

[1] 'This guilt is not the moral guilt of a human being who possesses freedom of choice between good and evil, but it is illusion, which is ultimately part of his existence. Man must become guilty. . . . From the limitations of human knowledge there follows human guilt . . . a guilt which is part of existence' (Article: ἁμαρτάνω in Kittel's *Wörterbuch*, I, 300). At the same time there is here a theory of Original Sin (Tantalus, Oedipus): 'the transgressions which have been handed down from our ancestors' (Eum. 934) are those which drive Eteocles to his horrible decisions (Rohde, *Psyche*, II, 229). Fate and guilt are one.

are combined with one another in a remarkable way. Behind the doctrine of re-birth, however, there lies as its presupposition the fundamentally Indian view that the physical, empirical world ought not to be (μὴ ὄν); and, accordingly, emancipation from Karma takes place essentially through ascetic self-redemption. The parallel with the Christian doctrine of Original Sin, therefore, is illusory; for the fundamental Christian idea is absent: the good Creation of the holy and loving God.[1]

Thus the power and the fidelity with which the fact of the contradiction (which, in some way or other, is always noticed in human existence) is held and interpreted varies greatly. But all the efforts to solve the problem, however different they may be, show one thing: the real contradiction, sin, cannot be rightly understood by man. Man sees the breach, but he does not see it fully. It is too deeply embedded within him for him to be able to see it aright. Rather, he experiences the contradiction unconsciously as an actual state of division, whose cause he does not know. The modern man, however, who denies this—in accordance with his monistic way of thinking—is forced to feel it all the more acutely in this unconscious manner as the conflict between the unconscious and the conscious, intensified in neurosis, and in some cases, in that final intensification in which the individual concerned has no conscious relation with real life at all, in that division of personality which characterizes actual mental illness and madness. We have no right, it is true, to assert that all mental illness has this origin; yet that the increasing frequency of neuroses and psychoses is not due first and foremost to the complicated nature of the life of modern civilization, but above all to that repression, to that evasion of the contradiction by its denial, seems to me an interpretation of the phenomenon which cannot easily be gainsaid; it is indeed one towards which

[1] The theory of *Karma*, which—with that of *Samsara* (never-ending cycle of successive existences)—determines Indian thought, is, so to speak, a metaphysical moralism, a doctrine of the cosmic causality of moral transgression. It is as impersonal as it is rigid, individualistic and remote from the world. The rent does not pass through man; it is man himself who frees himself from Fate, especially through asceticism.

modern psychiatrists, in their own way, are tending more and more.[1]

(c) *Certain Particular Phenomena which manifest the Contradiction*

A fundamental phenomenon of this kind, which indicates the presence of the contradiction, is fear.[2] The Bible teaches us that fear is the fundamental situation of man as separated from God, of the man who is not reconciled with God. The world has the very opposite of that state of mind which corresponds to faith, which is described as 'having peace.' Fear[3] is the feeling of not being at home, of feeling uncanny and lost in the universe. This fear dominates the life of man, not only exceptionally and in certain individuals who have a tendency that way, but absolutely, and in all human beings at every age. Fear is the air which man—in so far as he is separated from God—breathes, or does not breathe. Fear is difficulty of breathing—*angustiae*—the suffocating distress which the soul feels in its separation from God.

Most men are not aware either that they are afraid, or to what an extent fear rules their lives. Consciously, as a rule, they are not afraid; but their actions betray the presence of fear. Much of the intensity of human effort springs from the desire for security of every kind, that is, from fear. Fear in connexion with practical life is called anxiety. It would indeed seem to be more sensible to say that anxiety is the fundamental attitude of man; but what is anxiety except fear of life seeking for security? It is not by accident that the most important philosophical anthropologist of the present day conceives anxiety as the distinctive element of the life of man.[4] All fear, and all the efforts of anxiety to remove it, have their final ground in death, in the fact that our whole life is moving

[1] Cf. Maeder, *Psychoanalyse und Synthese* (*Arzt und Seelsorger*, No. 8) and *Die Richtung im Seelenleben*; C. G. Jung, *Wirklichkeit der Seele* (especially *Vom Werden der Persönlichkeit*, pp. 180 ff.).

[2] *Angst*: anguish, dread; fear; terror.—*Translator.*

[3] Cf. John xvi. 33. Heidegger, *Sein und Zeit*, pp. 184 ff., 266; his analysis of 'fear' or 'anguish' is secular and neutral compared with that of Kierkegaard, and is therefore less profound. To Heidegger the fundamental characteristic of existence is 'anxiety' (*Sorge*).

[4] See Heidegger, *Sein und Zeit*, pp. 180 ff.: *Die Sorge als Sein des Daseins.*

towards death. Not only the Egyptian pyramids, but the whole of civilization and culture, are an attempt to evade death, that death which is the wages of sin, that is, that death which we experience as connected with the contradiction in our existence.

Fear of life is the way in which, emotionally, we become aware of our homelessness, our banishment from our home. But a large part of our intellectual culture consists in concealing and suppressing this fear. How much of our present 'culture' is simply a sleeping-draught against fear of life.[1] This comes out most crudely in the use of chemical narcotics. But there are also mental narcotics which have the same purpose, and are equally effective in driving away, for a time, this fear of life. A particular form of this fear is that which Pascal describes as *ennui*, which we cannot translate simply as 'being bored.' It would be more correct to say that it means a weary sense of futility, of the sterility of life; it is the state of the empty soul, which feels its emptiness and cannot stand it without making an effort to fill the void.[2] This comes out very plainly in the phrase 'to kill time.' Time is the fundamental element in our existence, it is, so to speak, the substratum of our life. And this time one desires to—kill! Existence in time cannot be endured; people flee from it into a sham existence, into a life where they can forget themselves. Not only the greater part of our obvious pleasures, sport and play, but also a good deal of our highly intellectual pursuit of culture, is at bottom nothing more or less than a 'pas-time' of this kind, by means of which man hopes to be able to forget himself; it is a substitute with which—although it is impossible to satisfy the empty soul—it is at least possible to fill it; it is a narcotic with which the hunger of the soul is to some extent 'doped.' In

[1] Cf. Max Picard, *Die Flucht vor Gott*.

[2] 'Rien n'est si insupportable à l'homme que d'être dans un plein repos, sans passions, sans affaire, sans divertissement, sans application. Il sent alors son néant, son abandon, son insuffisance, sa dépendance, son impuissance, son vide. Incontinent il sortira du fond de son âme l'ennui, la noirceur, la tristesse, le chagrin, le dépit, de désespoir' (Fr. 131). 'Si l'homme était heureux, il le serait d'autant plus qu'il serait moins diverti, comme les saints et Dieu' (Fr. 170). Distraction is the greatest misery, for it prevents us from seeking the reason for our misery and our true salvation (Fr. 171).

such reflections we see the truth of the magnificent phrase of Augustine: 'Our soul is restless until it finds rest in Thee, O Lord. For Thou hast made us for Thyself.' This saying is the guiding principle of all genuine psychology; without it one wanders hopelessly in the labyrinth of the soul.

This unrest of the soul, which on its negative side is called fear, on the positive side is longing. Longing, therefore, like fear, is a fundamental state of our existence in which the contradiction, as contradiction, comes out perhaps still more plainly. We could not long, if there were nothing there to desire; we would not feel obliged to long, if this other were really ours.

Plato saw the immense significance of longing. Longing, *Eros*, the desire for the distant Beloved, namely the divine truth and goodness, is for Plato the wings by means of which the soul soars back to its origin. He saw longing correctly, but he has ascribed too much to it. The dream of the spirit—the vision of the Ideas—is not yet life in the spirit. Hence this spirituality, like mystical longing and mystical spirituality, does not lead to our fellow-man, to love, but it separates us from others, and leads us to seek solitude. Longing is not the way back but is merely the obscure remembrance of something which has been lost, and the fruitless turning to it in phantasy, in the dream of the spirit. Hence all ideal spirituality, the product of longing, understood as an ultimate, is just as much a substitute for the true 'bread of life' as 'distraction' and narcotics. The emptiness of the soul can be filled only by that in which and for which one has been created, the Word of God.

The whole emotional life of man, and thence the whole mechanism of the human mind, could be re-interpreted from the standpoint of fear and longing. It is a significant fact that Platonic love is called *Eros*, that is, it is described by the word which is used to describe the humanized form of the sex-instinct. Human love, in the sense of love between the sexes, should never be understood from the point of view of animal instincts, although it does include some elements of the animal instinct and of the animal function. It always has a specifically human element, the infinite element of imagination. Man always seeks much more in sexual love than it is really able to offer, because in *Eros* he is seeking the 'distinctive element' which can never be found in *Eros* but in love alone, that love of which the New Testament speaks. To a very great extent 'love' between the sexes is a misunderstanding of love, therefore it is an eternally unsatisfied longing.[1]

We owe a great debt of gratitude to psycho-analysis for showing us the immense importance of *Eros*—even if primarily only in the narrowly sexual sense. *Eros* is in fact connected with the whole life of man, and is not merely a partial function. It extends from the lowest plane to the highest. In a certain sense it is true to say: man is *Eros*. In any case it is as correct to say this as to say that man is spirit, or reason. The fact that Plato has connected them so closely with one another shows the incomparable depth of his philosophical conception. Which of the great Idealistic thinkers of later days is aware of this fundamental fact? Man is *Eros* to such an extent because he has been created by God in and for love, and because he has fallen away from God. *Eros* in its present dynamic is the product of the confusion of our existence. The account of the Fall and its emphasis on the first result of disobedience is not a 'naïve' idea, but profound wisdom: 'And the eyes of them both were opened and they knew that they were naked, and they sewed fig-leaves together and made themselves aprons.'[2] The attitude which took the sex-relation for granted has vanished, and shame and *Eros* show that the original order has been broken. The destiny of man for love now works out in a devastating dynamic of this 'love,' in which man is always impelled to seek without ever finding what he seeks, and what he cannot cease seeking in spite of all disappointment.

But there are also a whole series of psychological phenomena in which the contradiction is manifested, from which it cannot merely be deduced indirectly, as in the two forms which we have just discussed, but directly, indeed in which we become conscious of it as contradiction: doubt, despair and the bad conscience.

Doubt means that the mind is divided about what is true, good, right, just or 'valid.' At first it seems to be one psycho-

[1] Cf. my booklet, *Eros und Liebe*, Berlin. [2] Gen. iii. 7.

logical phenomenon among many, which, like others, appears under certain conditions, and then disappears again. But when we examine it more carefully we find something different. There is a 'chronic' kind of doubt—not merely in those rare individuals whom we call 'doubters,' or somewhat more academically 'sceptics'; but when we look at doubt clearly we see that, just like fear and longing, it is a fundamental element in human existence—to the extent in which the human spirit is awake. The fact that the spirit is alive shows itself in the keenness of its questions. A living mind cannot help questioning everything. The 'normal person,' it is true, does not doubt that twice one are two, nor that fire is hot, nor that lead is always heavy, nor that to-morrow morning the sun will rise. But where life as a whole is concerned, its meaning, its origin, its purpose, where we are trying to discover what is or is not permitted, what is commanded and what is prohibited, the nature of true happiness and of true human life, the question of what comes after death, and of what lies behind the veil of things seen and temporal—about all this man has no certainty, into all this doubt creeps and gnaws—as the grub of the cockchafer eats away the roots of grasses and herbs—and eats away the secret certainties of one's childhood. How can man come to certainty—save through the faith for which he has been created! Doubt also belongs to the *cor inquietum* which finds no rest until it has found the centre of life.[1] There are other religions than the Christian faith, it is true; and one is easily tempted to assert that that other faith is 'just as certain' for those who hold it as the Christian faith is for Christians. It is true that a Maori believes as firmly in his gods and his magic practices as a Christian believes in the Incarnate Son of God. But there is one incontestable fact: when reason awakens in the Maori, he begins to doubt, and can never again find rest. Reason destroys religion in all its forms, and 'philosophies of life' are very pallid and academic substitutes for the loss of a faith; from the very outset they

[1] Luther: 'We must lay great stress upon the word "doubt." For the Papists make faith a very slight matter and do not think that doubt is anything evil. But Christ lays all the blame upon doubt and makes us understand clearly that a doubter sinks' (after WA. 38, 581).

contain the seeds of doubt. It is a process which we see going on around us at the present day at a great rate. All religion is seized by doubt and destroyed—with the exception of that faith which is aware of the 'misunderstanding of reason within itself,' of that faith which knows that reason is derived from the Word of God, and is not its master. It is of course impossible to prove this statement; to the end of time it can only be proved by practical 'experiment.'

When doubt reaches the centre of man it becomes despair. Despair is no longer merely a state of uncertainty about what is valid, it is the earthquake which shakes the very foundations of our existence. The person who is in despair not only feels mental anguish, difficulty in breathing; spiritually he feels as if he were being suffocated. He has lost spiritual oxygen, that is, hope, faith in at least a possible solution of the problem of life, he has come to an end of everything; he is 'finished.' The idea of life—what he has expected from life, all that is meaningful, beautiful, good, desirable—and the reality of life are no longer connected; movement between the two has ceased and has become rigidity; they have become separated, the tension is broken, the nerve of life has snapped. This is the despairing man, that is, the person who—in full possession of his faculties, without being insane—is torn in two, into the 'true' man outside himself, and the 'actual' man, so that the unrest which usually passes from the one to the other is over. The point of absolute frigidity in existence has been reached, where all movement has ceased.

Possibly such despair as this is an extreme which no one ever reaches. What we usually call a state of 'desperation' is an approximation to a state of despair, a comparative hopelessness; it means rather that within a certain limited sphere everything is over; it does not mean that the person in question despairs of life as a whole. Of course it is evident that the man who 'makes away' with himself, because life has ceased to mean anything to him, is certainly very near this point of final, rigid despair. And yet—does any suicide lay hands on himself wholly in cold blood, without fear and without hope; without the feeling that in so doing, in some way or another, he has found a 'desperate way out'? Man, we may say, is never completely in despair so long as he breathes. It is as though the parable of the breathing of the soul were more than merely a parable, as if the final boundary of despair could not be combined with the act of life itself. On the other hand, there is more despair in the world than at first we are inclined to believe. It was no mere whim of Kierkegaard, when he undertook to try to represent the whole of human life—in so far as it is not in 'faith'—as despairing, and its phenomena as countless variations on the one theme of despair; and the book in which he does so has become one of the finest of his writings.[1] Let us not quibble about words. The point at issue is this: the state of mind which reaches its nadir in despair is the contradiction between man's 'true' and his 'actual' nature, between his Divine destiny in Creation and his self-determination in actual experience, and it is this conflict which not only runs right through human life as a whole, but is also somehow felt by all men, even if dimly and obscurely, as a sense of hopeless division, of being 'torn in two.' Even the happy and placid person is not so happy and placid as he thinks, or makes other people think, he is. Even he perceives, though dimly, that his life is torn, that he is inwardly bleeding from an unhealed wound at the centre of his personality, his heart. Even he observes that he cannot 'square' his own ideal of life and his actual life-experience, that things are out of proportion, the symmetry has been disturbed, 'something has gone wrong.'[2]

Every human being who is aware of his humanity at all, that is, who has some sense of responsibility, is aware that the order of life has been disturbed; this comes out in 'a bad conscience.' Of course people maintain that modern man never suffers from a bad conscience, but those who say this only show that their own view of life is superficial; they are only looking at the surface-consciousness. Man's knowledge

[1] Kierkegaard, *Die Krankheit zum Tode*.

[2] Luther speaks of a *fiducialis desperatio* (cf. the letter to Spenlein, 1516, *Zwischen den Zeiten*, 1923, 26 ff.), of a confident despair: 'Through confident despair in thyself and in thine own works thou wilt find peace.' But this despair is simply the abandonment of self-assurance of the autonomous self and the return to the original position: the self which is grounded in the Word of God.

of himself is far deeper than that of his 'consciousness,' and his 'consciousness,' again, is far deeper than his theories about himself. Theoretically, modern man is very often not aware of a bad conscience. For he has destroyed the sense of ought, and also the Idea of God. He explains what used to be called guilt and sin in a 'natural' way. As we have already seen, he possesses a monistic explanation which for him solves the contradiction. But all this only concerns the 'official reading'; the 'private,' secret reading is quite different. Of course, consciously, even to himself, man swears by the 'official reading'; but in experience he finds that his actual consciousness, and still more his soul as a whole, takes very little notice of this reading. The sense of guilt for example reacts extraordinarily promptly, and usually in an amazingly delicate manner, wherever he is concerned with the guilt of others which affects himself. It reacts, however, also continually secretly in himself; he has 'a bad conscience,' even when he swears over and over again that 'all that sort of thing is merely an ancient superstition.' He finds that it continually breaks through when the censor of theory does not intervene sufficiently swiftly. The bad conscience is like a dog which is shut up in the cellar on account of its tiresome habit of barking, but is continually on the watch to break into the house which is barred against him, and is able to do so the moment the master's vigilance is relaxed. The bad conscience is always there, it is chronic; but it is not always there with the same intensity, it only becomes 'awake' in the more intensive sense when it is aroused by special events. But then it not only takes up a position to this new particular occasion, but with the judgement on the particular, it also pronounces judgement upon the whole situation, even if a quite irrational and unintelligible one. It is a well-known fact that when people who have a strong alert sense of responsibility commit a slight fault this immediately raises the whole problem of existence, and awakens the whole sense of guilt.

The bad conscience is very closely connected with the fear of life and unconfessed despair. But in contrast to those other two phenomena, it is negative, the sense of the contradiction at the very heart of existence, at the point of responsibility.

The bad conscience announces that my responsible existence, that is, my distinctively human existence, is determined in a negative way—that is, 'being guilty.' But it is not the rational moral judgement: 'this or that is wrong.' It springs from a greater depth than that of the moral sense.[1] It is the place at which responsibility means the whole, thus it is concerned just as much with our relation to God as with our relation to our fellow-man and to the world. Like fear it is a sense of homelessness, but of a different kind, it is the sense of being cast out of one's home, and indeed of being cast out for one's own fault. That is the picture which is sketched for us in the pictures of mythological phantasy of the bad conscience, the phenomenon which the poets describe, and which every one of us, though in very different degrees of clarity, experiences in ourselves. No monistic theory can deal adequately with this fact of the bad conscience, any more than it does with the fear of death. In the bad conscience alone we experience the uncanny nature of our existence in its full wretchedness. Nothing makes us feel so lonely, so strange, so restless, as a bad conscience. Anyone who deliberately suppresses it will meet it again in dreams, in nervous disturbances, and finally perhaps in serious mental illness. This inhabitant of the house cannot be turned out simply by giving him notice to quit. The bad conscience is the way in which we, as sinners, experience the presence of God. It is, so to say, the negative Holy Spirit, the wrath of God as experience, life under the curse of the law as a psychological reality. That is why life must be reversed—from unbelief to faith, from sin to reconciliation with God—at this point; this is the witness of the Bible which was re-discovered by Luther in particular. 'God and the conscience cannot tolerate one another,' namely, the living God of love and the bad conscience, which is the central expression of our contradiction, that is, the central effect and the first result of sin. The fact that the actual man is to be understood only from this standpoint is a truth which at the present day especially forces itself upon the notice of those

[1] Cf. Kähler, *Das Gewissen*, 1878, and Kähler's article upon the conscience in the PRE³. Further, my book, *The Divine Imperative*, pp. 155 ff.; and G. Jacob, *Der Gewissensbegriff in der Theologie Luthers.*

who would like to help men out of their contradiction. Whether they believe that they themselves are able to remove this contradiction, or whether they recognize it simply to be what it is and expect its healing from some other quarter, will be the criterion by which the real soul-doctor will be distinguished from the soul-quack.

* * * * *

This then is the actual man, this being who lives in contradiction. Because man is in opposition to his divine origin in the Creation, daily renewing this opposition, he lives in opposition to his own God-given nature; therefore his present nature itself is: contradiction.

"Quelle chimère est-ce donc que l'homme? Quelle nouveauté, quel monstre, quel chaos, quel sujet de contradictions, quel prodige! Juge de toutes choses, imbécile ver de terre; dépositaire du vrai, cloaque d'incertitude et d'erreur; gloire et rebut de l'univers. . . . Connaissez donc, superbe, quel paradoxe vous êtes à vous-même . . . Si l'homme n'avait jamais été corrompu, il jouirait dans son innocence et de la vérité et de la félicité avec assurance; et si l'homme n'avait jamais été que corrompu il n'aurait aucune idée ni de la vérité ni de la béatitude. Mais, malheureux que nous sommes . . . nous sentons une image de la vérité, et ne possédons que le mensonge; incapables d'ignorer absolument et de savoir certainement, tant il est manifeste que nous avons été dans un degré de perfection dont nous sommes malheureusement déchus."[1]

[1] Pascal, op. cit., Fr. 434.

CHAPTER VIII

THE OBJECTIONS TO THE CHRISTIAN DOCTRINE, AND THE RETROSPECTIVE QUESTION FROM THE STANDPOINT OF ACTUAL EXPERIENCE

THE decision about the truth or untruth of the Christian doctrine of man is made in experience. This statement may be questioned from two points of view: from that of theology and religion, and from that of rational philosophy. The theologian, as the steward of the faith, may see in this statement an abandonment of faith in the Word of God or in the message of the Church, and he may feel obliged to protest that the truth of the Christian doctrine is being abandoned for an appeal to experience. For him, is not the Word of God, the Biblical Gospel, and thus also the Biblical doctrine of man, an *a priori*, and therefore never a product of experience? Does not the Church, the Bible, demand a 'blind' faith in its Message, that experience can neither prove nor disprove?

Here we come to a parting of the ways; hence it is very important to use words very carefully and exactly, and to avoid all catchwords. According to the teaching of the Bible there is no other faith save that which is itself 'experience,' namely, a real meeting with the real God. Faith in God's Word is never 'blind' in the sense that the one who believes does not know why he believes, or why he ought to believe, but simply that he is obeying the command of the Church to believe. Genuine faith is 'one's own' faith, it is an event in which 'I myself' am vanquished by the power of the truth of the Word of God. The Word of God, however, will never really vanquish anyone, never constrain him inwardly to faith, 'casting down reasonings,'[1] save through the message which is proclaimed to him in the Bible, in the message of the Church, in the pastoral ministry, which as God's Word discovers him in his actual condition, and through this becomes to him the Word of God. No man can rightly believe that he is a sinner

[1] 2 Cor. x. 5 (R.V.).

unless when that is said to him he equates his own actual state with this predicate 'being a sinner,' so that—as Paul describes it—he is 'convicted,'[1] as one who is accused in a law court who had previously obstinately denied his guilt is 'convicted' by the flawless evidence of the prosecuting counsel. Faith always means being convicted; this means that the soul feels that its true state has been discovered. The moment at which I feel that I have been discovered, when I say: 'Yes, that is what I really am,' and the moment at which I believe, is one and the same. The operation of the Word and the Spirit of God in me, who am affected by it, consists in this conviction. To know that one has thus been touched, the consciousness that the judgement of the Bible touches me *here*, where I really am, this sense of having been discovered, is not, it is true, the whole of faith; but it is an essential element of faith, apart from which faith would be merely a *fides historica*, a heteronomous acceptance of an article of doctrine imposed upon me from without. The Word of God does not lay claims on me which ignore the reality of actual experience, but it first of all makes me see my actual state, as it really is, in such a way that I know that now I am seeing myself as I really am. This means that the true experience of my actual state and faith in the Word of God are indissolubly intertwined.[2] I cannot see my actual condition at all save in the light of the Word of God, and I cannot believe in the Word of God save as it unveils to me my actual con-

[1] 1 Cor. xiv. 24 ff.

[2] Something right too has been killed by the slogan: the 'theology of experience.' Faith is not based upon experience, but upon the Word of God alone, upon Jesus Christ, and the promises of grace which run counter to all experience. But this being 'based upon' the Word, in the sense of being apprehended by the Word, and saying 'Yes' to the Word, this faith is certainly also experience, experience of the Holy Spirit. 'No one can rightly understand God or the Word of God save through the Holy Spirit. But no one can have the Holy Spirit unless he experiences, and is aware, and in the same experience the Holy Spirit teaches as in His own school outside of which nothing can be taught save unreal words and talk' (Luther, WA. 7, 546). He who removes the dialectic of faith in favour of the objective or the subjective aspects destroys—whether in an orthodox or a pietistic way—the mystery of faith. Cf. the chapter *Glaube als Erfahrung* in Loewenich: *Luthers theologia crucis*.

dition. The Word of God must 'strike the conscience,' as Luther says, in order that it may lead to real faith. The process by means of which the sinful, actual self is discovered by the Word of God, the knowledge that one is discovered and convicted, is repentance, the consent of the heart to the judgement of God which pronounces me guilty. This is the act in which the Word and my actual state are identified. The Christian message does not endeavour to evade this experience of reality; on the contrary, it seeks it. In this sense faith must become experience—it must be 'my' faith, the faith of the heart, no mere intellectual belief—otherwise it is merely theory.[1] Thus in this sense faith and the experience of reality are the same; in this sense, also for Christian doctrine, the postulate of critical experience remains valid. However far the promise of the Word of God may go beyond all that is experienced, faith in this promise can only come through man's discovery of his actual self based on the Word.

For exactly opposite reasons the rationalist, to whom the reason is the supreme court of appeal, may object to the above statement. He will say: the Christian anthropology is based upon such irrational assumptions that, without waiting to submit it to the touchstone of experience, I cannot accept it. Moreover, he feels it, so to speak, beneath his dignity to subject the statements of the Christian doctrine to the test of experience at all. He 'knows,' regardless of experience, that the Christian faith is false because it contradicts his reasoning. The Christian doctrine is based upon the 'absurd, mythological' presuppositions of the Creation and the Fall, and further, upon the no less 'absurd' presupposition of the personality of God, and finally—this is the most crude of all—upon the 'absurd mythology' of the Divine Incarnation. An educated and philosophically trained person of the present day cannot possibly consider a doctrine of this kind.

[1] Cf. my booklet, *Vom Werk des Heiligen Geistes*, pp. 28 ff.; Luther, *Ibi explora animum tuum an credas Deum esse tuum patrem* (WA. 43, 243). 'Should, however, a terror of conscience be suppressed . . . a divine power must belong to that, and not a thought, there must be something else within thee, that he (Satan) may find a power within thee which is too strong for him . . .' (WA. 33, 226).

Against this rationalism nothing can be said but that it is in the highest degree uncritical. It begins, for instance, with a statement which it regards as an axiom, but which the Christian faith maintains is false; the statement, namely, that the self-sufficient reason, complete within itself, is the final court of appeal where truth is concerned. It is *this* kind of rationalism that Christian doctrine describes as the πρῶτον ψεῦδος, as the Fall of reason, which separates reason from truth, instead of leading it to it. The quintessence of the Christian anthropology is that it denies this self-sufficient reason, this reason which is based upon itself, rendering account only unto itself, as indeed we have already pointed out in the previous chapters of this book. Christian anthropology also undertakes to prove why it must make this denial. This proof, however, cannot be achieved within the reason which is already thus severed from the Word of God, but only within that understanding of reason which starts from the Word of God. But in this 'proof' of the falsity of the rationalist axiom the Christian doctrine includes the indication of the human reality. Thus it summons the rationalist to examine his axiom in the light of reality, and prophesies that the result of his examination will be annihilating. But it also tells him that he can only see his actual state in the light of the Word of God.

The point, however, at which both reason and experience meet with faith—in such a way indeed that the meeting is actually a collision—is responsibility.[1] Neither the rationalist, nor the empiricist, nor the believer denies responsibility. On

[1] The point at which a Christian and theological anthropology and a non-Christian 'natural' anthropology come into contact with one another is that which Luther calls 'law-repentance,' which he defends against the Antinomians as a necessary preliminary stage on the way to the repentance of faith. The Disputations in connexion with the Visitations show on each side the concern of the pastor who has the cure of souls in face of the doctrinaire attitude of his ultra-Reformation opponents, who maintain that only the preaching of grace is necessary and not the preaching of the law. In that Luther turns against this error (for instance *Drews*, pp. 326, 330, etc.) and at the same time maintains the argument that the *lex* is integral to the state of man (e.g. pp. 312, 328, and elsewhere), he defends the point of contact with natural self-knowledge as a necessary *methodus* of all pastoral care and preaching. Cf. the Appendix II, p. 516.

the contrary, they must all recognize it. Thus the question can only be: who solves the problem of responsibility, that is, who speaks about responsibility in a way which is in accordance with the actual facts of the situation? Negatively, this means, who will speak about responsibility in a way which will not do violence to the facts? The Christian doctrine of man is simply a doctrine of responsibility.[1] It maintains that the Word of God alone makes visible the fact of responsibility, without adulteration, or ideology, or concealment. It is impossible to pass judgement on this claim by ignoring it—unless someone believes that for once he has the right to be uncritical and from the outset to use the *demonstrandum* as a *demonstratio*. If, however, he accepts the postulate of criticism in the light of experience, he will cease, at least at first, to declare that the presuppositions of the Christian doctrine of man are an impossible mythology; he will have to take the trouble to controvert the Christian doctrine from the point of view of experience.

At the present day this still seems to be easy to a good many people. And in point of fact it was easy so long as the Christian doctrine was wrapped up in its historical cloak. This 'record' of the Creation and the Fall certainly could not possibly be combined with the facts of history and of natural science. Just as little as the Biblical account of the world being made in six days, understood as an historical record, can be brought into harmony with the cosmogony of natural science, can the story of Paradise, of the first human beings, and their Fall, be combined with the facts as we know them to-day. But from the scientific point of view what is there to be said against what the poet who wrote the 139th Psalm says about the fact that God created him in his mother's womb? Here, while the empirical knowledge of man is fully maintained, a statement is made about the background of that which can be known empirically which eludes all empirical verification. In so far, however, as the religious statement, which belongs to another dimension, entirely different from that of empirical knowledge, also extends into the reality of experience—since it says, for example, that just because man is God's creation he is a

[1] See above, p. 50.

responsible being, and as a responsible being he also exists and is experienced—this aspect of the religious statement is certainly not opposed to any scientific statement; on the contrary, it describes a situation which, in some way or another, even the non-believer must recognize, and one which he too is striving, with more or less success, to interpret.

But even after the historical form of the Christian doctrine has been abandoned—for religious rather than for intellectual reasons—there still remain a number of objections which, whether from the side of philosophy or from that of science, are raised against the Christian doctrine. For instance, some object that this doctrine assigns to man a special position in the cosmos, a view which, in the light of the facts which we now know—in contradistinction to the ancient view of the universe—can no longer be held. Others maintain that the Christian conception of man contradicts the history of mankind as we have learned to know it in recent days. One objection is that the assertion of the Creation and the Fall does not take sufficient account of the facts of individual and general development; that which appears to be hopelessly divided may be explained after closer study, much more simply and rationally as a long story of development. Some claim that the Christian faith represents a dualism of body and soul, matter and spirit, which can no longer be brought into harmony with the present-day truths of psycho-physical life and anatomy and biology. Others say that the Christian doctrine schematizes man, and completely ignores the wide and deep individual differences between human beings, which makes a doctrine of man appear to be an artificial and worthless abstraction. Again, it is said that the Christian doctrine of man heightens the value of the individual to such an extent that it is opposed to the collective-generic form of man as one life-form among others. It gives him a freedom which he does not possess—this is the reproach from the one side; it makes him an enslaved being, whose responsibility is indeed asserted but is actually denied—this is the reproach from the other side. And finally, it is maintained that the Christian doctrine conceives man far too much as a personality, whereas in reality he is far more the resultant of the most varied forces; or again, this view destroys the unity of man and makes every healthy human being a schizophrenic.

Behind all these objections there are reflections and ideas which are undoubtedly very important; they raise problems with which a Christian doctrine of man would have to grapple even if it had not to deal with them as opposing opinions, for they are questions which continually arise for the Christian in his own struggle for faith, and which we meet therefore again and again in the history of Christian thought as well as in the history of Christian evangelization and pastoral work. Hence the description which has been given up to this point of the main features of a Christian anthropology does not exhaust what may, rightly, be expected of us. What we must now do is to take these fundamental principles and to examine them further in connexion with some of the more important problems, choosing only those which are more urgent than ever before.

We shall deal with all these questions which have been raised in order; only we shall follow the converse order. It will soon become clear why we are obliged to take this line. It is our opinion that this more detailed exposition of the fundamental doctrines of the Christian faith already includes within itself the elements of truth in these objections; this makes it unnecessary to enter into a particular polemical discussion. It will only be necessary to deal with the opposing opinions at all in order to bring out quite clearly the actual meaning of the Christian doctrine itself. Thus the second main section of this book will deal in greater detail with that which could only be sketched in outline in the first part; only by doing this will it be possible to show clearly the meaning of the fact that man has been created in the Image of God, that through sin he has fallen away from this origin, and that in so doing he has come into conflict with himself. The first part of this book can only be fully understood in the light of the second part.

MAIN SECTION II

DEVELOPMENT OF THE THEME

CHAPTER IX

THE UNITY OF PERSONALITY AND ITS DECAY

I. THE UNITY OF PERSONALITY

EVERY anthropology must deal with the question of the unity of personality; in one sense or another it must begin with this as a fact. But the method of treatment will vary considerably. The obvious starting-point is the unity of the physical *organism*. But even this unity, which distinguishes the organism from a conglomerate mass, is a problem for which a purely mechanistic, atomistic conception seems inadequate. The riddle of the organic structural unity already points beyond the visible sphere towards an invisible sphere, to a structural principle of unity, an entelechy, a dominant, or whatever we may call this 'X' which co-ordinates the parts into a whole. It is possible, as in American Behaviourism, to refuse to inquire into the basis of this unity and to confine our attention to the unified expression, the 'behaviour' of this given totality.[1] But even the most realistic, matter-of-fact observer cannot overlook the fact that this being, called man, reacts in a way in which other living beings do not react—or rather that he 'acts,' and does not simply re-act; to turn from the outward to the inward is seen to be inevitable. From the time of Aristotle we have been accustomed, even in scientific thought, to call this 'inner' entity the 'soul.'[2] But here again we are confronted by the same question: Is it a unity, or is the 'soul' only a collective name for a variety of psychical elements? Does 'the soul' really

[1] From the most extreme point of view: Watson, *Psychology from the Standpoint of the Behaviourist*. More moderate and therefore more instructive: Thorndike, *Educational Psychology*.

[2] The significance of Aristotle's *De anima* for the whole of European psychology is incalculable (cf. Siebeck, *Geschichte der Psychologie*; Dessoir, *Abriss einer Geschichte der Psychologie*). From the outset, too, this Aristotelianism has been at home in the theology of the Church. Tertullian, it is true, is more inclined to follow the Stoics, but the Greek Fathers have all learned from Aristotle. Psychology as a whole is one of the gates through which ancient thought entered into Christian doctrine. As such it is all the more important, since its influence was exerted more or less unconsciously, and was not supervised at all. Cf. Appendix I (pp. 499 ff.).

exist at all? Again and again, in spite of all atomistic efforts to the contrary, it has been recognized that we must at least assume something which cannot be further divided, and is therefore an inexplicable unity. We must do this partly in order to understand the unity of the organism, and partly in order to be able to understand the cohesion of the psychical processes themselves, both conscious and unconscious. Even the inquirer who has no use for metaphysics is forced to such an idea of unity, simply from the standpoint of purely psychological observation. Within modern psychology the most illuminating attempt, undertaken solely under the pressure of psychological necessity, seems to be that which tries to understand the whole of the psychical life from the one fundamental impulse of the *libido*. In so doing, of course, the necessity of distinguishing different kinds of *libido* immediately became evident.[1]

Ultimately, however, this psychological method of approach proves inadequate. The very science one employs in this approach cannot itself be understood simply as a psychological phenomenon, as an expression of the *libido*, and so on. It is itself based upon the distinction between valid and invalid, true and false statements. From the psychological way of approaching the problems there emerges the nöetic, from the 'soul' there arises the Nous, the reason, the mind, as the capacity to grasp truth, to demand and to produce that which is valid and in accordance with a norm, to perceive ideas, and through them to bring order into a chaotic mass of impressions, sensations, and instincts. Once more the movement goes a step further, either inwards or upwards. We perceive a unity 'behind' the psychical plane, a principle of unity, which co-ordinates the psychical realm into a structural whole, just as the structural principle (mentioned above[2]) co-ordinates the organism of the body: this 'unity' is the mind. Here all mere observation ceases. We do not reach this mind, its thought and creativity, save as we identify our thought and creativity with it. The philosophy of the mind penetrates behind psychology

[1] A powerful influence which counterbalances psychological atomism is provided by the *Gestalt* Psychology and by the Würzburg School, which is akin to it (Wertheimer, Koffka, Külpe, Messer, etc.).

[2] P. 215.

in order to be able to pierce to the heart of the highest unity of man, or in man, which dominates everything else. But it has scarcely set itself this task than it transcends the mind of man itself, and is directed towards a unity on a still higher plane, a unity which must not only be capable of explaining the agreement of the individual minds of men in one truth, or one idea, but, above all, which must be capable of explaining the valid truth comprehended according to its own unity.[1] So far as the definition of this ultimate unity is concerned, however, this unity which is enthroned above the minds of men, this all-inclusive principle of all truth and validity, of all meaning and relevance, men's views are hopelessly at variance, and have been so for nearly three thousand years, ever since the problem was first raised. In order to know what is the unity in man, we would have to know what is the attitude of the 'mind' to the 'minds' of men, how it, the mind, regards the totality of being, above all of material being, in which man participates through his body, and how, from that standpoint, the relation between body and mind, soul and mind should be understood. It is precisely this question of the unity in man which has given rise to all the problems of philosophy, and it seems as though they can never be settled.

Even the latest attempt to understand the unity of human existence as 'objective existence-in-the-world,' and in so doing as 'anxiety' and 'existence-for-death,' important and instructive as it is, is far from being a satisfactory answer to the question: in what does the unity of man consist, on what is it based, and how far does it extend? Perhaps its greatest advantage consists in the fact that it leads us back to that which the simple man, who knows nothing of philosophy or science, knows of his own unity.[2] The simple human being solves the problem

[1] From Plato onwards these problems dominate philosophy; the necessity for this enlargment of the horizon can be perceived especially clearly in the most recent times in the development of phenomenology.

[2] Heidegger, *Sein und Zeit*. With the concept of *Dasein* ('existence') Heidegger develops what is intended to be a formal structural anthropology, but he leaves a large number of the fundamental questions of anthropology entirely unanswered.

(On *Dasein*, cf. Nicolas Berdyaev, *Solitude and Society*, pp. 41–8, 51–2, 154.—*Translator*.)

with the two words: 'I myself.' That is the unity of personality in which he lives, of which, without reflecting upon it, he is aware, and perhaps knows more about than when he begins to think about it. And yet—who then is this 'I Myself'? What do these two enigmatic, pregnant words mean? Do they mean the same, or, if not, what is their relation to one another? We seek the answer to this question not in philosophy and not in psychology—little as we desire to depreciate the truth which we learn from both—but in the Word of God.

We shall never understand the unity of man, the enigma of the 'I-Self,' save in the light of man's Creation in and for the Word of God. Man has been created by God as a psycho-physical unity. This duality—(with the exact meaning of which we shall deal later on)—cannot and ought not to be removed, neither by materialism, nor by Idealism, nor by any theory of identity. But this does not mean that if we are Christian believers we cannot or ought not to understand man as a unity. We should and may know him as a unity, only not from himself or in himself, but solely from the truth of the Divine Creation. Here, too, is the basis of his 'hierarchical' constitution. Since God has created man in His image He has created him as person. It is not the mind, nor the soul but the psycho-physical whole, the person 'man' whom God has created in His own image. The unity of man is the unity of his personal being. But we can only perceive his personal being through faith, in the light of the Word of God, namely, as the creature which has been called to communion with God, and thus to responsibility-in-love. That is the Scriptural basis of the understanding of the 'I-Self.'

Man is in the Image of God, his personality derives from God's, yet just because it is from God his person is different from God's. God—the God known to us in His Word—is the unconditioned, the underived, the eternally self-sustained person, on no side limited, and, save from Himself, by naught determined, absolute and, to Himself, absolutely transparent Spirit. Yet this designation 'absolute Spirit' would forthwith land us in the bottomless and impersonal could we not at once add a second: He is to Himself self-related, one knowing and willing Himself in love, the

Triune God. Wherefore, only the Triune God is genuinely personal, for He is within Himself self-related, willing, knowing, loving Himself. The God not known in His Trinity—which is to say, not from the revelation in Jesus Christ—is not the God who within Himself is loving, therefore also not a God who within Himself is person. This Triune personal being of God is the original image according to which and for which man has been created. This Trinity is the basis of both facts: first, that man, like God, is person, and, secondly, that he is person in quite a different way from the way in which God is Person.[1] God, the Primal Word, is creative, self-existent, and self-sufficing love; man has been created by God as a responsive, reflexive love, that is, a love whose content is outside itself. With God, the 'I' of man has its 'Self' in the Word of God. In Himself God is love,[2] but man can only be love from God and unto God. His love can only be of the kind indicated in the words: 'Let us love Him, for He has first loved us.' Whenever man tries to love by his own efforts, or to love himself, in the same way as the Triune God loves, he distorts himself and splits his personality. Only in the love of God can man be loving, and therefore be himself. The fact that the love of God is the content of his being is the point at which he resembles God. In this he is the reflection of God. 'But

[1] Augustine's profound researches into the relation between the Divine Trinity and the structure of human personality—in his work *De Trinitate*—have never been rightly understood by Protestant theologians, because these theologians saw in them merely the danger of a speculative argument for belief in the Trinity. Yet in the mind of Augustine they were not intended primarily—if at all—as apologetics, but as Christian ontology. In this study Augustine is concerned with the question: How is the personal being of God related to the personal being of man? Thus understood, the work *De Trinitate* is an inexhaustible mine, and research in this direction is far more useful than any general observations on the theme of the *analogia entis*—which has a vogue at the present time; in my opinion, up to the present this line of thought has produced confusion rather than clarity.

[2] Nygren raises the extremely important question: Does the Fourth Gospel, by its emphasis upon love within the Trinity, weaken the contrast between the *Agape* of the New Testament (groundless love) and the Platonic *Eros* (love for that which is worthy of love)? (*Eros and Agape*, pp. 128 ff.). In any case the problem should be noted.

we all with unveiled face reflecting as a mirror the glory of the Lord, are transformed into the same image from glory to glory.'[1] But the fact that man has this content and meaning not in himself but in the Word of God, which gives him the love of God, means that he is absolutely unlike God, he is a creature. In the fact that, like God, he can say 'I,' he resembles God; but as soon as he truly desires to say 'I myself,' he must immediately refer himself to God as the ground of his selfhood, to whom he must be responsible; in this respect he is absolutely unlike God.

When theologians speak of the 'I' of man, and begin with 'knowing' instead of with 'love,' this is a relic of Greek thought, and is abstract and unscriptural. Love is the unity of willing, knowing and feeling, the sole total act of the person. Hence also the nature of the 'I' must not be defined from the point of view of knowing, nor from that of self-knowledge, but from that of God-given responsive love, of responsibility-in-love. The final ground of personality is not to be found in self-consciousness, nor even in the act of will; to begin there means to desire to understand man severed from God as person, and that means, to fall a prey to that primal misunderstanding about oneself. In contrast to all rational definitions of the Self the right religious self-consciousness of man is this: man becomes conscious of himself in the Word of God. The isolated self-consciousness, the *cogito ergo sum*, is the result of apostasy. The self-consciousness of man is 'theological' because man is a 'theological' being. The 'I' with which the philosophers tend to begin is, like the 'I' of God, an independent entity; this is why the 'I' philosophy, in some way or other, always leads to self-deification.[2]

It is the same with self-determination. It is true, of course, that self-determination belongs to the nature of person as person. But the self-determination proper to an original personal being created by God can only consist in being determined by God, as Kierkegaard finely puts it: 'The formula which describes the state of the Self, when despair has been completely eliminated: in the attitude to oneself, and since it wills to be itself, the self bases itself transparently upon the power which

[1] 2 Cor. iii. 18. See above p. 96. [2] Cf. on this Sannwald, op. cit.

created it.'[1] But this 'power' is simply the love of the Creator, and to 'base oneself transparently upon it' must simply mean that we gratefully say 'Yes' to this love, which we call the love of God or faith in God.[2] Thus even when the Self has been harmonized, when its faculties are in order, and all is quiet within, it is not dependent upon itself, but it rests in God and depends utterly upon Him; and thus it knows the 'peace of God, which passeth all understanding.'[3]

To be person is to be in relation to someone; the Divine Being is in relation to Himself; man's being is a relation to himself based on his relation to God. This concept of personality can only be gained from love, and not from the subject of the processes of knowledge. It is because natural knowledge does not and cannot know this—for one can only know this in the Word of God—that there is such an absolute gulf between the intellect and love in the natural understanding of man. When the effort is made to understand man from the point of view of the intellect, an abstract conception of the 'I' severed from the 'Thou' is developed, a monological, indeed a monomaniac intellectuality, whose first result is solipsism, an abstract, heartless, cold reason, where personality is expressed in almost mathematical or logical terms. When, on the other hand, love is made the point of departure, because there is still an idea that man is pre-eminently a being who wills love, then—owing to the fact that neither the origin nor the content of love is known—the result is an unintelligent and irrational idea of *libido* which conceives personality in biological or psychological terms.

It is the same with the relation to the 'Thou,' which is

[1] Kierkegaard, *Die Krankheit zum Tode*, p. 11.

[2] Nygren is particularly clear on the relation between faith and love. He shows how Paul has substituted the concept of faith for the Synoptic idea of love to God (op. cit., pp. 106 ff.) because he wants to make it plain that faith is receptive and love is that which gives. On the other hand, Luther, in his *Sermon on Good Works*, has shown how inseparable are faith and the love of God. 'Indeed, when we look at it aright, love is the first or is at the same time with faith. For I would not trust God if I had not thought that He would be favourable and gracious towards me, by which again I am moved to respond to Him with a heartfelt trust, and to ascribe all good to Him' (WA. 6, 210).

[3] Phil. iv. 7.

originally posited in the nature of the human personality. Rightly understood concrete personal being[1] is always the same as 'being-in-community,' a responsible 'existence-in-love.' Where man's origin is not known the person is either falsely isolated in an abstract intellectual individualism—the self-sufficient, autonomous rational 'I'; or the unified and independent personality breaks up into purely vitalistic relations. At the one extreme, man is a god, sufficient unto himself; at the other, man is a member of a species, the *animal homo sapiens* in the human herd.

Of all the thinkers who do not take their stand upon the Christian revelation probably Kant and Plato are those who come nearest to the Christian view, the one through his concept of the person as that of responsible being, and the other through his understanding of man from the point of view of the *Eros*. The comparison between the Kantian conception of personality and that of Christianity is most instructive. Since Kant, in accordance with his conception of reason, may not start from the divine love as the ground of personal responsibility, he defines his concept of responsibility as relation to the practical law of reason. This produces the following parallels and contrasts: Personal being[2] is understood, it is true, as being consisting in relations, but these relations are not personal; they are related to the law of reason and therefore ultimately —so far as motive and content are concerned—they are impersonal: self-respect as the motive, and a universal rule as the content. Personal being is based, it is true, in a kind of calling; this calling, however, is not the gift of the Creator but pure obligation; hence personality cannot realize itself in

[1] The word 'person' itself presents a complicated historical problem. (Cf. Hirzel, *Die Person. Begriff und Name derselben im Altertum*, Munich, 1914, *Sitzungsbericht der bayrischen Akademie*; Rheinfelder, *Das Wort persona, Geschichte seiner Bedeutungen*, 1928.) The allusion to the 'mask' should be used very cautiously, and the etymology *personare* should no longer be used.

[2] Kant has various conceptions of personality: psychological, moral, and that of the theory of knowledge. They are nowhere combined into a unity. But his conception of personality as the 'freedom of a rational being according to moral laws,' and, based upon that, 'freedom and independence of the mechanism of the whole nature,' is decisive. (Kehrbach, *Kritik der praktischen Vernunft*, p. 105.)

love, but only in obedience; hence, also, there is no connexion with the bodily nature and its inclinations. Body and mind are separated in a dualistic manner. Kant does recognize a claim on man which makes him person; but in the last resort this claim comes from himself, namely, rational self-respect, and thus leaves man without any relation to the 'Thou.' In place of the 'Thou,' both Divine and human, there is abstract humanity as an Idea.[1] In the second section of this book we shall see that this fundamental difference has also resulted in a profound difference in his conception of Evil.

Plato's conception of man is higher than that of the philosopher of Königsberg in the relation it establishes between spirit (*Geist*) and *Eros*, but it falls below it on the question of responsibility. It is more comprehensive than that of Kant, but it is less personal. The concept of *Eros* connects the spirit (*Geist*) with nature, reason with emotion (*Affekt*), even with corporeality. But this connexion is only achieved by means of the typically Greek conception of καλοκαγαθία, that is, by the predominance of the aesthetic element in the understanding of the spirit (*Geist*) or of the relation to the divine Idea.[2] In this concept of the Idea-Eros the complete contrast between Platonism and the Christian faith comes out most plainly. Plato cannot say: 'Let us love, for He has first loved us'; for his 'Idea of the Good' does not love, the loving is exclusively on the side of man, and is therefore different in character; it is not that of grateful humble obedience, but it is a sublimated form of human love: enjoyment of the eternal.

The *libido* theory of the latest modern psychology also presents an aspect which is both related and opposed to the Christian conception. Since it is attained entirely from the consideration of the emotional life it is very near to human life as it is actually lived; but then it is forced to leave the original-creation element and the sinful-fallen element side by side, undistinguished and unseparated, in an absolutely unexplained concept of *libido*-love, by which we may understand anything which

[1] See above, p. 190.

[2] Similarly Schiller's attempt to overcome the Kantian dualism by the aesthetic element. (*Die ästhetische Erziehung des Menschen.*)

has a positive relation to instinct or will. But as a testimony to the disintegration of human unity the view of this school is of particular value. This becomes plain when we study more closely the concept in which the Bible expresses its view of the personal existence of man in its central unity. This concept is: *the heart.* Where the Bible speaks of man as a whole, and indeed from the point of view of personal unity, it speaks of 'the heart.'

From the point of view of the Bible the 'heart'[1] is primarily the unified centre of all the fundamental functions of the *psyche.* Whatever a person wills wholly that he does from the heart,[2] whom one loves, to him one gives one's heart,[3] and one has him in one's heart.[4] The heart knows,[5] or perceives, understands,[6] ponders,[7] the heart is the 'storechamber of all that is heard and experienced';[8] 'they utter words out of their heart,'[9] to the heart are ascribed 'all degrees of pain, joy, dissatisfaction from anxiety to despair.'[10] The unity of will, thought and feeling 'as fully conscious means to be of one heart.'[11] But likewise the heart is the centre of the moral disposition and of man's relation to God, 'the source and the starting-point of all good and evil,'[12] of the love of God and of self-deifying arrogance.[13] The law of God is written[14] in the heart of all men; it is the 'field for the seed of the Divine Word,[15] it is the dwelling-place of the Holy Spirit.[16] It is 'the quiet chamber of secret communion with God,'[17] 'the central point of the whole man, the bearer of the personal conscious-

[1] The following quotations are taken from the *Biblische Psychologie* by Delitzsch (pp. 204 ff.), which indeed provides the most exhaustive and the best account of the significance of the *heart* in the Old and the New Testament, at any rate of anything which has been published on the subject down to the present time. The actual quotations are all from Delitzsch. (Cf. also Schlatter, *Herz und Gehirn im ersten Jahrhundert. Studien zur systematischen Theologie, Theodor v. Haering zum 70. Geburtstag,* 1918, pp. 86 ff.)

[2] Rom. vi. 17. [3] Prov. xxiii. 7. [4] Phil. i. 7; 2 Cor. vii. 3.

[5] Deut. xxix. 4. [6] Isa. xxxii. 4. [7] Luke ii. 19.

[8] Luke i. 66. [9] Job viii. 10.

[10] Acts ii. 46; John xvi. 6; James iii. 14; Acts vii. 54; Eccl. ii. 20.

[11] Jer. xxxii. 39; Acts iv. 32. [12] Matt. xii. 34.

[13] Ezek. xxviii. 2, 5. [14] Rom. ii. 15. [15] Matt. xiii. 19 ff.

[16] Eph. iii. 17; 2 Cor. i. 22. [17] Eph. v. 19.

ness,'[1] it 'is the medium of all relations and actions, both on the intellectual and on the physical side, in so far as they are due to self-consciousness and freedom of action.'[2] In a word, in the Bible the 'heart' is that which we have described as the unity of personality; the incomparable significance ascribed to it in the Bible as a whole is the clearest proof of the importance of the idea of personal unity within the Christian doctrine of man.

In the light of the Divine origin of man the heart is the receptive and re-acting centre of the Word of God and the love of God. Therefore 'with the heart one believes,'[3] 'with the whole heart' we are to love God,[4] even as 'the love of God is shed abroad in our hearts through the Holy Ghost.'[5] The heart which is thus determined is the human being as God intends him to be; this is the self as it 'bases itself transparently upon the power which created it'; this is the Biblical concept of personality. Hence, too, it is the heart which severs itself from God, which falls under the curse of sin and of the law; to it accordingly the saving grace of God appeals in the message of repentance andreconciliation.

As the 'heart' is the subject of unified personal being, so the grateful love which responds, faith, is the total act of this subject in harmony with its origin. For this very reason the actuality of human selfhood is no *actus purus*, but *actus* on the basis of a *passio*, an *actus relativus*. For man receives before he re-acts. He receives his being in, and from, and unto, the love of God through the Word of God; he receives at first in faith before he can answer by responsive love; or rather, the 'Yes' of the faith which gratefully accepts is indissolubly united with responsive love. The fact that the love of man begins with this believing and grateful act of reception distinguishes it profoundly from the Platonic *Eros*. The fact that the 'I' receives its Self, before it posits itself in self-knowledge and self-determination, distinguishes this 'I' from the 'I' of transcendental philosophy. The fact that love as an actual living human possibility comes from God, and that its responsive tendency towards God is also derived from this origin, distinguishes this

[1] Deut. iv. 29; vi. 5. [2] *Biblische Psychologie*, p. 207. [3] Rom. x. 10.
[4] Matt. xxii. 37. [5] Rom. v. 5.

love from the *libido* of the psychologists. In this love, but in it only, there is included, besides will, perception and feeling—the higher life of the mind and spirit—also the 'soul' as a whole, indeed, in a certain sense, even the realm of the unconscious. Here, therefore—and here alone—it is the whole man who answers.

This responsive love (this 'heartfelt faith') is primarily an act of *perception*. The word of God is received; an act of understanding is accomplished, the mind has perceived the Divine meaning. The love of God is perceived, and in it the meaning and the basis of our existence. In this act of perception, which is so simple that even a child can perform it, and in the performance of which the wisest of men has no advantage over the simplest, is disclosed the secret which the philosophers of all ages have tried in vain to penetrate. It is an act of the highest metaphysical dignity. The mystery of God—of the Triune God, the person who in Himself is Love—and the secret of man, of his origin, his nature and his end, disclose themselves in it. In comparison with this, all other knowledge is secondary. Love is thought, but it is an act of thought which in the strict sense of the word is reflection, receptive thought; for its content is election, its form is gratitude. Thanking is the most complete form of thought.

Secondly, this love is an act of *will*. God manifests His will to man in His Word, first of all that which He wills for him, and then—upon the basis of the former—what He wills from him. The love of God is the will of God, His free sovereign will as Lord, His Fatherly will which incomprehensibly imparts itself to us. Hence it is impossible to receive the will of God save by being drawn into this will as one who wills it after Him, and unites his human will with the Divine will. Love is the only voluntary act; thus it is the only will which is entirely *will*. Willing obedience is that form of human freedom which is harmony with man's origin.[1] This love is self-determination. It gives a uniform direction to the whole life, and it gives it wholly and entirely; it does not take anything away from it. This point may be compared with the words used

[1] It is thus that Paul expresses the aim of his whole missionary activity: sent forth "for obedience to the faith among all nations" (Rom. i. 5).

by Archimedes: δός μοι ποῦ στῶ; for the content of this will does not come out of the world but from above the world, not out of life but only into life. It is therefore 'pure will,' not moved by reasons from below, and yet it is not abstract or cold, but is a concrete and 'heartfelt' will. Its object is not an 'it,' neither of nature nor of the intellect; but it is the 'Thou' of God and of the neighbour, and all that is 'it' is only means and instrument. But this self-determination is not, like the Self of Fichte's philosophy, the act of self-creation; it is the act of self-reception.

Hence, thirdly, this love is *feeling*. The contrast between feeling and intellect which characterizes European thought about the higher life of the mind is not part of man's origin, but it is a product of his apostasy. Feeling therefore has its rightful place in man's 'experience' of his relation with God, because this 'experience' is something which man has received, and not something which he has himself created. To be apprehended by the love of God, means to be smitten in the very centre of one's being, to suffer it, not as pain, but as the supreme joy, as happiness and peace; that is, the Self knows that it is 'at home' in God, and that the 'I' and the 'Self' have become one. This does not mean that in love, understood as being loved and loving in return, feeling is the first or the most important element. Here, too, it is plainly the second; it follows the acts of perception and acceptance, but it follows them so swiftly that one might almost say that it is included in them. For in the moment at which the love of God is truly 'discovered' joy is already present. Indeed, should we not say that the character of this perception is precisely this, that it is a discovery-in-joy? Likewise this joy follows the act of willing obedience, and yet is included in it as that which characterizes the voluntary act of will. What is the love of God other than rejoicing in God?

What Calvin says of faith, namely, that it 'moves the profoundest depths of the heart,'[1] is also true here. The 'root' of the heart, however, is the 'soul' or the psychical realm, which extends down into the unconscious and thence penetrates the whole organism. 'When I awake I speak of Thee';[2]

[1] *Institutio*, III, 2, 36. Lit. 'roots.'—*Translator*. [2] Psa. lxiii. 7.

to the religious man of the Old Testament even his sleep is rest in God. True union with God penetrates into the realm of the unconscious, just as the unrest of the heart and the division of the personality in sin penetrates into the unconscious, and expresses itself not only in the face and in various gestures, but also in illness and in physical decline. The expression 'heart' as a picture of the unity of the personality, even though it is only pictorial, has not been chosen casually; it is an image which springs naturally out of experience. Its intention is to express the truth that the life-centre and the centre of personality are one. Man's relation with God, his origin, is on a higher plane than that of the antithesis between the intellect and the 'vital' principle, and there is no need for Christian theology to absorb this antithesis—which has dominated philosophy from the time of Plato—into itself. The Bible always thinks of faith as something which penetrates the 'joint and the marrow,' and causes such suffering that the physical heart is broken.[1] This brings us back to the point from which we started: God has created man as a psycho-physical unity, in a certain hierarchical order, which can only be understood in the light of a higher sphere, higher too than his own mind and spirit.

2. THE DECAY OF PERSONAL UNITY

In what sense does the destruction of the original relation between the Creator and the creature by the Fall mean the destruction of the unity of personality? And, in what sense does it not mean this? The concept of the 'heart,' in particular, which is used, both by the godless person and by the person who is united with God, to describe its unity and totality, makes this question necessary. Have we any right to speak about the 'destruction of the unity of personality by sin,' when even the sinner may be described by this personal unity designated the 'heart'? It is not said that through sin man loses his heart, but that sin has its seat even in the heart.[2] Thus the first point to note is that in a certain sense unity of personality still exists. The question therefore can only be put in this way: Is it true to say that it can be lost in any sense?

[1] Heb. iv. 12; Jer. xxiii. 9.

[2] Matt. xii. 34; Rom. i. 24.

and if so, how are the unity of personality which still remains, and that which has been lost, related to one another? Is the man who is living in sin as fully 'person' as he was when living in relation to his Origin? Or in what sense is personality lost? This is the first question to which we must now turn.

Just as personality is constituted at the centre, so also the disintegration of the unity of personality starts from the centre. Through the Fall man loses the content of his personal being, existence in the love of God. What remains over for him of the Original Source, is the form of his existence as man, personal being and human existence as structure; but this form is filled with a content which is the very opposite of the content which it originally contained. 'The desire of the flesh is enmity against God,[1] the *cor incurvatum in se*, the 'I' which seeks itself. Man is still related to God, he still possesses responsibility; but this relation to God has turned into enmity towards God and flight from God. Man's being is still responsible being; but this responsibility has become a legal demand. Through sin man does not become an animal, he remains *humanus*; but with the loss of the divine love and of existence in love he loses the distinctive content of humanity. All that remains to him of his original humanity is the formal element: creative power in virtue of the perception of ideas, self-consciousness and self-determination, as characteristics of man's being which cannot be lost.

Through the Fall the unity of being and destiny, or of the 'I' and the 'Self,' has been lost. Hence sinful man is forced continually to seek his Self or himself. Instead of circling round God the human life-movement now circles round the Self—lost and therefore sought. Hence the *cor incurvatum in se ipsum*. This fundamental egoism is both the manifestation of Original Sin and a fresh expression of it in concrete terms. This separation between the 'I' and the 'Self' is the central division of personality which characterizes the sinful man; it is that despair which Kierkegaard, in his *Sickness unto Death*, describes as the state of fallen man in theological ontology and psychology, as the decay of the original unity of the original elements of human existence.

[1] Rom. viii. 7.

The first result of the divided personality is the severance of responsibility from love. Obligation and desire are in opposition to one another. Since man has lost his being-in-the-love-of-God, and is severed from Him by his being-in-guilt and under the wrath of God—lost indeed, in such a way that no return to the Divine Origin is possible—his relation with God only exists in the form of a sense of obligation. The other aspect of sin, as we have already seen, is 'standing under the Law.' In theological terms, this is the most exact description of the sinner's condition. He is not simply severed from the will of God; he now knows the will of God only as law, as a demand, as an obligation. This obligation is the theological side, the aspect of formal personality which is related to God, which remains of man's original state even after the Fall. The reason on which humanity is based has, as its present centre, the divine law—even if this is not very clear. The practical relation with God of the 'natural' man is legalism. That is the common denominator of all non-Christian religions, and of all corruptions of the Christian faith. Legalism, however, is also the character of the non-Christian ethical relation to one's fellow-man. The contrast between law and inclination upon which the Kantian ethic is based, is the logical expression of a human existence which lives no longer in the love of God but only in the law.

The negative aspect of this religious and ethical legalism is lawless desire, love which has become godless. But the anarchy produced by man's apostasy means that this very desire is split up and torn in several directions. On the one hand there arises a desire directed towards oneself, self-seeking, greedy desire for oneself, being in love with oneself, narcissism. The self-will which should be embedded in the will of God now stands forth naked and unashamed. It sets the 'I' in the place of God, it makes itself an ultimate end, and the central point of all desire and activity; it is self-glorification, the *cor incurvatum in se ipsum* in its concrete direct form. But since the human 'I' is not constituted for the 'I' but for God, the man who no longer seeks God, but himself, is always seeking the void. Hence he must do one of two things: either he must intensify himself in a fantastic way, swell himself out to the dimensions of a god, or he must fill the empty 'I' with worldly material. The first process is accomplished in all forms of metaphysical, religious, mystical self-deification. The desire to be like God becomes the concrete content of life, not merely, as in the Fall itself, the final presupposition in the background. The second way is far more usual, the empty 'I' throws itself upon the world. At first this also takes place in religious form: the deification of nature and of the world, paganism. The honour due to the Creator is transferred to the creature.[1] But from this deification of the world there springs, further, the quite common greed for the world. This is so very usual that the natural man only knows sin in this form. The result of this greed for the world, however, is that the 'I' loses itself in the world; above all, it loses its freedom. In the Divine Love to have oneself and to lose oneself is the same thing; but in this greed for the world these two aspects become divided and then conflict with one another. Hence the man who has thrown himself upon the world, or is ready to do so, must continually withdraw himself from the world—and this is the content of all natural ethics:[2] self-control and self-assertion over against the world to the point of renunciation of the world—asceticism. Thus man is torn hither and thither by two opposing currents—he is drawn inwards to himself and then outwards to the world; he is torn between the desire for independence and the longing to abandon himself wholly to the things of this world, especially to those which minister to his pleasure; he is torn between arrogant and selfish isolation and self-abandonment to the world around him.

Man's relation to the other, in particular, is affected by this possessive attitude of his divided personality. Love which is no longer understood as responsibility, even where it is directed towards other human beings, becomes a passion which seeks to enjoy and to dominate: either a desire to dominate the other in possessive autocratic ways, or an abandonment which

[1] Rom. i. 21 ff.

[2] The Aristotelian ethic is the classical example of this. Its individualistic-ethical principle is that of self-preservation; its social-ethical principle is that of justice. Friendship is only for the man who is worthy of it. (*Nik. Ethik*, 1156b.)

becomes enslavement of oneself to the other. Alongside, however, there stands the moral law, which regulates the relation to one's neighbour with more or less success, or at least corrects it, and, as the overcoming of the anarchy of impulse, produces a ruder or a finer order. Above all, this takes place through the principle of justice, the main principle of legalistic social ethics, which at the same time makes the relations between human beings abstract and impersonal, and their attitude to one another self-righteous and loveless.

But it is not only the union of love and responsibility which has been broken, but also the unity of the fundamental psychological functions: will, thought, and feeling. Even the disintegrated, sinful, fallen man has an inner life. To be spirit, or rather to-be-spirit-as-well, is an essential part of the state of man as *humanus*, of the formal personality which he still retains. But the inner life which has been severed from love, from the personal Word of God, is necessarily impersonal, legalistic, abstract. The ultimate, the highest which it can attain, is the realm of Ideas. An 'inner life' which consists in the possession of high ideals apart from God, and legalistic reason, belong to one another. The will of God becomes the Idea of the Good, or the immanent law of practical reason; the self hidden in God becomes 'my divine self'; instead of 'I in God' we have *est Deus in nobis*. The Divine 'Thou' disappears in the abstract spirit, just as the human 'Thou' disappears in the idea of universal humanity and of the universal rational self. Likewise nature and spirit now break up into an irrevocable contradiction, into a contradiction which can only be 'removed' by some falsification either of the spirit or of nature; and to this metaphysical contradiction there corresponds the alienation of thought from the basis of life, to which there corresponds the division between sense impressions and thought. Thought, the more its purely rational aspect is developed, becomes increasingly hostile to life; desire and the 'vital' element become chaotic. The spirit becomes heartless, and the heart has no vision.

The same is true in the sphere of the will. The will which has broken away from the will of God, the more powerful it is in itself, the more it becomes arbitrary, self-willed, blind to the truth, a harshly assertive will, which treads feeling ruthlessly under foot. All that the will cares about is itself, that is, power. 'Will to power' is the correct formula for the will which has become godless, just as the self-deification of reason is the aim of emancipation of thought. Not the atheism of thought, but the atheism of the will, is the real antithesis to faith. It is this which says, 'If there were gods, who would hesitate to become a god?' (Nietzsche). It comes very close to the devilish *Hybris* which summons God to a contest as though between equals.[1] But where the will loses even this impulse towards higher things, negative though it may be, it becomes merely the lust for power; and it is only the peculiar futility of its lawless and capricious character which distinguishes it from ordinary greed for sensual and worldly pleasures. Here is the source of the cruelty of the man whose one aim is to carry out his own will at all costs. Finally, where the will unites with reason, it becomes, it is true, powerful in moulding events, but inhuman in its rigid adherence to principles. *Fiat justitia, pereat mundus!*

The same is true of feeling. Originally pleasure was spiritually connected with joy in God; through the Fall it has been, on the one hand, disconnected, and on the other, transformed into its opposite. The severance of pleasure from God means that it is abandoned to the world of the senses; for in the abstract life of reason there is little scope for it. It is indeed true that the Platonic *Eros*, the spiritual joy in creation and the delight of the vision of the Ideas is the proof that feeling and the higher life of the mind have not been wholly separated. But this Platonic *Eros* is itself more of an Idea than a reality, at least in actual life it is usually coupled with a shadowy partner. Indeed, in man's deepest being, where man seeks to find his way back to his—lost—Divine Origin, by thought or vision, we find that a very different feeling from that of pleasure predominates; it is rather melancholy, sorrow over existence and over man's destiny, or sometimes it is a passionate longing

[1] 'This wretched God of Christian monotono-Theism! This hybrid decadent picture of nothing, concept and contradiction, in which all the instincts of decadence, all the cowardices and fatigues of the soul have their sanction' (Nietzsche, *Antichrist*, Nr. 19).

for the 'moment' which might be seized with the cry: 'Abide with us! Thou art so beautiful!' Or it may express itself in a tragic sense of division, or in that protest against the evil, godless world and the meaninglessness of fate which has always been characteristic of those who have tried to pierce the mystery of human life. The loud and forced pæans of pleasure, with which the modern atheist protests against this pessimism about the pain of the world, scarcely avail to drown these deeper notes. The fundamental feeling of the existence separated from God is: profound sorrow and unrest.

Behind this sorrow there lies, on the one hand, disappointment over the fact that the meaning of life cannot be discovered —and how can it be found if the love of God be ignored?— and, on the other hand, the bad conscience, the anxiety of godlessness which is still dimly aware that it is wrong. In both man feels himself abandoned, helpless, 'thrown' into existence (Heidegger). Feeling does not participate in the personal self-determination, which is otherwise still characteristic of sinful fallen man. In his feeling he is completely passive; he has no power over his feeling, the disharmony of his existence comes out in his feeling, against his will, while in thought and will, to some extent at least, he is able to go beyond himself. His feeling as a whole is the total balance of his existence which is drawn up and presented to him without his will; no skilful intellectual speculation and no deliberate positing of an end for his will can alter this. This unstilled longing for life, this negative balance of life, is therefore in the Bible everywhere the most important point of contact for the Gospel message: 'If any man thirst let him come unto Me and drink."[1]

This, then, is the condition of the unity of personality in man's fallen state. Certainly, in so far as the disintegration has not taken the extreme form, in the pathological sense of the divided personality and the loss of the sense of unity in self-consciousness of insanity,[2] man is still a unity in the formal

[1] John vii. 37.

[2] Cf. the division of personality and the phenomena of dual and multiple personality which have been described by Ribot (*Les Maladies de la personnalité*) and Österreich (*Die Phänomenologie des Ich nach ihren Grundproblemen*).

sense of self-consciousness and of self-determination. But this shell of formal personality has no uniform content; on the contrary, it is extremely contradictory. The individual functions have formed different centres, and they develop like the different centres of government which exist at the same time in a civil war, each one at the cost of the others. It is true of course that all these centres are included in a uniform 'I will,' 'I think,' 'I feel,' which has not yet been disintegrated. It is still possible to recognize at least a comparative unity of personality in the 'heart.' But it is the *heart* which is torn, divided, contradictory. It is the *heart* which feels the disharmony of existence in its 'sorrow-of-heart.' The heart is divided into an upper and a lower sphere; impotently it strains after what ought to be, and yet it is dragged downwards by an opposing force, blind and powerful.[1] Out of the heart come thoughts good and bad, hence in the heart also there is waged that conflict of mutual accusation and defence which, according to Paul, manifests both the presence and the powerlessness of the 'law which is written in the heart.'[2]

Unity of personality—yes; but it is the unity of the person who has lost personal being and yet is ever seeking to recover it. Humanity, the being of man as the content of this personality—yes; but a human existence which lacks the distinctively human element, which always has a trace, and sometimes all the horror of *in*humanity about it. Unity—yes; but the unity of that which at bottom is in despair. This inward unity which still exists we call spiritual or psychological 'health' or 'normality,' to distinguish it from madness, or insanity. Yet all this health is in itself mad and insane. To place the central point of existence outside God, who is the true Centre, in the 'I' and the world, is madness; for it cannot be a real centre; the world cannot provide any resting-place for the Self; it only makes it oscillate hither and thither. Insanity—for sin is the product of an insane idea—the insanity of independence which has got rid of God and cannot help producing insanity, namely, all the substitute gods of a baser or a higher kind, substitutes for that happiness and peace

[1] Rom. vii. 14 ff.

[2] Rom. ii. 14 ff.; cf. Rom. vii.

which spring from being in the truth, all the substitute aims with which the empty soul tries to fill the 'aching void.'

Hence we can only speak of the original unity and of the decay of unity because, and in so far as in the midst of fallen existence unity is once more granted to us; this takes place in the fact that the Word of the Origin, which we have lost and cannot find for ourselves, comes to us once more, apprehends us in faith, once more gives us the love which we had lost, and thus restores man's original state. But we cannot pursue this subject any further at this point.

CHAPTER X

THE HUMAN SPIRIT AND THE HUMAN REASON

I. THE SPIRIT OF GOD AND THE SPIRIT OF MAN

MAN can be person because and in so far as he has spirit. Personal being is 'founded' in the spirit; the spirit is, so to speak, the substratum, the element of personal being. But what is spirit? And of what nature is this 'founding' of personality in spirit? The question of the spirit is, so it seems, a philosophical one, the problem of the spirit is the real subject of all serious philosophy. Having arrived at this point, then, are we to cease to inquire and to think in a theological manner? that means, to cease to inquire and to think from the point of view of God—the God who reveals Himself to us in His Word—and do a little philosophy for a change? We have no desire to depreciate the work of philosophy, or to set philosophy and theology against one another. Philosophers have not thought in vain, even for those who make faith their starting-point. But if it be true that man has been created in the image of God and thus—both in his original and in his fallen existence—can only understand himself from the point of view of God, and in God, then we must have the courage to approach the problem of the spirit as theologians, and we must use our philosophical knowledge to help us to see and understand our Biblical message better, and then to apply it. It will become evident that the question of the spirit will assume a different aspect when we look at it from the point of view of God, and not from that of man—in accordance with our basic idea that man is 'hierarchically' constituted, and thus that he can only be understood from 'above' and not from 'below.'

'God IS Spirit, and they that worship Him must worship Him in spirit and in truth.'[1] God *is* Spirit, man *has* spirit. God is *actus purus*. He has no nature.[2] He is not 'founded,'

[1] John iv. 24.

[2] It is the aim of Gnosis to discover some kind of 'nature' in God; nature in God is also the theme in the writings of Jacob Böhme, Oetinger,

posited, based on anything save Himself. He posits Himself, and is therefore completely transparent to Himself. But we are posited by Him, even as spirit; man receives spirit from the Creator. But he receives his spirit from the Creator in a different way from that in which he receives his body. When we read in the childlike narrative in Genesis that 'the Lord God formed man of the dust of the ground and breathed into his nostrils the breath of life,'[1] the statement suggests the truth which is the main view of the Bible, and also indicates the way in which the thought of the Bible is radically circumscribed in two directions. The spirit of man is not to be understood from below but 'from above,' the human spirit has a permanent relation with the Divine Spirit; but it is not the Divine Spirit. The spirit is not simply the 'power to think and will and feel.' This neutral psychological concept of spirit does not do justice to the nature of spirit. Every decent system of philosophy is aware of this, since it distinguishes the spirit from all that can be understood in a psychological functional sense by relating it to something beyond the existing sphere, the Idea, the *Logos*, Law, Value or the like. Spirit, in contradistinction from that which is merely functional and psychical, can only be understood as something 'transcending' the ordinary level, aspiring after something 'beyond the self,' an original actuality.[2] We may say indeed that spirit is that which thinks, wills, and feels, but the element of spirit is thought in contradistinction from mere imagination, willing in contradistinction to impulse, feeling in contradistinction to the mere sensation of pleasure or pain, and this difference springs from a consciousness of being adjusted and related to something valid, normative, something which ought to be, meaning, *logos*. The type of law which obtains in the realm of spirit is different from that which holds good in the psychical sphere; it is not a law governing sequence but the realm of 'meaning' and of 'norms.' Spirit only exists in relation to

Schelling, and—to mention a new and brilliant champion of this idea—in Berdyaev, for instance, in *Die Bestimmung des Menschen* (pp. 41 ff.).

[1] On Gen. ii. 7, cf. p. 99 and the Appendix on the *Idea of Humanity in the Ancient World*.

[2] See above Luther's conception of the spirit, p. 173, note 1.

meaning, or—as modern philosophy prefers to call it (in my opinion wrongly)—to 'Value.'[1] Hence a decent philosophy can never avoid forming the concept of 'meaning within the meaningful,' of a 'norm of all norms,' of a basis of value, or the like, in order to understand the spirit as spirit. It is this reference to a Beyond, the process of 'transcending,' which distinguishes the spirit and the spiritual from the *psyche* and the *psychical*. The highest concept which Greek philosophy forms to describe this transcendental unity, in reference to which alone the spirit as spirit can either act or exist, is that of the divine *nous* or *logos*, or the Idea of the Ideas.

We claim that this final point of reference, for which and from which our spirit as spirit exists, is the God who reveals Himself to us in His Word. And, more than this, it is the Spirit of God who reveals Himself to us in His Word, and in it creates us as spirit. This is the point from which we must start if we wish to understand 'the spirit in general' or 'the spiritual.' If even the philosophical concept of spirit is not purely psychological but one that can only be understood in 'transcending,'[2] this is still more true of the theological concept. In some way or another we must take account of the truths which philosophy perceives, the relation to the Idea, to value, norm, and law, and we must make room for them; but all this cannot be the final point of reference for the being of spirit. For the moment, in order to have a starting-point here and now we may say: in spite of the fact that the spirit is relation to Idea, norm, value and law, it is above all, and first of all, relatedness to God, as He reveals Himself in His Word, and indeed relatedness to the Word in which and for which we have been created. The spirit, in contrast to the

[1] Cf. the Value theories of Rickert, Scheler, N. Hartmann.

[2] Jaspers rightly lays decisive emphasis upon this 'transcending,' which lies in the nature of the human mind; but his point of view (*Sicht-von-unten*: lit. 'sight or view from below.' I have expanded this expression to give its meaning. Cf. *Contemporary German Philosophy*. Werner Brock, p. 106.—*Translator*)—which looks at the Ultimate, but from below, and clings to the given data in such a way that it does not reach the real transcendent —does not allow him to draw theological inferences from it. The case is different with Heinrich Barth, *Ontologie und Idealismus*, *Zwischen den Zeiten*, 1929, pp. 511 ff.

person, is that by means of which we 'relate' ourselves in thought, will, and feeling to the Word of God. That is why we said that personal being is 'founded' in spirit. By means of the spirit, in acts of the spirit, that relation to the Word of God which makes us persons, is accomplished. By means of the spirit we perceive the Word of God, by means of the spirit we believe and we love.

The language of the Bible about the 'spirit' of man is ambiguous. Paul, who here too is the actual fashioner of forms of thought, speaks both of the human *nous* and of the human *pneuma* as the organ which receives the Divine Word. Where he is dealing with the revelation of the Creation in the Works of God he uses the word *nous*. That manifestation of God in His Works becomes νοούμενα καθορᾶται,[1] just as in the Epistle to the Hebrews the Creation of the world by the Divine Word is shown as a *noumenon*, as something which is to be grasped by the *nous* in the act of faith,[2] and as in the Book of Revelation it is the *nous* to which the hidden wisdom makes itself known.[3] But where Paul speaks of the renewing revelation by the Holy Spirit he says that the Holy Spirit bears witness with our spirit (πνεῦμα) that we are the children of God.[4] Both, however, are also mentioned together in the expression that man is renewed in the spirit of the *nous*.[5] Through further reflections we hope to be able to throw light upon this differentiation; for the moment it is enough to state that in the Bible the spirit—whether the *nous* or the *pneuma* of man—in its acts is the organ which receives the Divine Word, the Divine Spirit. The relation of man to God is accomplished in spiritual acts; as a wholly spiritual act therefore, faith and love should also be understood.

This raises two questions. If we are to understand the spirit of man from his relation to the Divine Spirit as He reveals Himself in His Word, what then is the relation between the idea of God which our spirit—our reason—evolves by its own efforts, to the idea of God of faith? And how is the spirit, which is understood as the means of man's relation to God, the inward life as a whole—which is not directly concerned

[1] Rom. i. 20. [2] Heb. xi. 3. [3] Rev. xiii. 18; xvii. 9.
[4] Rom. viii. 16. [5] Eph. iv. 23.

with the Idea of God—to be understood? The first question is identical with that of the relation between reason and revelation; here, however, we shall only develop its subjective and anthropological aspect, and not its objective and theological aspect.

2. THE RATIONAL IDEA OF GOD

Apart from any special revelation, and indeed from a kind of inner necessity, the human spirit formulates the Idea of God, or something similar—the Idea of the Absolute, of a transcendental unity, and the like. Now whereas rationalism of all grades understands and estimates the revelation in the Word of God from the point of view of this 'rational and immanent' idea of God, the Christian faith, on the other hand, regards this rational, immanental idea of God as an indication of man's lost origin, of the original relation between the Word of God and the human spirit. The fact that man, whether he will or no, whether he believes or not, necessarily forms this idea of the Absolute, is a sign that even fallen man —in virtue of the fact that the Spirit of God still remains near to him, even when he, man, has become alienated from God —is still related to God. God holds him fast in the fact that he is obliged to think of the Unconditioned. At the same time, however, the abstract and sterile character of this 'idea of God' is a sign of the alienation of man from his personal Creator.[1] In this alienation from the living personal God the human spirit is that which we now know as the 'human reason.'

Rational thought necessarily produces an abstract idea of God, but for that very reason it never reaches the living personal God.[2] For this thought remains confined within itself;

[1] Cf. above p. 103, and also my *Religionsphilosophie protestantischer Theologie* in Bäumler's *Handbuch.*

[2] Cf. my book, *Gott und Mensch*, the first part. The customary contempt for thought which we find at the present time, even in theology, probably has more to do with the irrationalism of the tendencies of the day than with the truth of Christianity. Hence too the view that everything in Augustine which is Platonist or Neo-platonist is, for that very reason and for no other, un-scriptural, is erroneous. It is true Augustine will have been aware why it was that he gave up his Neo-platonism in the last period of his development, but not the truths which he had gained from Plato

it is a monologue. The two signs of rational thought, the close reasoning of a logical connexion, and autonomy, understood as autarchy, are the two aspects of this one situation. That which we think 'rational' must be within a logical connexion, it must be a statement rigidly based upon a closely reasoned argument. Reason itself can make no distinction between the irrational and the supra-rational. And, on the other hand, the knowledge of the reason recognizes nothing 'from the outside'; it will and must remain within the sphere of immanence. Hence it recognizes only a 'religion within the limits of pure reason.' Thus rational theology wishes to bring God into the reason, instead of bringing the reason into God and subordinating it to God. It identifies God with incontrovertible truth. The very Alpha and Omega of faith, the fact that God and man confront one another, the personal word of the personal God which creates persons, is a great stumbling-block to reason. Nowhere do we see so clearly as in Kant's posthumous metaphysical writings how a thinker, who knows that he is under an obligation to this demand of reason, and yet from his historical background knows the Christian idea of God, and cannot entirely escape from it, is baffled by the dilemma: Faith or Reason as the Ultimate. He thinks the God of the Christian faith, but he wants to think Him according to reason, and he does not want to believe in Him. Because his will to thought gets the upper hand he is ultimately forced to abandon the Christian idea of God.[1] The demand of reason —the principle of the immanent logical connexion, the principle of the unity of thought, the transcendental method of thought—destroys the content of the Christian conception of God. For this content cannot be conceived as a rational content; it can only be believed as a revelation. In reason man remains by himself, shut up within the self-sufficient reason; in faith, however, he is approached by the self-revealing

and Plotinus. The fact that he, even as a Pauline Christian, still dares to philosophize is for many a sufficient reason to reproach him with betrayal of the faith. This false separation of theology and philosophy is rightly levelled at us as a reproach by the Catholics. (Cf. Gilson, *L'esprit de la philosophie médiévale*, Chap. I.)

[1] *Kants opus postumum*, published by Adickes: *Kantstudien*, 1920, fourth part, second section, pp. 776 ff.

'Thou' who addresses him 'from without.' The rational God is the God whom I construct for myself; the revealed God is the God who speaks to me. This truth of a God who speaks to me 'from the outside,' this One who is the 'Thou' 'over against me' is seriously meant, in dead earnest, so that it is impossible to claim that in the last resort this 'I which speaks to myself' and the 'Divine Thou which says something to me' are the same. That is why we said: the autonomous reason is the spirit which remains shut up within itself, closed against the Divine revelation, and what it calls 'transcendent' is only a boundary which it has itself drawn, beyond which it recognizes nothing, because it has not been posited as rational by itself.

3. GOD AND IDEAS

It is from this point of view then that we are to understand the second question, that of the relation of the spirit to ideas. What is the meaning of those terms which that philosophical thought which knows nothing of revelation posits as the final point of reference of the spirit, within our theological understanding of the spirit? And how much truth do they contain? Can philosophical Idealism, as patristic theology assumed from the time of Justin Martyr onwards, be incorporated into the Christian understanding of God and become interwoven with it into a whole? Or is there here an Either-Or? Is it possible that there should be any 'Either-Or' here at all? Can we, for instance, understand the spirit without ideas, norms, values, laws of thought, *logos*? Is not the spirit distinguished from the *psyche* by this very relation? How can we think at all unless we formulate the concepts: true, valid, good, beautiful?

In point of fact, we cannot do so; and no Christian theologian would dream of thinking that he could do without this 'Idealism.' Were he to do so, what he *in thesi* denies *in praxi* he would be doing continually, unless he were to give up thinking altogether. The question is not whether we can get through without these terms, but how we are to incorporate them, and what final dignity we give to them.

Even in a definitely Christian theological anthropology there can never be any question of depreciating the reason, of hostility to reason, or of setting up a plea for irrationalism. If we must choose between two evils, then without stopping to reflect for a moment we would choose to be rationalists rather than irrationalists. The reason, 'the power of the idea' (Kant), is, even according to Luther's statement, the greatest gift of God that we possess.[1] The question is only whether we wish to understand God from the point of view of the reason, or the reason from the point of view of God. But as this question has already been answered, this means that it is our task to keep the reason within its own bounds, yet to give it its full rights within these bounds. It is not the reason as such which is in opposition to faith, but only the self-sufficient reason; and this means, the reason which sets itself up in the place of God, the reason which wills to understand God in itself instead of itself in God, the arrogant self-willed reason. There is war to the knife between faith and rationalism, but there is no war between faith and reason; by 'rationalism' we mean, not merely the superficial 'rationalism' of the eighteenth century, which usually bears this name, but also that titanic system of rational thought which is known as German Idealism, and that rationalism which we have inherited from Greek philosophy. The reason is right wherever it listens to the Word of God, and does not think that it is able to proclaim the divine truth to itself.

Reason is the abstract way of thinking which is concerned with argument; this is its character in so far as it refers to idea, law, value and norm. These abstract conceptions are not an ultimate for faith, but they are a pen-ultimate, without which we human beings cannot even approach the ultimate, or, more exactly, without which the Ultimate, namely, the

[1] 'It is beyond doubt that the reason is far and away the most important and the best of all things in this life, indeed that it is something divine. And after Adam's Fall God has not taken this glory away from reason, but rather He has confirmed it. Yet reason does not know of itself that it is such a majestic force but only from experience.' (Luther, according to WA. 39, T., p. 175.) 'Man is especially endowed with the glorious light of reason and intelligence, so that men have conceived and invented so many noble arts, whether it be wisdom, agility, cleverness, and all this comes from this Light or from the Word which was the life of men' (WA. 46, 562).

Word of God itself, cannot approach us. Even the Word of God is *Logos*, 'meaning,' which must be understood by us; that is, it must be received by us as something which has been thought, but not as that which has been produced by our own thinking. In all that is said to us in the Word of God which is true, good and beautiful, we always go beyond the words, cleaving in faith to the Person who is speaking to us, and in faith we open our hearts to receive what He has to say. The truth, conceived in an abstract way, separated from the Person of the God who speaks, is not the ultimate, but the necessary pen-ultimate, which, however, is based upon and proceeds from the ultimate. Our *nous* therefore is the vessel but not the source of the Word of God. Where it receives the Word of God it is called: faith.

When this is perceived, in principle the right integration of ideas has been achieved. All truth is divine truth, all good is divine good, all value is posited and given by God, all law is His law, every norm is the expression of His thought and will.[1] But while the Person of the God who speaks disappears from our sight when we withdraw ourselves from His Word by setting up our own thoughts and acting in self-will, the truth which He posits, the values which He gives, the laws and norms which express His will do not entirely disappear. On the contrary, what was said of the central truth, of the attitude towards the Good, with certain alterations is true of the spirit as a whole: man outside faith stands under the Law. To him the law, which was a penultimate, has become an ultimate; he is now at the mercy of the law, and stands under the curse of the law. Abstract legalism, abstract truth, abstract values and norms, are now all that he still knows about God;[2] and in this he experiences the perversion and the curse of legalism. The law itself however—and with that the idea—is divine and good. Indeed, it is the only represen-

[1] Not only Zwingli, but Luther and Calvin as well, have recognized that through the light of reason God has shown much truth to the heathen and that God is the Source of all reason. In support they adduce passages like John i. 4 and i. 9 (see above p. 79, n. 2).

[2] On the truth as abstraction, cf. Buber, *Die Frage an den Einzelnen*, and Grisebach's conception of truth as the identity of the thinking 'I' with itself.

tative of God for fallen man. The 'curse' does not consist in the fact that the law exists, but that man is shut up to it, that for him it is now the ultimate. The Moral Law is the will of God severed from the person of God, from His gracious speech to us. It is left to us, it is implanted in our spirit. It is the marrow of the moral reason. Through the law God maintains fallen humanity for faith and redemption.[1] The law is to be taken so seriously that God Himself only gives us His grace anew through the fulfilment of the law, that no human being returns to God, save by being broken down by the law and its demands.

4. THE CREATURELY ASPECT OF REASON

With the law as the norm of the will the heart of reason has been laid bare. Our rational thought is necessarily legalistic. Its legalistic character is its strictness, that which distinguishes thought from mere imagination and fantasy. Only that which has been thought in accordance with law, with a norm, has been actually thought. Behind the moral law of reason there stands logic. Without a logical law there is also no moral reason. Even theological thought is logical thought, or it would not be thought but mere babble. Indeed, even prayer comes under this rule of law. It too is rational speech with God, just as faith is a rational answer to the Word of God.[2] But the logical element is here in the service of another; it is not 'something said to oneself' but 'allowing something to be said to oneself.' In faith the monologue of thinking confined within the self is interrupted by hearing the Word from beyond ourselves; faith clings to the belief that the truth which is said to me is said to me by God, really said, and not invented by me. The truth of faith, therefore, in contradistinction to the truth of reason, is 'truth which is imparted,' 'from above,' not 'from within.' Here in faith, therefore, the turning from

[1] Rom. vii. 12; Rom. ii. 14; Gal. iii. 23 ff.

[2] Cf. 1 Cor. xiv. 15 ff. And Luther: *Sic etiam ratio* serves faith so that it reflects on a thing *quando est illustrata*; *sed sine fide nihil prodest nec potest ratio.* . . . *Ratio autem illustra* takes all thoughts from the *verbo*. *Substantia* remains, *vanitas* declines, *quando illustratur ratio a Spiritu* (Luther, *Tischreden*, WA. I, p. 191).

the law to grace is achieved. Faith is the reason which is opened to that which lies beyond reason.

But thinking confined within the self, so far as it goes, does not know this interruption; it marches forward under the steady guidance of the law of validity. The legitimate sphere of such thinking can only be indicated negatively: all that does not concern God Himself, but the world 'in itself,' and man 'in himself.' This 'in itself,' however, is not an isolated sphere, for there is nothing which is not related to God; but it is to be understood as a limited sphere. All being that is not God, has, as creaturely existence, a 'relative being' of its own, and can therefore be recognized in this being 'in itself,' that is, in its relative, creaturely independence. The astronomer as astronomer need not study theology, although it is quite certain that what he observes and calculates is God's Creation. But he grasps it first of all not as the Divine Creation but as the world. If he is a believer, however, he knows that this world is God's Creation, and he understands the laws which govern it as God's laws.[1] A natural scientist like Kepler, who is also a believer in God, relates that which he knows as scientist with that which he knows as a believer from the Word of God; indeed, he is in a position to recognize God the Creator in His Works; for *νοούμενα καθορᾶται*, says Paul of the majesty of the Creator. Thus also man himself, in his history, in his culture, in his bodily, mental and spiritual nature, is a creature, and thus a comparatively independent being, and therefore a being to be known in his distinctive nature. There is a completely legitimate, rational anthropology which is partly based on natural science and partly on the humanities. 'For who among men knoweth the things of a man (*τὰ τοῦ ἀνθρώπου*), save the spirit of the man which is in him?'[2] and this is explicitly distinguished from the Spirit of God, who makes known 'the things of God.' The creature, in its creaturely independence, in its own creaturely being, can be known by the human reason. This belongs to the right of dominion which has been granted to it. Where, however, personal being is concerned, the freedom and the responsibility of man, scientific neutrality ceases; there it is the whole that

[1] Cf. Calvin, opp. 22, 23, 100.

[2] I Cor. ii. 11 (R.V.).

matters, the truth, for which no specialists are competent, the truth which only becomes evident in the act of decision for or against the Word of God, the truth which is inevitably missed by the reason which desires to have the last word to say to itself. The more therefore that we are concerned with the 'personal heart' of human existence, the less sure is reason, the more limited is the autonomy which can be ascribed to it, the more sinister becomes its self-sufficient attitude and its claim to recognition.

5. THE VALUES AND THE CREATIVE ELEMENT

Man has been endowed by God in such a way that he himself can know and experience what he needs for life, what is of advantage to him and what is harmful, what also is useful and harmful for the life of human beings in all their relations with one another. He can form the concept of 'goods,' and through ideation he is able to grasp the idea of the 'values' which lie behind them. He can and ought to try to make clear to himself that spiritual being in ideas and ideals which can be grasped from the standpoint of his reason. But the 'higher' we ascend in this scale, the nearer we come to the sphere of that which is connected with the personal being of God and of man, which can no longer be perceived by reason but only by faith, the more we shall see that the self-sufficient reason is a source of error.

Culture is fundamentally the domain of the rational spirit. Its ultimate meaning, its ground, its limits and its dangers can only be understood in faith; but its immanent laws, its immanent meaning is to be understood also by the human spirit as that which has been brought forth by or is being brought forth by the human spirit. The power which creates culture is not faith but the rational spirit. This agrees with what was said above from the opposite point of view about formal personal being, which has not been destroyed by sin. In principle this is the situation; but in practice the reason is continually exceeding its rights in sinful arrogance and forgetfulness of God, and, as the creator of culture, in particular, it makes itself and its creations into idols. The creative power of man is one of the chief causes of sin in the realm of mind and spirit. The spirit which thinks creatively leads man astray into self-deification, into a confusion between the Spirit of God and the spirit of man.

The creative element in man, in the narrower, more usual sense of the word, is not so much abstract thought guided by the laws of logic, as imagination, the power of freely creating both inwardly and outwardly. Even the most rigid thought is not without this element, even the most arid conclusion is not possible without imagination, without understanding, without creative intuition. But this element is here assigned rigid limits. It is developed most freely in poetry and works of art. Here the—purely formal—similarity between the divine Spirit and the human spirit is greatest. For here man approaches existence in the freest way and creates something new, something which has never been there before. Here the spirit draws upon the depths of the unconscious and the richness of the emotional life. By means of this creative spirit man builds up for himself a world of his own, alongside that which has been created. Hence also this creative capacity is exposed in a special way to sinful misuse, and is a special occasion for self-glorification. Man makes use of this 'spiritual world' to escape from the real world, and as a means of evading its claims, for the concealment of his sinful perversity and poverty, and for self-deception about his own true situation. The prohibition of images in the Old Testament should not be understood only in its immediate sense, in its connexion with the cultus. It is a warning to the self-sufficient human being, pointing out to him where the very richness of his endowments may lead him astray, and where he may end in making self and the world his idols. The pagan creation of myth and artistic poetic symbolism are closely connected, and it is more than poetic licence when even modern poets so often play seriously with the world of the gods. Here the pantheistic deification of the self and of the world clothes and conceals itself in magical and deceptive garments. The higher the creative spirit of man aspires, the more surely, if he is not restrained by faith, he falls into the insanity of self-deification.[1]

[1] This serious and dangerous game with the polytheistic myth is played chiefly by Hölderlin; the magic of his language ought not to conceal from us the fact that here the most audacious self-deification is being carried on.

6. THE INTELLECT

But man is also threatened by danger at the opposite end. The spirit which turns away from the Ultimate, the Unconditioned, which turns towards the external world—in itself unavoidably and rightly—falls only too easily a prey to the temptation to venture to interpret existence as a whole from this narrow basis. As scientific intelligence it has been able in a definite way to master the world of things: here a certain way of thinking has proved successful, why then should not this way of thinking be the one which is correct as a whole, which is ultimately valid? A narrow intellectualism and a poverty-stricken positivism, if not indeed the most stupid of all 'world-views,' materialism, 'prove' to us that there is 'nothing higher,' that all that is 'supposed to be higher' are merely fantasy pictures of our imagination. Man—not to mention the heart—has become so unintelligent that he announces this 'world-view' with all the force of absolute truth and moral necessity, without even noting the opposition between formal absolutism and the material denial of the Absolute. But even behind this erroneous way of thinking there is a minute grain of truth; in view of an arrogant hybrid Idealism even materialism has some justification; and even an arid positivistic intellectualism has a certain right, as a corrective, when confronted by sweeping, undisciplined speculation.

For the rest we will recognize that even the most ordinary common sense is God's gift. Where ordinary daily life is concerned, ordinary common sense is in place. A deeply religious outlook may be combined with this highly practical way of thinking, which will not allow any confusion between an X and a U. Depreciation of the intellect as such is always a sign of lack of adaptation to the creaturely character of our existence.[1] The intellect is the power of perceiving the finite,

[1] Magnificent and true as is much in Fichte's protest against his bourgeois contemporaries (*Grundzüge des gegenwärtigen Zeitalters*), yet the sentiment and the Pharisaism with which the accusations are made can only be understood from the point of view of a thinker who at the same time advances the view that 'in reference to the doctrine of religion the positing of a Creation is the first criterion of its error . . . the denial of

especially the world of things and the like, and, with the aid of this knowledge the power to live and act in this finite world in a practical way. The Bible is full of respect for such astuteness, for such intelligence is needed by every human being in order to grasp the concrete purpose of his life. God's wisdom and love have more to do with this everyday practical sense, which understands how to make good and nourishing bread, than with all the highbrow speculations of great minds. But faith does not easily conflict even with the scientific intelligence which carefully observes the actual world, collects facts and inquires into the laws of events down to the very foundation. It is not natural science, nor empirical psychology, which leads us into opposition to that which God's word says to us, but the arrogance of a 'scientific' philosophy of life and of a pseudo-psychology.

7. FEELING AND MYSTICISM

A special word is required about the relation between spirit and feeling, which is too often neglected. When we remember what was said in the last chapter about the 'heart' as the centre of the person, it is obvious that we cannot accept the usual contrast between feeling and spirit. Feeling is related to the pleasure-pain sensation as the will is related to instinct and thought to mere imagination. Genuine feeling, as for instance sorrow or joy, is not possible without spirit. For such feelings arise only out of or in spiritual connexions. A good meal does not arouse joy; it merely gives pleasure; if I eat with joy it is because my spirit is turned in a certain direction, to that which is true, or good, or beautiful, which is connected with the act of eating, as indeed the Apostle is able to say: 'whether ye eat or drink, do all to the glory of God.'[1] Through joy pleasure is lifted to a higher plane since its subject is understood in a larger context.

The values, as their objective correlates, correspond to the feelings. We feel the values, but to feel value is never done

such a view is the first criterion of truth' (V, 191). Similar observations could be made about the Romantic contempt for the bourgeois element in general.

[1] 1 Cor. x. 31.

without thought, in which the meaning of the value is grasped.[1] Feeling accompanies the spiritual act; it is not itself, however, an act, it is a passive state in which the personality is determined by the content of that which is disclosed in the spiritual act. But—and comparatively speaking, this is the real point in the contrast between feeling and spirit—feeling always permeates the personal situation as a whole. There are therefore feelings of very varied depth, which may exist alongside, or, to put it better, inside one another at the same time. A person may be very happy about something 'on the surface,' and at the same time in the depth of his soul there may be a sense of profound sadness and suffering. This is why, constantly and involuntarily, feeling unites the different spheres—the centre of personality, the different levels of the spiritual life—with the purely psychical element, and makes it possible for them to penetrate one another.

For those of us whose relation to God is determined positively by faith, and negatively by sin, there is no occasion to ascribe any special significance to feeling in connexion with man's relation to God. Feeling accompanies but does not determine faith. It is true of course that faith is not only an act of understanding and will but that it is also a 'passion,'[2] and love in particular cannot be thought of apart from feeling. But feeling is not the distinctive element, the dominant and determining factor; it merely accompanies faith. In mystical religion, on the other hand, feeling plays the decisive part. The experience of union with the Infinite, with the All, the fusion of the divinity with man is sought in mysticism precisely in feeling. For objectivity is distinctive of thought and will; for thought and will there is something objective to be thought and willed. Union, fusion, cannot be attained in such acts, it must be experienced as a 'state.' This 'can' only happen in feeling, that is, this is the significance ascribed to

[1] The 'Christian' conception of God as the 'Supreme Good' always has something of Eudaemonism about it, which comes from the ancient doctrine of *Eros* and the mystical love of God; hence the Bible avoids it.

[2] That faith is also 'passion' has been taught us once more by Kierkegaard above all. Cf. *Fear and Trembling* and *Unscientific Postscript*. Faith is 'the objective uncertainty, in the appropriation of the most passionate inwardness.' (Postscript I, p. 278, German edition.)

feeling; a definite emotional experience is interpreted as the experience of union with God. This experience is ecstasy, an emotional state in which all definite consciousness, all objective thinking and feeling is drowned in a sea of emotion, where all the boundaries which separate the Self from the Other who stands 'over against' him disappear beneath this tide of feeling. It is impossible to deny the reality of this emotional state, or the possibility of such an experience; the question only is: what is the significance of this experience? How much reality does it contain? Faith opposes the mystical interpretation with a sharp, plain 'No.' The living God is not 'experienced' in such a way, whatever the content of this experience may be. The living God reveals Himself in His Word through faith, not in ecstasy. But it is not our business at this point to outline any theory of mysticism; all we wish to do is to make plain where we differ from it.[1]

8. THE SPIRIT OF MAN AND EVIL

In conclusion a word about the relation of the spirit to evil, unbelief and sin respectively. Idealism maintains that evil springs out of our 'lower' nature, out of our sense life, out of the fact that spirit is not present,[2] and thus that evil is really something negative. It reaches this position because for it the spirit as such, quite apart from its actual determination or tendency, the spirit as possibility, in the formal sense, is divine in its nature. To have spirit, to have reason is the same as participating in the divine Being, the divine Reason. The Christian faith counters this argument with the statement that even evil, sin, unbelief, have their seat and their origin in the spirit of man, hence that the more spirit there is the greater will be the sin. Idealism—often Idealism in the shape of Christian theology—has quite wrongly appealed to the Biblical antithesis between spirit and 'flesh'; for in the Bible evil and sin are certainly connected with the flesh; but the

[1] 1 Cor. xiv. and 2 Cor. xii, as well as other passages in the New Testament, show that even the ecstatic element is not foreign to the Christian life as a whole; but it is not the basis nor the aim of man's relation to God.

[2] i.e. if I could see the whole, evil would have no being, and would be non-being.—*Translator.*

Bible means something quite different from the 'capacity for base desire,' the sense nature, the instinctive forces turned towards the 'lower,' that is, the material sphere. This idea of the 'lower nature' indeed is foreign to the thought of the Bible as a whole. 'Flesh'[1] is rather: the creaturely element in contradistinction to the Creator—that is, that which in itself is impotent—or creatureliness in a false independence of the Creator. Hence sin is both: fleshly, and yet at the same time the act of the spirit. In the Bible sin is never anything other than a total act of the person, namely, self-determination which is opposed to man's real destiny, disobedience to the will of God.

This negative self-determination is called 'flesh' in order that it may be characterized in its nothingness, as something ending in death; then further because this self-determination against the Spirit of God necessarily entails the handing over of the person to the desires of the senses, to the world, to instinct, as its result; and finally, because it brings with it the loss of freedom, namely, essential freedom, freedom in the material, not in the formal sense of the word. 'Whoso committeth sin is the servant of sin.' The following chapter will deal with this point in greater detail.

In so far as, from the standpoint of the Word of God, we are always sinners, the whole of our 'higher life' is tainted with this 'fleshly' character. The central point of this 'fleshly' or 'carnal' nature is that self-sufficient, autonomous, emancipated reason, that reason against which Luther strove. Our reason, apart from its restoration through the Word of grace, is always sinfully self-sufficient, a reason infected with rationalism and unbelief. This is so even, and particularly, where it produces an irrationalistic philosophy. 'By nature,' that is, apart from redemption, we are always human beings who in their thinking cannot be and do not even wish to be open

[1] The concept of 'flesh,' σάρξ, in the New Testament presents us with an extremely difficult problem; it is a question whether Paul, who is the writer who uses this expression most, is completely unambiguous in his language. Cf. Gutbrod, *Die paulinische Anthropologie*, p. 153: 'As σάρξ man is defined as sinful, precisely because it, which is his nature, through his sin is itself sinful.' Cf. also Schott, *Fleisch und Geist nach Luthers Lehre*.

to the Divine Word. Our wish to be our own masters clothes itself in the noble garment of 'autonomous' thought or reason, by means of which we reject the revealed claim of the Divine Word as a temptation to irrationalism. In our treatment of the question of Humanism we shall be dealing with this self-defence of the self-sufficient reason in greater detail.

The more closely we are concerned with the centre, with man's personal relation with God and man's personal being, the greater will be the influence of unbelief upon the higher life of the mind and spirit. The further we move away from this central point the less evident does it become, and it is therefore still more difficult to recognize it. If a person studies anatomy or physics it will be impossible to tell from his scientific work, pure and simple, whether he is a Christian or an unbeliever. But his faith or his unbelief will come out very clearly in his way of thought and life as a man. The more that knowledge has to do with the world as world, the further it is removed from the sphere of sin, and therefore the more 'neutral' it becomes. But the will, which is always personal, is still connected with it, even where the trifles of everyday life are concerned. Thus if we had eyes to see, even in feeling we would discover the effect of sin as a fundamental joylessness, which always lies concealed under all other feelings, as 'un-peace' which, apart from the 'peace of God,' always dwells in us. But we have practised the art of concealment to such purpose that we have ourselves fallen victims to it. Without being fully aware of it we use the rich treasures and possibilities of our spirit in order to deceive ourselves about this inmost un-peace. The creative spirit in particular gives of its inexhaustible reserves for this end; but we shall be able to understand this best in relation to the problem of freedom.

CHAPTER XI

THE PROBLEM OF FREEDOM

I. THE PHILOSOPHY OF FREEDOM AND UNFREEDOM

THE problem of freedom is peculiarly 'the' problem of human existence, for freedom is the original element of personal being. Freedom is the specifically human characteristic. The Bible, too, is concerned with freedom: 'Where the Spirit of the Lord is, there is liberty.'[1] 'Ye, brethren, were called for freedom.'[2] 'If the Son shall make you free ye shall be free indeed.'[3] In Humanism freedom is the chief concern. It knows that in fighting for freedom it is fighting for the *humanum*. Freedom therefore ought to be the common ground on which the Biblical and the Humanistic thought of man should meet. In point of fact it is in the problem of freedom that they differ most widely from one another. Just as freedom is the quintessence of man's being, so unfreedom is the quintessence of sin. 'Everyone that committeth sin is the bondservant of sin.'[4] Sin is the opposite of freedom. Where the idea of sin stands in the centre of the understanding of man, there human un-freedom, the *servum arbitrium*, is the theme of anthropology. Can such a view possibly give sufficient weight to the concern of humanity for freedom? Will it be able to do it so adequately that it will become evident that the Humanist's protest is due to a misunderstanding?

Just as Augustine, in his Christian doctrine of freedom, was obliged to carry on a campaign on two fronts: against the fatalistic determinism of the Manichaeans with their false denial of freedom, on the one hand, and against a false assertion of freedom by Pelagian Humanism on the other, we also are obliged to do the same. Indeed, we may say that to-day the denial of human freedom by a naturalistic determinism is far more characteristic of the present 'spirit of the age' than the humanistic theory of freedom. Thus to-day, the drift towards determinism, which our Reformers in their struggle

[1] 2 Cor. iii. 17.
[2] Gal. v. 13.
[3] John viii. 36.
[4] John viii. 34.

against their sole opponents—the open liberalism of the Humanists and the disguised liberalism of Catholic theology—to some extent allowed to go unpunished, has become a far more serious matter. To-day our slogan must be: No determinism, on any account! For it makes all understanding of man as man impossible. If Luther had been obliged to grapple with a determinism of this kind, he would never have written his "*De servo arbitrio*' as he did—and possibly had to do—when faced by the liberalism of his own day.[1]

Naturalism, especially in its crass, materialistic form, sees in man only the object, the 'cerebrating-animal,' a living creature which is only distinguished from other creatures by the degree of differentiation of its organism, especially of its central nervous system. Whether naturalism actually interprets the life of nature in a materialistic manner or not, does not make any difference, so far as our question is concerned. Although man, like all other living creatures, and perhaps in a higher degree than they, may have a certain spontaneity, yet this vital spontaneity is still regarded as a given fact of nature, as a definite energy of a particular kind. In any case, man is a product of nature, both as individual and as species; his nature is wholly and clearly determined by the forces which have shaped him, and in his expressions of life, his so-called actions, he is equally clearly determined by the forces which compose his 'constitution.' Even when the extreme formula, *L'homme machine*, is avoided, it is still assumed that man is as fixed by his nature as the function of the machine is determined by its construction and its mass, and the energy supplied to it. This structure by which man is determined is called the 'character';[2] it is itself, however, the resultant of the forces which have created it. It is curious to note how this absolutely deterministic metaphysic is combined, in many minds, with an equally indeterministic ethic, which is absolutely and irreconcilably opposed to the metaphysical basis. In so far, however, as this contradiction is avoided, that is,

[1] Cf. Pfister, *Die Willensfreiheit*; Zickendraht, *Der Streit zwischen Erasmus und Luther über die Willensfreiheit.*

[2] Thus Kretschmer, *Körperbau und Charakter*. See also below, Chap. XIII, on the problem of Character.

in so far as man continues to think further and logically along the lines of this deterministic metaphysic, he cannot fail to arrive at a complete denial of responsibility.[1] Man acts indeed, as he must, just as a machine functions in accordance with its construction. To this type of mind it does not matter in the least to what factors the resultant 'character,' and the human behaviour proceeding from its activity, be attributed, whether to heredity or to environment, to general or to particular influences. In neither case can there be any question of responsibility. But if responsibility be eliminated the whole meaning of human existence disappears. Though the intelligent human animal may live differently from other animals, though owing to the complexity of his structure, which brings with it a certain vulnerability, he may need special measures of protection called 'civilization' and 'culture'; though, owing to the particular arrangement of his brain and his nervous system, he may be able to aspire far beyond the actual level of his life in daring wish-fantasies—yet after all, dreams are only dreams, and biological measures of protection remain bound to their biological ends. The phantasmagoria of a so-called 'spiritual life' have no real meaning, they are bubbles which appear for a moment on the surface of the ocean of natural events and then vanish once more, without aim or meaning. It may be impossible to prove freedom; in any case the meaninglessness of an un-free existence can be proved. By most of the champions of this determinism it needs no proof. From the very outset they refuse to consider the question of 'meaning' at all—evidently regarding it as futile.

Idealistic Humanism presents a far more beautiful picture of human reality than that offered by the comfortless theory which we have just outlined. Man is free, because he is spirit, because he is subject. Just as being 'object' implies, essentially, the state of 'being determined'—'forcible compulsion' (Spitteler)—to such an extent that 'being object' can actually be defined by this, so freedom belongs to the being of the subject, of the spirit, of the 'I,' to such an extent that both can be defined by each other. 'Object' is that which is what it is as the resul-

[1] Cf. my ethics, *Das Gebot und die Ordnungen*, pp. 21 ff. (English: *The Divine Imperative*, pp. 36 ff.)

tant of combined forces. 'Subject' is that which is as it determines itself, in which connexion, however, 'self-determination' is as much an act of thought as it is an act of will. To be 'spirit' is the antithesis of being 'a thing'; it is the exact opposite of all 'being object' which is conceived on 'thing' analogies. Perhaps—and on this point there is no uniform view in the idealism of freedom[1]—there is a middle term between being-object and being-subject, for instance, the spontaneity which is peculiar to all life, as something midway between freedom and necessity, and within this vital spontaneity again a series of degrees, middle terms, which lead from the zero-point of freedom in the thing by way of the spontaneity of the more highly organized animals to the plane of human freedom. If this were so, then in any case this phenomenon would have to be understood 'from above' and not 'from below,' that is, the whole scale of freedom would have to be understood from the point of view of freedom as the scale of reduced freedom, not from the point of view of un-freedom. For indeed it is possible to reach un-freedom by the decrease of freedom, but it is not possible to reverse the process and to attain freedom from necessity by a process of increase or intensification—of what? Strange as this may seem to us to-day, it is an incontrovertible fact that if we are ever to understand it at all, we must understand the animal from the point of view of man, and not man from the point of view of the animal.[2] The animal, the sub-human life as a whole, is 'only upon the way towards' freedom; the stages of this way describe the different 'stages' of this existence which is not yet human existence according to the graded order of their distance from man. There might be at the same time graded orders of participation in being spirit. Yet this is a problem which has remained

[1] Dilthey distinguishes the idealism of freedom (op. cit., pp. 348 ff.) from another kind which might be called objective idealism, or the idealism of 'Kultur,' which tends rather to Pantheism.

[2] Thus Schelling's natural philosophy, and also Schleiermacher in his philosophical ethics. The idea of ordered stages also dominates the Aristotelian and the Plotinian philosophy; in the one case it is optimistic and rational, in the other pessimistic and religious. The former has determined, in the main, medieval scholasticism, and the latter medieval mysticism.

controversial in Idealism from the days of Plato and Aristotle down to the present time.

In the spirit alone is freedom. Through the spirit man can detach himself from his present existence, as it is at this moment. He has the power of ideas, he is able to measure his existence by that which ought to be, his imperfections by the Perfect, the phenomena in their impurity by the purity of the idea or of the ideal. But man cannot merely think this idea as an ideal but unreal complementation of his actual being[1]—for if this were so the materialistic conception of the idea as mere imagination would be correct—he can also make this idea operative in his life. He can decide in the light of the idea, he can give shape and form to the idea, he can transform the idea into the actual stuff of life. The spirit proves itself as an operative principle, and in this effectiveness man experiences his freedom: the free shaping of that which does not yet exist into the sphere of being by means of the free activity of the spirit.

This certainly produces a quite different picture of the possibilities of human existence. From the very outset it has a meaning, that is, in this ideal possibility which is given by the idea. On the one hand, even the grasping of the idea as such, the vision, is a realization of meaning which is far more significant than any mere vitalistic course of life could be. Then, further, there is the possibility of introducing this meaning which has been perceived into the sphere of material reality by means of artistically or ethically creative action; this means: by the creation of works and by the building up of a human community shaped by spirit, and finally, by the ideal development of the individual person into a spiritual personality. But the primal element of this whole spirit-existence is: freedom.

Even the idealism of freedom, however, must take deterministic factors into account, factors which limit freedom, not merely the limitations imposed by matter, the material of freedom—for this limitation is at the same time the possibility of creation, of giving form to matter—but rather the limita-

[1] Thus in Friedrich Albert Lange, in his *Geschichte des Materialismus*, and in Vaihinger's *Als-Ob* philosophy.

tions which lie in the acting subject itself and are all due to the fact that the subject in an enigmatic manner is bound up with an object, the body. For the idealism of freedom, therefore, corporeality, as the limitation of freedom, is a stumbling-block, something which should not be, that troublesome 'double' whose co-existence with the spirit is not only a theoretical embarrassment, but a practical difficulty, σῶμα-σῆμα, the body a tomb![1] It is that in us which is not distinctively human, the lower, baser, earthly part; it is that aspect of man which is ignored when we are speaking of man's real being, his destiny and his meaning. Here, then, in the bodily nature of man, the centre and source of those limitations of the truly free, spiritual life, 'evil' as a whole, which the Christian calls 'sin,' is to be sought. For these restrictions cannot be derived from the spirit as freedom. Hence they do not really touch me myself, but rather 'me as not myself,' that strange element in me which does not really form part of 'me' at all. Hence we ought not to lay too much emphasis upon these limitations.

2. THE CHRISTIAN UNDERSTANDING OF FREEDOM

It is obvious that the Christian doctrine of freedom is far nearer to the view of Idealism than it is to that of materialistic determinism—a fact that has been freely admitted by the great teachers of the Church in all ages, by Kierkegaard, Calvin and Luther no less than by Augustine and Athanasius; and this fact ought not to be ignored, however strongly we may be opposed to this Idealistic view of freedom. In this view man's being may be wrongly defined, yet it is defined as human; the meaning of life may be misinterpreted, but it is admitted that life *has* meaning. We have no right to ignore this fundamental affinity, however great may be the difference in every other direction. Indeed, in so doing, the contrast is not weakened but is intensified. The great contrasts do not appear in a realm denuded of spirit, but in the spirit itself. There can be contrast only where there is some measure of likeness. The thinkers of the Church have never entered into

[1] 'We are imprisoned in the body, like an oyster in its shell,' says Plato in the *Phaedrus*, 250c.

a serious discussion of the materialistic conception of man because to them it seemed too remote from sense to be taken seriously. But the conflict with Idealism is so sharp because it contains so many elements of truth that even its errors become dangerous.

In Christian thought, freedom, as well as man as a whole, is considered from three different aspects: those of the Origin, the Fall, and the contradiction, and finally from that of restoration to our origin and of the final consummation. But the standpoint from which these three aspects are derived is always the same: the revelation of the Word of God. The doctrine of freedom as well as the doctrine of personality and of the spirit, must be developed from the centre of the Christian Faith, from Jesus Christ Himself.

The freedom from which, in which and for which man has been created is freedom-in-responsibility, freedom-in-and-for-love. In stating this we have already defined the decisive difference between the Christian and the humanistic understanding of freedom; this, however, is only the case when we understand this term 'created' in the actuality in which it has already been presented in this book. Pelagian Liberalism has grown out of a false, Deistic conception of the Creation, and still does so—though less in Idealism than in the indeterminism of 'common sense.' The original being of man is not anything which exists by itself, it is not substantial, but it is always derived from God and directed to God. It is never an independent existence; on the contrary, it is the achievement of dependence. In this fact, and not in any quantitative distinction, lies the difference between the freedom of the creature and the freedom of the Creator. The being of God alone is unconditioned, absolute freedom; that of the creature is conditioned, relative freedom, freedom in dependence. The more that any view of freedom ignores this primal fact of man's permanent dependence—up to the extreme case where man regards himself as the unconditionally free, world-creative Self—the more disastrous will the misunderstanding become.[1]

[1] The Greek-Humanistic idea of freedom is therefore different from that of the Christian idea, because it does not know God as the absolutely free.

The seeming paradox, namely, that man's freedom is based upon his dependence upon God, exists only so long as one holds the deistic conception of the divinely-created 'I' or the pantheistic idea of the divine 'I.'[1] Certainly to the extent in which the truth—this truth of our dependence upon God—seems alien to our reason, the Christian doctrine of freedom *is* a 'paradox.' For faith the paradox has disappeared. If the 'I' of man is the one who has been called by God to responsibility, and in this call is ever being created anew, then the misunderstanding of an 'I' which is based upon itself, of an independent *substantia cogitans*, falls away; man recognizes himself as the being who, in contrast to all substantial existence, remains in actuality, namely, in the *actus* of God and in his own act of response.

Because the being of man is actually based upon man's dependence upon God, upon the Call of God which chooses him and gives him responsibility, his freedom is only complete where he remains in this dependence, hence—to express this for once in quantitative terms—the maximum of his dependence on God is at the same time the maximum of his freedom, and his freedom decreases with his degree of distance from the place of his origin, from God. As a planet can shed warmth around itself in proportion as it is nearer the sun, so the nearer man is to God the more freedom he will have. Yet here all quantitative and dynamic images are dangerous; for here we are not concerned with a more or less, but with the Either-Or, namely, with being in God or being separated from God. We are concerned with the Primitive State and the Fall. The son who takes his share of the inheritance from his father does not linger about in the neighbourhood of his home, he 'goes into a far country.'[2] He has gone away, not more or less far away, but simply far away from home; the door has been shut behind him; there is no going back.

sovereign Lord, and because it misunderstands the spirit of man as *particula divinitatis*. Cf. the Appendix on the *Idea of Humanity in Antiquity* (p. 547).

[1] Hence Fichte's vehement protest against the idea of Creation. On the other hand, from this rejection of the idea of Creation alone do we perceive what he means by the relation between the human and the absolute self.

[2] Luke xv. 11 ff.

Of what kind, then, is the freedom which is grounded in dependence upon God? Certainly, freedom of the will, freedom of choice, freedom to say 'yes' or 'no.' This freedom, to be able to say 'Yes' or 'No,' points to an imperfection in the Primitive State in contrast to the perfection of the End. The freedom peculiar to the Primitive State was—according to Augustine's profound distinction—the freedom of the *non-peccare posse*; the freedom which belongs to the final state of eternal bliss is the freedom of the *non-posse peccare*; it shares in the divine freedom itself. In contrast with the latter the freedom of the origin is genuinely creaturely, a limited freedom, precisely in that which seems to make it especially free, the fact that it 'can' do something. There is a kind of ability to do something which is not a sign of freedom, but of the limitation of freedom, of imperfection. Man originally possessed not merely the power of decision but the necessity for decision—this could not be the distinguishing element in the state of eternal bliss.

It is not only freedom of decision, however, but also—and this is a further determination—a double necessity for responsibility. Man cannot do otherwise than say either 'yes' or 'no.' Whether he is a sinner or not, he must always keep on deciding. The evasion of decision does not help him in the least, for the very refusal to decide is decision. Inescapable—far more so than the law that he must breathe—is the law that man must decide, as long as he lives, and at every moment of his life. Nothing can alter this save a powerful act of God which alters the constitution of man—that mighty act which we call perfecting in eternal life, or that which we call damnation. Then alone does the necessity for decision, as well as the power to make decisions, cease. Then there will devolve upon man the negative or the positive faculty of decision, either necessity without any possibility of hope, or freedom without necessity for hope, eternal death or eternal life. Here, however, on this side of that ultimate state, at every moment man must decide, whether he will or not. He has not the freedom to decide or not to decide, but only that of saying 'Yes' or 'No.' For our later definition of unfreedom this will be of the greatest importance.

fact of individuality. Personal being is ethical, but the man who simply wants to be creative regards the ethical simply as a tiresome restriction. The claims of his neighbour cut across his creative activity, responsibility in the sight of God narrows the circle of that which is aesthetically possible, brings an 'Either-Or' into a life of possibilities in which all is still fluid, and turns the vague possibility of doing 'This' or 'That' into the plain demand that something definite should be *done*. The aesthetic person always considers the ethical element 'narrow-minded.' This 'narrow-mindedness' is precisely the personal element, the limitation of my otherwise unrestricted possibilities by the 'Thou.' As the *Eros* in itself is unrestricted and only through marriage—this narrow-minded monogamy!—finds its limits, so the free life of genius is limited by the claims of persons, and in this alone finds its personal meaning.[1] Unrestricted *Eros* belongs to the natural order; only as monogamy, where it becomes responsible, does it become truly personal.

The spiritual value of our life is always reached through limitation. Thinking is limitation of the infinite possibilities of mere imagination; willing is limitation of the infinite possibilities of desire; artistic creation is a limitation by selection; it is a process of elimination. Spirit means discipline: logical discipline, aesthetic discipline, ethical discipline. The highest discipline is that of belonging to God. Here all self-will is taken away from man, and in this alone does he become truly spiritual, genuine personality. This is the kind of freedom which God gives to man; in this alone does He make him really human. *Deo servire libertas.*

3. THE CHRISTIAN VIEW OF UNFREEDOM

The first statement with which a Christian doctrine of unfreedom must begin—if it is not to try to drive out the devil of a false freedom by the Beelzeboul of determinism—is this, that the un-freedom, into which man falls through sin, is unfreedom in freedom. It is true of course that he who 'committeth sin is the bondservant of sin'; but he never commits sin otherwise than by his own act of decision. On this point Augustine's

[1] This is the theme of *Either-Or* by Kierkegaard.

teaching is more accurate and careful than that of the Reformers —for the very reason that the determinism of the Manichees had shown him the danger of a false doctrine of freedom.[1] 'With free decision has God created me; if I have sinned, I *have* sinned. . . . It is *I* who have sinned, not Fate, not accident, not Satan because he has forced me into it, but *I* have consented to his transgression.'[2] 'Who of us, however, would like to assert that through the sin of the first man free decision has disappeared from the human race? . . . Free decision has been so little lost in the sinner that it is precisely by its aid that men sin.' 'Thus they were "free in regard to righteousness" (Rom. vi. 20) only through the decision of the will.'[3] Even the sinner is a human being, not an animal, not a thing; the form of his divinely-created existence, existence-in-decision, has not been destroyed. It is not sufficient to speak of mere desire as the Reformers do, we must speak absolutely of free will. We shall be speaking directly of the negative qualification of this freedom of the will, but it is only possible to speak of this after that deterministic misunderstanding has been excluded.

Indeed, it is possible to state categorically: with one exception only—a new limitation which is certainly of central importance, and one whose character still has to be defined —in principle at least, man has retained freedom in every form.[4] His thought, his activity, his spiritual life, do not lack that element of freedom which distinguishes the spiritual as such from the natural. Only by means of this freedom is he able to create art and science, civilization and culture, law and the State, and to produce the family, marriage, friendship, custom, and a moral order. He is still always a subject, with the capacity to detach himself from the given, he still has reason, and with that the power of grasping the idea and of measuring what exists by that as a norm. Since even as sinner

[1] On this cf. the excellent presentation and exposition of Heinrich Barth, *Die Freiheit der Entscheidung im Denken Augustins*, to which I am indebted for some essential help. The passages from *Augustine* which have been quoted above are in Barth, pp. 78, 82.

[2] Migne, 37, 37, 1938. [3] Migne, 44, 552.

[4] Cf. J. Gerhard (Loci v. 201), *in reliquis omnibus aliquam arbitrii libertatem in homine superesse dicimus.*

he still has that which the Reformers call the *justitia civilis*, so also he has retained a *libertas civilis*, that freedom which from time immemorial has been known as 'formal' freedom. This 'form' which is inseparable from human existence, the structure of human existence as existence-in-decision, has not been destroyed by sin.

Perhaps it would be more correct to say: it has not been destroyed *in principle*. For certainly the effect of sin penetrates into the sphere of that which characterizes man as human. The man who drinks himself into a state of unconsciousness can scarcely be addressed as a human being while he is in this drunken state; in the language of the law he is no longer 'accountable.' Even in the empirical sphere sin has an effect which destroys freedom and humanity. Even the creative faculties of a man may be inhibited and annihilated by sin—not only in the extreme form of physical injury as the result of vice, but also by the perversion of thought and will, by psychological conflicts, by the 'decadence' of the conception of culture, by inward repressions of all kinds. How many creative forces and how many creative works have been spoiled or destroyed by the sinful disintegration of the unity of personality and of community!

In spite of this, in principle we are bound to say that even the sinful human being has a free will; free will is the presupposition and the essence of his human existence. From the standpoint of the Christian faith this cannot and ought not to be denied. If Christian teachers often say otherwise, this is due to two causes: first, because to one whose thinking is controlled by the truth of man's relation to God, to whom God comes first, and everything else takes a second place, freedom of this kind seems insignificant compared with the freedom which has been lost; secondly, because this very loss of freedom is not perceived by the thought of the 'natural man'; hence it must be emphasized with vigour, and, if necessary, in a quite one-sided way. What, then, is this lost freedom?

In a word, it is the freedom which is based upon communion with God as such, which consists in that alone, and indeed is identical with it. Since man has separated himself from God by sin, as we have already seen, with the alteration of his attitude towards God there has also come a change in his nature. He lives no longer in God, but against God; he no longer has God for him but against him. He has been detached and alienated from his Creator, the Source of his life, from the Good, from love, which is his original life. He now possesses this Good no longer as a gift but only as an obligation; that is, he *has* it no longer, he merely ought to have it. The task of his life is now the hopeless one of squaring the circle; he ought to do the Good willingly, which, as a duty, cannot be done willingly at all. The Good which can only be done in the natural spirit of love has now become a legalistic demand! He ought—to love.[1] This nonsense is the result of the perversion of life's meaning and of man's relation with God. Man can only do that which is truly Good when he comes to it from God; now he has to do it while he is aspiring after God. He has to *do* good before he *is* good, or indeed, to put it still more sharply, he who is now bad must do good.

That is the fatal decision which has been made irrevocably: by falling away from God man has indeed fallen away from being good. Through sin he has become a sinner. The sinner ought to do good! The godless man, the enemy of God, ought to love God! This he cannot do; not only does this mean that he cannot do it wholly or perfectly; he cannot do it at all. This is so because the presupposition is lacking, existence in the love of God. How could he who is not in love, love? Just as a person who is no longer in the water cannot swim, or a person who is not in the air cannot fly, so a person who is no longer in love, cannot love. If, however, he cannot love—love as one loves in God—then he can no longer fulfil the meaning of his life, that which gives to his life its genuinely human character. He can no longer fulfil the divine meaning of his life, not only in part but not at all; and not only for a time, until he has regained it, but never again. The eye which has

[1] Kant: 'For a command that one should do something willingly is in itself contradictory'; *Kritik der praktischen Vernunft*, p. 101 (Kehrbach). That is the extreme limit of the ethic of duty which Schiller came up against, and which he tried to get round by means of the aesthetic element, that is, through a return to the Platonic *Eros* (*Die ästhetische Erziehung des Menschen*).

once been blinded can never see again; the connexion with God once broken cannot be reunited; the love of God which has been lost cannot be regained. And even if one 'could' do so, one may not. The Gate of Paradise is guarded by the Cherubim with the flaming sword. Above the gate there stand in flaming letters the words: guilt, the wrath of God, the curse of the law. Only he who has fulfilled the whole law is allowed to pass through the gate and enter Paradise, and even the very beginning of this fulfilment is impossible because the 'initial letter,' being-in-the-love-of-God, is absent. How can man as sinner be in the love of God? and how can man love God and his neighbour without being in the love of God? But how can one stand before God without loving God and one's neighbour? That is the vicious circle into which life has been drawn by sin. And this is the un-freedom with which Christian love is concerned.

It is the unfreedom of the *non-posse non-peccare*, the impossibility of not being a sinner. This impossibility is absolute, not relative. This freedom has been unconditionally, wholly lost. But this freedom is the real freedom, for it is that which decides the eternal meaning or non-meaning, the divine destiny of man. Where the divine meaning of existence is known, certainly, compared with the loss of this freedom, whatever freedom remains counts for so little that—in spite of its wealth of secular content—it is described as merely 'formal' freedom, and is denied any essential significance. For the essentially human element is man's relation with God. But the freedom which man still has, even as a sinner, does not suffice to save him from final disaster, from the Judgement and Eternal Death. What meaning is this, which ends in the loss of all meaning? What is a life worth whose result is death? So our first judgement is reversed. We no longer say: every kind of freedom is left to man save one . . . but we now say: man has lost his real freedom. The very fact that he is still a human being qualifies this negation, it is freedom to sin, it is freedom for eternal death.

In face of this situation, the fact that man not only has the capacity to create culture but also that he can still do that which is morally good, is, in the last resort, meaningless. For this morally good, even though it may be of the greatest use for the ordering of human relations, does not come under consideration 'before God,' in the presence of the final court of appeal. Sin, indeed, as we have seen, includes both the morally good and the morally bad. The inmost heart of personality, man's relation with God, has become corrupted, distorted, godless, *cor incurvatum in se ipsum*. Morality does not change this situation in the least. And if it finally alters nothing, then ultimately, it means—*nothing*. It means nothing which alters the negative verdict in the judgement. No 'righteousness of works' avails in the 'sight of God.' This one thing must be expressed before all else, incomparably before all else, as that which faith, and it alone, sees. But it must not be said untruly; it must not be said in such a way that what the actual man really sees and knows to be true is denied. How can good spring from exaggeration, how can untruth help the truth of God? But in any case it must be said so strongly that that particular misunderstanding will be excluded in which the original fall is continually repeated: the liberalistic misunderstanding of human freedom.[1]

For this conception of freedom, which is peculiar to sinful man, is so closely connected with the essence of sin that in touching it one touches sin itself. The false understanding of freedom is the very quintessence of sin. Sin is the desire for freedom and the illusion that it is possible to be free from God. It is this which constantly gives sin its most dangerous power, for it gives it a spiritual imprint, it leads man to imagine that he is obliged to defend one of the supreme goods of humanity against the inhumanity of religion. The seduction of sin springs from the liberalistic understanding of freedom; the humanistic misunderstanding of freedom is based upon the opinion that in the autonomous reason and in

[1] Of course we are not speaking here of political liberalism and its justifiable fight for certain rights of liberty. The liberalistic misunderstanding is that of Pelagianism. Its central statement has been formulated thus by Pelagius: *posse hominem sine peccato esse et dei mandata facile custodire, si vellit* (Harnack, *Dogmengeschichte*, III, 178). Kant expresses the same idea in very much the same way: 'It is still his duty to improve himself and thus he must be able to do so.' (*Religion innerhalb der Grenzen der blossen Vernunft*, p. 42.)

freedom the meaning of human existence, humanity, is being asserted and defended.[1] Hence the anthropological question is so important, so central, because in this self-understanding of man sin reaches its zenith. The most sinful thing in sin is the liberalistic, humanistic illusion of freedom. From it there springs the self-justification of sinful man in the name of the spirit. In the question of freedom, therefore, the decision is made between faith and godlessness; or, interpreted on the side of weakness, in the humanistic understanding of freedom man hides himself from the claim and the judgement of God. For this very reason it is so important not to provide him with a weapon by a false conception of the idea of un-freedom; for nothing makes evil so strong as injustice in fighting against it. On this point a great deal of harm has been done by the Church, and especially by the Reformed Churches, and the same fault is being repeated to-day. The religious truth of the unfreedom of sin is not served by the denial of moral and creative freedom.

4. THE HUMANISTIC OBJECTIONS

The main argument of humanism against the Christian doctrine of unfreedom is that it robs man of his responsibility.[2] If that were true, then at any cost we would all become humanists. For where responsibility is concerned, man and human existence as a whole is at stake. But this reproach is very wide of the mark; the converse indeed is true: it is the Christian Faith alone that in the last resort takes responsibility seriously. In support of this statement we would appeal to all that has already been said in this book. From beginning to end the Christian understanding of man is simply the doctrine of responsibility, and this can be said of the Christian under-

[1] It comes to a head in Cicero's saying: 'One will never thank God for a virtue as though he had received it,' to which the Pauline 'what hast thou that thou didst not receive?' is exactly opposed.

[2] Pelagius says: *si (peccatum) necessitatis est, peccatum non est, si voluntatis, vitari potest. Iterum quaerendum est, utrumne debeat homo sine peccato esse. Procul dubio debet. Si debet, potest, si non potest, ergo non debet* (in Gieseler, *Kirchengeschichte*, I, 2, p. 115). There is undoubtedly logic in the thought of N. Hartmann, namely, that in the interest of freedom (understood in this manner) atheism issues as a postulate.

standing of man alone. But through the Christian doctrine of unfreedom certainly the idea of responsibility gains a new and sinister meaning: guilt. The fact that all that man does in his present state makes him guilty in the sight of God does not remove the fact of responsibility, but it only shows how grave the whole question of responsibility is. We are responsible for the fact that we are what we are: sinners. We are responsible for the division which is the incurable disease which affects our whole life; we are responsible for the judgement which is passed upon us.

The second argument of Humanism against Christianity is as follows: if man's situation really were what Christians say it is, then all his actions would have no value at all. If he can do nothing but sin—what is the good of anything that he does? What shall we say in reply? We affirm the premises and deny the conclusion. Certainly, apart from God man can do nothing but sin—*per definitionem.* But there is something else that he can do, and this he ought to do—he can and should believe, that is, turn away from his false freedom and return to union with God.[1] That is the content of the Word of God which in Jesus Christ is addressed to him.[2] It is a Word calling him to repentance, to turn away from his false independence, and to return to the divine love offered to him in this Word. Within the godless state, it is true, there is no other alternative, sin is inevitable; but there is the alternative of returning to God in faith. The situation in which the Christian message places us is not that there is no other alternative, but that the alternative is: sin or faith; it is no longer virtue or vice, to do good or evil in the ethical sense of the word. The fact that man as sinner still has his existence-in-decision comes out positively in the fact that man is claimed for the Word of God, that faith is not possible save through the decision of man. In spite of the fact that faith is the gift of God, it is also true that faith is also human decision, and

[1] Luke xv. 18.

[2] The ability to believe may not be severed from the Word which creates this ability, nor denied by the reflection that this ability has been given. Cf. Appendix III, pp. 527 ff. Faith is indeed in itself the recognition that all that we are able to do comes from God.

indeed decision pure and simple, given by God, but a decision given by God through His claim on the human will. We shall be dealing further with this point later on.

The third argument of the Humanistic doctrine of freedom against the Christian doctrine of unfreedom is this: through it the Good that is in all, and especially in man, above all in his spiritual life, is depreciated. This assertion rests upon a misunderstanding. The truth that we are sinners does not in any way exclude the truth that there is much good in human life, both physically and spiritually as well as morally.[1] The reproach which is levelled at us by the Bible is not that we value this good but that we do not understand that it is the gift of the Creator, and that we do not see that by our sin we spoil it. The man who interprets his freedom in a humanistic sense is not a true protector and preserver of that Good, but one who destroys it. His false will for independence sows the seeds of disintegration in all the relationships of life. Through his severance from the will of God culture becomes an idol, the spirit becomes abstract and impersonal, desire becomes spiritless and lawless, the erotic becomes a demonic force and destroys marriage at its roots. In quite a different fashion from the emancipated human being the man who lives in the love of God would be in a position to make the earth subject to him, to order life, and to bring meaning and unity into the whole of the spiritual and cultural life of man. It is true that the culture we know is always impregnated with sin and therefore the judgement of God must fall upon it. But this does not mean that from the point of view of God as faith knows Him, culture, creative life, the life of the mind and spirit, is denied.

The final argument returns to the beginning: the Christian doctrine of unfreedom destroys the dignity of man. In point of fact the truth is the exact opposite. The Christian faith, or rather Christ grasped by faith, restores the human dignity which had been destroyed by sin. Certainly, if human dignity is the same as independence of God, then of course the Christian faith destroys human dignity from top to bottom. But that is only a false dignity, arrogance based upon a lie,

[1] On the recognition of a moral Good (*justitia civilis*) see above p. 153.

which always necessarily produces as its counterpart, as a reaction—cynicism. There is no other human dignity than this, that we are called to be the children of God. Where this vocation is accepted in faith, there arrogance and cynicism cease, there man receives a new pride and a new humility at the same time, the pride and the humility of one to whom God's love is given and who is called to communion with God. And in this he receives a new freedom, the 'glorious liberty of the children of God.'[1]

5. POINTS OF DIVERGENCE FROM THE TRADITIONAL DOCTRINE

But even if the objections of Humanism do not touch the substance of the Christian faith, still they are *partially* justified in the light of the historic form of the Christian doctrine. The way in which the Church has spoken about sin and unfreedom is not altogether free from the blame imputed to it in the never-ceasing protest of Humanism. By this I do not mean merely the occasional deflection of the doctrine of unfreedom into deterministic formulas, as happened especially with the Reformers when they were writing against Humanism, but the ecclesiastical doctrine of Original Sin as a whole. Through its historizing form, by which Adam and the man of the present day—in spite of the opposite intention—were severed from each other, and by its logical emphasis upon the idea of heredity, the Christian doctrine has been coloured by naturalistic and deterministic ideas quite alien to the thought of the Bible. The ambiguous idea of 'nature' has also helped to foster this way of thinking. The idea of 'sinful nature,' rightly understood the same as 'sinful being,' received an additional naturalistic meaning which greatly obscured the character of sin as decision. To be a sinner fell into the sphere of natural categories, and in so doing lost the plain meaning which it has in the Bible, that of being-in-decision. The Reformers were aware of this difficulty, and continually, by the idea of the sinful *person* and by the indication of our co-responsibility for the act of Adam, restored their Biblical content to the words 'sin' and 'sinner'; but for the reasons

[1] Rom. viii. 21.

which have been mentioned above they were not wholly successful.

The present tendency to re-emphasize the most massive formulas of the ecclesiastical tradition does not help us to deal adequately with the task which is set before us to-day. The immense influence which is being wielded to-day by deterministic thought lays upon us the sacred duty of finding a form for the idea of un-freedom which will not be open to the charge of having slipped into determinism. I do not venture to think that in this book I have been completely successful in this attempt; rather I believe that this can only succeed with the co-operation of the best forces at our disposal. It is already a great thing that at least we see clearly what should be done and that we admit it frankly.

CHAPTER XII

THE INDIVIDUAL AND THE COMMUNITY

I. INDIVIDUAL AND INDIVIDUALITY

We are mainly aware of the problem of the 'individual and the community' as a problem of ethics.[1] In the midst of the welter of practical problems at the present day, the following questions are central: Is individualism or collectivism to prevail, the right of the individual personality or the right of the social entities: the State, the family, society? The freedom and independence of the individual, or the higher authority of the 'whole,' to which the individual must submit? These questions are at the heart of all our modern problems, in politics and economics as well as in the sphere of private and personal life; everywhere they raise passionate discussion, and cause terrible conflict and suffering. But behind the ethical and practical problems there lie anthropological views, doctrines, and axioms. It is from them that the practical postulates are inferred. Behind Socialism or Communism, as well as behind the Totalitarianism of the State, and the programme of the Corporative State, there lie definite views of man from which the practical demands derive their power and justification. Is man essentially an individual or a collective being? Is his destiny, his dignity, his value, collective and social, or is it rather individual and personal? This is the question with which this chapter will deal; the ethical implications of this subject, although, indirectly, they give special point and force to our question, do not come under our purview. Does a characteristic view of the relation of the individual to the community arise from the standpoint of the Christian Faith? Or, to put it more exactly, Is there a characteristically Christian view of individual and social existence? Once again we must start from the highest point, from Jesus Christ, from the creation of man in the Word of God, in order that we may outline a doctrine of the relation between the individual and the community

[1] Cf. my ethics, *Das Gebot und die Ordnungen*, pp. 277 ff. (English version: *The Divine Imperative*, pp. 293 ff.)

which is not based on side-issues, but upon fundamental Christian truth.

Man has been created in and for the Word of God, and this makes him the being who is responsible. This fact unmistakably determines man as an individual. Responsibility is that which sets the individual as individual apart and makes him indedendent. Masses, collectives, species have no responsibility; they are not capable of assuming responsibility. The individual alone can decide in a responsible manner; in the strict sense of the word, the individual alone can be made responsible for anything. Even collective responsibilities are based upon the responsibilities of individuals. It is no doubt possible to extract a pledge from a community, but in the last resort this rests on individual guarantors. No romantic theory of the supra-personal subject—the 'spirit of a people,' the 'soul of a nation,' etc.—can blind our eyes to the fact that where decisions have to be made it is always the individual person alone who is concerned; his mind, his will is the source of all decisions. To the extent in which the Christian faith intensifies the content and the value of responsibility, as compared with the ordinary idea of responsibility, the content and the value of individual existence is also intensified.

At first sight individual existence, or 'being an individual,' seems to have nothing to do with responsibility. There are individual sheep which form one flock, or individual stones in a wall, or individual molecules in an atom, as well as individual human beings. Individual existence, in contradistinction from individual distinctiveness, which will be discussed in the next chapter,[1] that is, the fact that 'this' is not the same as 'that,' the fact that two things are not the same in contrast to the fact that they are not alike, is primarily a definition of all that exists, of all that is actual, in contrast to all that is merely thought. We think of all atoms of hydrogen as the same, yet each one is separated from the other by the fact that, although it is not different, it is still another. The difference between unlike and like is a relative difference, that

[1] In order to prevent the confusion of that which is not the same with that which is not like, Natorp has introduced the concept of individuation; unfortunately this has not been taken up.

between not the same and the same is an absolute difference. 'This' is absolutely not 'that,' neither more nor less. Thus this exclusive identity with itself, this unconditioned self-sameness, seems to refer, without any distinction, both to the realm of things and to that of spiritual existence. It was this thought which led Democritus to describe the atom with the conception with which we describe the independently existent as such: *in-dividuum, ἄτομον*.

And yet selfsameness, or the fact that 'this is I and not another,' that 'I alone among all these billions of individuals of all kinds am myself, identical with nothing but myself,' this fact that no human being can be exchanged for or confused with any other, has a quite different meaning in man from that which it has anywhere else; and only in the Christian faith, in existence in the Word of God, does this idea gain its full content.

Even an atom of hydrogen or a proton is 'this' particular atom, and no other. But it does not itself know that it cannot be exchanged for any other; the gulf between it and the other, the exclusive selfsameness and non-identity with any other, does not become actual. Also, so far as its content is concerned, it is entirely unimportant. What does the difference between atom number one and atom number two matter? What value has the difference between oak-leaf *a* and oak-leaf *b*? The fact that one cannot be exchanged for another plays no part in this, neither objectively nor subjectively. But as soon as consciousness and will of some kind are added to mere being, the fact that 'this' cannot be confused with 'that' begins to matter. It is important to this particular sparrow that *he*, and not that fellow over there, should be able to carry off this tasty crumb! He pushes the other aside. It is true that this atom here pushes the other aside; in spatial reality there is no interpenetration. That which is 'here' is not 'there,' and that which is 'there' is not 'here.' The fact that this is here prevents the other from being here too. But this 'pushing aside' is unconscious and unimportant. It gains importance only when it is conscious, and it becomes conscious only when it is important. Sparrow *a* does not allow himself to be confused with sparrow *b*; he 'protests' if he cannot get 'his' due.

But not only does this knowledge of exclusive identity with oneself become fully conscious in man alone, and therefore fully determines the will to self-existence, but here both gain an entirely new content, which makes the gulf which separates 'me-here' from 'you-there' infinitely more profound. From the point of view of man, all that cannot be exchanged in the 'lower' order of being seems unimportant, because it is valueless. The value resides in the fact that it is so, not that it is 'this-here.' It does not matter to me whether the gardener cuts this rose or that for me, if the one is as beautiful as the other. Just as it is a matter of indifference to me which particular copy of a particular book the bookseller gives me—all, as machine-products, are completely alike—so is it ultimately with all 'thing'-existence and 'natural' existence. In so far as we are not concerned with individual differences, non-identity plays no part. The individual members of the same species can be exchanged for one another; the fact that they have no metaphysical exchangeability, which is not denied, is unimportant. They are examples in which the species alone counts. The sheep *a*, *b*, *c*, are examples of the herd, of the whole species. So long as the condition is fulfilled that they belong to the species of sheep which are 'beautiful, fat, have plenty of wool, etc.,' the individual sheep does not count.

Only in man is it different. In so far indeed as a human being stands out above others by his talents or his genius, we are still on the natural plane, although here, through the differentiation of individualization, classes shrivel up into individuals. A genius like Rubens only occurs once, although Rubens is not the highest type of genius. But this kind of uniqueness is only relative, as we see at once in the case of mere 'talent.' 'Talents' are possessed by all kinds of people. But the transition from talent to genius is a relative one; thus the fact that the genius cannot be exchanged for any other is also something relative. The value of genius is a value of individuality, hence it is relative, like all that is connected with individuality.[1]

[1] The next chapter deals with this more fully.

2. THE GROUND OF SELF-VALUE

Where personal value is concerned the situation is quite different. This is absolute. It makes no difference to the gardener if I desire 'one of his roses.' But if I go to a father and say that I desire 'one of his daughters' for my wife, because 'they are all the same to me,' the father, and above all each of the daughters, has a right to be offended! The human person, as person, cannot possibly be exchanged for anyone else; the person is not an example of a species, he is unconditionally this person and no one else. To the manufacturer, it is true, it is a matter of indifference who tends the machine, if only the person who does so does his job properly; he is exchangeable. The manufacturer, as manufacturer, has no personal relation with the man who tends the machine; for him, this workman is simply—to use the honest English phrase—a 'hand.' But while the workman may possibly accept this position so far as his labour-relation is concerned, yet, so long as he still has a spark of human dignity, as a human being he does not admit in the slightest that he could be 'exchanged' for anyone else. He knows this: 'as a human being I cannot be exchanged for any other, although as a "hand" I may be'; the more 'personal' relations become, the more it is recognized that one human being cannot be 'exchanged' for another. 'No one is indispensable' is the language of impersonal thinking. 'No one can be replaced,' is the language of personal thinking. As person man is unconditionally and exclusively this particular person and no other.

But what is the deepest reason for, and the full content of, this truth that persons cannot be exchanged? of this unconditional, non-relative value of the self? The 'natural man' cannot really give any answer to this question. He appeals to the idea of personal being, of personal human existence; but he cannot adduce any reason why self-existence should be unconditional; for it is not derived from the idea of reason as such.[1] If man is person only as the bearer of reason, or as

[1] In his idea of the monads Leibniz made this absolute distinction of one individual from another as such the fundamental principle of his metaphysic. It is no accident that Greek philosophy does not know this

self-conscious mind, then his being as person is *not*[1] selfness which cannot be exchanged. Then all that matters is 'spirit in general,' 'reason in general'; the individual existence as such has no significance. Thus in the philosophy of reason, for instance in Hegel, we see how little significance is ascribed to personal self-existence. This consciousness of the unconditional value of the person as person cannot be derived from any rational philosophy. Where, however, there is some feeling for this, there is—though more potential than actual—a recollection of the Origin in the Creation.

I am a self, I, as this particular person, cannot be exchanged for any other, simply and solely because God, the Self-personal, knows me, this person as this person, because He 'called me by my name,'[2] when He created me,[3] because He loves me, not as an example of a species, but as this particular human being, from all eternity, and destines *me*, not humanity as a whole, for an eternal goal, namely, for a personal end, for communion with Himself, the Creator, because He values me unconditionally and will never exchange me for any other, because He never confuses me with any other, nor depreciates me at the cost of someone else, because He gives me this supremely personal life in His supremely personal Word of election.[4] In the electing word of God I have my person, my self. The divine eternal election is the ground, and indeed the sole and sufficient ground, of my unconditional self-value. There is no personal value in itself,[5] but the value of the person

idea; it is only possible from the point of view of the Christian conception of personality, even though in the thought of Leibniz it has not the full content of the Christian idea of personality.

[1] The whole of Idealism, from Plato down to Hegel, has not been able to give a metaphysical basis for the individual personality as such. Leibniz is an exception; but in his system the distinctive element of personality is made questionable by the idea of continuity—the merely relative distinction of the human personal-monad and the sub-human atom-monad. This cannot be otherwise because Leibniz does not start from the personal will of God as love, but from the mere consciousness or 'imagination.'

[2] Isa. xl. 1; xlv. 4. [3] Psa. cxxxix. 13 ff. [4] Gal. i. 15.

[5] Nygren is justified in objecting to Harnack's doctrine of the 'infinite value of the human soul,' because it suggests that it is this 'value' which is the object of the love of God (*Eros und Agape*, p. 62). But it is true to say that *through* the divine love the human soul gains this infinite value.

as person is based upon the fact that man has been created in the personal word of God. This alone is the reason why I am not an example of a species, a number, but that in the unconditional sense I am an individual. The metaphysical self-sameness which is also ascribed to the atom only becomes the self-sameness of the person where its value is unconditional and its consciousness absolute: in the value posited by God and in God's consciousness. 'What is man that Thou art mindful of him? And the son of man that Thou visitest him?'[1]

Through this personal call of God, however, our responsibility also becomes unconditional, and in the consciousness of this unconditional responsibility our personal being, the unique character of our existence, becomes clear to us. That to which God calls me from all eternity, He has not called another; and to that, in all eternity, He will not call another. He gives me an unconditional 'calling' which cannot be exchanged for any other; that which through His gift is my task[2] no other person, in even the very least degree, can take away from me. Neither the Platonist nor the Stoic nor the Neo-platonist philosophy knows this independence.[3] This independence, this impossibility of exchanging the task appointed for one's life, is the correlate of the Christian idea of Election and Creation; thus we see that where the Christian faith declines, this sense of value which cannot be exchanged for any other, and this sense of responsibility which cannot be handed over to anyone else, also disappears. The fact that I, unconditionally, must remain at my post, and that no other can take my place—even when in the technical sense of the word there are plenty of competent people who would be well able to replace me—this sense of the seriousness of my calling can only be understood from the point of view of the personal call of God. This independence, this absolute impossibility of

[1] Psa. viii.

[2] The usual play on the words *Gabe* (gift) and *Aufgabe* (task).—*Translator.*

[3] Plato clearly recognizes a certain differentiation among human beings; it lies at the basis of his order of classes. But it is at the same time a metaphysical inequality in value. The Stoics remove this inequality in value in the concept of Reason which is everywhere the same, but with it there disappears the differentiation of the life-calling in an abstract, non-historical idea of humanity.

being exchanged for anyone else, creates an absolute isolation. This emerges, above all, in the idea that I must come before the Judge of the world quite alone. There, as Kierkegaard puts it, all corporate life ceases and I am unconditionally: this individual. Here is absolute, eternal, fathomless solitude, here too no Christian fellowship is any help—we do not pray for the dead!—here am I, quite alone, in the presence of God, face to face; alone. As I myself must believe, must decide,[1] as I myself must hear the electing Word, the Call of God—and no Church, no priest, no Pope, and indeed no word of the Bible can take from me my responsibility for listening to this call—so I myself must stand before the Judge; and no other can take my place—none save Himself, the merciful God, who Himself provides the 'Advocate.'[2] So solitary, so absolutely independent does the Christian faith make us.

3. SELF-RESPONSIBILITY AND ITS NEGATION

It is not only in faith that man possesses this self-responsibility. As we have already said, whether he will or no man must always answer for himself. Even if he evades his responsibility, even if he throws responsibility on to the shoulders of other people, even when he says, 'I do not know what the situation is—the priest, the Church, the Pope, must decide this for me, or Fate, or the future, or death, or something else will decide it,' yet it is he himself who speaks thus; and in the Judgement he himself will have to bear the responsibility for this decision. No one can escape from his responsibility, not even when he denies it. His denial of responsibility is a responsible action; it is 'up to him' to see whether he can really be responsible for it! Man must take a position, and he does so even when he refuses to take one. Even his refusal is his 'position.' Even when he hides himself behind collectives, and hands over his responsibility to them, he does this upon his own responsibility.[3] He must be responsible for it at the last

[1] Catholic doctrine, and still more Catholic practice, does not dare to place the individual over against God Himself; hence the mediators and mediations; hence too their prayers for the dead.

[2] 1 John ii. 1.

[3] No one has said this so urgently as Kierkegaard (cf. now: Buber, *Die Frage an den Einzelnen*). This has no connexion with either individualism or

Judgement; he must be responsible for it every day of his life before the God who has created and called him, even when he denies Him and will not listen to His Call. Just as the factory whistle calls the lazy and careless worker who does not wish to hear it—and he is held responsible even when he asserts that he did not hear it—so also the call to responsibility comes to every human being, and it is 'reckoned' to him even when he ignores it.[1]

This responsibility is the basis of our freedom. No one can rob me of this power of deciding for myself. No one can force me to say 'yes'; the Power which alone could do so will not do so, because He waits for my personal answer. No human being, no creature has any power over my decision; to me alone has God given this power of personal decision;[2] He has given me this power through the Creation, and He continually gives it to me afresh through His Call to responsibility. The moment that I could no longer hear the Call of God, when the knowledge of the law of God would be completely eliminated, I would cease to be a human being at all. I would still be, it is true, an example of the species *homo sapiens*, but I would no longer be *humanus*. The peculiar element, the specific element of the species *homo sapiens* is this, that it is not a species in which the individual is an example, but *humanitas*, in which the individual is person. It belongs therefore to the peculiarity of this 'species' that the individual is able to abandon it and to deny it, that—at least within certain limits—he can become an 'in-human' human being. That is the dangerous freedom which belongs to this independence.

Humanly speaking—must not the hand of God have trembled

subjectivism; for to this certainty of the individual there belong as correlates the objective revelation and the community. It is true that in the thought of Kierkegaard the idea of 'community' does not get a fair deal, but in principle it is included in his category of 'the individual.'

[1] Rom. i. 21; ii. 14 ff.

[2] The ἀντεξούσιον plays a great part in the doctrine of the Early Church; but as a rule it is understood in a rationalistic and individualistic way, from the point of view of the rational *imago*-concept (Justin, *Apol.*, II, 14; Iren., IV, 4.3; Tertullian, *c. Marc.*, II, 5; Joh. Damasc., II, 12). Cf. Engelhardt, *Die Gottesbildlichkeit des Menschen* in *Jahrbücher für deutsche Theologie*, 1870, p. 31.

when He created man with this independence? For—apart from the angels, of whom we know practically nothing from experience, and very little more from the Bible[1]—it is the most dangerous, and indeed the only dangerous element which God has created.[2] He created that by means of which His Creation, although not destroyed, could still be spoilt and distorted. The fact that man has been made in the image of God has really 'gone to the head' of the man who decides independently, and has made him mad. Man has turned the word of the Creator, 'You must yourself say "yes"; I will not force you,' into, 'I can say "yes" or "no," just as I will.' Man has turned, 'you can and you ought to decide,' into, 'I can myself determine.' Man turns the independence checked by God's determination into an independence which knows no bounds; thus he turns genuine responsibility into a sham responsibility, or self-responsibility. In modern man, in particular, this sin reappears in its original form; genuine responsibility is replaced by self-responsibility, the idea that 'I owe it to myself.' Man only owes himself anything because he alone owes himself to God.

The 'misunderstanding of the reason with itself,' the primal sin, is the misunderstanding of independence. This misunderstanding comes out as a misunderstanding and a lie in the fact that through this presumptuous independence man does not become free or independent, but, on the contrary, he becomes enslaved and dependent. Promethean defiance drives man either into madness, or into the most wretched bondage to the world and to men, or into both at the same time. In the last resort how false was the prophetic independence of Nietzsche! How even this Titan longed, in his solitude, for human recognition; how easily his pride was offended, and

[1] On the doctrine of Angels, see below, p. 414 (n. 2).

[2] In this emphasis upon the freedom of "being made in the Image of God" lies the point of greatest nearness and at the same time of contrast to Berdyaev's profound Christian Gnosticism; his doctrine of the 'eternal birth of God out of groundlessness' (*Bestimmung des Menschen*, p. 47), of 'uncreated freedom,' of the non-being which precedes being (p. 80), and the emphasis upon the creative element as that which is distinctively human (p. 51), show the typically Gnostic-dualistic features which mar what is otherwise a deeply Christian view.

how unhappy was his solitude! And yet he was a rare and exceptional case. For the majority of men break away from their connexion with God in order to give themselves up to some pleasure or ambition, to the satisfaction of strangely inhuman, enslaving passions, or to some kind of infatuation. Schiller's saying, 'Tremble before the slave when he breaks his fetters, but not before the free man,' is deeper than he knew. This revolt of the slave is the sin of emancipation. But the only free man, whom there is no need to fear, is the man living in man's Origin, the man who possesses a truly royal freedom, whom humanity has beheld once, and once only.

The man who has become alienated from God lost his true independence when he lost his self which was made in the image of God.[1] His independence, in the strict sense of the word 'exaggerated' independence, the 'desire to stand independently over against God,' actually makes him dependent. He falls a prey to the world, he becomes the slave of human beings; this is true even when he appears to rise above them and to dominate and control them. The apparently independent, dominating man can no more exist without those whom he dominates than the herd-man without the herd. The 'free spirits' have always been dependent in the highest degree on the recognition of an *élite*. The love of fame and the vanity of 'independent' people, of geniuses and individualists, is well known. Most people, however, live in dependence on the collective body, on 'one'[2] in all its[3] forms, on the spirit of the age, on the fashion, on that which 'one' says, thinks and wills. But the moment that a human being begins to live with God, he first awakens to independence, to his own responsibility, to his own powers of thought and will. This, too, is the moment when he begins to know the true meaning of community.

4. VARIOUS FORMS OF ASSOCIATION: COMMUNITY

For this is the paradox of the Christian idea of independence: the same things which give man his absolute value as a self,

[1] Rom. vi. 16, 20; vii. 14. [2] Cf. Heidegger, *Sein und Zeit*, pp. 126 ff.

[3] By '*man*' ('one' or 'they') Heidegger means the easy, shallow life of the average society or business man in Western civilization during a period of prosperity.—*Translator.*

and in so doing make him an individual, in an individualization which cannot be compared with any other, also place him just as absolutely in community, and give him an incomparable association with others.

All that actually exists, in spite of the gulf which lies between 'this' and 'that,' is connected existence. The atom is 'here' and not 'there,' it is true; and where it is, there is no other. And yet, in a *coincidentia oppositorum* which can never be completely understood, the opposite also holds good; the atom is always there, where it is not, and 'that' is also where 'this' is. This is the mystery of mutual influence, the invisible bond which binds that which is separated through the separation of space.[1] Even the hard pebble which lies beside its neighbour has a remnant of association, a force of attraction, which, however minute it may be, proceeds from the one to the other. But apart from this minimum we distinguish the living from the dead by the fact that they are outside one another, not in one another, and not with one another.

In the living organism there is the mysterious interconnexion of parts, the union of all to form the whole. By a similar, although far looser bond, living individuals also are connected with each other by community of blood. The hen defends her chickens as her own blood, every mammal watches jealously over her brood, she is bound up with it in the community of life. The animal only knows real community with another being under the influence of man. Man alone knows the union which extends beyond the biological relation of procreation and community of blood, the union of free choice. Only through free decision does living together become community, just as only through the vow of fidelity do two lovers become a married couple. From the point of view of human community all that nature knows as unity may be described as non-community. Community is a specifically human phenomenon. Now what is the basis of genuinely human, genuinely social community? It is not sympathy; for sympathy, while it is certainly a powerful element, is also an unstable and 'partisan' element, which is only able to create an unstable, arbitrary

[1] It is well known that for Lotze it is this enigma of mutual influence which is the metaphysical place of his Idea of God.

and unreliable unity.[1] Even reason does not create real community. Reason may, it is true, create higher 'communities with a special aim in view,' ideal associations, cultural societies and States, but their purpose is not so much union with other persons as the common furtherance of a spiritual cause. The fact that persons come together to do this is a very secondary matter. Greek philosophy regards friendship[2] as the distinctive element in, and, at the same time, the model of community. But owing to the fact that friendship is conditioned by 'value' and by sympathy, on the one hand, and to its exclusiveness on the other, it cannot be taken as the realization of absolute community. Unconditional community is union through that which the New Testament calls 'love.'

5. BASIS OF GENUINE COMMUNITY

God has created man to be a self, an individual, but He did not create him to be alone, to live for and by himself. In the same fact in which He gives him his selfhood, He also gives him his being-in-community: that is, in calling him to His love. God has created man primarily and chiefly for communion with Him, the Creator. Hence in his Origin man is never alone, even when he is 'solitary.' He is always in converse with his Creator. Intercourse with God, genuine prayer, is the vital act of man in his Origin. Prayer is the final and sole confutation of solipsism. That which makes man truly independent is precisely communion with God, just as communion with God only exists in complete independence. Only in communion with God can man realize his independence, his self, for indeed he has his self in God. Thus the realization of the self is identical with complete dependence upon God. 'God is our nearest relation,' is a profound saying of Pestalozzi.

Existence in God, however, as existence in the love of God, is also necessarily existence in love to the whole creation. He who affirms the divine will of the Creator cannot do otherwise

[1] Cf. Max Scheler, *Wesen und Formen der Sympathie* and *Der Formalismus in der Ethik*. The boundary of the personalism of Scheler (of that period!) is his idea of God and of love determined by Neo-platonism (*Eros*).

[2] Typical of this is the Aristotelian conception of friendship. Above p. 231.

than love God's creatures, because God loves them. God has created man not only for communion with Himself, but also for communion with his fellow-creatures. He has created man, from the very outset, not only as an individual, but as a member of the most comprehensive human community. Election, as the call out of the world to Himself, is at the same time that which calls human beings together, the κλῆσις is necessarily connected with the ἐκκλησία, its correlate.[1] The goal to which God calls the individual, and to which one comes only as an 'individual,' as one who is responsible for himself, as one who answers for himself, is the Kingdom of God. Thus the obverse of Divinely given responsibility is the most universal and absolute community which we can imagine. Responsible existence is communal existence; existence connected with community; love, in the New Testament meaning of love.[2]

6. COMMUNITY AND SELF-EXISTENCE

Accordingly, man can only be fully 'himself' when he lives in love. Only in love does man do what he does quite willingly. Apart from love he is always under some kind of compulsion, either of natural law or moral law. There are many kinds of compulsion, even of spiritual compulsion; from the compulsion of physiological automatisms to the compulsion of passion, of the artistic or scientific desire to create, of the emotional experience of ecstasy. But none of these varieties of compulsion is accompanied by complete willingness; likewise in none of these varieties of compulsion is the action and existence of man fully personal. Love alone is a completely willing compulsion, and therefore fully personal existence and action. 'In obedience I always felt my soul most beautifully free,' says Iphigenia in Goethe's poem. But only in the love of God, which lays hold of us in Christ, is this love which is wholly obedient and wholly free. 'Where the Spirit of the Lord is there is liberty';[3] but this spirit is the Holy Spirit,

[1] Therefore in his *Genesis* lecture Luther makes the Church begin in Paradise (WA. 42, 72).

[2] The Christian idea of *agape* is as different from every other idea of love as the message of the Cross is different from all mythology and philosophy.

[3] 2 Cor. iii. 17.

the love of God which is shed abroad in our hearts.[1] It is the same Spirit who creates the 'Christian community,' that kind of union in which alone it is fully true that one member suffers and rejoices with the other,[2] because they are all joined to one another and to the Head in a living whole,[3] where individuals grow like the branches in the Vine[4] in Him who gives them the common life.

All that is human is disposed for this community by the Creator. God has created man in such a way that the individual can only become 'I' through the 'other,' that the 'I' can only become the 'I' through the 'Thou.' The husband can only become truly husband through his wife, the child gives paternal character to the father.[5] It is only because we are made for one another that the values of the individual differences develop in such a fashion that the peculiar quality of the individual members is determined by their functions for the organism as a whole. Human life is intended to be a mutual exchange in giving and receiving; it is thus that it is consummated when man lives in contact with his Divine Origin, hence, too, it is consummated in the 'communion of saints.' This is the *communio sanctorum*, which is also a *participatio omnium bonorum*. Only in such community can true independence be developed.[6]

That is the basis of that fundamental law of the Gospel which sounds such a paradox: 'For whosoever would save his life shall lose it; and whosoever shall lose his life for My sake shall find it.'[7] Personality and sacrifice, and indeed, self-

[1] Cf. Luther: 'Let *charitatem* not be such a mean thing, *quia charitas* is God Himself. . . . Hence he who has love must have God and be full of Him' (WA. 36, 422, 427). Love is the Holy Spirit Himself: Rbr. II, 140, 20 ff.

[2] I Cor. xii. 26. [3] Eph. iv. 15. [4] John xv. 4.

[5] This dependence on the other is not Gogarten's discovery, it is true—for Buber and Ebner preceded him in this—but it was first perceived in its significance for the whole Christian message by Gogarten in his book, *Ich glaube an den dreieinigen Gott*, and still more clearly in *Glaube und Wirklichkeit*. Cf. Cullberg, op. cit., p. 74.

[6] Luther: 'I believe that in this community or Christendom all things are common, and each one owns the other's goods and no one has anything of his own' (WA. 7, 219; WA. 6, 131). In Althaus, *Communio sanctorum*.

[7] Matt. xvi. 25.

sacrifice, belong to one another. The only authentic exposition of the real nature of love is that which was given by Him who desired nothing for Himself, and gave His life 'a ransom for many.' True independence is realized in self-denial. But true self-denial must not be confused with the morbid desire for suffering (masochism). Genuine love is characterized by a strict sobriety, which challenges the one for whose sake one makes the sacrifice, summoning him to follow and to repent. Self-denial does not mean throwing oneself away; it is not renunciation of the value of one's own existence—not even the value of one's physical existence. Love seeks not her own, but 'the good of her neighbour'; yet she does not throw away 'her own.' She does not defend it as justice does, since the latter measures its claims according to a rational principle of equality; she realizes her own when of her own free will, in view of the divine End, she goes forth to meet the other to the very limits of self-emptying. She does not make a rigid line of demarcation between what belongs to herself and to the other, but she lives in the other, as a member of the body in which she herself is a member. She knows no other sacrifice than that which takes place in truth, and for the sake of truth, which also includes the 'Thou.' Love combines the strictest sobriety with supreme emphasis upon personality.

Hence love is the opposite of 'being in love.' Those who are 'in love' are possessive; this state is an ecstatic form of self-love. To be 'in love' means the loss of independence, whereas love is precisely its assertion. 'Being in love' is to be enslaved; it is a binding dependence upon the other, but love is free self-positing in perceiving the claim of God which meets us in the other. Love is the highest act of the spiritual personality, but 'being-in-love' is being enslaved to the other by instinct.

7. COLLECTIVISM

Just as the destiny for selfhood may be misunderstood, so also the destiny for community may be misunderstood. A misunderstanding of this kind is collectivism in all its forms, the subordinating of personal being to natural or abstract spiritual forces. Collectivism is a perversion of the hierarchical divine order of being, which subordinates everything, the natural and the spiritual, to personal being. The possibility of such perversion consists in the fact that man has both a bodily and a spiritual nature. This nature—the spiritual as well as the physical—places him within a supra-individual context which constitutes the basis of his personal existence, which is its presupposition, but, as such, is subordinate to it. The individual human being comes into existence in connexion with the life of nature, and especially in connexion with the life of the human species. Through vital connexions, through sexual union, the family, the clan, the people and the race, the individual existence ascends towards its personal destiny. As person the individual frees himself from these ties of blood. Where this process of emancipation is hindered or arrested by the super-ordination of that which is subordinate, by the elevation of that which is a means to be a self-end, the personal is swallowed up in the natural existence; community becomes natural collectivism. Something similar occurs where the artificial ties which have been, and must be, created for the preservation of life, the associations of civilization, the economic order and society, are turned from means into super-ordinated ends, where personal community is subordinated to or sacrificed to the impersonal process of socialization. A kind of collectivism also arises where human personal life is subordinated to its spiritual means, its culture and the institutions which serve it, where the individual is regarded merely as so much compost to enrich the cultural dung-heap.[1] This occurs in the most dangerous manner where the most powerful of all forms of community, the State—in whose formation both spirit and nature participate equally, which arises equally out of vital and spiritual connexions, the associations of blood as well as of ideas—claims to be the self-end of human existence; that is, where man becomes a mere instrument for the purpose of the State. The State has the power to crush the personal life utterly. As an absolute state it misuses the sovereign power which is granted to it for the protection of

[1] Cf. Berdyaev's 'idolization of the collective' in *Fate of Man in the Modern World*, pp. iii ff.

the personal life, to annihilate it. But we must not forget that it is always man who wills a collective of this kind. The State is not a natural product but an historical entity; it is the fruit of human decision and human action. It is never a disastrous Fate without being at the same time disastrous sin.

Still more terrible, however, than this injurious demonic influence over the community by the State, is the danger to the soul from the side of the Church. In the New Testament the Church is never anything other than the community of believers, based upon the divine election, and granted to man in his effective calling. *Est autem ecclesia communio sanctorum. . . .* Hence in the genuine Church nothing and no one has authority save 'the Head,' Jesus Christ, His own spirit, His own Word; no priest, and also no synod, no confession or dogma, not even the Holy Scriptures; the latter has authority only in so far as it is the Word of God, not in itself, and therefore never as an entity which is at the disposal of theology or ecclesiastical law. Clericalism, however, makes the means which Jesus Christ uses to rule His Church into self-sufficient idolatrous authorities: either those of a sacerdotal hierarchy, or of a dogmatic orthodoxy. They set up an interim-court taking the place of the Word of God but clothed with divine authority—a Pope, a dogma—by which necessarily the Church becomes a collective body rather than a community, which suppresses or spoils the order of the Holy Spirit in order to make room for the secular laws of an ecclesiastical code and a scientific theology. It is not the ecclesiastical office, nor the function of the *Credo* which we question, but the fact that they are clothed with absolute divine authority, binding on the conscience. When this takes place the correlation of the individual and the community is destroyed, and its place is taken by a subordination of the individual to the collective power of the Church. This is the most terrible thing that can ever happen; the sanctuary itself has been defiled; it has been infected with the demonic.

8. THE UNDERSTANDING OF COMMUNITY OUTSIDE THE CHRISTIAN FAITH

Now from this point of view it is also possible to perceive the alternatives to the Christian understanding of self-existence and existence-in-community in all their extent and significance. Naturalism in all its forms knows no independence of the individual at all. To it the category of 'the individual' is a closed book, for it knows man only as a member of a species. Humanity is only a branch on the Tree of Life as a whole, a special zoological species. Naturalism does not possess the pre-supposition for the recognition of a self-existence, namely, knowledge of freedom, of responsibility. In place of the recognition of the self-existence of the individual it sets individuality, as, indeed, individuality is that which is characteristic of all natural existence. Individuality, however, is the correlate to the universal which characterizes the species.

Hence Naturalism understands man's being, essentially, as a collective entity. As in animal life, so here too, in the life of man, everything is directed towards the preservation of the species. The individual has no self-end, his end is absorbed in the purpose of the species. The meaning of life is adaptation to biological and other existing conditions, mainly the adaptation of the needs of the individual to the needs of the species. Morality—in so far as this is considered at all—law, civilization, and culture are said to be derived from this source. The conscience and the religious consciousness are regarded as the hypostatization of this purpose of the species. Actually, however, the product of such a view will be neither morality, nor culture, nor religion; at its best it would only produce a utilitarian kind of civilization. The exposure of the individual and his independence to an extremely sterile collectivism would be unavoidable.

In Idealism the problem is posed quite differently. The main thought of Idealism gives rise to very different possibilities of relating the individual and the community to each other; as indeed in Plato we have already seen the development of two different ideals of life, an individualistic and a collectivistic, alongside of one another, even though in a clear gradation.[1] There is an Idealism of freedom, in which the independence of the individual as the bearer of spirit is the higher end. Its conception of personality, gained from the moral law, is sufficient to serve as a basis for and to postulate a claim of this kind

[1] Cf. Groethuysen, op. cit., p. 29, *Die beiden anthropologischen Typen.*

for the individual personality. Thus there arises the view of life of idealistic individualism. The individual as the bearer of reason contains within himself all that is essential for a human existence. In the last resort he has no need of the other. The sage, to whom the vision of the divine Ideas is the real content of life, or the free spiritual personality which shapes itself and its life according to the commands of reason, has no primary necessary relation to community, but on the contrary, as Plato's *Phaedo* shows, the tendency towards isolation, the desire to be alone.[1] The creative artist, as such, also has no need of community. 'A talent is cultivated in quietness,' the creative person is not directly connected with others in his work itself. But through his creative work the creative human being always emerges from his solitude, his work means publicity, he needs others to look at and enjoy his work.

Above all, however, to the extent in which the ethical law becomes prominent, our relation to our fellow-man becomes important. The community is here represented in the idea of a humanity ordered by the law of reason, of a 'kingdom of reason.' And yet here, too, there is no real understanding of community. This ethical idealism knows 'justice' it is true; the individual is connected with his fellows by respect; but here, too, there is no genuine community. For the individual persons as such—not merely as bearers of the rational self—are not really united to one another; love is lacking. In the system of the idealism of freedom there is no room for love.[2]

[1] In Plato the link between the purely spiritual existence of the sage and the State is the fact that human life is conditioned by the senses and the body. The State, however, for Plato, as for later Hellenism, is the proper community, the only necessary community, the only one which is to be taken quite seriously. As a purely spiritual community, the only one that could qualify for this was the school based upon the philosophical *Eros* or the circle of friends. Yet in Plato this was scarcely the case. Man as a spiritual being is one who beholds the Ideas, and as such he is solitary.

[2] How little Kant's 'kingdom of ends' (Kehrbach, *Grundlegung zur Metaphysik der Sitten*, second section, p. 70) is really to be regarded as community comes out already in the definition 'systematic association of different rational beings through social laws'; 'it is thus that man necessarily imagines his own existence . . . and it is thus that every other rational being imagines his existence . . .' (p. 65). Man is not man by

Different again is the relation of the individual to the community in the system of objective Idealism. Here it is not the idea of freedom which predominates, but that of the universal life of Spirit, of the 'objective Spirit.' The subject is only—in itself an insignificant—bearer and producer of this spiritual development. The essential bearer of this spiritual being is not the individual but the State; but the State from the spiritual point of view. Over against the ideal of the solitary sage, Plato sets the idea of his State, from which, however, it follows, in the logic of his thought, that in the last resort the State exists for the sake of the sage, and not the sage for the sake of the State. To Plato the community of the State is of less value than the individual's contemplation of the Ideas. In Hegel it is quite plain that the universal outweighs the personal. The personal life is subordinated to the abstract forces of Spirit. In his system of Idealism, 'culture'[1] does not exist for the sake of man, but man for the sake of 'culture,' and indeed above all for the sake of that form of 'culture' in which also the vital element is brought under the domination of Spirit: for the sake of the State.[2] No attempt is made to conceal the fact that the individual life is inferior. Its value is to be measured by the contribution it makes to the development of 'culture'; its significance within spirit as a whole is subordinate, and ultimately—in the eschatology of this idealism—transitory. Only 'Spirit,' not the individual person, has eternal value and eternal continuance. In objective Idealism there is neither a truly personal nor a truly social existence. Both are absorbed in an abstractly impersonal and non-social spirituality. Common participation in a 'culture'

relation to the other, but through the reason which dwells in him, especially through its law. The dependence of the Thou—and thus of the community—moreover becomes plain in Fichte. 'The concept of the Thou arises out of the association of the "It" and the "I"' (*Werke*, III, p. 86); in this derivation no further attention is paid to the Thou. Only later is the Thou understood as a practical postulate of the I. (Cf. Cullberg, op. cit., p. 26.)

[1] *Kultur*.

[2] 'All that man is he owes to the State; in that alone he has his being. All value that man has, all spiritual reality, he has alone through the State,' for the divine element in the State is the moral idea as it exists upon earth (Hegel, *Werke*, ed. Lasson, vol. viii, pp. 90 ff.).

of this kind is not community but—understood as an aim—spiritual unity. Unity, however, is not the consummation but the antithesis of community. This idea of unity corresponds to the monistic fundamental conception: the final reality is the One Spirit, not the 'over-againstness' of a divine person and of human 'creaturely' persons. Objective Idealism is pantheism or monism of the spirit, which knows no personal Other confronting it, but only the merging of all in one Spirit. Here above all it becomes plain that personal being and existence-in-community belong together. As the God of Hegel's philosophy is ultimately impersonal Spirit, so also there is no communion with Him and through Him, but only the disappearance of all that is personal in this All-Spirit. Community and personal selfhood only exist through the fact that the personal God, who in Himself is Person, the Triune God, calls His creatures whom He has created by His word of love—through this word of love—to communion with Himself, and in so doing gives them a community existence, as fellowship with one another, through this love.

CHAPTER XIII

CHARACTER AND VARIETIES OF CHARACTER

I. CHARACTER AS ACT

PERSONAL being, spirit and freedom are definitions which apply to man as man; one participates in each through the mere fact that one has been created a human being. And yet all three are of such a kind that they exclude pure existence. Person, spirit and freedom are only real *in actu*. They include self-knowledge and self-determination. Where we speak of man as 'person,' who has spirit and freedom, we speak of him as of one who necessarily exists in decision. This means that we can take the *fact* of decision for granted; the way in which this takes place and the content of this decision is still open.

Since we have related these three fundamental conceptions of human existence to the contrast between Creation and Sin, the all-important question 'what' and 'how' to decide is already implied in the merely formal fact of decision. Personal being is not an unlimited possibility; on the contrary, it is limited in two directions, by the twofold destiny of Creation and Sin, in the same way in which we saw the same process at work in the conception of the 'un-freedom of the free human being.' Man is still 'in decision' or he would no longer be man; but behind his present acts of decision lies the truth that the fundamental or primal decision has already been made. The quality of this primal decision, its content and its character, is the abiding element in all his further decisions. That is the content of the idea of *peccatum originis*. Both the Divine image which has been imprinted upon man by the Creator, and its destruction by sin, together constitute—without ceasing to be 'act'—the primal act which determines all that follows and the primal imprint of man's nature.[1]

[1] Kant distinguishes between the empirical character, which is the object of perception, and as such strictly causally determined, and the intelligible character which 'indeed can never be known directly because we can perceive nothing save in so far as it appears, but yet must be thought in accordance with the empirical character' (Kehrbach, *Kritik der*

But this imprint is common to all men; every man is 'Adam,' the creature who has been made in the image of God, and has fallen away from God. But if we pursue this thought further and are confronted by the great variety in human beings, then, as we know from experience, it is fatally easy to leap directly from the realm of spirit into that of nature, and to conceive that which distinguishes men—who are all 'Adam'—from one another, simply as the differentiation of the natural individuality. In so doing, however, not only is an important middle term ignored, but the personal being of the actual man is denuded of its concreteness. The individual human being would then be, on the one hand, from the point of view of God, a being made in the image of God and a sinner, and on the other hand, from the point of view of man, a natural individuality. Thus that which makes human beings distinctive would be a mere existence, and the actual, decisive element would belong to a sphere above that of concrete historical existence and its present, actual decisions. The middle term which is missing is that of character.

Character is certainly not a directly theological category; indeed in the Bible it is not regarded as of supreme importance. The Bible, it is true, both in its narrative and its teaching, evinces a clear grasp of that which distinguishes human beings from one another as characters. There is not much in world literature which can be compared with the Old Testament for power of characterization. We need only think of the story of Joseph and his brothers, or the narrative of King David, to be certain that what we mean by the Greek concept of 'character' is not alien to the thought of the Bible. Also there is no doubt that the Bible is aware of the connexion between character and spirit, freedom and personality, and that it does not confuse character with individuality, as a naturalistic type

reinen Vernunft, p. 433). Whether by this Kant means something similar to the thought of Schopenhauer, for whom the intelligible character is 'an act of will outside time, and therefore indivisible and unalterable,' which appears in the empirical character, is doubtful. A clear definition of the relation between intelligible and empirical personal being is excluded by the whole structure of the critique of reason. The idea of Schopenhauer, however, breaks down on the fact that he makes the empirical and historical life of man into a mechanism.

of thought, especially that of our own day, tends to do. But the fundamental distinction—for or against God, faith and sin, origin and contradiction—is so prominent in the thought of the Bible that it is true to say that the differentiation of human beings from the point of view of character recedes into the background. The Bible has no special interest in the question of character. The following pages will show why this is so.

If we still consider this question, in spite of the fact that the Bible does not lay any particular stress upon it, we are not doing so simply because, as 'moderns,' we are interested in those elements which characterize and differentiate human beings from one another; were this our attitude it would mean that we had abandoned our fundamental position to enter the sphere of philosophical anthropology in general. No, we are studying this question because it is only through the illumination of this middle term that we can fully clarify those fundamental ideas, Creation and Sin; we do so, further, because only thus is it possible to identify man as we now know him with his twofold primal destiny. For the actual empirical human being, whom we know here and now, is understood from the point of view of spiritual decision: character. Character is the empirical totality of man as act, understood as a unified act of decision.

By character we understand, first of all, that which distinguishes human beings from one another, not however merely 'natural' differences—or differences of individuality—but those which are due to self-determination, to the imprint which is due to a man's own reaction to life as a whole. Individuality is inborn, but character is not. It is true that character, like individuality, is something which precedes and determines the particular act. Action in the form of a single act springs from character. But the character itself is the product of an act, and indeed not merely in the sense of a final gathering up of all constituent elements, as a river delta is the result of affluvium, or as a habit grows out of constant practice, but in the sense of a systematic unity, of a 'constitution.' Character is the product of self-determination. In what sense, and within what limits, we shall be studying in closer detail. Primarily, we are concerned with ascribing character essentially to the spirit, to freedom, to personality, and in so doing to distinguish it from all mere natural existence. In saying this we do not deny that character has a certain relation to the natural existence.[1]

Even when we ignore the Ultimate, the background of the *imago* and the *peccatum originis*, and thus remain in the sphere of the empirical and the relative, every human being is a totality with a special 'imprint.' Even a person who is said to be 'without character' has his own imprint, namely, the fact that he is unreliable and capricious. We can rely upon the fact that he is unreliable. But the fact that we actually speak of a person as having 'no character' certainly points to the fact that this totality cannot be taken for granted,[2] that it comes into existence through an act, which—at least apparently—could be omitted. Character is a constitution of the self; it is a deliberate choice of a certain direction; it is self-determination for some particular purpose; and indeed it is 'constitutive' fundamental, self-decision. Character—even if only in a relative sense—is a total act; it is, to put it more correctly, the 'constitution' which comes into being through a total act of this kind, out of which spring 'as a result' further acts which are less 'total' in character.

This fact has seldom been seen aright; rather it has tempted even deep thinkers into the sphere of determinism. Determination is certainly present here, and, indeed, in a double sense. Character is both that which determines and that which

[1] The anthropology which is based upon natural science has the right to conceive character first of all and primarily in a purely biological and deterministic fashion, as for instance Kretschmer does in his *Körperbau und Charakter*; only the natural scientist must not forget that in so doing he is only stressing one aspect, namely, that which we describe by the word 'individuality.' Thus we analyse the 'imprint' of character into that which already exists by nature and that which is due to personal self-determination. The *vinculum substantiale* (Leibniz) will always remain a mystery to us. According to Kant, character is 'the practical and logical way of thinking in accordance with unchangeable maxims' (Kehrbach, *Kritik der praktischen Vernunft*, p. 182).

[2] In anthropology Kant uses the idea of character both in the sense of positive valuation as well as in the neutral sense; but he always means by this 'not that which nature makes of man, but what man makes of himself' (*Anthropologie*, § 94).

is determined. It is a determinant in the fact that actions follow from it with a certain necessity. But they do not 'follow' causally or logically. What is meant is a relation *sui generis*: namely, the result of the individual act of the will springing out of the fundamental tendency of the will; likewise it is the result of the individual view springing out of the fundamental view. This determination is the exact opposite of the causal kind; what it means is the power of freedom to force the individual to come under it, to work itself out in the manifold stuff of life as a synthetic force creating unity. It is the power of synthesis over against associative isolation, and over against the isolating of moments of time, *durée réelle*, thought and will as a force creating unity. It is determination from the point of view of personal existence and not from that of natural existence, similar to the 'determination' exercised by a king over his land and people.

But character is also determination in the sense of that which is determined: character is not that which posits itself but it is that which is posited; but this takes place in such a way that the two can scarcely be distinguished, or at any rate they are not to be separated. A pseudo-deterministic, causal idea is operative where this fundamental view, this self-direction is ascribed to any natural element. When this happens it means that the nature of freedom, which is the original element in character, has been misunderstood. Character is created by freedom; it springs from the will which cannot be derived from any further source. Always on the assumption that we are remaining on the middle plane of the relative and the empirical, the statement of Fichte is correct: *man is what he loves*. But why he loves this rather than that—that is the irrational primal datum of the will. Derivation from natural causes, for example from bodily dispositions, is a complete *μετάβασις εἰς ἄλλο γένος*, a gross error of thought; but in saying this we do not in any way wish to deny the close relation to such physical facts.[1]

[1] According to our present knowledge of natural science we might just as well say that the type is a function of the character as the opposite (cf. v. Monakow's discoveries in neurological research).

2. CHARACTER AS A MIDDLE TERM

The concept of character, as has already been suggested by the phenomenon of 'lack of character' which we have mentioned in passing, is not an obvious quality, it is something relative and fluid. Such 'totality' and such active quality of character varies in degree; sometimes it is more, sometimes less. There are human beings with little or almost no particular imprint. Further, there is no fixed boundary between a 'fundamental' and a 'consecutive' act. Even the 'consecutive' act still has the character of a decision. It may indeed 'follow' from such a character that one acts in a particular way; in spite of this, however, this action does not 'follow' as a clap of thunder follows a flash of lightning; the manner in which the action is accomplished is rather that in which we perform our less important actions, as for instance, when a subordinate carries out the orders of his superior, and yet, when he so acts, he is not acting like a machine but like a person, who wills and decides, even though in this case his freedom for decision is restricted. There are many middle terms between the individual action and the character as a whole.

No individual action is absolutely 'individual,' and no character is an absolute totality. Both conceptions are signposts rather than entities which can be clearly defined. This is connected with the further fact that character is not an absolute unity, but only an approximate unity. There are degrees of totality, from the individual act to the total act which is character; but, as we shall see, it belongs to the very essence of character itself that it cannot be an absolute but only a relative unity. The degrees of totality are at the same time levels of personal depth. But personality itself is always far deeper than character; for personality itself is determined by the *Imago Dei* and by the *peccatum originis*, and is not in the least affected by 'character,' or by any merely human distinctions.

A classic instance of the nature and the limitations of character is that famous phrase from *Richard III*: ' . . . I am determined to prove a villain.' It is not 'something' that Richard decides at this moment—as when we decide to do or not to do this or that trifle, here and now, or when we decide to carry out this or that important act or not, at this moment. Rather, at this moment Richard determines his 'constitution,' from which his further actions will follow with a certain necessity. The 'depth' of this fundamental decision, which touches the very being, is quite different from that of those 'consecutive' decisions. This depth determines the 'range,' the extent of the decision which is made here and now. It also affects a third element: the *permanence* of the imprint on character. The more fleeting and superficial are the decisions to 'do' this or that, the more easily can they be reversed. But if a person has decided, like Richard, 'to be a villain,' he cannot reverse this decision at the next moment with a mere wave of his hand. It is not merely habit which gives a permanent imprint to character, but it is also the depth of the decision. The character which has been thus 'chosen'—within certain limits which will be mentioned shortly—is Destiny.[1] Something has been fixed which abides. Richard is *now* a villain. His decision has a fateful result.

It is true, of course, that the process here indicated by Shakespeare could not ever be actually observed as a psychological fact. What the poet here shows us is seen through a reversed time-lens, as it were, greatly foreshortened from the point of view of time, and therefore at the same time in a certain schematic abstraction. Self-determination of character is not so 'simple' as this; for one reason, Richard is not creating himself out of nothing, for even in 'Richard before this decision' there was something which moved him to decide in this way, and in no other. We say, rightly, that a decision 'ripens'; this decision of Richard, too, has ripened; this means, however, that it gathers up many decisions, made at various moments. But this schematic representation has the advantage of making the nature of the process itself plain to us, namely, that character is based upon decision, and indeed upon 'fundamental decision.' The psychological refinement of the description must not obscure this fundamental fact—as is usually the case.

But just as it is necessary to contrast character as fundamental

[1] Ἦθος ἀνθρώπου δαίμων, 'character is the destiny of man,' says Heraclitus (*Diels*, Fr. 119).

decision with 'consecutive' or 'partial' decisions, especially with those which lie wholly upon the surface, so also it is necessary to recognize that in character we are concerned only with something which is relatively 'total' and relatively 'fundamental.' The totality of the decision which is attainable by us empirically is limited in two directions: by the Creation and by Original Sin. First, by the Creation; man can only determine himself within the limits which have been appointed by the Creator. He cannot determine to be something other than a human being—as the magic which operates in myths and fairy-tales maintains he can. Hence he cannot decide to refrain from deciding, to flee from the actuality of being obliged to decide; even the flight into passivity is not an escape from the sphere of decision; it only means that one slips away from the brightly lit centre of decision into the dim circumference of the sphere of decision, into a twilight condition of languid decision, which, however, as a human state, always retains the quality of responsibility, and therefore itself still bears decision within itself.[1] Nor can man decide to be God, although in his madness and illusion he may imagine something like this, and thus aspire far beyond himself. In so doing he cannot burst the creaturely bounds of his personality; even in his arrogant desire to 'deify' himself he remains a mortal creature, conditioned by a thousand accidental elements.

Man's empirical freedom of decision is, secondly, also limited by the negative decision which has already been made, which always lies behind every conscious decision registered in the empirical realm. Perhaps Richard can really decide to be a villain; for the villain is a definite type of sinner. But he cannot decide that he will not be a sinner, that is, that he will be a saint—save in faith, which is not primarily decision, but the reception of a decision which has already been made, apart from us. This does not lie within the realm of empirical-human possibilities; it is rather the Divine possibility, which, from our human point of view, is an impossibility. This decision to be sinless, pleasing to God, 'righteous' in the Biblical sense of the word, has become impossible for us owing to Original Sin. Indeed, the doctrine of the *peccatum originis* means pre-

[1] Cf. Rev. iii. 15.

cisely this, that this possibility, which, from the point of view of Creation, is the one intended by God to be distinctive of humanity, has been taken from us, and that this is not due to Fate or Destiny, but to that original decision which has already been made, once for all. Thus empirically, in the sense of the fundamental decision of character, we can only decide within the space which is bounded by Creation and Original Sin.

But, just as we said about Richard III, this statement must not be regarded as an abstraction; it must be translated into the concrete terms of psychology and physiology; we have not only been created as 'man,' in the general sense of the word, but also as individually different, and therefore definite human beings. The Creation is embedded in our empirical growth. Nor should original sin be conceived in an abstract, schematic manner; it too is mediated empirically. Historical and physical inheritance, historical and natural influences mediate to us both that which comes from God's creation, and also that abalienation which is due to the solidarity of humanity. But this does not mean that all freedom of decision has been taken away from man—neither the freedom of the surface, individual decision, nor the freedom to determine character in the sense of Richard III—but only that our freedom is limited by these factors.

3. THE AMBIGUITY OF CHARACTER

Now it is inherent in the limitations set up within the empirical sphere as such, that even a fundamental decision in which we 'ourselves' decide, as Richard III decided to be a villain, can never be a total decision, since owing to the contradiction between Creation and Sin we are already divided. To put it rather bluntly, we never complete a total act; we are incapable of doing so. It is indeed characteristic of the nature of the sinner, as sinner, that he is always divided in himself; Paul's description, in a classic passage, is always true of him, namely, that he is always in conflict with himself, since his 'spirit' wants something different from his 'flesh,' since the divine law, which is written upon his heart, and therefore always in some way or another helps to determine his will, is opposed to his fleshly, self-centred will. Man is despairing,[1] he is always divided, even when he does not know this himself. The strongest expression of this despair, of this 'division,' is the incapacity to will anything wholly.

It is true, of course, that we often say: I will this or that 'with my whole heart'; this is correct within the limits of this 'something'; but it is impossible to will 'something' 'with one's whole heart.' The whole heart cannot be concentrated upon one point, it never has one point only.[2] We always want several contradictory things at the same time, even when we are not fully aware of the fact. This is true in evil as well as in good. God's preserving grace does not allow us to desire evil with all our heart. The doctrine of the Church maintains that this is the privilege of the devil; experience, in any case, teaches us, in agreement with the Bible, that man cannot simply become devil, even if he wishes to do so. In this earthly life, in any case, this extreme negative possibility is denied him by divine grace, even though the Bible reminds us, by expressions like 'the sin against the Holy Ghost,' 'which will not be forgiven,' the 'hardening' of the heart, or 'sin unto death,' that even in this temporal experience there is a negative *definitivum* as an extreme instance.[3] Nor is it empirically possible for us—by our own efforts, apart from the redeeming action of God—to decide with our whole heart for the Good; for our heart is evil, although there is that room for decision between good and evil in the relative sense, to which we have already alluded. If we were able to will the Good 'with our whole heart,' we would be redeemed. The fact that we have to be redeemed means that this possibility does not actually exist for us. We are human beings with divided and not with whole hearts, who can never will good and evil 'wholly' but only half-heartedly.[4]

[1] *Ver-zwei-felt*: a play on words here, containing the idea of being 'divided' in 'two,' or 'torn in two.'—*Translator.*

[2] This is, of course, not opposed to the central Scriptural statement of the evil heart of man; for the evil heart is precisely the divided heart.

[3] Jer. v. 6; Heb. iii. 13; Matt. xii. 31 ff.; 1 John v. 16.

[4] 'He who wills one thing which is not the Good does not really will one thing; it is a deception, an illusion, a self-deception that he wills one thing; for in his innermost soul he is and must be divided' (Kierkegaard, *Purity of Heart*, an address for a Day of Penitence).

Even Richard III cannot decide with his whole heart to be a villain. Hence that monologue has a certain quaint, almost amusing flavour about it. Rumpelstilzchen alone, in the fairy-tale, was able to tear himself into two pieces. We ordinary mortals, Richard III included, cannot do this. Even the villain in his evil existence is still vulnerable at certain points; at some points even he is like a child who would rather not be naughty. Apart from the extreme instance of complete 'hardening of the heart,' man remains 'ambiguous' and thus plastic. 'The whole Richard' was not involved. He, too, still had an unquiet heart, in him too, however hidden, there was still the unrest of conscience and the longing for something better.

Hence, because here the claim to totality, which lies in all self-determination of character, is to some extent fictitious, there belongs to character as such an element of deception, indeed, even of deliberate self-deception, or pose. As soon as a human being becomes aware of his character and deliberately maintains his character, then necessarily he becomes a *poseur*. Character becomes a kind of mask, which one assumes; even in Richard III we do not fail to feel this; it is a part which one is playing. One plays it with seriousness and constancy, indeed for life or death; and yet one is not completely honest about it. Every human being, in all that he deliberately wills and for which he strives, in that which he most seriously determines to be, has something of this *poseur*, of this mask of the *persona*; even the most genuine people are no exceptions to this rule; for instance, did not most people feel that Goethe was playing a part all the time? And is not the same true of Napoleon? And even he who imagines that he wants to be simply *himself*, to be as 'real' as he can, is no exception to this rule; he too, poses as the natural, undivided human being who is in harmony with himself.[1]

This means nothing less than that character is in itself necessarily ambiguous. Man is not a sufficiently natural being

[1] That which Jung calls the *persona* (for instance, in *Die Beziehungen zwischen dem Ich und dem Unbewussten*, pp. 63 ff.) has some affinity with what I mean here, save that I would see *persona* of this kind, where Jung already sees 'actual individuality,' or the Self (p. 64).

to be able to be what he naturally is in accordance with the given order. For his being 'man' and his having a 'man's' destiny is part of this given order. No self-chosen attitude towards life sets us free from Creation and sin. On the other hand, man is not sufficiently free actually to make himself what he can inwardly wholly affirm. For he could only 'wholly affirm' his original divine destiny, and this he cannot do because he is a sinner. The ambiguity of character consists in the fact that we cannot avoid trying to order our lives 'in accordance' with 'something,' in accordance with some idea of what ought to be, or of that which is suitable for us, and yet sin prevents us from actually carrying out the aim we have set before ourselves. Not only has all character something of 'pose' about it, but it also has something strained and feverish; this explains why some people give up all attempts to achieve any distinctive character at all. But such a proceeding is not so honest nor so free from 'pose' and strain as people sometimes imagine.

Why is it that character has this ambiguity? Because it is a substitute, a human surrogate for our God-given destiny. A 'character' without pose or strain would be a person who realizes in his divinely-given individuality the universally human destiny of love. If a person were to live in the love of God, at the place appointed to him in accordance with his individuality, he would not play a 'part' any longer, he would cease to have a 'character.' In point of fact—what sort of 'character' has Jesus, the Christ? From the point of view of the divine destiny every character not only has that ambiguity, but it also contains an element of caricature. We feel that distinctly in people who are 'characters,' they lend themselves easily to caricature, because their one-sidedness, which emphasizes some particular element in them, makes them caricatures. But this is true of every character save that which would no longer be any character at all, because here self-decision would fully harmonize with the divine determination. Hence here, too, we would point out that faith, to the extent in which it really determines man by love, removes this element of 'caricature,' and also of 'character,' replacing the latter by love, the completely individual personality, or—and this is the same—the completely personalized individuality, which binds itself wholly with that which already exists by nature. Men and women in whom Christ has taken form victoriously[1] no longer possess a striking type of character; the only 'striking' thing about them is their naturalness. In order to illuminate what has just been said we may assume that we reach this faith only by laying aside the mask of character, by ceasing to 'play a part' in life, by becoming wholly transparent, not only before God but also in the sight of men; this is indicated by emphasis upon repentance and confession. The hardest mask to lay aside—and this is in the nature of the case—is that of piety; the Pharisee in the New Testament is not simply a hypocrite, but the ὑποκρίτης, the actor, who seriously plays a pious part. This brings us to the question of varieties of character.

4. VARIETIES OF CHARACTER

Character is the result of a fundamental decision made by the self about 'something.' This 'something' about which man may make a decision may, indeed, vary greatly; but this variety of possibilities is not unlimited; on the contrary, it is extremely limited. Although humanity has a wealth of possibilities of character, its actual stock-in-trade of 'theatrical producer's properties' is not unlimited; in contrast to the infinite variety of divinely-created individualities it can at least be quickly surveyed in a schematic manner, with the assistance of two schemata, one of which I will call the horizontal and the other the vertical. The more familiar schema, the horizontal, consists in a different 'blending' of the fundamental elements of man's being in self-determination; this variety is a parallel to that of the natural temperaments, with this difference, that there the blending is one which is already given to us, while here it is self-made, and indeed has come into being through a decision made by the Self. The vertical schema, on the other hand, is a graded order, corresponding to the 'height' of the 'something' at which one is aiming; in so doing the measure of the 'height' is taken to be the difference between spirit and nature. It is this second element with which I propose to deal

[1] Gal. iv. 19.

first of all, but in order to avoid misunderstanding, I would again remind the reader of my remarks in the earlier part of this book about the 'official' and 'unofficial' dominant.

Every human being exercises self-determination, more or less consciously, for some purpose. He makes a picture in his mind of what he 'really' is and 'really' desires. Then, more or less logically, he plays this part, while his real self—and indeed not only his natural individuality but his will—plays a second unofficial part in the shadow of the semi-conscious, and this, too, in a more or less logical manner. This contradiction, which is simply the incapacity of the unredeemed man to be a whole, now creates a whole multitude of special problems of character, which are very attractive to the poet, but of no further interest for us. For us it is sufficient to have pointed out this difference between the conscious 'official' aim and the semi-conscious or unconscious 'unofficial' aim in order that what follows should not incur the reproach of a non-psychological abstractness and remoteness from reality.[1]

The vertical schema, the graded order of characters, results from the fact that man, since he determines himself with a particular end in view, determines himself either in the sense of natural or of spiritual being. The characteristic forms of life which result I have described elsewhere in some detail;[2] here I must confine myself to a few illustrative remarks.

For instance, a man's aim may be merely that of self-preservation; this being so, his life, and also he himself, will bear the stamp of a purely utilitarian civilization; all his powers of thought and will are concentrated on securing what he needs for his external life; hence he is enmeshed in the net of the finite. Tillich aptly describes this character, that of the thoroughgoing 'Philistine,' as 'finitude based upon itself.' Only here we ought to note that no human being is simply what he determines to be; there still remains operative within

[1] Heidegger's (cf. Translator's note on p. 19, see op. cit., pp. 306 ff.) contrast between *Eigentlichkeit* and *man* goes back to the freedom concept of Fichte and of the Stoics, only here it is provided with a negative sign.

[2] *Das Gebot und die Ordnungen*, pp. 6 ff. (English version: *The Divine Imperative*, pp. 21 ff.)

him something of the original divine determination, and also of original sin. No human being is *merely* a Philistine, as 'man' he is always far more, both for Good and for Evil; even if this 'more' may be only operative in a hidden manner, in feelings that are either unconscious or not understood. Another example, again, is that of the man who regards himself from the point of view of 'spirit' and determines to live in accordance with this; he leads a 'spiritual existence'; but this spiritual existence is merely understood in an aesthetic manner. It is merely playing with spirit; it ends in the category of that which is interesting, creative, and beautiful. This character bears the stamp of aesthetic spirituality; such people are usually either amiable and unreliable, or splendid and irresponsible. This kind of character always sees possibilities, any of which might well be chosen; the character has not yet been stiffened by the challenge, so 'limited' to such minds, of ethical decision: Either—Or. Here man still regards himself as one with all that is high and noble, and indeed with the supreme, without noticing that he does not really live on this plane at all, but that he merely has a vision of it, in admiration and ecstasy. This aesthetic spirituality, therefore, has as its unconfessed, denied, dim 'second self' a purely instinctive, wholly unspiritual element alongside of itself, which is only with difficulty concealed by the aesthetic façade. And behind all, or below all, there lies that *cor inquietum*, a secret awareness that 'all this' is not enough.

We could make similar observations about the character based on 'sensible infinity'—the 'daemonic'[1]—or about the moral, or the mystical character, each of which occupies a quite definite plane in life, and one which can be clearly defined; here, however, we must cease to study this question in greater detail. One thing only should be added: from the Christian point of view the conception of a 'higher' plane is a dialectical one; that is, that at any particular moment the 'higher' plane may indeed, on the one hand, be a closer approach to the original purpose of Creation, to man's divine destiny, while, on the other hand, as a misunderstanding of the claim of the spirit, it may also constitute a dangerous

[1] *The Divine Imperative*, p. 23.—*Translator.*

divergence from man's true purpose. The primitive man—as the Biblical view of the child shows—is in a certain sense closer to the original divine order than all that is 'higher'; although, on the other hand, he is remote from it, owing to the absence of the spiritual element.

The fact that every picture of character of this kind represents a certain abstraction has already been indicated by the fact that this first, vertical, schema may and must be completed by the second, horizontal, one. Here the variety of characters is shown by the fact that each is conceived as an exaggeration or one-sided emphasis upon one of the basic elements of human nature, thus, as one-sidedness, as hypertrophy and atrophy, as caricature.

Kierkegaard has outlined this characterology in his book entitled *Sickness unto Death*, with the help of categories such as: the finite and the infinite, freedom and necessity, consciousness and unconsciousness, in a way that surpasses all that already has been attempted in this sphere.[1] Deepest of all perhaps—to take one of the most important examples—is his inquiry into the 'despair at not willing to be oneself'—despair as weakness—and 'despair at willing to be oneself'—despair as defiance, that is, the 'despairing misuse of the eternal in the Self. . . . But just because it is despair about the eternal the True lies very near to it; and just because the True lies very close to it, it is infinitely far away from it. . . . In order to will in desperation to be oneself there must be consciousness of an infinite self. . . . By the aid of this infinite form, the self in desperation wills to dispose of his own self, or to create his own self, to make his own self into that self which he desires to be, to determine what he will admit and what he will not admit as a constituent of his concrete self . . . he will not clothe himself in his own self, will not see his task indicated in the self that is given him, he will construct it for himself by the aid of the infinite form.'[2]

[1] Cf. the excellent survey in the *Charakterologie* by Seifert, in Bäumler's *Handbuch der Philosophie*.

[2] Kierkegaard, *Die Krankheit zum Tode*, pp. 65 ff. Cf. Lowrie, *Kierkegaard*, p. 124.—*Translator*.

5. THE OVERCOMING OF CHARACTER IN FAITH

This whole characterology of Kierkegaard is based upon the Christian understanding of man; all these characters, these caricatures of real human existence, are measured by that self-existence which 'is transparently based upon the Power which created it.' Kierkegaard has not himself drawn the conclusion, but it is obvious: character is always and necessarily ambiguous, strained, and 'posing' so long as the element of 'character' has not been overcome and replaced by the purely human, namely, that man instead of giving himself a Self, receives it from the hands of the Creator, and thus is a believer. We are 'characters' only so long as, and in so far as, we are not in faith, in the Word of God, in Christ. The moment that the 'I' receives its Self from the hands of God, instead of, as previously, giving it to himself, the feverish effort and the pose of the man who is playing a part ceases. Compared with this, all differences of character are irrelevant. No part played by a character is so near to faith, and yet so far from it, as that of the Pharisee, one who plays the part of the moral and religious man, with strain and effort, and a certain artificiality, and with serious conviction; yet behind and beneath everything there is an element of falsity. As Richard III was 'determined to prove a villain,' so this pious man decides in his own strength that he will be a man who is well-pleasing to God. He does not notice that to do this 'in his own strength' is fundamentally opposed to his divine destiny; thus he does not notice that his self-determination, however religious it may be, is included in original sin, and is indeed its highest expression. And yet he has some sense of this, for he is continually intensifying his efforts to overcome his inner unrest, until he reaches a climax, either in resignation and compromise, or in despair, or—through the stage of despair—in faith. Faith, however, consists in the fact that man recognizes that his desire to do everything by his own efforts is sin; he sees that his religious and ethical character is merely an assumed rôle, and thus that it is hypocrisy; he throws away his mask and becomes honest in the sight of God and man, accepts the Divine decision upon himself in place of his own decision for God, and thus receives his Self from the hand of God as a gift. This is what Paul calls the 'righteousness of faith.'[1]

Now alone do we perceive why the concept of character is not a directly theological one, and yet, for the sake of theological definitions, must not be left out of account. It describes simply the different forms in which the sinner appears, in which men are different from one another, not as created but as sinful beings. In a purely secular ethic, and therefore in practical everyday thinking, character has a relative right, it is true, and is of great importance. But it belongs wholly to the sphere of the *justitia civilis*, to that middle sphere where, within the limits of sinful human existence, there is a difference between the good and the bad, where one can speak of people who are less good and less evil in various degrees, which every description of human life takes into account. From all that has already been said it is evident why character must not be confused with individuality, which is an endowment given by creation. Character is something which is destined to disappear, lying as it does midway between the two conceptions of man's being: being in the image of God and sinful being, on the one hand, and natural individuality on the other. Individuality, however, in so far as it is the God-given, natural basis of man's being, will not be extinguished, even in eternity. Now we must turn to the consideration of this natural endowment.

[1] Cf. my book, *Das Gebot und die Ordnungen*, Chap. VIII. (English version: *The Divine Imperative.*)

CHAPTER XIV

INDIVIDUALITY AND HUMANITY

1. THE GENERAL PROBLEM OF INDIVIDUALITY

THE problem of individuality, the question of the significance of individual peculiarity, and especially the stress laid upon this individual distinctiveness of man, is characteristic of modern thought in the realm of anthropology. As a rule the thinkers of antiquity and of the Middle Ages paid little attention to this question. It was not until the Renaissance that it became prominent;[1] to-day it dominates the thought of man to such an extent that the element common to humanity as a whole is almost completely concealed. In the consciousness of nationality, and in the nationalism based upon it, it has become a supreme force which is moulding history. If all the signs of the present day are not deceptive, this question will affect the future still more strongly, in the form of the race problem. As the question of personal individuality, and of the significance of the difference between the sexes, it stands in the very centre of the present interests of psychology. How is that which distinguishes human beings from one another related to that which is common to them all? Thus our question must be: Does the Bible and the Christian revelation provide us with a particular solution of this problem?

The ancient statement, *principium individuationis est materia*, must be altered, from the point of view of the Christian faith, to *Principium individuationis est voluntas Dei creatoris*. There is a great gulf between these two statements. The first statement is essentially pantheistic and monistic. Behind it there lies the view that being as such is universal being. The essential is the same as the general—a view which dominates our thought all the more that as a rule we are not conscious of it at all. It is the fundamental thought of Greek philosophy that real being is ideal being, a general spiritual existence and a spiritual

[1] Cf. Dilthey, *Menschenkunde und Theorie der Lebensführung im Zeitalter der Renaissance und Reformation*, op. cit., p. 423.

universal existence.[1] Matter is then a principle of individuation as a negation, as a limitation in the sense of depreciation of being. The most universal being is the actual, the ὄντως ὄν. The less universal, the less being. The extreme limit of this universal being, the boundary towards non-being is then the individual, that which no longer participates in the universal. The individual element, from this point of view, is the non-essential, that which is accidental and insignificant, that with which it is not worth while occupying oneself.

Faith in the Divine Creation[2] confronts this whole ontology with the following statement: All that is actual, as created, is individual. Individuality is the sign of created, creaturely —but not material—actuality. All that is created has not only been created as individual, as 'this' which is not 'that,' of which we spoke in Chapter XII, but also as individuality, as 'this' which is different from 'that.' The difference in individuality, the difference between like and unlike (other) does not go so deep as the difference between identity and non-identity. Identity and non-identity is a contradictory antithesis; being like and unlike is merely a contrary antithesis.[3] Wherever the antithesis is merely contrary, not contradictory, there are transitions, a sliding scale from a maximum of unlikeness or likeness to zero. The non-identical cannot be exchanged for anything else, the unlike is only more or less inexchangeable down to the extreme instance of non-distinguishability.

All that is actual is individual being, it has individuality. We see how misleading is the statement that 'matter is the principle of individuation' in the fact that the more a being approaches the material realm the less individual it is. The boundary of individual differentiation is doubtless the being of the material 'atom.' Two atoms of hydrogen—or two protons—have only an extremely minute minimum of 'distinctive imprint.' The higher we ascend in the scale of being the more significance does individuality gain. Mammals are

[1] Cf. Zeller on *Aristotle*, op. cit., II, 2, pp. 312 ff.

[2] Here too we see the necessity for a Christian ontology, determined by the Biblical idea of the Creator and the creature.

[3] Hence Bergson's derivation of the nothing out of the Other is a complete reversal (*Évolution créatrice*, pp. 295 ff.).

far more highly individualized than infusorians. Individualization only reaches its maximum in personal being, in 'personal individuality.' It is not matter that individualizes but life, and still more than life, the spirit. The more spiritual people are the less can they be exchanged for anyone else, the more 'distinctive imprint' do they possess.

Hence it is also questionable whether we have any right to regard individuality simply as a natural endowment. In contrast to personality, certainly, individuality is that in which man simply finds himself where, at first sight, the freedom of his self-determination has no influence. This comes out most plainly in physical individuality. I am either blue-eyed or dark-eyed, either tall or short, either 'pyknic' or 'athletic' (Kretschmer), or however these physical types may be described; my freedom has nothing to do with this kind of physical type; it is simply given to me as a matter of fact.[1] This applies also to my psychical structure. The psychical type and the psychical peculiarity do not belong to my own sphere of self-determination; I 'am what I am' as I have been created. Here there is a constant, which precedes all the variable elements which are determined by the decision of the Self as psychical material for spiritual determination.

This applies, thirdly, to the 'spiritual or mental aptitude.' Talents, spiritual capacities, are inborn, and absolutely given, and the fact that they have been bestowed upon us from the very outset means that they form the fixed capital with which the personality can, and indeed must, carry on its affairs. This inborn physical, psychical and spiritual endowment as a whole is given to every individual human being as something different, something peculiar to himself. We may indeed sum up these differences, these individualities in types; that is, we may group together points of non-resemblance in resemblances of a lower grade, but within such a type there are an unlimited number of individual differences. No oak-leaf exactly resembles any other; still less resemblance is there between two human beings of the same physical or psychical or spiritual type! Actually, here it is never possible to exchange one for the other; it is only the superficial glance which does

[1] Matt. vi. 27.

not see the distinctive element in each person. Twins whom the stranger cannot distinguish from one another are never confused with one another by their family or their friends.

Although this is quite true, it is not the whole truth. The individuality, even the spiritual individuality, is, it is true, in some way or another—the more exact meaning we still have to seek—absolutely given and posited by the Creator, but it is not that only. It is at the same time a product of history. We see this most clearly in the individuality which is determined in a negative sense. There are degenerate individualities in whom we can still see clearly the factor dependent on human action which lies in personal decision. A specially familiar and sad instance is that of the drunkard's child, a particular type of individuality, which has its origin in the human act, the father's abuse of the enjoyment of alcoholic drinks, and certainly not in the will of the Creator. As man is able to breed varieties at will, so the historical life possesses this possibility, both positive and negative, of breeding for its own purposes.[1] The will and the thought of man enter into the circle of factors which determine the individuality which is absolutely given to the individual. The history of the aristocracy, of urban families, and also of cultures, civilizations and religions, provides a wealth of instances of such determination of individuality by the human will, by human action and omission.

But history also, action and inaction, the thought and the decision of the individual themselves affect the individuality. The free decision of man as person may, within certain limits, re-group the existing relations between the psychical and spiritual elements which form the individuality at its outset. Personality influences temperament, which is the psychical mechanism of reaction included in the elements composing the individuality with which we have been endowed by nature. The various typical temperaments, the 'psychological types,' alter with the personal development of a human being, for instance, with his outlook on life as a whole, with his faith or

[1] A. Huxley's *Brave New World* gives the horrible picture of a future in which human individualities (and even characters!) are manufactured by a systematic treatment of the embryos.

his unbelief. The stronger the personal element in a human being becomes, the more does the natural individual peculiarity in him recede, but it does not disappear altogether. The personal life operates by toning down the natural aspect of individuality, and by intensifying its spiritual aspect. These reflections may preserve us from hastily describing individuality as a natural matter, and also from connecting it too plainly with the Creation. Sin, too, has a share in individuality.

What, however, is the significance of individuality from the point of view of the idea of Creation? This remains true: the Creator creates an individualized creature, individuality is the token of the creature as such. But what is the meaning of this? When we reflect upon the Divine revelation, instead of receiving a plain answer we receive several answers. The *first* meaning of the individualized creation is that of the manifestation of the Divine Creator Spirit in His richness and in His freedom.[1] God creates what He wills, great and small, powerful and weak, simple and complicated, the infinite variety of species and kinds, sub-species and varieties;[2] He creates also the still more infinite variety of individualities in the narrowest and most rigid sense of the word, because He wills to do so. This individual creation is for us absolutely 'contingent,' accidental, in the sense that we cannot see its meaning. In it the Creator proves His freedom and the inexhaustible nature of His 'invention.'[3] The difference between the gift of the Creator which has been granted to us and His Creator-Spirit is made visible in the infinite number of His created works. The variety of human individualities also shares in this irrational variety of the created world.

The second point which I wish to emphasize is connected with what has already been said about the being of the individual as individual. God the Creator does not create humanity, but He creates each individual human being separately, He has 'called thee by thy name,'[4] He knows you 'personally,' 'specially.' Hence you are not an example but a person, a self which cannot be exchanged for any other. The Creator knows you as this particular person. This is the

[1] Thus in Psa. civ. 24 ff.
[2] Gen. i. 21 ff.
[3] Psa. cxlviii.
[4] Isa. xliii.1.

basis of our identity, for ever. God would know us, and He would not confuse us with any other even if we were all completely alike. For Him our selfness, the fact that we cannot be exchanged for anyone else, also means that each one of us is distinctive, that one cannot be confused with another. But He wishes to carry this distinction and uniqueness out into the sphere of human relations, He clothes our selfness with individuality, in order that we may know each other as distinct individuals. Thus individuality, the fact that we are not all alike, becomes the form in which selfness, the fact that we are not the same, appears. Individuality is the garment of personal independence. Hence it is important, but not too important; we should be aware of it, but we should not lay too much stress upon it. It is that which exists of itself if personal being is in right condition. Hence it grows with the personal self and yet is re-absorbed into the personal self.[1] The more we are person, the less emphasis will we lay upon individuality, the more, however, will we have an individual imprint.

The third consideration concerns the connexion between the self and the community. God has created the self for self-existence in community, as a non-self-sufficient self, which ought not to exist for itself, and cannot exist for itself. This is why God gives us such individuality which forces us to depend upon one another that we may complement each other. The most important instance of this is sex-individuality, man and woman. Here individuality contains not only the natural meaning of reproduction, but also the personal meaning of 'two-ness,' as an indication of community of life.[2] It is implanted so deeply in human life in order that man may not misinterpret himself as a self-sufficient being. If, in spite of everything, he does this, then the sex nature above all revenges itself upon such exaggeration. The human being who confuses himself with God is reminded of his creatureliness, of the fact that he is not intended to be alone, by nothing so much as by his sexuality. The basis for the two sexes is stated in the

[1] Gal. iii. 28; Col. iii. 11.

[2] Gen. ii. 18. And also the parable of the body and its members in 1 Cor. xii.

phrase, 'it is not good for man to be alone.'[1] But all human individuality is in this sense an education for community. It is because human beings are so different that they can, and must, complement each other, and thus share a common life. Only through this differentiation of individualities can they be united into one 'body.'[2] The organism requires differentiation of the organs and the functions. The one body of humanity, seen in the light of the origin, is composed of differentiated organs, in which its particular function is appointed to each. Individuality of being is the presupposition of the peculiarity of the personal calling, or, to put it more exactly, the presupposition of the concrete realization of the special calling. Thus in the origin individuality and the personal calling become one. But individuality must not be understood merely in the sense of natural differentiation; it must also be understood in the sense of historical differentiation. Nature and history, in respect of individuality as well as of the calling, must be thought of together, as indeed we have already seen that *de facto* they cannot be separated.[3]

Only now do we perceive that the Christian understanding of individuality is completely different from that of Idealistic Pantheism. Idealism, which is dominated by the idea of the universal, can only understand individuality as a tiresome limitation of spiritual being, as something negative; the belief in the Creation, however, understands it positively, both in view of God Himself and in view of the being of man. Certainly individuality is the characteristic of that which is creaturely and limited—God Himself has no individuality—but it is only a 'tiresome limitation,' a negative determination, for one who 'cannot endure not to be a god' (Nietzsche). From the point of view of the personal creature individuality is, on the one hand, emphasis upon the selfness of the person, and on the other, on the fact that the personal life is related to the community. Only as individualities, as persons, which are distinguished from each other as individuals, are we really 'selves'; at the same time, however, it is this which forces us

[1] Gen. ii. 18, and also 1 Cor. vii. 4, 5. [2] 1 Cor. xii. 4 ff.

[3] 1 Cor. vii. 20 ff. The Pauline parable of the body makes no distinction between the natural and the historical individuality.

to depend upon one another, and thus makes us capable of community. If we were all alike, how could we exist for one another and give to each other? Individuality is fulfilment of our creation as persons destined for community.

2. THE GENERAL PROBLEM OF HUMANITY

From this point of view, then, how are we to understand the element which is common to all human beings, that of humanity? It cannot be taken for granted that this element exists, but it is a truth which is only gained through history, which might perhaps even be lost again after it has been perceived. Where man understands himself as a purely natural being, there is little occasion for the formation of the concept of that which is 'common to all mankind.' Looked at from the point of view of the physical nature of man, the distinctiveness and unity of the human race, the element which is common to all human beings, and to them alone, is not particularly striking. The idea of humanity does not grow so much out of the physical as out of the spiritual and personal aspect of man's being. But it would be an error to believe that the idea of humanity as such is a specifically Christian idea. It was there before Christianity, and it is powerful also outside the sphere influenced by the thought of the Bible and of Christianity. Outside Christianity we know it above all in the form of the thought of antiquity, especially the Stoic doctrine of humanity. Here for the first time[1] it is both fully formed and firmly established. But both the basis and the content of this ancient philosophical idea of humanity is very different from that of the Christian faith, in spite of the fact that it has many points of contact with it.

The ancient idea of humanity[2] is, naturally, based on the philosophy of religion. The Greek is too clear a thinker not to be aware of the transcendental content of this idea. There

[1] Still it would be well to inquire whether and to what extent here (as for instance in Posidonius) there has already been a certain amount of Jewish influence.

[2] Cf. the Appendix on the *Idea of Humanity in the Ancient World* (p. 547). How far even Plato was from a universal idea of humanity can be seen in his *Republic*.

can only be humanity, a *humanum*, where there is a divinity, a *divinum*. But ancient Humanism bases the connexion between both on a rational doctrine of immanence, namely, on the idea of a divine-human Reason, the divine-human *Logos*. Man, in virtue of his reason, has a share in the divine *Logos*. The spiritual being of man is based upon the immanence of the Transcendent, of the Divine. It is true of course that in many of its expressions Stoic Pantheism comes very near to the personalistic Biblical idea of God; but the rational origin of the idea of humanity, or of the *Logos*, always prevents it from gaining a truly personal idea of God. The truly personal idea of God cannot be found through thought, it can only be given in revelation through faith. In the last resort, the God to whom we attain by way of our own thought is necessarily impersonal.[1]

The same is true of the understanding of humanity which is always the correlate of the understanding of God. Like the immanent God of human reason, so also the man who through his reason has a share in the divine existence is ultimately conceived impersonally. His deepest ground is not individual and personal, but universal rational being, the universal *Logos*-Spirit. In this *Logos*, or spirit, which indwells us and is universal, in this Divine Reason—as we have already seen[2]—according to the conception of Humanism, the human existence has its ground, both its being as self and also its being as humanity. The *humanum* is based upon participation in the Divine *Logos*, in the Divine Reason. It is this which lifts man above the animals, which is peculiar to him as man, and therefore also binds all human beings to one another. Through this indwelling Divine Reason human beings are related to one another, although otherwise, from the point of view of race, they may be foreign to one another.

The Greek rational idea of humanity by which Western Humanism is determined is, therefore, abstract in a threefold sense. Firstly, it creates no positive relation to the other as 'Thou.' Our relation to our fellow-man is based on the idea that the Other also is a bearer of the same Reason as I am

[1] Cf. my book, *Gott und Mensch*, first paper.

[2] See above, pp. 258 ff.

myself; thus between him and me there exists a relation of identity in view of the essential, to which there corresponds, subjectively, respect but not love. Unity may exist between us it is true—unity in the one identical Reason—but not personal community, love to the 'Thou' of the Other. Secondly, it is abstract, in the sense that it is not related to the emotional aspect of human nature; the rational idea of Humanity is without personal warmth. For the dualism of reason and emotion is unavoidable, where the purely rational concept of humanity is logically thought out. The Stoic's contempt for all that is affective and emotional (ataraxia) is typical of this. Thirdly, it is abstract, in the sense that it provides no possibility for a positive valuation of the individual element as such, of that which is peculiar to the individual. It is egalitarian—it puts everyone on the same level. All human beings are essentially alike; their unlikeness is the accidental, unimportant element; the individual difference is to be estimated as a limitation and restriction of the one identical reason in a wholly negative way. On the other hand, the strong side of this concept of Humanity is its understanding for all mental and spiritual achievement, for all that reason brings forth, for culture and all that promotes culture, for the tasks of the domination of Nature, for superiority over Nature, manifested both in knowledge and in creative achievements, in short, for all that we have previously described as 'formal' Humanity.[1] It is 'formal' spirituality which constitutes the basis of this 'Humanity.'

There is not a great deal more to say about the Christian understanding of humanity—in general—since all that has already been said about 'man,' both of his selfhood and of his being-in-community, was simply the development of this *humanum*. In summing up we would only draw attention to this one point. In contrast to rational Humanism the Christian idea of humanity, because it starts from the personal and

[1] We call it 'formal' in so far as it is only the presupposition of spiritual acts of decision and thought, and is thus not yet determined materially by such acts. Of course this is the modern use of the word 'formal,' which is very different from that of the Thomist and Aristotelian use of it, and is not the scholastic and medieval use of the word.

social determination of Creation, is orientated from the 'material' and not from the 'formal' point of view. Here the content of humanity is not the creative nature of man as such, nor his superiority over nature as such, but that which has been entrusted to us as a gift and a task, as the ultimate meaning of the being of man, who is endowed with these creative powers: the material aim, namely, responsibility-in-love, community, being in the love of God, and union with one another through this love. The decisive point is not the fact that man is self-conscious mind, and that he creates culture, but *how* he lives as self-conscious mind, what he desires to create in his creation of 'culture,' and to what goal he directs his existence as self-conscious mind and his creation of culture, his self-existence and his creative existence, as their end. Self-conscious mind as such does not make him 'human'; indeed, even if he is a genius he may use his mental powers in an 'in-human' way. Measured by this content the whole potential power to create culture shows itself first of all as a possibility and not as an actuality of human existence, all cultural realization only as a presupposition, framework and means, but not yet as the content of human existence. For the Idealist to be 'spirit,' as such, is already the Divine; in the Christian view, however, to be 'spirit' means being as open to the satanic possibility as to the Divine. The deepest contrast is not that which lies between spirit and nature but that which lies between the use of the spirit in harmony with or in opposition to God. By the very use of that which distinguishes humanity from the rest of the creation—by means of reason, the spirit, culture, spiritual achievement—man has the power of utterly denying the meaning of human existence, and of destroying the image of man and making it unrecognizable. Indeed, not only can man do this, but he does so, and is continually occupied in carrying on this work of destruction. Hence as a Christian one cannot be enthusiastic about humanity, and speak with enthusiasm about humanity and its possibilities, since immediately the memory of the misuse of all these possibilities arises in our minds, reminding us of all those influences which tear humanity in pieces, instead of uniting it, which allow conflicts to break out within mankind which are unknown in every other part of the creation, conflicts in which mankind can achieve complete mutual annihilation. In point of fact, a high degree of abstraction would be required if—in spite of all this—we were to work up any enthusiasm for the word 'humanity'! Enthusiasm for humanity disappears when we remember what man can accomplish in the way of madness, lies and destruction—and all this not by means of his instincts, but by means of his mind and spirit.

Nevertheless, there is a genuine, Scriptural and Christian Humanism, and an idea of humanity which springs directly out of the centre of the Christian faith: the idea of the unity of the human race in its origin and its goal which is based upon the Divine Creation and the Divine Revelation, to be perceived in the Incarnation of the Son of God, and created anew through the Divine Redemption.[1] In Jesus Christ we see not only the picture of the true (ideal) man, but also the origin and the goal of the humanity created by God, and destined by Him for communion with Him and with one another. The revelation of true divinity is both the revelation and the basis of true humanity, of man's true being and of true mankind. The loss of man's true being through sin does not cancel the divine plan for the creation of a humanity

[1] To support this statement with individual passages from the Bible would be as unnecessary as it is impossible; we would need to write out the whole Bible. In the Old Testament the idea of the unity of all men based upon the divine Creation and plan for the Kingdom only gradually gains definite and clear expression; the history of the people of Israel stands in the foreground. In the New Testament the vision of unity which was only begun or suggested in the Old Testament is fulfilled. The New Testament is concerned with the old and the new Adam, with 'man' and with 'all men.' They have all been created by God after His image, they have all become sinners, the message of redemption is intended for them all—whether they accept it and thus participate in it or not. The aim of redemption is absolutely universal and for all mankind, and in view of this all other differentiations fall out of sight. 'Ye are all one in Christ Jesus.' It has one limitation only, namely, that which it contains itself: that one does not accept it although it is offered, that one does not believe. From this one goal of redemption the gaze is directed back to the Origin, to the unity of the Creation-Logos for all. On Him the unity of mankind is based, as through Him it is revealed. (Eph. i. 9 ff.)

founded on and unified in Christ. Each human being has been created for this *humanitas*; this ground of creation, which is at the same time the goal of creation, defines every human being as *humanus*, even in the midst of the contradiction of sin, and mankind as a whole, in spite of all its conflicts, as the one *humanitas*. It is only from the point of view of this absolute common element that the conflicts due to sin, and the differences of individuality which are based upon the creation and upon sin, can be rightly understood. Yet this will come out most clearly in view of the particular problems of individuality.

There are two reasons which make it necessary to discuss some particular problems of individuality: first, because they are urgent practical problems, and secondly, because the truth of the Christian idea of humanity can be clearly brought out only in wrestling with these problems. The two are very closely connected. At the present day there are certain definite practical tendencies which, in a quite general way, raise doubts in people's minds about the truth of any 'idea of humanity,' either Christian or Idealistic. The will to build up human communities on definite narrow lines is so strong that in order to achieve its own ends it ruthlessly pushes aside all that humanity has learned about its unity in the course of history. Certainly, in order to complete this statement, we ought to add that, conversely, this practical anti-humanism only has such a powerful influence because for a century past a crude naturalism had undermined every kind of belief in a special, higher destiny of man. As in all other spheres, so here too theoretical and practical unbelief go hand in hand. Out of the great variety of the problems of individuality which are especially urgent at the present day—and are indeed always very important—we will choose some as illustrations; certainly they are the most important: the problems of race, mass civilization, personal individuality, and, finally, in a special chapter owing to its special difficulty, the problem of the sexes.

3. RACE AND HUMANITY

The modern race problem has a twofold origin. It springs first from instinct and emotion, out of a half-unconscious knowledge and recoil from a different race, which when it becomes conscious, seeks to give legitimate reason for this recoil; secondly, from a romantic and aesthetic theory of individuality, which makes use of certain modern biological discoveries, and then condenses them into a pseudo-scientific philosophy of race-values. Contact with a human being who does not belong to one's own race arouses a natural instinct of repulsion, a feeling which might be thus expressed in rational terms, 'This is a human creature of a different kind from myself; I do not want to have anything to do with him, and I ought not to have anything to do with him either.' This feeling of repulsion is, of course, mixed with other feelings: curiosity, amusement, fear and a sense of something uncanny, etc. What is the significance of these natural feelings? And how far are they spiritually justified?

The first point to note is this, that 'we must use the concept of race very cautiously because we are still in the dark about the origin of the various races in nature, with their many variations in type.' 'Race is a concept of natural science and not of historical science.'[1] Secondly, it is a fact which can be proved that the race-instinct, that feeling of repulsion, varies a good deal among 'races' which from the point of view of 'blood' are very nearly related, as for instance the Jews and the Arabs. Here it would seem as though historical, rather than racial and blood characteristics and attitudes were operative. Thirdly, we must distinguish between facts which can be established by natural science, and a wild mythology of race, springing from a source which is very far from scientific, but which apes the appearance of science;[2] as a rule it is the latter which hardens into political slogans, programmes and actions. The practical problems do not arise so much in the fact of race itself as in that romantic race-philosophy and mythology which has just been mentioned; it is this which—combined, however, with fundamental historical facts, at least in the sphere of 'white' civilization—creates practical problems. What then, from the point of view of the Biblical knowledge of God, are we to think of the race problem?

[1] W. Classen, in *Religion in Geschichte und Gegenwart,* IV, col. 1704.

[2] According to the view of the experts, Günther's well-known work, *Rassenkunde des deutschen Volkes,* belongs to this category.

So far as the actual empirical situation is concerned, in this, as in other questions of natural science, we must not expect to find any special doctrine in the Bible. We must be quite prepared for the possibility that, as a result of scientific research, it might be established that the human race is not a unity, that indeed it may have had a plural and not a single origin;[1] although, until the present day, certainly, very little has been proved to have been established as 'truth' by science. Neither in this nor in other questions which affect the growth of man[2] may we conduct an apologetic for the Biblical narratives; and we must not allow ourselves to be led astray by the fact that the New Testament,[3] in this as in other cosmological questions, simply follows the Old Testament. It is from science and not from the Bible that we must learn about the racial origin of peoples and races, with their blood-relationships and their empirical qualities.

But so far as the *significance* of these facts—which have been ascertained empirically and scientifically—is concerned, the whole situation is quite different. Although we are not justified in deducing any kind of palaeontological anthropological science from the Bible, it is clear, on the other hand, that the view of the human race as a unity is a fundamental, essential, absolute 'dogma' of the faith based on the Scriptures. All the chief Christian doctrines which concern man, beginning with the central dogma of the Incarnation of God in Jesus Christ, by which the whole human race, with all its races, is included in the redemption, the doctrine of the *Imago Dei* and the *peccatum originis*, either have no validity at all, or have absolute validity, which means that they exclude every kind of racial discrimination. 'In Christ' there is not only 'neither Jew nor Greek, Barbarian nor Scythian,[4] but also there is neither black nor white nor yellow. From the very outset the Christian Church has held this view in its missionary practice, and since

[1] Cf. the informing report on the latest anthropological research in the sphere of natural science by Titius, *Natur und Gott*, pp. 538 ff. Also Bavink, *Ergebnisse und Probleme der Naturwissenschaften*, fifth edition, pp. 468 ff. 'Man stands indubitably in the line of descent from the animal world' (p. 477), but 'real religion has nothing to do with this question of man's genealogy' (p. 478).

[2] Cf. Chap. XVII.

[3] Cf. Acts xvii. 26; Rom. v. 12, 18.

[4] Col. iii. 11.

then it has never been in any doubt about it for a moment. The question is only: what is the relation between the two views, which seem at first to be opposed to one another, of the unity and non-unity of the human race? And what are the consequences, especially the practical consequences, of each of them?

To this question we must reply first, that the religious belief in the unity of the human race through the Creation, in and for the Divine image, is completely independent of all biological, palaeontological, scientific results. The story of Adam in Genesis expresses, in historical form, it is true, a fact which in itself is super-empirical and super-historical; the biological genealogical question has very little to do with belief in the unity of the creation. That which is a unity from the one point of view may, or may not, from the other point of view, be a non-unity. We declare, as those who take their point of view from the truth of the Bible, that we are completely indifferent to the question of biological genealogy. The unity of the divine creation of man lies upon a quite different plane. Humanity is not necessarily a unity from the zoological point of view; it may indeed be composed of different species of differing origin or it may not. It is, however, beyond all doubt a unity, a *humanitas*, through the *humanum*, its one origin and its one destiny in God's creative Word and plan of salvation, spiritually given to man by God Himself.

This does not mean that all races or all peoples—however the concept of the 'people' (*Volk*) may be more exactly defined, and the origin of a nation (people) be conceived—have the same mental and spiritual endowments. The one and the same *humanum*, the fact of being created in and for the image of God, and the fact that man has fallen away from God through sin, is undoubtedly differentiated and graduated in different ways in individual groups. Speaking quite generally, there are races and peoples which are more or less highly endowed than others, just as there are more or less gifted individuals. There is thus a general differentiation and gradation of talents. To this we must add at once, however, that there are also differences in the types of gifts and talents and that the distribution of these again is more or less 'accidental' and irrational. The Greeks are not in every respect the most highly gifted people in world history; the white and the yellow races are not superior to the black in every respect.

Not only is there a racial, and perhaps also to a certain extent a national, differentiation of cultural gifts, but there may possibly be also a different 'average endowment' in the moral and religious sphere. But this differentiation takes place entirely in the relative realm, that of the 'more or less.' The elements which compose the *humanum* are blended differently, and they are represented in a different degree. But the essential elements are never wholly absent, and they are everywhere limited. They bear a different imprint, but at bottom they have in common that which is essential and fundamental. Every race is capable of civilization and of culture, though not to the same extent, nor in the same way. Every human being, to whatever race he may belong, shares in the common treasure of the *humanum*; he is able to understand all that is essentially human; there is a common human understanding —of concepts like joy, fidelity, well-doing, justice, of course also of all logical categories—and of valuation. The decisive point, however, is this—for here alone lies the origin of being-a-self and of being-for-community, of the materially human —that no race and no people is unable to understand the message of Jesus Christ, of the Divine plan of salvation.

The missionary work of the Church proves this a thousand times over.[1] None of the languages of the negro peoples, not even the most primitive, has proved unsuitable for the translation of the Bible; in no race and no tribe has the Church in the mission-field met with a hopelessly closed mind to the message of God, the Creator and Redeemer. However great the initial difficulties may have been, yet missionary zeal and effort, supported by the love of Christ, have always and everywhere been rewarded by indubitable success, sometimes amazingly great and sometimes modest. This means that no kind of race or people forms a definite hindrance to the true

[1] Cf. for instance Warneck, *The Living Forces of the Gospel*, and the paper on *Race Problems in Missionary Work* in *Religion in Geschichte und Gegenwart* IV, col. 1706 ff., and Oldham, *Christianity and the Race Problem.*

Biblical-Christian self-understanding of man. On the contrary, in this decisive fact—in comparison with which all cultural differences fade into insignificance, one point stands out above all others (and this has been proved repeatedly), namely, that the true development of man as man, which springs from the original being of man in accordance with the aim of the Creation, is completely independent of his intellectual culture. The race differentiation which is comparatively great where culture is concerned, is wholly unimportant in the question of essential humanity. Whether the black or the yellow or the white races are more capable of faith and love in the sense of the Gospel, and thus of genuine human existence, is a question which may be shelved as a misunderstanding, both from the point of view of experience and of that of the fundamental truths of Creation and Redemption. Every one who bears the human countenance can be addressed by the Divine Gospel, whereas in principle, and also from the explicit statement of the Bible, the animal cannot be thus addressed. The only limitation which we know is not that of race, but that of the completely pathological individual nature, on the one hand, and, on the other, the mystery of the divine and the human personal decision of which we can never have any final knowledge.

4. THE PSYCHICAL AND MENTAL INDIVIDUALITY OF THE INDIVIDUAL

The individual psychical and mental distinctiveness of the individual human being is the favourite anthropological theme of modern individualistic man, out of all proportion to the objective importance of this question. All that the human being who has forgotten the real point of human life knows of the fact that 'everything does not come to the same in the end' is this unimportant point: all human beings are not alike, but are unlike. For our part, however, we must not fall into the opposite error and treat individual differentiation as a negligible quantity. That would be in opposition to our view of the significance of individuality which we gained from the idea of the Creation. But from the outset we must bring the question into proportion with others. The individual difference is not unimportant, but it is a secondary fact, not only for anthropology in general, but also for every individual human being. We cannot regard it as ultimately very important, but we can only regard it as of second-rate and even third-rate importance. Within this clear delimitation, however, it must not be ignored, because were we to do so it would certainly feel obliged to exaggerate its importance by over-emphasizing the relative justification which it does possess.

Psychical differentiation is intimately connected with physical differentiation, but it extends into the spiritual realm as well. Since the *Characters* of Theophrastus, and the theories of the 'temperaments' of Hippocrates and Galen, and, in particular, since the characterological efforts of the Renaissance psychologists, the distinction between typical individual differences has been a favourite theme of psychology. Hippocrates' theory of the four temperaments is an attempt—still worthy of respect at the present day[1]—to understand the differences in human beings from their emotional reactions. There may be more psycho-physical wisdom in his theory of the relation between 'temperament' and 'body-juices' than in recent times one has been willing to admit. But in any case this is not the only possibility of psychological formation of types. At the present time, in particular, Jung's attempt to create a new psychological typology has rightly gained consideration.[2] The distinction between the introvert and the extravert, the types of feeling, thought, emotion and intuition, and the recognition of the complementary spheres of the 'conscious' and the 'unconscious,' with all the variety of cross-possibilities to which this gives rise, actually provides an instructive schema for the understanding of the countless varieties of psychical types. On the other hand, in Jung especially, we see how difficult it is not to confuse psychical individuality with the results of personal decision. Psychical individuality must primarily—in spite of fluid transitions—be distinguished from personal character. A man has his psychical type from the day of his birth, but not his character. A man

[1] The fact that a thinker like Kant paid great attention to this theory (cf. his *Anthropologie*) is decidedly in its favour.

[2] C. G. Jung, *Psychologische Typen.*

or woman is born with a definite 'temperament,' but not with a definite attitude towards life.

Now, however, it becomes evident that in the light of the 'temperaments,' as well as in that of modern psychological types, a person's 'psychological make-up' has some relation to the spiritual and personal aspect of his nature. An extremely 'sanguine' temperament, for example, or an extreme type of extravert, is incompatible with a 'deeper' fundamental personal attitude. This cannot mean that a human being of this kind would not be capable of a deeper attitude; it can only mean the exact opposite, namely, that entrance into faith, and living in faith, will have a retrospective action upon the innate psychical type, and will transform it. The innate element, therefore, is not absolutely unchangeable. The inborn typical or individual element is only a relative constant. It will, it is true, remain operative as an initial constant through all personal changes, but it will always be one which will never be perceived from the outset, nor will it ever be definitely grasped.

We have already pointed out that the rigid contours with which the psychical types are distinguished from one another in the state of nature are dimmed by a strongly personal and spiritual life, and are replaced, or, to put it more correctly, superimposed by an imprint of a quite different kind and one which is not natural. Thus the effect of the spiritual life on the one-sidedness of temperament and on psychical peculiarities, is that it smooths out differences. The more a human being has a genuinely personal life, the more that he lives in faith and love, the less will one perceive in him of a special temperament or of a pronounced psychological type, while he now has far more 'personality' of a distinctive kind than he had when he did not possess this personal element. His inborn individuality has been fused, it is true, with this personal imprint; but in being fused it has also been transformed. On the other hand, development in the other direction, that is, sin, causes the harsher aspects of the natural psychical peculiarities to stand out more plainly, and, as we saw in the previous chapter, it turns them into characters which are almost caricatures. This could be easily illustrated by pictures like those of Daumier.

In the psychical type, in the psychical individuality, personal differences are as it were dimly pre-formed; every psychical peculiarity, every psychical type has, so to speak, an affinity with a definite spiritual attitude. But this affinity must not be misunderstood as an absolutely determining factor. The person is concealed within this psychical form; it may identify itself with it, it *may* come completely under its sway—it then always becomes something different, namely a definite character—but it is not obliged to do so. The attitude expressed in the phrase, 'Well! this is what I am!' implying that there is no hope of alteration, is always a sinful misunderstanding of man, a denial of his personal self. Only an animal would have the right to say this; but the animal does not say so because it knows nothing about it. The psychical individual disposition is always detached from the person not only by faith, but also, even if in a different way, by sin. Even the unbeliever has the possibility of 'moulding' himself, of altering the general tendency of his life with which he was born. But in faith alone does man gain the right relation to this natural psychical tendency. He makes a fundamental distinction between the nature which is derived from the Creation and nature which has been influenced by sin; he does not deny that which exists by nature, but he also does not absolutely identify himself with it. He understands this nature of his as a world connected with his existence, and indeed specially ordered for it, which is for him, as for everyone else, both a gift and a task, something which has to be moulded and transformed, something to be accepted with gratitude, and yet at the same time in penitent obedience to be rejected. He does not rebel, like the man who regards himself wrongly as a purely spiritual being, against his creaturely being, which is what it is, and cannot be altered; but he also does not capitulate to it, like the man who regards himself, wrongly, as a mere product of nature. But how he does either the one or the other belongs to the sphere of ethical rather than of anthropological problems.

5. GENIUS AND THE "AVERAGE MAN"

Genius is a kind of spiritual individuality. The spiritual endowment which, when it reaches its highest form, is called genius, is, as the words 'gifted' and 'genius' suggest, something given by nature, something which one receives at birth. In our post-Romantic age it is particularly necessary to emphasize the relative character of the distinction between genius and non-genius, or as in romantic arrogance it is expressed: genius versus the 'average man.' Genius is a special degree of mental endowment, so great that it may even appear to be a new quality. In reality every human being, to a certain degree, and in some particular direction, has genius, and especially every child. The creative endowment may be very great or very small, but to a certain extent every human being possesses it. Hence there is no fixed boundary between the man who has genius and the man who has not. In cases where there seems to be a complete absence of every spark of creative power, this is always due to either the loveless superficiality of our vision or to a lack of opportunity for the development of dormant faculties. The teacher in special classes for backward children knows something of the wealth of creative ability—even if of a very modest kind—in the most dull and backward children. Yet there is a boundary line which is also the boundary of all human existence known to us: the idiot.

The element of truth in the romantic concept of genius as a special quality, is this, that genius is not so much a wealth of gifts, and not even a supreme measure of one particular gift, but—in contrast to great talent—an 'all-round' spiritual alertness, a general quality of originality in seeing and in thinking. Yet even this is relative. It exists certainly in a great number of degrees and grades, and it is not lacking in any 'normal' human being as a whole. Every human being who has not become rigidly fixed within systems of convention and training, thus every person who has remained natural, every human being in whom the child has not wholly died out under the artificialities of civilization and culture, has something original, which is connected with genius. Geniuses and children love one another. The most important element of genius is a naturalness which cannot be dragooned. Here, however, we are particularly concerned with this question: What has this question of the degree of mind, of its quantum, or the degree of originality of vital intellectual power to do with man, with personal being in the sense of the Christian faith?

It is clear that where humanity is measured by cultural rather than personal standards, genius must be immensely over-estimated. The genius is then pre-eminently 'man,' and the non-genius is a kind of 'throw-out.'[1] This aesthetic standpoint makes us, as we know, ignore the essential element of humanity. The genius may be really inhuman, while a very simple person without genius may be truly human. The degree of mental endowment has nothing to do with the distinctively human element. It is merely a dynamic sign of human or non-human existence. If the man of genius is truly human, in the sense of personal being, then certainly his humanity will be something far more impressive and powerful, and historically more effective than that of the man without genius. Hence—and this is the other side of the question—we must always make a distinction between that which is remarkable about a person which is due to faith and love, and that which is due to the fact that he is a genius. The estimate of personalities who have been prominent in the history of Christianity is very often obscured by the confusion of the two standards. A man may play an influential part in the history of the Church because his faith was combined with great genius, without his faith having been at all extraordinary. Kierkegaard, in particular, has pointed out the possibilities of error which lie in this situation. In his own person he learned to know the difference between 'an apostle and a genius'[2] in all its range and existential depth, and he brought this out very clearly with humility and passion.

[1] Cf. Lucka, *Grenzen der Seele*, second part, p. 191: 'Genius . . . is a higher synthesis of nature and freedom, it is a superlative, an ideal of the human, it is the necessary man, to whom there clings no longer anything accidental. In the genius there comes before our eyes a fortunate solution of the tragedy of humanity.' This is the necessary consequence of the conception: 'Human nature in the highest sense is productivity; and so the maximum of the human can only lie in unconditional productivity' (p. 192).

[2] Kierkegaard, *Das Buch über Adler* and *Über den Unterschied zwischen einem Apostle und einem Genie*, edited and translated by Th. Haecker under the title *Der Begriff des Auserwählten.*

On the other hand, however, the fact of idiocy shows us that we have no right to make a dualistic distinction between the being of man and his intellectual endowments. Without a certain measure of intellectual gifts it is impossible to be human. Without that mind which at its zenith is called genius, man cannot even understand the fact that he is man, and he cannot make decisions in the sense of personality. The mind, as we have already said, is the basis of being person. One does not need to have a great mind to be a person who truly believes and loves; but if one has no mind—as an idiot—one cannot even believe. The presupposition for the understanding of the Word of God is understanding in general, the understanding of words, in the general, purely human sense. What that poor creature which, in the extreme case, so far as we know, has not a spark of intelligence means in the Family of God, we do not know; we only know that it is inaccessible to the message of the Word of God, thus that in this life it cannot become a believer, because it cannot understand human speech. It is, however, more than probable that even the most vacant idiot can be approached in some way or another by real love, and thus is not without a glimmer of personal being. In spite of this, such cases are extreme instances, whose significance we cannot understand.[1]

A man is 'born' either as a genius or a non-genius. No schooling, cultivation, discipline, labour, either of his own or of someone else, can make the man who is not a genius into a genius. The capital of mental capacity which is at our disposal for life cannot be created by human effort or even be increased by it. On the other hand, it can either be destroyed, or more or less 'cultivated,' that is, developed. Human faculties are far less limited on the negative than on the positive side. As we are able to annihilate life but not to create it, so

[1] Since the Bible clearly presupposes the *nous* of man as the place and organ of faith, and the *meta-noein* is contained in the process of faith itself, it is not permissible to emphasize the creative power of the preached Word of God to such an extent that the relation to the receiving *nous* and to the understanding act of the thought of man is left out of account, in order not to be obliged to admit that there is a point of contact. The point of contact is indeed precisely characterized as a dialectical one by the *meta-noein*. Cf. Appendix III.

also we are able to destroy mind but not to create it. The vicious man may for ever ruin his genius, his intellectual and artistic powers. But there is also the opposite possibility of developing these gifts. The sum-total of that which we have the ability to do, in order to develop the creative endowments which we possess, we call 'education.' It is possible, by mental practice, by the absorption of influences outside ourselves, by the active use of our faculties, to promote, to a high degree, mental capacity and vigour, just as, on the other hand, it is possible to allow it to wither away by ignoring it. But this does not alter the fact that the endowments themselves, as such, are not in our hands at all. We can only cultivate that which is already there; cultivation is not creation. Through cultivation one becomes cultivated, but not a genius. Even the highest cultivation can never replace genius, just as the converse also is true. Both, close as they are to one another, are incommensurable.

Hence Carlyle's contention,[1] that genius and personal humanity are ultimately the same thing, that the great man, in the sense of the genius, must also be a truly great human person, contradicts the truth, as indeed it is contradicted by the actual experience of life. Through personal self-determination, through character and the content of humanity, an endowment or a genius may gain a definite tendency, but it is itself independent of it. It is and remains a mental natural power, a quantum, which man cannot increase by his own efforts. And yet between the two there is at least an analogous and indirect relation. Genuine love has something of an affinity with genius, in its own way it is creative. 'Love makes us inventive' is said even of natural love. The phrase is still more applicable if we refer to it that love 'which is shed abroad in our hearts by the Holy Spirit.'[2] For this love touches the roots of the personal life; indeed it is its deepest root—of that Self which is hidden for us in the Word of God. Not in vain does the New Testament call this love 'living water,' describing it as the beginning of eternal life.[3] Through faith we participate in the Divine life, and thus in some way we also participate in a creative life.

[1] Carlyle, *Heroes and Hero Worship*. [2] Rom. v. 5. [3] John vii. 38.

It is true, of course, that no one becomes a mathematician or an artist or a thinker of genius simply because he is a genuine believer. But when he becomes a believer powers are released which he did not know he possessed before. If in Jesus Christ 'all the treasures of wisdom are hidden,'[1] the believer gains a perception which, without being on that account 'genius,' pierces more deeply into truth, and soars to greater heights than all wisdom and philosophy. Through love, above all, he receives a kind of alertness about all that concerns human existence which amounts to genius, an alertness about all that concerns the personal life, or his neighbour, a keen and profound insight for that which his fellow-man 'really' is, and what he needs most desperately and what he lacks; a wisdom which in its absolutely original, unschematic, unique, individual and personal character presents a remarkable analogy to genius. Through faith man is set free from all that is legalistic—in such a way that this freedom, conversely, is a standard of faith—and in this experience is set free from much that prevents the truly natural, truly creaturely life from natural development. Through faith therefore human beings with a very modest outfit of intellectual powers often develop amazingly, reaching an extraordinary degree of mental independence and freedom of spirit, wisdom and clearness, compared with which a far greater intellectual ability looks meagre. The fine phrase of Schiller: 'Man grows with his great ends,' here gains a wonderful confirmation upon a higher plane—presupposing always that here, where the highest 'aim' of all is concerned, he is really, and with all his heart and soul, concerned with the 'one thing needful.'

This, however, cannot be our final word, but rather that 'what is foolishness in the sight of the world, that God has chosen to confound the wise.'[2] The 'wisdom which is from above' and the 'wisdom of the world' are of two kinds, although even the latter has its ground in the Divine Creation. It is not for us to pay special attention to the fact that faith 'may thus in some way or another make us far more intelligent'—if anyone were to strive after this he would be bitterly disappointed—our aim rather should be to see that through

[1] Col. ii. 3.
[2] I Cor. i. 27.

faith, and through it alone, we return to the divine destiny of man, which in our own wisdom we are continually leaving, that faith is only given to those who perceive the nothingness of all human gifts in view of the one thing that matters, and who join in the act of praise of the Lord Himself: 'I praise Thee, Lord of heaven and earth, that Thou hast hidden these things from the wise and prudent, and hast revealed them unto babes. Yea, Father, for so it seemed good in Thy sight.'[1]

* * * * *

Thus there is a 'Christian Humanism,' by which we do not mean that combination of ancient Humanism with the Christian faith whose patron and example is Erasmus of Rotterdam, but the knowledge of and insistence on the unity of humanity, and of the particular dignity and divine distinctiveness of man's being which is based upon the centre of the Biblical revelation. Genuine Christian Humanism is based upon the fact of the Incarnation of the Son of God, which, for its part, points back to the creation of man in the image of God. Even sin—and in the counterpart of the Divine revelation: the Cross of Christ—does not alter the fact but rather confirms it, that man is singled out by the Creator in an unparalleled way as the one in whom the Creation has reached its summit, whose redemption, therefore, is also the aim and the meaning of the whole of history. Man—not the Aryan, not the male, not the civilized man, not the bearer of spiritual values, not the superman of the future—but all who bear the human face. There is only one distinction which is decisive, this indeed decides for time and eternity: 'that all who believe on Him should not perish, but should have everlasting life.[2] In the end, the only differentiation which matters is this: whether man returns to his origin or remains in his alienation, in his opposition to the Word in which he has been created. It is not the formal humanity upon which Humanism builds, but this content which is decisive; hence the meaning of man's being is not secured in something which cannot be altered, but it is a matter for decision.

[1] Matt. xi. 25.

[2] John iii. 16.

CHAPTER XV

MAN AND WOMAN

I. THE SEX DIFFERENCE AS CREATION

THE problem of the sexes and of sexuality is primarily one of the phenomena of the problem of individuality. A human being is individualized just as much by the fact of being male or female as by the fact that he or she belongs to a particular race, or has a peculiar psychical 'make-up,' or by his or her intellectual endowments; the human element is differentiated in a definite way by the fact of belonging to the male or the female sex. In spite of this, however, we are not dealing with this question in that context; the reason is that the sex difference penetrates far more deeply than all individuality, and that the problem of sexuality is far more fundamental than that of individual characteristics. We cannot say that humanity is divided into the 'sanguine' and the 'choleric' temperament, into extraverts and introverts, into white or coloured races, into geniuses and non-geniuses; but humanity certainly is divided into men and women, and this distinction goes down to the very roots of our personal existence, and penetrates into the deepest 'metaphysical' grounds of our personality and our destiny. Just as the problem of marriage is the crucial point and the fateful question in ethics, so is the problem of the sexes in anthropology. And the sex difference has this fateful significance not only for the philosophers, who from the very outset only have 'man' in view[1]—and as a rule this means the male—but for the poets of all

[1] Still philosophers like Schelling, and especially Wilhelm von Humboldt, have said some valuable things about sex as an anthropological problem (cf. the work by the latter entitled *Über die männliche und weibliche Form*, *Werke*, vol. I). It is well known that Goethe's thought from beginning to end continually revolves round this problem, and that it is determinative in Dante's vision of the world. In Plato it is indicated, and after him it scarcely plays any part in ancient philosophy. (In Posidonius it is at least mentioned, in connexion with cosmic sympathy, Reinhardt, op. cit., p. 127.)

ages and all kinds, for the folk-soul which forms myths, that is, for the living 'natural man' as such. Has the Bible anything distinctive to say about this problem?

'So God created man in His own image, in the image of God created He him; male and female created He them.'[1] That is the immense double statement, of a lapidary simplicity, so simple indeed that we hardly realize that with it a vast world of myth and Gnostic speculation, of cynicism and asceticism, of the deification of sexuality and fear of sex completely disappears. It seems so incredibly naïve to couple the statement that 'man was made in the image of God' with the statement that God 'created them, one man and one woman.' And yet in the whole long history of man's understanding of himself this statement has only been made *once* and at this point. Otherwise, in a hundred different ways, man has always said something else which contradicts this statement; sometimes he says too little and sometimes too much; sometimes one aspect or another of the problem has been over-emphasized; at other times men have cursed the fact that it exists at all. On account of this one statement alone the Bible shines out among all other books in the world as the Word of God. So there is a connexion between these two statements: God created man in His image, and, He created him as man and woman. It will be worth while thinking deeply about this, that we too may say neither too much nor too little about it.

It is well known that it is not correct to say that bi-sexuality is characteristic of all natural life. There is life which is not sexually differentiated, there are asexual creatures which are reproduced by division into cells, and there are bi-sexual creatures which have the sex differentiation in themselves. It is not a foregone conclusion that man should not belong to these creatures but to those which pair. To use zoological terms, for once, man is the one perfect mammal, since that tendency which we recognize in the mammalian species the more highly it develops as its biological idea is expressed quite clearly in man alone; I mean, the fact that the partners

[1] Gen. i. 27. For this whole chapter see the important book by Otto Piper, *Sinn und Geheimnis der Geschlechter.*

remain together, and that the young remain with their parents; permanent pairing and permanent provision for the young. In man, however, marriage and the family turns out to be something which cannot be realized on the natural plane, but is only possible as an ethical institution. Only in the personal relation of marriage is the biological meaning of the natural pairing fulfilled. Even from this one fact we perceive that the sexuality of man is not a merely natural fact, in the biological sense of the word.

Certainly man is primarily a sex-being in the sense of natural disposition and function. But this sexual disposition is not something purely natural—as is, for instance, the digestive system. It helps to determine the whole psychical and even the spiritual nature of the man and the woman. Just as the whole physical nature of man is connected with and indeed penetrated by the organic sex function, so also is his psychical and spiritual being. Conversely, the spiritual and psychical human quality permeates the sexual function, so that we may even venture to say that man does not know the animal sex instinct. The sexuality of man is always, in some way or another, connected with love,[1] and it is the love element which characterizes it as either spiritual or demonic. The animal does not know love, because it has no ideas, and above all, because it can know nothing of love as personal fellowship. On the other hand, even so-called 'primitive' people know nothing of animal sexuality; in some form or another their sexuality always contains an ethical, personal element. The complete elimination of the personal love element and of the personal ethical element is not characteristic of human nature; it is a phenomenon of a decadent civilization. But we would be sentimentally romantic about nature and shut our eyes to facts if we were to believe in a condition of pure 'nature,' for instance, among primitive peoples. Just as the specifically human element is never completely absent from the sexuality of man, everywhere there can be found something of that unnatural demonic deformation of sexuality which is lacking in the animal, as well as the distinctively

[1] German: *Erotik*. The meaning of this term is fully discussed in *Eros und Liebe* by Emil Brunner.—*Translator*.

human element.[1] But the more that man comes to consciousness of himself the more he feels his sexuality as a problem, as an experience in which pleasure and pain, light and darkness, freedom and slavery are mysteriously intertwined. Here too the experience of man himself forces us to lay emphasis upon the twofold point of view: Creation and sin.

2. THE RENT, SHAME AND LONGING

The statement that God created them, man and woman, implies that the myth of the androgynes is an impossibility for Christian thought. This ought to be specially emphasized because—as has happened frequently in the past—there is at the present day a Gnostic tendency which represents the fact of the two sexes as a result of the Fall. This view is of Greek and pagan, not of Biblical origin.[2] But we do not deny the important truths which lie behind this old Gnostic doctrine. The sexuality which we know from human experience does in point of fact bear witness to a vast rent which runs right through human nature, and comes out in this particular sphere with special poignancy. There are two facts which accompany all 'love'—and especially all genuinely human 'love'—in the sense of sex attraction: a shame which cannot be overcome, and a longing which cannot be satisfied. Sexual shame is not, as a superficial materialism would suggest, something which is artificially produced, something added, but it is a genuine human feeling, founded deeply in human nature. To know nothing of this sense of shame is not a sign of a specially high kind of humanity, but is a token of perversion. Man is not merely ashamed of the sexuality which is forbidden to him morally, but shame accompanies him even into the completely personal sex-relation in marriage, and indeed the more he determines himself as person, the more spiritual his existence, the more is he aware of this. We cannot think of our Lord as married, although we are not in the least jarred by the fact that He ate and drank like the rest of mankind. Even

[1] It is enough to recall the story of the destruction of Sodom (Gen. xix).

[2] The most important champion of the Gnostic myth of the androgynes in modern times is Berdyaev. Cf. his *Destiny of Man* (German translation, pp. 89 ff.).

the doctrine of the Virgin Birth points in this direction—whatever we may think about it from other points of view. It would appear that in sexuality there is something which is fundamentally and irreparably out of order, that is, out of the divine order.

But the immense longing, the longing which cannot be stilled, which is expressed in the love lyrics of all ages and peoples, also points to this fundamental rent. Certainly, it is first of all longing for the beloved, for full union with him or her. But is that all? Does there not lie behind all fulfilment, and indeed within it, that longing for something more complete? Is it not true that here the phrase 'enough is not enough' is very apt? Thus is there not here a division which no intimate communion with one another can overcome, even if neither the physical nor the mental and spiritual element of union be lacking? Finally, may it not be possible that the myth which teaches how wrong it is to say that man and woman are two, when they really should be regarded as one, may have some truth in it? Is it perhaps the case that sexual polarity is a cosmic potency far beyond all sex experience, a metaphysical principle of duality which indicates a metaphysical division at the very source of life itself?

The Bible says, however, in the simplest and plainest language that one can imagine: God created them, man and woman. Then what is the meaning of this duality? And from this point of view how are we to understand that complex of facts which leads so many—even Christian—thinkers to the myth of the androgynes? The first question we can best answer in the negative. The desire for the overcoming of sex duality belongs to an (openly or hiddenly monistic) way of thinking. In the Platonist idealism of the Spirit the thought of the androgynes is fully justified;[1] in the thought of the Bible it is

[1] Plato conceals his own view behind the poetical and mythological speech of Aristophanes in the *Symposium*; but the fact that in this way he suggests the myth of the androgynes is more than a merely poetic whim. The theme recurs in W. v. Humboldt in his 'idea of pure and sexless humanity' (*Über die männliche und weibliche Form, Werke*, I, p. 351). Through the revival of the interpretation of myths by Bachofen, and the neo-romantic philosophy of the 'cosmogonal Eros' of Klages, this has once more become a subject of ardent philosophical discussion.

not. Why? The argument from the fact of nature as such we refuse to employ. God could have used both ways and means to fit man out in such a way that his species could have been handed on without the apparatus common to all mammals, without procreation through pairing, just as God has actually freed man from many of the laws to which the animal series is subject. It was not to be so, He willed it otherwise, somehow more humblingly for man. It is not a necessity of nature, but His will, which is the reason for this state of affairs; and we may reverently make the attempt to understand this will from the Scriptures as a whole. God creates us as finite, creaturely beings, dependent upon each other, unable to exist by ourselves, not as autonomous, self-sufficient beings. Precisely in this function, in which the Creator most fully allows us to share in His creative work, we are to experience this fact, that we are made for and depend upon one another. 'It is not good for man to be alone.'[1] It is good for him, in view of the constant danger of confusing himself with the Creative Spirit, that, as a creature, he should have a part in that arrangement which most fundamentally binds two beings to one another, and thus makes each one dependent upon, and needing to be supplemented by the other. The arrogant idea of the self-sufficient individual person is here most effectively eliminated.

Then what is the source of shame and longing? To this the answer of the Bible comes quite explicitly and plainly: the Fall. The first effect of the Fall on the pair of human beings created by God was: shame.[2] It is only now, after man and woman have sinned, that a rent goes right through their sex nature and makes them ashamed of themselves. It is not their sexuality in itself which is the reason for their shame—before the Fall we are told explicitly 'they were not ashamed'[3]—but the nakedness unveiled by sin, which previously, like the terrible majesty of God, was veiled from them by God's loving Word which united them. This does not mean that sexuality, the sexual difference, and the polarity of man and woman, is sin, but that sin has entered into the sex relation in such a way that the sex nature and the personal life, sexuality and

[1] Gen. ii. 18. [2] Gen. iii. 7. [3] Gen. ii. 25.

spiritual destiny, the sex creature and the spiritual creature have become separated. Shame is the expression of this separation, surprise at the fact that man is both the one and the other. Man now feels, and rightly, that the personal-spiritual element and the sexuality which he now has are incompatible, and thus he feels that from the point of view of personal existence sex does not belong to him; it is low, and base, humiliating animal nature. In shame, however, there is also, with the feeling of surprise, the fear of something uncanny and at the same time a curious desire for it.

This forms the bridge to the second element, to *longing*. 'And thy desire shall be to thy husband'[1]—that is the curse which follows the Fall. It is not the sexual desire in itself which is regarded in this light—the suggestion that husband and wife should cleave unto one another, and that they should become 'one flesh' comes before the story of the Fall[2]—but what is wrong is greedy desire and unsatisfied longing. Longing, by its very nature, is unquenchable, whereas the natural instinct can be satisfied. Man alone, by means of his spiritual nature, knows what longing is. The relation between the sexes which has fallen away from genuine love, from the realm of the personal, cannot satisfy; it leaves a profound desire unsatisfied, not the aspiration after union, but the desire for true community. In the actual union itself there is division, caused by sin, hence it does not satisfy, but leaves behind it an unsatisfied desire. But man, as sinner, is not capable of rightly interpreting this desire, and sin is so deeply rooted in his nature, that even the correct interpretation alone would not help. Only the complete return to love could banish this division; but this return cannot take place fully in any earthly-historical life, since man, even as a believer, remains at the same time a sinner, since even in the believer that disintegration, that separation between personal being and sexuality is still to some extent present.

The whole complex of problems connected with the question of sex is based upon this dualism of person and sex; the impersonality of sexuality is that which causes man so much trouble; at the same time it is that which arouses his desire because it

[1] Gen. iii. 16. [2] Gen. ii. 24.

seems mysterious and rather frightening, and yet attractive. When the *Eros* has become fully personal this mysterious attraction, with its almost magical appeal, disappears. That is why the prostitute makes herself as impersonal as possible, that is why sex desire 'needs' depersonalizing secrecies and obscurities in order to be effective. The Venusberg is lighted with artificial light, the sexual deities are night-deities; this whole sinfully-depersonalized *Eros* seeks the *clair-obscur* of the semi-conscious and derives its force from this region. The struggle arises between the Light God 'Apollo' and the 'chthonic'[1] deities,[2] between the brightness of the spirit and the darkness of passion, a struggle which, from the point of view of man, can never end, because even the spirit is no longer originally personal, but it has become abstract, part of the realm of mere ideas. Neither Apollo nor the dim earth-gods are 'right,' for this rationality lacks warmth, just as that hot atmosphere lacks light. The severance of spirit and nature by sin has now become above all the separation between spirit and sex.

3. THE MASCULINE AND THE FEMININE NATURE

The depth of this division shows how deeply sexuality has been implanted in the nature of man by the Creation. Man is not a sex being in addition to that which he is otherwise, but the sex difference penetrates and determines the whole of human existence. The man is not only man in his sexual function, but he is man in all his thought and feeling. The same is true of the woman in her existence as woman. The differentiation of the biological sexual function in the man and the woman has its exact counterpart in the mental and spiritual[3] nature of both sexes, although—in accordance with what has already been said about the relation between individuality and genius in a previous chapter—it recedes in

[1] Deities dwelling in the interior of the earth.—*Translator.*

[2] Bachofen's *Das Mutterrecht* (1861) was a first brilliant attempt to take this mythical contrast seriously; but it needed the force of Nietzsche (*Geburt der Tragödie*) and his theory of the 'Apollinische' and the 'Dionysische' to bring out and set in the right light the—rather different—theory of Bachofen.

[3] i.e. the 'psychological make-up.'—*Translator*

exact proportion to the measure in which the spirit, and the personal spirit in particular, becomes strong. Within this limitation it may be said that also spiritually the man expresses the productive principle and the woman expresses the principle of bearing, tending and nourishing.[1] The man turns more to the outside world, the woman turns more to the inner realm; the man inclines to be objective, the woman to be subjective; the man seeks the new, the woman preserves the old; the man roams about, the woman makes a home.

One result of this particular kind of differentiation is that the man's connexion with the natural sex function penetrates less deeply than with the woman. The woman, through her natural calling as wife and mother, carries a far heavier burden than the man does, as husband and father. The growth of the new human being forms part of the life of the woman far more than it forms part of the life of the man. The wife must give her heart's blood to the new being; she must bear it, she must bring it into the world not only with pain, but with danger to life itself, and she must nourish at her own breast that which she has brought into the world. By this natural determination she is far more closely connected with the natural process of life, impregnated with it, restricted, but also preserved by it. Far less than her husband can she order her own life as she would like; but this is not her husband's doing; it is simply due to the fact of her motherhood. This difference penetrates into the very depths of her nature.

Man and woman are both sinners, just as both have been created in the image of God. But they are sinners in different ways. Their otherness gives even their sinfulness a different stamp. The man, the one who roams about freely, sins above all on the side of freedom; he is arbitrary, dominating, masterful, arrogant; he cannot brook any interference, he will not accept ties, he is presumptuous; he does not lose himself so much in nature as in his own creations, his culture and his

[1] Cf. Humboldt's delicate characterization of the sexes in his paper, *Über die männliche und die weibliche Form* (*Werke*, vol. I, pp. 335 ff.). It is in accordance with Humboldt's harmonistic view that he sees rather the positive and complementary aspects of the question than the negative and contradictory.

civilization; he not only makes things objective but he makes everything an object. He brutalizes the creature and treads it under foot; he places himself in an arrogant manner above its ordinances and imposes on it his arbitrary order. He is the one who imposes his will by force and he is the destroyer. But he does not lightly forget that he is destined for freedom, that he is called to make the earth subject to him. Even when he is fettered by the senses, he does not easily yield to their domination, he does not accept this simply as his destiny. The sin of the man is generally speaking so violent and obvious that he has less difficulty than the woman in admitting that he is a sinner.

The woman, on the other hand, will not so easily deny and destroy the creaturely bond. She remains closer to the creation as a given fact, and she tends to preserve this relation; but her sin is that she often forgets and inwardly abandons the freedom which so often she does not possess outwardly. She adapts herself, she does not rebel against evil; she sinks down into her natural calling, she does not rise above the level of ordinary existence, she loses herself in nature-mysticism, she emphasizes the sex relation in her existence. For her the relation between husband and wife is far more central than it is for her husband; in this she loses her universal human destiny, her spiritual task, she allows herself to be persuaded by her husband that she 'belongs to the home and has no other responsibilities outside.' She lays far more emphasis upon the fact of sex, she is far more sexual than the man, although the instinct within her, from the purely organic point of view, is not so acute and passionate. If the husband is falsely free she is falsely bound; and if the husband is impersonal and intellectual, she tends to be personal and natural in a wrong way.

Such a theory of sex types is, of course, like all such theories, to be accepted with all due reserve. The modern woman, in particular, will not see her own portrait in this picture. But she may be asked not to forget that we are not speaking of woman since the year 1850, but of woman since 'the days of Adam,' of woman among primitive peoples, in antiquity, in the Middle Ages, of the Eastern woman, of the unemancipated woman of the present day, who still represents more than nine-tenths of the women who are alive at the present time. The emancipated woman of the present day generally tends to regard the sex difference—in so far as it is unalterable —as a purely biological matter, while she regards the psychical and spiritual differentiation partly as a mere figment of the imagination, and partly as the result of education under male domination. She will not allow that the same difference of structure which is evident in the physical sphere is also found in the psycho-spiritual nature of woman, and that this is due to nature, and is not the result of education. This is the exaggerated one-sidedness which colours all movements for the emancipation of woman. This modern psychology of woman is not tenable in the light of the testimony of history and of the literature of all countries.

But behind this view there is a concern for truth which ought not to be overlooked. In point of fact, man, as the actually dominating shaper of history, culture, the conditions of the law and of public education, from selfish and short-sighted motives, has artificially riveted woman to her natural destiny, and has hindered the free development of her mind and spirit, to which she, as well as the man, as one who has been made in the image of God, has been called. He has shaped her according to his desire of what woman should be. Even at the present day, and to a far greater degree than we usually realize, woman is still the slave of man, even the woman in the higher classes, even the educated woman. Hence her real nature cannot yet be clearly discerned. It is still concealed behind the picture of woman as man wants her to be, and by the woman who is the product of the masterful will of the man. The right of woman's emancipation is not got rid of by a cheap allusion to its exaggerated forms and extravagances; woman has still a long way to go before she attains her real freedom. At the present day we can only say what woman 'really' is in a very cursory manner and with reserve. The man has had every opportunity to show what he really is; he has indeed—and this is a part of his self-manifestation—shown what he is in the very fact that he has deprived woman of the same possibility.

4. SEX AND HUMANITY

The man could not do this without first of all outlining a theory of the nature of woman which made his action legitimate. This is the theory of the metaphysical, essentially inferior value of the woman.[1] It is connected with that misunderstanding of man about himself, it is part of that falsely abstract conception of the nature of the spiritual which we have already described. If, as the man usually does, we expound human existence from the point of view of his power to create culture, of his creative capacities, thus as 'formal' and not as 'material' humanity, then certainly the woman is less human than the man. For the woman's mind is less creative than that of man. This has a deep connexion with her natural destiny. In the contrast between 'Apollo' and the 'gods who dwell in the interior of the earth,' the man is undubitably more on the side of Apollo and the woman on the side of the earth-gods. As we have already said, however, the struggle between these two deities, these genuine idols, is endless, because it is a conflict caused by sin. For it exactly reflects that misunderstanding of the life of the mind which deals only in abstractions, which is concerned with culture and work, and not with persons, and makes this the standard of the life of the mind and the spirit.

If, however, we start from the Biblical concept of spirit, from the material concept of humanity, which understands the meaning of existence not as impersonal culture, but as being-in-love, being-in-community, then our view of the relation of the sexes to the destiny of humanity becomes quite

[1] There is an explicitly misogynous tradition in philosophy. By this I do not mean the 'Apollonian' rational thought of the man, which takes for granted the depreciation of woman, and the quite open contempt for woman which appears in Greek philosophy from Socrates onwards, but the strongly emotionally emphasized, in part passionate suspicion and caricature of the feminine element, which in some way or another is connected with personal suffering due to the sex problem. Schopenhauer's cynical misogyny belongs less to this tendency than does a book like that of Weininger—a book which is at once brilliant and absurd—*Geschlecht und Charakter*; the work of Strindberg; certain often quoted expressions of Nietzsche, and also similar ones by Kierkegaard (cf. Geismar, *Sören Kierkegaard*, the chapter *Mann und Weib*, pp. 585 ff.).

different. Instead of a difference of degree we have a difference of kind; instead of thinking in terms of stages we think in parallel terms. Woman is human and inhuman in a different way from the man, but she is no less human than the man. Her personal existence is less 'intellectual' but also, for that very reason, it is less abstract than that of the man. Her danger and her error is that of being on the merely psychical plane, while the man's danger is that of leading a merely self-willed and rational intellectual existence. The 'Apollonian' masculine principle is just as much a deviation from the will of the Creator as the 'chthonic' feminine principle; the abstract and concrete intellectuality of the man is just as sinful as the unintellectual concreteness of the woman and her narrowly personal nature.

Hence, because there is right and wrong on both sides, there is the eternal struggle between man and woman, which is waged on both sides with passion, but by very different methods. The man fights against the woman by trying to dominate and tyrannize over her; the woman fights against the man by fettering and 'entangling' him. This struggle, far more mighty than all the wars of which we hear in world history, operates further as a 'breeding factor'; moreover, it stamps the character of the man and of the woman with one-sidedness and a false differentiation. The man develops his masterfulness still further, and the woman develops her typical feminine arts which she uses as her weapons; she becomes more and more the kind of woman who as a slave dominates her lord; she develops her effective defence tactics. She conquers in being conquered and is defeated in the fact of this victory. She revenges herself upon man for the inferiority which is ascribed to her by accepting this masculine picture of woman, and thus she becomes for him the 'dangerous female.'

It is not only sin which is at work in this sphere, but also the divine original destiny of man, the *Imago Dei*. Man never loses the idea of the 'true woman,' just as the woman never loses the idea of the 'true man.' Even in the midst of his sinful masterfulness, by means of which man subjects woman to his will, man knows that there is more in woman than that which his sin shows him as something to be both desired and feared. This idea of the true woman is somehow operative in his longing, and never allows him to find satisfaction in the woman whom he desires and who satisfies his desires. Alongside of the type of Eve the temptress, there is the type of Mary the holy Maid. It was not only for woman, but above all for man, that the picture of Mary was introduced into the cult of the Catholic Church. The ascetic ideal of chastity and monasticism was developed by man and not by woman. In this we see, even though in a fresh perversion, the Original ideal.

5. THE PROBLEM OF ORDER

The primal truth, however, is this: God created man in His own image; male and female created He them. This truth cuts away the ground from all belief in the inferior value of woman. The Creator has created man and woman not with different values but of different kinds,[1] dependent upon one another, a difference in kind which means that each complements the other. Together with their different natural destiny—which as an original Creation should be taken seriously and not regarded as a secondary matter—man and woman have received a different stamp as human beings, as persons, which extends to their existence-for-community. Both are called to be persons, to live in love, in the same degree, but in different ways. The man is the one who produces, he is the leader; the woman is receptive, and she preserves life; it is the man's duty to shape the new; it is the woman's duty to unite it and adapt it to that which already exists. The man

[1] It can scarcely be contested that the low view of woman which prevailed in pre-Christian Judaism casts a certain shadow over the New Testament as well. The expressions used by Paul in 1 Cor. xi. 3 ff. cannot be explained merely by speaking of a differentiation between the sexes, and therefore that the leadership is put in the hands of the man. It is undeniable that here there is a certain element of depreciation of woman. Along with other elements this forms part of the garment of the times in which the message of the New Testament is clothed. But it is a disappearing element. It is not only overcome by the truth of Gal. iii. 28, but even in the missionary practice of Paul it plays scarcely any part. The way in which Paul speaks in his letters of and to his women fellow workers bears scarcely any traces of the metaphysic of 1 Cor. xi.

has to go forth and make the earth subject to him, the woman looks within and guards the hidden unity. The man must be objective and generalize, the woman must be subjective and individualize; the man must build, the woman adorns; the man must conquer, the woman must tend; the man must comprehend all with his mind, the woman must impregnate all with the life of her soul. It is the duty of the man to plan and to master, of the woman to understand and to unite.

In these distinctive qualities there lies a certain super- and sub-ordination; but it is a purely functional difference, not a difference in value, it is not a scale of values.[1] The special call to serve where love is perceived as the meaning of life, is rather a privilege than a humiliation. This different attitude is maintained in the Bible, even in the Creation narrative. A 'helpmeet'[2] is given to man. In our corrupted world that means 'a subordinate, dependent, less important person,' but originally this was not the intention; this is how it is interpreted by masterful people who want to be like God, positively by the man, and negatively by the woman. For mutual service is the supreme proof of fully mature and well-developed human life. From this centre there should issue a transformation of all values, derived from Him who came 'not to be ministered unto but to minister,'[3] and who by that very fact has revealed the meaning of human life.

As husband and wife—with their different structure and their different functions—are one in the physical fact of sexual union, so they ought to be one in all their life together;

[1] The fact that in the New Testament the function of leadership does not denote masterfulness or *dominium*, but a *ministerium*, may be deduced from the whole context of that very passage which for many is the greatest stumbling-block at the present day, Eph. v. 22 ff. The way in which the man is to have the leadership in marriage and in the Church, is determined by the Christian community, through the example of the relation between Christ and the Church. Christ rules by love; He rules only through the call to freedom, in the creation of personal responsibility. We see from the *Letter to Philemon* how Paul transforms the master-relation of a slave owner into a personal relation of community; how much more then here! The historical limits of this idea have been indicated above. On the whole question see my book, *Das Gebot und die Ordnungen*, pp. 358 ff. (English: *The Divine Imperative*, pp. 356 ff.)

[2] Gen. ii. 18.

[3] Mark x. 45.

through all the differences of mind and spirit, they should be one in all they do and are, for one another, and for their whole environment. The husband, for instance, simply because he enters into contact with the outside world, is not the only one who is related to the whole. Just as the wife is of equal value as a member of the Church, of the community of the faithful, so she also, like her husband, should bring her own contribution to the welfare of the nation, and of humanity as a whole. Only her contribution will always be more intimate, less evident to the outside world, more hidden and individual than that of the man. If our analysis be correct, then both extremes are equally wrong: complete 'equality' in public life, and the 'private' life to which woman has been relegated in the past. If woman is to give her best, and is to make her specific contribution, there must be, even in her public service, some measure of differentiation from man's way of doing things, some space for the more intimate and personal element.

There will come a time when all these questions of differentiation, and the problems to which they give rise, will disappear entirely. 'They shall be as the angels in heaven.'[1] That super- and sub-ordination of man and woman is destined for the period of this world, not for eternity. For 'in Christ there is neither male nor female.'[2] We must make a distinction between the original Creation and the aim of redemption. Even the divinely good origin, the divine Creation, is not the divine and blessed End. All that is gradually being prepared here, within the sphere of history, for the final End, shall there be perfected. Hence Jesus Christ, the Redeemer, has nothing to do with the whole question of the difference between the sexes. He is not shown to us as an ideal and honourable husband, but as One in whose Person the end of all things, the end even of all orders which are intended for this earthly world, and also are good and necessary for them, the end of the order of marriage and of the family is foreshadowed. Marriage and the family and the whole of sexuality is related to the process of becoming, but not to that of fulfilment. Sexuality is the divinely willed manner in which humanity is permitted to come into being, to give us all existence. This

[1] Matt. xxii. 30.

[2] Gal. iii. 28.

growth will come to an end one day, and with it sexuality and its differentiation of existence and of function. The sex element belongs to the sphere of earth, not to that of heaven, to the temporal, not to the eternal. Therefore even the most perfect possible order of the relations between the sexes is only a penultimate, not an ultimate matter.

CHAPTER XVI

SOUL AND BODY

1. SOUL AND SPIRIT

As personal being is rooted in the mind, so also mental existence is rooted in the soul. The mental life is composed of soul-material. As such, this 'soul' or psychical element is not a special subject of Christian anthropology, any more than the body, as such. The one fact of decisive importance is this, that man is a whole consisting of body, soul and spirit. So far as the soul is concerned, this is expressed in the fact that the Bible very often uses 'soul' and 'spirit,' 'soul' and 'heart' as equivalent expressions. This again is only possible because the Bible does not take the 'soul' into account, as it differs from the spirit—that is, it takes no account of the 'psychical material'; it regards the 'soul' only from the point of view of the spirit or the person. In this sense the Bible, both the Old and the New Testament, is not in the least psychological; the psychical element as such is almost unknown, or at least it is regarded as entirely uninteresting.

The following question has often been discussed: Is the thought of the Bible a dichotomy or a trichotomy? That is, Is there only one principle outside the body, namely, the soul?—which is, in some way or another, bearer of the spirit—or are there two principles, soul and spirit, soul and reason, which should be regarded as constituting the nature of man? The question is insoluble so long as one fails to note the way in which soul and spirit are related to one another.[1] The soul,

[1] The question of dichotomy or trichotomy has only been able to play such a large part in the theology of the Church because already the Biblical view of personality had been obscured by the influence of a Platonic dualism through the interest in the *anima immortalis*. Certainly the Platonic trichotomy encouraged this interest, since it set the spirit, as the higher, the immortal soul, against the psychical vital function. The idea of an *anima rationalis* is fused with that of the *natura rationalis* (Irenaeus) into a unity in that of the *anima immortalis*, which in death becomes separated from the body. The soul which after death ascends up to heaven, that is, after its severance from the body, is that Platonic

in and for itself, is that which inheres in all that lives; it is not the distinctive characteristic of man as man; the specifically human element is mind and spirit. The relation between the two, however, is complicated by the fact that the soul is regarded as both the basis of the spirit and as one with it. The soul is the substratum of the spirit;[1] the spirit is the soul, determined by sense-acts. The spirit therefore is that in which the relation to the *Logos*, to God, and to all that is Truth, Law, Norm, etc., operates; the soul, on the other hand, is that which connects all that lives, as such, even the living body.[2] Indeed, the soul is itself the life-principle of the body, just as the soul is the life-principle of the spirit. As a rule the Bible does not distinguish between these two aspects of the soul: that which is turned towards the spirit, and that which is turned towards the natural life. The question of dichotomy or trichotomy is therefore an idle one. So far as the human soul as such—in contrast to the animal—is understood from the very outset as disposed for acts of the spirit, outside the body there is only one element: the soul, the bearer of the acts of the spirit, and through them of the whole personal life. In so far, however, as the spiritual act as such is distinguished from the psychical—that is, so far as the specifically human element is concerned—of course even in the Bible

element which has penetrated most deeply into the *faith* of the Church—and not only into its theology; even to-day it is the predominating metaphysic. If, on the contrary, we start from the Biblical idea of personality, then the question: *dichotomy versus trichotomy* becomes pointless. The same human being who has been created by God has physical, psychical and spiritual functions, which as such are absolutely distinguishable, but which cannot be distinguished metaphysically. There is no *anima immortalis*, but only a personality, destined by God for eternity, a person who is body-soul-spirit, who dies as a whole, and is raised as a whole. The corporeal personal existence characterizes human creatureliness, not the mortal in contrast to the immortal, nor the 'lower' part in contrast with a 'higher' part. Cf. on this point the excellent observations of Gutbrod: op. cit., pp. 31 ff.

[1] *Geist*, here taken in its broadest sense.—*Translator.*

[2] Cf. Luther's famous *Magnificat* passage: 'The Scripture divides men into three parts . . . and each of these three together with the whole man is also divided in another way into two parts. . . . The other, the soul, is the same spirit according to nature, but yet in another work.' The spirit is 'the house wherein dwells faith and the Word of God,' the soul is that 'which makes the body alive' (WA. 7, 550).

a threefold nature is recognized: the body, the soul, which man has along with all that lives, and the spiritual or personal element, the reason and the 'heart.'

In this connexion the constitution of the soul is only relevant —like the constitution of the body—in so far as it concerns the personality as a whole. The fact that our spiritual acts and our lives as persons consist of psychical elements stamps them as creaturely. God has no soul, the absolute personality has no psychical constitution; it is pure actuality. The psychical element, however, determines our spiritual existence at the same time as a natural existence. Our will has as its basis, impulse, our thought, sense-perception and imagination, our emotion, the feeling of pleasure and pain, proper to all the higher animals. Thus it is always possible for man to neglect or ignore that spiritual life for which he is destined. When this happens he immediately relapses into the animal and natural sphere. The spirit always comes into being by rising above the merely psychical existence, by 'work.' Indolence, unwillingness to work, the failure to rise above the inward existence, is, so to speak, the 'natural state of equilibrium.' This qualification as the 'natural' is, however, only correct when seen 'from below'; when seen 'from above,' that is, from the point of view of divine destiny and of responsibility, from that of true human existence, it can only be understood as apostasy, as self-alienation. From the point of view of physics inertness is evident, and needs no explanation, while motion is the problem; from the point of view of the mind the situation is the very opposite, because the mind is activity, matter is inertness.[1] Hence the mind—ultimately the 'I,' the person—must 'awaken' the soul to its mental activity; left to itself, it sleeps. Severed from mental activity the soul sinks down into animal, and even into vegetable passivity, that is, into a lower kind of activity, which, although it does not lack spontaneity, lacks that spontaneity which we call freedom.

[1] The idea of Fichte, that indolence is the primal sin, is typically Idealistic; from the point of view of the Bible we should rather say that indolence is one of the effects and phenomena of sin, that is, of the destroyed union with God. Where the 'heart' is not united with God, it falls a prey either to abstract spirituality or to the sense-life.

Hence it is easy to understand why the mind has been called the 'adversary of the soul' and made responsible for all evil.[1] In point of fact, the mind and it alone is responsible for all evil. But this is not to say that the fact that the mind, or freedom, exists, is an evil; what is evil is the fact that the mind, or rather the person, has made a false use of freedom. The determinative element, the ἡγεμονικόν, whether false or true, is always the spirit, the 'heart,' the 'I.' But the element of truth in that romantic theory of the mind as the adversary of the soul is this: that the mind, when it determines itself sinfully, also corrupts the soul, and indeed that it is precisely the soul which is rendered ineffective and is not allowed to come to life. That which is peculiar to the 'soul' is its connexion with the creaturely life as a whole.

The soul unites man with the world of nature and of things, by means of the body, which directly connects the person with the world. The sense impressions and the inner impulses which set the body in motion are the extreme boundary of the soul in its relation to the external world. But the connexion with all other living creatures is not only of this external, objective character, but it is also accomplished in a quite different way—it is sympathetic and instinctive. The conscious is only a small part, it is like the summit[2] of the iceberg which emerges from the ocean, whereas the other ten-elevenths remain hidden in the ocean of the unconscious. Through the unconscious the past is present to our minds, both to that of the individual as well as—in ways which are still little known—to the whole human race; and indeed, perhaps, in some way or another, even to that of the whole of living nature. The conscious mental life is only that part of the soul as a whole which is illuminated by the 'I,' which otherwise loses itself in the collective, just as the lower part of the individual mountain loses itself in the mountain chain, and in the 'skeleton of the earth' as a whole. Bodily 'independence,' the detachment of the animal organism from its environment, easily deceives us, and makes us forget that we are not only 'of the earth earthy,' but that we belong, in all our life and soul, to the life and soul

[1] Klages: *Der Geist als Widersacher der Seele.*

[2] Lit. 'eleventh part.'—*Translator.*

of the whole; the discovery of the 'collective unconscious' by means of psycho-analysis has explicitly reminded us of this bond with the world of creatures, although in itself it has been a well-known fact for a long time.[1] Although the question, 'How is our conscious life connected with this unconscious psychical life?' is undoubtedly of great importance, it is still only part of the larger question: How is our personal life as a whole conditioned by the psychical element? And how does this react upon the latter?

The mind as 'the adversary of the soul' is the mind which alienates the soul from its twofold original destiny in Creation, the restoration of the connexion between personal life and created life as a whole. In accordance with the purpose of the Creation man is embedded in the incredibly rich soil of the creaturely world, not in order to sink down into it, but in order to draw from it the forces for his own personal life, and to give back to the creature that which it has taken from it, but re-moulded by the spirit. In this connexion with the natural life the human life ought to work out its own laws, which are different from the life of nature, and yet themselves 'natural,' with a different rhythm and in quite other dimensions, and yet still in contact with the rhythm of the life of nature as a whole. Here, in these unconscious depths, the human creator-spirit should have a fathomless provision of insights and awarenesses, he should secretly listen to the secret of the divine work of creation, and gaze, as it were, into the divine workshop, in order that he himself, as God's apprentice, is his own small way may exercise his own activity in the way in which God works.[2] The human spirit should

[1] Jung's theory of the collective-unconscious and of the 'arche-types' (cf. *Die Beziehung zwischen dem Ich und dem Unbewussten*) is still at a tentative stage and cannot therefore be simply accepted; but it points to situations which have always been seen as, for instance, by I. H. Fichte, Schubert, Carus, which we might indicate by the phrase 'cosmic-psychical connex.' Semon's *Mneme*, the racial memory, also belongs to this context.

[2] That is the justifiable concern of theologians like Oetinger, Auberlen and more recently Köberle (*Die Seele des Christentums*). The Bible directs us towards and does not warn us off the study of the wisdom and the will of God even in the natural orders, which He has created, not in order that we may base our faith upon them, but in order to recognize God in His

reach down thither with the unconscious roots of his soul in order to bring this obscure element out into the spiritual light, and express it freely in intellectual or artistic terms, or in practical forms of work and service. The command 'make the earth subject unto you' is not to be understood as that violent act of domination which seeks in all that is 'not I' only 'material' for the active Self; man was placed in the Garden of Eden, not in order to brutalize the created world, but in order to 'cultivate and preserve it,' and in order to give to each one of these creatures its own name.[1] The intimate connexion between man and the creatures is not only a dream of romantic people who are weary of culture, and disappointed with life; it is an original destiny appointed by the Creator. This is how man's human existence should be, and would be, if rightly ordered. We perceive this truth only when it is contradicted, that is, when we see how human life is injured when this is not the case.

We have already spoken frequently of the abstract character of human personal and spiritual life which is the result of that original perversion of man's nature. We see this in its most extreme form when man is regarded as a 'cerebrating animal,' that is, the man in whom the 'brain' has been developed at the cost of the 'heart.' We do not mean this primarily physiologically, but pictorially. Yet it is difficult to translate this picture into conceptual terms. False abstractness, which is the result of man's emancipation from the Creator, works out above all in the fact that the soul, in the function in which it unites us with the creaturely element as a whole, becomes

works and to respect His Ordinances. In Romans i. 19 ff., Paul is not saying anything new; it is all familiar to every reader of the Old Testament. It is just as irreligious as it is unscriptural to ignore this revelation, and to maintain that God can and will speak to us only through the revelation in the Word (cf. Eichrodt: *Theologie des Alten Testaments*, II, pp. 52 ff.; L. Köhler: the same, pp. 84 ff.; Dillmann, the same, II, pp. 285 ff.).

[1] Gen. ii. 15; ii. 19. *Aliud in Adamo lumen fuit, qui statim, ut inspexit animal totam ejus naturam et vires habuit cognitas* (Luther, WA. 42, p. 90). In this connexion perhaps it should be noted that the primitive man has an intimate knowledge of nature which is no longer at the disposal of the civilized human being. (Cf. Lévy-Bruhl: *L'âme primitive*.)

severed from the mind, and in so doing sinks down into the unconscious. To look at the mind first of all, this separation may express itself in different ways. The mind becomes arid, concept and view are severed; the purely conceptual, in its extreme form, the reckoning element, the empty logically mathematical form, remains without the irrational living content. There remains a naked brutal will without feeling, without sentiment. Thought becomes rigid, since it lacks creative imagination; the will becomes hard, since it lacks the softness and vitality of feeling. Man can only think in an objective way, and as the final product of this objective way of thinking he produces the idea of a world mechanism in which he himself no longer has any meaning, and a technical civilization which robs life of all spontaneity. The 'cerebrating animal' can do no more than build machines and see mechanisms. The man who has forgotten that he also is a creature along with other creatures, to whom the creature is only a thing, an object, must necessarily also dominate it. To him indeed the creature is only material, a quarry for his own creations.[1] He is himself caught in his own illusion of reason; the final product of this elimination of the 'soul' and the 'creaturely' element from the sphere of mind is always such an 'objectivity' that man forgets that he is subject, and makes himself an object, that is, materialism both in theory and practice.

Romanticism is always justified in protesting against the mind, the dominating tyrant. It always defends the relative right of motherhood against the arrogant father, the right of the night chthonic deities against the all too bright Sun god Apollo, whose rays, if received directly, singe all living things. The inhabitant of the city of iron and concrete is not without reason a lover of the East and one who longs for Nirvana. The mind which denies its creaturely origin necessarily becomes poor in its angularity and its insistence on principles; its rationality destroys life and corrupts instinct. The human personal life must be filled with vital force, or else it will become

[1] That is an idea which has been championed of late especially by Martin Buber both passionately and competently. Cf. his paper with the title: *Die Kreatur*. And also Berdyaev's *Cinq méditations sur l'existence*. (English translation, *Society and Solitude*.)

a mere phantom. The Creator has not made man to have a reason for everything that he does; it is not intended that he should make a clear diagram beforehand of all that he plans and wills to do. The spirit of calculation and the spirit of love are enemies; the creative faculty and the extreme brightness of conceptual clarity do not agree. God the Lord, who has made us body and mind, also wills that the soul, the creatureliness which is turned towards the higher life of the mind, and the mind which is turned towards nature, should come into their rights. It is not necessary to fall a prey to a romanticism of 'blood and soil' which is hostile to the mind, to recognize the danger of a one-sided intellectualism. What will become of marriage if men have no longer a healthy instinct? What will become of our orders of life as a whole if man is no longer aware of the secret rhythm, the beating heart, and the pulsing life of nature? Even if it be proclaimed a thousand times over, it is still untrue to say that the Bible forbids us to seek the will of God even in the orders which the Creator has given to nature.[1] We are bidden to 'consider!'—and not to refrain from 'considering'—'the lilies of the field.' He who has given us a living soul also wills that we should observe the laws of all that lives, the laws of creation of all living existence. The separation between the life of the mind and nature, even if it be achieved by theologians, and based upon theological grounds, is to despise the will of the Creator. It necessarily reveals its opposition to the Creation in the fact that it produces a theology which is without heart or real sentiment, which makes human beings heartless and hard.[2]

[1] That which is against nature is for Paul also against the will of God and therefore it is sin (Rom. i. 26 ff.); the fundamental order of marriage is based upon the natural fact that we have been created for each other (Gen. ii. 24) and this order of creation is explicitly distinguished from the Mosaic Law which is connected with sin (Matt. xix. 4–5).

[2] There is a pseudo-logical misunderstanding of 'the Word of God' just as there is a pseudo-dynamic one. The Bible stands above this contrast. The same Christ who is called the Word of God is also called the Life, and the connexion with Him is described not only by 'faith in the Word' but also in the simile of the Vine and the branches, the Head and the body, the Spirit and the temple, which point to an indwelling power, etc. This throws light upon the meaning of the Sacraments.

But the soul which has been forcibly suppressed in this way revenges itself upon the mind which exerts this pressure upon it by the fact that it tyrannizes over man all the more from the place to which it has been banished, namely, from the Unconscious. The result of that over-cultivation of the intellectual element,[1] of the abstractly intellectual, is an uncontrollable activity of the unconscious and of psychic activity. The lunatic asylum, the nursing home for nerve cases, the host of nerve specialists and the endless number of nerve 'cures' of all kinds, are evidently the fruit of our soulless rationality. The creaturely nature which has been overcome has not been killed, but only 'suppressed,' and now it expresses itself quite irrationally and obscurely. The emotional and instinctive life in particular is most fully exposed to this invasion from the unconscious. A highly developed abstract intellectuality has as its sinister opposite pole a morbidly sensitive sexuality, a wildly erotic world of instinct and imagination which either breaks into the conscious life or agitates it with its symbols.

The more the intellectual life is invigorated and nourished by the soul, and the more it penetrates into and absorbs the soul, the less will there be of these phenomena of division and repression. It is the sign of the 'natural' intellectual life in the good sense of the word, that it is not menaced, disturbed and destroyed by complexes arising from the unconscious. But this extreme case is merely an idea, not a reality. This 'natural' intellectual life does not exist, because we are all sinners. Rather among us all there exists a comparative—greater or smaller—separation between the mind and the soul, and therefore a state of complex, unconscious-conscious psychical disturbance of the intellectual life. The danger for the soul is not the fact that the mind develops, but that in sinful human beings the mind necessarily develops sinfully,

[1] 'The present eccentric preponderance of the life of the brain is, on the one hand, the result of a one-sided intellectual progress, by means of which we have far outstripped the ancient world, on the other hand, of a one-sidedness of mental and spiritual life by means of which we have fallen far behind the ancient world.' That is the view of Delitzsch on the basis of his Old Testament study (op. cit., 220).

in a one-sided manner, in a false abstractness; that is the danger which is at least perceived and—even if falsely interpreted—defined as a problem in the slogan 'the mind the adversary of the soul.'

Only through a misunderstanding, however, can one speak of an *essential* contradiction between soul and mind. Originally, in the purpose of the Creation, the soul is as much there for the mind as the body is there for the soul; the soul is disposed for the mind. As in the process of development the life of the spirit arises out of the purely psychical life, in a creative act of freedom which cannot be explained, without on that account setting itself in opposition to the latter, so ought the relation of soul and mind as a whole to be one of reciprocal orientation. The animal and psychical element in man is disposed for the life of the spirit, for the personal, just as the life of the spirit, the personal, needs the animal and psychical element for its realization. Human instinct must become will, imagination must become thought, perception must become feeling; will, thought and feeling, however, are dependent upon the fact that instinct, imagination and perception exist. Certainly there arises in the psychical element through the coming into being of the mind something like an alienation, a division. The childlike, naïve, spontaneous, is broken up and divided into thought and will, in the mental process of maturing and development, just as the husk is burst by the fruit. The process whereby the unconscious becomes conscious, and the process of the taming and moulding of the primeval savage element, will never seem wholly a gain but also a loss. 'Progress' from a primitive stage of existence to a higher culture, from the natural-psychical plane to that of the personal, will always also involve a loss of vitality, vigour and elemental fullness.[1] But this is not due to the process *in itself*, but to the wrongly intellectual manner, the arbitrary and one-sided way in which the mind takes the natural existence

[1] That is the relatively justifiable element in the saying of Rousseau: *Retour à la nature,* in all vitalistic philosophy—even in that of Nietzsche—in Bergson's contrast between instinct-intuition and intelligence, and in a word, in the romantic reaction against intellectualism. The vitalism of the present day is the reaction against European-American rationalism.

in hand as its material and shapes it. The intellectual development of the genius may serve as an indication of the fact to how small an extent intellectual ability and psychical fullness and vigour are necessarily mutually exclusive. The genius is a man whose mind comes to maturity without losing the original natural vitality of the psyche; in whom, on the contrary, intellectual maturity brings with it an increase of psychical vitality. From this illustration we can dimly guess what was 'originally intended': how the mind should help the soul to come into its own, how in the higher life of the mind the soul should develop a fullness and power which neither can have alone. The human being who is most fully developed in mind and spirit, that is, a real *person*, will also be most full of soul. The soul can only become complete as 'heart,' that is, in the totality of personal being.[1]

This means, however, that in principle faith represents the original unity of mind and soul. For here that self-sufficient intellectuality which wrongly elevates itself above the level of existence is abandoned; man once more accepts his 'creaturely' status; he does not stake everything upon his intellectual activity, he also allows for that which is simply *there*, which has been transmitted to him, he is passively receptive in activity and active in his receptivity. Hence, although faith is an act of the mind, it is that act which, since it receives personal being from the hand of God, takes it into and allows it to operate right down 'into the roots of the heart' (Calvin), deep down into the 'soul,' even into the unconscious. Faith re-integrates the personality which is divided in mind and soul; through faith the mind which has lost contact with the soul can be re-invigorated. In anthropological terms, faith is the quickening and interpenetration of mind and soul. Faith therefore penetrates into the depths of the soul, which neither philosophical nor scientific thought, nor artistic creation, can reach. Hence the operation of the Holy Spirit manifests itself precisely upon the higher levels of the life of faith in phenomena which are not known to the normal consciousness and the normal experience. Paul is not

[1] Hence it is no accident that the Bible describes the 'heart' and not the 'head' as the centre of the person.

using language which belongs to the realm of 'primitive' thought when he recognizes the 'gift of tongues' in the Early Church as a manifestation of the life of Christ both in the Church and in the individual; he is uttering words of profound wisdom when he recognizes that this 'gift' is of divine origin; at the same time, he warns the Christian community against over-emphasizing its importance. Again, throughout the Bible it is taken for granted that faith should produce healing miracles; it is regarded as a normal effect of the new life that personal and spiritual power should extend its influence into the natural physical sphere.[1] In this restoration of the connexion between the soul and the mind, the *particula veri* of the magical view of existence disappear: in the Bible miracle is regarded as the obvious or natural result of the new life, and this refers especially to miracles of healing. This shows the original continuity between the soul and the mind, and between the soul and the body.

2. THE BODY

If we cannot expect to find a special Christian doctrine of the constitution of the soul, still less can we expect to find a doctrine of the physical constitution of man.[2] The Bible is only concerned with the integration of the body and of the corporeal nature into the whole of the personal life. The Christian faith is dualistic in the sense that it teaches the inevitable 'two-ness' of mind and body.[3] The mind is not to be understood as a modification of, or emanation from, the

[1] In Pauline thought it is the one life-creating Spirit of God who creates the miracle of faith and the miracle of the charismata of the most varied kinds, and both are inseparably united. Cf. Gunkel: *Die Wirkungen des Heiligen Geistes*.

[2] How much significance may be ascribed to the Biblical doctrine of the physical powers, which Delitzsch develops, may be left an open question; it seems to me that here theosophical speculation is mingled with genuine insight into the Bible.

[3] This is true, in spite of what was said above (Note on p. 362) about the totality of the person. Ontologically man is a unity, phenomenologically, mind and nature, and especially mind and body, are to be strictly distinguished.

body, nor does the body emanate from the mind. God, the Creator, took a clod of earth from the soil, and out of it He formed the human body into which He breathed the spirit and thus formed it into a living personal being.[1] This childlike point of view expresses a fourfold truth: body and mind belong equally to the nature of man, neither is to be deduced from the other, the spirit is 'from above' and the body 'from below'—and, this is the most important, they are both destined for each other, and in a definite way adapted to one another.

The body is the means through which man communicates with the world, by which he is connected with it, adapted to it, and conditioned by it. Therefore the body is the most solid and impressive manifestation of the creaturely character of man. That which has a body, in any case, is not God, and —whatever else it may be—it is a finite creature, localized in this world of time and space, at this point, *here* and not there, *now* and not then, determined by its 'environment,' both in the temporal and spatial, as well as the causal sense. Man is a product, a structure of the natural process, and at the same time he is a piece or element of it. The body therefore is not merely the means of communication with the world, a means of expression for the mind in the world, an organ of the mind's contact with the external world; but the body is at the same time a limitation both of man over against God, and of individual human beings from one another. Perhaps there exists a creaturely boundary without corporeality,[2] but in any case the body is the boundary which cannot be ignored; it is so solid that it forces itself upon our attention. Therefore it is that which is most offensive to the human being who wants to be like God; it is that which he wants to get rid of and treat as though it did not belong to him; therefore, conversely, in the Bible—where to wish to be like God is *the* sin *par excellence* —there is no depreciation of, or contempt for, the physical nature. Hostility to the body—which since the days of Nietzsche many regard as a token of Christianity—penetrated into the Church from late Hellenistic thought, and is wholly foreign

[1] Gen. ii. 7.

[2] Upon the world of angels, see below p. 414.

to the thought of the Bible,[1] so foreign indeed that the man of the Bible still thinks of eternal life in bodily terms, which leads to 'the resurrection of the body.' Christian thought is so 'materialistic,' because for it the body as well as the mind is God's good creation, although at the same time the body is that which is intended to distinguish the being of the creature from the Being of the Creator, unto all eternity.

3. THEORIES OF THE RELATION BETWEEN BODY AND SOUL

The inter-connexion of body and soul, the *vinculum substantiale* (Leibniz) will for ever remain for us an insoluble enigma. If we could see through it we would be like God. The impossibility of understanding man's constitution is an integral part of the creaturely character of human existence. Hence all the theories of the relation between body and soul which have been evolved down to the present time have been unable to solve the riddle. Each man can only point to one aspect of this relation. The materialistic denial of the independence of the mind points to the fact that the physical nature is an independent form of existence alongside the life of the mind, and it also points to the other fact that the physical element is the underlying basis of the life of the mind, that the soul and the organically functional have a material basis. Man, and not merely his body, consists of carbon, hydrogen, oxygen, nitrogen, calcium, phosphorus, etc. Man, and not merely his body, weighs so many ounces and pounds, and has a volume of so many cubic centimetres. The physical and material element is not merely a case or a framework which contains the real human being, but the material element extends right into the centre of the mind itself. The modern discovery of hormones provides us with a fresh example of the delicacy and depth of the connexion between the mental and the chemico-physical element in man. These elements of our material body, so minute in size, which have only been more fully known in recent years, and are chemically so highly

[1] The view of the body as the prison of the soul is also completely remote from the thought of Paul. He too knows a prison-house of man—but this is —the Law (Gal. iii. 23), a kind of divine 'protective custody' for the sinful human being.

complicated, determine the life of the soul and mind as well as the purely physical life. The removal of the sex-glands—that is, the sex hormones—from the organism as a whole alters not only the sexual but also the whole mental life of a man or woman. Inevitably men try to explain—from this standpoint—the whole mental and spiritual nature as a purely chemical matter; and this view is bound to reappear from time to time. It is equally evident, however, that this attempt is bound to fail, owing to the peculiar character of the mental processes which belong to a totally different dimension, of which physics and chemistry have no idea. Since they are non-spatial they cannot be explained in spatial terms, close as the relations between the two may be. Materialism as a total view of human existence is the nearest and shortest blind alley in which human interpretation can lose itself.

Idealism takes the opposite line, which is apparently more promising; it regards the bodily and material element as a degraded, reduced existence of the spirit, or even as a mere illusion to which the spirit falls a prey. Does not the latest development of physics actually provide the best basis for this more daring attempt at interpretation? If energy and not substance is the last word in physics, if a heavy mass and an inert mass are expressions of one and the same fact, if electricity, or something like it, is the final element of physical reality which can be discovered—then was not Leibniz right, as against all materialism, when he conceived the so-called material atom as the least spiritual and the least free, the most lacking in spontaneity, but still always as a spiritual monad? Was not Plotinus right who represented the whole realm of being as a hierarchy of decreasing and increasing spirituality whose one positive pole had to be the pure spirituality of the Deity and whose other negative pole was empty space? Materiality and spirituality therefore are merely relative concepts, opposite termini of a continuous series of ascents, whereby certainly only the life of the spirit would be the real, and its absence would be simply the minus coefficient of reality.

[1] Cf. Medicus: *Die Freiheit des Willens und ihre Grenze*; Eddington: *The Nature of the Physical World*, pp. 293 ff.

It is evident that from this point of view it is impossible to estimate the value of corporeality. But it is plain that this theory breaks down whenever it is confronted by the irrevocable boundary between material and psycho-spiritual existence. In any case this minimum of spirit, which we call matter, exists in its own peculiar and characteristic way, and that is all we can say about it. It exists as the material bodily nature of man which can never be resolved into non-material actuality. In whatever way we may interpret the body, it is *there* as something other than the mind (*Geist*) as a form of existence which is alien to the mind, impenetrable, and impossible to master by thought.

The third main theory, that of psycho-physical parallelism—as a rule connected with a pantheistic philosophy of life—starts from the fact that the physical nature always has its counterpart in the life of the mind, and vice versa, thus from the fact that material and mental processes correspond to one another. Its favourite illustration is that of the physiognomy and the work of art: spirit, which appears in a material form, matter which expresses spirit, visible soul and 'ensouled' matter. In the last resort is not all existence like the expression on a human face, that is, both psychical and material, so that every material process corresponds to a psychical process, and vice versa?[1] The strongest argument for this theory is a negative one: the impossibility of conceiving the influence of the non-spatial upon the spatial or of the spatial upon the non-spatial. How can mind affect matter? How can it do so, since the effect upon matter can only be of a material kind? Could any part of a mass be affected by anything save that which comes into actual contact with it? And can that with which it comes into contact be anything other than something in its vicinity, that is, something material? And conversely: how could a spatial section of a mass affect something non-spatial, for instance, a thought? How could the gulf between subject and object be bridged?[2] To-day, however, in the age of wave

[1] Cf. the chapter *The Sacramental Universe* in the valuable Gifford lectures of the Archbishop of York, W. Temple: *Nature, Man and God*, pp. 473 ff.

[2] On the problem of body and soul there is an immense literature. Cf. Busse: *Geist und Körper, Seele und Leib*, and the article: *Leib und Seele* by

physics, these arguments are not so convincing as in the period when the classic theory of atoms was accepted, and direct daily observation of the—unintelligible it is true—mutual influence of mind and body always allows the fourth view, the *common-sense* theory of mutual influence, finally to gain the upper hand.

In a way which we cannot understand the mind influences the material body, and through it the material world as a whole; and, conversely, the world of objects, through the body, influences the mind. The simplest example of the former is the arbitrary movement of the muscle, of the latter that of sense-perception. The mind commands the arm to lift itself in a certain way; the world impresses upon the mind this or that to be seen or heard. Common sense will continually return to this—theoretically unsatisfactory—scheme of interpretation, which is, however, the one which does most justice to the facts of the actual situation, although naturally it does not solve the problem. But, on the other hand, this hypothesis expresses more naturally than any other the twofold situation, the fact of mutual dependence which experience forces upon us. We do not write a letter or a book because our nerves are itching to do so in a certain manner, but because our thought imposes upon the hand which writes this movement and no other. And we hear the crashing of the thunder, not because through some mental association we are ready to hear a clap of thunder, but because the contingent happening, outside in the material world, penetrates through the gates of our sense apparatus, breaking into the process of our thought and disturbing it. How this happens we do not know—*ignoramus ignorabimus*.[1] All the refinements with which the processes on both sides have been pictured have not made the gulf between within and without any smaller, not even by the width of a ray of light. It remains the gulf which separates subject and object.

Titius in *Religion in Geschichte und Gegenwart*, III, col. 1545 ff., with an ample bibliography. The Bible teaches that which springs naturally from the idea of personality: that the physical, mental and spiritual elements are absolutely interwoven with one another.

[1] Cf. with Du Bois-Reymond's famous *Ignoramus, ignorabimus* the *Geschichte des Materialismus* of F. A. Lange, vol. II, p. 196 ff., observations which are still quite relevant.

On the other hand, in a different sense, a certain approximation has taken place. After a period of extremely mechanistic experiment we perceive possibly more clearly than ever the non-mechanical character of the organism, and, on the other hand, we have learned to see traces of organic wholeness even in that which is apparently non-organic, namely, in the atom itself. The human organism, like every other organism, cannot be constituted mechanically by a number of separate pieces, but it is a functional whole, and indeed, in contradiction to the machine, a living functional whole, where, in principle, every part is and represents the whole. Every human cell,[1] indeed every chromosome, every part of the heart of every cell, has a special human character. The whole is present in every part, which at least in the lower stages of life is expressed by an almost boundless power of regeneration of the individual organs. Hence the wonder of the whole is not to be explained through the structure—which in itself is not a whole—out of sectional pieces, but each part, each section of protoplasm contains somehow the unity of form of the whole in itself. Here, however, we have no desire to identify ourselves too closely with views which are still open to scientific criticism. But, from the standpoint of a Christian doctrine of personality, we can never speak about the human body in terms of a machine. The machine which has been invented by man, and can be understood by man, is not sufficient to explain the divine wonder of creation of the living body. Indeed, at the present day it looks as though the mechanistic conception cannot hold the field even in physics. So much at any rate is certain: to-day even the purely material happening looks far more mysterious and is far more difficult to understand than in the days of Democritus, or in the days of the great metaphysicians at the beginning of the modern period.

4. THE MEANING OF THE BODY IN THE LIGHT OF THE CREATION

It would be the task of a Christian ontology to inquire into the different spheres of being according to the special mystery of creation which they contain, the special manner in which

[1] Cf. the amazing results of Driesch's experiments on the egg of the sea-urchin; Titius, op. cit., pp. 468 ff.; Bavink, op. cit., pp. 528 ff.

they contain the divine Presence, so far as this is possible for us, from the standpoint of faith, but at the same time continually taking experience into account. We have confined ourselves to the one supreme and innermost sphere: human personal being. We have treated the second sphere, that of spiritual being in general, very indirectly from the point of view of theology; and we have not attempted to study the psychical, the organic or even the physico-material existence in its special relation to God. But of all existence it is true, even if in different ways, that God's omnipotence, God's working is present in it.[1] Even in the being of the atom we come upon the mystery of the divine Presence and power. Hence, because there is absolutely no existence outside God, there is no existence without mystery; therefore behind every form of being, even that of a simple atom of hydrogen or of an electron, there lies the whole mystery of the Divine Omnipotence. 'Thou hast beset me behind and before.'[2] The resistance which my foot experiences from a simple stone in the gravel is a resistance which God's will opposes to me; how much more is the mysterious power which shapes the organism of my body, and combines its parts into a whole, power which springs from the omnipotence of God.

The meaning of the body is a God-given possibility of expressing spirit and of realizing will. Someone who is completely paralysed, who has no possibility of making himself known to the world, of taking part in its activity, will realize the force of this truth better than anyone else. It would not be correct to say that he is condemned to pure passivity, for he might have a very active mind; but he is certainly condemned to an inactive, non-creative life. The connexion between him and the world has been broken, because the connexion between his mind and his body, the motor nervous system, has been destroyed. The fact that I can 'command' my hand, my foot, my tongue, to move in one way and not in another, so that it

[1] Calvin: *Fateor quidem pie hoc posse dici, modo a pio animo proficiscatur, Naturam esse Deum*; but he immediately perceives the danger of this doctrine: *Potius Natura sit ordo a Deo praescriptus* (*Institutio* I, 5, 5). Similarly Luther's phrase: 'All creatures are masks of God' (WA. 40, 1, 174).

[2] Psa. cxxxix. 5.

expresses my mind, or an alteration of the world willed by me takes place, this is the great gift which we have received from the hand of the Creator as an incomprehensible wonder. It may indeed be true that our spirit is the real source of the creative element within us; but without the body the work which the mind sees is not actual, it remains merely a thought, undifferentiated from mere phantasy. Work and act spring from the spirit, it is true, but—mediated through the psyche—they are accomplished by means of the body.

It would be strange if a Christian anthropology should not point to the special element, the endowment of the human body which corresponds to the wealth of the spirit. Present-day research—apart from all questions of origin[1]—here sees far more plainly and simply than that of earlier generations the peculiarity of the human organism as compared with the animal organism. What does even the one fact peculiar to man of the grip with opposing thumbs mean? or the fact that man alone has a supporting foot which makes it possible to walk upright? above all, however, the immense development of the central nervous system and of the brain, upon which is based physiologically the possibility of mental and spiritual activity! The physical nature of man is in a wonderful way adapted to his personal existence, as on the other hand it is also an expression of it. At least in passing it may be noted that the human organism, of all mammal organisms, is that which, from the biological point of view, is the least one-sidedly specialized, and thus is the richest in possibilities.[2] All these are facts which, from the point of view of faith, are certainly not without significance, although it is certain that they would not be sufficient to form a basis for this faith or to serve as a proof for it. Even in the organism, in the corporeal aspect of man, his special position, his special destiny is indicated beforehand. How much more is this true of the psychical mechanisms which serve as a basis for the life of his mind and spirit, and serve as direct material for it.

Yet here too we see the effects of the rent which goes through

[1] See Chapter III (p. 40).

[2] Thus Dacqué: *Urwelt, Sage und Menschheit*, p. 64. Also Rüfner: *Die Natur und der Mensch in ihr*, pp. 75 ff.

the whole of human nature. Indeed, here and here in particular, they are so clearly perceptible that the human intellect constantly falls into the habit of regarding the dualism of body and mind as the reason for, and the starting-point of, all the troublesome contradictions which man meets in the course of his ordinary experience. Through sin we all have a body which does not willingly obey the mind, which seems to have its own code of laws, and does not trouble about the meaning of the higher life of the mind and spirit. And we have a mind which often seems to have no power over the body, but which experiences its impotence in the bodily sphere in particular. Within that fundamental original mutual relation of body and mind there is this state of division, which means that body and mind are regarded either as parallel (but never meeting), or as in opposition to one another; and it is this distortion of the original relation which gives us so much trouble. We see our mind and spirit exposed to the accidental elements of the structure and the functions of the body, and its 'freely creative' activity hindered by some glandular disturbance. We see our disposition affected by disturbances of the muscles of the heart, the secretion of the liver, and the activity of the kidneys. Above all, we see those facts which might give us cause—wrongly—to make the body responsible for all the moral disorder in life: the exaggerated desire for pleasure of all kinds, a greediness, an impossibility of satisfying the senses in the sphere of sex, at least in the direction of a constant desire for change, unknown among the lower animals. Which of us does not understand what Plato says in the *Phaedo*[1] when he expresses the view that if the mind could get rid of this tiresome partner, the body, it could and would give itself to the undisturbed contemplation of the Ideas: eternal Truth, Beauty, and Goodness?

And yet this is an illusion! We say, indeed, that it is the body which gives us so much trouble, but in reality it is the mind which gives the body so much trouble. For this disintegration starts from the mind and not from the body. Sin does not issue from the bodily instinct and then enter into the mind and spirit, but it comes from the mind and enters into

[1] Plato, 64E, 67A.

the bodily instinct. Once again, this argument that it is the mind which is the real adversary and disturber of the peace is true. Only this does not mean that there is a constitutional opposition between mind and body—as though it were of the nature of the mind to disturb the functions of the body—but it means that the mind does not hold fast its God-given destiny, but chooses its own destiny in addition. The 'pre-established harmony' of body and mind has been disturbed by the false self-determination of the mind and spirit, and in so doing the bodily function itself is disintegrated. But this disturbance should not be conceived merely as an individual act, as though every individual were simply and solely responsible for the relative disintegration of his organism. Here if anywhere we have to come back to the fact of *Original Sin* in the most solid sense of the word.

The problem of heredity stands to-day in the centre of scientific research,[1] and in spite of all that is hypothetical in this rather new science, it is possible to speak of certain definitely new truths which were not at the disposal of earlier generations. In particular the Mendelian laws which were discovered by a purely inductive process, after many experiments, methodically carried out, and on the other hand, researches into the nature of chromosomes, carried out with the aid of the microscope, have thrown a great deal of light on this sphere, which was formerly so obscure. Christian theology has no right to ignore these discoveries. The result of scientific research merely confirms, however—even if only in its most general features—the Biblical view, namely, the great importance of the factor of heredity in the determination of the human individuality. For instance, the teaching of modern research into the problem of heredity on the basis of inquiries into identical twins, about 'crime as destiny,'[2] sounds like a scientific paraphrase of the words of the Bible: 'who visits the sins of the fathers upon the children unto the third and fourth generation.'[3] Earlier inquiries into the descendants of inebriates brought out the same truth with appalling clarity.

[1] Titius, op. cit., pp. 483 ff., gives a very detailed account of the position of the natural science theory of heredity.

[2] Bavink: op cit., pp. 348 ff.

[3] Exod. xx. 5.

And yet, as we have already pointed out, it would be wrong to draw deterministic conclusions from these facts. We must not forget that the Biblical phrase about the 'third and fourth generation' adds, 'of them that hate Me.' It is not the physical inheritance which is the absolutely determining element, but it simply gives a pre-disposition in that direction; the individuality, even the moral individuality, is only one side of character. So long as man is still man, the fact remains that man's existence is existence-in-decision. Character-dispositions may be inherited, but never the character itself. Where physical inheritance through the transmission of the genes by means of procreation is concerned, there too—even upon the basis of the scientific knowledge of the present day—the determination is not unconditioned, but it is always very limited, that is, it is one which in no way excludes an element of freedom. In so far as the *peccatum originis*—as in the classic doctrine—is brought into direct connexion with the fact of heredity, the Zwinglian modification is more correct than the strictly orthodox conception.[1] So far as the inherited disposition is concerned, the individual has quite as much freedom as he has the pre-disposition to be influenced by it. No one is born with the drunkard's fate hanging over him as something he cannot escape; his 'heredity' means that over-indulgence in strong drink will be his particular temptation. The fact that the *peccatum originis* cannot be evaded lies upon a different plane from that of the empirical inheritance of qualities which can be proved, although it is certain that the former is an important indication of the latter.

This truth can indeed be proved *positively*, as well as negatively, although—for the reasons which have just been mentioned—it will never be possible to show quite plainly the connexion between sin and bodily disorder. Faith gives a new basis to personal existence, that is, the will of the

[1] Zwingli bases his doctrine (as will shortly be proved by a Zürich dissertation) upon an exegesis of Rom. v. 12 ff., which is freed from the ecclesiastical traditions, and his view certainly is nearer to the present system of exegesis than is the Augustinian doctrine of Original Sin. The Pauline θάνατος corresponds to his 'inherited malady.' The idea of inherited guilt cannot be proved with any certainty from the Bible any more than that of inherited sin. See above, p. 119.

Creator, and we see how this alters the whole situation; frequently, as a result, not only psychological but physical troubles disappear completely. Thus we see divided elements in a personality being re-united; a new beginning has been made for that harmony of body and mind intended by the Creator; we see too that the believer is able to control his appetites in a way not known to the unbeliever; all these experiences may be summed up in Paul's daring words: 'Even so reckon ye yourselves to be dead unto sin.'[1] The dominance of physical appetite, which as a rule the 'natural man' finds it impossible to overcome, can be overcome by faith, once the far more deeply rooted sin, false independence and distrust of God, has been overcome.[2]

But this does not mean that we hold the view that only through faith can the human mind control the instincts which have become uncontrolled and independent. It is precisely this part of ethics which is also accessible to the rational moralist or the Stoic sage. His independence of the desires of his instinctive nature and his dominion over the body is precisely that in which he—supposedly—experiences the divinity of his spirit and upon which his whole ethic of self-redemption is built.[3] There are bodily difficulties, there is a 'fleshliness' from which even the man who knows nothing of the God and Father of Our Lord Jesus Christ can become free, just as, on the other hand, there are bodily disturbances which no amount of Christian faith can overcome. Here we are moving in the sphere of the relative, and at the same time in

[1] Rom. vi. 11.

[2] The fact that the Church takes too little account of the healing power of the Holy Spirit should be clear to us once for all when we remember the teaching and experience of the Blumhardts, father and son; this has also been a limitation of the Reformation doctrine of the new life. On this cf. Ellwein's informative synoptic presentation of the teaching of the Humanists and Reformers: *Vom neuen Leben.*

[3] In all the ethical teaching of the Stoics the idea of progress is of central importance, which is to be understood in this sense, 'that the Stoics have never denied the possibility of moral perfection in theory, but were convinced that the same . . . has been attained by individuals and that in principle it could be attained by everyone.' Bonhöffer: *Die Ethik Epictets*, p. 148.

the sphere where the fate of the individual and of humanity are indissolubly united.

5. NATURE AND CREATION

Here also, therefore, the content of the idea of 'the natural' receives a special definition. Not only the Cynic moralists but also the Stoics[1] use the phrase: *Naturalia non sunt turpia*. But the question is, what are *naturalia*? If by Nature we mean our present *Physis* then from the point of view of the Christian faith, the statement is certainly false, because nature itself is disturbed and thrown into confusion by that which is un-natural, by the contradiction which comes from the mind and spirit of man. Our nature has become un-natural. Not culture in general, but *our* culture, not intellect in general, but *our* intellect, has sinned against nature and made us all 'un-natural.' Every civilized human being is a little perverse, and every further step into the intellectual realm—we being what we are—makes us to some extent more un-natural. Even the intellectuality of the believer does not fully escape from this, because it is the intellectuality of a believing human being as sinner, although in principle true faith brings with it the right attitude towards the bodily nature. What seems natural to us over-cultivated human beings in our natural existence is indeed not always a divine order of creation, and the goodness of the Creator, but it is frequently absolutely opposed to nature. The history of religious as well as of secular movements brings this out very clearly. The 'emancipation of Nature' at the Renaissance and the Enlightenment led to much unnatural perversity, and many a religious movement which was undoubtedly genuinely Christian led to sheer denial of the purpose of the Creation. Possibly it is as difficult to discover what is truly natural, as it is difficult to find out what is truly spiritual or intellectual. To confuse God-created nature and physical existence can only occur to one who knows nothing of the rent which runs right through the whole Creation.

Therefore we must be on our guard when we relate physical

[1] On the rapprochement between the later Stoics and the Cynics, cf. Zeller, op. cit., iv, p. 751.

existence—for instance, the bodily organism—and the Divine Creation to one another; but at the same time we must never cease to do so. For God wills to be praised in His works of Creation, especially also in those of His human creation. To lay so much stress on sin that we refuse to give Him this praise from the Creation, and to assert that even we who know His will from His revelation, can discover nothing of His work in Creation, is a very strange way of showing our fidelity to the Bible![1] Indeed, such an attitude seems to be more in harmony with typically modern agnosticism than with the Christian faith and with the Bible. Even the idea of sin finally becomes wholly abstract, and therefore empty, when we no longer measure sin by the order of Creation and renounce the definition of the content of both. In any case the Bible gives us the opposite example. Certain things it names as 'against nature'[2] and in so doing stamps them as at the same time contrary to God. In point of fact, in this sense the Stoic phrase 'naturalia non turpia' is valid, only here a concept of nature is used determined by the revealed faith and therefore always orientated by the Creation, which is suitable for an ethical norm.[3]

This brings us back to the centre of the Biblical doctrine of man, to the idea of the *Imago Dei*. For centuries commentators on Genesis i. 26 ff. have argued whether the fact that man was made in the image of God applies only to his soul or also to his body. The purely spiritual conception of God of the New Testament seems to decide the question in a negative sense.[4] In reality this negative decision was not due to the

[1] How little in this matter we can appeal to the Reformers—in spite of Luther's expressions about the 'Madensack' ('wretched carcase')—let Calvin himself say: In spite of his sinful corruption man is *eximium quoddam inter alias reaturas divinae sapientiae, justitiae et bonitatis specimen: ut merito a veteribus dictus sit* μικρόκοσμος (opp. 23, 25). In spite of sin *manere adhuc aliquid residuum, ut praestet non parva dignitate homo* (ibid., p. 147).

[2] Rom. i. 26 ff. Also Rom. ii. 14.

[3] An example of how little we can do without the conception of the order of creation in the ethic of marriage for instance is given by Thurneysen's excellent observations on the question of birth-control in the *Mitteilungen des Schweizerischen Pfarrervereins*.

[4] Ecclesiastical exegesis in general is guided by the endeavour to divert interest from the corporeal understanding of the *imago*, which in view of

realistic thought of the Bible but to the abstract thought of Greece. Actually, man in his psycho-physical totality is an image of God. Even in his bodily nature something of his special destiny which the Creator has given him has been expressed. Man, who does not crawl on the ground like the other animals, but holds himself upright, and therefore goes through the world holding his head high, with a wide horizon and a free outlook, man whose whole physical quality points symbolically to his personal existence, and serves as an instrument for it, has 'been created in the image of God,' although we certainly would not ascribe to God a corporeal nature, as do some Christian Theosophists. Even man's *body* expresses the 'hierarchical' structure of his nature, and this can be understood solely from the fact that his created nature is in the image of God. His blood-relationship with the ape may be an actual fact or not; the first and the chief impression which the sight of a healthy human being makes upon us is not this relation, but, on the contrary, the complete difference of man from all other *zoa*.[1] One only needs to see man to know that this being has a different species and destiny from that of any *animal*.

At the same time, however, our present bodily nature is a clear expression of the transitory character and the mortality of our sinful existence. The greatest abstraction which Greek thought achieved, in order to be able to maintain its enthusiasm for man, was the ignoring of death. These glorious bodies which to it were objects of divine reverence have all decayed; the youthful athlete who served as a model for Praxiteles died, perhaps after a long period of weakness, as an aged man bowed down with the weight of years. To isolate one element in life always betokens lack of vision; it is always a sign of a sinful lack of vision to dwell on the marve of the body without fear of death, and all that belongs to preparation for death. It is not without significance that the

the impossibility of a corporeal conception of God is justified, but which obscures the symbolical significance of the human body, which undoubtedly is also intended in the Old Testament (cf. Eichrodt, op. cit., p. 60).

[1] Heraclitus: 'The most beautiful monkey is ugly in comparison with the human species.' Diels, Fr., 82.

picture of a dying man is the sacred sign of Christendom. It is not beautiful, but it is a true picture. The Man of Sorrows shows us in a 'counter-picture' the significance of the fact that we have been made in the image of God, not only for our spiritual, but also for our bodily life. The word 'death' describes the final stage of our human pilgrimage along the roads of earth—and it is with this that we are concerned; where man refuses to look at this 'final stage' in our earthly existence, he fails to see the reality of human life at all; in its stead he beholds a—more beautiful—abstraction.

CHAPTER XVII

THE GROWTH OF MAN AND THE DOCTRINE OF EVOLUTION

I. THE THREE FORMS OF THE IDEA OF EVOLUTION

It is very difficult for the modern man to understand the Christian doctrine of man, especially if his training has been on the lines of modern science; this difficulty arises mainly from one idea, which he has come to regard more or less as a dogma—and, still more important—which has become a habit of thought, namely, the opinion that all that *is* can be best understood from the point of view of its growth. This genetic thinking, quite alien to the thought of earlier generations, is one of the chief characteristics of the modern mind.[1] The fact that the genetic postulate has almost become an axiom and a dogma is not without reason. In point of fact, especially in the sphere of the natural sciences—but not only there—this key has unlocked many doors of knowledge, and has brought with it an immense enrichment of our knowledge. The category of growth or development has therefore, in several spheres of knowledge, been set up as the standard, so that 'to comprehend something' and to 'understand something in its genesis' have become identical notions. The geologist who 'understands' something of the structure of the earth's surface of a country or of a continent, does so by 'explaining' by what processes of folding and faulting the present structure has come into existence. The doctor of medicine diagnoses a disease by reconstructing the process—of the infection for instance—by means of which the present condition has developed out of an earlier one. Genetic thought is a great attempt to grasp the unity of all being. The impressiveness of this idea

[1] The idea of development is indeed not wholly foreign to the thought of antiquity; but, on the one hand, as a principle of explanation, and, on the other hand, as the integration of all that happens into the time-series, it was not known to Heraclitus, nor to Empedocles, nor to Aristotle. It is the product of the secularization of the Christian view of history. From Christianity comes the idea of a time-series extended in one direction.

of understanding what exists from the processes of growth, comes out, among other things, in the fact that it has proved itself independent of the fundamental metaphysical tendencies of various philosophies of life, and in each of them has been able to assert itself in a characteristic way. There is both an Idealistic and a Naturalistic theory of development, and even the Romantic pantheistic tendency of thought, especially of late, has accepted this in a form peculiar to itself.

The naturalistic theory of evolution tries to grasp all that now is as a product of a causal process, which, beginning with the simple and elementary as the original existence, through the operation of the natural laws of physics and chemistry, has led to the differentiation of the present variety of dead and living bodies. The Idealistic theory of evolution understands all that which now exists in the converse direction from the end for which it develops, teleologically, as a development of spirit which at first is only latent, as a gradual development of spirit. The Romantic theory of evolution finally tries to penetrate to the heart of the mystery of reality by the introduction of a semi-spiritual, semi-natural principle of formation, as the theory of *évolution créatrice*,[1] which is in harmony with the universal character of the fundamental idea of Romantic pantheism.

All these three forms of the idea of evolution are not only metaphysical hypotheses, but they have proved themselves to be fruitful working principles, and indeed, each of them in a different sphere, the first principally in the sphere of astrophysics, geology and—within certain limits—of biology; the second within the sphere of thought; the third is on the point of replacing the purely causal in the sphere of the living. In each sphere an attempt has also been made with the two others, but with less success; the causal theory of evolution has not accomplished much more in the sphere of history than the Idealistic view has achieved in that of research in natural science.

[1] Bergson's idea of the *évolution créatrice* goes back to Schelling. The emphasis on the time factor—of the *durée réelle*—distinguishes Bergson's metaphysic from that of Neo-Platonism, with which otherwise it has many affinities.

It is obvious that man as a microcosm, as one who belongs to both, or to all three, worlds, has also become an object of the three theories of evolution. Even in connexion with man each of these three forms of the idea of evolution has proved fruitful, leading to real knowledge, whether applied to the individual human being in his individual growth, or to humanity as a whole. Here, however, it is impossible to state in a general way what we should regard as knowledge, and what as hypothesis; but we must beware of two errors: first, that of regarding real knowledge as mere hypothesis, and, secondly, that of regarding mere hypothesis as real knowledge.

2. HYPOTHESIS AND KNOWLEDGE

It is real new knowledge and not mere hypothesis—and indeed knowledge which has its own significance for the problems of Christian theology—that every human being comes from a male sperm and a female ovum. For centuries nothing was known of the latter, because it is so minute; hence the rôle of the wife, in the process of procreation, was conceived as merely passive, receptive and fostering, which, in view of the question of the equal value of the sexes, makes a good deal of difference.[1] To-day we know all the phases and stages of bodily development through which the human embryo passes to the point of birth, and we are able to estimate these phases from the point of view of comparative anatomy in a way unknown to earlier generations. The connexion of these individual phases of development with the stages of the development of man as a whole is evident to everyone who has studied the subject. In spite of this, to-day we are not quite so confident as in the days of Haeckel that we can speak of a 'fundamental biogenetic law,' namely, that 'ontogeny recapitulates phylogeny'; hence, it was argued, each individual phase of development has its phylogenetic counterpart, so that the one course of development could be reconstructed from the other.

[1] The fact that this view also formed a presupposition for the early Christian view of the Virgin Birth of Jesus is evident. The mother of Christ is the purely passive vessel containing the divine Seed of the Spirit.

But even the mere fact that there is a development of the species as well as of the individual, and that this also in some way or other must begin with the primitive and the elementary (i.e. in itself, and apart from any more exact definition of this beginning and this series of development), was a truth of revolutionary significance in anthropology. The champions of the Christian theological doctrine, in particular, resisted these conclusions with might and main. For this theory seemed to shake the very foundation of Biblical and ecclesiastical anthropology, of that which the Church had taught from time immemorial about the Primitive State and the Fall. If 'Darwinism' they asked,—understanding the word in the widest sense—is right, what will become of both those doctrines which are so fundamental for the whole of Christian dogma? The Church's attempt to refute this theory took the form of the distinction—in itself necessary—between a metaphysical hypothesis and scientific knowledge. But the longer this went on the more it became evident to those who were familiar with the subject that in this struggle the Church was the loser.[1] What at first seemed to be hypothesis transformed itself more and more into stable knowledge, and made it increasingly evident that the Biblical narrative of Paradise and the Primitive State was untenable. Historical science too became the ally of natural science; palaeontology or prehistory could elevate the 'hypothesis' of a primitive, a-historical period preceding the historical life of man to the rank of an indubitable certainty. To-day two facts are firmly established which bring us into irreconcilable conflict with the traditional form of theological anthropology: historical man, with whom alone the ecclesiastical doctrine reckons, has a long prehistory, covering thousands of years, and this pre-history shows us a human being who, the further we delve into the past,

[1] An instance of such an apologetic is Zöckler's book: *Die Lehre vom Urstand des Menschen*. Roman Catholic dogmatics still follows these lines. Cf. Bartmann: *Lehrbuch der Dogmatik*, para. 73. A sentence like this: 'The age of mankind is now reckoned by Catholic theologians . . . as at least ten thousand years,' shows plainly the old kind of apologetic—but in retreat. On the other hand, since the time of Schlatter and v. Oettingen Protestant dogmatics, with its Biblical emphasis, has been fairly free from this apologetic tendency.

resembles still less the man of the present day, and indeed—this is the decisive point—in the sense of becoming more and more 'primitive,' that is, he is less clearly differentiated from sub-human creatures. Christian theology must come to terms with these facts, just as it had to adjust itself to the Copernican upheaval, and the vastly enlarged picture of time and space given to us by the newer astro-physics and geology. In this picture of development (which is not a hypothesis) derived from established truths of historical and natural science, there is no longer any room for the traditional view of the Church of the temporal beginning of the human race. That is a situation which the theology which centres in the Bible has never yet squarely faced.

On the other hand, the distinction between hypothesis and scientific discovery remains in force; again and again we see how necessary it is to recognize the formation of hypotheses proceeding from natural and historical science as such, and to remind 'scientific anthropology' of its limitations. To-day it is certain that the pedigrees of the human race, by means of which it was believed that we could trace the descent of man back to the amoeba, were over-hasty hypotheses, which could not stand the process of critical examination, that the physical and psychological pictures which were drawn of primitive man were derived rather from a monistic dogma of development than from exact research into facts, that to-day we know far less about the pedigree of the human race than the generation before us believed it did, that to a great extent phenotypic analogies were taken for relations to hereditary characters. Even if we cannot regard the picture of the genesis of mankind which has been sketched by Dacqué—a man who was both learned and the possessor of a fertile imagination—which departs to a very large extent from that of accepted science,[1]

[1] It would be absolutely prejudicial to theology to contend with the theories of Dacqué against the Doctrine of Descent. For that which Dacqué finally comes to is at bottom only a variant, even if a veiled one, of the Doctrine of Descent. His 'Adamite human being' would be 'according to his own expressed opinion outwardly quite like an amphibious creature or a higher mammal; . . . It is a private pleasure of Dacqué's to describe such creatures as human beings because their great grandchildren became such later.' (Bavink, op. cit., 483.) On the whole problem of evolution

as an established result of scientific research, yet it remains important as a warning against too swift an acceptance of hypotheses, which often proceed more from prejudice than from strict lines of scientific enquiry. We must indeed be on our guard against decrying the Doctrine of Descent as a product of materialism, but we also have no reason to accept it simply in its present form as an established result of science, so long as it is still so largely hypothetical, and the metaphysical prejudices of most of its defenders are so evident. But even if through further research it will become unshakable certainty, have we as Christians any occasion to be uneasy about this? This question leads us to some fundamental considerations.

3. THE LIMITS OF GENETIC THOUGHT

First of all, we must remember that the significance of every genetic explanation has its limits, and that the different kinds of genetic explanation mutually limit each other. This may be illustrated by a simple example. The coming into being of a work of art, as for instance that of the *Moses* of Michelangelo, is doubtless open to a causal-genetic explanation. With the aid of the causal idea used in physics we can 'explain' 'how *Moses* came into being': how the block of marble was hewn out of the quarry at Carrara, how by mechanical means it was transported, set up in the studio and there fashioned with hammer and chisel, that is, was reduced in a definite way. An absolutely accurate report of the mechanical causal events leads from the first stroke of the hammer to the completion of the work of art, and thus 'explains' 'how the *Moses* of Michelangelo came into being.' This account of the process by which this work of art came into being is no different in principle from that which describes the way in which a sand-dune has come into being, or from a geological description of the formation of a particular 'folding' in a mountain range. It leaves out nothing save the one point which interests us: namely, how the work of art, the meaningful structure,

from the point of view of natural science cf. Tschulok: *Deszendenzlehre*, an objective presentation of the average view which is accepted at the present time and the arguments for it.

the manifestation of the idea, 'Michelangelo's *Moses*' came into being.

For the understanding of this 'object,' or of this aspect of the same object, the Idealistic view of development is far more significant. The *Moses* of Michelangelo has grown out of the inner picture, out of the idea of the artist. This it was which led him to the marble quarry, it was this which determined his choice of the block of marble, which guided his hand, which moved the hammer towards the chisel; this was 'the cause'—and yet something quite different from that which the student of physics means by 'cause'—of this piece of sculpture, which is one of the most precious treasures of civilized humanity. The 'development' of this piece of reality can only be explained from the idea, not from physical causes. We do not understand a work of art, a scientific book, a work of technics, or even an association, a society or a community from the causal scheme of development, but from the final end, not from causes, but from ends or formative ideas. Yet we cannot understand even the development of an organism simply from mechanical causes,[1] but only with the aid of a principle of another kind, namely, of that third idea of development, which we called the romantic: through the idea of the organic totality, of the shaping and creative potentiality which is operative in nature itself, of the 'entelechy,' or whatever we may wish to call this mysterious 'something' which co-ordinates the parts into a coherent whole, and gives to each part of this 'pre-forming' whole its place and its function.

Hence we must always look at man in the light of different ideas of development. There is certainly more to be learned about the growth of European culture from Hegel than from Darwin, although certain principles of development of the natural science which works on causal lines—as, for example, to take the most important, that of selection—can also be usefully applied even here. Wherever we are concerned with something which has spiritual meaning there both the causal

[1] Titius, op. cit., pp. 503 ff., describes the limits of the mechanistic doctrine of evolution recognized to-day. The arguments which Bergson brought forward against the mechanistic evolutionary theory were of epoch-making importance.

and the romantic ideas of development break down; where we are concerned with an organic, planned structure, there the latter in particular throws most light upon the question.

Secondly, not only do the different theories of development limit each other mutually, but they are also all limited by other ideas. Mathematics, logic, ethics, etc., may either make no use at all of the idea of development or at least only in a very indirect manner. For the perception of the meaningful as full of meaning, of that which is in harmony with the norm as normal, of the understanding of the beautiful as beautiful, of the Good as good, of the True as true, of the Holy as holy, the genetic idea cannot help us. I do not learn what art is—or at least certainly not in any essential way—from its growth; on the contrary, in order to understand the development of art, and to interest me in it, I must first of all know what art is. And I shall certainly not learn this from the study of the most primitive beginnings of art, but only by immersing myself in the study of the most finished works of the most mature kind of art. To try to come to terms with such things with the aid of the idea of development—of any variety—is an absolute perversion of thought. No human being would imagine that he could learn the nature of mathematics from the beginnings of mathematics among primitive peoples, or in the study of the child. We learn from the great mathematicians what mathematics is. Thus only one who has himself no original understanding of religion will want to explain the mystery of religion in an evolutionistic way. Indeed we may say—though with a certain exaggeration—only where the subject is itself not understood do we begin to study its genesis. The meaningful, in any case, is not understood from its genesis but from its meaning, from its *logos*.

Thirdly, we must not confuse development with history. Development, or the account of a process of growth, may be, but need not be, historical. In the strict sense of the word man alone has history, and it is misleading to speak of 'natural history,' for example, of the 'history of the mammal.' The mammal as animal has no history. This point will be dealt with in the following chapter. The essential element in history is not 'becoming' but action. The true historian will not report how things have become what they are—that is already an evolutionary falsification of real history—but how they were, how they happened. He reports the deeds of men, not their development. The fact that history has become so genetic at the present day does not belong to the essence of history, but is due to the modern mind, and it shows the power of the genetic idea. Even history has taken possession of it, certainly not to its own advantage. History, instead of being a scientific narrative—as it ought to be—has become an explanatory narrative, by which it is falsified. The fact that the genuinely historical is not 'becoming' as such is due to its unique character. Growth, however, is continuous, and is not unique. The Idealistic, the Naturalistic, or the Romantic idea of development, if it is to become a dominating conception instead of being merely a subordinate idea, will inevitably spoil every historical presentation. It is the duty of the historian, as Thucydides and Tacitus knew: to report and not to explain.

4. EVOLUTION, CREATION AND SIN

These preliminary considerations were necessary in order to answer the question: what significance have the truths of modern genetic research for the understanding of man? or, to put it more exactly, in what way do they affect or modify the Christian understanding of man? In order to answer this question, we shall once more divide the Christian anthropology into its two main statements, and contemplate each in turn.

From the assertion that God created man in a definite way, namely, as one who has been determined by the Divine image, and thus has been created good, there arises the question: what is the relation between this good creation and the fact of growth? This question forces us to leave the statement about the Creation quite uncomplicated, leaving out of account the various stages in the growth of mankind. The man who has been created by God as good is not the Neanderthal man, nor the Heidelberg man, nor the Peking man, nor the *homo sapiens*, but simply 'man' in general. As Christian theologians we have no special knowledge of the growth of man, neither individual nor general, which the natural scientist or the historian for instance would have to take over from us. The actual, spatio-temporal growth of man is not an article of faith but of natural—scientific—experience. But what we learn about man from experience is interpreted by the perception of faith in a definite way; its meaning and its relation to the will and the action of God is unveiled by the revealed knowledge of God, as the Psalmist[1] brings into the light of the thought of Creation the fact which everyone knows—the pagan as well as the Hebrew—of the growth of the embryo. The Bible cannot claim to impart a special, revealed knowledge of the growth of humanity in the empirical sense; conversely, however, the empirical science of the growth of human beings cannot solve the riddle of the growth of persons—either individually or generally. It can only describe the individual phases through which this process of human growth passes.

The same must be said of the second main statement of the Christian faith, namely, that man who was created good by God has 'fallen' through sin. The Fall, too, is not an event in the story of the growth of humanity; it is no more an empirical event than the Creation; it lies behind or above the empirical plane. The antithesis between 'created good—fallen' has nothing to do with the difference between 'earlier (in the empirical time-series) or later.' Abraham is no nearer the good Creation and the event of the Fall than I am, because he lived at an earlier time. To trace the story of the growth of humanity back into the past does not bring us finally to the Fall and the Creation. The difference between 'primitive' and 'developed' has no more connexion with the content of the Christian statements than the difference between the child and the grown man. In so far as the child is a human being, it has a share both in the Creation in the image of God and in the Fall; and the same is true of the 'primitive' human being who lives in our own day, or who lived before us.

So the question of the relation between the pre-historic period and the Primitive State and the Fall of Man can only be answered negatively. The doctrine of the original human existence and of the Fall has no special relation to the pre-historic period, any more than the individual sin has a special

[1] Psa. cxxxix; see above, p. 89.

relation to childhood. Even in childhood, from the very moment that the child in the actual sense of the words is a human being, sin is already present, but not in a special explicit way as 'the Fall';[1] and precisely not in an explicit way, but only in a rudimentary and dim way. The same is true of the child-stage of humanity as a whole. We shall not expect any illumination on the nature of original human existence and of the Fall from the prehistoric period. On the contrary, we shall give up all attempts to discover somewhere in that field the event of the Fall, and after that of Paradise, the way of life of the original man. Rather we may say that both the child and the primitive human being, our original ancestor, back to the Peking man or the Java man, are further removed from Original and Fallen man than we are.

This makes it clear that the idea of development should not be used for the explanation of Christian concepts, nor should it be set up in opposition to them. The former is what modern theology, since Schleiermacher, has tried to do; the second was the opinion both of the opponents and of the defenders of the doctrine of the Early Church. We have already become familiar with the essential thought of Schleiermacher. He tried to conceive the meaning of the ecclesiastical doctrine of Original Sin in evolutionary terms by applying the idea of the after-effects of the earlier stages of evolution to the present stage of evolution.[2] It is not our intention to deny this fact as such, nor to depreciate its importance. Genetic individual psychology shows us in an impressive way, in the example of 'infantilism,' the actual existence of such after-effects of a more primitive stage of development; likewise there are enough instances—provided by paleontological research—of physical and psychical relics of earlier stages of development, of 'atavistic' elements which have been left behind. So also the history of custom shows us how some old

[1] In his work, *The Concept of Dread,* Kierkegaard seems to wish to ascribe a very special significance to the first sin of the individual, as if this itself were the Fall of Man. This would be a psychological misunderstanding, which would be on a level with the historical misunderstanding against which he is contending.

[2] For further details see my book, *Die Mystik und das Wort,* Chapter X; *Die Sünde als Atavismus und als Schuld.*

custom or tradition may be handed on for centuries without being understood, long after its meaning has disappeared and been forgotten. Finally, too, psychological research into the 'collective-unconscious,' and the archaic types which appear in the latter, also point in the same direction. The actual fact which lies behind Schleiermacher's theory must be admitted. Still more: even its relation to sin ought not to be denied. In all sin there is something of atavism or archaism and 'infantilism.' What we know to-day about our past from the empirical scientific point of view is not without significance for our knowledge of sin. But it does not explain sin, neither the common sin of humanity as a whole, nor individual 'sins.' To explain sin causally in such a way would mean denying it altogether. The actual situation of atavism or infantilism is a psychological element of the concrete fact of sin, but it is not its origin; for this lies in decision, in a spiritual act of self-determination, not in psychical causes. Sin, as Kierkegaard discusses it in his *Concept of Dread*, is something *new*; in contradistinction from all genetic psychological conditions it is a leap; it is that element in decision which cannot be explained.[1] Thus the fact that infantile or atavistic tendencies are in operation in the nature of man at the present day is not to be contested. But they only become sin when man in his moral decision, in his self-determination, makes room for them, or allows them to remain. Thus our knowledge of the growth of humanity or of the single human being may possibly enrich our conception of the actual, concrete forms of sin, but they can never in the slightest degree make any contribution to our knowledge of the nature of sin itself, the fact of the sinful decision as such. Both man's creation in the image of God, and also his 'contradiction,' are facts which do not lie upon the empirical plane, but through the genuinely historical they impinge upon it, and manifest themselves within it.

This also clears away the second misunderstanding, namely, the view that the doctrine of the Origin and Fall of Man is in opposition to the facts of human development maintained by science. This opinion, as is well known, is held not only by orthodox Christian theologians but also by orthodox Darwinian

[1] Kierkegaard: *Begriff der Angst*, p. 25.

natural scientists and their still more orthodox pupils: 'either Moses or Darwin,' 'either the Christian Faith or the idea of evolution.' It is true of course that there certainly is an irreconcilable opposition between the ancient ecclesiastical form of the doctrine and the idea of evolution. But purely from religious considerations we have already rejected this traditional form of the doctrine as a fatal misunderstanding, as a corruption of the real thought of the Bible.

The theologically purified doctrine of the Origin and of the Fall, on the other hand, can neither be proved nor disproved by the findings of empirical science. For the Creation and the Fall are happenings which cannot be introduced into any empirico-historical picture, thus they cannot be affected by any changes in the empirical picture of growth. The genetic picture of the growth of humanity or of the individual human being may show how the specifically human element, whether in the positive or in the negative sense, either as the image of God or as sin, begins to appear on the plane of that which can be empirically perceived. It may perhaps describe the beginnings of human existence—so far as we can trace them; but it cannot explain personal existence as such, nor that negative element by which it is determined—sin. It merely shows us: from this point of view we see living creatures with the perhaps still very dim and primitive characteristics of that which is distinctively human; but how personal existence and sin come to be lies beyond all that empirical genetic description and research into causes can prove. Equally little, however, can the theological statement about the Origin and the Fall of Man contain an element which prejudices the picture of the story of the growth of man. It merely says that wherever there are human beings there too you will always find both the divine Origin of Man and his Fall: the image of God and its destruction, that is, 'man in contradiction.'

Thus the Christian doctrine of Original Sin and of the Fall, rightly understood, is no more opposed to the fact of evolution than the beauty or the ugliness of a picture is opposed to the chemical qualities of its material—the canvas or the colours. The beauty or the ugliness of a picture has certain chemical substances as its substratum. It is not beautiful or ugly without these chemical elements, but it is not beautiful or ugly because of them, but only 'through' them. This may serve as an analogy for the disparity between the statements which concern growth and those which concern personal being, thus Creation and Sin. The specifically human element, personal being, is not a fact which can be proved either empirically or rationally, in either its positive or its negative aspect. Every view of man which does not start from the Word of God and from responsibility must ignore precisely the essential element of human existence, its character of decision. So also every theory of development, whether it be the Idealistic, the Romantic or the Naturalistic, must also ignore it. How man comes to be, so far as this real element is concerned, has no essential importance for that which he is, unless we understand by its 'growth' his growth from God and from his decision in opposition to God. But this is not what is usually called 'growth.' That has far more to do with his history than with his development. A later chapter will deal with this question.

5. GROWTH AND SPIRITUAL BEING

Human existence, the fact that man has been created in the image of God, and the fact that he has set himself in opposition to God, cannot be understood from the fact of his development, but it is embedded in the fact of his development. It is part of human existence as we know it—even of that part which has been created by God—that it is not there from the very outset, but that it grows. There is no theological reason why we should regard the process of growth as such—birth and growth—as something which ought not to be, as something which is contrary to the purpose of the Creation. Even the process of growth with which we are familiar participates in the Creation as well as in sin. The suspicion of the process of development as ungodly in itself, as something which cannot be reconciled with the Divine Good, is an idea of Greek Idealism, not of the faith of the Bible.[1] It is rooted

[1] By the equation *Urzeit gleich Endzeit*, which Heim sets up in the first edition of his *Glaube und Denken* (p. 387) and which is based upon the identification of the Fall and an objective, temporal world-form (p. 379), growth is opposed to the act of creation; in spite of all modifications, this

ultimately in the protest against creaturely-finite existence as such, in the rebellion of man who wants to be God, against the fact that he has been created at all. From the being of God certainly, all growth, all possibility of growth or necessity for growth is excluded; but growth belongs to the nature of the creature as such. The necessity for development is a fundamental destiny of all, also of human creatureliness. The Biblical narrative of the Creation takes into account the human process of reproduction, and therefore it regards the procreation of children and the process of birth as a law of the good Creation, not of the Fall.[1] The fact of being unfinished—which belongs to the process of growth as such—ought not to be regarded as a manifestation of evil. From the very outset a process of human growth and development has always been taken for granted.

We know this human growth of man primarily as a fact of the individual life. The specifically human element in man is not there from the very outset—in the infant or even in the embryo, in the fertilized ovum—but it develops in connexion with and in a certain parallel to bodily and psycho-physical development. Even the Bible takes account of the fact that man is first of all a ψυχικός and not a πνευματικός,[2] that is, that the fully human element is not present from the outset but that it is added to that which first existed.[3] The infant,

is the idea of the Fall due to Plato and to Origen, with the consequence that Redemption does not bring in anything new, as against the Original Creation, thus that the whole of history can begin anew. The Augustinian distinction: *posse non mori* and *non posse mori* is here abandoned, and in so doing time which was going in one direction has again become a cycle. That is the 'Achilles' heel' of Heim's presentation which is otherwise so fine.

[1] Gen. i. 28.

[2] Cor. xv. 45 ff.

[3] Whether Rom. vii. 7–9 has this biographical meaning or not is questionable. Zwingli understood the passage in this sense, whereas most modern commentators see here a parallel to Rom. v. 14, that is, not an autobiographical reflection at all but one which is concerned with the history of humanity. It is beyond doubt that Jesus Himself takes into consideration a relative innocence on the part of the child (Matt. xviii. 3; xix. 14). The Church has not kept to the lines laid down by the Bible when it has regarded the infant as a sinner, although it is quite right to insist that every human being to whom the Word is proclaimed is a sinner.

just as he is not able to use human speech, is not capable of understanding the Word of God. This human element in man, whether in the formal or in the material sense, is indeed never to be understood by the idea of development; on the other hand it is something which we learn to know only in the process of development. Not only in the sphere of the body, but also in that of the mind and the spirit, do we see the process of growth in human life; man *grows* as long as he lives. Even of our Saviour it was said: 'He increased in wisdom and in stature.'[1] Growth is characteristic, not of sinful existence, but of the earthly world and the earthly existence.

But just as certainly as we can observe this fact of growth, register and describe its stages and phases, so also we lack all insight into the connexion between human growth and the being of man. The growth of even the simplest logical fundamental conception, for instance, the idea of 'where' or 'what' is an enigma to us. For these categories are not constructed from various elements, thus they cannot be analysed or fitted together; but suddenly they are *there*, at one bound, so to speak. 'It flashes upon us' what this means: 'why,' 'who,' 'where,' 'what,' etc. No one can tell another; each person must see it for himself, and he must see it in a flash. And yet actually it does not happen 'in a flash,' and the teacher, the one who imparts, plays an indispensable part in this process. As the body, and above all the brain, must be prepared for the psychical functions, so must the latter also be prepared for the mental and then again for the personal act. This preparation requires time, in it development takes place; the act itself, however, happens, when it happens, suddenly, in such a way that we can only conceive its relation to time in a negative manner. It comes in time, indeed even with time, and yet is itself, by its very nature, above time. It comes with growth, in the process of growth, and yet it is itself either wholly there or not at all. We cannot 'understand' the question of 'why' in part—half or three-quarters for instance—we either understand it all at once or not at all.

What is true of the formal structure of the mind is also true of material personal existence. Responsible self-determination

[1] Luke ii. 52.

cannot 'grow.' It is or it is not. Love happens or it does not happen. And yet that which itself cannot grow happens in the process of growth and takes a share in growth. Just as the question 'why,' although it is an indivisible whole, may be thought more or less powerfully or profoundly, so also man may accomplish the personal act of responsible self-decision more or less powerfully and 'decidedly.' There is a personality which is childlike, and another which is masculine, there is a childlike faith and a vigorous masculine faith, a childlike and a masculine way of committing sin. To deny this state of affairs is just as dangerous as to over-estimate its psychological importance. Even the spiritual life, even man's relation to God, is embedded in the process of growth, both in its negative and in its positive form. There is a development in sin and in faith, in spite of the fact that man is either wholly a believer or wholly a sinner. The two aspects must be held by us continually side by side, and can never be equated with one another—the logical aspect of the 'wholly' 'total' which knows no 'more or less,' and the psychological aspect, in which the 'more or less,' the 'ever more' and the 'ever less' are the standard.[1] But as we shall never be able to understand how it is that body and mind exist together, so also we shall never be able to discover that which, in the nature of the case, cannot be fitted together, but while it is an indivisible whole, at the same time can be something which grows. It must be enough for us to know that this is the case, and that both these two points of view are justified.

We are not aware, however, merely of the fact of an individual growth of man, but—and this is the new element as compared with previous generations—also of a general

[1] This is why the question whether faith is to be conceived psychologically or not can neither be answered with No nor with Yes, but can only be answered with both No and Yes. It is therefore not right to place faith on its psychological side as something comparatively immaterial. In theology pseudo-logic is as bad as pseudo-psychology. This must be said against my own observations in *Die Mystik und das Wort* (pp. 18 ff.), which only emphasize one side. Faith stands above the opposition between *Logos* and *Dynamis*. It is a looking away from oneself but 'a whole-hearted looking at Christ' and therefore the 'growth' of faith plays such a large part in the New Testament.

process of growth. The human race as a whole, as a human race, is not simply from the beginning *there*, finished; it too, like the individual human being, has grown out of primitive origins. Here again we must accept a certain parallel between the physical and the mental. The meagre—but significant—documents of the mental life of the more primitive stages of humanity, which testify to early human civilization, art and religion, are, it is true, not sufficient to give us a picture of the mental life of man in his earlier days; but they do give us a right to extend the parallel between the bodily and the mental development which we know from individual experience to humanity as a whole. The study of the 'primitive' life of the present day, in order to supplement our knowledge about the origin of mankind, has been continually shown to be justified by the study of palaeontology, although a good deal which at first sight looks 'primitive' in reality is not 'primitive' at all, but is a product of degeneration.

Why, then, should not Christian theology boldly admit the fact that even mankind as a whole—like the individual—has developed not only physically but also mentally out of 'embryonic' human conditions to childlike human existence, and from that to historical human existence? This fact was not admitted on the side of the Christian Church for so long because on both sides there was misunderstanding and confusion. To admit mental development from primitive origins does not mean that we *explain* mental life from these origins. Individually as well as generally, the being of man as human is a divine new creation, and can no more be explained from its antecedents—as will be shown in more detail further on—than the mental can be explained from the psychical or the psychical from the physical. The fact that the mental, both individually and generally, runs parallel with the physical development, does not in any way exclude the other fact, that it is something completely *new*. Why should not that which in principle is new appear only gradually, by degrees? Even the most striking and clear proof of the way in which man has developed out of the animal series would not alter the fact in the least that man, as compared with all other creatures, is something new, something which cannot be deduced from and understood in the light of it, but that man is a being *sui generis*. Up to the present time science has not yet provided such a proof, although the 'missing link' has become ever shorter, and not a great deal is now lacking to make the strict proof possible. No Christian ought to deny to-day, on account of his Christian faith, the extreme probability of the Doctrine of Descent, and no theologian ought to deny it on account of his theology. The controversy which on the side of theology has been carried on against the theory of evolution is certainly nothing to be proud of in the history of Christian theology, and it has done a great deal to shake people's faith in the genuine truthfulness of the teachers of the Church. If it has pleased God the Creator to allow mankind to develop out of the animal series, just as He allows the human individual to develop out of a fertilized ovum—why should we rebel against this? Does this alter anything in the special significance of the creation of man? What does it alter in the statement of the Bible, that man has been created in the image of God and through sin has fallen away from Him?

CHAPTER XVIII

MAN IN THE COSMOS

1. THE THREEFOLD BOUNDARY

A DISTINCTIVE feature of the Christian understanding of existence is the fact that in it not only is the boundary between God and the world, God and man maintained, but also that the distinction between man and the world is kept very clear and sharp, as something which must never be allowed to become blurred. Man is not a bit of the world; he stands over against all creaturely existence as something special, as a new dimension. It is not due to *naïveté*, but is the necessary consequence of the Biblical idea of God that the Biblical picture of the world is absolutely anthropocentric, to such an extent indeed that in the Bible the world and man are frequently interchangeable ideas. The world of which the Bible speaks is always the world for man, the world in which the fate of man is of supreme importance. Man is in the centre of the world, in spite of the fact that God is His Creator and Lord, as He is the Creator and Lord of the world. God has placed man as lord over the creatures, He has ordered the world for him. In this respect the Bible is in opposition to both the ancient and the modern idea of the cosmos, where man is integrated into the cosmos as a dependent element. Since God appoints man lord of the created world and 'places all things under his feet,'[1] He places him over against the

[1] Psa. viii. 7. This central position of man is not removed by the New Testament interpretation of the Psalm as applied to Christ; it is only made still clearer: only through the *Logos*, the Christ, 'in whom are gathered together in one all things in Christ, both which are in heaven and which are on earth' (Eph. i. 10), has man a part in this centre of the world; but for that very reason he *has* a part in it, and his part in it is due to the Christ. The tendency to deny this special position of man, plainly expressed in Barth's *Credo*, where (p. 30) it is said that it is seemly for man as a creature 'to recognize his own insignificance and smallness also within the sphere of creation,' is non-Scriptural. On the other hand Augustine may stand as the representative of the view of the Church as a whole: *In homine omnis propemodum creatura; breviter, creationis et naturae centrum est* (quoted in J. Gerhard, op. cit., IV, 239).

world, makes him the goal and the purpose of the whole creation. This 'anthropocentric' idea of the world, however, is in opposition both to speculative Idealism and to mysticism, which ultimately equate the spirit of man with the Divine Spirit, the human reason with the divine Reason, with the idea of the correlation of God and man, which the Cherubinic Wanderer, a singer supposed to be Christian, expresses so bluntly:

> That God so holy is, and lives without desire
> He has received from me, as I from Him,
> I am as great as God, He is as small as I,
> No higher I than He, nor I than He less high.[1]

Here the three dimensions are not distinguished from one another, here the absolute boundary between God and man, and also that between the world and man, has become fluid. The mysticism which sees God and man as a unity, since it is pantheistic, necessarily also regards God and the world, and man and the world, as a unity.

The distinctive element in the Biblical idea of the world is this, that man, for whom the world is ordered as its summit, its goal and its end, is also himself God's creature, servant and not master; one who receives and not one who sends; a reflection, not an original light; a dependent and not an independent being. It is the creaturely being, man, who has been created out of nothing, who is not eternal, not unconditioned, who is wholly dependent, whom God makes lord over His Creation. Man is master of the world because and in so far as God makes him so, because through the fact that God creates him only in His own image, He allows him to have the privilege of being subject and being spirit, of freedom and of creative activity, and endows him with those powers by means of which man can actually 'make subject unto him' 'that which is under him.'

The fact that man has been created in the Divine Image singles him out from all other creatures; by means of this

[1] *The Cherubinic Wanderer* is a long poem by Angelus Silesius (Johannes Scheffler), 1562–1677.—*Translator.*

quality, which is assigned to man alone, among all the creatures with which we are familiar, he is a dimension of his own. By means of this Divine image, through the Word of God, which is the ground of his personal being, he participates in the manner of the divine being—that is, in being subject, in which the sub-human creation, the world, has no part. He alone is person, even if—in contrast to the Creator Himself—he is a person who is not unconditioned but conditioned, not autonomous and self-sufficient, but wholly dependent on the positing of God. It is through his personality that, in virtue of the divine positing, he is lord of all the other creatures, and is the meaning and the end of the Creation.[1] For he alone, who is created as person, can give back to the Creator with a self-actuated, loving response the love with which he has been loved. The Creator, whose power is in all that exists, and who preserves all in existence, can be in communion with man alone. Man has this special position in the created cosmos in spite of his fall from God and the perversion of his nature.[2] Even as sinner man does not cease to be subject, to be person, in contrast to all else that exists. He remains, even as sinner, in a distinctive, even if negative relation to God; before and afterwards alike, even if in another, that is, an altered sense, namely, changed by sin and law, he remains responsible. Hence even as sinner he still remains over against the world, knowing it and acting in it, making it, theoretically and practically, an object. He dominates it, he 'makes it subject to himself,' even though in a way which is not in harmony with the divine will, but in one which is contrary to it, which leads finally to the fact that he himself becomes dominated. But even his tyrannical and brutal way of making his fellow-creatures subject to himself is a proof of his original exceptional position, just as it is also a proof of his fall into sin.

[1] J. Gerhard thus sums up what Christian theologians—except Karl Barth—have always taught: *Sicut factus homo propter Deum, ut Deo serviret; ita mundus factus propter hominem ut homine serviret*, IV, 239.

[2] This *dominium* is regarded by the earlier theologians, including Luther, as spoilt indeed, but not as lost, and precisely in this they see that 'relic' of the image of God.

2. MAN IN THE CENTRE OF THE WORLD

Through his double attitude to the world, namely, that, on the one hand, he is set within it as a bodily creature, and that, on the other hand, he stands over against it as a spiritual-personal being, man, as even the very earliest theologians noticed, occupies a curious position midway between 'heaven' and 'earth.' He is somehow the pivot of the creation; his destiny is not only his own, but it also determines that of the created world as a whole. The world around him, according to the Biblical view, does not seem so objectively independent as the naïve realism of common sense—often wrongly appealing to the word of the Bible—assumes. The manner in which the world exists which man 'has' is somehow 'covariant' with his own manner of existence, with his attitude to God; according to the Biblical view the counterpart of the sinful existence of man is a world which is very different from human existence as originally created by God.[1]

Primarily man is a microcosm, a being in whose structure all the stages of existence of the world can be seen: the inorganic, the organic, the vital, the animal element. The human body, like every body which occupies space, is composed of protons, atoms, molecules, and crystals; his body, like every organic structure, is a totality with 'self-direction,' a vegetative structure, which nourishes itself by assimilation, grows through the division of cells and differentiates itself; from the point of view of comparative anatomy he belongs to the mammal species of the vertebrates, with whom he has in common not only the main features of the morphological structure but also most of the biological functions. Thus man, in spite of his distinctiveness, is primarily also a compendium of the whole created world.

But, as has already been emphasized by Gregory of Nyssa, there is no special reason to extol man as a microcosm; for he shares this quality with 'every mouse.'[2] The pre-Christian

[1] Thus according to the usual conception of the meaning of Rom. viii. 20. Here too Schlatter and others certainly understand κτίσις as said of man, namely, of the unbeliever, in contradistinction to the children of God.

[2] Thus Gregory of Nyssa, *De hom. opif*, c. 16. Luther: *Nam in ceteris creaturis cognoscitur Deus ceu in vestigio, in homine autem, praesertim in Adamo, vere cognoscitur . . . ut recte dicatur μικρόκοσμος* (WA. 42, 51).

Greek thinkers laid so much stress upon the idea of the microcosm because for them the cosmos was divine, and thus in their conception of 'microcosm' they intended to express the fact that man had a share in the divine existence. Within Christian thought it merely expresses the fact that the higher state of existence always includes within itself the lower, but is not contained in it. We may understand the lower stage from the higher, but the opposite is not the case, although genetically the higher stage develops out of the lower. We can understand repose as the extreme limit of motion, but we cannot reverse the order and understand motion as springing from repose. We may regard the dead as the limit of the living, but we cannot reverse the order and understand the living from the dead. Thus we may also understand the irrational life of the *psyche* from the rational life of the *psyche* but not the other way round. That which is rich in dimension helps us to understand that which is less rich in dimension, but not vice versa. For the new 'dimension' is not the result of an increase or combination of previous dimensions, but is indeed something which in itself is inexplicably new. The fact that this new dimension only gradually emerges out of the realm of the previous one, beginning with a minimum, may lead a superficial mind to think that the new dimension can be explained from the previous one and thus as a mere transformation of the old. Precisely this, however, is the sign of the new 'dimension,' that this possibility of transformation does not exist. The new quality cannot be attained by any new combination or increase of that which previously existed. It is a new creation, although the new may fit smoothly to the old; just as the points which switch over to the other line are connected so harmoniously that the transition is easy. A mechanistic theory of evolution has to a large extent obscured insight into this situation, and in so doing has raised a host of problems which are not real problems at all, but could be solved with a right *exercitium logicum*.

This significant idea of the graded order of being, which cannot be reversed, is already expressed in the Biblical narrative of the Creation. The fundamental truth that all, the dead and the living, the higher and the lower, are equally creatures, created beings, dependent entities, does not rule out the other truth that this created existence is an organic whole which has been created by stages, whose summit is man, the creature which has been endowed with reason or spirit. The fact that alongside of this Biblical doctrine there is also a Neo-Platonist and Aristotelian doctrine of the graded order of being,[1] which was combined by Thomas Aquinas with the Christian idea of Creation, and made into a central idea of scholastic philosophy and theology, does not mean that we need reject the simple idea of the Bible itself. It is not the idea itself, but the use of the scholastic argument which is dangerous. According to the teaching of the Bible, in his personal being man is the summit of an hierarchically ordered world of creation, whereas his material, his organic and his animal existence connects him with the whole of the rest of the created world, gives him a share in its existence, whether material or biological. This summit itself, however, towers above the sphere of the created world; his personal being, as we have seen, is only to be understood as being-in-the-word-of-God, as responsible being.

The Bible indeed suggests that not only man but also other beings endowed with reason have a share in this distinctive position, created spirits, which do not belong to the life of earth; but the Bible tells us so little about the 'angels' that in any case it is not sufficient to give us any clear knowledge about these beings whom we meet neither in our natural nor in our religious experience.[2] What the Church has taught on

[1] The Aristotelian *scala naturae* (dead matter—plants—lower animals—higher animals—man) is first of all simply that which every thinking human being perceives; but it is combined with his metaphysic of *nous* and *hyle* in such a way that it is in opposition to the Christian idea of Creation. The 'lower' is for Aristotle a product of the limitation of the spirit, even as in Neo-Platonism it is a depreciation of existence. Cf. Zeller, III, pp. 426 ff. Scholasticism has tried to weave all three *motifs* into a unity; hence the Catholic ethic is determined by the contrast between the 'lower' and the 'higher,' which is completely absent from the thought of the Bible.

[2] Whether the following statement of Schlatter: 'for those who speak to us in the Scriptures, man did not stand at the summit of creation, but above him they saw a manifold kingdom of spirits' (*Das christliche Dogma*, p. 92) is tenable in view of such passages as 1 Cor. vi. 3; 1 Pet. i. 12; Heb. ii. 16, is extremely questionable. On the other hand, we gladly agree with him that the idea 'makes clear to us the glory of God.' The specu-

this subject from time immemorial should rightly belong rather to the realm of speculative imagination than to that of the truths of faith. In any case there is no occasion for us to give any more attention to this subject in a doctrine of man; the mere fact that it has been mentioned will be sufficient.

Although man is not the centre, he is *in* the centre of the cosmos, because he has been created in the Word of God. The Word of God, the *Logos* 'which was in the beginning'[1] and 'through whom all has been created,'[2] 'the Son who upholds all things by the word of His power,'[3] 'for whom all was created,'[4] and 'in whom all things cohere'[5] is the centre of the world. He is also the 'true Light which lighteth every man'[6]—the Word of God, apart from whom man would not be man, and would not be a responsible being. Through his participation in this Word—which sin does not destroy although it corrupts it—man is capable of placing himself over against the world and of making his fellow-creatures subject unto him. Hence, because man—whether in a right or a wrong relation, whether saved or doomed—has a share in this Word, he himself, though indeed not the centre of the world, is *in* the centre of the world. Hence we cannot imagine any other world, and we do not know of any other world, save that which is 'for us,' the subject of our knowledge, and the object of our domination.

We express the same truth from the opposite angle when we remind ourselves that God became man and not an animal. It is not an arbitrary fact that God reveals Himself to us as man and not as an animal. It is contrary to the revealed meaning of the Creation when it is asserted that God could have revealed Himself just as well as animal as man. The fact

lations about the angels which are such a favourite theme in scholastic, and also in Protestant, theology (cf. J. Gerhard, all the nineteen chapters) are in strange contrast to the relative unimportance of this theme in the New Testament.

[1] John i. 1. [2] John i. 3. [3] Heb. i. 3.

[4] Col. i. 16. [5] Col. i. 17.

[6] John i. 9. When Luther says of man that he is *praestantior creatura quam coelum, quam terra et omnia, quae in eis sunt* (WA. 42, 87), that is to be understood, like all Luther's thought on creation and man, of existence in the Word of God.

that God became man, and the fact that man alone has been created in the image of God, are inseparably connected.[1] In the light of the first we perceive the second. Only from the standpoint of the Incarnation do we perceive that this is the case with man; but in the light of the Incarnation we perceive that this connexion with man is due to the Creation, that this distinctiveness has been given to man, which not even the Fall destroys, indeed that even the Fall itself—even if in the negative form—can only re-emphasize it. The Incarnation takes place —not only but also—in order to restore the picture which has been destroyed; the Divine Incarnation—not only, but also, and necessarily—is the renewal of that which took place in the creation of man in the image of God. Human personal being alone is a suitable means of revealing the personal Being of God. The revelation of the Divine person in the God-Man is at the same time the revelation of the originally true, personal being of man.

God reveals Himself to us in Jesus Christ as the Man-God, as the 'God for man,' just as He reveals Himself to us as the 'Man from God and for God.' The Incarnation of the Son of God is *both* the revelation of God who is the Centre, and of man, who through the creation of God has a share in this centre; it reveals to us, as the divine goal for the cosmos, a theanthropic end, the divine end, which is at the same time the end of man.[2] The Rule of God which is the purpose of God is at the same time the Redemption and the consummation of man, which is the purpose for man. In His revelation God confesses Himself on the side of man as the aim, and therefore

[1] Luther: *Et tamen, quia est conditus ad imaginem invisibilis Dei, occulte per hoc significatur, sicut audiemus, Deum se revelaturum mundo in homine Christo* (WA. 42, 66). It is one and the same revealed will of God which lies behind the creation of man in the image of God and the Incarnation of the Son of God in the Man Christ Jesus. Cf. Rom. viii. 29 and Eph. i. 10.

[2] Thus Luther, speaking explicitly of present, fallen man, classes together the creation of man and the aim of the Kingdom of God, since he calls men the highest and best creatures of God, for whose sake all has been created and to whom God has given all, and indeed whom He has appointed to be His children and His heirs (cf. Köstlin: *Luthers Theologie*, II, p. 97). In the New Testament the Kingdom of God is always first of all perfected communion between God and humanity.

also as the central point, of His creation. Ultimately everything turns on the destiny of man. Even the dumb creation waits 'for the revealing of the sons of God.'[1] The whole cosmos is only a framework for the history of mankind, which has its central point in the God-Man. The cosmos moves, as it were, in harmony with the history of mankind—in destruction as well as in restoration and consummation. The history of mankind, from the very outset, is connected with a cosmic and super-cosmic dimension, because it is based in the God who is in Himself the Loving One, and thus the One who wills community, the Triune God. If it be true that God is Love, that this one Word alone can fully and rightly express the nature of God,[2] then this means that God is a God-Man, and His creation is a creation for the sake of man. Hence in the Bible there is so little about the world of nature, the sub-human world. The Bible is concerned with God's dominion over man—as the meaning and end of the whole cosmos. This truth must be strongly emphasized because at the present day even theology shows a tendency to depreciate man as much as possible—supposedly for the sake of the glory of God, of the God who reveals His plan for the world as a plan for humanity, and who in order to reveal Himself became man!

This Biblical idea of the relation of the cosmos to man is quite foreign to the modern mind; the whole conception is regarded as a relic of bygone ages, when man, in his naïve way, had a fantastic idea of his own importance, fostered by his 'myth-forming imagination,' projecting as it were the cosmos into this view of himself. But the 'imagination which creates myths,' which is supposed to be the cause of this anthropocentric idea of the world, does precisely what the Bible, when it speaks of man, never does: it eliminates the boundary between man and nature, man and things, man and the animal creation, whereas the Bible always maintains this boundary inviolate. The 'myth-forming imagination' leads to the Pantheistic, but certainly not to the Christian, idea of

[1] Rom. viii. 19.

[2] John iv. 16. Also Luther: *Immo deus est aliud nihil quam charitas . . . Qui deum cognoscit iratum, inimicum . . . ille non cognoscit deum, quia non cognoscit charitatem in deo* (WA. 20, 755).

God and the world. For the Bible the unconditional separation of the three dimensions, and their strictly categorical relation to each other, is characteristic; the relations between God, the World, and Man cannot be altered. Hence the derivation of the Biblical idea of the cosmos from the 'myth-forming imagination' is untenable. On the other hand, there is a second question which ought to be faced: has the alteration of our view of the world by science, above all, the knowledge of the descent of man from the animals, and the abandonment of the geocentric, and even of the heliocentric picture of the world, made the Biblical view of man for ever impossible?

3. MAN AND THE ANIMALS

The discussion of the question of the development of man has made us familiar with the idea that even man is to be co-ordinated into the great continuum of the development of life. In spite of the famous 'missing-link' between man and the primates, the fact of a continuity between man and the animals cannot to-day be left in any doubt at all. The difference between man and the highest kind of mammal, from the morphological and physiological point of view, is far less than that which exists between a higher and a lower mammal, not to mention that between a mammal and a living creature of the lowest kind of organism, such as a jelly-fish or even an amoeba. We must also admit that these differences do not refer merely to the physical organism. The idea of Descartes that only man has a 'psyche,' and that animals have none,[1] has proved wholly untenable. Everyone who knows animals knows how differentiated is the psychical experience of a higher animal—as for instance, a dog. Even the long-established distinction between animal instinct and human intelligence, the singling out of man as the *homo faber*, has proved impossible to carry through completely. At the present day we have some experimental knowledge of the intelligence of animals. In any case the boundary between man and the animals cannot be sought at this point.

The boundary lies rather where the Bible sees it: in the fact that man has been created in the image of God, in the

[1] Cf. Windelband: *Lehrbuch der Geschichte der Philosophie*, p. 344.

spiritually-responsible personal being of man. It is not the intellect, but the spirit related to God, which distinguishes man from the animal. Even the highest animal does not show a trace of spirit, that is, of the possibility of ideation, of the transcending of that which exists in experience by something unconditioned, normative, perfect. In the animal we do not see even the smallest beginning of a tendency to seek truth for truth's sake, to shape beauty for the sake of beauty, to promote righteousness for the sake of righteousness, to reverence the Holy for the sake of its holiness. Here too all attempts to maintain the principle of continuity prove to be misrepresentations, whether of the non-spiritual as the spiritual, or of the spiritual as the non-spiritual. The unconditional self-end of the spirit, the spiritual norm, and decision in accordance with the spiritual norm, is something which is wholly and entirely foreign to the animal.[1] The animal knows nothing 'above' its immediate sphere of existence, nothing by which it measures or tests its existence. Montaigne,[2] one of the first who thought it his duty to depreciate man to the glory of God, was simply being witty when he said that when man plays with his cat he cannot be sure that his cat is not playing with him. We cannot penetrate into the soul of a cat, it is true, but all spiritual existence expresses itself in spiritual act, spirit has as its necessary form of expression, culture, humanity, religion. Of all this, animal life, even upon its highest levels, does not show the least trace. We may assign to the animal a minimum amount of a certain kind of civilization, especially technical, the use of the artificial tool for the satisfaction of biologically existing needs; to be *faber*, 'tool-user,' is not the exclusive privilege of man.

[1] The results of the later psychology of animals is thus summed up by Titius: 'that every action according to general principles or even according to ideas, as it finds its universally human and simplest expression in the creation and observance of customs, law and religion, goes absolutely beyond anything which can be observed in animals,' etc. (op. cit., p. 566).

[2] Montaigne, *Essais*, II, 12. The comparison of Montaigne and Ecclesiastes in Vischer's book certainly has something to be said for it, but, like the whole 'wisdom of the Preacher,' certainly does not indicate the essential element in that which the Bible has to tell us about man (W. Vischer: *Der Prediger Salomo im Spiegel Michel de Montaignes, Jahrbuch der theologischen Schule Bethel*, vol. 4).

But culture, the creation of significant works, which are intended to manifest, and do manifest the spirit, is alien to the animal, and is unconditionally characteristic of man as man. Man alone, and every man, even though in different degrees, knows this possibility and this need. The same might be said of speech. The animal may indeed make signs to the members of the same species, but he cannot talk with them, he cannot exchange ideas with them. If the animal had mind he would be obliged to express it, he would be impelled to create culture. Instead of this we see that even animals with the highest forms of organization use their intelligence to maintain their own life and the life of those like themselves. All that goes beyond this belongs to animal fables; it is a pantheistic or materialistic removal of the boundary which the Creator has set between man and beast, since He has created man—and man alone—after His image. To-day, after two hundred years of the most intensive effort to remove it, this boundary is as sharp and clear as ever. The difference between man and beast amounts to a whole dimension of existence,[1] just as that between the living and the dead amounts to a whole dimension of being. The fact that this new element, this special element, is often present in such a slight degree that it is almost nil—when, for instance, the mind is weak to the very extreme of having almost none at all—only provides the apparent possibility of turning the actual stage into a continuum. There is still a vast difference between 'having very little mind' and 'having no mind at all.' The most empty-headed human being is entirely different from the most intelligent animal. The sinner, too, is not a middle term between the animal and the true human being—sin as atavism—but he is wholly a human being, just as much as the perfect saint, although he is a perverted human being. Sin does not consist in the fact that man becomes animal—this confusion of thought does injustice both to the animal and to man—but it consists in the fact that the specifically human element is determined negatively instead of positively. An 'inhuman' person is not an animal, and an animal is not 'inhuman.' It is indeed characteristic of man that he can pervert his nature, that he

[1] Cf. Th. Haecker: *Was ist der Mensch?* an 'order' of being, p. 9.

can become 'inhuman.' There are no foxes and geese whose nature is perverted in this way, but there are 'inhuman' beings—and it is precisely this, sin—which is the fixed gulf between man and beast. Indeed, this gulf between non-personal and personal being is greater than any other difference within the created universe. There is only one difference which is greater still, that between the created universe and the uncreated Creator Himself. Because the Bible regards this difference as such, as the greatest within the created universe, it also perceives the special position of man in the cosmos: namely, that all creatures are subject to man, that all that is not personal is subject to the personal. The basis for this distinctive position, however, is that which makes us responsible: the relation of the human person to the Divine Person, the fact that man has been made in the image of God.

4. MAN IN INFINITE SPACE

But opposition to the Biblical idea of the cosmos does not only and primarily arise from the idea of evolution, but from that revolution in cosmology which is connected with the names of Copernicus and Giordano Bruno. The anthropocentricism of the Bible, so it is said, is connected with its geocentric attitude, but geocentricism was once for all annihilated in the year 1543. Thus anthropocentricism also, the ludicrous arrogance of puny man, with his belief that he is the central point of the world, must also fall to the ground. The cosmos of the ancient world was, so to speak, a 'homely' dwelling for the human race, which corresponded to the proportions of man. The cosmos of modern astrophysics and geology, both from the point of view of time and of space, has become essentially an 'unhomely'[1] world. Is it not madness when man, this tiny speck of the dust of the earth, in the midst of a world in which even the solar system is a minute point, asserts that the world has been created for his sake, that the Incarnation of the Son of God and the history of man is the real meaning of the universe, when the history of man,

[1] There is a play on words here; '*heimlich*' = 'homely, familiar'; '*unheimlich*' = 'weird, uncanny,' something which makes one feel uneasy.—*Translator.*

from the temporal point of view, has become merely a second in cosmic time? What a comic figure man cuts within this world which has become so infinite from the temporal and spatial point of view, man who maintains that he is a matter of such great concern to the Creator of the world! It is quite evident that this 'removal of the roof of the world'—to use Karl Heim's vivid phrase[1] describing the Copernican revolution—has made, and is still making, a very deep impression upon modern man, filling him with that awe and fear of the Infinite first expressed by Pascal, more eloquently than by anyone else who has come after him![2] For the modern man the new view of the cosmic infinity of space and time constitutes a serious obstacle to faith and is a powerful cause of doubt; we theologians in particular ought to be quite clear about this, and we ought to take it into account.

Yet all this uneasiness is simply a sign of panic, a kind of cosmic giddiness which prevents us from seeing things clearly. In this matter a great deal could be learned from Kant.[3] In proportion as man decreases as *object*, and loses significance as part of the world, he increases as *subject*, because his cosmos becomes larger. For it is *man* who measures this universe, it is *man* who inquires into its laws, it is the world of *man* which he now finds so strange and 'un-homely.' Still, as in the days of Thales, it is man who comprehends the cosmos with his mind, and reflects upon it. It is indeed true that he reflects 'upon it,' for the world is beneath him, as an 'object,' 'cast at his feet.' There is no need to proclaim all this aloud with the sentiments of a Fichte, but it is true nevertheless. Only the man who seeks his greatness in the spatial dimension has become a ludicrous figure—unspeakably ludicrous; and this is the comic element in our own day, that, while it perceives with consternation the hopeless disappearance of man in space, it seeks its triumphs mainly in the overcoming of spatial dis-

[1] K. Heim: *Glaube und Denken*, second edition, p. 39.

[2] Pascal: *Qu'est-ce qu'un homme dans l'infini? . . . Pensées*. Fr. 72.

[3] The most important attempt to make this second Copernican upheaval fruitful for a Biblical theology is that of Karl Heim in his *Glaube und Denken*. The Kantian idea (we always see only 'our' world) is here fused with a philosophy of existence and the Christian belief in Creation into a magnificant synthesis.

tances—like someone who has not caught the express train and runs after it for a bit, as if he could still catch it up. Truly such a person is hopelessly ludicrous!

But who has told man that he should seek his greatness in space? Man has dimensions which the universe, with all its cosmic proportions, does not and never will possess, even if it were enlarged a million times. Man as a piece of the world has really become nothing; but has the man who by the Word of God has been called to communion with the Creator, as person, as made in the image of God, been in any way affected by the enlargement of the structure of the world? On the contrary is not this the situation? Is it not because he has forgotten what it means to be man, created in the image of God, that the Copernican enlargement of the cosmos has made him afraid, and has made the universe so strange and 'un-homely'? It is not due to Copernicus that he has lost his home, but it is because he has lost his home that the discovery of Copernicus has been too much for him. It is because he has no firm standing ground that he becomes giddy when he looks at the vastness of the universe.

. THE WORLD AND ITS MEANING

Certainly, with the ancient view of the world the Biblical view too has gone for ever. But the ancient view of the world is only the alphabet in which the man of the Bible, who had no other, had to write down the Word revealed by God. We no longer use this alphabet of the ancient cosmography; we have a new alphabet, with letters inserted by Copernicus, Newton and Einstein. But what a fool anyone would be to think that when the old alphabet was destroyed the Divine revelation was destroyed as well. It will give us a good deal of trouble to make right use of the new alphabet in order to proclaim the old truth of revelation in a new way. Theologians, preachers and believers as a whole still cling far too much—and how can they help it?—to the historical picture of the Creation of the World and the Fall of Man. They are still trying to do something impossible, to fit cosmic history into this historico-chronological history of mankind and thus to include billions of years within thousands of years. Once for all, this apologetic business has become quite hopeless. There was a time when people believed that the history of mankind and cosmic history were co-extensive. All the Biblical authors had this restricted view of time and space. This view has been destroyed for ever. With the disappearance from the scene of the geocentric picture of space the anthropocentric picture also has gone for ever. As man is an insignificant point in world space, so also his history is a minute fragment of world-time. In point of fact, to disturb this equation means to turn the wheel of history backwards, to ignore the revolutionary movement of knowledge of the last four hundred years—a quixotic act which would expose one to hopeless ridicule! And more than this! The God who has created this vast world of time and space, and who through science places this vastness of His Creation before our eyes, is not honoured if we stand still and will not move away from an earlier, more limited picture of time and space. He expects that in these greater expanses of Creation we shall also learn to adore Him as Creator. Let us broaden our imagination! It cannot do our faith any harm, it can neither diminish nor increase it. It can scarcely be right to say that through this expansion God becomes 'greater' for us; for what has the Greatness of God to do with ways of measuring space? Nor is it true that the personal being of God will be injured thereby, as though the Lord of so great a world were less sovereign in consequence. The personal being of God and of man has nothing at all to do with the standards of measurement of the world of time and space, any more than the meaning of a word is altered by the fact that it is written with smaller or larger letters. The dimension of 'significance,' 'meaning,' 'Logos,' is untouched by changes within the dimension of time and space. 'For a thousand years in Thy sight are but as yesterday when it is past, and as a watch in the night';[1] and the same is true of millions of years. Eternity transcends a thousand millions of years, just as much as a thousand years; the Word of God, the eternal original picture of the creation of man cannot be affected by changes in our ideas of time and space.[2]

[1] Psa. xc. 4.

[2] Cf. Karl Heim, op. cit.; the chapter: *Das Problem der Transzendenz* and *Die Überwindung der Alleinherrschaft des gegenständlichen Weltbildes.*

Hence the content of our human existence is independent of changes in our temporal and spatial environment. What does it matter to us that the astronomers calculate time in billions of years! Does this alter the fact of our personal responsibility by one iota? Does this in the very least affect the contrast between personal and impersonal, subject and object, love and hate, meaning and meaninglessness, human and inhuman? In short, is anything which concerns either our relation with God or our relations with one another affected by all this? If we reflect upon these questions quietly for a little while we then become aware of the truly insane panic of numbers into which modern man has allowed himself to fall. He has fallen a prey to a kind of cosmic fear of space; not because the universe has expanded so greatly, but because he has lost the real standing-ground of his human existence. For the man who knows no other standing-ground than that of the world of time and space, certainly the effect of the knowledge of the extension of the world is a catastrophe. It absolutely annihilates him. A humanity which is tied to the external world is hopelessly lost in the external world as we now know it through the telescopes of Mount Wilson. But, let us not deceive ourselves—this humanity was lost the moment that it became tied to the external world. Man as a piece of the world, even in the supposedly 'homely' structure of the world, did not cut a very dashing figure, even the man in the ancient world felt uneasy, not 'at home.' We only need a little solitude in the High Alps to be convinced of our nothingness; we do not need the calculations of the astronomers to make us feel this. Man as a piece of the world is in any case a nonentity.

6. THE HISTORICAL AND THE NON-HISTORICAL VIEW OF THE UNIVERSE

But man, who has been created in and for the Word of God, who has his self not in himself but in the Eternal Son, is above the world and in the centre of the world, whether this world is measured by the small scale of the ancient world or by the gigantic one of the modern view of the universe. In this transitory world of time and space this Word has been revealed; our changed view of the world of time and space does not in the least alter the significance of 'saving history.'[1] The fact that man stands in the light of this history, whose meaning is eternity, lifts him right above all temporal happenings—not into a timeless Platonic world, where there are no events, where being alone exists—but into a history of another kind, a history which takes place between God and man, which cannot be inserted into any system of chronology, ancient or modern.[2]

From Plato onwards Idealism has been dimly aware that man, as one who participates in the *Logos*, is above the cosmos. Hence even in modern times Idealism has helped a good many people over the shattering effects of the Copernican revolution. From the point of view of Idealism existence in space and time is indeed only apparent, whereas true existence is above time and space. But to the extent in which Idealism frees man from bondage to the cosmos it also severs him from history, and in so doing destroys the decisive character of human life. The eternal life which for the Christian is a divine gift, which man must receive in the decision of the obedience of faith, is to the Idealist that which already is in being, that which in itself is true, in contrast to mere appearance, which man only needs to perceive through the process of thought. Idealism rescues the content of eternity of human life from cosmic nothingness by sacrificing history; the Christian faith, however, conceives the eternal meaning of human life in the fact that in it history becomes decision. In history, in Jesus Christ, the decision has been made; here it becomes for me, what it is there, through the decision of the obedience of faith. This history, however—the history of salvation and the history of faith—is not part of the cosmic time-series, but it is a qualification of the cosmological time-series from a point which, while it lies within it, derives its special character from another sphere, from that point where eternity became time and time became eternity. From this point of view all other

[1] *Heilsgeschichte*: lit. 'history of salvation.'—*Translator.*

[2] Cf. the important paper on *Zeit und Ewigkeit* by K. Heim in the work: *Glaube und Leben*, pp. 539 ff., and his critical discussion of H. W. Schmidt's book *Zeit und Ewigkeit* in *Glaube und Denken*, pp. 381 ff.

points can be perceived which determine the plane of faith as such: Creation and the Fall, Reconciliation and Redemption. They all—in contrast to the Idealistic conception—describe a real happening, and indeed a happening which is related to our world of time and space, and yet does not lie upon the plane of space-time events. We have really been created to enter into this world of space and time—but we have not been created within it; we are really sinners in this world of time and space—but we did not become sinners at any given point of time in the history of the world; the Son of God really became man in this temporal world, and was crucified 'under Pontius Pilate'—but that which took place then only becomes redemption to me because it confronts me as a present fact; and I make my decision of faith upon this earth and within this time-series—in the seventy or eighty years which, even if we live so long, are granted to us—and this decision is made for eternity; but it is made anew at every moment, and in such a way that the 'decisive element' is not the moment at which it is made, but the decision which is made for me in eternity. The redemption and consummation is the redemption and consummation of this world in which we are now living, but it is promised as one in which 'heaven and earth will pass away,' and 'God's Word' alone will 'not pass away.'[1] Thus the Divine event, although it affects this cosmic world, affects it in such a way that the meaning and content of the event lie beyond the world of time and space, 'there, not here,' in the Eternal Word, in the Eternal Son, in the eternal election, in the mystery of the Triune God, in the divine plan for the world which is fulfilled in the *consummatio mundi*, in a 'new heaven and a new earth.'[2]

We human beings are players in this cosmic world-theatre of time and space, formed of the stuff of this earthly world, and the stage is this infinite cosmos with its mysterious systems —like the Milky Way—as they hurry along with their billions of years. But the light in which we stand and play our part does not come from this cosmos, and the piece which we play cannot be understood from the point of view of the cosmos. In the world of time and space we are 'playing' 'a heavenly

[1] Mark xiii. 31. [2] 2 Pet. iii. 13.

drama'—a drama of heaven and hell, a drama which, just because it means the decision of heaven and hell, is not really a play at all but is the only thing that matters. That which issues from the cosmos cannot be truly 'serious,' because it can have no meaning. There is one point about which we must be quite clear: the sole meaning which the cosmic element has as such, is death, nothingness, absolute meaninglessness. 'The world passeth away and the lust thereof.'[1] The meaning comes *from* the world beyond, but it is not only *in* the world beyond. The Kingdom of God is not of this world, but it has come into this world, and it is meant to fulfil the meaning of this world, just as Jesus Christ, who is not of this world, has come into this world, in order that we, like Him and through Him, may become united to the eternal God, as He is united with Him.

Thus the fact that our life has a significance, an origin and a goal which spring from the world beyond, makes us 'strangers'[2] in this cosmos. In point of fact we are 'behind the times' as Nietzsche says mockingly in his *Zarathustra*.[3] In this 'behind' the meaning, the only possible meaning, of human life, is preserved. But this meaning must be worked out in the world. The meaning of the 'star performance' is that we are to 'produce it' in this temporal world as that which has its origin and its destiny 'there,' not 'here,' and we, the players, out of God's love, have been created for the divine love. The 'background'—the eternal word of the Triune God—has been brought into the foreground in Jesus Christ. The background is continually being brought into the foreground where men in faith come to belong to this Christ, where that responsibility which is always the background of human existence is realized through communion with God and men.

But what will happen to the cosmos as such we do not know. 'Heaven and earth will pass away but My words will not pass away.'[4] This cosmos is not so solid as it looks. It too has its background in the Word of God and is 'upheld by His divine Word.' It too 'coheres' 'in Him,' in the eternal Son, and in His Word.[5] In spite of the fact that while we are playing our

[1] I John ii. 17. [2] Heb. xi. 13.
[3] Nietzsche: *Zarathustra, Von den Hinterweltlern, Ausg. Kröner*, p. 41.
[4] Matt. xxiv. 35. [5] Col. i. 17.

part in the cosmic drama it seems an independent reality, and must appear so, with an infinity of time and space which frightens us and threatens to swallow us up, in reality it is not an independent entity, but it is there 'for us.' All that the best philosophers have said about the phenomenal character of the world is—even from the point of view of the Bible—no fantasy. We know absolutely nothing of a 'world in itself' or of the 'thing in itself.' We only know that this stage with its infinite spaces and its billions of years belongs to our play. What this stage is 'in itself,' apart from our play, does not concern us at all. All we know is this: even this world of time and space, this cosmos, precisely in its infinity, which makes us shrink into insignificance, is given to us as a stage by God, and therefore, just as it has its beginning in God, it also has an end in God—a beginning and an end which cannot enter into its own system of time and space. The stage, to whose empirical nature it belongs to have no beginning and no end, will, together with this infinity, come to an end. But this 'coming to an end' will not be a 'cosmic' event, but—if I may repeat what I have said already—a theological event. We shall be 'like unto them that dream';[1] this infinite world-stage will be no more, but there will be a 'new heaven and a new earth.'[2] This is all we can say, but this is all that is required.

7. THE MODERN MYTH

But all this has carried us far beyond our proper subject: man as he actually is. We were obliged to do so, for the cosmos is the environment of the actual man. It is part of the destiny of man as he actually is, that he belongs on the one hand to the supra-cosmic plane of Creation, while on the other hand, he is profoundly involved in the cosmos, and in the travail of the cosmos. 'In the world you shall have tribulation[3]—but be of good cheer, I have overcome the world.'[4] Our subject is the man who has as yet no share in this victory, even though

[1] Psa. cxxvi. 1. [2] 2 Pet. iii. 13.

[3] The German word is *Angst*; possibly the English word 'anguish' would be the best rendering in this context.—*Translator.*

[4] John xvi. 33.

we can only see this man from the point of view of that victory. The actual man in the cosmos is the one who is at the mercy of the cosmos. Fear of the world is no new sensation, it is as old as humanity. It comes out most clearly in the pagan religions. The whole of mythology is penetrated with this cosmic panic, and is indeed derived from it. Pagan man has no standing ground above this world because his gods or his divinity are not themselves above the level of the world. They are themselves interwoven with the cosmic process. The mythological Pantheon, like the myth itself, is a cosmic projection of the pagan fear of the world—a shattering confirmation of the word of Christ: 'In the world ye have tribulation (or anguish).'

The *ratio* of the modern man has indeed made an end of this myth and this mythological world of the gods; but it has not been able to get rid of the fear of the world. It impels men to set up a system of securities called civilization, by means of which the intelligent human being thinks he can evade the cosmic forces of destiny. But the fear itself he cannot banish, and new myths take the place of the old. What is the modern pantheistic philosophy—we might rather speak of a pantheistic sentiment of life—other than the myth of the de-personalized God,[1] the myth of the deification of nature which brings God down to the level of Nature? It is believed that the impersonal Idea of God fits more easily into the view of the world which has been created by modern science. In reality behind it there lies the old pagan idea of the identity of God and Nature, the naturalistic idea of the pagan conception of God. The fact that the abstract reason inclines to this de-personalized idea of God is true; but to allow the abstract reason to go too far is the πρῶτον ψεῦδος. The abstract reason is that which is already severed from God, the falsely autonomous, falsely independent reason, the reason of the man whose self has become isolated. All this has as little to do with science as has the Homeric world of the gods. Neither making reason into an absolute, nor the deification of nature, is necessarily connected with the truth which modern research has disclosed to

[1] Cf. my book *Der Mittler* (English, *The Mediator*), Chapter XIV, Appendix: *On Christian Mythology*.

us. The connexion is purely psychological, it is not concrete at all; it simply means the extension of the sphere dominated by human rational knowledge from the conditioned to the unconditioned. Rational metaphysics—so we see from the standpoint of faith—is not a whit better than irrational mythology. From the scientific point of view the claim that reason is the supreme court of appeal is an axiom which cannot be proved; from the point of view of faith it means the arrogance of the man who has severed himself from God.

The result of this modern mythology—of rational metaphysics of every shade, from the doctrine of speculative Idealism, that all is Spirit, down to the crudest materialism, to the deification of the atom—is necessarily the weakening of human responsibility. Neither in pantheism nor in materialism is there any real responsibility left to man. To whom should he give an answer? To what court is he responsible? The annihilation of the personal in the idea of God brings with it necessarily the annihilation of the personal element in the idea of man, and with this, as the theoretically necessary but practically rarely admitted consequence, the denial of responsibility. Perhaps, however, this causal series should be reversed: man will have no lord over him because he himself desires to be master. He wishes to give an account of himself to no one but himself; he will not be responsible. 'If there were gods who would not be a god? Thus there are no gods' (Nietzsche). A very modern thinker has called this 'postulatory atheism.' He must have touched the deepest motive of all impersonal metaphysics: for the sake of his 'freedom,' because he desires to be free not merely in a creaturely, conditional way, but unconditionally, there shall be no God. For it is true to say: either God or Man can be unconditionally free, but not both.

8. PANTHEISM AND RESPONSIBILITY

But the idea that the impersonal view of the world of rationalistic metaphysics is far more worthy of the intellectually developed human being than the 'somewhat primitive,' 'somewhat childlike' idea of a personal God, the mystery of the world, the All, the World-soul—or however we may express this divine *It*—is 'more,' 'greater,' 'more divine' than the Biblical Lord God, this idea[1] which is supposed to be so modern and so superior, is simply the evasion of responsibility and the arrogance of reason. It is so much more comfortable to have a pantheistic philosophy of life than to believe in a Lord God, because a pantheistic philosophy does not commit you to anything, but faith in the Lord God means obedience to His will; just as in the days of Elijah it was far easier to serve 'Baal,' a nature-deity, than the Lord God of Israel, because it was possible to placate the gods with sacrifices; but this was not the case with Yahweh.

A God who is neuter makes no claims; He simply allows Himself to be looked at. A 'philosophy of life' instead of faith means aesthetic enjoyment instead of obedience. The world-soul, the mystery of the world, does not desire anything from me, it does not intervene in my life in a masterful way. Modern pantheism—the substitute for faith—allows us to evade decision in an aesthetic manner, and in so doing it asserts that it has the advantage of a higher cultivation. For it is so much more intellectual to 'hold a view' than to obey. That is the secret of the supposed expansion of the idea of God into the Impersonal: the extension of the conscience into the unlimited, the transformation of the ethical into the aesthetical.

But this evasion of decision works out its own revenge. The consequence of leaving the question of existence open is that this open universe swallows me up. It robs existence of its meaning—all meaning is limitation; of seriousness—all seriousness presents a challenge to decide for or against; of its goal—for a goal is something clear; and in so doing it robs us of hope. Pantheism proves its affinity with pagan mythology in the fact that in it too ultimately all happenings are cyclic: eternal recurrence. Nothing actually happens, the infinite ocean of the All seethes and tosses up and down, its waves rise and fall, but all that happens sinks again down into the All-One, always the same, and the fact that it has happened has no significance, for what comes afterwards is the same as that which was before. The decisions of life have no eternal content. The practical consequence of the 'All-is-One'

[1] For the usual philosophical arguments against the personality of God see D. F. Strauss: *Die christliche Claubenslehre*, p. 33. *Von der Persönlichkeit Gottes.*

doctrine means that everything comes out to the same thing in the end.

9. THE ELEMENT OF DECISION

Everything does not 'come to the same thing in the end' only if life has a genuine quality of decision, if it is concerned with an ultimate Either-Or. Only then in the strict sense of the word can we speak of responsibility and of meaning. Both mean: decision which extends into the realm of the eternal. That exists only if my life must answer a personal claim, if God is not 'It' but my Lord, if the final truth is not impersonal but personal, the supreme and final court of appeal, if it is not the cosmos which includes the *Logos*, but the *Logos* which includes the cosmos, if the Word is not finally subordinated to a neutral element, but if it is the eternal Word of God, who from eternity is personal Person, that is, love. To have one's existence in this Word means to be responsible. To decide against this Word means to be a sinner, to be seized and re-created by this Word means to believe. And of this faith alone is it true: 'it overcometh the world'[1]—that world in which we have tribulation.

Fear of the world, world-panic, is the result of the severance of man's connexion with the Word of God. As the disobedient child who, in spite of the fatherly prohibition, could not resist breaking away from the peaceful environment of the paternal estate into 'freedom,' now in the midst of this strange outside world suddenly feels afraid, because he feels that he is at the mercy of this 'unchartered freedom,' so is it with the man who would like to have more 'freedom' than is fitting for the creature, and than it is able to bear, who wants to be free of the father's restraints, and now in the infinite extent of the world is at the mercy of its meaninglessness. The meaning of the world is identical with the will of God which establishes limits. Unlimited existence is for God alone. The creature which, attracted by the glamour of unbounded and unrestrained freedom, steps over the boundary falls a hopeless prey to the dizzy sense of the cosmos, the fear of the universe. All now becomes 'uncanny,' God and the world, the All and

[1] 1 John v. 4.

human existence. This uneasiness cannot be overcome by anything—this is shown by the history of religions and philosophies. The way back is blocked, not merely lost. It cannot be rediscovered; it must be reopened. The fact that this has taken place is the Christian message of Redemption.

CHAPTER XIX

MAN IN HISTORY

1. THE PHILOSOPHY OF HISTORY AND THE CHRISTIAN UNDERSTANDING OF HISTORY

THERE is no Christian philosophy of history,[1] but there is a Christian understanding of history. Indeed, the special understanding of history is so interwoven with the nature of the Christian faith that we might well say: the Christian faith is a peculiar understanding of history, the understanding of man as historical. If we are to understand man from the Biblical point of view it is essential to understand him historically. The Bible does not regard man as an isolated individual or as a member of a species; it sees the individual human being as part of the history of mankind as a whole. On the other hand, in this view history is neither a mere succession of cause and effect nor an ideal process of evolution; thus it does not regard history as development but as the sphere of personal decision, based on a Divine act of revelation. The Christian idea of the person and the Christian idea of history are complementary; each requires the other. Indeed, in the last resort, they are identical, since the historical event, Jesus Christ, is both the revelation of and the basis for the true personality of man's being and of true history.

The understanding of man from the *ratio*, the rational *Logos*, is essentially, and necessarily, non-historical.[2] It must and will

[1] Troeltsch in *Der Historismus und seine Probleme* saw that Augustine was not a philosophical historian; but when he classes him among the 'compilers and dogmatic writers' who 'sketch a framework for all that happens, which is composed of miracles and of the historical scholastic convention of antiquity' (p. 15), he merely shows how little understanding he had for the magnificent unity and distinctiveness of Augustine's view of history, which in essentials was derived from Paul (cf. Schrenk, *Die Geschichtsanschauung des Paulus auf dem Hintergrund seines Zeitalters* in the *Jahrbuch der theologischen Schule Bethel*, vol. iii).

[2] Post-Christian philosophy shows the influence of Christianity in the very fact that—in contrast to pre-Christian and non-Christian philosophy—it finds history, in some way or another, a problem. A (certainly somewhat

derive all that is changeable from the unchanging, all that is moving from the stable, all that is merely factual from principle. The irrationality of the absolutely factual, and the conformity to logical laws which is everything to thought, are hostile to one another. At the same time—so far as history is concerned—it does not matter whether this conformity which thought seeks is teleological or normative, the value-essence, the idea, or the causal law. Whether man is understood, Idealistically, from the point of view of the Idea, or causally from that of Nature: in each case he is understood non-historically. He is integrated into an order of being—whether of a spiritual or a natural kind—whose laws are the essential thing, whereas that which cannot be summed up under this must be regarded as 'accidental,' and therefore of little account. In neither order is there any room for the really vital element in history: the deed, the decision. It slips through the meshes which thought provides for the grasping of reality: the historical event, the 'stuff of which history is made,' eludes the thought which is controlled by abstract principles, unless it is transformed by it into development. Development in the sense of the causal process, or in the sense of ideal development: these are the two categories with which rational thought tries to master history. Both omit the essentially historical element in history: the deed, the decision.[1]

antiquated) survey of the history of the philosophy of history is presented by de Rougemont, *Les Deux Cités* (2 vols.), which, however, loses sight frequently of the real subject, and the first volume of Rocholl's *Philosophie der Geschichte*. Troeltsch's brilliant work only deals with the nineteenth and twentieth centuries.

[1] In his monumental work Troeltsch has provided a complete typology of the various modern views of the philosophy of history, which would be suitable to illustrate that which has only been briefly indicated above, as for instance the pointed description of the positivistic conception of history as *histoire sans noms, soit de personnes soit de peuples* (p. 406), the justified criticism of the Hegelian dialectic, which 'makes the attempt to rationalize the dynamic of the Historical and of existence as a whole' (p. 273), the deviation of the Marxist dialectic from that of Hegel by its 'connexion with . . . revolutionary prophecy' (p. 433), its naturalization (p. 339), its connexion with the economic sphere (p. 342), and 'the dissolution of the logical contrasts . . . into actual and materially interested contrasts of life' (p. 350). Troeltsch himself failed to achieve the impossible: to conceive the properly historical in a philosophical way.

Very closely connected with this is the fact that the rational habit of mind, which is controlled by principles, cannot conceive man as a social being. Community is the second fundamental element of historical life. The individual human being, in so far as one tries to understand him from the point of view of reason, becomes either the object or the subject of this universal reason. In both instances he is incorporated into a larger context, but this larger whole is not community but unity. In the one case it is the larger context of the realm of Nature; man is incorporated into the world of nature as a dependent member of it, as its product, and at the same time as one of its many phenomena. Man stands in the context of nature, but the context of nature is not community, but causal unity. In the other instance man is understood as the bearer or manifestation of the world of the Idea, of Spirit, of the One, eternal reason. The individual human being is not isolated, he is connected with all rational creatures through the one reason, common to them all. Man stands in the context of Spirit. But that too is not community but unity; that which is essential in the one human being is essential in the other. This one essential element, therefore, in the last resort, makes the one independent of the other. He can always 'tell himself' what the other could tell him. He has no need of the other. The unity of reason is ultimately a principle of independence, of self-sufficiency; to it, to be dependent upon others and connected with others seems to be something accidental or transient. Thus community is not established. The Spirit understood as Reason does not create community, but unity of agreement, the unity of the identity of that which has been thought.

From a third point of view, also, we see the non-historical character of thought based on abstract principles, of rational thought, which depends upon itself alone. Thought wills *unity*, thus it desires to resolve contradictions; this means, however, that the result it desires to achieve is this: that which at first sight appears contradictory is finally recognized as a unity. Thus thought tries to prove that the contradictions are not real, and to dissolve them into merely apparent contradictions. The contradictions are to disappear under the influence of the systematic nature of thought. Thought itself is the dissolution of contradictions, they do not need any dissolution in act, in actuality. The system of the thinker takes the place of history; that is, of that history which actually either resolves those contradictions which cannot be resolved by reason in act, or shows that they are insoluble. The thinker who starts his process of thought from the ultimate principles of the *ratio*, transforms the real dialectic of historical reality into a merely logical sham dialectic of concepts.[1] The *real* movement of history, which passes through act and decision, is presented to the rational interpretation of history as a *logical* movement, in which, properly speaking, nothing is done, because everything was already there from the outset. It does not matter whether it was already 'there' in a teleological or in a causal sense. In both cases something which was already there is inevitably unrolled like a map which has been rolled up, or a film which was already complete. Here there is no room for the element of real history, for the solution of contradictions in act and decision.

The Christian understanding of history is of a totally different character.[2] Here we are not concerned with any kind of *a priori* idea, which is merely made concrete, or, as it were, illustrative in history; history as a kind of picture-book illustrating the formulae of thought is an idea of the Lessing period of the philosophy of the Enlightenment, which, in a more profound form, was repeated in the Hegelian parallels between logic and the philosophy of history. No, in the Christian view, we are dealing with history itself, in all its reality and its mystery—which it is not for us to construct ourselves—which does not

[1] Cf. the powerful destructive criticism of the most impressive of all philosophies of history, the Hegelian, in Kierkegaard's *Unscientific Postscript* (2 vols.).

[2] Cf. the penetrating work *Geschichte und Existenz* by H. Thielicke, which, in spite of several deviations in detail, is close to the view which is presented above; further, Hirsch's *Grundlegung einer christlichen Geschichtsphilosophie*, which is strongly influenced by Idealism; Schrenk, op. cit., Lilje, *Luthers Geschichtsanschauung*; Scholz, *Glaube und Unglaube in der Weltgeschichte* (on Augustine's *Civitas Dei*); Althaus, *Die Gestalt dieser Welt und die Sünde*, in *Theologische Aufsätze II*; my paper *Das Einmalige und der Existenzcharakter*, in *Blätter für deutsche Philosophie*, 1929, pp. 265 ff.

symbolize or illustrate an eternal truth, but in which the actual contradiction between the temporal-sinful world and the eternal Will of God is actually overcome by real, concrete events. To the extent in which the contradiction is seen as something real, as something which can never be solved by thought, by regarding it as a mere illusion—as sin, which really separates man from God—the overcoming of the contradiction, redemption, can only be sought in a real event, which is not merely the removal of an error, namely, in the real divine *Act* of redemption in Jesus Christ. It is not the *idea* of redemption, but redemption itself, which has actually happened, as an event, which is the content of the Christian message. The content of the Christian faith—what an offence to everyone who has the Greek habit of mind!—is an 'accidental truth of history' (Lessing), a genuine external fact which can and must be fixed chronologically, a fact which could very well be the subject of a police report: Jesus of Nazareth, 'crucified under Pontius Pilate.' That is, indeed, 'to the Greeks foolishness.' But this is not all. Not only is the content of faith an historical event of this kind, but the manner in which we attain this knowledge of faith is wholly historical: the hearing of a message, the announcement of this event, apart from which there is no possibility of being a Christian.[1] The Bible gathers up both these elements, namely, the historical content, that a real act of redemption has taken place, and the way of knowing it, that it is the hearing of an historical report, in one phrase: faith in the Good News, the *εὐ-αγγέλιον*. It unites them also in such a way that it calls Jesus Christ 'the Word made flesh' and says that through Him 'came the truth.'[2] Truth which has come into being; that is indeed the rock of offence at which Greek thought stumbles. Hence there is no Christian philosophy of history—in so far as philosophy can only be based upon principles and not upon historical facts—but there is a Christian understanding of history, which starts from an historical fact and relates everything to this one Fact, to the Divine Word made flesh. It is from this point of view that we must understand both the historical character of personal being and the personalistic character of history.

[1] Rom. x. 14 ff. [2] John i. 17.

2. THE PERSON AS HISTORICAL

The Romans, that nation of the ancient world which had the most historical sense, invented for that which we call history the apt expression: *res gestae*. By that they mean action as the element of history. The characteristic element in history is not that something happens—even in the clouds all kinds of things happen, but there is no history there—but that something is *done*. We must express still more clearly what the Romans meant by their distinction between the idea of action and the happenings of nature. So we say: History is made where decisions are made. It is the decisions which give the character of uniqueness and unrepeatableness to the historical in contradistinction from the happenings of nature.[1] Decision separates the historical element from that rhythmical, cyclic process of nature ever returning to itself, where nothing really happens, because the end always returns to the beginning. Decision separates definitely that which took place afterwards from that which took place before. The fact that events cannot be reversed is absent from nature—seed-fruit, fruit-seed, summer-winter, winter-summer—because in it no decisions are made. It is these which give to the historical element that clearness of direction which leads from 'before' to 'after.' *Iacta est alea*—Caesar knows what history is; where 'the die has been cast,' there, and there alone, does history take place. Thus the historical quality of existence must be the same as the quality of decision.

Hence the Christian understanding of the person is historical. Here the person is not thought of as a being in the sense of that which is eternally, that which is in repose, nor yet in the sense of that which grows naturally, as organisms grow; it is not *dynamis*, an element in the play of forces, or a potentiality, the source of creative possibilities of development. Person is understood as being-in-decision; human life is a decisive answer to a destiny full of responsibility. This gravity of decision of the Christian idea of 'person' comes out very clearly in its attitude towards the past. For the Greek thinker the past is nothing. Since it is past it no longer exists nor has

[1] Cf. my paper *Das Einmalige und der Existenzcharakter*, loc. cit.

it any meaning. For the Christian the past is the guilt which I bear. I am now determined by my past, because the past has decided, and the decision is not a mere nothing; it is everything.

One who does not take the past seriously always thinks that he can continually re-start from the beginning; thus he does not believe in the seriousness of decision. To take the past seriously as guilt, for which I am now responsible, which is not only one element in my life, but which irrevocably determines my present existence, shows the seriousness of the decision, and thus shows the seriousness of irrevocable history.[1]

If the Christian does not despair about this fatality of his existence, about the irrevocable fact of guilt, it is due solely to the fact that he knows of a second decision which removes that first fatal decision. It is not a decision which he makes himself—for in so doing he would be presuming to decide his life twice over, and thus would infringe the seriousness of the decision which has already been made; but it is a counter-decision against his decision, decreed by that authority against which his first decision was taken. The human decision which is called sin and is fixed as guilt, is answered by the divine decision, which is called forgiveness, and is also fixed as decision: *cruci-fixus*, the divine acquittal through the reconciliation which has taken place, as an actual event. Paul has expressed the twofold character of this decision in a wonderful way: Christ has forgiven us all our sins, in the fact that He has nailed the accusation against us to the Cross, and in so doing has annulled it.[2] Our decision has been 'fixed' in the accusation; but since this accusation has been 'fixed' in a new way, it has at the same time been rendered null and void. The decision which was made *there* has been wiped out by the decision which has been made *here*. So we may begin afresh, without any danger that this new beginning will minimize the seriousness of our guilt. But this new beginning, on the basis of the decision made in Christ, is once again a decision which cannot be reversed: a decision for Christ, and for the will of God which has been revealed in Him. That is the new, the Messianic quality of decision of the Christian life.

[1] Cf. my pamphlet, *Vom Werk des Heiligen Geistes*, pp. 11 ff.
[2] Col. ii. 14.

What Christ has done governs the perspective of all that becomes the subject of Christian thought. From the point of view of this world-decision alone does the whole of human life gain its quality of decision. The idea of something 'unique, which cannot be repeated'[1] is a concept which is not taken seriously outside Christianity. Strictly speaking there is no such thing as an event which takes place once for all, for 'there is nothing new under the sun';[2] everything, in some way or another, has already been there before. The historical, understood in the usual sense, is characterized by a relative uniqueness but not by an absolute novelty or uniqueness. Within the sphere of empirical happenings there are no final decisions. *Iacta est alea*—yes, but the die will still be cast many a time, long after the departure of Caesar from the scene; even during the lifetime of Caesar it will have been cast several times. What are usually called 'historical decisions' are relatively irreversible, relatively unique, relatively decisive events. Decision must be a happening, an event, which separates world history into a 'before' and an 'after,' an event in which not merely 'something' is decided but everything! Strictly speaking nothing deserves the name of 'decision' save an absolute reversal of the order of the world. In this sense the Christian faith alone can speak of one decision, namely, the reversal of the world order in Jesus Christ, in whom not only earthly history but also all that happens, from its beginning derived from eternity and its end in eternity, eternally receives its centre, and in this centre its qualification—the event which the witnesses in the New Testament expressly testify has taken place 'once for all.'[3] All that stands outside this one thing is qualified as negative, all that is within it is positive. Indeed it is only from this centre that the beginning and the end themselves gain their meaning, and indeed their absolutely unchangeable meaning, which excludes all idea of an 'eternal return.' Only through this decisive event is it impossible to turn Time into a myth, and the idea of eternal cycles is

[1] *Das 'Einmalige'*: that which only happens once; can never be repeated. Cf. *The Mediator*, p. 25, n. 1.—*Translator.*

[2] Eccles. i. 9.

[3] Cf. Rom. vi. 10; Heb. vii. 28, ix. 12, x. 10.

eliminated. The last prophet of this 'cyclic' theory knew this, and that is why he described himself as Antichrist.

Through our relation to this unique and decisive event our past is plainly stamped as guilt; but it also stamps our present as a period of decision, and the future as that which is definitely decided, the Judgement, which severs Heaven and Hell. Thus only through our relation to the decision in Jesus Christ does it become clear that responsibility cannot be severed from ultimate decision. So long as the idea of responsibility is still free from the idea of the Last Judgement, it is still harmless, it is merely a dream of responsibility. It only gains its full weight from the thought of the divine decision for or against us. The idea of judgement is certainly known outside Christianity; but where it occurs elsewhere—as for instance in Zarathustra or in Plato's *Gorgias*[1]—the division in man has not yet been perceived; it is not yet understood that, so far as man is concerned, he has already made a negative decision, and therefore that judgement, in a negative sense, ought to have been passed upon him already. The Christian faith alone can look at everything at once: the negative decision upon our side, the positive decision of God for us, who are judged; and finally: the new decisive quality of our present decision (derived from this), as decision in the obedience of faith, as a share in the Messianic world-decision.

We have said that *one* element of history is decision, and that the *second* is *community*. The individual as individual has no history. History consists in the fact that my existence is interwoven with the existence of others.[2] History is a community of destiny as much as it is a community of decision. Where a people, acting together, receives the fruit of its common action in a common solidarity, there is history. We might call that the relatively historical character of existence. An essential element of history in this sense is the continuity between the generations, the historical heritage—whether in

[1] The fact that the conception of judgement in Plato's teaching springs rather from the Orphic religious tradition than from his Theory of Ideas may be assumed to be generally accepted at the present day (in spite of Zeller's protest; op. cit., II, p. 708). (Cf. Rohde, *Psyche*, II, pp. 275 ff.)

[2] Kierkegaard, *The Concept of Dread*, pp. 22 ff.

the form of an inherited blessing or an inherited curse. No historical consciousness arises without a strong sense of tradition; the tradition, however, is simply the sense of the connexion between the generations. One who disowns his own past will take still less account of the past of earlier generations. Conversely: individualism, the habit of thinking of oneself as an isolated individual, must necessarily also destroy the historical sense, the understanding of oneself as historical.[1] The meaning of being historical is: solidarity.

In this sense Christian thought alone is completely historical. It overcomes individualism by the absolute solidarity of mankind in creation and in sin. We are all the same Adam, and indeed the 'Adam' who has been created by God as well as the 'Adam' who has become sinful. We know that we are united in a solidarity of guilt not only with those human beings who are now alive upon this earth, but also with all the generations which were before us, as far as human beings in time and space ever existed—and now exist. 'All one in Christ Jesus.'[2] The doctrine of Original Sin expressed this powerfully, although in a dubious manner. In Christ we confess ourselves to be a society of debtors who are all united in their indebtedness. We do not make any attempt to separate ourselves as individuals from one another by singling out our individual share of guilt. From the very outset we renounce this individualistic calculation because it is as impossible as it is pharisaical. Sin is, it is true, an individual matter, but it is also an affair and an act of the community. To know this means to think historically, and to think historically simply means this. At least this kind of thinking alone should be called unconditionally historical, while certainly alongside of this there is a relatively historical way of thinking which knows nothing of this idea of unconditional solidarity.

But just as the seriousness of man's knowledge of guilt is confronted by the divine decision as forgiveness, so also the solidarity of guilt is matched by the solidarity of redemption. Not only 'in Adam' are we one, but above all 'in Christ.'

[1] An outstanding instance is the philosophy of the Enlightenment, whose lack of historical sense is as striking as its rationalism and its individualism.

[2] Gal. iii. 28.

Even that negative perception of truth was only possible from the standpoint of this positive truth. Only in the light of Christ do we become aware of our solidarity in guilt, where we also perceive our solidarity in redemption.

This positive truth of our solidarity, however, also works itself out practically in unconditional willingness for community, in the new responsibility in love over against every other human being. Radical historical thought necessarily leads not only to a humanistic point of view, but also to a human ethos. We are united with every other human being, through love; not by *our* love—how could we be capable of this!—but through the love of Christ. That is the marvellous meaning of that much abused phrase 'for Christ's sake.' Decision for the Christ means practically: being present for, and at the disposal of, everyone who needs us. This practical and ethical position in the community is therefore also the proof whether the historical character, that is, the character of decision, of existence, is taken seriously or—height of nonsense—whether the decisive character of existence is merely a beautiful theory!

3. THE PERSONAL MEANING OF HISTORY

The theme of history as the object of thought is remote from the philosophy of the ancient pagan world, and even in religion—with the one exception of Zoroastrianism[1]—history plays no part. In Greek thought, whose incomparable energy otherwise mastered practically all subjects worthy of study, as Windelband says, the predominance of the idea of *physis* and of the *cosmos* was so strong 'that the temporal course of events was always treated as something merely secondary, in which there was no real metaphysical interest. At the same time Greek thought regarded not only the individual human being, but also the whole human race, with all its destinies, deeds, and sufferings, as an episode, as a passing, transitory particular phenomenon, of the cyclic world process which takes place eternally according to the same laws. The question of a meaning for the history of humanity as a whole, of a systematic plan behind the course of historical development, was never raised as such; still less did it occur to any of the ancient thinkers

[1] Cf. above p. 191.

to regard this as the real nature of the world.'[1] It is Christianity which has forced the recognition of this subject on thought, and has indeed given it historical direction[2] as a whole.

The eminent writer of the history of philosophy who has just been mentioned does not only rightly lay emphasis upon the fact as such, but he also gives the reason for it: 'Christianity found, from the very outset, the nature of the whole course of the world in the experiences of personalities; to it external nature was only the stage upon which the relation of person to person, and above all that of the finite spirit to the divinity was played. To that was added a further determinative principle: the principle of love, the consciousness of the solidarity of the human race, the deep conviction of universal sinfulness and faith in a common redemption. All this led to the fact that the story of the Fall and of Redemption was regarded as the true metaphysical content of the world-reality, and that instead of an everlasting process of nature the drama of world history as a temporal course of freely willed activities became the content of the Christian metaphysic.'[3]

There is a vital connexion between the personal and history. Where, as in recent times, the sense of the personal begins to fade, in place of genuine historical understanding comes the transformation of the interpretation of history by the two fundamental schemata of our thought: causality and the development of meaning. The product of historical thought influenced by Christianity, and the non-historical character of the natural *ratio*, is evolutionism, whether of the mechanistic and naturalistic kind or of the idealistic teleological kind, 'Darwin' or 'Hegel.' Mechanistic or causal evolutionism, the 'Darwinistic' philosophy of history, understands history as a course of events determined by causes, on the analogy of the geological process of 'folding,' or of the formation of valleys by erosion; the idealistic teleological view understands it as a

[1] Windelband, *Lehrbuch der Geschichte der Philosophie*, p. 212.

[2] After what has been said above (p. 440) it is not surprising that it was the Roman Cicero—certainly no philosophical genius—through whom the 'value of the Historical for the first time attained full philosophical valuation' (Windelband, op. cit., p. 147). It is the Roman and the statesman who, so to say, forces this subject upon the attention of philosophy. But that is true only within the limits of that which has been said above.

[3] Windelband, ibid.

logical process of the development of ideas, like the coming into being of a book or a work of art. In both cases[1] man is the point of transition and the means of an impersonal process, either one which has no meaning at all, as in the first instance, or one which has its meaning outside the realm of the personal in an abstract spiritual goal.

An instructive parallel to this is provided by the pagan myth. In contradistinction from rational philosophy the myth knows the category of personal happening. Indeed, the happening itself seems to be its proper element. Indeed, is it not full of action, of surprising and sensational events? But if we examine it more narrowly we find that the actual events are not so seriously meant as would appear at first sight. It is true that all kinds of things are going on; gods enter into time and act and suffer, the heavenly world manifests itself within the world of earth, there is an unbroken process of coming and going from above to below and from below to above. But the striking thing about this process is that again and again it begins from the beginning, and that even in the most exciting happenings—as related in the myths of Adonis or Osiris—nothing results which had not been there already. In the last resort the myth does not take really seriously the heavenly-earthly, the divine-human happenings, which it narrates, or it takes them seriously in a relative sense only, as incidents within a process, which finally returns to the starting-point. In spite of many important revelations and deliverances—in the end, according to its own view—it stands precisely where it stood at the outset. History has gone round in a circle and begins anew. Eternal recurrence, repetition, the reflection of the rhythmical process of nature, the circle as the essential and inclusive symbol, the end, which again becomes the beginning, the non-unique, the non-historical—that is the essence of the myth. This is so because here too, in spite of all

[1] This is of course an over-simplification of the possibilities of the philosophy of history when it is measured by the wealth of the typology of a man like Troeltsch; but it is a simplification which does not omit anything which is essential for what is here said on this question. A detailed study of the possibilities detailed by Troeltsch would have to show on the other hand precisely that 'ultimately' everything falls into these two main categories—the causal and the logical—at the best their romantic synthesis—the organic principle.

the plastic anthropomorphic character of the actors, the truly personal is lacking.[1]

It was the people of Israel which from its very beginning—since it was created by the Mosaic revelation of God—understood its relation to God as historical, and its history as the result of its relation to God. Yahweh is the Covenant God, and the covenant of God with Israel and of Israel with Yahweh is the content of its history. History is that which takes place between the personal God and His people. No other nation, either before or after Israel, ever understood its history in this way. In accordance with this truth, therefore, even at the stage of the early Mosaic revelation,[2] the life of the people of Israel was conceived in personal terms. In the national life of Israel the main concern was not with culture, civilization, technique, world-conquest or political power—although these motives certainly often predominated very strongly in actual fact—but with one thing only: the obedience of the nation to its God, and the union of the members of the nation to one another in the community, based upon this relation to God. From the very outset the ethos of Israel is strictly personal and social. The opposition between good and evil is not sought in the two metaphysical principles of sense and spirit, but in the relation to one's fellow-man, in the contrast between right and wrong, lovelessness and the brotherly spirit, obedience or disobedience to the will of God. The great twofold commandment stands already in the Old Testament: 'Thou shalt love the Lord thy God,'[3] and 'thou shalt love thy neighbour as thyself.'[4] Thus too, more and more, in view of the non-realized will of God, the whole of life comes to be seen *sub specie futuri*—or as we more correctly say in German, in the light of the *Zu-kunft*:[5] the real Divine Covenant still waits to be realized:

[1] On this cf. Frick, *Das Evangelium und die Religionen*; and my own work, *Die Christusbotschaft im Kampf mit den Religionen.*

[2] Cf. Martin Buber, *Königtum Gottes* (second edition), a book which shows what history is better than any philosophy of history.

[3] Deut. vi. 5.

[4] Lev. xix. 18.

[5] In my article already mentioned on *Das Einmalige* I have called attention to the fact that the German word *Zu-kunft* (future) was originally the translation of *parousia*, the Return of Jesus Christ, and that, in contradistinction from *futurum*, it is an historical eschatological word.

the unity between God and the nation and the members of the nation themselves, and indeed of the world of nations as a whole, is the final Messianic goal, in which alone the divine plan of God in the Creation will be fulfilled.[1]

But this personal understanding of history, like the whole of the knowledge of God of the Old Testament, is only completely fulfilled in and through Jesus Christ. History does not only mean the history of a people with God, but a history of humanity derived from God and going to God, in which every individual is a fully qualified member of the whole, and where the decision of each individual alone incorporates him into the whole, as a 'member' in the 'body.' This 'people of God'[2] is no longer bound to any presuppositions of natural contact, and every appearance of bondage to a collective-destiny, or of the opposite, has been finally dispelled. It is not a kind of final cosmic catastrophe which brings in the new way of existence, but a historical personality, Jesus of Nazareth, 'crucified under Pontius Pilate.' His act of love, His obedience and His sacrifice is the foundation of the New Covenant. In Him, in His judging and forgiving, in His condescension and His championship of the Divine honour, the holy loving will of God, the divine plan of world redemption is revealed, which at the same time includes the consummation of the divine work of the creation of the world. He Himself, Jesus Christ, is the Word of God, History and Eternity have become one in Him, just as in Him Humanity and Divinity have become one. In Him, the Eternal Son, there is shown to us both the origin of the world and the goal of the world; the *Logos*, 'in whom, through whom and for whom the world has been created,'[3] He, the 'Son of His love,'[4] is the meaning of history, and He is a Person, not an abstract principle, not an Idea. In His love, which He gives to those who believe in Him, communion between God and man, and of all human beings among themselves, is realized. This *recapitulatio*, this 'gathering up into one head' by means of which 'all that is in heaven

[1] Cf. the remarks of L. Köhler, *Jahwe der Geschichtsgott*, op. cit., pp. 62 ff., and of Eichrodt, *Gottes Eingehen in die Geschichte*, in contrast to mythology, abstraction and individualism, op. cit., I, p. 266.

[2] 1 Pet. ii. 9. [3] Col. i. 16. [4] Col. i. 13.

and upon the earth'[1] becomes one body: that is the goal which is disclosed in Him, and indeed in principle is already realized in Him, towards which the whole history of humanity and of the cosmos is tending.[2] A human life—the only human life in which the personal meaning of the person, love, has really been lived—is not only the disclosure of, but at the same time the foundation of, the actual realization of the meaning and the end of all history.

The fact that a definite event within history is understood as the turning-point in the history of the world, and as the centre of history, which divides the whole of history into a 'before' and an 'afterwards,' determines the direction not only of human happenings but of all happenings. The cycle of eternal recurrence has been broken, the line of time is extended,[3] it has a beginning and an end; this end, moreover, is a real end, a serious one—it is not the starting-point of a new cycle—but it is a goal which is an end, a final goal, the 'fulness of the time'[4] in eternity. Between this Ultimate End and the present lies the 'Judgement,' that event which closes the period in which life is the 'period of decision,' which fixes the decision and makes it 'definitive.' All that lies beyond this point is not decision; it has been decided.

The meaning of world history is Jesus Christ and the Kingdom of God, which is grounded in Him, in the eternal Son, the Son of His love. That is history understood in the personal sense. To this, however, another element must be added, one in which both the personal meaning of history and the historical meaning of personality coincide, namely, faith. It is only in the light of this which has been finally decided, by the decision of faith or unbelief[5] in the message

[1] Eph. i. 10.

[2] The first great outline of a theology of history, that of Irenaeus, is, more plainly than that of Augustine, determined by the thought of *recapitulatio in Christo* (cf. Harnack, op. cit., I, p. 562).

[3] Even modern physics is aware of the 'one-way property of time,' of 'time's arrow' (Eddington, op. cit., pp. 75 ff.) in connexion with the law of entropy—an extremely gloomy eschatology of final 'chaotic changelessness,' and thus of a cosmic repose silent as the grave.

[4] Gal. iv. 4; Eph. i. 10.

[5] Scholz has rightly connected his presentation of Augustine's *Civitas Dei* with *Glaube und Unglaube in der Weltgeschichte*, for that is its theme.

of Christ, that human time is qualified as 'high time,' as the Messianic time of decision. A time of growth, a time of maturing, of education, is not 'high time,' just as it is not truly personal time. 'High time' only exists where heaven and hell are decided. Only where each individual personally, by becoming a member of the body of Christ, by being incorporated into the Messianic Kingdom, becomes world-historical in the full sense of the word, is he, the individual, truly person, and his time is truly historical. It is true that life outside the Christian revelation does not lack a wealth of individuality, originality and spontaneity; but it lacks the tension of decision, and it lacks the breadth of horizon of world history. 'In Christ' life gains both these elements, in the true responsibility which is grounded in Him alone.

4. WORLD HISTORY AND REDEMPTION

If the meaning of history is that which is revealed to us in the Biblical history of the Old and the New Testament, then what is the meaning of non-Biblical history—of the builders of the Pyramids in Egypt, and of the wise Emperors of China, and of all world history down to Napoleon and Lenin? What is the connexion between the history of the *civitas terrena* and the *civitas Dei*?[1] If the meaning of all history is the Kingdom of God, that is, the rise, the extension, and the consummation of the fellowship of believers in eternal life, then what is the meaning of that history which has no relation with the Biblical knowledge of God, or whose relation is merely negative? The following points seem to me relevant for any attempt to answer this question. First, we must distinguish between three forms

[1] That is the statement of the problem in Augustine's *De Civitate Dei.* His solution of the problem, in spite of its grandeur, cannot satisfy us to-day; on this point we must admit that Troeltsch is right. But we are not satisfied with Augustine's solution, not because he seeks it in the Christian faith, but first of all because—as a dogmatic theologian—he sees the whole question in too simple a manner, and further, because his knowledge of history is too fragmentary and his view too uncritical. But the *question* he raises is still waiting for our answer; we need urgently a Christian doctrine of history. There are important rudiments of such a theory—in addition to those mentioned on p. 455—in the work of the Roman Catholic writer, Th. Haecker, *Der Christ und die Geschichte.*

of existence: first of all, the distinction between an existence which is before Christ, outside of Christ, and hostile to Christ; secondly, we should note the fact that even the human being who is hostile to or outside of Christ is still one who has been created by the God whom he does not know, or *will* not know; thirdly, there is the fact that history is not only decision, but that there is a kind of history which is not history proper—the growth of the responsible subject, the history of the presuppositions of actual history—and finally, that likewise, just as there is a great variety of created individualities, a variety which, from *our* point of view, seems wholly irrational, so also there is a completely irrational variety of historical actualities. All we can do here is to develop these points quite briefly; their application to the concrete material of history must be reserved for a Christian doctrine of history.

We will begin with the point which was mentioned last. The Christian understanding of history takes into account that which is absolutely obscure in two ways. The first thing which we cannot understand is the variety of the created universe as such, even in the sphere of history. Faith cannot explain why all that exists and happens in history exists at all, any more than reason can explain it. We do not understand how all this is ordered for the divine End; Christian faith knows the *fact* of the divine rule of the world; it knows also of the final End towards which all that happens is directed, but it does not know 'the ways of God' in detail. This Divine rule, however, is based upon the fact that God is both Creator and Redeemer. The mysterious variety of the historical creation, like that of the physical creation, is the work of the same God who has revealed to us His plan of redemption and of fulfilment in Jesus Christ. That is all we know. The second point to which faith directs our attention is an irrational factor of another kind: evil. We do not understand why evil exists, particularly those manifestations of evil which fill the actual historical life, any more than we understand the variety in creation. What faith does teach us is that evil is due to man's sin, that it springs from disobedience to the Will of God. But we are either wholly, or to a very large extent, ignorant of the reason why human beings are disobedient, and especially why they are disobedient in these particular ways which we see in history. There are, however, two things which we know in faith: first, that, so far as our experience extends, evil is that which is contrary to meaning *par excellence*; secondly, we know that God is able to make use of this evil which is contrary to all meaning and sense for His purpose, in a way which we cannot possibly understand. The most meaningless event in world history, the death of Christ, through the divine wisdom has become the most meaningful, indeed the revelation of, and realization of the final divine goal. But this paradox does not make it possible for us to give paradoxical interpretations of history in detail. The certainty 'that to those who love God all things work together for good,'[1] is not a principle of a Christian logic of history which can be applied to all cases.[2] If there were a convincing 'theodicy of history'[3] for thought, even for Christian thought—we would not need redemption. For then the contradictions of existence would be resolved by thought, and we would not need to wait for their solution by

[1] Rom. viii. 28.

[2] The appeal to a hidden decree of God which would contain something different from the revealed decree of salvation, and the subsumption of both decrees under the concept of the glory of God—so that God wills to be glorified in Hell as well as in the Kingdom of God—is an idea which, in spite of Calvin, is foreign to the Bible, and is one which destroys the unity of the divine nature, in spite of all assertions to the contrary. If we would teach, with Calvin, that from all eternity God has predestined and created some for eternal life and others for eternal damnation (*Institutio*, III, 21, 5), then logically we would have to teach that there is in the nature of God alongside of love a Primal Wrath, as has been done by certain Gnostics. The Biblical doctrine of the hiddenness of God in the course of human history has nothing to do with this; the will of God is not hidden, but what is concealed is the way in which that which is contrary to sense, that which is opposed to the aim of His Kingdom, is used as a means for His revealed aim. (Rom. xi. 33.)

[3] Th. Haecker, in his beautiful book *Schöpfer und Schöpfung*, has ventured to make an 'attempt at a Theodicy' (pp. 24–87); I have very little to say against his ideas, only for my part I would maintain that all this is not a theodicy. He who makes faith in the God who acts, in love, in an unfathomable way, whose rule of love in history can only become intelligible beyond history, his central point has in so doing ceased to regard it as allowable to construct a theodicy. The 'nevertheless' of faith means that we give up all attempts to 'justify the ways of God to men.'

the divine redeeming action. Either theodicy or eschatology! Eschatology, the certainty of the future consummation of redemption and of the eternal consummation of all things in the Kingdom of God, is the sole Christian theodicy; this means, however, that we do not know how the irrational is incorporated into the divine plan, but we look for this incorporation solely and simply from the Divine action. The 'system' will only be disclosed in eternity. In faith, we only see so much of the divine meaning in actual life as is necessary for action in obedience to God.

The second point[1] is the recognition of a subordinate historical element, growth as the preparation for the personal-historical. The child, for instance, before it becomes a person who thinks and acts for himself, has no proper history but a pre-history. It is the same with humanity as a whole. The growth of man is not the theme of history but of pre-history. It is no accident that the Bible shows us the beginning of history not as a growth but as a decision. The story of growth is always quietly presupposed behind the Bible narrative. Only legend, not the Biblical message itself, has for instance an interest in the growth of Jesus.[2] But this story of growth is recognized as something willed by the Creator. The Bible itself, which tells us so little about children, has given a special dignity to the child.

The history of man is embedded in a natural process, which is not itself historical in character. But, further, the whole historical life is accomplished, so to speak, within non-historical material, which also has its own logic, as a something which lies midway between nature and history, between the realm of nature and personal being.[3] The whole of civilization and of culture is not itself historical, but it is the sediment of

[1] Point three on p. 452.—*Translator.*

[2] We must recognize as the result of criticism that precisely Luke ii. 42 ff. does not contradict this.

[3] This conception has some affinity with the argument of Rickert, that historical science as research into and presentation of history has to do with the *Einmalige* (the unique and the non-recurrent) (cf. *Die Grenzen der naturwissenschaftlichen Begriffsbildung*); but because in an idealistic way he relates this 'unique' element to a system of abstract values by which alone the unique gains significance, the idea of 'uniqueness' does not gain its full significance. Cf. also Hildegard Astholz, *Das Problem Geschichte untersucht bei J. G. Droysen*, 1933.

history, and the means of expression of historical man. Civilization and culture are, so to speak, the fingerprints and footprints of historical man. They have therefore a 'history' of their own kind. We can only speak very loosely and incorrectly of a 'history of art,' or of a 'history of culture,' or even of a 'history of technique and science.' Its relation to history proper, to the acts of man as man is purely instrumental.

These two facts stand in a context which I can merely indicate here. The process through which man becomes human, his development to spiritual maturity, takes place by means of civilization and culture, and conversely, it is precisely this maturity of man as man which manifests itself as civilization and culture. Hence here there exists a continuity which resembles that of organic growth. Here, in point of fact, there is something which we may describe as 'progress.' The more we are concerned with that which is only instrumental the more we can speak about 'progress.' The history of technique for instance is the history of an indubitable march forward. One generation makes use of the discoveries and inventions of another. There arises a cumulation of technical possibilities which 'develops' in an almost unbroken line from the first stone tool to the modern technique of steel and concrete, on the analogy of the development of a child to a man. The more, however, that the means and forms of expression of personal being are 'personal,' the more we are concerned with culture and not with civilization, with that which cannot be handed on, the less can we speak of 'progress.' In the historical itself, in personal decision, the concept of 'progress' becomes meaningless. Progress only exists to the extent in which there is growth or transference or cumulation, thus progress is excluded to the extent in which there is personal decision. Since, however, the historical life is wholly embedded in this natural element, on the one hand, and in the instrumental on the other hand, it is not possible to separate the 'sphere' of progress from the 'sphere' where there can be no progress.[1] This natural growth and technical progress accompany history, without themselves being history.

The third and the fourth points[2]—(in the preceding enumera-

[1] Cf. the chapter on *Success and Progress* in *The Divine Imperative*, pp. 280 ff.

[2] On p. 452.

tion the second and the first)—are directly theological. Every human being is God's creature, whether he believes it or not, whether he is a Christian or not. Every human being, therefore, owing to the fact of his creation through the Word, is related to God, and is therefore responsible. It is upon this that his personal being is based, it is for this that his historical character is intended. But it belongs to the nature of the 'natural' man—of the man who is outside the sphere of the Biblical revelation of God—that his knowledge of God is perverted by sin, and therefore that his personal being itself is also perverted. He is indeed person, but as we have frequently explained—impersonal person; he is still a human being, it is true, but his existence is not fully 'human' and 'personal.' Sin is being human in an inhuman way, it is impersonal personal being. So also man's historical being is not truly historical. Before Christ man is indeed responsible, but he is not fully responsible. Pre-Christian, and in the strict sense of the word, non-Christian history—for instance, the historical existence of a Red Indian before the advent of Columbus—is called in the Bible 'the times of ignorance which God has overlooked,'[1] although even there responsibility exists. History, in the proper, strict sense of the word, has only existed since, and by means of, Jesus Christ. Only since He came has human time become time of decision, in the full grave sense of the word, because only since He came is there the possibility of deciding in view of the challenge to decision with which we are confronted. The pre-Christian period, when compared with this character of existence, has something relatively 'simple' about it; the pre-Christian human being is not yet fully awake, he cannot be fully 'serious,' because in his world there is nothing pre-eminently serious—or at least not in the full sense. The pre-Christian human being is not personal in the same sense as the post-Christian human being, because he does not know of personal being in the same way, just as he has not a fully historical existence because he is not aware of the historical[2] in the same full sense.

Through Jesus Christ alone has the world become an

[1] Acts xvii. 30; Rom. iii. 25; Acts xiv. 16.

[2] Kierkegaard, *Sickness unto Death*: 'Hence the selfishness of paganism . . . is not nearly so qualified as that of Christendom, even though there

historical world, in the full sense of the word. Hence this alteration of historical existence affects not merely believers but unbelievers. Through Jesus Christ something has happened which affects even those who do not believe on Him. This can already be seen in the fact that to-day everyone, whether believer or unbeliever, asks about the meaning of the world process as a whole, and is aware of the existence of world history. This question, this category, unknown to the pre-Christian period, cannot now be removed from the mind of man. It is there; whether one believes in Christ or not does not alter this fact. We cannot help thinking in terms of world-history—and no amount of Nationalism in the present day alters this one jot—and we cannot help thinking of humanity as a whole. In theory we may deny this wholeness, but it is there, spiritually as well as in the technical and economic sense. It is there as a recognized task as well as a fact. It is known as a task in a different way from the way in which it is known as a fact, but both are irrevocable.

With Jesus Christ, wherever His Word, or the news about Him, has come, directly or indirectly, there a new consciousness of existence has begun, both for believers and unbelievers. The man who has heard the message of Jesus Christ can only do one of two things: he can decide against Him or for Him, but he cannot ignore Him without making a decision. Hence the manner of existence of the unbeliever or of the man who believes something other than Christianity has no longer that comparative harmlessness of the pre-Christian heathen. Even in its negative form this existence is burdened with the seriousness of the decision of the Bible. The atheism of the present day is not merely a-theistic, but it is always at the same time anti-theistic; non-Christian existence is anti-Christian, paganism is not naïve, but it is consciously and aggressively pagan. But also in a positive sense we may speak of an influence of the message of Christ upon non-Christian humanity—a fact which has often been noted. A great part of our heritage of

too there is selfishness; for the pagan does not see his Self over against God' (p. 78 in German translation). 'Greek intellectuality was too happy, too naïve, too aesthetic, too ironical, too witty, too sinful, to be able to conceive that anyone could deliberately refrain from doing the Good' (ibid., p. 87).

intellectual culture which everyone uses, whether believer or unbeliever, is of Christian origin; it is secularized Christianity; even the unbelieving man uses Biblical-Christian concepts, views, categories, forms of expression, which by way of Augustine, scholasticism and the Reformation, especially through the translation of the Bible, have become the common possession of Western man. The non-Christian man bears a Christian imprint, whether he likes it or not, and this imprint is a *character indelebilis.*[1] Indeed, not only the Western man but also the Eastern man who consciously rejects Christianity, unconsciously absorbs Christian influences into himself. A Buddhism which founds 'Young Men's Associations' on the model of the Y.M.C.A. is Christianized, even though in other ways it may behave in orthodox Buddhist fashion; an Indian Woman's Movement, even though quite Hindu in character, is due to the influence of the New Testament. Through a thousand hidden channels there flows into humanity down the centuries a way of thinking, willing and feeling which is derived from the message of the Gospel, without anyone necessarily being conscious of the fact. Above all, however, humanity cannot get rid of one thing: the Christian idea of personality, the Christian idea of humanity. It is still alive in the most anti-Christian Communism; it is this which gives to modern atheism its particular sharpness and passion. Neither Marx nor Nietzsche can be imagined without the Bible. From it they drew most of their strength to combat Christianity. Of course, we must not overlook the fact that the inherited

[1] Here we are not merely concerned with the fact that man since Christ, even if he is not a Christian, has 'all kinds of Christian ideas,' but that his understanding of himself, his sense of personality—even if it were in extreme opposition to it—is only possible from the point of view of the message of Christ. The liberalistic sense of freedom of Renaissance Humanism and of German Idealism truly is not Christian (cf. the excellent observations on this point by Gogarten in the epilogue to his edition of Luther's *Vom unfreien Willen*), but it is not possible without the emancipation from bondage to the cosmos, which determines the whole of humanity in the ancient world, which has taken place through Jesus Christ. Between the Kantian–Fichte and the Platonist concept of the Self—even if we can speak of such a thing at all—there stands the Christian message of the God-Man. Fichte's philosophy of the Self is far more titanic than that of the ancient world owing to its opposition to Jesus Christ.

Christian capital is not inexhaustible. The feeling for the personal and the human which is the fruit of faith may outlive for a time the death of the roots from which it has grown, but this cannot last very long. As a rule the decay of religion works out in the second generation as moral rigidity, and in the third generation as the breakdown of all morality. Humanity without religion has never been an historical force capable of resistance. Even to-day, severance from the Christian faith, wherever it has been of some duration, works out in the dehumanization of all human conditions. 'The wine of life has been poured out'; the dregs alone remain.

On the other hand, much which is to-day regarded as a special sign of Christianity would reveal itself on closer examination as the product of a spirit which is remote from that of the Bible. Even the Church has 'alien and still more alien stuff imposed upon it.' The stream of the life which has sprung from the Gospel has carried along with it much of the historical soil through which it has flowed. In saying this we are not thinking only of the history of the Catholic Church but also of the Protestant Church. Not only the so-called 'visible Church,' but also the actual norms by means of which the 'empirical' and the 'true' Church have always been distinguished from one another, are permeated with a spirit which has been influenced by Platonism, Stoicism, Neo-Platonism, and also by the Roman, Germanic, and Romance spirit, so that even devout Bible reading never takes place solely under the influence of the Holy Spirit, but also under that of the 'spirit of the age,' which is 'the spirit of men themselves.' I do not imagine that this book is any exception to the rule.

Hence for us the problem of the *civitas Dei* and the *civitas terrena* has become much more complicated than it was for the great Father of the Church. There is a great deal of heathenism even in Christian speech and doctrine, and there is also much Christianity in the most godless anti-Christianity.[1] This does

[1] Again and again Christendom has forgotten that to believe in a Christian doctrine does not mean that one is a Christian believer, and that, on the other hand, much real faith in Christ may be hidden behind a doctrine which may be theologically quite incorrect. That is the grain of truth in Rothe's questionable theory of 'unconscious Christianity.'

not mean that even to-day the 'Yea' to Christ is not a 'Yea' nor the 'No' a 'No,' nor that even to-day one can only become a member of the Christian community by the genuine 'Yea' of faith and in no other way, and that without this 'Yea'—whether by saying nothing or by saying 'No'—one places oneself outside the Christian community. But it is a reminder that it is not so easy to distinguish the genuine 'Yea' from the false one, and that often the 'No' lies nearer to it than would appear. The parable of Jesus of the paradoxical world Judgement upon the unbelieving believers and the believing unbelievers remains as a warning, above all confessions and creeds, and as a reminder of the hidden judgement of God, above all unbelief.[1] The Kingdom of God is indeed invisible in the midst of the godless world; and even of the godless world it is said that 'God so loved the world. . . .'[2] Even there, when the veil is drawn back the first will become the last and the last first.

But in fundamentals this does not alter anything; the fact remains that the Kingdom of God in the midst of time is there—even if concealed and struggling—where Jesus Christ is with His Word and Spirit, in the faith, love, and hope of His true Church. But it is essential to the Kingdom of God as it grows within time, that where it is, it is only in the way of decision, and has not yet been decided. 'Wherefore let him that thinketh he standeth take heed lest he fall.'[3] The fact that the *ecclesia* is called *militans* does not mean primarily that it must defend itself against the world around, but that every one of its members is permanently engaged in a struggle with himself. The Christian is not only, as Luther says, always growing, but he is always making decisions.[4] 'To live by his faith' means to live in decision. But as a believer he is not alone, he is a member of the Body of which Christ is the Head. To believe means to be in fellowship, in that com-

[1] Matt. xxv. 37 ff. [2] John iii. 16. [3] 1 Cor. x. 12.

[4] Stomps (op. cit., p. 126) rightly lays emphasis upon the fact that the Lutheran *semper homo est in non esse, in fieri* does not mean a growth in the sense of development, of progress, but that it means actuality absolutely; but it is an actuality which is connected with that which is not yet completed, with that which is destined for death, and thus with faith as distinguished from sight.

munity or fellowship which is the meaning of all history. 'The Kingdom in which we are citizens is in the heavens.'[1] The meaning of history lies where history itself has been overcome and fulfilled.

[1] Phil. iii. 20 (following German version).—*Translator.*

CHAPTER XX

MAN IN HIS EARTHLY LIFE; AND DEATH

I. THE NATURAL UNDERSTANDING OF DEATH AND OF ETERNAL DESTINY

WE cannot think rightly about man as he actually is without continually reminding ourselves of the fact that man must die, that the character of this whole existence is temporal and transitory. 'Dust thou art, and unto dust shalt thou return.'[1] The whole of human existence is an 'existence unto death';[2] as a whole it is shadowed by death; as a river rushes towards the cataract, so human life is flowing towards death; by death is it attracted and moved. We can judge whether a doctrine of man is realistic or merely in the clouds by the way in which it sees and emphasizes this fact.

But we do not understand this mortality of human life, this 'existence for death,' if we do not also emphasize the claim on eternity as an essential characteristic of human life, which, in some way or other—*how* will be shown a little later—belongs to the life of man as a spiritual being, and is continually re-asserting itself as part of this spiritual being. The contradiction which we have recognized as the characteristic of the actual empirical human existence comes out in a peculiarly painful and shattering way in the fact that man does not die as other creatures die, and that his life, which is destined for death, also contains within it a desire to disbelieve in death, a revolt against death, even a desire to escape death, which cannot be explained simply by saying that it is due to the instinct of self-preservation known to every living being. Even,

[1] Gen. iii. 19.

[2] It is Heidegger's merit that, unlike most modern philosophers, he has taken the problem of death seriously, and indeed that he has set it in the centre of his thought; only we must not imagine that his understanding of death is a kind of 'neutral ontology' or even—which is something different—that of the simple human being. It is rather a pessimistic metaphysic of death, a view like that of Fichte transformed into the negative, *Eigentlichkeit* (see Translator's Note on p. 19) understood as 'resolution for death.'

and especially, in face of death man cannot simply place himself on a level with the other creatures. There is within him something which revolts against this equation with the rest of creation, and at the same time something which makes his dying so much more terrible than that of any of the other creatures. For man is not simply part of the world, he is not simply a living creature; he knows that as a bearer of spirit, as subject, as person, he has a 'soul' of a different kind from that of all other 'ensouled' creatures.[1] However he may explain this to himself, he is aware of the fact, even if he denies it in theory. Even though he may deny it time after time, he can never feel his death as something 'natural'; he feels dimly that there is a real difference between the death of a human being and the death of an animal. Creatures come to an end; man dies. But then can a person, can that which is spiritual, die? The mystery of his personal being breaks out in the mystery of his dying, in the fact that he can never console himself by thinking that now all is 'over.'

This contradiction reveals itself also in the fact that to man death is an enigma, which he can never solve, and which he has tried to solve in very different ways.[2] The 'simplest' solution is to forget the spirit altogether; man manages—at least in theory—to forget entirely that the being of a person is something different from that of the being of any other creature. In some way or other he succeeds in repressing his inner knowledge which tells him the opposite; having done so, he believes that he can accept death as something quite 'natural,' and as a 'matter of course'; this means that he succeeds in regarding himself as an object, and in transferring to himself the experience which he makes of all that is objective in the world. If man is simply one organism alongside of all the

[1] The imperfection of the Old Testament shows itself especially in the way in which, in contrast to the New Testament, it speaks of man's death. Cf. Koehler, op. cit., pp. 134 ff.

[2] Cf. Rohde's *Psyche*. There is the idea of a shadowy continuation of life in the underworld; all kinds of ideas of the Beyond, the doctrine of re-birth and of final redemption into Nirvana (which probably no non-Indian will ever understand). In the text we take into account only the actual alternatives to the Christian faith which are now operative among us, the 'Epicurean' and the 'Platonic.'

others then there is no enigma in death. For in all organisms, once their life-force has been expended, the process of growing old will reach its acute and final stage, and the gradual failure of strength will become complete decay; rigidity and dissolution then reaches its highest point and causes the destruction of the living unity of the individual. 'Death is the natural end of a development which starts even with the beginning of life.'[1] And then? What shall be 'then'? When a beautiful soap-bubble has burst do we ask what has happened to 'it itself'? Man *was*, and now he is no more. As a totality he has been dispersed in the elements out of which he was composed. These elements will perhaps be used again for the upbuilding of a living whole, perhaps even of a human being. 'Death is the stratagem of Nature to have much life' (Goethe). 'Imperious Caesar,' so philosophizes the cynical grave-digger in *Hamlet*, 'dead and turned to clay,' 'Might stop a hole to keep the wind away.'

Then is the personal life of humanity nothing more than a poor little soap-bubble which shimmers for a year or two with wonderful colours and then one day bursts and dissolves into nothing? Then is the spirit of man nothing more than an 'epiphenomenon,' a phenomenon which accompanies organic processes? Then is the subject nothing more than a certain aspect of the object, is man simply part of the world and nothing more? Because this answer—in spite of the undeniable fact of death and the corruption of the human body—is so evidently false that everyone who has preserved even a glimmer of knowledge of personal being cannot believe in it, the human spirit has gone to the other extreme and claims that death is not the destruction of man; on the contrary, that it is a release, the emancipation of the soul from the prison of the body, the setting free of the soul from the burden of its base material partner. In this phenomenon it is not death which is the important thing, but the immortality of the soul, which it manifests and expresses.

This idea of the immortality of the soul was born not of philosophy but of mystical religion,[2] but it was eagerly seized and appropriated by philosophy, which was more profound.

[1] Article on *Death* in the *Grosse Brockhaus*.

[2] Rohde, *Psyche*.

Plato was the first to combine philosophy, his theory of Ideas, with the Idea of the immortal soul, as he knew it from the Orphic tradition, and to weld them into a wonderful unity. Scarcely any other idea in philosophy has had such an effect as this. Nothing shows more clearly the power of this idea than the fact that it was able not only to penetrate into Christianity, but that for nearly two thousand years it was regarded as a Christian idea, although, as we shall show directly, it is alien to the genuine thought of the Bible.

It is not very easy to answer the question: how did Plato think of the Immortality of the Soul, and upon what did he base his view?[1] but so much is certain, that according to Plato, immortality is regarded as belonging to the nature or essence of the soul, that it has its basis in its special relation to the world of Ideas, especially to the Idea of the Good, that for that very reason it is indissolubly connected with the idea of the eternal pre-existence of the soul, and that it manifests itself in the *anamnesis*-character of the ideal knowledge. Accordingly, the immortality of the Soul, as Plato understands it, must not be confused either with the Biblical idea of Creation or with the Neo-Platonist pantheistic idea of emanation. For the rest, the fact that Plato deliberately clothed his ideas about immortality in the form of myth makes it impossible to give a clear answer to all the questions which Plato's thought is bound to raise in the mind of the critical philosopher or the Christian theologian.

According to the Platonic conception the soul is an entity which is in opposition to the bodily existence, which could only come into this existence by means of a 'Fall,'[2] from which

[1] Zeller (op. cit., p. 697) rightly calls attention to the lack of unity of the Platonic doctrine of Immortality, and to the impossibility of abstracting the pure philosophical kernel from the husk of myth. But the main lines of thought are clear. 'Life belongs to the nature of the soul. Thus it cannot allow any approach of the contrary, death; it is therefore immortal and incorruptible.'

[2] Most drastically in the *Phaedrus*. The metaphysical doctrine of Immortality should further be distinguished from the ethical existential doctrine of dying, whose distinctiveness against all speculative theories Bultmann rightly emphasizes (article on θάνατος in Kittel's *Wörterbuch*, pp. 10, 12). His doctrine of Judgement, which does not fit in with his metaphysic of the soul, is connected with the latter. See above, p. 170.

it must and can only be set free by the right knowledge, by the philosophical way of life, by a progressive detachment from all that is of the sense life, and non-spiritual. Only that part of the soul therefore is immortal which is turned towards the world of Ideas, or, to use Kantian terminology: reason as the 'power of the idea.' It is this rational, spiritual being of the soul by means of which it is immortal, pre-existent, gifted with the power of *anamnesis*, and capable of self-redemption. By its higher being, by that through which it is in opposition to corporeality, it is immortal. This idea was varied in many ways in later Greek philosophy, in early and later Stoicism, in the syncretistic philosophy influenced by the thought of the East, in the popular philosophy impregnated with the Roman spirit, in Gnosticism and in Neo-Platonism. But through all these variations the decisive element remains: the immortality of the soul is its very nature, its unchangeable metaphysical essence. Even in its connexion with the Biblical idea of Creation, which begins with the earliest Christian theologians, this fundamental idea remains: the soul is immortal in virtue of its nature—even if it is not an eternally pre-existent but a divinely created being. This idea is intimately connected with the doctrine of the *Imago Dei*. The *Imago Dei*, distinguished from the *similitudo*, understood as an essential similarity to God, has as its most important characteristic, and one which it can never lose: immortality.[1]

This synthesis of the Platonic doctrine of the soul and the Christian doctrine of Creation dominates the whole of patristic literature, was developed still further in Scholasticism with the aid of Aristotelian concepts, and passed on, with only slight modifications, into the early Protestant theology; it has not only dominated the development of theological thought in the narrower sense of the word, but it has also become an integral part of the piety of the Church, of

[1] The doctrine of an *imago* which cannot be lost—alongside of the *similitudo* which can be and has been lost—brings into the statements of the Fathers a certain fluctuation with regard to immortality. On the whole, however, the view prevails that immortality belongs to the nature of the *imago* which cannot be lost, which for its part, however, is regarded as a gift of the divine grace of Creation.

preaching, religious instruction, the liturgy, and ecclesiastical hymnology.

2. THE ETERNAL DESTINY

There can be no doubt at all to-day that the Bible[1] does not contain this idea of a metaphysical immortality grounded in the nature of the essence of the soul. Its fundamental view of man as a divinely created unity of body and soul, on the one hand, as also its fundamental view of the actual foundation of personal being in the creating Word of God, on the other hand, cannot be combined with this doctrine of the essential immortality of the human spirit, and of the emancipation of the spirit from its prison, the body, any more than it can be combined with the former naturalistic theory which wholly forgets the special being of man as person.[2] It is certainly no mere accident that the Christian idea has continually been linked with the Platonic doctrine, but never with the Epicurean theory—artificial and dangerous as that synthesis may have been.

The destiny of man as something special is determined by the special nature of his being. If man is that which we have recognized him to be from the teaching of the Bible: personal being founded in the Word of God, being-in-responsibility, being-for-love, then also the perversion which has taken place, through sin, in the original created human nature cannot result in the fact that man dies just like any other creature. The error of Idealism is not that it brings man, on account of his spirit, into relation with eternal being; what is wrong is the way in which it does this; that is, that it attributes eternal being substantially, naturally, or essentially to man as the manner of his spiritual being, that it regards eternity as something which can be taken for granted, as part of the spiritual being of man, as the result of his divine kind of being.

[1] Cf. the discussion between Althaus and Stange, especially with regard to Luther (Althaus, *Unsterblichkeit und ewiges Leben bei Luther*, 1930, and the bibliography there).

[2] Althaus rightly protests against a tendency in the theology of the present day to deny the distinctiveness of man's being which is supposed to be 'to the greater glory of the Christian faith' (*Die letzten Dinge*, p. 102).

Originally—so the Bible tells us—man was not destined for death but for eternal being. Death is something foreign to this original destiny in the creation, something added and hostile, it is an intruder.[1] The man who is destined by the Creator for communion with Himself, the Eternal, in so doing is himself destined for eternal life. This destiny is the *telos*, which the Creator has given him, and without this *telos* the nature of man cannot be imagined; the *telos*, the destiny, and the being of man are, it is true, not the same—the ecclesiastical doctrine has expressed this rightly from the days of St. Augustine, in the distinction it makes between the *posse non mori* and the *non posse mori*, that is, the destiny for the Eternal in contradistinction from eternal being—but neither can be severed from the other, as if being were something by itself, and destiny something by itself. The eternal destiny is impressed upon the being of man with the gift of personal being, to such an extent indeed, that, just like personal being, it does not simply disappear even with man's hostile self-determination against God.

Luther—just as he separated the doctrine of the *Imago* from its idealistic form with a sure feeling for the original Biblical idea—has also wonderfully clearly distinguished this idea from the ecclesiastical and idealistic idea of immortality, and has seen both the eternal character of man's destiny and its complete dependence upon the will and the word of God. 'Where, however, or with whom, God speaks, whether in wrath or in grace, the same is certainly immortal. The Person of God who speaks, and the Word of God show that we are creatures with whom God wills to speak even unto eternity and in an immortal manner.'[2] 'And because the divine Majesty speaks with man alone (*cum solo homine*), and man alone recognizes God (*agnoscit*) and perceives Him, so it follows necessarily that there is another life after this life.'[3]

The eternal does not reside in a spiritual nature, in a neutral and impersonal spiritual being, but in the Word of God and in the personal destiny—wrath or grace—which it contains. But this being in the Word of God is the being of man, whether

[1] Rom. v. 12, 14; Rom. vi. 23; 1 Cor. xv. 26.
[2] According to WA. 43, 481.
[3] According to WA. 42, 61.

he be a believer or an unredeemed sinner, thus whether he is standing under the wrath or under the grace of God; he may be in the Word of God in a perverted way and he then stands under wrath; but it is impossible for him not to be in the Word of God at all. Just as his being is always an actual 'being-responsible' so also it is always an existence in the Word of God, whether in the Word of grace or of wrath. Being under the word of wrath, however—and so the circle is closed—is the same as being under the law, which once again is an 'existence-for-death,' but now an existence for eternal death, an existence in condemnation.

Luther does not consider that the unbelieving man ceases to exist at death, any more than does the New Testament.[1] The fact that man, even when he dies, does not simply cease to be, but that then in particular the perversion of his being, sin, comes out, is not merely an inference, but a necessary element in the Lutheran—and that means also in the Biblical—understanding of personality. The fact that man's being is decision gains its final and its most serious expression in this truth.

From this, too, we see why it is that the man who does not really 'know' God, who only 'knows' Him in an idolatrous way, and who therefore does not see himself aright (either as he is in his true nature or as he actually is) is uncertain about the significance of death, and oscillates between the naturalistic-nihilistic understanding of death and the Idealistic-sentimental view of it. This also makes it clear why it is that the actual facts of human life are such that they may lend colour first to one interpretation and then to the other, so long as man has not penetrated through all questionings to

[1] Althaus, in his presentation of the Biblical doctrine, rightly lays stress on the fact that we must make a distinction between relation to God and communion with God. Stange's contrary assertion, in spite of Luke xiv. 14, cannot be regarded as the view of the Bible. On the contrary, we must admit that in the New Testament a continuation of human existence beyond death is expressed without an explicit mention of the resurrection; for instance, Luke xvi. 23; Rom. ii. 5–13. On the other hand, 'the idea of the sleeping soul is foreign to the thought of the New Testament,' whilst to some extent the Old Testament view of Sheol is developed further (article on *Hades* in Kittel's *Wörterbuch*).

the fundamental truth of his origin, of his being in the Word of God.

On the one hand, spiritual being, which indeed even fallen man knows, points to the Eternal. We cannot think of the spiritual as such absolutely together with 'death.' Plato was not simply giving rein to his imagination in a phantasy when he calls the world of Ideas an eternal existence, but he saw something essential. Behind the Ideas stands the divine Truth,[1] and in the act of grasping ideas man does not remain simply imprisoned within himself but he participates in divine Truth. Indeed the act of thinking—in the broadest sense of the word, of the grasping of ideas—is itself, although it is certainly immersed in time, also something timeless; in the act of synthesis the distracting effect of time ceases—otherwise the 'synthesis' would never be reached, no thought would ever be formulated. Hence the fundamental law of all thinking, of all mental activity in general, is the Law of Identity, which constitutes the boundary between the psychological current of life and intellectual truth or meaning. The act which grasps truth and meaning participates in the timelessness of truth; that is the relative truth of Idealism.

3. MORTALITY AND EXISTENCE-UNTO-DEATH

On the other hand, however, to infer the eternity of our being from this timelessness of the Idea is that paralogism[2] upon which Kant has rightly poured scorn, the confusion of our human existence—or 'soul'—with the content of thought. Our spiritual life participates both in the eternity of truth and in the transitoriness of creaturely existence. No Law of Identity helps us out of the misery of forgetfulness, which is indeed the clearest proof of the fact that our spiritual existence is deeply embedded in 'the world which passeth away.' There is certainly a deep meaning in the fact that the Greeks described the truth as *Ἀ-λήθεια*,[3] as not-forgetting. Forgetting is tran-

[1] See above, pp. 243 ff.

[2] *Kritik der reinen Vernunft, Von den Paralogismen. d.r.V.*

[3] *ἀλήθεια* means first of all the act of not concealing; the connection with *Lethe* may not belong to the etymology, but it belongs to the spirit of the Greek language.

sitoriness in knowledge, death beforehand, so far as it affects the mental life, the non-*durée-réelle*, perpetual dispersion, the tearing apart of that which should be united. Death in the mental life, however, takes on the most varied forms: mental indolence, dullness of mind, susceptibility to illusions of all kinds, 'forgetfulness' in not holding fast the truth which is already known, in the assertion of contradictory statements and the like.

But far more important than all this, is that which does not affect the spirit *in abstracto*, 'the spiritual,' but that which affects the person. That is the theme which is treated in the Bible;[1] it has to do with *man*, not with 'the spiritual' or with 'spiritual being' in itself. The Bible does so by co-ordinating, strictly and indissolubly, the three fundamental concepts which characterize the existence of man outside the redeeming revelation: Sin, law and death, so that these three very nearly become interchangeable ideas. The severance of man from living union with God is expressed as a state of being 'fallen' under the power of death, and at the same time as a state of having fallen under the law. 'Death'—this death, the death of human beings, which is both curse and damnation,[2] is 'the wages of sin.' 'The sting of death is sin, but the power of sin is the law.'[3] Here death is no longer regarded as a natural event—the question of the origin of this purely creaturely death appears at the most on the verge of Biblical thought, in a characteristically 'human' light[4]—but death is closely connected with wrath and judgement.

Fear—*human* fear, and not creaturely fear—is connected with this view of death. The thought of this death cannot be separated from the thought of the wrath of God. 'For we are consumed in Thine anger, and in Thy wrath are we troubled. Thou hast set our iniquities before Thee, our secret sins in the light of Thy countenance. For all our days are passed away in Thy wrath.'[5] This fear is the effect of the 'sting of sin.' Without this sting possibly death would be something 'natural' —perhaps simply a 'going to sleep.' We do not know. We

[1] Cf. the excellent article on θάνατος by Bultmann (op. cit.).

[2] Rom. vi. 23.

[3] 1 Cor. xv. 56.

[4] Rom. viii. 20.

[5] Psa. xc. 7 ff.

only know that as sinners we are aware of this 'sting of death,' and therefore that the death of man is something quite different, something far more terrible than that of any other creature. Behind this fear there lies, as we have heard, fear of the God who judges man.[1] The evil conscience and the fear of death cannot be kept apart from one another. Sin, the bad conscience, law—that is, the God who makes merciless demands—and the wrath of God are inseparably and existentially connected.

It is peculiar to man that because he has spirit, he anticipates death. Even the animal that is led to the slaughter—so the peasants assure us—has some dim suspicion of the terrible thing towards which it goes. Its whole life is orientated towards self-preservation, towards keeping death at bay. Within the limits of its subject-existence even the animal anticipates death. But it has no knowledge of the Eternal, it knows nothing of responsibility, of guilt and sin, nothing of being destined for God. But man knows all this, even as sinner—even if his knowledge is perverted. Hence his 'being-in-sin' and his 'being-under-the-law' is also a 'being-unto-death,' which is certainly not exhaustively defined in the platitude: 'all finite existence is transitory.' Fear of death permeates the whole of human life. Fear of life is always fear of death. 'In the world ye have tribulation' or 'fear,'[2] namely, of death; but this does not simply mean the fear of fading out or of ceasing to be, but still more, the fear of not fading out and of not ceasing to be.

But death has not only rooted itself to this extent within the subject of the person. It dominates the whole of personal existence. The undying honour which humanism seeks as compensation for death is indeed a feeble gesture of protest, a phrase, just like the talk about 'immortal works.' What do two centuries or even a thousand years matter which some

[1] The phenomenon of 'dread' in its connexion with death, sin and the bad conscience has never been so clearly grasped by anyone as by Luther. Cf. his description of the terror of death of the first human beings after the Fall (WA. 42, 137 ff.).

[2] John xvi. 33. Humanity stands under the influence of death, due to wrath, through its godlessness (Rom. i. 20 ff.); the sorrow of the world is standing in the shadow of death (2 Cor. vii. 10; cf. Bultmann, op. cit.).

supreme human achievements attain in the opinion and understanding of posterity! The history of humanity is a symphony—or a cacophony—on this theme with variations: all that exists is worthy of destruction. 'All is vanity.' The Preacher certainly sees human life in a one-sided manner, but what he says is true. His reminder of the nothingness of all that man does and creates cannot be refuted. History as a whole is a 'mixture of error and force'; 'vain,' however, also —apart from the hope of redemption—is the individual human life.

It is true, of course, that much that is wonderful, great, glorious, amazing and beneficial has been produced by human beings in the course of human history, and what we call 'ordinary life' still produces it daily. That picture of history which modern Idealism has outlined, that happy vision of a world of spirit gradually maturing towards its fulfilment of meaning, of a humanity which gradually finds itself, and gradually unveils its human countenance, is not, any more than the idea of timelessness, a purely insubstantial vision. The idea of history as the 'becoming human' of man is no mere phantasy, although it is far from being the truth.[1] In the midst of the actual fallen world it is a trace, which can still be discerned, of the original meaning of history—of the individual, as of humanity as a whole: this earthly life as a time of growth, as time which is being fulfilled. Here and there in the history of mankind or in the history of an individual human being something of this meaning suddenly shines out for a moment, like a flash of lightning, and it seems as though it could be seized. But then we turn over the next page in the book of history and—it is gone, this meaning, hidden, buried, destroyed by utter nonsense. But the quintessence of utter non-sense is—death, nothingness as the common heritage of all that lives, the final goal of all 'meaningful'

[1] This view of history has been possibly most clearly outlined by Herder and Humboldt. Kant's judgement was essentially a more sober one. 'The history of nature begins with the Good, for that is the work of God, the history of freedom from evil, for that is the work of man.' Still he believes in infinite progress. (*Mutmasslicher Anfang der Menschengeschichte*, *Ausgabe Cassirer*, vol. iv, p. 334.)

developments, the fruit of all maturity—this terrible 'Nothing.' Hence the final conclusion is this: so far as we are concerned, the result of this human life is that 'we bring our years to an end as a tale that is told.'[1] All is vanity.

4. ETERNAL DEATH

But faith, in its seriousness, knows something more than this: death means falling under the Divine Judgement. 'It is a fearful thing to fall into the hands of the living God.'[2] 'Therefore indeed a Christian is a particularly miserable creature, above all that can be called wretched, . . . and always he must have a frightened, weak, trembling heart as often as the thought comes to him of death and the severe judgement of God'; while others die 'as though a cow had died' (Luther).[3] 'Existence-for-death' reveals itself as an existence for eternal death. The Christian understanding of death is the most serious—and thus the most terrible there is—because it alone is truly personal. It does not treat death lightly, in either the naturalistic or in the idealistic sense of the word—in the sense of simply ceasing to be, or of henceforward being divine. The serious way in which Christianity treats death shows its serious view of personal responsibility. Death is neither the negative nor the positive metaphysical event, but it is *the* personal event, in which the perversion of the personal attitude of man over against the Creator is finally manifested—in so far indeed as man sees himself under the aspect of his perversion, that is, in so far as he stands knowingly under the law. 'The law worketh wrath.'[4] 'It is the law' which, in point of fact, 'works death'; 'its letter kills, so that the office of the law is the service of death.'[5] For the legalistic will is the 'way of the man who wants to live by himself instead of in dependence on God.'[6] Thus the believer understands existence in unbelief, 'under wrath,' 'under the Law,' in sin: as 'being lost.'

5. THE CONQUEST OF DEATH

But this is not the only thing and not the main thing that the Christian knows about death. It is thus that he under-

[1] Ps. xc. 9. [2] Heb. x. 31. [3] WA. 36, 538.
[4] Rom. iv. 15. [5] Bultmann, op. cit. [6] Bultmann, op. cit., p. 16.

stands his existence as that of an unbeliever, as a human being who knows the Word of God only as a word of wrath and not as a word of grace, as a word which corresponds to the Law and not to the Gospel, as a word which causes wrath and not as a word which dispenses life. Faith, however, may take that Word 'which the Person of God speaks' as a word of grace. There, where, for the sinner, death stands as the sign of the divine wrath, stands for the believer the Cross of Jesus Christ, as the Sign of the Divine Mercy, and of the newly granted share in eternal life. If human death—in contrast to death as a natural event—is the effect of sin and the divine wrath, that is, of man's perverted relation to God, then conversely, the consequence of the newly established communion with God in Christ is the re-establishment of 'existence-unto-eternal-life.' Jesus Christ is the great Transformer: He reverses the perverted meaning of human existence and once more gives it its original meaning, the meaning which it had in the intention of the Creation. This is precisely the significance of His death upon the Cross. As the coming of God into the curse of our sinful existence[1] not only reveals to the sinner the unconditional love of God, but also provides a new ground of existence, so also His acceptance of death and His passage through it in the Resurrection is not only revelation, but it also constitutes the new possibility for every believer, the beginning of the realization of eternal life. 'He that believeth on Me, though he die, yet shall he live.'[2] 'We know that we have passed from death unto life';[3] we are again united with our Origin, in 'existence-for-eternal life,' through the fact that we are once more, in the right sense, in the Word of God, that is, through faith. The point here is not merely that through Jesus Christ the Christian receives the certainty of eternal life, nor that through Jesus Christ his immortality is assured afresh; it is rather that Jesus Christ is the Saviour from death, and that faith in Him is already the beginning, the 'dawn' of Eternal Life.

Even Christians must die; outward death confronts them too, and this dying will be a dying of the whole man and not merely of the body. The whole man must pass through an

[1] Rom. viii. 2. [2] John xi. 25. [3] 1 John iii. 14.

experience of annihilation which affects the whole man[1] since the whole man is a sinner. It would be strange if the spirit in particular, the personal centre, the 'heart,' which, just because it is the centre of the personality is also the seat of sin, did not feel the effect of sin. Man owes this death to God. But through Christ this death has lost its sting, for indeed the sting of death is sin, and this has been removed by Jesus Christ; it stands no longer between me and God. The power of this sting was the law; but the law has been removed by grace. Man's relation to God is now no longer a legalistic one; but in faith man lives again on the generous love of God, the self-giving love which God Himself pours out upon us, out of His fullness.

Hence the fear of death has been removed. 'This terrible death, which the Scripture calls the second death, is now taken away from believers by Christ, and is swallowed up in His life, and there is left behind a little death, indeed a sweet death, when a Christian dies according to the flesh.'[2] 'Such a death is sweeter and better than any life upon earth. For all the life, the goods, pleasures and joys of this world cannot make us so happy as to die with a good conscience, in certain faith and comfort of eternal life' (Luther).[3] 'O Death, where is thy sting? O Grave, where is thy victory? But thanks be to God which giveth us the victory through our Lord Jesus Christ.'[4] 'Having the desire to depart and to be with Christ.'[5] Thus understood, death becomes the happy event, the stepping over the threshold which lies between this transitory suffering world, which is full of death, and that world of eternal life, as the mystics and the Platonists call it; and yet here we mean something quite different. It is not in virtue of something which is in the human soul, but in virtue of the Christ, in virtue of the divine saving act that man gains eternal life. There is a fight, and indeed a fight in which it is not the spirit of man which conquers, but God.[6] Hence it is not the

[1] Schlatter: 'We rise again, but only after our self has come to an end' (quoted by Althaus, op. cit., p. 108). [2] EA. 9, p. 154.
[3] Ibid. (cf. W.A., 41, p. 372). [4] 1 Cor. xv. 55. [5] Phil. i. 23.
[6] 'It was a wondrous battle,
When death and life did strive,
But life has been victorious,
It swallowed death alive,' sings Luther (WA. 35, 444).

entrance into a world which is 'all spirit,' but the entrance into perfect communion with God and His creatures.

In any case, both for the believer and for the unbeliever, whether one knows it or not, recognizes it or not, death is the decisive sign of human life—either my own death as the final stage, the sign of nothingness, or the death of Christ as the sign of positive fulfilment. Without faith man cannot come to terms with death. He cannot look it in the face. Either man must forget that he is any more than a beast, or he must forget that he is something other than a god, in order to be able to endure death. It is not merely difficult actually to die as man; but it is literally, in the exact sense of the word, impossible. There are human beings who die bravely, who refuse even in death to have any illusions. But they do not really 'pull it off'; they all die in an illusion which makes death harmless. For the only possibility of not making death harmless, but of seeing it as it is, and yet of not going mad with terror, is faith in Him who in His death has revealed the whole horror of death, and at the same time the still greater glory and power of the divine love.

EPILOGUE

THE REMOVAL OF THE CONTRADICTION BETWEEN MAN AS HE ACTUALLY IS, AND MAN AS HE IS INTENDED TO BE

As we look back over the road we have travelled, we see that the theme of this book was man as he actually is; that is, man in the contradiction between Creation and Sin. This contradiction is not 'something in' the actual man; it is himself. Only in the light of this contradiction do we see man as he actually is; then, too, we see how he differs from all other living creatures. Only he who understands this contradiction understands man as he actually is, and only he who comprehends the depth of this contradiction comprehends the depth of man as he actually is.

Up to this point we have emphasized two truths: first, that this contradiction cannot be understood from the point of view of an *a priori* philosophy, but only from the standpoint of faith; that is, that in order to look into these depths we must take up that position above man which would be impossible to us in our own strength, namely, in the Word of God. This position is given to us by the Incarnation of the Son of God and by the Spirit of God; to take up this position means to believe. From the point of view of faith we can understand the contradiction in man in such a way that we see him as he really is, namely, as one who stands between the creation in the image of God, the original union with God, and sin, the false independence of man. That was the first point.

The second was the proof, worked out in detail, that solely from this standpoint can we see aright—that is, without distortion—the phenomena of human existence, about the interpretation of which religion and philosophy have always been concerned; thus we have endeavoured to show that the Christian view of man is the only realistic one, and that every other view, in some way or other, distorts or conceals the picture of man as he actually is.

Having gone so far, we might consider that our task had been completed. From the point of view of the Bible there would still be a great deal to say about man: about Atonement, Restoration and the final consummation. But that is no longer the doctrine of man, but the doctrine of Jesus Christ and His atoning and redeeming work. This would bring us to the real central theme of Christian doctrine, to the Gospel of the Kingdom of God. But this does not belong to the sphere of our present inquiry. To speak of that at all adequately we would need to develop the whole of Christian doctrine, whereas all that we intended to do in this book was to deal with a definite section of Christian doctrine, the subject of which is the pre-supposition for the Message itself. And yet to break off our presentation of the subject at this point would be to incur the danger of a terrible misunderstanding; in conclusion we must speak of that other truth which lies beyond our present field of vision. This we do for the following reasons.

The truth of the actual man, as a truth of faith, is not something 'objective,' neutral, it is not one which offers a picture which speaks for itself, but it is to the highest extent subjective, that is, it is one which can only be gained in the existential decision of faith. As a realistic war report can only be given by a war correspondent who himself enters into the war zone and exposes himself personally to the danger of death in the trenches, so the report of the actual man, which the Christian gives, is only gained by the fact that one surrenders oneself to the decision of faith. Further, the perception of the actual man is even an integral element in faith itself. No one can be a believer without—in the main—seeing himself as we have described him in this book. This view is a decision of faith, and the decision of faith is this view. In other words: this view of the sick, divided man is also the beginning of the process of healing; and the beginning of the process of healing of the sick man is precisely this view of himself. Hence we must not take this truth out of the context in which alone it can be attained—otherwise we would immediately turn it into something else; it is part of the 'optical experimental condition' without which this 'picture' cannot exist: the seeing is part of the struggle, of the process of healing, of the process of recovery.

We said that this view of 'man-in-contradiction' is only possible to faith. But faith itself emerges from this contradiction. Faith is itself the power to say 'yes,' and to feel impelled to say 'yes,' once more, to the originally-creative, eternally-electing Word of God. Faith is not a 'view' (*Anschauung*) or 'opinion'; it does not mean regarding 'something' as true, it is not a theoretical attitude; but faith is saying 'yes' to the Word of God as the existential decision, it is man's return from his enmity against God to his Origin; it means resolving the contradiction by saying 'yes' to the Primal Word. Faith is the 'No' to the contradiction, the 'No' to sin. It is not virtue which is the opposite of sin, but faith, just as it is not vice which is the essence of sin, but unbelief. The original ground and the original nature of sin is the severance of man from his origin, from the loving, gracious and generous Word of God, which makes him free while it binds him, which gives him life in the very act of requiring it from him.

In his insane desire to be independent and autonomous, man denies this dependence. The autonomous reason, the man who makes himself autonomous in his reason, 'captain of his soul,' this proclamation of his own glory, and of reason as the final court of appeal, is the real core of sin, the secret heart of the contradiction in the nature of man. For in point of fact the reason is *not* autonomous; man, even in his reason, is *not* equal with God, he is *not* his own Creator and Master, and above all he does *not* gain freedom but the opposite when he severs himself from the ground of his freedom, from the Word of God. This freedom is a lie, and this lie manifests itself in the contradiction in his nature.[1]

Because this is what sin means, faith is able to overcome it. Faith is reason subject to the rule of God, reason as perception, the return to obedience, to the Word of God, and

[1] The whole of the more recent history of philosophy—indeed, the whole history of the modern mind—is the parable of the Prodigal Son, as told by André Gide: the son who severs his relation with the Father, because he wants at last to become independent, free, and thus a human being, without noticing that in so doing he falls into falsity and misery.

trust in the grace of God which is 'sufficient,'[1] that is, that in it all life is included and guaranteed. Distrust, indeed the fear of missing something, the view that one must help oneself to a full and satisfying life, is the source of sin, that whisper of the serpent, that God, by binding man to Himself, wills to deprive him of something. Both the distrust which springs from fear, which leads us to try to help ourselves, and the renunciation of obedience and of dependence upon God, which springs from arrogance, are inseparably connected. So too in faith—which is opposition to the contradiction—two things are inseparably connected: trust in the life-giving Word, and willing and joyful obedience to the bond which it contains, to the will of the Creator.

But this faith is quite different from that which the simple faith of the origin would have been. It means the elimination of the contradiction between the 'Origin' and the 'Now'; it is remorse, repentance, the sense of sin and guilt. The sinner cannot come back to the beginning as though nothing had happened. Hence faith is a twofold movement; first of all one must retrace the whole false path to the beginning, and then obey the original Word of God. That is the 'No' to the 'No' before it can become the 'Yea' to the 'Yea.' It is *mortificatio* before it can be *vivificatio*. 'I will arise and go to my Father and will say unto Him: I am not worthy to be called thy son.'[2] Faith does not allow the past to be treated as nothing. The past lies like a block of stone in the way between God and me. I could not go back, even if I wanted to, unless this block were removed out of the way. My past is so closely connected with me, that there is no new present and no new future for me unless this past is annulled.

But I cannot possibly find the way back by myself. My repentance cannot annul the past. My repentance only has meaning as the recognition of the truth that by His forgiveness God wipes out the past. God's primal word of love comes to me as a new event, by means of which God wipes out my past as though it had never happened, through His act of reconciliation. It is not I who go all the way back but God; He takes the whole consequence of my falling away upon

[1] 2 Cor. xii. 9. [2] Luke xv. 18.

Himself. God comes, so to speak, towards me, through all my apostasy, laden with the whole burden of my falling away, suffering from the whole curse which my fall has caused as an objective fact. My faith, therefore, can only go back the whole way because God's Word comes to me in this way: in Jesus Christ the Crucified, in God's act of atonement which blots out my past, my guilt. Hence faith is now no longer the simple childlike acceptance of the 'man made in the divine Image,' but it is first of all a painful process, in which I have to say 'No' before I can say 'Yes'; that is, I must acknowledge my guilt and my sin, and I must admit the necessity for the Divine Atonement. We can only perceive in this Divine light what we really are; it is only in the Word of the Cross, which actually brings out our contradiction to our Origin—just as the Origin is actually present within it—that we see ourselves in our true light.

This shows how seriously God treats us. He does not treat our past as nothing—which in virtue of His Omnipotence He can overlook—over which He leads us swiftly back to the beginning. The contradiction has weight, not only for us, but also for Him. It is because God takes us seriously, even in our contradiction, that the Word of the Origin comes to us burdened with the whole weight of the contradiction. The less a being has significance, the less importance has his past. The more a man takes his life seriously, the more seriously he takes his past. But God takes us more seriously than we take ourselves, hence He takes our past absolutely seriously. The Cross of Christ shows us how seriously He takes our past, and thus how seriously He regards us, ourselves.

It is only because He takes us so seriously that we also can do this on our side. Only in faith in Jesus Christ, the Crucified, as the eternal Word of God, can we perceive and know the full weight of our guilt, can we thus also perceive the contrast between our Origin and our opposition to it; that is, can we know ourselves. Only thus can our false autonomy be broken. The Word of the Cross is foolishness and an offence. This 'folly' and this 'offence' correspond exactly to our arrogance of autonomy and our insane pretensions to it. The more self-assurance and self-confidence we have, the more is the Cross of Christ a stumbling-block. With our faith we must pass through these Caudine Forks, because only thus can our pride of reason be broken, because only thus do we perceive our contradiction, take back our past, and regain our origin. The Cross of Christ is the objective point at which the contradiction between the true and the actual man is concentrated; hence for the actual man—until the miracle of conversion takes place—it is that which he hates the most. What he hates in it is the truth about himself, about his estrangement from God.[1]

But where the miracle of return to God takes place, this is what happens: man allows himself to be told his real state, he goes back to his Origin, in the 'recapitulation,' in the objective 'anamnesis' of this past, in the Cross of Christ.[2] In this faith man finally renounces sovereignty over himself, self-assertion, and all trust in his own efforts; in this faith he accepts life purely as a gift. He accepts it as the word of reconciliation with the God who stretches out His hand to him, the rebel, ignoring his rebellion, and setting him once again at the place for which he was created. The nature of man is—this was our main thesis—identical with his attitude to God. If man is once more united with God, then he is restored; the rent has been healed, the contradiction has been set aside, the original intention has become the new reality. The Truth and the Actuality of man have once more become a unity. In Jesus Christ, the God-Man, the original image has been restored, in faith in Christ this restoration is continually being reflected. This faith is the *restitutio imaginis*.[3] Faith is the re-birth of man out of a 'carnal' state—that is, the effort to achieve self-realization in one's own strength—into a 'spiritual' one, that is, one which lives on and in the Word of God.

To see oneself as a sinner, the perception of the contra-

[1] Cf. Goethe's observations on the Cross during his journey in Italy.

[2] Away from God—back to God, that is the Platonic and Neo-Platonic way of the soul; the movement is thereby exclusively on the side of the soul. The Gospel: through the Incarnation of the Son of God estranged humanity is 'brought back,' and at the same time God's work is completed.

[3] Col. iii. 10; Eph. iv. 24. *Nec sane aliud est regeneratio piorum, quam reformatio imaginis Dei in illis* (Calvin, 51, 208).

diction, is the negative element in this restoration. The restoration is above all a process of breaking down; the breaking down of the arrogant and insolent independence of the autonomous will and of the autonomous reason. This 'breaking down' does not actually take place anywhere save 'in Christ.' It is true of course that mysticism attempts something similar: the self must be wholly 'emptied' in order to receive the divine life. But because mysticism is never concerned with guilt, but only with becoming like God, it never really succeeds in 'breaking down' man's arrogant self-will; for it never perceives the conflict between the Origin and man's opposition to it. The mystic never takes upon himself the burden of his past. He seeks to find the way back by himself, and to effect this reconciliation by his own efforts—this shows that he still cherishes the insane illusion of independence, characteristic of the autonomous self.

Even the Platonist has perceived something of this contradiction, and tries to find his way back to the Origin. But he too will not take the past upon himself—even he, like the mystic, only in a more rational way—wishes to find the way back to the divine primal existence, by himself. Even he will not allow himself to be humbled by the knowledge that God alone can take back the past, through forgiveness and reconciliation. It is true, of course, that even the Idealistic philosophy speaks of a 'reconciliation of the contradiction' as the theme of the whole of world history. But this reconciliation is not the taking of guilt upon oneself, therefore it is not the divine act and gift, but it is the human spirit trying to find its way back to the Origin through thought. Here too man is spared humiliation and the arrogance of his autonomy is not broken.

This is the reason why 'modern man' does not wish to know anything about the Christian faith. He does not want to give up his autonomy, he does not wish to pass through the Caudine Forks of the Cross, he does not want to bend and take upon himself his past as guilt which he cannot repair. It is true, of course, that in some way or other he sees the contradiction in human nature—how indeed could anyone overlook it! But he tries to interpret it as simply as possible, so that the vexatiously humbling words 'guilt,' 'expiation,' 'forgiveness,' 'Cross,' may be avoided. He may perhaps desire to have God in some fashion, but he has no desire at all to accept his life as God's generous gift of grace. He is indeed willing to be 'responsible,' and yet he does not perceive that the only real responsibility consists in responding to generous love with responsive love. He does not see the connexion between the lovelessness which he too would like to condemn and the independence which he does not want to give up. Few people are as clear-sighted and as honest as Nietzsche. He saw clearly to the bottom of the modern desire for autonomy, and stood for it as one of the very few people who are entirely logical and radical. He did not—like the majority of modern folk—deny the Christian faith and affirm Christian love, but he perceived the connexion between the Cross and self-denying love; therefore he spurned both with the same hate and scorn. Indeed, he even ventured to mock at conscience and to regard the sense of responsibility as the fundamental evil. His 'transvaluation of all values' is an attack on the Christian ideal of love, and on all bonds imposed by the claims of the other. Hence he calls himself, knowing what he is doing, Antichrist.

The Word of God approaches man as a call to repentance and as a promise of rescue and fulfilment, as a Word which punishes and breaks man, and as One which woos and redeems him. Above all, however, it comes to him as the Word of the Origin, the Word which was in the beginning, in which all has been created.[1] He came to His own property, to His Own.[2] If He is rejected as a stranger—'His own received Him not'—it is not because He is a stranger, but because 'His own' have become alienated from Him, and wish to remain so.[3] But the opposite may happen—they may 'receive Him,'[4] they may perceive that they have become strangers, and they may recognize His right of ownership over them. Hence faith, this return to man's origin, is never a new beginning out of nothing, but it is a *renovatio imaginis*, a re-storation. But when the Word really reaches man through the proclamation of Jesus Christ and the revealing activity of the Holy Spirit,

[1] John i. 1–3.
[2] John i. 11.
[3] Col. i. 21; Eph. ii. 12.
[4] John i. 12.

then in Him man really perceives the Word of his origin, in which he finds his true self, and the meaning and content of his life. Then follows: his return to the knowledge of God, and his restoration to Him.

Faith is a miracle, but it is not magic. Where word and understanding are concerned, there may be miracle, but there cannot be magic. Here, in this central question—Miracle or magic?—the confessions part company. The *opere operato*, physically operative grace, is magic; the grace which is grasped and appropriated in the knowledge and the obedience of faith is miracle. But even where in the act of faith man is made into a mere object, to whom grace is applied, the miracle of grace is misunderstood as the magic of grace. Even in faith man is still man, not to be compared with anything else; he is responsible subject, person.[1] It is his personal centre, his 'heart,' which receives the Word of God; it is his spirit which understands it, since it is the Spirit of God who makes him understand. What else is faith save this, that in God's Word the heart of man learns to know the ground and the meaning of his life? As it is the heart which turns away from God in sin, so also it is the heart—the same heart in which the divine law is engraved—upon which the divine seed of the word is sown,[2] it 'hears and understands,[3] it is the heart in which Christ dwells by faith,[4] into which God has poured the Holy Spirit,[5] in which the peace of God rules,[6] in which the light of Christ shines forth,[7] in which the love of God is shed abroad by the Holy Spirit.[8] It is with the heart that we say 'Yes' to the Word of God, 'for with the heart man believeth'[9]—just as unbelief has its seat and its source in the heart.

Faith is the personal act through which the 'I' knows itself and recognizes itself in the Word of God. In faith—to use Kierkegaard's formula once more—'the self bases itself transparently upon the power which created it.' Faith is life on the Word of God, life in the reception and the acceptance of the divine love, complete freedom from self-seeking, dependence

[1] See the Appendix III, pp. 527 ff.
[2] Matt. xiii. 19.
[3] Matt. xiii. 23.
[4] Eph. iii. 17.
[5] 2 Cor. i. 22.
[6] Col. iii. 15.
[7] 2 Cor. iv. 6.
[8] Rom. v. 5.
[9] Rom. x. 10.

upon the God who seeks us. In faith our original destiny is realized as life-from-God. Faith therefore is both the renunciation of autonomous independence, and in so doing being set free from the Law. Man lives under the law, because, and so long as, he does not live on the generous love of God. Faith dares to make union with God the starting-point of life, not the goal to be attained; faith dares to begin with God, to see the self in God's Word, thus outside oneself instead of in oneself. *Nostra theologia ponit nos extra nos.*[1] In faith man ventures to be most daring, to identify himself with Christ, because Christ identifies Himself with him.[2] Faith ventures to take God's gracious Word seriously: 'thou art acceptable in My sight,' in spite of all experience to the contrary; faith dares to regard the true being in Christ as the only valid being which can be set against man's actual existence, his existence in contradiction, not in virtue of his own aspirations, but in virtue of the condescension of Christ to man. 'In so doing the Christian receives a self-consciousness which is wholly independent of all self-introspection.'[3] *Non debeo niti in mea conscientia, sensuali persona, opere, sed in promissione divina.*[4] Through faith the new person is constituted—the person which was created by God in the origin, whose content is the divine loving. 'I have been crucified with Christ; yet I live; and yet no longer I, but Christ liveth in me; and that life which I now live in the flesh I live in faith, the faith which is in the Son of God, who loved me, and gave Himself up for me.'[5]

Faith, therefore, is the threshold of love, or perhaps it would be more correct to say that it is the act of stepping into the divine love. In faith man, since he takes his life from the hands of God, does not desire anything more of his own, but only that which God wills. But the will of God is love.[6] Love is the

[1] Luther, WA. 40, 1, 589.
[2] Gal. ii. 20.
[3] Schott, *Geist und Fleisch in Luthers Theologie*, p. 39.
[4] Luther, WA. 40, 1, 589.
[5] Gal. ii. 20.
[6] Luther, *Immo proprie sola charitati tribuit Apostolus presentiam simul et donationem spiritus cum ipsa.* (Luther on Rom. v. 5. Ficker, II, 140.) I quote once more: 'let *charitatem* also not be such a small thing, *quia charitas* is God Himself. That is right, *quid sit charitas . . . qui diligit habet deum, qui deum habet, habet omnia*' (WA. 36, 422). 'Hence he who has love must have God too and be full of Him' (ibid., 427).

meaning of the revelation of Christ; therefore love is the content of the existence of the believer. Love is therefore 'greater' than faith[1] because God is love, but He is not faith. Faith is saying 'Yes' to the divine love. The act of saying 'Yes' is not the life itself, but it is the reception of the life. Faith takes the divine life which is love, and in so doing gains love as the content of human life. Through faith man receives his original position over against God, the one which was destined for him at the Creation, and in so doing he gains his own genuinely human life. Through this, then, responsibility is realized as life in community, life in service. But faith and love can scarcely be separated; for to say 'Yes' joyfully and gratefully to the Word of God who gives us life, is this faith in God, or the love of God? Is there anything else wherewith God's love could be received than by responsive love?

We can only make a distinction between faith and love to this extent, that faith is always the 'yes' of sinful man to the forgiving and loving God. Here is the limitation of the statement that faith is the restoration of the image of God. It is true, certainly, that in Christ faith grasps the primal image, the divine ground of creation of his existence: he says 'Yes' to the Original word, and in this 'yes' the division is healed. Man becomes sound and whole in this 'Yes,' he has once more found his position-in-God. The Spirit of God, of *one* nature with the Word of God, is the power of the new life. All this—this integration of the unity of the personality—takes place, truly, in faith. But the whole man is not faith; faith struggles to free itself from unbelief, from sin, it strives to wring union with God out of the contradiction, the new nature out of the old nature, the 'Yes' out of the 'No.' The actuality of faith is the new man; yet the eggshells of the old nature still cling to him as something which has been overcome, but still also as something which has to be overcome again and again. The old nature was not merely actuality, but it made itself substantial as 'flesh'; its movement was arrested; in the act of tearing itself away it became rigidly fixed as *habitus*. As *peccatum originale* indeed, it was no longer merely act, but it was at the same time something which had

[1] I Cor. xiii. 13.

become rigidly fixed; it was an actual state of being united with sinful humanity as a whole. The decision, however, which has been made in Christ is total and universal. It is a whole reconciliation, and reconciliation for all; but the decision by means of which we appropriate that Christ-decision in faith, by which, as it were, we take it over, is not in this sense total, not definitive, but it is a process which is still going on, and is not yet completed. The life of decision is not finished, as the act of reconciliation by Christ is 'finished'; as believers we are still growing, the *factum* there is here only a *fieri*, the *perfectum prateritum* there is here a *perfectum praesens*, a continual 'I have said yes,' which lasts as long as life itself.

The new nature, which is the conquest of the contradiction, consists in the struggle against the old nature, and through this the contradiction in the old nature becomes particularly acute. Not only do Christ and faith make the contradiction in the old nature explicit and evident, but Christ also brings it to that state of crisis, to a head, in which it fully breaks out at the very moment at which it is overcome. Faith alone creates the crisis in the 'sickness unto death'; only through it indeed does the sickness break out fully; but this total outbreak is already the beginning of the process of healing.[1] It is not merely that through Christ the contradiction in humanity becomes accentuated—before Christ there was no Nietzsche—but it is also that in the individual Christian, through faith alone, or rather in conflict with faith, evil gains a depth which it did not previously possess. *Christus facit nos peccatores*: this truth, of course, is not on the same plane as the other truth, that Christ makes us free from sin; but it is also true. The Christian is menaced by a danger of sin of which the pagan has no idea. The sin of the pagan is still too dull to be quite serious.[2] He does not yet stand in the full sense in the presence of God, hence he cannot sin in the same way as the Christian. Still, we must not forget that when the Christian sins, he does

[1] Kierkegaard: 'despair is . . . the disease of which it is true that it is the greatest misfortune never to have had it, a real gift of God to gain it, although it is the most dangerous illness of all' (*Sickness unto Death*, p. 23). The 'gain of infinity will never be attained save through despair' (p. 24).

[2] See above, p. 456.

not do so as a believer, but as an unbeliever, as one who falls away from Christ. Hence the *simul justus et peccator* is not to be understood to mean that nothing happens to sin save that it is recognized and forgiven; it is also overcome, set aside, even this real conquest of sin is one which is always only just beginning, one which in this life is never ended. The Christian is a new creature,[1] although the eggshells of the old nature still cling to him. He walks by the Spirit and not in the flesh,[2] even if again and again he is in conflict with the flesh and that means with self-will and a false independence—and must renew the struggle again and again. The contradiction has been overcome[3] even if it is always ready to break out afresh. For participation in the victory of Christ is not merely 'believing in it' but standing and living in it—even if as such it is at the same time a resistance-to-evil, a fight. Integration of personality is an actual fact, even if it is not yet completed, but is being continually shaken by the contradiction, and is therefore still imperfect.

Faith—so we said—is different from love. Faith is a continually renewed effort of love against lovelessness, but it does not proceed 'from the law,' from mere demand, but from the new life, from the Spirit of God. Love—pure, perfect love, would be an existence without conflict, it would be a life of natural and unbroken fellowship with God and with our neighbour, whereas while faith must break out in such love, the point is that it must *break out.* A true Christian actually has a quite different way of living with his neighbour from a non-Christian; but this new way of living is constantly checked and obscured by the old nature, so that we are forced to ask again and again whether it really is a new way of life, or merely a new form of development of the old nature. This imperfection of the new existence, of the wholeness and soundness of the new life, belongs to the 'state of faith' as opposed to 'sight.'[4] As the new skin forms under burnt skin—and yet even it is not finally clean, it too will peel off, it too has scars of the burns—so also the new integrated man of faith, who is being formed under the old nature, is one who is only being formed.

[1] 2 Cor. v. 17.
[2] Rom. viii. 1, 9, viii. 4.
[3] 1 John iii. 14; John v. 24.
[4] 2 Cor. v. 7.

The manner in which the contradiction is overcome in faith is: the Atonement. Atonement means: the re-discovery of man's original position, his restored position in God. This status is expressed as a condition or state; but only the status, not the state, is completed. The knight has been dubbed knight, his patent of nobility has been issued, but the knight is still, in his condition, a 'commoner,' his nobility has not yet permeated his whole nature; redemption is not to be separated from atonement, it is true, but it is not yet completed. Man still awaits the consummation of Redemption; this consummation would mean the transition from faith to sight, complete deliverance from this 'body of death,'[1] from all that is contradictory in our present state, from that participation in the curse which even the man who has been reconciled to God still bears; for as a member of the human race he shares in the sin of all. Redemption therefore can only be consummated on the other side of this earthly existence. Death, which stamps its mark upon this earthly life, does not belong to that life for which we have been created. This death must cease, there must be a form of existence which no longer, like this one, is controlled by the goal of death, and indeed in all its movements is moved by the approach of death. Life in communion with God is intended to be eternal life. Complete redemption means being set free from all that contradicts the eternal and the perfect. Eternal life is life as pure simultaneity.

He who stands in faith knows something of the pure simultaneity of life. That life in the Spirit, in love, the new life into which we are born again by the Word of God, is simultaneity; for it is 'peace with God.'[2] We are unable to live in the present because we are weighed down with the guilt of the past and anxiety for the future. The power which robs life of its complete simultaneity, and makes it something which is half in the past and half in the future, is un-peace, which proceeds from sin. For the 'natural' man, who has no part in Christ's life, life is either something which is already over, something which 'has been,' for which he mourns and which oppresses him, something fatal, which always makes his present already seem old, outlived, pre-determined, in which, so to speak, the

[1] Rom. vii. 24. [2] Rom. v. 1.

past merely continues to roll on farther; or, it is a 'not yet,' an everlasting planning and hoping, longing and expecting, straining after a goal, springing from branch to branch without stopping anywhere. In every present moment one is already ahead, one is already no longer there, because one is already at the next step. The only thing which would be real life—the full, tranquil present—*that* is absent. It has been crushed into powder between the upper and the nether millstone of the past and the future until nothing remains. The dream of Faust that he 'would like to say to the passing moment, stay awhile . . .' never becomes reality. The wine is turned immediately into vinegar, one does not like it any more, almost before the present has arrived, one is tired of it. But all this is changed where a soul has found God and 'has peace with Him.' And this peace brings joy in its train. Hence 'the Kingdom of God is peace and joy in the Holy Spirit.'[1] It is only the sick who wants to be different; only he who is not at home suffers from homesickness. But he who has found God is indeed at home. Hence too he is present for his neighbour. He has time for him, he can bear with him. Just as a mother can be at the bedside of her child without wanting anything else save simply to be there, so too genuine love can 'hold out' with his neighbour without wanting to hurry away. One must indeed no longer seek oneself. The heart which has been turned in upon itself and closed has been opened for the 'Thou.' Not only has one peace with God, but also peace with man, and this 'peace which passeth all understanding'[2] is pure simultaneity.

But—this peace is constantly threatened by un-peace, it has to struggle again and again to rise above the conflict; it does not yet *exist*, but it is *coming into being*. Hence the believer is aware of his own imperfection; therefore he looks for a final end where the struggle will cease and the victory be assured, where the present is a *nunc aeternum*: not standing still, but the full release and movement of life; 'love which wells up and springs forth' (Luther).[3] For it is not the struggle with death which is full life; but only beyond this conflict will life be full and complete. The fight with death is half life. But the man

[1] Rom. xiv. 17. [2] Phil. iv. 7. [3] WA. 36, 352 ff.

who is separated from God is able to deceive himself to such an extent that he imagines that this actual struggle between life and death is the true life. He does not believe that life is all the more living, the less it is affected by the contradiction. He confuses the tension which comes from the contradiction with the tension which is peculiar to life itself as such. Is then the sick man most alive because he is struggling with death? Does the artist create most freely who has to struggle most of all with his medium? What a cowardly lie—to regard the frustration of life as necessary for life! Love is life, which needs no contradiction to express itself in life, it is 'a stream of living water.' The Divine love is not the longing of a needy soul for fulfilment—that is *eros*, not *agape*. The Divine love is the welling up of the Perfect. It is the love of the Triune God which needs no other in order to love because in Himself He is all-sufficient love.

For this love, for this eternal Life man is destined. Only where this love—which no longer knows any contradiction—realizes itself, is the meaning, the truth of man, realized. Hence this love is not the goal of the individual but of humanity, as the final goal of the divine Creation as a whole, as the perfect Kingdom of God, the *regnum Gloriae*. The true man is not an individual *qua* individual, but he is only an individual in perfect communion with the other creatures through communion with the Creator Himself. Jesus Christ has not only grounded and revealed anew true man but true humanity. He is not only the Redeemer of the individual but He is the Head of the Body, the Church. By this is meant not an abstract idea of humanity, but the concrete community of humanity as both a universal and a personal reality. Christ is not the idea of the true humanity embodied, but He is the personal Founder of the true community of real human beings. He removes the antithesis between actuality and truth by removing the antithesis between the individual and humanity. For this is the Divine plan of Creation and of Redemption: 'to sum up all things in Christ as Head, the things in the heavens and the things upon the earth.'[1] *Omnia instaurare in Christo*—'that they all may be one.'[2]

[1] Eph. i. 10.

[2] John xvii. 21.

Faith in Jesus Christ is not an interpretation of the world, but it is participation in an event: in something which has happened, which is happening, and which is going to happen. These three dimensions of time are in faith indissolubly connected, but they are not one. We are not yet living in the eternal Now; even as believers we are still living in this time-era where the past, the present and the future fall apart. But we live in faith in the future and in the light which streams to us from the future which will be an eternal Now. We do not only believe in eternal life; in faith we already have our share in it. But we have our part in it only, in the strict sense of the word, for the moment. In faith we have part in it in so far as faith is really life in the Word of God, a new way of living, not merely a new view of the world and life. Faith is real communion with the Creator, hence it is not merely a direction towards something future, but it is also a fulfilled present; for the love of God *has* been shed abroad in our hearts through the Holy Spirit.[1] But this love is the 'substance' out of which eternal life is made, the essential nature of that *nunc aeternum*. 'But we have this treasure in earthen vessels.'[2] Hence faith is not merely present communion, but it is the expectation and the certainty of the final consummation of communion with God.

Love which is self-imparting is the content of that Primal Word which was in the beginning, in which we have been created, in which we have our life. This love is life. It is not an attribute added to life but it is life itself. Failure to love is failure to live. We know gradations of life from the natural point of view: even a plant lives, but it does not live in the same way as a living creature whose proper characteristic is spontaneity. Then does man live more like an animal? The answer is 'yes' and 'no.' Everyone recognizes that in man a higher degree of spontaneity is present, that freedom of the spirit by which he rises above and confronts all that exists, understands and determines himself.

But we hesitate to ascribe to man a higher kind of vitality because in man death has permeated life in a way which no other creature knows. Man is the only being who lives in

[1] Rom. v. 5. [2] 2 Cor. iv. 7.

conflict with himself, and is, so to speak, in a state of perpetual self-destruction. This destructive element arises at the same point where the special vitality of man arises: in his relation to God, upon which his freedom is based. The self-destroying use of freedom is that which the Bible calls sin. It is therefore in league with death, it is destruction of life. But it is so owing to the fact that it has turned the meaning of life into its opposite. Out of the life which delights to share, it has produced the greedy spirit; out of surrender, self-assertion; out of giving, taking; out of confidence, anxiety and the fear of life; out of the wonderful circle 'from God to the neighbour,' to the 'arrested development' of the self-centred, which indeed is no life but only death in life.

God alone is life in the absolute sense of the word: He 'who only hath immortality';[1] He who alone 'is love.'[2] In some sense or other that is a truth taught by many religions; but none of them know what love is. The possessive man's misunderstanding of his own nature lives also in them. They do not know that unfathomable love is self-giving. They may seek life in God; but they do not know that the truly divine life can only be reached when God Himself gives it to sinful man. They do not know this, because they do not know what has happened. It has only happened in Jesus Christ, and therefore one can only know it in Him. Through Him, however, it began alone to act in us. We are still living 'in the flesh,' in a way of existence which is determined by separation from God, which in faith, in principle, but not in its actual consequences, has been overcome. Death still clings to us; it still waits for us; we still have to pass through it. The absolute living life can only be where death, and all that is connected with death, has been purged away. 'The last enemy that shall be abolished is death.'[3] 'And death shall be no more; neither shall there be mourning, nor crying, nor pain, any more; the first things are passed away.'[4] 'That God may be all in all.'[5] 'For of Him and through Him and unto Him are all things. To Him be the glory for ever.'[6]

[1] I Tim. vi. 16. [2] I John iv. 16. [3] I Cor. xv. 26.
[4] Acts xxi. 4. [5] I Cor. xv. 28. [6] Rom. xi. 36.

APPENDICES

APPENDIX I

THE IMAGE OF GOD IN THE TEACHING OF THE BIBLE AND THE CHURCH

(1) THE doctrine of the *Imago Dei*, if one equates the phrase with the truth for which it stands, does not play a very important part in the Bible. That is true, however, not only of the *Imago* doctrine in particular, but of the doctrine of the Primitive State as a whole. The allusions to the Primitive State in the Old Testament are few, and even in the New Testament they are not very striking. For the New Testament, however, we may claim that, like the doctrine of Creation, it is a natural presupposition. Every Christian recognized the Canon of the Old Testament, which begins with the narrative of the Creation and of Paradise, as the Word of God. The objective significance of the doctrine of the Primitive State—and also that of the *Imago*—must be measured by the fact that the message of Redemption of the whole of the New Testament is retrospective in character; although Redemption is not *only* restoration, it is always also, and primarily, re-storation, renewal. The fact that God created man good and that man is now evil: these two statements are the presupposition of the message of the New Testament, a presupposition which can never be removed from New Testament thought, and one which is always operative.

(2) The doctrine of the *Imago* in the Old Testament is explicitly stated only in the following three passages: Gen. i. 26 ff.; v. 1; ix. 6; to them we must add two references in the Apocrypha: Wisdom ii. 23, and Ecclesiasticus xvii. 3. In all these passages the *Imago Dei* describes a dignity conferred on man, one which is somehow like God (*kidemutenu*), which distinguishes man from all other creatures. Whether this dignity is loosely defined as the 'Elohim-nature which is proper to man,' the fact that man 'is a creature whose nature does not originate from below,' a reflection of the divine glory (cf. Rad on εἰκών in Kittel's *Wörterbuch*), or whether it means the self-

conscious, self-determined personality, the free 'I,' the dignity of man as man (thus Dillmann, Oehler, König, and recently Eichrodt in their works on the theology of the Old Testament), or whether it says nothing at all about the nature of man, but merely about his power of dominion and his dominating position in the realm of nature (Köhler in his *Alttestamentliche Theologie*), is not a matter of decisive importance for our problem. For, so far as I can see, all modern expositors of the Old Testament are agreed in this, namely, that the *Imago Dei* describes man as he now is, and that it is never applied to a way of human existence lost through the Fall of Man. The doctrine of the Reformation cannot appeal to the Old Testament, while the Catholic doctrine, on the other hand, at least so far as its exposition of *imago* = *Zälem* is concerned, has the Old Testament more for it than against it. 'The Old Testament knows nothing of the idea that henceforth the image of God in man has been lost' (v. Rad, op. cit., p. 390). Likewise there seems to be general agreement in the view that the fact that man has been made in the Image of God, is primarily expressed—even if it does not consist in this—in man's position of pre-eminence which he now holds in the created world (now—empirically—) as is expressed in Psalm viii (so also Cremer RE³ 5, 114). Luther too—although he himself created a different idea of the *Imago Dei*—had recognized this state of affairs (see below, p. 503). Judaism, also, interpreted the passages in question in this sense, although among the Rabbis it was debated whether individual human beings might have lost the *Imago* through special wickedness (Kittel in his *Wörterbuch*, p. 391).

(3) The *Imago* is also mentioned in the New Testament in a similar sense in two passages: 1 Cor. xi. 7 and James iii. 9. 'The man,' whether a Christian or not, is the bearer of the *Imago*—'the image and glory of God' (1 Cor.)—and for that reason man should never be cursed (Jas.). Indeed, in Acts xvii. 28, Paul even summons the heathen as witnesses to this relation with God of all human beings; for in point of fact, the *Imago Dei*, understood in this sense, is the most important testimony to the revelation of the Creation, and—since, as such, it is not

destroyed—is the starting-point for a 'natural' knowledge of God. In the New Testament, however, in addition to these passages there are some others which are of decisive importance, which give an entirely new meaning to the idea of the *Imago*. The most definite are the following: Rom. viii. 29; 2 Cor. iii. 18; Eph. iv. 24; Col. iii. 10. In this connexion Cremer (op. cit.) rightly points also to the passages in the New Testament where sonship to God is spoken of as likeness to God, of the 'imitation' of God, of 'being holy as He is holy.' Thus, with the idea of 'sonship,' or of being 'children of God,' the *Imago* doctrine, especially in connexion with the doctrine of the original 'sonship' of Jesus Christ, comes into the very centre of the New Testament message. 'To be like Him' (1 John iii. 2) becomes absolutely the sum-total of the hope of salvation, and thus of the message of the New Testament as a whole. From this point of view alone, therefore, can we understand why the concept of the *Imago* has gained such an outstanding position in Christian doctrine, and especially in that of the theologians of the Reformation. In the New Testament—as has already been shown above, in the text—through the relation of the *Imago* to the Primal *Imago*, Jesus Christ, to the Word of God, and thus to faith, the concept of the *Imago* is torn out of its Old Testament structural or morphological rigidity, and the dynamic understanding of the *Imago*, as being-in-the-Word-of-God through faith, is established, which is the basic idea of my whole work. In my detailed exposition of 2 Cor. iii. 18 (above, p. 96), I think that I have made the Biblical basis of my view quite clear.

(4) Now the presupposition of this new doctrine of the *Imago* —that is, the doctrine of the New Testament—in contrast to that of the Old Testament, is the following: the fact that man has been created in the Image of God has been lost, that it must be renewed in man, so that the whole work of Jesus Christ in reconciliation and redemption may be summed up in this central conception of the renewal and consummation of the Divine Image in man.

The contrast, however, which certainly exists between the understanding of this truth in the Old Testament and in the

New—which, as we have seen, is even continued into the New Testament itself—makes two things clear:

(*a*) that here, as elsewhere, a Fundamentalist appeal to the Bible, such as is being renewed to-day, will not help us; for the Catholic doctrine, so far as the doctrine of the *Imago* is concerned, has as much right to be called a Biblical doctrine, in this sense, as the doctrine of the Reformation;

(*b*) that already in the Bible itself the problem with which we are wrestling in a systematic manner, lies there unsolved: how, namely, the *Imago Dei*, in the formal sense, (this is how von Oettingen, before me, describes in his *Dogmatik*, II, Part I, p. 385, the Old Testament conception and the patristic and Catholic conception of the *Imago* respectively), that is, in the sense of the special endowments of human nature, as they can be perceived even in the sinful human being (personal being, dominion over the other creatures, reason, free choice in the moral sense) is to be related to the *Imago* in the material sense, that is, in the sense of the fact that life is determined by the Word of God, in the sense of the *justitia originalis*, to which man is renewed by Jesus Christ, which will only be consummated by the final Redemption.

Even in the thought of Paul, as we have seen, the ideas lie alongside of one another, disconnected, or at least not clearly connected. Even Luther perceived the difference between the two ways of putting this truth in the Scriptures. In what he dictated for his Lectures on Genesis, on Gen. i. 26, he writes:

'*Duplex est similitudo: publica et privata. Paulus loquitur de similitudine privata, sed textus videtur sonare de publica: similem nobis i.e. scil. in gubernandis rebus. Haec similitudo manet sub peccato adhuc, non abstulit eam similitudinem ab Adam.* But Paul goes further: *eam similitudinem abstulit peccatum, scil bonitatem, justitiam. Ego autem proprie puto loqui Mosen de similitudine publica.* A woman is like our Lord God, but she is like Him not with breasts or navel, *sed quod habet dominium in familiam. De hac imagine loquitur Paulus in Cor: vir est gloria et imago Dei. In summa hic locus vult*, fish, bird, etc., ought to have a master, but the same should not be a fish or a bird *sed homo. Sicut ego sum deus et dominus hominum et nihil habeo illarum rerum quas ipsi habent*, have no noses, eyes, etc.' (WA. 42, 51).

Later expositors have not had the same feeling for exegesis and the same courage as Luther: henceforth *Imago* must always mean in the Bible what dogmatic orthodoxy chooses.

Therefore it is also incorrect to say that the later differences 'have their basis in the fact that the doctrine of the nature of man as made in the image of God involuntarily became the doctrine of the Primitive State' (Cremer, op. cit.); for the connexion with the Primitive State is also present in the distinctively New Testament doctrine of the *Imago*. Here we are really concerned with 'regaining the image of God in accordance with the Creation' as 'identical with the restoration of communion with Christ' (Kittel, op. cit.). Thus the problem can neither be solved nor shelved by an appeal to the Bible, it is rather a standard example of the necessity for systematic theology alongside of Biblical theology.

(5) We cannot go into the question of the development of the *Imago* doctrine down to Irenaeus in any detail. The material for this has been fully collected and well sifted in Struker: *Die Gottebenbildlichkeit des Menschen in der urchristlichen Literatur der ersten zwei Jahrhunderte*, 1913. Its strong point is that it brings in Gnostic and Jewish literature; its weak point is the view that philosophical ideas only become operative in Christian literature after Irenaeus (p. 2). I would simply call attention to the following four points in this book:

(*a*) The concept of the *Imago* has not yet any place in the body of doctrine as a whole, and—apart from the Gnostics—is not often mentioned.

(*b*) It is used almost exclusively in the formal sense, *imago* = the *humanum* (reason, freedom, speech, special position of man, etc.). The extreme on this side is represented by a sentence in Melito: *Deus autem omni tempore vivens currit in mente tua; mens enim tua est ipsa eius similitudo* (essentially based upon the invisibility of the spirit),

Apol., c. 6, in Struker, p. 42. The comment of Struker, 'The idea *Deus currit* etc. has some resemblance to the formulae of Stoicism,' is a very mild term to apply to a state of affairs which is not to the liking of a Catholic author.

(*c*) At the opposite extreme stands that which is said about the *Imago* in the *Epistle to Diognetus*; it is related entirely to the self-imparting love of God. Struker, p. 14.

(*d*) The distinction between the *Imago* and the *Similitudo* which appears henceforth, from the time of Irenaeus onwards, and becomes the standard, springs from Valentinian Gnosticism (but in Irenaeus it is otherwise interpreted). It also plays a part in the Pseudo-Clementines.

(6) The creator of the doctrine of the *Imago* which the Church was henceforth to recognize as the standard one, was—as has already been indicated in the text—Irenaeus, the first great genuine theologian, and possibly the most Scriptural of all the theologians of the early Church. We might almost call him the 'Fundamentalist' among the early Fathers. In spite of this, however, even in his thinking the spirit of Greek rationalism was at work, and precisely in his doctrine of the *imago-similitudo*, which otherwise represents an important theological achievement (cf. on this point the careful study of the Catholic Klebba: *Die Anthropologie des heiligen Irenaeus* in *Kirchengeschichtliche Studien*, Münster, 1894, which is a valuable work, in spite of the fact that its point of view is entirely Catholic). His anthropology is Gnosticism purified by Scripture, with a strong element of general Greek philosophy. The first important point, and indeed the decisive element in his doctrine, is the conception of the *Imago Dei* as man's natural endowment of reason. For Irenaeus certainly God Himself is Reason proper, hence the rational nature of man is a *participatio Dei*. But that view does not go further than the Stoic idea of the human rational nature: (Human) reason is conceived wholly in the sense of Greek rationalism, as something which is intelligible in itself —not as something which is actually related to God. The starting-point is the Aristotelian distinction between man and the creatures which are not endowed with reason. Man has

been 'created as gifted with reason and accordingly like God, as free in his will, and his own master, the cause of himself' (IV. 4, 3). But Irenaeus is too much of a Christian and a Biblical theologian to be satisfied with this rationalistic idea of the *Imago*. Hence he combines it with a second idea, which, in connexion with Gen. i. 26 (although in a complete distortion of the meaning of the passage), as *Similitudo* (ὁμοίωσις) he sets over against the *Imago* (εἰκών). The *Imago* means the human nature which cannot be lost; the *Similitudo* means man's original relation to God which may be lost, and, since Adam, has been lost. This is mediated through the Divine Spirit. As it only emerges, rightly, in Christ, and not in Adam ('it was not yet shown, for the *Logos* was still invisible, after whose image man came into being, and therefore he so easily lost the likeness,' V. 16, 2), it is related to soteriology rather than to the doctrine of Creation, and in general is conceived rather as the goal of development than as the Primitive State. Since Irenaeus does not conceive the first man as an almost perfect being (as was done later by Augustine and after him by the Reformers (cf. for instance *De civitate Dei*, XII. 23; XIII. 19–21, and *Luther's Commentary on Genesis*, WA. 42, 46 ff.) but rather as a big child, it is difficult to say in what the loss which was caused by the Fall is supposed to have consisted. Man could not lose the *Imago* which was his nature, but the *Similitudo* was only present in germ, and was rather a promise for the future than a present reality. In any case, this distinction implies the standard Catholic doctrine of nature and supernature, although the word 'supernature' is not used until the rise of Scholasticism (in Augustine primarily as *gratia* in contrast to Nature, here already the concept of the *adiutorium*; it is only modern Catholicism which is able to speak explicitly and emphatically of the 'concrete supernatural gift of God,' Bartmann: *Dogmatik*, I, 290). At the same time we ought to note that this distinction between the *Imago* and the *Similitudo* makes it possible for Catholic theology to ascribe to unredeemed man complete freedom of the will, since it belongs to the *Imago* which cannot be lost, as is also done by the Greek Fathers quite openly, and by the later Latin Fathers and the Scholastics more or less under cover of Augustinian formulas.

(7) Augustine's doctrine of the *Imago* is distinguished from that of Irenaeus first of all by the conception of the Primitive State as a state of complete Perfection—not only in regard to the *justitia originalis*, but also in view of man's physical, psychical and spiritual endowments. Since, however, he took over the distinction of Irenaeus between the *Imago* and the *Similitudo*, he was obliged to introduce the idea of *vulneratio in naturalibus* which, although since then it has been incorporated into Catholic doctrine, plays a very uncertain part. Secondly, in Augustine we now see, under the influence of his new ideas on Grace, a new conception of the *Imago* being formed, as it were beneath the covering of the old idea, which was bound finally to explode the old traditional dual schema. The rational structural idea of the *Imago* is replaced by the actual and pneumatic idea. The human spirit is increasingly moulded according to the image of God, the more it allows itself to be determined by the divine Truth. (*De Trinitate* 12, 7.) It is not the threefold character of the psychological functions as such which is the image of the Trinity, but it is the fact that the spirit, by means of this structure, is reminded of God, understands Him and loves Him (ibid., 14, 2). It is rightful self-love if the spirit loves God, through whose working the divine image not merely exists but is also renewed (ibid., 13). Hence this divine image can be almost (even if never wholly) extinguished (ibid., 4). Here certainly the Biblical truth is coloured by Neo-Platonism, but Augustine has grasped the central problem: that man's being as a whole, both original and fallen, should be understood from the point of view of being-in-the-Word-of-God. The elements which *De Trinitate* provides for the solution of the problem have never been adequately recognized by theology, because the problem itself has never been seen aright. Especially the conception of love as that which unites the original picture and its reflection, and the relation of love to the Divine Trinity on the one hand, to the human structure of the mind on the other, is here developed in a way that has never been done anywhere else in Christian theology, not even in Luther.

(8) In principle Scholasticism did not introduce anything new, but through its Aristotelianism it developed the distinction

between the *Imago* = *anima rationalis* and the *similitudo* = *donum superadditum supernaturale* into a universal system of Nature and Supernature. In so doing it intensified the dualism of Irenaeus, by making a sharp distinction between the state of nature and the state of supernature (in Irenaeus the idea was rather that of elements in the same state which could be distinguished conceptually from one another) and to this state of *pura naturalia*—thus, of the *Imago*—a certain element of concupiscence was also added, which emphasized the fact that by sin man did not lose the *Imago*, but only the *dona superaddita*. Above all, however, Scholasticism developed systematically the Aristotelian rationalistic and individualistic conception of the *Imago* as *anima rationalis*, and in so doing finally brought out the full meaning of the ancient heritage. For Scholasticism it is rationalism, not supra-rationalism, which is the decisive element. Scholastic theology in part itself drew the following conclusions from its *Imago* doctrine, and in part prepared the way for them:

(*a*) a rational natural theology is possible;
(*b*) a rational natural ethic is possible;
(*c*) free will has been left to man;
(*d*) good works are possible also apart from grace;
(*e*) thence there arose necessarily the condemnation of Augustinian doctrine in the doctrine of Bajus, for instance, of the statement (27) *Liberum arbitrium sine gratiae adiutorio non nisi ad peccatum valet.*

(9) It was an act of far-reaching significance (indeed a history of thought of the Reformation might be written from this point of view) when Luther broke through the tradition of thirteen hundred years and removed the division between the *Imago* and the *Similitudo* by the declaration: *Similitudo et imago Dei est vera et perfecta Dei notitia, summa Dei dilectio, aeterna vita, aeterna leticia, aeterna securitas* (WA. 42, 46). With the one sentence: 'If the *Imago* consists in that power of the soul (in the *anima rationalis*) then it would follow that Satan too would be formed according to the image of God, since in him these natural qualities are far stronger' (ibid.), he breaks with the

whole tradition and returns to the New Testament (in the same context stands his distinction between the *Imago publica* and *privata*!). The *Imago Dei* is the same as the *justitia originalis.* The nature of man is again understood theologically and not philosophically, man as man is once more a 'theological' being, that is, as man he can only be understood in the light of the Word of God. That is Luther's achievement. That is his main concern. For himself, it is true, the negative and polemical aspect is in the foreground; that is, the rejection of the conclusions (*liberum arbitrium*) which Catholic theology drew from its *Imago* doctrine (which were on the lines of indeterminism) (ibid., p. 45). It is easy to understand that this led Luther to follow the Augustinian view of the wonderful, perfect endowments of Adam (ibid., *intellectus fuit purissimus.* Eagles' eyes . . . *potuisse uno verbo imperare Leoni* etc.). Now all the more difficult —as has already been shown in the text—was the question: How is the *humanitas* of fallen man to be explained? All that could be said was: 'Relics of the *Imago.*' Everywhere we see how reluctantly Luther admits this—but what else can he do? We see Joh. Gerhard wrestling with the same difficulty, only in still greater measure. The definition of the *Imago* as *justitia originalis* and—following from that—the doctrine of the complete loss of the *Imago*, is always followed again and again by the painful addition: down to a 'small relic' which remained. But this little relic becomes the bearer of great things. Upon this relic is based the whole *humanitas*, and with it that which man still has of freedom, the *justitia civilis*, the *naturalis cognitio Dei*, which already plays a considerable part in the thought of Gerhard (*quod libenter concedimus, est enim alique naturalis dei notitia, sed languida et imperfecta, novit ratio aliquam particulam legis divinae, potest ex κοιναῖς ἐννοίαις et libro naturae discere, quod sit deus, quod justus sit quod sapiens.* . . . V, 140), the *dictamen conscientiae* (*est particula quaedam imaginis divinae quam in nobis ipsis vereri debemus*! IV, 292), and finally (at the end of the whole chapter, op. cit.): This relic has been still preserved to us by God, in order that these truths which have still been left to us may be "*rectrices externae disciplinae qua velut paedagogia quadam utitur ad instaurationem imaginis suae partam nobis per Christum*"—thus here even the doctrine of the point of contact is present, questionable as the argument for it may be. J. Gerhard is then also aware that there are two possible conceptions of the *Imago*, one of which (formal) he sees represented by the Calvinists; but, although he does not absolutely reject this, he describes it as *non principalis pars imaginis* (IV, 292). In this he was right—but in saying this the problem was not solved; it had not even been seen.

(10) In essentials the same position is taken by Calvinistic theology, at least in so far as it is determined by Calvin. But now it is in accordance with the special historical mission of Calvinistic theology that—within the common doctrine of the Reformers of the *justitia originalis* and of the *corruptio totalis*—the concern of the *humanitas* is perceived more clearly and urgently than within Lutheran theology, without, on that account, becoming Humanistic.

Calvin follows Luther, since in principle he ascribes the *humanitas*—which characterizes even the empirically fallen man—to the 'relic' of the *Imago*. At the same time he 'solves' the problem—like the Bible itself—simply by making use of a dual conception of the *Imago*. Hence the fluctuations of his statements about the *Imago* and its significance. The fact that he suggests that the *anima immortalis*—which also belongs to the sinner—is derived from the *Imago* ought not to be regarded as a peculiarly Calvinistic view, for the Lutherans also took this for granted; and, even when Luther was in conflict with Rome, he never forgot this (WA. 42, 63). It may be said, however, that Calvin developed the idea of the formal *Imago*, *imago* = *humanitas* (that is, that which belongs to man as man, whether man in his origin or man after the Fall), in a very casual manner: 'We have ideas of justice, integrity and honesty. . . . The seat of these ideas must be a spirit . . . the image of God reaches out to all in which the nature of man surpasses that of every other species . . . the *Imago* includes within itself all that has any relation to the spiritual and eternal life' (*Institutio*, I, 15, 1–6). In this connexion he mentions with approval Plato's idea that the soul is a picture of the divine (ibid., 6). He also united the ideas of reason with that of the spiritual *Imago*: 'The more that a man tries to come near to God, the more he shows that he is endowed with reason' (ibid.).

But he still maintains that the original *Imago* was not 'wholly extinguished and destroyed, it is true, but yet that it is so entirely defaced that all that is left is terribly deformed' (ibid., 4). Even he does not extricate himself from this dilemma: the reason belongs to the *Imago*, which (in the main) is destroyed, and yet we are still rational creatures. He 'solves' it with the suggestion that we have a defaced reason (II, 2, 12 ff). But since Calvin cannot help recognizing reason in its own sphere, he asserts the principle: the higher the reason aspires, the more it errs (at this point, again, he is in essential agreement with Luther). Neither Luther nor Calvin has solved the problem: How is the central doctrine of the loss of the *Imago* (= *justitia originis*) to be combined with the recognition of the fact that the *humanum* which cannot be, and has not been lost (freedom, reason, conscience, language, etc.), belongs to the *Imago Dei*? In the attempt to answer this question Augustine has gone further than the Reformers, although, on the other hand, he had not such a profound understanding of the nature of the *justitia originalis*, being in the Word of God.

(11) The theologians of the post-Reformation period did not contribute anything essential towards the solution of the problem; they depended wholly on Luther, Calvin and Augustine, and soon began to revert to the twofold scholastic and patristic conception; this process was facilitated by the fact of the re-acceptance of the concept *Imago* = *anima rationalis*, the rationalistic Aristotelian idea of reason.

Later theologians, as a rule, have not understood what this question involves. Their whole attention has been absorbed in the questions raised by modern science; on the one hand, some of them try to save an impossible doctrine of the Primitive State by means of apologetics, while others abandon the historical form altogether as impossible, and in so doing they lose the meaning of the doctrine of the Primitive State as well.

Vilmar (*Dogmatik*) develops a picture of the Primitive State which is wholly free from the influence of historical and scientific criticism; his view is in entire accordance with Lutheran orthodoxy—from his own premisses he rightly defends the Primitive State as genuine being against every attempt to reduce it to a mere 'determination' ('a form of being complete in every direction,' I, p. 340); this, however, inevitably raises the question: What then distinguishes an existence of this kind from that of the redeemed? That is, in what did the *posse peccare* consist?

Frank (*System der christlichen Wahrheit*) takes the opposite line; he understands the *Imago* in a purely formal way in the sense of possessing selfhood, and the 'filling of this form with moral and religious content'—the *justitia originalis*—as something which is added to the nature of man, and further is only recognized as embryonic existence (p. 349 ff.), and thus goes back directly to Irenaeus.

Von Oettingen distinguishes the 'so-called "formal"—that is, that which belongs essentially to the form of man's being, and is on that account impossible to lose, and is actually not lost—aspect of likeness to God because made in His image' (II, Part I, 363), the 'spiritually personal nature of man' from the 'so-called ethico-material aspect of being made in the image of God' (p. 373)—which further he only regards as a tendency (*Anlage*) of primitive man. To this extent he too accepts the dual division of Irenaeus. Since, however, he relates both to the self-imparting love of God, he comes very near to a solution of the problem, though without actually doing so, and indeed without being actually aware of the problem at all. Kähler also begins with the personality of man as 'being of the same nature with God,' and describes this as the form of 'being made in the image of God' which cannot be lost. From this he distinguishes the 'task' of 'filling it with the corresponding content' (*Die Wissenschaft der christlichen Lehre*, pp. 270 ff.); thus he too simply seems to return to the twofold schema of Irenaeus. But the further development of his thought shows that at least dimly he has discerned the problem, and that he wishes to regard the formal and the material as both derived from one common principle, namely, from the divine will of Love, and —this is the essential point—that he already regards the formal element as an actual relation to the divine will of love, or at least as a disposition thereto. In particular, his emphasis upon the historical nature of human existence as such, works against the traditional rationalism in the definition of personal being, and places him among those thinkers who are on the path towards the new understanding. Schlatter (*Das christliche Dogma*), on the other hand, has no interest in the problem of the Primitive State, nor in that of the *Imago Dei*; he dismisses it with the remark that 'no certain perception leads us back to man's origin.' What he says further about the historical conception of the Primitive State is absolutely correct (p. 278), namely, that a long period of pre-history preceded the history known to us, but that at one point in history the human 'I' was present as something new. But this does not exhaust the meaning of the concern which lies in the idea of the *Imago Dei*; it is strange that a man who has given more thought to the fifth chapter of Romans than many others should overlook this.

The attempts to deal with the problem on the part of liberal theology have already been treated in the text.

The new understanding of the problem of anthropology begins with Ferdinand Ebner, Martin Buber, and Friedrich Gogarten; Heidegger has only made a very remote contribution to this question—essentially as one mediating the thought of Kierkegaard. Since, however, none of them have wrestled with the problem of the *Imago Dei* in the narrower sense, I must here content myself with expressing my very deep gratitude to these pioneers (cf. my small contribution in the *Ferdinand Ebner Gedenkschrift*, Verlag F. Pustet). A good critical survey of these works which I regard as preparing the way for the new solution which is attempted in this book, is given by the Swedish writer Cullberg, in his book: *Das Du und die Wirklichkeit* (Uppsala, 1933).

(12) In conclusion, a word about the relation between the view represented in this book and that in *Natur und Gnade*. I assume that what I stand for both here and in that work is exactly the same, but here I have tried to say the same truth in different words, because it is evident that to a very large extent this theological generation is deficient in that logical training which is necessary for the understanding of such a concept. Otherwise how could a theologian make the objection that 'after all, my conception of the formal *Imago* turns out

to be something with a good deal of content!' 'Formal' and 'material' are relative ideas. What the ancients, for instance, called 'formal freedom' is certainly something which has a great deal of content; but it is 'formal' in view of that with which they were then concerned: the power to be righteous in the sight of God. My concept of the formal *Imago* is formed on the analogy of this concept of formal freedom; it describes the human as human, the imperishable structure of man's being which cannot be affected by the conflict between the Original Creation and Sin. But in opposition to Barth, and in agreement with all the previous theologians of the Church, and also with the Reformers, I conceive this formal element, man's being, as something which is not only far from being a commonplace, but, on the contrary, as very relevant for theology; the Reformers expressed this truth in the rather dubious notion of the 'relic' of the *Imago*; and I, on the other hand, express this as a dialectical relation between the *Imago*-origin and the humanity-of-the-sinner. The content of my concept 'formal *Imago*' is exactly the same as that of this 'relic' of the *Imago* in the thought of the Reformers.

Although in using this terminology I am making no innovation—in addition to those who have been named above I could also name other precursors in this sphere—I have now renounced the use of this expression 'formal *Imago*.' First of all, in order to avoid giving further occasion for the misunderstanding—into which Schlink and others have already fallen—that I defend the Catholic doctrine of a double *Imago* (*imago-similitudo*), whereas I regard this doctrine as the fatal, fundamental error of all the anthropology of the Church, and thus reject it; and secondly, in order not to give further offence to theologians who are unable to understand that something 'formal' may have a rich content, and even theological relevance.

Over against the Catholic doctrine and that of Irenaeus (which, as I have shown, many Lutherans have taken over from orthodox Scholasticism) I maintain: there are not two elements—an *Imago* which can never be lost, and a *Similitudo* which can be lost, of which the one is a natural quality, while the other is an actual relation with God; but the nature of man is to be understood as a *unity*, from the point of view of man's relation to God, without the distinction between nature and super-nature; this unified 'theological' nature is perverted by sin, but in this perversion it still always reveals the traces of the image of God in the human structure, so that it is actually the formal 'human' element which betrays man's lost origin.

Over against the doctrine of the Reformation I maintain: my whole aim is to renew their fundamental conception—which both the orthodox Lutherans and Barth have lost, although in different ways—namely, that man as a whole must be understood from the standpoint of God, and therefore that man's being as sinner is man's being in a corrupt form, but that, for that very reason, even the *humanitas* which still exists must be understood in the light of the original image of God, or of man's relation with God.

Thus, like Luther, I teach that this present *humanitas* is a mere 'relic' of the original *humanitas*, but that, for that very reason, that element in it which is inalienable—that which distinguishes man as man—is not a *profanum*, nor a trifle, but that it should be understood only from the point of view of the original *Imago*, and thus in a theological and Christological manner.

The present *humanitas* is not, as Catholicism teaches, the truly original human nature (since all that it lacks is the *dona superadditum*), nor is it, as Barth teaches, a secular matter which is of no interest for theology; but, precisely in its merely formal character, it is that which man has retained of his original relation with God. But it is not sufficient to describe this element that remains—as the Reformers do—merely quantitatively as a 'relic'; it ought to be understood dialectically: namely, as the present structure of man's being which is based on law, dialectically related to the Gospel, which, firstly, has some power of creating order in human life, and, secondly, necessarily preserves man in his relation with God—although it is perverted; which, thirdly, serves the Gospel as a point of contact; which, however, at the same time, fourthly, is the point of supreme contradiction and that which repels. I have never taught that there was any other point of contact than this dialectical one; for the past twelve years (see my article on the Law in *Theologische Blätter*, 1925!) the central point of my theological thought—which has been unchanged—just as it is that of the theology of the Reformers, has been, and is, the dialectic of the Law and the Gospel.

APPENDIX II

ON THE DIALECTIC OF THE LAW

'It is the opinion of St. Paul that in Christendom both by preachers and Christians a certain difference should be taught and understood between the Law and faith, between the Command and the Gospel. . . . For this is the highest art in Christendom, which we ought to know, and where one does not know this thou canst not be thoroughly sure of the difference between a Christian and a pagan or a Jew. For everything hangs upon this difference.' (Luther, WA. 36, 9.) At the present day, too, 'everything hangs upon' this difference; this present work should be a testimony to this. But this distinction is still, as it was in the days when Luther had to wrestle with the Antinomians, the 'highest art,' and the confusion is great.

Karl Barth has ventured to reverse the traditional order and to say: the Gospel and the Law. For in the Gospel 'the Law is hidden and enclosed as in the Ark.' 'In order to know what tha Law is' we must 'first of all know what the Gospel is, and not the other way round' (*Evangelium und Gesetz*, p. 3). Then were the Reformers mistaken when they so obstinately and plainly insisted on the reverse order? Or must we perhaps with Otto Wolff (*Gesetz und Evangelium*, *Evangelische Theologie*, 1936, pp. 136 ff.) play off Luther against Luther, 'illuminated by the most original intentions of Luther' (p. 139), in order to get rid of the traditional 'dualism in which *justitia* and *gratia* are either left side by side, or the one comes after the other,' in favour of a 'creative, living and unified synthesis of *justitia* and *gratia*' (p. 143)?

The concern of Barth and Thurneysen (*Die Bergpredigt*) is clear and fundamentally Scriptural. 'How could the sovereignty of Jesus Christ be proclaimed without the proclamation as such being a summons to obedience?' (Barth, op. cit., p. 10.) 'The very faith in the *articulis stantis et cadentis ecclesiae*, in the word of the justification of the sinner through the atonement made by the Blood of Christ, means purification, sanctification, renewal, or it means nothing at all' (Barth, p. 11). The one concern is the Word of Jesus Christ, and nothing else at all, and in that God's summons to us is, in point of fact, 'hidden and enclosed.' Would anyone have anything to say against this argument, from the point of view of the Bible? The fact that in the writings of Barth and Thurneysen we do not find sufficient emphasis laid upon the renewing work of the Holy Spirit, which creates real—though rudimentary and imperfect —obedience, is another question. Nothing can be taken away from this their main Christocentric thesis. This is the message of the Bible: the message of the grace of God in Jesus Christ, which, as such, lays claim on our obedience. Who would question the fact that the Reformers knew this too, and that they taught it with such power and conviction that we can even learn it afresh from then! Why, then, did they still say: the Law and the Gospel? Why did Luther in his Disputations against the Antinomians repeat this order of words hundreds of times, and why did he defend this with all the force of his theological power and authority? Is it possible that we can really know better than he what he 'originally' intended? Or perhaps, as so often happens in discussions: are we missing the point entirely because we are using the same words with a quite different meaning?

In reality, Luther means something fundamentally different from Karl Barth, when he speaks of the 'Law,' and his whole doctrine will only become intelligible to one who knows what Luther meant by 'Law.' He alone will understand why Luther reckons the law among the 'powers of wrath,' why he so often classes it with death and the devil. He is, namely, always speaking of the law of which Paul says explicitly, that it has been abolished by Jesus Christ—'If ye are under the Spirit ye are no longer under the law'; 'we are free from the law and have died to the law.' Christ has come to 'ransom us from the curse of the law'—Christ is the 'end of the law.' Thus when Luther speaks of the Law, he is speaking of something with which the Christian, as a believer, has no further connexion, of which, from the standpoint of the Gospel, one can only speak in antithesis—without on that account becoming an *ἄνομος*—just as St. Paul does.

Barth, too, knows of this law, 'which Paul—not universally, but as a rule—calls the *Nomos*, against whose "righteousness" and "bondage" and "curse" he warns his churches most urgently . . . of which it has been said, and must be said: either wholly the law and then death, or wholly the Gospel and then life. . . . It is the law which has been dishonoured and rendered void by sin, which with the power of the wrath of God still is and remains His law' (p. 25). But while Barth passes on swiftly, as though there were very little to say about this law, Paul, on account of this very law, wrote the Epistles to the *Romans* and to the *Galatians*; and the whole of Luther's theological thought revolves round this 'law' in particular, and its dialectical relation to our Gospel. Luther only begins to think deeply about the Law at the point where Barth stops.

Now this *Nomos* is not something which one can easily pass over as a simple, even if unfortunate, misunderstanding; it is not something which merely concerned the Jews of that day; but this law is the fundamental principle of the natural self-understanding of man. It does not matter whether it is the Jewish Law, or the law written in man's heart; it is all the same (Rom. i and ii); in any case it is clearly opposed to the righteousness of faith (Rom. iii), although 'in some way or other' it is God's own law. For this very reason, because it stands in this antithesis to the righteousness of God, and yet at the same time is God's Law, there exists between the Law and the Gospel a remarkable dialectical relation.

The Jewish Law as such has no longer much interest for Luther. But he is intensely interested in that which Barth would fain ignore, that is: the law which is written in the heart of man, which he also describes by the phrase *lex naturae*, which comes—through the patristic literature—from the Stoics. *Neque tamen Moses autor fuit decalogi. Sed a condito mundo decalogus fuit inscriptus omnium hominum mentibus* (*Disputationen*, Drews, 378). Indeed, this law is the criterion of the law, valid for us also. in the Old Testament. 'Where now Moses' law and the law of nature are one thing, there remaineth the law and it is not removed outwardly, save spiritually through faith' (WA. 18, 81).

Thus the problem is posed of the Categorical Imperative which indwells reason; for the 'law of nature,' for Luther, is always a law of obligation, even where it meets us as the Word of God in an order of creation. '*In omni iure* must the *debet* be' (cf. E. Wolff: *Natürliches Gesetz und Gesetz Christi bei Luther*, *Evangelische Theologie*, 1935, p. 317). In the Disputations in particular Luther again and again sets up this equation (for instance, pp. 378, 337 ff., 312, etc.). He is concerned to establish an antithetical but immovable dialectical relation between the immanental self-understanding and the Christian revelation, corresponding to the antithetical dialectical relation between the natural (and legalistic), and the revealed knowledge of God, or, to use the phrase of Kierkegaard, between the immanental 'religion A' and the 'paradoxical' Christian faith.

This law and sin belong together. It is true of course that the law is placed in our hearts from the Creation, *lex nobiscum nata* (*Disputationen*, 483). But the fact that we understand ourselves from this law, instead of from the generous will of God as Creator, is not due to the Creation but to sin. Sin in its centre is precisely this legalistic self-understanding, with its self-justification of man. Hence the effect of this law is bondage, curse and death—again: not of the law as such, but of the self-understanding which is derived from it. Therefore the law as the point of reference of this natural self-understanding of man belongs to the 'powers of wrath.' It does not reveal the grace but the wrath of God (*revelatio irae*, *Disputationen* 306; 336).

If, however, that were all there is to say about it, it would be a simple matter—that is, just as simple as Barth would like to make it out to be. But it is not so simple as all that. For we have heard that this law 'is not removed through faith.' This law is not a plain and simple entity, but, in the most rigid sense of the word, it is ambiguous. It has a dialectical relation to the revelation of grace. Of *this* law it is said, that it is *ostensio peccati seu revelatio irae; sunt termines convertibiles*, or correlates, as we would say (op. cit., 337). Hence this law plays a part in the process of salvation. It is not to be valued simply negatively. It is and remains the divine factor in the lost situation of the sinner. It accuses and disquiets man, it 'accuses thee through thine own conscience' (WA. 36, 386). Precisely that comes from God, although it certainly is not

God's *opus proprium* but His *opus alienum*, just as the wrath of God shows us not the true face of God but the face of God altered by our sin.

This law—which everyone knows to some extent, even if not very clearly—(for instance, see *Disputationen*, 337–9)—has primarily a secular meaning. Its *usus primus* is *coercere delicta, atque haec coercitio est mundi seu carnis justitia quae habet suum praemium et gloriam. Sed coram Deo nihil est* (*Disputationen*, 365). By means of the knowledge of this law even the heathen have some knowledge of the divine ordinances, even if they do not know the One who created them. So this law also remains 'outwardly'—that is, in secular matters—even where it has been 'spiritually abolished' by faith. It is the—also critical—principle of natural righteousness, for instance, political righteousness (cf. E. Wolff, op. cit., p. 317). As a whole, however, it is what we may describe as a moral norm. For it is not in the content of the law that there is the difference between the Bible and heathenism or the natural man; rather what the law of nature teaches is precisely what also the Bible of the Old and the New Testament teaches: the love of God and of one's neighbour. 'Nature teaches, as love does, that I ought to do what I would like to have done to me' (WA. II, 279). 'But where thou dost shut thine eyes to love and nature, thou wilt never be able to please God' (ibid.). Although this natural law written in the heart may be 'dimmer' than that which is revealed in the Scriptures, yet here there is no difference in principle. As we have heard, the natural law is even the criterion for that which is valid in the Old Testament doctrine of the law.

But this, important as it is, is not the most important. What is most important is the fact that this law—always this same *Nomos* separated from grace—is at the same time a necessary element in the process of salvation. It is only here that the dialectic of the law begins. That is the second *usus legis. Secundus usus est, de quo dicit Paulus, quod lex sit paedogogus ad Christum* (*Disputationen*, 365). Man may look away from the law and ignore it; and that is even the usual attitude. He evades the law. Indeed, in his own strength he cannot help doing so. At this point, however, God intervenes. Not first of all, through grace, but by holding before man's eyes the death-dealing, merciless law. It may be true that all men have the law in their hearts, but they do not all feel it. '*Lex omnibus est communis, sed non omnes sentiunt ejus vim et effectum.*' It is rather God who does this, but *per sensum legis* (267). It is through the law that one comes to the knowledge of sin and of despair. For this very reason this law—the *nomos* apart from grace—is necessary. Here we are yet not thinking of repentance, but of the terror of conscience. '*Lex arguit sine spiritus sancti dono*' (269). Here, too, the Spirit of God is at work, but it is God in His majesty, *adversarius noster*. So the *Lex* is not '*donum, sed Dei aeterni omnipotentis verbum qui est ignis conscientiae*' (268).

In itself the despair which thus arises is not that which does the soul good. Rather it is ambiguous. If it is to become healing the grace which acquits must be added to the law which condemns. Thus—as I have already said elsewhere (*Zwischen den Zeiten*, 1932, pp. 505 ff.)—there is no continuity upwards from man to God, but only downwards from God to man. He, and He alone, makes the law a *paedagogus* (*Disputationen*, 286). In itself the effect of the law is absolute annihilation, '*lex redigit ad nihilum*' (270). But without this *redactio ad nihil*, thus without this merciless law and its condemnation, there is no conversion, no faith (268 ff.). This is the origin and the content of the dialectic of the law. This is the extremely indirect but extremely important connexion between man's understanding of himself from the immanental point of view and from the point of view of faith.

Viewed from man's standpoint all we can say is: Lost! No immanental dialectic leads us beyond this terrible negative conclusion. But in the Hands of God this same law, which in itself only works death, becomes repentance. It is the divine work of grace that repentance arises out of this terror of the law; but repentance must pass through this terror in face of the merciless law. That is the divine 'pedagogy.' Thus there is a *prius* and a *posterius*; this order of the Law and the Gospel, so far as Luther is concerned, is not a misunderstanding. This is the genuine teaching of Luther; this is his real position, which he defends with all his might; it is not an 'element in his early teaching which he afterwards reversed.' All the

Antinomian Disputations turn on this point. In ever new forms (in the work of Drews this occupies two hundred and fifty pages!) Luther repeats the one statement: it is not the Gospel as such which creates this *redactio ad nihil*, but the Law.

All that 'kills' in this way is law; for the Gospel alone 'makes alive.' But God 'kills' through this law in order to lead to life. He uses the law as a *paedagogus*. Repentance begins with the Law, not with the Gospel (254); it is not grace which creates *contritio*. '*Mortificatio ante fidem est contritio. Sed haec fit per legem quia lex occidit*' (326). But through this law-repentance God leads when and whom He wills to faith, to Christ. This takes place in the fact that He awakens the desire for mercy. 'The law is a sermon which sin makes, it is a thirsty preaching, it makes hungry souls, frightened, sorrowful, thirsty hearts and souls which sigh after the grace of God' (WA. 33, 443). '*Lex docet quid habeas et quo careas, Christus dat quid facias et habeas*' (WA. 2,500). Why is this? '*Quia Deus sic statuit convertere homines ac praeparare ad suscipiendum Christum. Paedagogus in Christum, verbum solatii, est propriissima et jucundissima legis definitio*' (*Disputationen*, 364). Thus there is a twofold *desperatio*: the *desperatio* of the man who remains under the Law, and therefore also under wrath, the *desperatio diabolica*, and the *desperatio evangelica, ad quam lex adigere debet*, through which God Himself *praeparat ad concipiendam fidem in Christum* (351).

This is Luther's concern in his defence of the law, and indeed of the law which kills, of the law which in Paul emerges as the *Nomos*, which leads to condemnation, which, however, at the same time he acknowledges to be the παιδαγωγὸς εἰς χριστόν. There is one more objection to be met: Is it then really the law which creates repentance, and not the preaching of the Gospel? To that too Luther gives a clear, even if not a simple answer. *Sive jam lege sive evangelii rhetorica veneris ad poenitentiam, unum et idem eris* (320). Jesus Christ and the preaching of the Cross also lead to repentance. *Non omnes eodem modo vocamur ad Christum* (346). Christ too may exercise this office, although it is not *ejus proprium* (ibid.). *Est quidem ex cruce seu passione Christi homo ducendus ad poenitentiam, sed inde non sequitur quod lex ideo prorsus inutilis, inefficax et in totum tollenda.* The way of the Gospel is different from that of the

Law; it depends upon the circumstances which of the two is the best in the individual case (318). 'It doth not matter through which it cometh' (320). It is the *rhetorica evangelii*, not the Gospel itself which creates *contritio*—which is necessary for faith, and precedes it. Here the Gospel works not as the Gospel but as the Law. For it is the office of the law and not of the Gospel to kill. Luther is not concerned about the means, but about the truth itself. That which kills is according to its office, law. And through this death one comes to Christ, even if it is the message of Christ which leads along this way of the law. To Christ Himself, however, one only comes through the message of forgiving grace, through which the Holy Spirit works and creates free obedience (270, 280, 284, 302).

This is the *methodus* of God, and *haec methodus summa diligentia conservanda est* (259). *Cum ergo prophetae Christus, apostoli hac methodo usi sint, debemus eos sequi, praecipue insensatos et impoenitentes, ut discant agnoscere magnitudinem peccati. Hoc ubi per legem fecimus, habemus mandatum divinum, ut iterum erigamus per evangelium pusillanimes. Sic verum et proprium officium legis est accusare et occidere, evangelii vivificare* (260). In the Third *Disputation*, too, Luther openly admits that he had previously taught otherwise; but then the times were different. He had terror-stricken people before him, to-day through the preaching of the Gospel they have become presumptuous (478; and also 306). But he also gives another reason why the law is necessary: the law, from its own standpoint, must affirm the reason (WA. 36, 368). 'Otherwise, where it is not naturally written in the heart, we would need to preach and teach for a long time before the conscience would take it home to itself. Thus it must find it and feel it by itself' (WA. 18, 80). The self-understanding of the natural man from the standpoint of the law must come to its own end; and with it the independent human being. Hence the work of the law is the *opus alienum* of God; God as it were goes after man along his path, and leads him to the end of it, before He can show him the other right way, the way of grace, which leads man back to his original being, to his being in the gracious Word of God. That is why there is this order: the Law, and then the Gospel. Hence the knowledge of the law, when God gives it in this way, is the *praeparatio* (316); it is not that man can thus prepare himself, but he is thus prepared by God.

There is one further point to be noted. Through faith 'we are no longer under the law.' *Ubi cessat peccatum; cessat lex,* and Luther adds, providentially, for the theology of the twentieth century: *et in quantum cessavit peccatum tantum cessavit lex, ut in futura vita simpliciter debet cessare lex* (354). 'But if ye are ruled by the Spirit ye are no longer under the law.' Luther, like the New Testament writers, believes that Christ really rules men by His Spirit, that He really creates in them a new will and obedience, the willingness of obedience and of love, even if at first these may be very imperfect, so long as we live in the flesh. *Et ita Christus expellit Adam de die in diem magis et magis secundum quod crescit illa fides et cognitio Christi, non enim tota infunditur, sed incipit, proficit et perficitur tandem in fine per mortem* (WA. 2, 146). Life in the righteousness of faith creates a new man—'a different feeling, a different way of looking at things, a different way of hearing, working and speaking' (EA. XI, 200). A great deal is said in the *Disputations* about the fact that although the Christian is exposed to temptations he triumphs over them in faith *per spiritum sanctum, qui novos motus parit et voluntatem imbuit, ut vere incipiat Deum amare et peccatum detestari in carne reliquum* (302 ff.). Much might be said about this in discussion with the Ultra-Kohlbrüggians of our own day. Yet this is not the place for this (cf. my pamphlet: *Vom Werk des Heiligen Geistes*).

But true as it is that as a believer the Christian is no longer under the Law, as a sinner he continually comes under it. This is the final dialectic of the Law and the Gospel. Even faith itself is never without that element, which was mentioned at the beginning, of being claimed by God; but in faith this divine claim is revealed as His generous grace, and therefore it is not law; and yet in it in particular the *Nomos* fulfils its meaning; rather, in it alone could the true will of God be discerned, which under the *Nomos* was only perceived in a hidden and indirect manner and as broken by sin. In this dual sense Christ is the 'end of the law.' He has made us free from the law by leading us back to the gracious primal claim of God. Hence Paul can call himself an ἔννομος χριστοῦ, one who is obedient to Christ, particularly where he says that he is no longer under the law (1 Cor. ix. 21).

In so far, however, as sin—in the Christian—is concerned, the law remains operative; for sin must die, it must be judged and condemned, even and particularly, where one stands in faith, in the new life. For that very reason Luther insists, in his campaign against the Antinomians, that the Law must remain, not merely for 'blockheads' but also for believers, in order that they should not fall into a false security. It is not the fact that man is apprehended by God, which belongs to faith as such which is meant, but the death-dealing Law, which is different from the Gospel, which indeed in its office and work is opposed to it—in order that man may learn more and more to live through faith alone, on the generous grace of God alone.

Both are summed up in the Cross. The Cross is both the 'strangest work' of God, the condescension of God towards the world of sin and hostility to the law and the fulfilment of the 'demands of the law' (Rom. viii. 4), and in this very fact it is 'the most proper work' of God, the overcoming of the law, and redemption from its curse. In the Cross God follows man upon his way of law which leads to death, to the bitter end (Phil. ii. 8), in order to put him on the other way, when he has reached the end of his own way, the original way of life which, through the conquest of the contradiction, has now become a new way from and in the generous Word. That is the dialectical doctrine of the Law of the Bible and of the Reformers and the legalistic self-understanding of the natural man. It is in exact agreement with the doctrine of the *Imago Dei* and of sin. Man, even as sinner, is always responsible to God; but as sinner he necessarily has a wrong idea of his responsibility, that is, a legalistic one. He understands it wrongly because he understands the Word of God which gives him life, since it lays its claim on him, as law, which in his own strength he should and can fulfil. Thus precisely in his legalism he is one who lives in conflict with God and with himself. But in this very conflict he is to be understood only in the light of his origin and his original nature, that is, of the *Imago Dei*. That he *can* be a sinner is due to his origin; that he *must* be a sinner is due to his falling away from his origin. The fact that he *knows* the law of God springs from his origin, the fact that he has *a wrong understanding* of it is due to sin. Hence emancipation from the curse of the law is the same as the restoration of the image of God; hence both the 'relic' of the *Imago* and the *Nomos*, precisely in their dialectical ambiguity, are the critical points in the Christian doctrine of man, by which it is proved whether a theology is dialectical, that is, whether it is in harmony with the Christian message.

APPENDIX III

THE PROBLEM OF 'NATURAL THEOLOGY' AND THE 'POINT OF CONTACT' (*ANKNÜPFUNG*)

OWING to a somewhat unfortunate use of terms in my pamphlet *Natur und Gnade* I am myself partly to blame for the curious fact that to-day many people regard me as the champion of 'natural theology' in the usual sense of the word, although actually I hold the diametrically opposite view. In spite of Barth's remarks about my 'retrograde development' (*Brunner einst und jetzt*, in his *Antwort*, p. 46) I have always been opposed to a 'natural theology' of this kind, and I still am. The unfortunate phrase is the following: *christliche theologia naturalis*. Apparently the phrase 'natural theology' was so impressive that the addition of the significant word 'Christian' was overlooked, and, in the heat of the controversy, the distinction I make between a *theologia naturalis* in the subjective and in the objective sense (of which more anon) was completely overlooked, although everything hinges upon it. Further, some twenty times or so Karl Barth quotes from my pamphlet the words *Offenbarungsmächtigkeit des Menschen*[1] which I not only have never employed at all, but which I, as much as he, detest as heretical. The phrase I did use was that of the *Wortmächtigkeit* (capacity for speech) of man, that is, I took the usual phrase which describes the fact that man is endowed with the gift of speech and understanding, and turned it into a noun with the same meaning.

The difference of view between myself and Barth comes out, in the main, at two particular points: (i) that I, in opposition to Barth, but in agreement with the Scriptures and the Reformers, maintain that God is still revealing Himself in His work of Creation at the present time, and (ii) that I do not regard the distinctively human element in man as a trifle, but that I regard it as a theologically relevant fact, which can only be understood from the point of view of the truth that man

[1] Lit. 'man's capacity for revelation,' i.e. that man can provide his own revelation.—*Translator*.

has been created in the image of God. In the following remarks I hope that I shall be able to make my thought so clear that such misunderstandings as those which have occurred with Karl Barth may no longer be possible.

1. THE SIGNIFICANCE OF THE PROBLEM: NATURAL THEOLOGY

The events in the German Church Struggle in particular have shown how fundamental for the existence of the Church is the *right kind* of *theologia naturalis* (*Natur und Gnade*, p. 44), that is, the doctrine of general revelation or revelation through Creation which is based upon the Bible, and of the being of the natural man as being in the denial of this original revelation (*Natur und Gnade*, p. 12). The position of the 'natural man's' knowledge of God and of himself from the point of view of Jesus Christ is a theme which must necessarily stand at the centre of theological discussion at the present time, not because in itself it is the centre, but because it is the point at which the contrast between 'modern' thought and that of the Bible comes out most clearly. We have also seen how this problem, quite apart from all external controversy, penetrates into the ultimate propositions of exegetical, dogmatic and practical theology. How can *man* understand the Word of *God*?—a problem of exegesis; how can *man* with his concepts sum up the Word of *God* in doctrine?—a problem of dogmatics; how can *man* proclaim the Word of *God* to man?—a problem of the practical work of the Church.

2. RATIONAL KNOWLEDGE

The doctrine of sin must not be conceived in such a way that it excludes the possibility of 'natural' knowledge, that is, the competence of our reason for knowledge in general. Certain statements of the period of the Reformation cannot be absolved from the reproach of suggesting this view. A depreciation of the power of the human mind to know is not Biblical; it is not true. The recognition of rational knowledge within its own sphere is part not only of the doctrine of the Bible, but also of the Reformers. Without this recognition of a certain competence of the reason even the value of theological work will be wholly illusory. For that which distinguishes the theologian from the simple old Christian woman is not his greater faith, but his greater power of thought in the service of the faith. This competence of the reason, which ought to be recognized, is a graduated one: the reason is more competent to know the world than to know man; it is better able to discern the bodily than the spiritual quality of man; apart from the Word of God it is not able to perceive the true being of man because this is not possible without the knowledge of the true being of God. According to Luther, the reason is not wholly unfit for the knowledge of God—namely, in the negative sense (cf. Köstlin, *Luthers Theologie*, I, 328), but the more we are concerned with the knowledge of the Divine Being and the Divine Will, the less competent is reason. It may know something of the Divine Law (see below), but it knows nothing of God's forgiving grace (cf. Schlink: *Der Mensch in der Verkündigung der Kirche*, p. 249). So far as the natural knowledge of God is concerned, this is the position: 'Sin dims man's vision to such an extent that in place of God he sets up and "knows" or imagines gods; that is, he turns God's revelation in Creation into "images" of false gods, or idols' (*Natur und Gnade*, p. 14).

3. THE REVELATION IN THE CREATION

The question of general revelation or of revelation through the Creation (in *Natur und Gnade* described as the 'objektive theologia naturalis') must be distinguished from the natural or rational knowledge of God (described in *Natur und Gnade* as 'subjektive theologia naturalis'). Save for Karl Barth there was a consensus of opinion in the Church—Böhl, the follower of Kohlbrügge, is no exception—that there is such a general revelation, or revelation through the Creation, just as it is not contested that it is taught in the Scriptures of the Old and of the New Testament (for instance, Romans i; cf. too the excellent observations of Bornkamm in the paper: *Neutestamentliche Wissenschaft*, 1935, pp. 239 ff.; and of Schlier, *Evangelische Theologie*, 1935, pp. 9 ff.). It is equally clear that the Bible expects us to consider this revelation through the Creation, and that to ignore it is condemned as the great sin of the heathen; likewise, it is evident that the Bible bases the responsibility of all men, and thus the sin of idolatry, upon this possibility of knowing Him, given by God Himself. The denial of this revelation through the Creation in the latest theology empties the Biblical idea of Creation of meaning—the Creation is a manifestation of the wisdom and the Godhead of God, the 'natural revelation is not over with the Fall of man' (Bornkamm, p. 249)—and also, wrongly, denies man's relation to God, and with that the responsibility of the godless man.

It is equally clear that sin prevents man from seeing this revelation through the Creation aright ('the Christian alone has the right natural knowledge of God'—*Natur und Gnade*, p. 15), that we need the Scripture as guide (Calvin) if we are really to recognize God and not idols in the works of the Divine Creation (see above the quotation from *Natur und Gnade*, p. 14). Thus according to the Scriptures we must distinguish between the revelation in Creation, or in Nature, which has not in any way been destroyed by sin, and the actual knowledge of God which is required by Him, but actually frustrated by sin; that is, between the general (nature) and the special (historical) revelation, and finally between that which the believer and that which the unbeliever knows of the revelation in Nature.

4. THE KNOWLEDGE OF THE LAW AND THE ORDERS OF CREATION

The fact that there is also a certain knowledge of the Divine Law outside the Bible is the teaching of Scripture; this is expressed by the Reformers in the traditional phrase: the *lex naturae*. It is upon it, above all, that the doctrine of the responsibility of the 'natural' man is based, and also of the *justitia civilis*, and of the competence of the reason in such matters as the legal system, the State, and ordinary morality. But this knowledge of the will of God through the reason is subject to the same restrictions as the knowledge of God from the works of Creation. The bond between both is the divine orders of Creation. Also from them the natural man has a certain knowledge, but 'they can only be understood in their real meaning from the standpoint of faith' (*Natur und Gnade*, p. 17; Schlink, pp. 153 and 195 ff.). The Reformers express this, for instance, by making a distinction between the commandments of the Second Table, which, as such, can be known by the reason, and those of the First Table, which can be understood only through faith in Christ. Their view is that the reason here recognizes the fact, but does not know the 'Whence' or the 'Why' of it, because it is not able to know the Lawgiver Himself. Further, the legalistic rational understanding of God is also the exact opposite of the evangelical truths of faith (cf. Appendix II, pp. 520 ff.). But in so far as the external keeping of the Commandments is a fulfilment of the Divine Law—within the limits of the idea of the *justitia civilis*, of being morally good—it is possible for the natural man to fulfil the will of God—in such a way, however, that this takes place within the realm of sin, and thus in spite of all stands under the wrath of God, and does not justify man in the sight of God. For the rest, the more exact understanding of the relation between the natural law and the law revealed in the Bible is, even among the Reformers, one of the most obscure and difficult problems and has not yet been solved (cf. Bohatec: *Das Recht bei Calvin*).

It is Scriptural doctrine that through faith the good Creation of God, in contrast to sinful corruption, and thus also the divine orders of Creation in contrast to their corruption—at least to a certain degree—may be known, and that not to know or recognize the manifested will of the Creator in the Creation is sin. Just as it is contrary to Scripture to conceive the idea of sin in such a way that it excludes the competence of reason altogether, so too, is it against Scripture to conceive it in such a way that it excludes the possibility of knowing the Creation and the orders of Creation. This supposedly Biblical agnosticism is a doctrine which has never before been heard in the Church (I cannot think of any theologian, ancient or modern, within the Church who could be held to represent this view), and it is an innovation which would make all concrete knowledge of sin impossible. For it is precisely the distinction between the divine orders of Creation and their sinful corruption which gives the idea of sin its concrete content. Thus, for instance, the content of the Seventh Commandment is this: to protect the order of creation of marriage from all disorderly sex relations. The Bible itself indicates that (Matt. xix. 4 ff.) the order of Creation is the ground of the Commandment. Thus the Scripture itself requires that we should not stand still at the 'it is written,' but that we should allow ourselves to be guided back by the Scriptures to the order of Creation as the basis of the concrete content of the commandment. There is no Scriptural basis for this new doctrine that the divine Creation and the orders of Creation cannot be perceived even from the standpoint of faith; this view is rather an offshoot from Kantian, Ritschlian and neo-Kantian ideas. With the rejection of this new theory we are upon the firm ground of the Reformation, and there is no reason—and above all no Scriptural reason—to allow ourselves to be led away from this Reformation position by the statement that in this matter we ought to go further than the Reformers. There is no need to be disturbed by the further charge, that if we hold fast to this doctrine—which is taught both by the Bible and by the Reformers—we are 'Thomist' reactionaries; for it is quite easy to prove, from the history of dogma itself, that this is not the case.

5. HUMANITY AND THE IMAGO

Theologically all the negative and positive statements about the possibilities of reason must be taken into account. From time immemorial ecclesiastical theology has done this in connexion with the doctrine of the *Imago*. In this respect the doctrine of the Reformers is no exception. The undeniable fact of the *humanitas*, which also belongs to sinful man, is ascribed by all the Reformers to a 'relic' of the *Imago Dei*. This view, even if somewhat awkwardly expressed, brings out the idea that the *humanitas* has some connexion with the original relation of man with God, and thus that the formal structure of human existence as such, which cannot be lost, contains a relation to God. The fact that both Luther and Calvin held this idea firmly, although it did not fit in with their main doctrine of the complete loss of the *Imago*, shows that the perception of the connexion between the *humanitas* and man's relation with God was very deeply rooted.

Objectively the Reformers are absolutely right: the *humanitas* is only a relic of the original being of man in accordance with the Creation; that is, it is that which points back to the Origin, even in the sinful being of man. But this must not be understood in a quantitative sense, but in a dialectical sense, as indeed has been done in this book. The expression: 'formal *Imago*' should thus be expressed in precise terms: the relation to the original being of man or to the *Imago* which lies in the formal, personal structure of human existence.

6. THE 'POINT OF CONTACT' IN THE ACTION OF THE CHURCH

Here Schlink's book (*Der Mensch in der Verkündigung der Kirche*), although it has not provided a solution, has made one possible. All that Schlink writes about '*die Bemühung um den Menschen*' ('effort to get into touch with man') I can only affirm, and recommend most cordially to my readers. This 'effort to get into touch with man' is God's command to the translator of the Bible, the religious teacher, the preacher, and the pastor. As Schlink rightly says, it is not a matter of course but a divine command (p. 243). But there are two points raised by Schlink, one big and the other small, which are curious and dangerous.

First of all, Schlink claims that this effort for the sake of man, this wrestling for the understanding of a foreign language, in order that the Bible may be rightly translated, this wrestling to understand the other in the distinctiveness of his being and of his situation, in order to discover the point 'at which he must be touched if he is to understand that it is *he* who is meant' (249)—all this, because it has been commanded by God (243) must not be called a 'point of contact'! As if God could not command that we should make use of the 'point of contact' to get into touch with man! But let us leave this word *Anknüpfung* alone—for it is certainly not a classical expression, nor is it a particularly good one—(although I have found it used in theological language of at least a hundred years ago, in J. Müller: *Lehre von der Sünde*, II, p. 320). By *Anknüpfung* I mean nothing other than that which Schlink describes in those pregnant pages as the effort to get into touch with man which is commanded by God, and thus the 'divine claim to lay hold of an anthropology outside theology in the interest of theology itself' (p. 243).

Secondly, however, and this is the most amazing thing of

all—this effort which God commands, is said to be 'fruitless' (p. 244 ff. especially pp. 251, 253). It is true of course that this effort in itself, without the special co-operation of the Holy Spirit, cannot attain its end, that is, place man under the Word of God. It is quite correct to say that this effort is 'limited in three directions': by the Scriptures, by the Creed, and by the problems connected with the knowledge of human beings. But the conclusion which he draws from all this is wholly unscriptural and false, namely, that because it is *man* who speaks, and because this man is sinful, even if he speaks as an evangelist or pastor, he speaks in vain. 'The command to make disciples cannot be carried out.'

Here then the ultra-Reformation idea of sin of a certain theological group has reached such a pitch of intensity that it becomes sheer nonsense. For this 'fruitlessness' no longer refers, as at first, to efforts made for man as such, but to the accomplishment of the divine missionary command as a whole. If the idea of sin is to be understood to imply that no command of God can be carried out because we—even those who believe and have received the grace of God—are all sinners, then the effort to translate and interpret the Scriptures falls under the same condemnation, then it too, and also the preaching of the Word which is achieved through the preaching of sinful human beings, is 'fruitless.'

If we are prepared, in principle, to draw this conclusion in every direction, in that of theology as well as in that of anthropology, in the same way, then I could accept it as a somewhat exaggerated expression of a central truth: namely, that apart from God we can do nothing, that without the Spirit of God all human activity for the Kingdom of God is 'fruitless'; for the Spirit of God alone can build the Kingdom of God. He alone can speak God's own Word.

But once the idea has been developed so far, immediately the exaggeration becomes clear. For the Kingdom of God, in spite of the fact that it is built by human action, and in spite of the fact that all human action is sinful, is actually never built otherwise than with the help of human action in teaching, preaching, pastoral work, and the administration of the Sacraments. The dualistic severance of the instrumental human action and the divine self-action is opposed to the experience and the teaching of the Church, as well as to the Biblical doctrine that God builds His Church through the instrumentality of human activity and human speech. Without the Spirit of God we cannot fulfil His Commands—neither the command to 'make disciples of all nations' nor any other. But this which in itself is impossible becomes possible through the Spirit of God; and that it actually takes place through us, and actually can be experienced through us, is the teaching which meets us, so to speak, on every page of the New Testament (I would only remind the reader of Paul's expression: 'workers together with God.' 1 Cor. iii. 9).

God builds His Church, He makes disciples, through human action alone, which He uses as His instrument. Thus in principle 'effort for the sake of man' and 'effort for the Word of God' are on exactly the same plane. In themselves, without the blessing of the Spirit, neither can succeed, both are 'fruitless' —the theological effort as well as that of the missionary and pastor; through the blessing of the Holy Spirit not only *can* both succeed, but this success is explicitly promised, even as the Apostles give explicit testimony to actual achievements of this kind in particular instances (cf. 1 Thess. ii. 1, 'hath not been in vain'). The Bible, however, in contrast to this theological school, does not lead us to reflect on the lack of success of our activity which takes place under the command of God, but, on the contrary, the Bible leads us to the confidence that an action which takes place in faith, even if this faith is imperfect, and although the men who perform it are sinful, is accompanied with God's blessing, and will never be fruitless, even if it does not lead to positive success, to the actual making of disciples; for He who has commanded us to 'make disciples of all nations' (Matt. xxviii. 19) has also given us the promise: 'I am with you all the days' (Matt. xxviii. 20).

If we take the opposite attitude, and exaggerate the conclusions to be drawn from the Biblical doctrine of sin, we do not remain within the sphere of Biblical truth, and we merely give the opponents of the Christian message a certain right to call the Christian idea of sin morbid and destructive. In actual fact such a doctrine of the 'fruitlessness' of human action *is* destructive.

Schlink's book goes further than the previous discussion in the intensity and thoroughness with which that exaggerated unscriptural idea of sin is pressed to its utmost conclusion; it attacks the very starting-point itself. This doctrinaire kind of theology makes theology, as well as all other forms of human activity, useless. If all human action be fruitless, then theology also is useless; if all the effort of sinful men for the Kingdom of God is futile, then the effort to proclaim the Word of God, whether in teaching or in preaching, as well as everything else that we do, is also useless, because it is the work of sinful human beings. At this point we see clearly how untrue it is to make this division between divine and human action as the logical conclusion drawn from a false idea of sin. It is the mystery of that faith which worketh through love that both the divine and the human word are united (Gal. v. 6). Human reason and divine revelation are not merely related to one another in a negative manner; they are also in a positive relation to one another. The positive relation may be described by the word 'instrumental.' Every good theological book, as for instance Karl Barth's *Dogmatics*, is a proof of this positive relation, since it is a document of human rational effort and of capacity for thought in the service of the Gospel. The question is not whether there be such a positive relation between human reason and divine revelation, but in what it consists. To recognize this point in our own day is a great gain, and to express it in the theological world is a proceeding which is fraught with a certain amount of danger. This brings us to the question of the 'point of contact.'

7. THE POINT OF CONTACT

By this we mean all that the God who deals with us in His Word and by His Spirit apprehends in man, in order to give him the gift of faith. And again all that He thus apprehends is created by Him, by His Word and His Spirit. He only apprehends what He has already created. When the word of the Gospel, through its proclamation, approaches the sinner, his life is apprehended by God in the following order: first of all, his outward presence and the external act of hearing, the act of understanding, in the logical and grammatical sense, then his rational and personal being, above all its centre, the knowledge of responsibility. Here I cannot refrain from quoting once again a decisive passage from Luther which I have quoted elsewhere: 'But if the natural law were not written and given by God in the heart, we would have to preach a very long time before the conscience would be reached; we would have to preach to an ox or a horse or cattle for a hundred thousand years before they would accept the law, although they have ears, eyes, and a heart just like a man, they can also hear, but it does not enter into their heart. Why? What is lacking? Their soul is not formed and created for this so that they can accept it. But if a man in confronted with the law, he soon saith: "Yes, it is so; I cannot deny it." We could not persuade him so quickly were it not that the law is written in his heart. Because it is already in his heart, although in a dim and obscure manner, it is awakened again by the Word' (WA. 16, 447). Further, to this we may add the passage quoted above (Appendix II, p. 523) 'otherwise were it (the law) not naturally written in the heart, we would have to preach and teach for a long time before the conscience would apply it to itself.' This is the Biblical view of the 'point of contact'; the Bible contains no actual doctrine of the 'point of contact,' but this applies to many other questions as well. This 'point of contact' is the presupposition of the Pauline message; hence Paul places it at the beginning of his Letter to the Romans which deals with the question: with whom does the man who preaches the Gospel have to do? The Bible teaches us that the Word of God is set in our hearts in order that it might be received by the reason, by the responsible human being who could know something of God. The Word of God does not presuppose man as a *tabula rasa*, nor does it make him into a *tabula rasa*!

It is entirely contrary to the Biblical doctrine that in faith —as the Formula of Concord says—man should be 'wholly passive,' or, as Amsdorf puts it, should be like a clod of earth or a stone. Definitions of this kind are not Biblical theology, but bad philosophy. The Biblical statement is that man receives grace, and also faith, purely as a gift. But it does not say that in faith man is to be wholly passive, but something very different. The Bible never regards man, and least of all in the process of faith as *truncus et lapis*, as an object which is treated as a piece of wood which is planed by the carpenter, but it always regards him as a responsible subject. This responsible subject is not first of all created in the preaching of the Word, but is presupposed before the preaching takes place. It is not the subject Paul who is created anew by the Word of God—it is rather presupposed by the Word of God—but the new person is created by the historical Word of God; a believer is made out of an unbeliever, the self-righteous is turned into the Paul who depends wholly on the grace of God; that which we have called material personality becomes new. This creation, however, takes place through the use of the mental acts of understanding, thus with the use of the reason. The new creation consists in the fact that out of the *cor incurvatum in se ipsum* there arises the heart which is opened to God, so that not merely is there a new content of the spirit, the reason, the heart, but a new way of being, a new 'person' has come into existence.

Now a false anthropology has defined this relation between God and man, which is presupposed by the preaching of the Word on the one hand (formaliter), and at the same time (materialiter) is created anew, in such a manner that it inevitably leads to insoluble dilemmas, and, what is worse, to a false conception of faith itself. The relation between God and man was, namely, conceived *causally*. This meant that there was nothing for it but either to seek causality purely upon the side of God and to make man into a *truncus seu lapis*; or to distribute causality between both, although in unequal proportions, which endangered the truth of the sole power of the grace of God. The views of Flacius led to the first conclusion and Synergism led to the second. All this is not in the Bible at all. The Bible always places man over against the Word of God as a responsible subject and understands the operation of the Word always as a process *sui generis* which is achieved as speaking and hearing, being apprehended and being obedient. Hence it places the two statements alongside of one another: that God alone does everything, and that man must believe, that he must receive the message, that he must 'come' to the feast which God has prepared, that he must 'put on' the Wedding Garment, that he must 'sell all' and 'buy' the Pearl of Great Price. Thus in spite of the fact that God gives us His grace purely out of groundless love, in this whole process man is not presupposed as passive, but, on the contrary, as extremely active. The action of God is achieved by apprehending the highest activity of man, which, however, in its meaning (but not in its psychological form) is *passio*: to surrender oneself, to surrender all, to give oneself over to death, to look away wholly from oneself to the Word of God alone, and so on. The action of God takes place by claiming human personal acts, and indeed, the sole possible total act of the person, to which there corresponds in concentrated activity nothing save the total act of sin—and this only within certain limits—faith.

Thus the structure of the being of man is always pre-supposed, which indeed, as we now know, is an actual, not a substantial responsible being, being in decision. In the Bible this structure is never regarded as lost—indeed how could this be so, since even the sinner is still a human being?—rather even in the act of faith it is presupposed as operative, and as such it is shown parabolically ('coming,' 'selling,' 'drawing'), as well as in purely logical conceptions. This personal structure as actual being is that which is always proper to man, and this, in the general sense, is the 'point of contact.' To put it more exactly, that which makes this personal structure personal is responsibility—that which in the passage above quoted from Luther is called 'conscience'—the point of contact in the narrower sense of the word, and therefore the act of 'making contact' of the preacher or pastor consists in seeking for the point at which the hearer is to be 'met' in the sense of responsibility, or in accordance with his conscience.

But this situation is now complicated by the fact that the same reason which on its formal side is always a presupposition, in its material aspect as material personality, is always defined as sin, and thus in opposition to the Word of God. Hence the very same point which is the real 'point of contact' is also the point of the greatest contradiction: namely, responsibility as the sinful human being understands it, the legalistic understanding of God and oneself. Legalism, too, is a kind of responsible being, that is, the function of responsibility is reversed, and becomes responsibility in the 'un-real' sense, being which is in opposition to the Word of God, as, conversely, faith is the right kind of responsibility, that which corresponds to the Word of God which calls man, is real being in the Word of God. Thus while the structure of responsible being as such is presupposed—only men, in any case only beings endowed with reason, can hear the Word of God—the material aspect of this being of man, that is, man as godless, or sinner, or 'under the law' is that which cannot serve as a 'point of contact,' but is denied. The soul that passes through this process of allowing the self-centred, autonomous reason to be broken up, comes out into the light of faith. The passive endurance of this painful process is what the Bible describes as 'repentance.' In it man is extremely active, but his activity consists in *passio*, in self-denial, in the abdication of the sovereign 'I,' of that 'confident despair' which clings to the divine promise of grace. The defiant 'I' is overcome by the love of God, surrenders itself as a defeated captive, and at the same time exults in the fact that it has been taken captive. For now it knows that it has once more become what it was originally, and to which it was in opposition. But how this activity of the human heart is awakened and aroused to such a pitch of intensity, in the divine *actio*, which the *actio* of man apprehends as *passio*, is possible, and how it takes place, is, and remains, a mystery. What matters to us is the preservation of the character of this happening: that from the point of view of the content it is God's sole act and gift, that from the side of man it is the supreme, and indeed the only total act, and that both these truths are united from the very outset, and in accordance with the Creation, because this active quality of the being of man is already grounded in the divine action. Because man's being as a whole, as responsible being, whether that of the sinner or of the believer, is being derived from the Word of God and destined for the Word of God, and this remains irrevocably, for curse or blessing, in the love or in the wrath of God—therefore the turning from sin to faith, from falling away from God to return unto God, is God's new creation of man's original state, and is at the same time the apprehension of that way of being which, even when turned in the wrong direction, is still the being, or the nature of man, and here this means: responsive actuality.

The old dogmatic theologians of the Reformation, once more following Augustine, expressed this in their teaching that sin is not the 'substance' but the 'accident' of sinful human existence. But the Aristotelian distinction between substance and accident is not adequate. It is just as dangerous to affirm the substantial nature of sin like Flacius, as it is to deny it, like the protagonists of the Formula of Concord. Personal being cannot be compressed within this schema of ideas; God's action in man is not causal, and the being of man is not substantial. If, however, that is understood we shall then again return to the personal type of doctrine of the Bible—which seems so paradoxical to abstract thought—which simply places these two thoughts side by side: God alone must do it, but man must 'work out his own salvation with fear and trembling.' Faith comes from God alone, but if faith does not come into being man alone is to blame. God gives faith freely, from pure mercy, yet faith does not come into being save through the obedience of man. Every attempt to go beyond this dualism, which yet plainly expresses the priority of God, and to reach a unified formula, destroys the personal understanding of the relation between God and man and changes it into something material. The relation between God and man cannot be described by the formula of the sole causality of God, or of the sole operation of God, because God's creation of man has from the outset created a relation of 'over-againstness' which—this is God's will—has the result that even the divine action in man always respects the fact that man is subject. Even the divine action of grace is not an arbitrary action, but it is intercourse or personal communion, and indeed the only real intercourse which is the only pure contrast to any arbitrary treatment, because it consists in the fact that God's word of love changes man's defiance into voluntary obedience. So great is God's gracious approach to us, so very much is it the opposite of any coercion that it is the self-surrender of God for us. God is greatly concerned that man, even as sinner, shall not be overwhelmed, but addressed as one whom God confronts. The most decisive thing which can be said about the 'point of contact' is the fact that the divine operation in man takes place through God's speaking to man.

APPENDIX IV

PHILOSOPHICAL AND THEOLOGICAL ANTHROPOLOGY

THE discussion of this theme has entered upon a new phrase with the rise of the 'Existenzphilosophie,' that is, with the entrance of Kierkegaard into the sphere of philosophy. The ontology of Heidegger is the point at which it has crystallized. If at the moment we are hearing less about it, this does not mean that it has been completed, nor does it mean that it has proved unproductive. The reason why this discussion has been arrested is purely a practical one. Like so many important theological problems, it has had to stand aside for the moment in order that all the effort may be concentrated on the defence of the existence of the Church itself, and the preservation of a position in which the Bible is central. But the urgency and the importance of this theme is as great as ever.

The question, which, on the side of the philosophers, has been discussed by Löwith and Kuhlmann (in spite of the 'Theological Anthropology' written by the latter, he must be reckoned among the philosophers and not among the theologians), and, on the side of the theologians, has been discussed by Bultmann, Heim, Schumann and myself, primarily concerns the relation between philosophical ontology and theology (cf. chiefly No. 5 in the *Zeitschrift für Theologie und Kirche*, 1930, and No. 2, 1931; also Bultmann: *Glaube und Verstehen*; Schumann, *Um Kirche und Lehre*). Here it is impossible to discuss the views of the various authors in detail, but I must confine myself to the effort to make my own position quite clear; this is all the more necessary since in many respects I have advanced beyond what I have said in earlier books.

1. Whatever the claims of philosophy may be, I maintain that faith must never renounce its own ontology. Being—not merely the existent—as being created, and indeed as being created by and in the Word of God, is equally a being of its own kind as the Being of God is the ground of all that exists,

and of His manner of being. There is absolutely no definition which is more 'original' than this: Creator and creature. God is the Creator not only of all that exists, but also of all the forms of existence, just as there is no reason which is higher than God in which the Divine Being might have a share—God is the Creator also of the reason. If I had space to develop it, this could be illustrated most plainly by means of the idea of contingency which seems to be a purely philosophical idea. In reality, this idea is an offshoot from the Idea of Creation; at least the pre-Christian idea of contingency (Aristotle), like all Greek thought, betrays the pantheistic idea of continuity as its background; thus it is not radical like the Christian idea. The same is true of the idea of Being in general. The thought of the being of the existent is fundamentally different according as the idea of the Creator lies behind it or not. There is no neutral being. Every idea of being already betrays its background, whether it be that of metaphysics or of faith.

2. This becomes particularly clear in the *Sein des Daseins*.[1] The definition 'creaturely being' applies absolutely to the character of being as such, and is thus an ontological and not an ontal category; all the more is the historical, or 'being-in-decision,' the contrast between *Eigentlichkeit* and *Uneigentlichkeit*,[2] etc., not only accidentally—through the never complete objectivity of the thinker, as I used to believe—but necessarily, an ontological category, the content of which is completely different, according as one thinks from the Christian point of view or not. It is a leading idea of my book that the structure of the being of man, as such, is to be understood theologically, and not (or not merely) philosophically. Being-in-responsibility, being-in-decision, being-in-freedom, and all the further definitions which depend upon this fundamental one, of guilt, etc., are such that, formal though they may be, they are conceived quite differently according as they start from the Christian idea of Creation or not.

In any case I would feel obliged to reverse Heim's statement

[1] See *Contemporary German Philosophy* by Werner Brock, pp. 109 ff., for Heidegger. cf. *God Transcendent*: Karl Heim, pp. 140 and 149.—*Translator.*

[2] See Translator's Note, Chap. I, p. 19.

that 'every theology which believes in a personal God applies ontological presuppositions about the structure of the "I-Thou" relation to the relation between God and man,' and to say: every philosophy of the present day which deals with the 'I-Thou' relation uses, perhaps without being aware of the fact, Christian categories, while thinking that they are using purely rational philosophical ideas. It is no accident that the Existential philosophy was created by the Christian theologian Kierkegaard;[1] further, it is no accident that Heidegger, in his attempt to set himself free from the Christian presuppositions of this philosophy, has already given a different meaning to the fundamental ontological concepts of Kierkegaard (for instance, to the idea of the 'existential'). I hope that in my book I have proved that it is precisely the understanding of the structure of existence as such from the standpoint of the Christian idea of God and Man which alone makes it possible to perceive the true connexion between Humanity and Faith, and solves a mass of theological problems which are only 'problems' when viewed superficially, or apart from the real clue.

3. I believe that I am aware of the danger of this point of view. It lies in the fact that theology threatens to become a universal science. And indeed what is there left for unfortunate philosophy if even the formal is no longer left to it? And what will happen to theology if it even presumes to produce its own logic? I believe, however, that it will not be too difficult, at least in principle, to avoid this danger. Of course there is no special science of Christian logic or mathematics as such, although—following some hints thrown out by Leibniz—I am not so sure that the Christian faith could not throw light upon certain problems of mathematics. The less a truth has to do with the centre of personality, the more autonomous is reason within it; that is, the difference, or the contrast between the point of view of the believer or of the unbeliever, comes out in it less and less. But in the problem of the being of man as responsible being, the formal and the material are originally, in harmony with the purpose of the Creation, one.

[1] See *Contemporary German Philosophy*, by Werner Brock, on *Kierkegaard*: pp. 82 ff.—*Translator*.

This, indeed, is the really revolutionary meaning of Luther's doctrine of the *Imago*. There is no neutral idea of responsibility into which the Christian content could then be incorporated; but the idea of responsibility itself is either a Christian or a non-Christian idea; it is either legalistic and autonomous, or it is in harmony with faith. In the thought of Heidegger it is secretly derived from the philosophy of Fichte; in that of Kierkegaard it is explicitly Christian. Through the Fall alone does the separation between formal responsibility (and accordingly: Humanity) and its closer determination as content arise. Formal *humanitas* is not the presupposition of being-in-the-Word-of-God, but the opposite: it is that which is left of being-in-the-Word, even after the Fall.

The statement of Bultmann: 'since there is no other existence (*Dasein*) than this which constitutes itself in its freedom, the formal structures of existence which are shown in the ontological analysis are neutral, that is, they are valid for all existence (*Dasein*)' (*Glaube und Verstehen*, p. 312), is therefore the πρῶτον ψεῦδος. The understanding of freedom is quite different when it leads to the concept of a freedom in itself (as in the thought of Heidegger), or as in the thought of Christianity, to that of freedom in God, which as such is never neutral, but is always defined as either negative or positive, as sin or as faith, as either a lost freedom or a real freedom. If, however, as Bultmann says, faith 'leads back to the original Creation'—how can a non-believing philosophy know of this possibility?—even, as Bultmann says, as meaningless?

4. But the problem has been rendered still more complicated by the fact that man is never without some knowledge of God; whether rightly or not, to some extent he is always aware of Him. Rational ideas about the being of man are always, secretly, theological ideas, however formal they may seem to be, namely, ideas of a reason which is set free from God, and therefore one which regards man from a legalistic point of view, that is, from the point of view of reason which misunderstands. This is particularly true of the idea of freedom. This idea certainly is that with which we think first of all; it is the pre-understanding of the right understanding which is in

harmony with faith, to which therefore preaching, but always polemically, appeals. Even the *formal* concepts of every philosophical ontology are positions of *sinful* reason, from which, it is true, not *reason* but *sin* must be eliminated. From the standpoint of methodology this means: we always have already a philosophical ontology of some kind before we have faith; but it would be a hopeless undertaking to try to create the right philosophical ontology without faith. Rather, the right ontology of the being of man arises—approximately—through the critical sifting of rational concepts from the standpoint of faith; that means, through a fundamentally Christian philosophy. It was as a Christian philosopher that Kierkegaard created the 'Existential' philosophy, it was as a Christian thinker that Ebner discovered the theme of 'I-Thou'—no Greek, however great a genius, would have ever understood such a theme—it was as a Biblical thinker that Martin Buber recognized the significance of the contrasts between 'I' and 'It,' 'I' and 'Thou.' It is as a Christian thinker that Karl Heim has established his theory of dimensions which in essentials is simply the attempt to create a Christian ontology.

The fact that there are subjects about which in point of fact—at least approximately—there is neutral philosophical thought, ought not to lead us astray to the point of believing that there is also a neutral ontology of being or of existence. Where we are dealing with ultimates—and the concept of Being is truly an ultimate—there can be no philosophical neutrality. Belief in the division of labour between philosophy and theology, which also colours much of the theology of the Reformation, must give place to the view that between theology and philosophy, or, to put it more correctly, between rational thought and thought governed by faith, there is a dialectical relation, which simply reflects the dialectic of the Law and the Gospel, that is, a view of man which is either legalistic or believing. So long as this is not perceived, we shall continue to miss the point, while we argue as 'Humanists' or as 'Reformation Christians,' and each will see his advantage in the—rightly perceived—weakness of the other. How much my book contributes to the solution of this problem, I do not know. But of this I am sure: the problem lies where I have seen it.

APPENDIX V

THE UNDERSTANDING OF MAN IN ANCIENT PHILOSOPHY AND IN CHRISTIANITY

THE conception of man in antiquity is a problem which I am not competent to treat adequately, as a whole. Here all I can do will be to discuss what everyone knows from some points of view which are suggested by comparison with the Christian understanding of man. In addition to the original sources themselves—so far as I am acquainted with them—I have made use of the following books: Jäger: *Paideia*; Groetehuysen: *Philosophische Anthropologie, Part I, The Ancient World*, op. cit.; Schneidewin: *Antike Humanität*; Mühl: *Die antike Menschheitsidee*; Reitzenstein: *Werden und Wesen der Humanität im Altertum*; Bonhöffer: *Die Ethik des Stoikers Epiktet*; Bonhöffer: *Epiktet und das Neue Testament*; Deissner: *Paulus und Seneca*; Nygren: *Eros und Agape*; Reinhardt: *Kosmos und Sympathie*; Rohde: *Psyche*; Bultmann: *Das christliche Gebot der Nächstenliebe*; as well as the works on the History of Ancient Philosophy by Zeller and Uberweg-Praechter which have already been mentioned. The aim of this comparative presentation of this subject is not in any sense historical, it is exclusively theological and practical; what I want to do is to show as clearly as possible the contrast between the view of man in ancient philosophy and that of the Bible and the Christian faith. At the same time—as has already been said in Chapter VII—the presupposition of all this is the fact that Ancient Humanism, in spite of, and precisely *in* this contrast to the Christian understanding of man, is one of the clearest 'traces of the *Imago Dei*' which can be seen in fallen man from the point of view of faith.

1. In spite of the various modifications which the ancient idea of man underwent in the course of the six or eight hundred years of Greek and Roman thought, it does possess a certain common element, which, especially when compared with the Christian conception of man, strikes one immediately, and makes the differences appear less important. Formally, this

distinctively common element is rationalism—that is, the rational understanding of man—materially, it is Pantheism, understood in a very broad sense.

2. Ancient Humanism, like all other forms of humanism, has a religious background; to the extent in which the religious background disappears, the distinctive character of man, as distinguished from the rest of the natural order, also disappears, becoming at first unimportant and insignificant, till at last it fades away altogether. The distinctive element in man, upon the perception of which theoretical Humanism, and upon the assertion of which practical Humanism is based, is the *humanum*, which for Greek thought is also a *divinum*. The *humanum* is based upon a *divinum*. This is the common element in the idea of man both in ancient philosophy and in Christianity. The contrast lies in the sphere of the content, and the manner in which this *divinum* is based on this *humanum*, and how the relation is determined between these two entities.

3. The *divinum*, on which ancient humanity knows itself to be based, is an idea of God which is either pluralistically-personal or monistically-impersonal. In Homeric polytheism the relation between the *humanum* and the *divinum* is extremely uncertain (cf. the work, still very instructive, of Nägelsbach: *Homerische Theologie*); in some way or another men come from the gods; but the relation between both is not really essential, or such that it constitutes man's *nature*. Accordingly, the distinctive element in man, as against nature, does not stand out very clearly. Man is still to a very great extent conceived as a natural being. Similarly, the unity of mankind is either questionable, or it has not yet become a problem.

It is only in the sphere of philosophical reflection that the relation between both conceptions comes clearly into the field of vision. The *divinum*, however, which emerges in this philosophical reflection—which is certainly mostly still connected with religious and irrational elements—is on the one hand a more or less rational, on the other hand a more or less pantheistic conception of God. All Greek thinkers, from Plato to Plotinus, speak about the divinity in a manner which, as

Bonhöffer says of Epictetus, "represents a mixture of Theism, Pantheism and Polytheism, which is scarcely intelligible to our modern ideas' (*Die Ethik Epiktets*, p. 82). This, however, is no accident, but it is in the nature of the case—namely, in the rational idea of God. What is disclosed to thought cannot be the living personal God of faith and of revelation. The reason, by its very nature, cannot get beyond the idea of spiritual laws, of the *Logos* of reason which pervades the All. Reason can only posit that which is in accordance with the law which is the presupposition of rational thought; to it everything else is 'exaggerated.' On the other hand, the idea of reason as the essential sign of divine Being leads to a kind of personalism; the divinity is represented as thinking and willing. Here is the same oscillation which we have seen in the thought of Kant (see above, p. 113). In so far, however, as these thinkers still —or like Posidonius and Plotinus, once more—stand within a religious tradition, their rational philosophical ideas are also always interwoven with religious and personalistic *motifs*, which, on their side, are mingled with polytheism. Even Epictetus, who 'perhaps comes closest to the Theistic idea of God, of all philosophers before and after Christ' (Bonhöffer, loc. cit., p. 81) and the Roman Stoics, Seneca and Marcus Aurelius, are no exception to this rule, although in them all the purely practical purpose of their thought makes room for the emergence of the personalistic element. 'Seneca also teaches that every name can be applied to the divinity—this reminds us of Goethe's words in *Faust*, *Name ist Schall und Rauch*—for him God, Fate, Providence, Nature and World are identical conceptions.' To the question: What is the divinity? he answers, in a wholly Pantheistic manner: 'the soul of the All . . . all that thou seest and all that thou dost not see. Then alone will its peculiar greatness be perceived beyond which nothing greater can be conceived, if it alone is all, it dominates its work from without and from within' (*Natur. quaest. lib. I. Praef.* 13 in Deissner, op. cit., p. 19). The same is true of Marcus Aurelius. 'Usually by God he understands the *Hegemonikon* (ruling part) of the All, the World Reason,' or, more naturalistically expressed, 'All-Nature' (Bonhöffer, op. cit., pp. 246 ff.). The great classical philosophers, like Plato, have a still more impersonal idea of God than these later, popular philosophers. In Plato, for instance, we find the same confusing blend of polytheistic myth, used half playfully and half seriously, of the rational World Reason which pervades the All, and monotheistic elements of the Idea of God. Plato speaks of the world Creator (*Timaeus*, 30 B) only in connexion with obviously mythical ideas; in the same Dialogue he also says that the world has become God, and that the constellations have become gods (*Tim.* 40 D). In Heraclitus, as in other older Stoics, the pantheistic and impersonal element far outweighs the theistic personal element, although the idea of the *Logos*, as the World Reason, understood as an active idea of the world, is continually pressing towards the idea of a Divine Self.

4. In exact accordance with this is the way in which the *humanum* is understood as grounded in the *divinum*. Here too there is the same oscillation between the ideas of creation, emanation and immanence, in the sense of 'being part of.' So far as the human reason is concerned—and that is the real *humanum*, that distinguishes man from all other beings—the idea predominates that it is itself of a divine nature, and indeed that it is identical with the Divine Reason. It is the idea of affinity with God which, in various forms, constitutes the fundamental idea of ancient Humanism. First, it is solely this 'affinity with the divinity which makes man capable of the knowledge of the divine, as only the eye which is accustomed to the light can bear the rays of the sun' (Posidonius, according to Mühl, op. cit., p. 67). The theoretical possibility of the rational knowledge of God is based upon this presupposition of the identity of the human and the Divine Reason; at the same time, however, the limitations of human knowledge are recognized. Thus the human reason is a fragment, a spark, a splinter, of the Divine Reason; nevertheless, here there is similarity of nature. The same thought is also expressed as the indwelling of the divine in the human reason; in the spirit of man as such—in the reason as such, in rationality—the Divine Spirit is immanent. The concrete idea of spirit of the Stoics in particular allows such an identification of the divine and human reason, even if only in a partial way; the human

spirit is *particula Dei.* This means that the *humanum* does not consist so much in a personal relation to the divinity as in a nature, that is, in the rational nature. The Reason is the divinity which lodges within man, in the slave as well as in the nobleman (Seneca, *Epist.* xxxi. 11). (That in Plato the actual relation is at least foreshadowed, see above, p. 99.)

Here is the root of the idea which has had such a disastrous influence upon the anthropology of the Church: man as a rational *substance.* Think, for example, of the idea of personality of Boethius: *persona est naturae rationalis individua substantia* (*De duobus naturis et una persona Christi*, c. 3). Being divine is ascribed to man as a natural quality, in virtue of his rational nature. This nature cannot be perverted like an act; it is what it is in virtue of its present being. There is no decisive importance in the content or direction of this spiritual act as compared with this formal structure. Here the idea of sin cannot develop.

5. Hence it follows that the Divine is always potentially present in man; all that is needed is to make the knowledge actual. Man must become aware of his relation to God. *Anamnesis*, or introspection, or reflection upon oneself are all that is required to make the divine-human possibility into a reality. Here there can never be any idea of a real contrast between God and man, between the will of God and human self-existence; evil can never consist in anything other than either in not knowing—that is, the latent possibility is not actualized—or in the fact that the physical nature or the domination of the senses either does not permit or actually hinders the spirit from expressing itself. For ignorance is due to mental inertia, which, again, is due to the fact that the sense-life is a drag upon the higher part of man. Thus evil never springs from the higher part of man—from the mind or spirit—it is simply due to the fact that the spirit is not wide awake, which again is the fault of the sense-nature. Evil, therefore, is not a personal but a metaphysical principle; it is not act, but nature. If the positive relation with God is not conceived in a personal way, but as part of nature, then the negative relation also must be understood in the same way; here, indeed, we can scarcely speak of a negative relation with

God at all. Evil is not enmity against God, but it is imperfection, weakness, indolence; in short, a defect, not an act of the spirit.

6. The positive relation with God, however, the right understanding of oneself in the divinity, is realized as knowledge of man's participation in Divine Being, and therefore leads quite logically to the characteristic idea of middle and later Stoicism, of a republic 'common to man and gods, of a great commonwealth guided and directed by the *recta ratio* as by a Divine Law" (Panaetius in Mühl, op. cit., p. 77), a thought which characteristically returns once more in Kant (cf. the *Grundlegung zu einer Metaphysik der Sitten*, Kehrbach, pp. 75, 95, 104 ff.).

7. If then the *humanum* as formal-rational being, or spiritual being, is by nature substantially based upon the Divine Reason, then in relation to man it must work out as the recognition of that element which is common to all, of that which is alike in all, and thus in an egalitarian manner. To do this it is not necessary to deny differences of individuality; their value will differ in accordance with the view one holds of the physical part of man. But so much at least is clear: the individual element is the non-essential, it is that which is based on physical being, not on spiritual being. All that is essential is solely that which belongs to the species, that which is typical, the same, the universal, that which is rational and in accordance with laws. The relation to man which, as the 'Humane,' results from this, is that of respect, which, however, can well be combined with a certain enthusiasm, and, where the pantheistic idea is coloured with mysticism, may become a 'cosmic sympathy,' or an emotional awareness of a universal affinity. All human beings are related to one another, and should, as such, love each other. 'Humanity' arises on the one hand as philanthropy and on the other as a sense of world citizenship.

But just as the personal character of the Idea of God is uncertain and fluctuating, so is it too with the idea of love. The legalism of the reason does not really admit anything more than recognition in the sense of respect on the basis of equality. It would then be more correct to speak of enthusiasm for humanity than of the love of one's neighbour. *Homo sacrares homini*; this saying of Seneca describes most beautifully of what ancient Humanism is capable (*Epist.* xcv. 33). 'Each enjoys my favour because he bears the name of man' (*De Clem.* I. 1, 3). Both sayings describe the recognition of the divine origin of every other human being, and in that his inviolability; but there is here no trace of the ideas of love as self-sacrifice, or living for others. Philanthropy should be accorded to man in so far as he is worthy of it, not according to his need. The idea of universal cosmic sympathy may indeed produce something which resembles what Paul expresses in his parable of the 'Body of Christ'; but this 'cosmic sympathy' has no sense of a sacred obligation. Just as the idea of God oscillates between the pantheistic idea of the All-One and the rational world law, so also our relation to our fellow-man oscillates between mere respect, in rigid accordance with law, and love in a rather aesthetic sense, *Eros*. The Stoic cannot really be united with the other man because he is sufficient unto himself, he is independent. He recognizes, it is true, that the other also possesses reason; but he has no need of the other, since in his own reason he has access to the highest goods, and because to him the supreme good is the preservation of his independence and his freedom. As Humanism is rationalistic, it is also liberalistic, and therefore also individualistic.

Even in Plato the relation of the spiritual man to the community is something secondary; it is a concession. Actually, he ought to sever himself completely from society, in order to give himself up wholly and without interruption to the contemplation of the Ideas, to the way of redemption through thought. The connexion with the *Polis*, with the State, is only recognized because he who knows guides the State. In the philosophy of the Cynics and of the Stoics the connexion with society was still looser. Here we have the world citizen; the cosmopolitan ideal is the consequence of the rational idea of humanity which has been thought out logically. For the real philosopher—in contrast to the statesman who is a dilettante philosopher—however, this world-citizenship is not real citizenship, it does not entail concrete political responsibility. The Roman Stoic, however, is too much of a Roman, that is, a political person, to become logically a Stoic sage; he tries to find a compromise between political and social obligations to the community and philosophical isolation and self-sufficiency.

In the Stoic idea of the sage, however, as understood and expressed by the later Greeks, the self-sufficiency of the individual as the bearer of the Divine Reason is based. Certainly—so far as he has to do with the other man he must meet him in a way proper to the dignity of man, as one who is spiritually related, as a bearer of the same Reason which dwells in himself, and he must even do him good. But this social task is a parergon; the Stoic sage is an occasional philanthropist, he practises love of his neighbour by the way. His main calling is the cultivation of his own virtue and its preservation under difficult circumstances. But these difficult circumstances all issue from the *physis* and from external Fate; his task is *ataraxia*, the power to remain undisturbed, and thus ultimately to be self-contained.

8. One final consequence we have not yet noted: the self-sufficiency of man over against God. The relation to the deity, as we have seen, is not conceived as an actual relation, but as a substantial one, as similarity, affinity-in-being. Here, however, there is an oscillation between the mystical and pantheistic and the rational and legalistic pole. The rational line of development leads to the idea of self-redemption through *anamnesis*, through philosophical reflection, through soaring to the heights of the Divine. The Platonic philosophy knows a 'way of salvation' (Nygren) which corresponds to the myth of the soul. The soul which has fallen out of its heavenly existence into the earthly existence, once more aspires to rise upwards, and finds the way back through the contemplation of the Ideas. The soul redeems itself by means of right thought. Thanks to its rational nature it has the power and the possibility of cleansing itself, and of once more uniting itself with the Divine Being. This religious *gnosis* is simply self-redemption.

In speculative mysticism man's relation to the deity is rather different. Here the emphasis is rather on the rational being which belongs to the soul, its own rational nature, than upon a continual participation in the divine life of the spirit. Even in Ancient Greece mysticism—to speak of a 'Roman mysticism' would be a sort of *contradictio in adjecto*—has something which at least resembles the New Testament doctrine of Grace. In reality, here too there is a contrast which is no less sharp, but it is hidden. All mysticism, even the Hellenistic mysticism of Posidonius, and that of Plotinus of late antiquity, seeks union with the deity in the experience of ecstasy, or in the surrender of contemplation. But—especially in the mysticism of the ancient world—the initiative in this divine experience is always taken by man. The movement goes forth from him, his search for God, and his absorption in God is the *movens*. 'A God does not hold intercourse with a man' (*Symposium*, 203 A). Even as mystic the Greek never abandons the fundamental idea of *αὐτεξουσία*. Greek mysticism, and mysticism in general, knows nothing of the forgiving love of God. Hence here, too, the mystical relation with God is little affected by the contrast between the Divine command and the guilt of sin. The rigidity of the rational is not overcome by breaking the autonomy of the Self, but by an aesthetic softening. Here, too, we see that between God and man there is no real relation of 'over-againstness' but only that of immanence, thus not real dependence but affinity of nature, not a personal and actual relation, but one which is natural and substantial.

9. The characteristic element of ancient Humanism, however, is not mysticism but the idea of the world law, and of the *lex naturae* which naturally belongs to human nature. The Greek spirit can only bear a certain amount of the influence of Oriental mysticism; if it goes beyond this it becomes estranged from itself and the Humanism peculiar to it. Then, too, it is the *lex naturae* which has had the greatest practical influence both on antiquity, and also, through the Fathers and the Scholastics, upon the Middle Ages, and on later times. The doctrine of the *lex naturae* not only formed an important element in public opinion which, through the educated classes, penetrated into the life of the people at large—exercising a liberating, civilizing, uniting influence, softening the harshness of human destiny, and affecting the social life of antiquity as a whole; but, above all, through the Roman Law it has influenced

men's views of law as a whole—the legislation, the legal practice, and the political life of Europe—as one of the main factors in the history of Europe. It is that idea which sums up most fully and comprehensively all that has to be said about ancient Humanism, and shows most simply what it was.

The three elements which we have recognized as essential are contained in it: the rationalism of the *lex*, the pantheism of the *natura*, and the natural immanence of the divine in man. The *lex*, the Divine Law which prevails in the cosmos is the main concern. The question whether this is a law related to facts, or to the moral order, cannot be answered. It is both, and it is neither. It is related to facts, in so far as the Divine Law effectively determines and orders the world, quite apart from the will of man; it is related to the moral order in so far as man ought to live ὁμολογουμένως τῇ φύσει, as that, in particular, is the sum-total of all attitude to law, and thus the 'law of nature' is the supreme norm of all ethics and all law. But it is not a law related to facts in the sense in which we use the phrase 'law of nature'; it is not a law related to the moral order in the sense in which we, within the Christian tradition, are aware of 'obligation.' This oscillation between what is and what ought to be in the idea of law is a characteristic expression of the ancient idea of the cosmos, in which God and the world, what ought to be and what is, are one—a unity which has been destroyed by Christianity. The fact that for us the law of nature and the law of the moral order have been separated so widely from one another, that we can no longer reduce them to a common denominator, is the effect of Christianity, or to put it more exactly, of the Christian Idea of God and of Creation.

The rationalism of the idea of God is, firstly, based upon the fact that this *lex* includes the possibility of the knowledge of God immanent within itself; the rationalism of the order of internal human relations is grounded in the fact that this *lex* is the practical fundamental law. The rational, legal knowledge of God can never be truly personal; the legalistic relation to one's fellow-man can never be truly personal. The barrier of the one is the barrier of the other. To the impersonality of God there corresponds, on the one hand, abstractness in our relation to the other man—the abstract ethos of humanity (respect), the abstract unity of humanity (cosmopolitanism), and the abstract idea of equality—on the other hand, the barrier between man and man in general, the principle of autarchy. If I possess the essential in myself, I have no need of the other. If I have the essential in myself, the main task of my life will be to preserve this inward possession, to defend my inward freedom and my inward balance against all disturbance from without.

Secondly, there is the Law of Nature. God and Nature are one. All attempts to assert the sovereignty of God over the world are always swallowed up in the thought of this identity. Hence God cannot be really known as the Creator of the world, and therefore not as really personal; accordingly there is no real personal relation with Him. Man's relation with God is exhausted in a kind of being, namely, in an affinity with Him and an awareness of this relation. The necessity to perceive these relations brings a certain actuality into man's relation with God; here decisions can be made; here there is an Either-Or. One may see it or not see it, one may obey or disobey that which one has seen. But once more: all attempts to assert this actuality ultimately crumble into nothingness owing to the idea that man is already divine, that his divine nature is secured to him in his nature, hence that, in the last resort, the decision cannot be a matter of life or death.

This brings us to the third element: immanence. The divine being of nature is, in a natural way, that is, as a natural being, peculiar to man. Reason as such, as a possibility, as a formal element is already the divine. The divine therefore cannot be lost—thus the decision is not really serious. We can no more lose this reason than we can lose the divine patent of nobility; all we need to do is to remind ourselves of it continually. But the divine which is in man is also from the point of view of content essentially the same as the divine of the deity itself. *Est deus in nobis,* not through grace—grace which includes within itself the human decision of faith—not through historical events in the world, and not through Nature. Man has God in himself in virtue of his being as man, in virtue of his birth as man. This idea is, so to speak, the very opposite of the

—equally non-Biblical—idea of the ecclesiastical doctrine of Original Sin, namely, that man, in virtue of his birth, in virtue of his nature, is a sinner. The negative idea of nature of Christian theology is the assertion of the truth as against the penetration of the positive idea of nature into the ecclesiastical doctrine, from the Stoics, from the *lex naturae* (Pelagius). The Augustinian idea of the natural inherited curse corresponds to the Stoic idea of the natural inheritance of the divine nobility defended by Pelagianism, an idea which holds that the divine inheritance cannot be lost, and does not leave any room for a serious idea of sin.

10. From what has been said both the relation to, and the contrast to, the Christian idea of man's being will have become clear. The common element is this: man can never be understood apart from his relation to God. Man is always, irrevocably related to God. But in Christianity this relation to God is an actual relation, responsibility as the answer in faith and obedience to the word of the generous Creator. Hence, although it is true that man's relation to God as such can never be lost, the right relation may be, and indeed is, lost by sin. The relation to God therefore always stands in decision, it is never nature, because God is person and creates man as person. Through the primal decision, the personal act of the *peccatum originis*, the right relation has been lost; through the free decision, free choice, the generous grace of God in Jesus Christ, this relation is once more restored, but in such a way that it must be once more appropriated by man in an act of decision, in faith. Hence, because here everything depends upon the personal and the actual, the relation to man also becomes personal and actual love which cannot be summed up in any law. Greek Humanism, from this point of view, is the great misunderstanding of true humanity, great too in its misunderstanding. At the present day we are striving to remove this misunderstanding; that is why it is so important to perceive the contrast aright. It is falsely conceived when the relation of sinful man to God is denied; when the *humanum* is made a *profanum*. The error of ancient Humanism did not consist in the fact that it regarded the *humanum* as divine, but that it

defined the *humanum* as divine *by nature*. Hence a truly Biblical theology will be opposed both to the dehumanizing of man and to his divinization. Man is not divine in virtue of his nature; but God has given him from the beginning the divine destiny which, if he acts against it, becomes his curse, but which is given to him once more now in faith and later in sight, now as something imperfect and later as a perfect 'being like unto Him' through Him who is equal with God from all eternity, through the eternal Son who restores to us our lost sonship and perfects it.

INDEX

WESTMAR COLLEGE LIBRARY